Praise for *The Jewish Heroes of Warsaw*

"With *The Jewish Heroes of Warsaw*, Avinoam Patt takes his place among the ranks of the top Holocaust scholars on the academic scene today. In this deeply researched, sharply thought out, and skillfully written book, Patt provides a way for readers, both within and outside the academy, to learn about this much-mythologized event and this iconic place in public memory."

—Hasia Diner, Paul and Sylvia Steinberg Professor of American Jewish History, New York University

"Patt has produced a detailed and well-written account tracing these different commemorative narratives of this epic event, revealing the conflicts and complexities of memory work. He highlights the overriding imperative of ensuring the future of the Jewish people and forging a meaning of the tragic and heroic past. In this impressive work, Patt weaves together a tapestry of the postwar political, emotional, and cultural narratives of the uprising which enables readers to reflect on how history is used to create meaning in the present."

—Dalia Ofer, the Max and Rita Haber Professor of Holocaust and East European Studies at the Avraham Harman Institute of Contemporary Jewry at the Hebrew University of Jerusalem

"This is the best account of one of the major pillars of Jewish collective memory of the Holocaust, the Warsaw Ghetto Uprising of 1943. Patt offers a superb analysis of a fraught and complex story: how the uprising was interpreted in a postwar Jewish world that struggled to recover from a national catastrophe."

—Samuel D. Kassow, Charles Northam Professor of History at Trinity College and author of *Who Will Write Our History: Rediscovering a Hidden Archive from the Warsaw Ghetto*

"As this new and detailed account reveals, already during the war the Warsaw Ghetto Uprising of 1943 became a worldwide symbol of Jewish resistance, while at the same time Jewish organizations abroad struggled to respond to the news of the Nazi extermination campaign in occupied Poland. Enabled by a close reading of an abundance of original sources, Patt aptly illuminates the contested political makings of The Jewish Heroes of Warsaw by survivors and Jewish factions in Palestine/Israel, Poland, and the United States during the first decade after the uprising and even today."

—Wolf Gruner, author of *The Holocaust in Bohemia and Moravia: Czech Initiatives, German Policies and Jewish Responses*

"*The Jewish Heroes of Warsaw* provides a comprehensive overview of the complex ties between Zionism and the Holocaust and of the Holocaust's central place in the life of the State of Israel. Avinoam Patt's brilliant analysis challenges accepted notions of nationalism, identity, and commemoration and offers new insights and understandings."

—Hava Dreifuss, historian of the Holocaust in Eastern Europe at the Department of Jewish History at Tel-Aviv University

THE JEWISH HEROES OF WARSAW

THE JEWISH HEROES OF WARSAW

THE AFTERLIFE OF THE REVOLT

Avinoam J. Patt

Wayne State University Press
Detroit

ISBN 978-0-8143-4835-2 (paperback); ISBN 978-0-8143-4516-0 (hardback);
ISBN 978-0-8143-4517-7 (ebook)

Library of Congress Control Number: 2020945643

Wayne State University Press
Leonard N. Simons Building
4809 Woodward Avenue
Detroit, Michigan 48201-1309

Visit us online at wsupress.wayne.edu

On cover: *Pomnik Bohaterów Getta*, the Ghetto Heroes Monument, Warsaw. Photo by Avinoam J. Patt. Cover design by Mindy Basinger Hill.

Photographs on pages 95, 103, 177, and 335 are included courtesy of the Historical Jewish Press collection, National Library of Israel.

To Eidel Sara,
always and forever

Contents

Acknowledgments

This is a project many years in the making. The idea for this book first began when I was writing my dissertation and discovered that the Hashomer Hatzair youth movement in postwar Germany had decided to name its kibbutz groups after ghetto fighters like Tosia Altman, Mordecai Anielewicz, Yosef Kaplan, Shmuel Breslaw, and others. How quickly did a heroic ethos develop after the war? To my surprise, I found that this process of competitive mythmaking began immediately after the revolt during the war. Like the young members of the kibbutz named after Tosia Altman I was captivated by her persona, her heroism, and her tragic death. And yet, I still wondered, why were some names remembered while others were forgotten? This book is first and foremost dedicated to the Jewish victims and survivors, to those whose names are remembered and to those whose names have been forgotten.

I have benefitted from the shared wisdom of many teachers who have assisted and encouraged me at various stages of this project. My graduate advisor at NYU, David Engel, encouraged me to examine the role of the surviving ghetto fighters in writing the history of the revolt and graciously read and commented on early drafts of manuscript chapters. Thank you for the "lifetime service contract." My sincere appreciation also goes to Atina Grossmann, who has been a mentor, colleague, and friend, and who also read early drafts of chapters. And a special thanks to Hasia Diner, whose pioneering work on early American Jewish postwar memory of the Holocaust spurred me to examine why the Warsaw Ghetto uprising became the prism through which American Jews remembered the Holocaust. Deborah Lipstadt, who first introduced me to the field of Holocaust studies at Emory University, encouraged me to "just get the thing done." Havi Dreifuss was incredibly generous in sharing her deep knowledge of both the history of the Warsaw ghetto and the Jewish fighting organization, along with many suggestions for further research. Her book on the last year in the life and death of the Warsaw ghetto offers fascinating new insights into this history and challenged me to rethink certain parts of my argument. Natalia Aleksiun has been a source of advice and support since we were graduate students together at NYU; thank you for the many suggestions to help improve the final manuscript, cousin. To my traveling road show partners, Gabriel Finder and David Slucki, we make a great team! Other scholars (and I apologize if I forget anyone) have offered insights, suggestions, and comments throughout the research and writing process, both directly and indirectly, including Sam Kassow, Dalia Ofer, Nancy Sinkoff, Laura Jockusch, Boaz Cohen, Wolf Gruner, Samantha Baskind, Victoria Aarons, Kasia Person, Richard Freund, David Roskies, Bella Gutterman, Daniel Soyer, Nick Underwood, Graciela Ben-Dror, and Phyllis Lassner. I am especially grateful to the two outstanding reviewers at Wayne State University Press whose comments and suggestions only served to strengthen the final book. As always, while I am grateful for the advice and support, any mistakes in the book (and I am sure there are some) are mine and mine alone. Over the past seventy-five years, multiple generations of scholars and survivors have preceded me in writing this history. To paraphrase Rabbi Moses Isserles, they have prepared the table, I have just come to lay a tablecloth.

Feedback at various conferences where this research has been presented over the years has helped spur my thinking on various aspects of the project, including the annual or biannual conferences of the Association for Jewish Studies; the Association for Israel Studies, Lessons and Legacies; Beyond Camps and Forced Labor, a conference on the legacy of Rachel Auerbach at the Fortunoff Video Archives for Holocaust Testimony at Yale University; a University of Toronto conference on the aftermath of the Holocaust in 2018; the Future of Holocaust Testimonies conferences in Akko (2016) and at the University of Virginia (2017); and a 2013 conference on Jewish resistance sponsored by Moses Mendelssohn Center for European Jewish Studies, held at the German Resistance Memorial Center in Berlin, which served as the initial impetus to write this book.

In the Talmud (Ta'anit 7a), R. Chanina is quoted as saying, "I have learned much from my teachers, more from my colleagues, but from my students I have learned more than from all of them." I am grateful to many colleagues and students at the University of Connecticut, the University of Hartford, Clark University, Trinity College, and Voices of Hope/HERO Center, as well as to colleagues on the Jewish responses to persecution project at USHMM, which spurred my thinking on the nature of Jewish responses to the Holocaust and the spectrum of Jewish resistance in ghettos large and small throughout Europe. I have been privileged to hold the Philip D. Feltman Chair in Modern Jewish History at the University of Hartford and the Doris and Simon Konover Chair in Judaic Studies at the University of Connecticut. I am grateful for the critical support of Judaic Studies as a respected discipline in American universities. I hope that this work makes the Feltman and Konover families proud. Arnold Greenberg has long been a trusted supporter and advocate since I first arrived in Hartford in 2007—thank you for all you have done to support my research, writing, teaching, and community engagement. I have been fortunate to work with two wonderful program assistants at the University of Hartford and UConn; to Susan Gottlieb and Pam Weathers, thank you for all of your assistance over the years. I was fortunate to receive multiple Cardin grants at the University of Hartford for research and writing to complete this book project and also benefitted from serving as a Jewish Theological Seminary Fellow, which enabled me to present this research to multiple audiences.

I am grateful to the archival staffs at multiple institutions who offered invaluable assistance at various stages of the project (even in the midst of a global pandemic). Digitization projects at many of these institutions have made it possible to access and read materials that never would have been available otherwise. The Ghetto Fighters House Archive is a treasure trove and in many ways the materials housed there helped lay the foundation for this book. Thank you to Anat Bratman-Elhalel and the archival staff at Lochamei Ha-Geta'ot for the invaluable assistance. Thank you to Judith Cohen, Caroline Waddell, Vincent Slatt, and Ron Coleman at USHMM; Linda Levi, Jeff Edelstein, Misha Mitsel, and Anat Kutner at the JDC Archives in New York and Jerusalem; Fruma Mohrer and Vital Zajka at the YIVO Archives; Eliot Nidam-Orvieto and Sharon Kangisser-Cohen for assistance in locating materials at Yad Vashem; to Chana Pollack for digital research assistance at the Forward Archive; Melanie Meyers for assistance in securing images from the American Jewish Historical Society; to the staff at the Wagner Labor Archives at the NYU Library; to the Jewish National Library in Jerusalem for digitizing the Historical Jewish Press (another treasure trove); to the Jewish Telegraphic Agency for making historical bulletins available online; to the Steven Spielberg Digital Yiddish Library for making Yiddish treasures from the period during and after World War II available online; and to Gregg, Michelle, and Shlomi Philipson in Austin, Texas, for always being so generous with your one-of-a-kind collection.

The Wayne State University Press team is simply the best in the business. I appreciate you and am so happy you are all there. Thank you for your dedication to academic publishing. Special thanks to the team: Kathy Wildfong, Annie Martin, Kristin Harpster, Emily Nowak, Carrie Downes Teefey, Jamie Jones, and Kristina Stonehill. I also want to acknowledge the incredible work of the one of the most amazing copyeditors I have ever been privileged to work with, the other A-Patt, Amy Pattullo. Thank you for your careful and detailed reading.

As the writing of this book was completed in the midst of a global pandemic, the bonds of family were reinforced, even as we tried to transcend time and space virtually. Thank you to my parents, Nurit and Yehuda Patt, for instilling a lifelong love of history, for always being interested in my research and writing, and for poring over lines of poetry by Natan Alterman (and even enjoying it as much as me). To the Einstein, Weinstein, and Neustat clans, thank you for the support and love. To my siblings, Iddo, Hanoch, and Suzie Patt and your beautiful families, I have to think some of the questions posed here go back to those long discussions around the dinner table on Friday nights long ago. We were raised in a family culture of debate, discussion, and intellectual curiosity. I hope we can continue this tradition for our families, too. To my amazing children, Maya, Alex, and Micah—you have been surrounded by this history much too early and for far too long. Thank you for your patience, your love, and your support (and for the much-needed grounding, distraction, and occasional games of basketball). And finally to my beloved wife, Ivy, who has supported and encouraged me in countless ways since we first began discussing Jewish identity, Holocaust studies, and much more at Emory University in Atlanta in 1996; words cannot express my gratitude for decades of love, support, and inspiration. I dedicate this book to you, my hero.

Introduction

Warsaw, A Place in Jewish History

The Warsaw Ghetto Uprising, the largest mass revolt in a major city in Nazi-occupied Europe, is the defining symbol of Jewish resistance to Nazi oppression during World War II. By the first anniversary of the revolt (April 19, 1944) Jews around the world seized upon it as the basis for Holocaust commemoration activities, and the dates of the uprising have since been linked to annual Holocaust commemoration events in countries around the world. Israel's Knesset selected the 27th of Nisan as the date for Yom HaShoah vehaGevurah (Day of Remembrance of the Holocaust and Heroism) in 1953 to correspond with the timing of the uprising.[1] The Warsaw Ghetto Uprising has occupied a central place in the history of the Holocaust and of the Second World War; as a military encounter, its significance may seem relatively minor, having resulted in a small number of German dead and wounded over the course of the one month that the Jewish resistance fighters managed to battle German forces in the ghetto. Nonetheless, the revolt in the Warsaw ghetto had a major impact on Jewish communities elsewhere in Eastern Europe and on German procedures in the aftermath of the uprising as well, and this impact has been well documented.[2] And from the perspective of Jewish history, its significance has been tremendous, representing perhaps the most well known Jewish response to Nazi persecution during the war, serving both as the counterargument to the myth that the Jews of Europe had been "led like sheep to the slaughter" and conversely, reinforcing the mistaken view that the Warsaw Ghetto Uprising represented the only case of armed Jewish resistance in Europe. Why, despite representing the best-known case of Jewish resistance during the war, has the Warsaw Ghetto Uprising continued to reinforce the paradigm of passivity and resistance, of martyrs and heroes, and why has this motif been such a persistent part of how the Holocaust is remembered?

Recent literature on the subject reinforces a continued fascination with the topic of Jewish resistance, while also suggesting a perceived need to continue arguing against the stereotype of Jewish passivity, to, in the words of one author, "demonstrate definitively that Jews during the Holocaust did not go to their deaths passively like sheep."[3] While scholars frequently critique Raul Hilberg's argument that "preventive attack, armed resistance, and revenge were almost completely absent in Jewish exilic history,"[4] a review of early commemorations and historical treatments of the war reveals that the poles of passivity and resistance were established very early—in fact, they were fixed even before the war.

In November 1942, after learning of the deportations from Kraków to Belzec, Aharon Dolek Libeskind, a leading member of the prewar Akiva movement and leader of the Jewish underground in Kraków, called for armed resistance in Kraków, arguing "we are fighting for three lines in history . . . it will not be said that our youth marched like sheep to the slaughter." Postwar depictions of the Warsaw Ghetto Uprising by surviving ghetto fighters likewise contrasted resistance with the "sheep (sent) to the slaughter." After the war, the Yishuv and its emissaries sought to capitalize on the heroism of movement members, and the surviving ghetto fighters themselves also presented the choice to resist as emerging from a place of deep Zionist ideological immersion. This notion of sheep to the slaughter, however, not exclusive to members of Zionist youth movements, had an important prewar precedent and was not merely a postwar interpretation by Zionist leaders.[5] The phrase had its origins in Psalms 44 and Isaiah and was also cited in the Talmud (Gittin 57b), where the phrase was invoked to celebrate acts of *Kiddush Hashem* by Jewish children who refused to be enslaved by the Romans and went willingly to their deaths to sanctify God's name.[6] Nonetheless, in the context of pogroms in Europe in the nineteenth century, the phrase evolved from a celebration of martyrdom to sanctify God's name, to a source that evoked the manner in which Jews were degraded and humiliated by such persecutions. In Zionist ideology, the notion of a passive diaspora mentality that needed to be vanquished in the negation of the Diaspora was given its strongest depiction in the work of Haim Nachman Bialik, who in his famous poem "City of Slaughter" indicted the victims (and survivors!) of the 1903 Kishinev pogrom.[7] The pogrom in Kishinev (then part of the Russian empire, now Moldova) and the seemingly passive response of the Jewish public to the attacks gave rise to bitter indictment, particularly in Zionist circles, of Jewish behavior and the willingness of victims to go to their deaths "with necks outstretched."[8] With the outbreak of violence in Palestine in 1920, leaders of the Yishuv appropriated the phrase, but this time to indicate that Zionist pioneers would refuse to go to their deaths passively. Thus, for example, Zalman Rubashov (later Shazar—third president of Israel) proclaimed: "The brothers of the Tel Hai heroes will not be led as sheep to slaughter. The Land of Israel will not become a gallows [*gardom*] for the people of Israel."[9] After a 1929 pogrom in Safed, *Ha'aretz* described Jews as "going to the slaughter like sheep."[10] As expressed by Yudka in Haim Hazaz's *The Sermon* (written in 1942) Jewish diaspora history was nothing but a series of persecutions and oppressions to be ignored and forgotten. "It's simply because Jewish history is dull, uninteresting. It has no glory or action, no heroes and conquerors, no rulers and masters of their fate, just a collection of wounded, hunted, groaning, and wailing wretches, always begging for mercy."[11] In Zionist ideology, the notion of diaspora Jewry as passive, depicted as "mice," "scurrying roaches," "wailing wretches," and "sheep to the slaughter" exercised a powerful influence on movement members in the Yishuv and in the Diaspora who sought to elevate their spiritual and historic standing. These historiographical parameters were reinforced in texts composed during the war.

It was not only ghetto fighters who invoked the language of "sheep to the slaughter" to summon the will to resistance. Emanuel Ringelblum, historian and creator of the Oneg Shabbes underground archive in the Warsaw ghetto, writing in his diary on June 17, 1942, reflected on the passivity of the Jewish masses in the face of destruction after hearing of the deportations from Biała Podlaska to Sobibor, "left to be led as sheep to a slaughterhouse. . . .

Not to act, not to lift a hand against Germans, has since then become the quiet, passive heroism of a common Jew."[12] Reflecting again in October 1942 on the Great Deportation, Ringelblum would ask: "why did we allow ourselves to be led like sheep to the slaughter?"[13] Echoing Abba Kovner's call for resistance in Vilna on New Year's Day in 1942, the Jewish Fighting Organization (Żydowska Organizacja Bojowa—ŻOB) in Warsaw, which proved powerless to prevent the Great Deportation of July and August 1942 that decimated the ghetto,[14] called on the remaining Jews of Warsaw to resist deportation six months later in January 1943: "Jewish masses, the hour is drawing near. You must be prepared to resist, not give yourselves up to slaughter like sheep. Not a single Jew should go to the railroad cars. Those who are unable to put up active resistance should resist passively, meaning go into hiding. . . . Our motto should be: All are ready to die as human beings."[15]

So when reports began to emerge of the heroic uprising in Warsaw—not the first or last ghetto to revolt (the Lachwa, present-day Belarus, *Yizkor* book [memorial book] adopted the title *Rishonim LaMered*—First to Revolt—to honor the September 2, 1942, revolt there), but the most famous—it is not surprising that it was seized upon by Jews around the world from all movements. Reports emerging from the Warsaw ghetto framed the choice to engage in armed resistance as proof that Jews could in fact "fight for the honor and dignity of the Jewish people." The timing of the revolt, coming as it did in the midst of a transition to mourning the destruction of European Jewry, and its framing as proof that Jewish heroes could overcome Jewish passivity, would shape the nature of Holocaust memory for decades to come.

Historical writing on the Warsaw Ghetto Uprising developed rapidly both during and after the war. Historical frameworks, in place before the war, also influenced writing and documentation projects during the war. Journalists, historians, surviving participants, and writers of fiction began to create historical accounts of the "battle of Warsaw's Jews" almost immediately after it occurred. Document collections that presented eyewitness testimony, underground reports, and other tantalizing details of the event were already published in 1944; examples discussed in this book include the Bund's *Ghetto in Flames*, the publication of Shloime Mendelson's 1944 lecture at YIVO, and *Warsaw Ghetto Rising*, written by Melech Neustadt and published by Poalei Zion in 1944. Melech Neustadt also compiled one of the first document collections on the revolt, published in the Yishuv in 1946 as *Churban ve-Mered shel Yehudei Varsha*. The testimonies of surviving ghetto fighters (like Marek Edelman, Vladka Meed, Zivia Lubetkin, Tuvia Borzykowski, Yitzhak Zuckerman, Stefan Grajek, and others) also found a broad audience soon after the war, as did one of the earliest popular historical treatments of Jewish resistance during the war, American writer Marie Syrkin's *Blessed Is the Match* (published in 1947). In a review of literature on the "Jewish Catastrophe" by Philip Friedman and Koppel Pinson published in *Jewish Social Studies* in January 1950, the scholars pointed to over three hundred books, memoirs, and document collections dealing with the Warsaw ghetto and the uprising that had already been published.[16]

As a rich historical literature on the revolt developed in the first decade after 1943 (in Yiddish, Polish, English, and Hebrew) several key patterns in the historiography began to emerge. All reinforced the centrality of the Warsaw Ghetto Uprising as the *key* focal point of Jewish collective memory of the war—but also as an event sufficiently flexible as to be incorporated into multiple postwar Jewish political and historical frameworks. The 1954 publication of the anthology *Martyrs and Fighters: The Epic of the Warsaw Ghetto* captured this duality—both the division of Jewish responses between an emphasis on martyrdom and heroism, and the bifurcation of the Jewish world between Israel and America. As a response to Nazi persecution, the revolt symbolized the determination of the Jewish people to endure, persevere, and preserve their faith and traditions, whether in Israel or America. The revolt symbolized the defense of freedom and democracy *and* the collective ethos of the Jewish people. The editor of the anthology was Dr. Philip Friedman (1901–60), a Polish Jewish historian who trained in Vienna and taught in Warsaw, Lodz, and Vilna before the war began. Friedman survived the war in hiding in Poland and became the director of the Central Jewish Historical Commission in Poland after the war, later testifying at the Nuremberg trials before directing the educational department of the JDC (American Jewish Joint Distribution Committee) in Germany and then teaching at Columbia. In his introduction, Friedman argued that the "Jewish revolt in Warsaw is almost unique in its historical significance." While it had "no more military effect on the course of the war against the Germans than did the heroic resistance of the three hundred Spartans at Thermopylae," its "deep moral impact" demonstrated that the "vigorous will of free men" could overcome the "ruthless and coldly calculated crimes of totalitarian regimes."[17] For Friedman, writing and teaching in English in New York in December 1953, the connections were clear: the Warsaw Ghetto Uprising symbolized the ability of free men to stand up to the evil power of totalitarian regimes, whether represented by Nazi Germany or the Soviet Union. Friedman, who had published a detailed "Bibliography of the Warsaw Ghetto" in *The Jewish Book Annual* (vol. 11, 1952–53) based his selection in the anthology on a wide range of sources in Yiddish, Polish, German, and French, which included testimonies of eyewitnesses, ghetto fighters, members of the Jewish Fighting Organization, and reports written by Rachel Auerbach, Adolf Berman, Tuvia Borzykowski, Marek Edelman, Bernard Goldstein, Zivia Lubetkin, Vladka Meed, Simcha Rotem, Emanuel Ringelblum, Hillel Seidman, Wladyslaw Szpilman, David Wdowinski, Szmuel Zygielbojm, and others, along with reports by SS general Jurgen Stroop and the Polish underground courier Jan Karski, that reflected a broad array of viewpoints translated into English for an American audience. Even though a broad range of sources was already available (with some translated into English and Hebrew) on Jewish life in the Warsaw ghetto, the revolt and the subject of death in the ghetto remained the primary focus. *Martyrs and Fighters*—the two poles of Jewish behavior in the ghetto—would be reinforced repeatedly in representations of the uprising and in historical literature on the war.

In Israel in the 1950s, too, the two poles of Jewish behavior also seemed fixed, determined by a pre–World War II Zionist worldview that determined the standard Jewish response in the face of destruction, to be defined by a complete lack of self-defense and armed struggle.[18] The Ghetto Fighters House, founded on April 19, 1949, worked to counteract the myth of

Jewish passivity during the war by focusing on specific examples of Jewish resistance and Jewish heroism. *Sefer Milhamot Ha-Getaot* (The Book of the Ghetto Wars), edited by Yitzhak Zuckerman and Moshe Basok, published in 1954, contained more than 150 testimonies and parts of original sources from the Ghetto Fighters House Archives, and more than 40 percent of the book was devoted to the Warsaw ghetto, especially its underground activity and rebellion.[19] Other sections highlighted underground work of pioneering Zionist youth in Kraków, Będzin, Białystok, and Vilna, while testimonies by members of the Jewish Socialist (non-Zionist) Bund and the Revisionist Zionist youth movement Betar were largely excluded (with the exception of a brief excerpt from the Bundist Marek Edelman). *Sefer Milhamot Ha-Getaot* devoted very little space to the activity of the partisans.[20] The introduction to the volume explained:

> ghetto wars means fighting for life, if only to die with honor, to die a death different from that the enemy has decreed. Fighting means every action taken against the interests and edicts of the violent invader, actions taken in public and in secret, by groups of people and by individuals, organized and planned or suddenly at the last moment, armed and even by taking a daring stance by protesting in a brave voice.

Although *Sefer Milhamot Ha-Getaot* offered an expanded definition of resistance—defining ghetto wars as fighting against the decrees of the invaders (in a form similar to Bauer's later use of the term *amidah*—literally, "standing up against" or defiance of Nazi decrees)—the volume reinforced a divide that had existed between the ghetto fighters themselves, the leaders of the Jewish councils, and the rest of the ghetto population as a whole. The book focused primarily on physical struggle as the supreme form of Jewish rebellion and highlighted calls by the underground for the Jewish population not to go passively to their deaths, while also stressing the alienation felt by the underground from the rest of the ghetto population, which they perceived as helpless and passive.[21] Nonetheless, as seen above, the motif of "sheep to the slaughter" employed by the ghetto fighters in their calls to resistance, and reinforced in the dichotomy of passivity and resistance after the war, had important prewar precedents that shaped perceptions of the nature of Jewish behavior during the war.

In his 1961 opus *The Destruction of the European Jews*, Raul Hilberg focused almost exclusively on how the Germans organized the Final Solution, generally ignoring Jewish responses and Jewish source material.[22] Hilberg presented the uneven confrontation between the forces of SS general Stroop and Anielewicz's Jewish Fighting Organization as a military battle in the chapter on deportations. He based his evidence largely on the Stroop report, while also relying on the ŻOB report reprinted in Friedman's *Martyrs and Fighters*, as well as testimonies by Edelman, Goldstein, and others that had been printed in English. All the same, Hilberg's assessment of the Warsaw Ghetto Uprising measured its significance from the perspective of the history of the development of the Final Solution:

> the largest single clash between Jews and Germans occurred in the ghetto of Warsaw. For the further development of the destruction process, this armed encounter was without consequence. In Jewish history, however, the battle is literally a revolution, for after two thousand years of a policy of submission the wheel had been turned and once again Jews were using force.[23]

For Hilberg, the Jewish councils were part of the machinery of destruction, part of the Jewish tendency to submit to the power of the oppressor, "composed of precisely those elements of the community that had staked everything on a course of complete cooperation with the German administration." The resistance, on the other hand, was organized by "a new hierarchy that was strong enough to challenge the council successfully in a bid for control over the Jewish community." Formed from the political parties that had been "represented in the prewar Jewish community machinery" and had managed to survive in the ghetto by looking out for their members, these "now banded together into a resistance bloc."[24] For Hilberg, the revolution in Jewish history was as much a manifestation of resistance against Nazi oppression as it was a determination to throw off the yoke of two thousand years of Jewish submission to passivity and compliance. Hilberg only covered armed resistance briefly, focusing almost exclusively on the Warsaw ghetto but ignoring other cases of resistance, because, in the end, it bolstered his thesis that resistance did nothing to alter the fate of Poland's Jews or the outcome of the Final Solution.

In the same year that Hilberg published *The Destruction of European Jewry*, the trial of Adolf Eichmann commenced in Jerusalem on April 12 (the day before Yom HaShoah vehaGevurah). Just a week later, Gideon Hausner, the Israel Attorney General, read the indictment in the name of "six million accusers. But they cannot rise to their feet and point an accusing finger toward him who sits in the dock and cry: 'I accuse'. For their ashes are piled up on the hills of Auschwitz and the fields of Treblinka, and are strewn in the forests of Poland. Their graves are scattered throughout the length and breadth of Europe. Their blood cries out, but their voice is not heard."[25]

Surviving ghetto fighters like Yitzhak Zuckerman, Zivia Lubetkin, and Abba Kovner testified at the trial in May 1961, again seeking to offset the notion that Jews had gone passively to their deaths. Adolf Berman and Rachel Auerbach also testified, offering evidence on education and social welfare efforts in the Warsaw ghetto. Auerbach, who had been part of the Oneg Shabbat underground archive project and then an important figure in the postwar Historical Commission before emigrating to Israel and founding the oral history department at Yad Vashem, also played a central role in convincing the prosecution to incorporate the voices of so many survivors in the case, raising general awareness of the Holocaust that had not existed before among broad audiences.

Reporting on the Eichmann trial, Hannah Arendt cited the distinction between "Israeli heroism and Jewish submissive meekness" as one of the primary lessons David Ben-Gurion sought to convey to an Israeli audience. He also wanted diaspora Jewry to understand that "four-thousand-year-old Judaism, with its spiritual creations, its ethical strivings, its Messianic aspirations, had always faced a hostile world," and that in the face of Nazi persecution, the Jews had degenerated until they went to their death like sheep.[26]

In Arendt's reporting, she singled out this "contrast between Israeli heroism and the submissive meekness with which Jews went to their death" as a telling point of the trial, noting that in his cross-examination of witnesses, Hausner seemed to emphasize the behavior of Jewish victims. Arendt concluded, "the deliberate attempt in Jerusalem to tell only the Jewish side of the story distorted the truth, even the Jewish truth. The glory of the uprising in the Warsaw ghetto and the heroism of the few others who fought back . . . confirmed the known fact that only the very young had been capable of taking the 'decision that we cannot go and be slaughtered like sheep.'"[27]

Despite increasing evidence of a broad range of Jewish responses to persecution during the war, the historical literature on the uprising itself continued to reinforce the view that the revolt in Warsaw served as the counterpoint to a history of Jewish passivity. Yuri Suhl's *They Fought Back: The Story of Jewish Resistance in Nazi Europe* was published in 1967 to counteract the "unchallenged myth that European Jews went passively to their deaths." Suhl's volume, which provided details on revolts in Białystok, Lachwa, Tuczyn, Minsk, Vilna, Sobibor, Treblinka, Auschwitz, and elsewhere sought specifically to correct the record: "[T]he world knows little or nothing about the other side of the Holocaust picture: Jewish resistance—how the Jews struck back at their tormentors. The epic Warsaw Ghetto uprising is famous, but it is not generally known that in practically every ghetto and in every labor and concentration camp there existed a Jewish underground organization that kept up the prisoners' morale, reduced their physical sufferings, committed acts of sabotage, organized escapes, collected arms, planned revolts, and in many instances, carried them out." As Suhl argued, the disproportionate focus on the Warsaw Ghetto Uprising as the prism of Jewish memory and the focal point of historical writing on the war had obscured most other aspects of Jewish experiences during the war (and if it had overshadowed all other cases of armed resistance, it had most certainly obscured almost all other forms of Jewish experience during the war). The Warsaw Ghetto Uprising has a curious place in historical literature on the Holocaust: invoked as the counterargument to the notion that Jews went passively to their deaths during the war, it simultaneously reinforces this idea, by being presented as the only case of armed resistance during the war.

Speaking at a conference at Yad Vashem dedicated to the subject of "Jewish Resistance during the Holocaust," convened on the twenty-fifth anniversary of the revolt in Warsaw to present a much broader array of resistance activities (including Jewish education, underground political work, the role of youth movements, Jewish partisans, documentation projects in ghettos, the struggle for daily life, Jewish involvement in allied resistance movements, rescue work, and more), Dr. Yosef Burg (Minister of Social Welfare for the State of Israel) brought greetings on behalf of the nation, less than a year after the momentous turning point in Israel's history, the Six-Day War. Burg, one of the founders of the National Religious Party in Israel and an Orthodox Jew, presented the choice to engage in resistance as a major transformation in Jewish self-understanding.

> I am certain that this conference will show how large a role the individual, isolated Jew, as well as the Jews organized in group frameworks, played in the struggle against the demonic oppressor. We must remember that this struggle marked a departure from the *traditional passive martyrdom and Kiddush Hashem* to a new active "sanctification of the name"—a process which involved a difficult spiritual revolution. It was a departure from the historical passivity of the believing Jew, but only a Jew who believed profoundly in the future of the Jewish people could make the transition in our generation from self-sacrificing Kiddush Hashem to the Kiddush Hashem of armed resistance. Thus our generation is a direct continuation of all the previous generations who believed in, and suffered for, the eternity of the Jewish people.[28]

Yitzhak Zuckerman, one of the leaders of the Jewish Fighting Organization, who had been stationed outside the ghetto to secure weapons when the revolt began, also spoke at the conference, offering reflections twenty-five years after the event. While great armies engaged one another on the battlefield and mass revolts in European cities would erupt later in the war, Zuckerman explained the call to resist as a choice between two alternatives: "death in Treblinka, or battle." While most of the Jews in the ghetto did not understand the gravity of the situation in the summer of 1942, the Zionist pioneering underground called for resistance as the last stand of an isolated people on the precipice of destruction. He cited Mordecai Tenenbaum-Tamaroff's stark call to make a last stand in June 1942 as if in a "fortress under siege."

> The spirit in which we act each day must be that of Masada. All other matters must be set aside for the sake of this one over-riding question: life or death. And this must be done not only in moments of stock taking, but coolly and calmly, with systematic preparation, with daily reappraisal, with precision, with the desperation of a Polish Jew in a German ghetto in the month of June 1942.[29]

The inability to understand the grave danger facing the Jewish masses would later erupt into bitter rivalry between Zionist groups in the ghetto who would argue that they called for the organization of armed resistance in the spring of 1942, and the socialist and generally anti- or non-Zionist Bund, who contended that lack of weaponry and outside support made the call to revolt premature. But for the members of Zionist youth groups, this isolation, the sense of being cut off from any hope of outside support, was also confirmation of an ideology that renounced the possibility of future coexistence in the Diaspora. Thus, as we will see in subsequent chapters, leaders of the Zionist underground like Yitzhak Zuckerman and Zivia Lubetkin would claim that it was only the youth of HeHalutz, of the pioneering Zionist youth movements, who could organize the resistance. Zuckerman would argue at the twenty-fifth anniversary symposium that "it is not remarkable that it was the Zionist pioneering youth who rejected the Diaspora, who had no faith in Jewish survival in a foreign land, who had left their homes to prepare themselves for a new life in the Eretz Yisrael—that it was precisely these young people who upheld the case for struggle within the ghettos and clung to the ghetto walls."[30] Such arguments were not the product of twenty-five years of historical research on armed resistance by Jewish groups in occupied Europe, however. Instead, as this book will show, the opposing viewpoints on armed resistance, which focused almost exclusively on the role of Zionist youth affiliated with the Labor Zionist movements (and excluded members of the Bund, Communists, and the Revisionist Zionists) were the products of prewar and wartime debates that colored the writing of the history of armed resistance in Warsaw at the time, in the immediate aftermath of the revolt.

According to this approach, the Warsaw Ghetto Uprising culminated a process that not only represented the destruction of European Jewish life, but also reflected the Zionist determination to throw off the passivity of almost two millennia in the Diaspora. Lucy Dawidowicz, born and raised in New York, briefly trained at Columbia University before studying and working at YIVO in Vilna before the outbreak of the war. She dedicated her major work on the history of the Holocaust, *The War against the Jews*, to the relatives of her husband, Szymon Dawidowicz, including Toba (Tobcie) Dawidowicz, who died fighting with the Bund and the ŻOB in the Warsaw ghetto, and Zarek Dawidowicz, killed at Treblinka in 1942, "two of the six million," a dedication that again reflected the duality of "heroes and martyrs." News of the revolt in Warsaw had a profound impact on her in 1943, and the culmination of Dawidowicz's highly popular historical treatment of the Final Solution and the Holocaust (the two parts of her book) was the Warsaw Ghetto Uprising (essentially concluding the book in 1943, even though the volume covered the years 1933–45). Explaining the armed resistance organized by the youth in the Jewish political movements, Dawidowicz argued that "the young people in the Zionist and Bundist movements, reared in the ideals of secular modernity, rejected the traditionalist values and modes of behavior that had sustained Diaspora existence for centuries. Contemptuous of the long tradition of Jewish accommodation, they sought ways—whether nationalist or socialist—to combat Jewish powerlessness."[31] For both Zionists and Bundists, according to Dawidowicz (and in contrast to Yosef Burg), "the Jewish tradition of martyrdom, Kiddush-hashem, was the epitome of the Diaspora fate against which they rebelled. To them, nonbelievers, martyrdom did not mean bearing witness to God, but merely signified Jewish helplessness, passivity in the face of destruction." United by a drive for revenge against the Germans, all members of the Jewish underground engaged in resistance, not merely as a form of self-defense, according to Dawidowicz, but as "an act of desperation, whose Jewish paradigm was the suicidal stand of the zealots at Masada against Rome's imperial legions. Masada had been incorporated into modern Zionist myth under the influence of Yitzhak Lamdan's epic poem: 'We have one treasure left—the daring after despair. Since hope for survival had been abandoned, one must die gloriously'." Concluding her account of the Warsaw Ghetto uprising with the final gassing of the ŻOB headquarters at Miła 18, Dawidowicz says, "they began to kill themselves and each other, in a scene that must have rivaled the mass suicide at Masada. Mordecai Anielewicz was among them." Thus, while the Warsaw Ghetto Uprising reflected the end point of the Jewish experience of the war, the final act of the Holocaust, whose participants saw it as throwing off the yoke of centuries of Jewish passivity, the destruction of the Warsaw ghetto also marked the end of one historical time period: "there were no Jewish communities anymore, no synagogues, no Jewish schools, no Jewish life to sustain. Blood-soaked debris of Yiddish and Hebrew books at the banks of the Vistula were all that remained of the thousand-year-old civilization of Jews in Poland."[32]

Dawidowicz also sought to incorporate Jewish points of view into her analysis, an implicit critique of the work of Raul Hilberg, which had relied primarily on German sources. This approach included an analysis of Jewish responses in Germany, life and death in the ghettos, actions of the official and unofficial Jewish leadership (the Judenräte and the underground), and the organization of self-help. Even so, by presenting the Warsaw Ghetto Uprising as the final act of the Jews in Europe that "must have rivaled the mass suicide at Masada," Dawidowicz reinforced a tendency in the literature to present armed resistance, and specifically the case of the Warsaw Ghetto Uprising, as the counterargument to Hilberg's notion that "preventive attack, armed resistance, and revenge were almost completely absent in

Jewish exilic history" and "the Jewish reactions to force have always been alleviation and compliance."[33]

Later scholars in Israel continued to refute what was seen as the tendency to dismiss Jewish resistance as insignificant, not only by bringing to light lesser known cases of armed resistance that took place beyond Warsaw, but by expanding the definition of the term "resistance" to encompass a much broader spectrum of Jewish responses to persecution. In his study of the development of resistance in Warsaw, Israel Gutman (born in Warsaw in 1923 and a member of the Jewish Fighting Organization in the ghetto who also testified at the Eichmann trial) sought to provide a comprehensive overview of the development of armed resistance within the context of life in the ghetto from 1939 to 1943.

As he noted in the preface to *The Jews of Warsaw*: "one cannot detach the acts of resistance and the armed uprising from the broader character of Jewish public life as it took shape during the periods of the occupation and the ghetto. . . . It is impossible to understand the significance of the resistance and the uprising without appreciating the tensions and human and social conditions that existed during the Holocaust."[34] Gutman was among the first historians of the Warsaw Ghetto Uprising to make use of the materials collected by Ringelblum and the Oneg Shabbes archive to situate the development of armed resistance against the broader context of the Jewish struggle to survive in the ghetto. Rather than limiting himself to the reports of those involved in the military or underground action, Gutman's comprehensive study offered a synthesis of the available source material in German, Polish, Yiddish, and Hebrew, to overcome the challenge of relying on only one viewpoint or the tendency to overlook the broad range of Jewish responses before revolt. Still, by largely overlooking the experiences of those not affiliated with the ŻOB during the revolt (both the ŻZW [Jewish Military Union] and the majority of Jews who endured the final battle in the ghetto on their own) and by making the revolt the endpoint of his study, Gutman did not question the centrality of the Warsaw Ghetto Uprising as a turning point in Jewish history or the ways in which the collective memory of the revolt was shaped by those who survived it.

Nonetheless, along with Yehuda Bauer, Gutman's work helped expand the scope of research on Jewish responses to persecution among Holocaust historians in Israel, who began to broaden the definition of "resistance" and *amidah* beyond armed combat.[35] Bauer also cautioned against overemphasizing the degree of resistance, both armed and unarmed, physical and spiritual, that took place under German occupation, noting that despite many forms of *amidah*, "life was hell, the people were starving to death, and that when survivors tell us that inmates of the Lodz or Warsaw ghetto made attempts to educate their children, for instance, these attempts were heroic, but they did not encompass all or even most of the children, and they were part of a constant struggle against impossible odds."[36] The impact of resistance should not be measured according to the effect it had on German policies, but according to its effect on those Jews who fought and on postwar Jewish consciousness. Nonetheless, as Bauer argued, "the motivations of the rebels were several" and included the desire for revenge, escape, a drive to participate in the fight against a murderous regime for the liberation of a common homeland, to "make a moral and political statement as Jews by taking up arms against the murders of Jews," and finally, in the defense of Jewish honor to convey a message to Jews in the free world: "for three lines in history that will be written about the youth who fought and did not go like sheep to the slaughter it is even worth dying."[37] Bauer's call to explain the origins of the "instinct for Jewish resistance" indeed demands further investigation: Was the call for armed struggle a "Jewish response"? Was it a secular, modern response that threw off centuries of *Kiddush haShem*? Is it even possible to categorize the broad range of motivations that led Jewish rebels to fight back?[38] And was armed resistance the culmination of all other forms of underground activity? Bauer suggests that if we can understand the motivations of those Jews who engaged in resistance, we might be better suited to interpret its meaning and message for the future.

Nonetheless, in his popular history of the Warsaw Ghetto Uprising, *Resistance* (1994), Gutman reinforced the notion that "the Uprising was literally a revolution in Jewish history."[39] Gutman framed the revolt in Jewish terms as an event that transcended history:

> The Warsaw Ghetto Uprising is a historical event, but it also has become a symbol of Jewish resistance and determination, a moment in history that has transformed the self-perception of the Jewish people from passivity to active armed struggle. The Uprising has shaped Israel's national self-understanding. It is viewed as the first Jewish rebellion since the heroic days of the Bar Kochba revolt in 135 CE. The Uprising has become a universal symbol of resistance and courage.[40]

And in his detailed account of the uprising, Dan Kurzman writes that the "military encounter" in the Warsaw ghetto "symbolically ended two thousand years of Jewish submission to discrimination, oppression, and finally, genocide. It signaled the beginning of an iron militancy rooted in the will to survive, a militancy that was to be given form and direction by the creation of the state of Israel."[41]

Here we have the historiographical parameters within which the Warsaw Ghetto Uprising is interpreted—from the perspective of World War II history, while understood as the last, desperate act of a doomed people, it was an event that had little impact on the course of the war. From the perspective of Jewish history, however, the event came to be explained as the most significant event since the Bar Kochba revolt of 135 CE, celebrated as a revolution in Jewish history, as the counterproof to the myth that Jews did not fight back, and generally linked to the struggle for the creation of the Jewish state after the war.

In responding to the notion that the Warsaw Ghetto Uprising was rooted in an iron militancy that was given form by the creation of the State of Israel, more recent literature in Israel has questioned the role of the Jewish state in shaping a particular Zionist memory of the Holocaust. This approach analyzes the role of the state and sociocultural structures in shaping collective memory, thereby influencing the way in which history is written and remembered.[42] According to Yael Zerubavel, in the shaping of collective memory, "the master commemorative narrative thus presents these events as *turning points* that changed the course of the group's historical development and hence are commemorated in great emphasis and elaboration. In turn, the selection of certain events as turning points highlights the ideological principles underlying the master commemorative narrative by dramatizing the transitions between periods."[43] In this sense, the Warsaw Ghetto Uprising is presented within the Zionist master commemorative narrative as a turning point in Jewish history, which changed the course of the Jewish nation's historical development.[44] In the case of the Warsaw Ghetto Uprising, the actors who participated in the uprising, the ghetto fighters who lived to tell the tale, the writers, journalists, politicians, and historians all played a role in shaping a particular collective memory of the revolt. However, as this book will demonstrate, the process of shaping a particular memory of the war did not take place in the decades after .the war; instead this process began contemporaneously, as events unfolded in the ghetto.

This reexamination not only applies to the ways in which the Holocaust has been reinterpreted in the shaping of Israeli national tradition. We must also reexamine the ways in which Holocaust history, memory, and awareness developed in the United States, especially among Jews, and the timing of these developments. Peter Novick, for example, argues that collective memory of the Holocaust in the American context was exploited for Jewish political needs, usually in support of Israel, and that it did not develop until the 1960s.[45] In response to Novick's argument that American Jews paid little attention to the Holocaust until the 1960s, Hasia Diner categorically refutes the myth of silence, demonstrating that American Jews publicly and privately commemorated the Shoah in a multitude of ways between 1945 and 1962; and while she notes that the Warsaw Ghetto Uprising became the prism through which American Jews "performed the memory of the six million," she leaves as an open question why this might have been:

> Why did the Warsaw Ghetto become the prism through which American Jews performed the memory of the six million? Did the heroism of the ghetto fighters offer them something to be proud of rather than something that caused shame? Did they use the Warsaw Ghetto as a magnet for the

community mourning because other images of the Holocaust inspired in them embarrassment and discomfort?[46]

Diner disproves Novick's thesis that the Holocaust was marginalized in early postwar years, clearly demonstrating the early and frequent invocation of the Holocaust in American Jewish life.[47] But does this refute or reinforce Novick's thesis of political instrumentalization of Holocaust memory? Certainly as survivor testimony has proliferated since the 1980s, offering a much broader spectrum of Jewish experiences during the war, historical accounts have focused on the diverse range of experiences. The diversity has found its way into popular culture, with a broad range of books and films. And yet the dualities of martyrs and fighters, passivity and resistance, contintue to delineate the spectrum of response.

Because in many ways the major frameworks for understanding Jewish history have not changed after the Holocaust, the categories of passivity and resistance have endured. As David Engel's research has shown, the Holocaust (and the uprising in Warsaw) was certainly not a revolution in the writing of Jewish history. Speaking in 2002 at the Maurice and Corinne Greenberg Inaugural Lecture at the United States Holocaust Memorial Museum (USHMM), Engel argued that the "one area of humanistic study where the Holocaust has *not* exerted any notable influence has been the study of *Jewish* history."[48] Accordingly, Engel argues in *Historians of the Jews and the Holocaust* that the major parameters for interpreting and understanding Jewish history were shaped before the Holocaust and did not change during or after the war. The existing frameworks for interpreting Jewish history have largely framed the ways in which events (like the Warsaw Ghetto Uprising) were interpreted at the time and subsequently. More recent works on the history of the Holocaust, such as Saul Friedlander's *The Years of Extermination*, seek to correct some of the oversights of previous generations of historiography by writing an "integrated history" of the Holocaust that should, according to Friedlander, "include the reactions (and at times the initiatives) of the surrounding world and the attitudes of the victims, for the fundamental reason that the events we call the Holocaust represent a totality defined by this very convergence of distinct elements."[49] Friedlander's account provides a more balanced assessment of the meaning and impact of the revolt in Warsaw, too, which he interprets in light of Yehoshua Perle's harsh judgment of the Warsaw ghetto population in *Khurbn Varshe*. Perle, a Polish-Jewish novelist active in the Yiddish underground cultural organization in the Warsaw ghetto, YIKOR, wrote *Khurbn Varshe* for the Oneg Shabbes archive in October 1942 after the deportations to Treblinka, and condemned Jewish behavior, and especially Jewish leadership in the ghetto, writing that "each one (in Warsaw) was out to save his own skin. Each one was ready to sacrifice even his own father, his own mother, his own wife and children."[50]

According to Friedlander, then:

> The events of April 1943 introduced a new perspective. Of course the Warsaw fighters did not seek even a minimal success in military terms. Whether they wanted to redeem the image of Jews facing death, and to erase, so to speak, Perle's terrible verdict, is not certain, either. They knew that most of a leaderless, hungry, and utterly desperate mass could not but passively submit to unbridled violence, before the uprising and no less so in its wake. Not all of them meant to send a message to their own political movements in Eretz Israel or to the socialist community: For a long time already, many had given up on the active solidarity of their comrades outside Europe. They just wanted, as they had proclaimed, to die with dignity.[51]

All the same, Friedlander's work makes a potent suggestion: if the war and the relentless persecution led to a complete breakdown of Jewish social structures and any notion of Jewish solidarity, if in fact Yehoshua Perle was correct in his assessment that "each was out to save his own skin," then what was revolutionary about the revolt was not that it represented a throwing off of the yoke of Jewish passivity through a revolt against Nazi oppression; instead, the uprising literally represented a revolt against patterns of Jewish behavior and Jewish leadership that had developed under three years of

Nazi rule. The fact that a small group of Jews reflecting diverse political viewpoints were able to maintain Jewish solidarity under extreme persecution is noteworthy by itself.

Most recently, Havi Dreifuss's work, which expands on the experiences of thousands of Jews who remained in the ghetto until its final destruction (and were not affiliated with the Jewish Fighting Organization, which counted fewer than five hundred members) adds to a broader understanding of the final weeks and months of the ghetto. This approach again raises the question of Jewish solidarity there: Did the ghetto fighters see themselves acting on behalf of the Jewish masses or did they construct reasons for their actions in opposition to the behavior of the masses?[52] It is remarkable that in a field as rich as Holocaust studies, in a subject that has probably been examined more than any other, Dreifuss has identified a critical gap: What were the experiences of the forty thousand Jews left in the Warsaw ghetto after the deportations to Treblinka—those Jews who constituted the vast majority of the surviving Jewish population in Warsaw but were not members of the ŻOB or ŻZW? For decades, the historiography focused on the revolt, a process set into motion by the ghetto fighters themselves, who began writing reports of the uprising soon after the event, in the summer of 1943. By the end of April 1943, the revolt had seized the attention of the Jewish world and these reports found an audience eager to learn the identities of the "Jewish heroes of Warsaw." But these accounts did not tell the stories of the "Jewish masses," the surviving Jewish public unable to join the fighting organizations. Dreifuss's book corrects a major gap in the literature by telling their stories. Her new analysis challenges the distinction between "fighters" and "sheep to the slaughter" by offering a much broader context for resistance activities, challenging the notion of an armed underground responsible for the revolt (because for the revolt to succeed it needed the participation of the Jewish masses; the revolt did not succeed despite the Jewish masses), and instead reinforcing a point that actually emerged in early reports about the revolt in Warsaw—that it was distinguished by the fact it was a broad popular uprising. The revolt, Dreifuss argues, must be understood as the determined resistance of those thousands of unarmed Jews in the ghetto who resolved to go into hiding, defy deportation orders, and force the Germans to round up each and every Jew to complete the liquidation. Turning the historiography on its head, Dreifuss makes the convincing case that we have misunderstood the significance of the revolt for generations: it was not the battle of the armed fighters that made this such a unique historical event. As she argues: "There were those who emphasized that next to the armed struggle there was another struggle, the struggle of the masses of tens of thousands of Jews who hid in hiding places in the burning ghetto. Nonetheless the masses of the Jewish public—who in their lives and deaths gave the revolt its popular character—have never stood at the center of research and their fate has been ignored."[53]

The tens of thousands of Jews who lived in the Warsaw ghetto in its last months focused on one singular objective: survival. In doing so they also resisted German actions by resisting German attempts to exterminate them. This was distinct from the efforts of the underground, which was not focused on survival and not focused on victory but instead was focused on revenge. And yet, even if the revolt in the Warsaw ghetto was in fact distinguished by its broad popular character (and this book will point to numerous contemporaneous descriptions that supported this conclusion during and immediately after the event), we still need to understand how and why a particular memory of it was shaped in its aftermath.

All the same, even as the contours of this debate become apparent—whether the uprising in Warsaw reflects the Jewish ability to fight back, whether it was a revolution in Jewish history reflecting the determination of the Jewish people to reject the passivity of the Diaspora and embrace the need for the creation of the Jewish state, or whether it was a broad popular uprising of the thousands of Jews who remained in Warsaw determined to defy Nazi deportation orders—one common theme is clear: the specific identities of those who resisted in the ghetto became less significant than the idea that resistance had occurred. The names of certain Zionist leaders like Anielewicz, Zuckerman, and to a lesser extent Lubetkin, Altman, Kaplan, and Breslaw, became synonymous with the revolt, while the identities of hundreds and indeed thousands of others were forgotten. In a pamphlet issued by the World Jewish Congress on the tenth anniversary of the revolt, Dr. Itzhak Schwartzbart, who had served as a member of the Polish National Council in London and been among the first to receive the secret messages from Warsaw that relayed the news of the revolt, recalled the names of a series of fighters who died in the Jewish resistance: Mordecai Anielewicz, Michał Klepfisz, Aharon (Dolek) Liebeskind (leader of the Akiva Resistance Group in Kraków), Yitzhak Goldstein, Tosia Altman, Eliezer Geller, Shlomo Alterman, Rubin Rosenberg, Rifkah Glanz, Leib Grusalz, and Leib Rotblat. In the first year after the revolt, one name, that of Michał Klepfisz, became most associated with the revolt. Today his name, along with those of the other "Jewish heroes of Warsaw," is largely forgotten. History records the names of actors and events; collective memory determines what and whom we remember and forget.

There has been a tendency to see the Warsaw Ghetto Uprising as the paradigmatic example of Jewish resistance during the Holocaust and, at the same time, as the prime case of Zionist manipulation of history to suit its own ideological ends. To be sure, the Zionist movement did indeed make use of the uprising for political purposes, transforming its heroes into symbols of the Zionist revolt against diaspora history. But this book will show that the interpretation of the Warsaw Ghetto Uprising as a symbol of Jewish resistance had its roots in the period *before* the war. That is, the frameworks for understanding the significance of the resistance were shaped before the Holocaust, not in response to it or to certain events.

When the news of the uprising first reached the outside world, it was interpreted as an event of mythological proportions, standing outside of history. The timing of the revolt coincided with a Jewish awareness of the mass destruction of European Jewry, anger at the apathy of the surrounding world, and intense feelings of powerlessness to stop the destruction and arouse the conscience of the so-called civilized world. This context shaped the ways in which news of the revolt would be interpreted at the time, laying the foundation for a transnational collective memory of the revolt. If Jews in the outside world perceived the event from the perspective of complete abandonment and annihilation, the Jewish fighters of Warsaw did so to an even greater extent, and there was no way to convey the trauma of what they had endured to the outside world. Even so, participants in the revolt worked to shape the historical narrative. In the first year after the revolt, the Jewish Labor Bund seized credit for organizing and leading it. By the second anniversary, in response to reports drafted by the surviving Zionist members of the underground in Warsaw, the Zionist movement began to claim leadership, arguing the revolt was part of the struggle for the creation of the Jewish state. The dynamic interplay between the accounts of witnesses to the final liquidation of the ghetto, the frameworks for understanding the destruction of European Jewry at the time, and the subsequent memory of the revolt will be the focus of this book. The chapters that follow focus on the ways in which the Warsaw Ghetto Uprising was first reported in April and May of 1943 and subsequently interpreted and commemorated in the first ten years after the revolt, primarily in America, the Yishuv and then Israel, the Jewish displaced persons camps of postwar Germany, and by the surviving ghetto fighters who remained in Poland.

1

The Centrality of Warsaw

Warsaw was not the first ghetto to revolt but it would become the most famous case of Jewish resistance during the war, and in some ways would come to obscure almost every other case of armed revolt and resistance, despite the efforts of the surviving ghetto fighters themselves to highlight resistance elsewhere. As events unfolded in Warsaw, the ways in which they were reported, perceived, and understood at the time would influence subsequent historical writing on the revolt. In order to understand how this process worked, it is necessary to examine the factors leading to the development of armed resistance in Warsaw and the ways in which information was able to travel from Warsaw, through occupied Poland, to the wider world.

What was it about Warsaw that captured the attention of the Jewish world? In 1939, Warsaw was the second largest Jewish city in the world; only New York had a larger Jewish population at the time. Rapid industrialization and urbanization in the nineteenth century helped turn Warsaw into a major Jewish center, making it the largest Jewish city in Europe (Warsaw's population of 337,000 Jews in 1914 was equal to the Jewish population of France).[1] Warsaw became the capital of an independent Poland after World War I, and Jews from parts of the newly created Poland that had formerly been part of the Austro-Hungarian empire (like Galicia) or the Russian empire streamed toward the new capital, eager to partake in the economic, educational, and political opportunities it offered. As the population of Warsaw grew in the interwar period, so did its Jewish population, although the number of Jews as a percentage of the overall population declined (by 1938, the 368,394 Jews in Warsaw constituted 29.1 percent of the total population of 1.265 million).[2] Following emancipation in the nineteenth century and the removal of legal restrictions on Jews in Congress Poland in 1862, Jews were allowed to live wherever they wished in Warsaw, but the northwestern section of the city, especially Muranów, became the cultural, economic, social, and religious center of Jewish life. In 1938, Jews comprised no less than 90.5 percent of all inhabitants in the Muranów district alone.[3] While Jews were increasingly dispersed around the city, the center of Jewish Warsaw remained around the Nalewki, a hectic thoroughfare awash with shouting peddlers, artisans, the unemployed, and those employed in legal and illegal ways.

Over the course of the 1930s, and especially after the death of Marshall Pilsudski in May 1935, the situation of the Jews in Poland (and of Jewish Warsaw) deteriorated, as public expressions of hostility against Jews increased, along with calls for the emigration of Jews from Poland, the establishment of separate seating for Jews (ghetto benches) in the universities, and a general increase in violence against Jews. At the same time, as prospects for migration to Palestine decreased with the growing "Arab revolt" after 1936, the political influence of Zionist parties declined and the Bund (along with the more radical right-wing Revisionist Zionists and the Communists) enjoyed greater popularity among the Jewish population of Warsaw.

The Bund's platform, which called for a culturally autonomous Jewish people living in a socialist state, increasingly focused on specifically Jewish issues in the interwar period, as the Bund played a central role in organizing Jewish trade unions, representing Jews professionally as workers and nationally as Jews. The Bund came to see itself as representing the "Jewish masses" more broadly and enjoyed most of its electoral success on the local level, winning seventeen of the twenty city council seats taken by members of Jewish parties in the Warsaw municipal elections of 1938; in December 1938 it won fourteen seats (61.7 percent of the Jewish vote), as opposed to five seats for the Jewish National Bloc, which included both Zionists and Agudas Yisroel, and one for the Democratic Zionists.[4]

Ideologically, the Bund was completely opposed to Zionism, which its leaders understood as representing only the interests of "bourgeois" Jews and offering false promises to solve Jewish problems "there" (in Palestine) not "here" (in Eastern Europe), which Jews had made their home for centuries. In general, the Bund refused to collaborate with any of the Zionist parties (with the exception of the socialist Left Poalei Zion); as will be seen, such internal divisions within the Jewish community, between political parties and youth movements, would have implications for the development of the Jewish underground during the war. During the war, however, the Bund continued to maintain connections to the Polish government-in-exile, as well as to party leaders in New York, and Bund reports smuggled out of Warsaw would be an important factor in the spread of information about the war in Poland and development of the Final Solution.[5]

From the Outbreak of War to Creation of the Ghetto in Warsaw

In August 1939, just before the outbreak of the war, the 375,000 Jews in Warsaw made up approximately 30 percent of the city's total population. While some Jews in Poland assumed that events in Germany were still distant, more and more Jews in Warsaw and throughout Poland anxiously tracked developments in the German Reich over the summer of 1939, as it became increasingly clear war was likely to break out. With the outbreak of war on September 1, 1939, Jews and non-Jews alike suffered from the indiscriminate bombing of the Luftwaffe. A JDC (American Jewish Joint Distribution Committee) report in Warsaw estimated twenty thousand Jews were killed in the first month of the war, with seven thousand Jews killed in Warsaw alone in September 1939.[6] In the first weeks of the war, Warsaw's Jewish population fluctuated as a result of mobilization, flight to the East, and the arrival of refugees fleeing the advancing German army; by early 1940, the Jewish population of Warsaw swelled to some four hundred thousand as Jews from areas annexed to the Reich were deported to the *Generalgouvernement*, and refugees crowded into Warsaw.[7] This only further compounded the scarcity of housing, food, and medical supplies in the city.

Adam Czerniakow, who had served as deputy chair of the Jewish community before the war, was appointed head of the Jewish community by the mayor of Warsaw, Stefan Starzynski, on September 23. He would subsequently be named head of the Warsaw Jewish Council (*Judenrat*) under the Nazis. At the beginning of the war in September 1939 most of the official Polish Jewish leadership fled east from Warsaw and the other major cities of Poland, bound for Vilna, the Soviet Union, or abroad, while others were captured, imprisoned, and executed. Among the leaders who fled at the beginning of the war were the leaders of all of the major Jewish political parties and movements in Poland: from the General Zionists, Moshe Kleinbaum (Sneh), Apolinary Hartglas, and Moshe Kerner; from the Bund, Henryk Erlich and Victor Alter; from Poalei Zion Z.S., Anshel Reiss and Abraham Bialopolski; from Mizrachi, Zerah Warhaftig and Aaron Weiss; from Left Poalei Zion, Yitzhak Leib and Nathan Buksbaum; from Agudat Israel, Yitzhak Meir Levin; and from Betar and the Revisionist party, Menachem Begin.[8] The flight of the leadership during the first week of the war left Warsaw without most of its political leadership (from across the political spectrum) and most directors of Jewish relief organizations.[9]

After the start of the war, however, a number of Zionist youth leaders who had managed to flee to the east made the decision to return to occupied Poland. This was the case among the youth movement leadership of Warsaw, many of whom had fled to Vilna in order to escape the Nazi invasion in September 1939. The leaders of Hashomer Hatzair (including Haim Holtz, Zelig Geyer, Yosef Shamir, Yitzhak Zalmanson, and Tosia Altman) decided that "as long as there is a Jewish community in Poland, the movement must be there."[10] Taking refuge in Vilna at the start of the war (Vilna would fall under German occupation after June 1941), movements like Hashomer Hatzair shifted their focus from solely training an elite cadre of movement members for *aliyah* (emigration) to the Land of Israel, to a broader effort to represent the wider Jewish public in the struggle against Nazism, and to an ideological position that would enable them to support the Soviet Union in this struggle.[11] The Hashomer Hatzair movement leadership sent emissaries from Vilna back to the occupied zone of Poland, first sending Tosia Altman, later to be followed by Yosef Kaplan, Mordecai Anielewicz, and Josef Kaplan.[12] Likewise, the Dror movement decided at a secret conference in L'vov on December 31, 1939, to send Zivia Lubetkin to Warsaw; she was followed several months later by Yitzhak Zuckerman.[13] While much of the leadership of the Bund fled Warsaw, Abrasha (Abraham) Blum (1905–43) was one of the few Bund leaders who remained in Warsaw and would eventually become a member of the Jewish Fighting Organization (ŻOB) and one of the leading figures in the revolt. As the Bund's veteran leadership left Warsaw, younger leaders like Abrasha Blum, who were members of the Tsukunft youth movement, helped prevent the complete disintegration of the party.

The youth movement leaders who returned to Warsaw were motivated by a sense of responsibility as local leaders, not only to their young *chanichim* (movement trainees) but to the Jewish community as a whole. These youth movement leaders (like Zionists Mordechai Anielewicz, Zivia Lubetkin, Yitzhak Zuckerman, Josef Kaplan, Frumka Plotnicka, Tosia Altman, and Shmuel Breslaw; along with Abrasha Blum, Marek Edelman, Leon Feiner, and other members of the Bund) would play a key role in the formation of the ghetto underground, and eventually, the Jewish Fighting Organization, or ŻOB. On the other hand, it was a group of Jewish military officers who had participated in the defense of Poland in September 1939, including Kalman Mendelson, a Revisionist and former officer in the Polish Army, Henryk Lipszyc-Lipiński, and Szymon Białoskóra (Białoskórnik), who would form the core nucleus from which developed the Revisionist Zionist fighting organization, the ŻZW. Later, along with Leon Rodal, members of Betar, the Revisionist Zionist youth movement, including Peretz Lasker and Pawel Frenkel, joined and helped to further organize the group.[14]

By September 28, 1939, the siege of Warsaw was over, with fully one quarter of the city's buildings having been destroyed, and as many as fifty thousand citizens killed or injured.[15] As the Wehrmacht entered the city and organized soup lines for the starving population, Jews quickly experienced the changing dynamics of Polish society under German occupation. In addition to the rapid process of social isolation and extreme persecution that quickly unfolded in Warsaw and throughout occupied Poland, the official establishment of the *Generalgouvernement*, which replaced the German military administration under the leadership of Hans Frank, soon subjected Jews to special decrees that limited them to two thousand zlotys in cash, blocked their access to bank accounts, limited Jewish use of trains and public transport, instituted the "aryanization" of Jewish businesses, and subjected Jews between the ages of fourteen and sixty to random seizure for forced labor.[16] By December 1, 1939, Hans Frank had decreed that all Jews over the age of ten residing in the *Generalgouvernement* must wear white armbands with a Star of David on the right sleeve of their clothing.[17]

Szmuel Zygielbojm, the Bundist leader and member of the first Warsaw *Judenrat* (Jewish council) (before his escape from Poland in February 1940, first to France, then New York, and finally London), detailed the efforts of the *Judenrat* to intervene and prevent random kidnappings of Jews for forced labor in the fall of 1939 as Jews young and old were seized in the streets to perform hard labor, enduring terrible torture in the process:

> The Warsaw Jewish Community approached the Gestapo with a proposal: if the German occupation authorities need people for labor, they should obtain them in an organized fashion; but the kidnapping of people in the street must stop. . . . From that time (November 1939) the Warsaw Jewish Community did, indeed, provide two thousand Jews a day for labor service. But the kidnappings of Jews from the streets did not stop.[18]

The Jewish council, which had sought to end the indignity and harassment of random kidnappings, had now obligated itself to provide two thousand workers for the Germans daily, even as random seizures continued. For the Jewish public in Warsaw, this seemed to make the *Judenrat* complicit in German policy, eventually opening a space for an alternative underground leadership in Jewish Warsaw to emerge as the Nazi policy of persecution continued and increased.

Following the occupation of Warsaw, German military leaders discussed the idea of creating a ghetto in Warsaw, although the idea was initially shelved for economic reasons, partly in response to petitions from Jewish leaders in the city, who argued that imprisoning the Jewish population in a ghetto would lead to the rapid spread of disease. On March 27, 1940, however, the Warsaw *Judenrat* received orders to begin the construction of walls around a "plague-infected area" in the Jewish residential section of Warsaw, and, as noted by Czerniaków in his diary, on April 13, 1940, the Jews of Warsaw were even ordered to pay to build their own ghetto walls.[19] By the beginning of June at least twenty sections of the wall had been erected and in August 1940, German authorities issued an official announcement that the city would be divided into German, Polish, and Jewish quarters.[20]

On Yom Kippur 1940 (October 12), the Jews of Warsaw were informed by announcements made over street megaphones that all Jews in the city would be required to move into the ghetto by the end of the month.[21] As Chaim Kaplan put it in his diary, the Jews of Warsaw were gradually being imprisoned in their own dungeon, walls rising before their very eyes.

> In all the thoroughfares leading to the Aryan quarters, high walls are being erected. . . . Before our eyes a dungeon is being built in which half a million men, women, and children will be imprisoned, no one knows for how long. (November 10, 1940) What we dreaded most has come to us. . . . We went to bed in the "Jewish quarter," and the next morning we awoke in a closed Jewish ghetto, a ghetto in every detail. (November 17, 1940)[22]

On November 15, 1940, German authorities ordered the Warsaw ghetto in the *Generalgouvernement* sealed off, creating the largest ghetto in both area and population in Poland. Over 350,000 Jews, approximately 30 percent of the city's population, were confined to about 2.4 percent of Warsaw's total area. Over 120,000 additional refugees would later be sent to the city, bringing the total population of the ghetto to nearly 500,000.[23]

The population of the ghetto fluctuated over the course of 1941, both as a result of the influx of refugees from smaller cities and towns in the Warsaw district and as a result of the staggering death rate within the ghetto as a result of starvation and disease. Approximately 43,000 inhabitants (10 percent of the ghetto population) died over the course of 1941, marking the period before the initiation of the mass deportation as the period of "gradual extermination."[24] The sealing of the ghetto left Warsaw's Jews completely isolated and without access to sufficient nourishment—food shortages became the primary concern of the ghetto's inhabitants. The *Judenrat* assumed a position of significance that the prewar *kahal* (Jewish community council) never had, directing all aspects of daily life in the ghetto and forming the Jewish administration within the ghetto. The areas of *Judenrat* responsibility included basic nutrition, public health (and prevention of the spread of disease), sanitation (removal of garbage from the ghetto), public order (police and firefighting), housing, and registration of the ghetto inhabitants. The *Judenrat* not only had to administer daily affairs, but also to ensure compliance with German regulations. It oversaw the establishment of hospitals and clinics, cultural activities and education, welfare and mutual aid institutions, and orphanages.[25] By using the *Judenrat* as their conduit to control Jewish life in the ghetto, the Germans also successfully deflected much of the direct rage of the population at the abominable conditions in the ghetto onto the *Judenrat* itself, and onto the other hated Jewish institution in the ghetto, the Jewish police. The Jewish police, headed by Jozef Szerynski (a Jewish convert to Catholicism), numbered 1,635 policemen, and was responsible for directing traffic, supervising trash collection and sanitation, preventing crime, and adjudicating disputes between Jews in the ghetto.[26] While the Jewish police were subject to the supervision of the Polish police, over time it became clear that the Gestapo and the *Sicherheitsdienst* (security service, or SD) would pass orders directly to the Jewish police; this became abundantly clear during the mass deportations in July 1942, when the *Judenrat* was sidelined by the Jewish police, who supervised the roundups in direct communication with the German authorities. (One of the first actions of the Jewish underground after the period of the Great Deportations was to take revenge on perceived collaborators among the Jewish police). Beyond the Jewish police, Abraham Gancwajch headed Force 13 (so named for the address of its headquarters at 13 Leszno Street) a unit established under the supervision of the German security police as the Office to Combat Usury and Profiteering in the Jewish Quarter of Warsaw. While Gancwajch engaged in a bitter power struggle with the *Judenrat*'s Czerniakow to assume power in the ghetto, arguing that Jews must understand that the Germans would win the war and operate accordingly under this new reality, his office was nonetheless eventually shut down by Heinz Auerswald (German Commissioner of the Jewish quarter in Warsaw).[27]

Grass Roots Social Welfare in the Ghetto

Under the extreme conditions created in the ghetto—the food crisis, the economic crisis, the housing crisis, the public health crisis, and the refugee crisis—the work of social welfare organizations to address all of these issues became critical. Voluntary Jewish organizations that existed before the war to aid the weak and the needy continued to function, augmenting and often exceeding the efforts of the *Judenrat* to provide for the Jewish public. The Jewish Self-Help (Żydowska Samopomoc Spoleczna [ŻSS]; renamed ŻTOS in October 1940, then ŻSS in November 1941) was funded by the "Joint" (the JDC), and worked in cooperation with the *Judenrat*.[28] The JDC also transferred funds from American contributors to local self-help organizations like TOZ, a health and sanitation organization and CENTOS, which cared for orphans.[29]

The Warsaw Aleynhilf (literally, self-help) organization was the name for the Jewish relief movement that grew out of the Warsaw-based Coordinating Commission of Jewish Aid and Social Societies in the first days of the war. Emanuel Ringelblum played an important role in the work of the group, which assumed even more prominence in the ghetto, coordinating the grassroots Jewish relief efforts of the house committees and other groups.[30] The house committees were centered in the inner courtyards of the large apartment buildings in the Jewish quarter, which seemed to offer more security from the dangers of the street. As Samuel

Kassow suggests, "the house committees quickly became the basis of public life in the Warsaw ghetto," providing communal kitchens, child care, shelter for the sick, and a safe place for social interaction.[31] By April 1940, 778 such committees had been set up in the Jewish quarter of the city, and eventually this number would reach 1,518, covering more than two thousand houses. The committees received contributions from their members as well as from the ŻSS and other organizations.[32] The JDC also worked to alleviate the suffering of Warsaw's Jews and feed the starving population. Because of its international status, access to American resources, and experience on the ground and in cooperative projects, the Joint served as the most important source of support for all Polish Jews. In Warsaw alone between October 1939 and September 1940, the Joint counted 10,101,963 meals distributed.[33] In the course of 1940, the Joint spent almost fifteen million zlotys on relief work before dropping to a mere eight million in 1941. After the American entry into the war in December 1941, JDC funds from the United States became largely unavailable, although through the efforts of David Guzik, Isaac Gitterman, and Emanuel Ringelblum, the Warsaw office of the JDC continued to operate.[34]

Cultural, Religious, and Educational Activity in the Ghetto

In addition to the organization of social welfare, an active cultural, educational, and religious life continued in the ghetto, despite the abominable conditions and a German ban on most educational activities. Elementary and secondary schools functioned, and vocational training and university-level lectures were still being conducted. Although religious services in the ghetto were officially banned, Jews continued to worship in secret, even as maintaining Jewish religious law became increasingly difficult, and visibly observant Jews were often singled out for the harshest persecution. Emanuel Ringelblum helped found a society for the advancement of Yiddish culture (Yidishe Kultur Organizatsye—YIKOR) in the ghetto. His most important initiative, however, was the creation of the Oneg Shabbes underground archive—the secret archive of the Warsaw ghetto. Begun as an individual chronicle by Ringelblum in October 1939, the archive was transformed into an organized underground operation with several dozen contributors after the sealing of the ghetto in November 1940.[35] Ringelblum organized the Oneg Shabbes archive around the networks of the Aleynhilf—using the refugee points, soup kitchens, house committees, and underground schools to provide the information, documents, and testimonies for the archive. After July 22, 1942, the archive documented the Great Deportation, collecting posters that had called on Jews to assemble for transport and the desperate appeals from those waiting to board deportation trains (to Treblinka). These records were crammed into milk cans along with later posters calling for armed resistance in 1943. Two of Ringelblum's young collaborators on his documentation effort, Josef Kaplan and Shmuel Breslaw of Hashomer Hatzair, would become early leaders of the armed resistance in the Warsaw ghetto.[36] Hersh Wasser was the secretary of the underground Oneg Shabbes archive; together with Rachel Auerbach, he was one of only two of the primary activists to survive and help recover the archive after the war. The materials collected demonstrate that despite the hardships of life in the ghetto, Jews believed they could maintain elements of communal life under such circumstances, holding out hope for survival until the war ended.

Youth Movements and the Formation of the Ghetto Underground

Under the German occupation, Jewish youth, especially those organized in Zionist and Bundist youth movements, worked to better understand the needs of a wider Jewish public. Whereas before the war, the activities of Zionist youth movements had been focused on the "elite" among Jewish youth training for *aliyah* to Palestine, during the war their sense of responsibility and range of activities broadened. As part of their educational efforts, Zionist youth movements established kibbutz groups and underground schools in the ghettos throughout Eastern Europe. Through continued activity during the war, communication between ghettos, and the establishment of an underground press, Zionist youth groups maintained better organization than other political groups (which collapsed or were greatly weakened under the weight of German persecution and exterminatory policies). Through the broader scope of underground activities during the war and a network that facilitated the dissemination of knowledge despite the extreme isolation of the ghetto, the youth movements were well suited to emerge as an alternative leadership in the ghetto, and eventually organize the resistance movement in Warsaw.

Before the scope of the Nazi plan to exterminate European Jewry became evident and the underground began to focus on organizing armed resistance, youth movements within the ghettos worked to improve Jewish morale and rescue what they deemed to be an increasingly alienated, isolated, and demoralized youth suffering bitterly from the persecution and privations of the occupation, forming study groups, schools, and collective social frameworks, while also providing food and shelter to children and adults. While numbers are difficult to establish, Dror Hechalutz counted an estimated three hundred members in Warsaw: Hashomer Hatzair, eight hundred; Hanoar Hatzioni, 160; and Betar, probably several hundred—one of Betar's eight Warsaw groups had eighty *chanichim* (or trainees).[37] Youth movement activists like Frumka Plotnicka, Mordecai Tennenbaum, Yitzhak Zuckerman, Tuvia Borzykowski, and Zivia Lubetkin helped to establish a broad educational-political-underground system which adapted to the new circumstances in the ghetto. As part of the wartime transition the youth movements began to change their view of the Jewish street and their responsibility to the Jewish masses, feeling increased solidarity with the plight of their fellow Jews (and not just the elite) struggling under the burden of decrees, starvation, and death. Tuvia Borzykowski, born in Lodz in 1914, spent his childhood and youth in Radomsk, where he was located at the start of the war. In the middle of 1940, Tuvia was called to the Dror HeHalutz central offices in Warsaw and participated in the organization of illegal seminars and development of widespread educational activities among the youth. As he wrote in the underground newspaper of the Dror youth movement in 1940, the youth movement sensed that it had a responsibility to take the broken and demoralized youth of Warsaw and save them from a "spiritual calamity" by providing them not only with education, but more importantly, with a secure social framework in a "warm, friendly environment."

> To instill the feeling of solidarity and responsibility . . . to awaken in them national feeling, give them a socialist consciousness, to activate them socially to all aspects of Jewish life, to familiarize them with all of the spiritual creation, which the Jewish people have formed throughout time. And finally, to concentrate the best segment of the Jewish youth, which have already received their instruction in our branches, as a front-line avant-garde of the Jewish youth.[38]

Such dedication to the spiritual state of the youth, while instilling solidarity and camaraderie among the members, would suit the movements well when the call for resistance came after the Great Deportation. Even so, the movements were focused on a small cadre of youth, and it is difficult to establish how widespread their impact was on the broader ghetto population.

Warsaw functioned as a central point of information gathering for youth movement members across Poland, with women playing a crucial role as underground couriers traveling between ghettos under false identities. Over the course of 1941, movements like Hashomer Hatzair and Betar managed to reopen prewar agricultural training farms, which they adapted to wartime conditions by obtaining permission from German authorities to identify agricultural work on the farm as a work camp (Hashomer Hatzair in Zarki, near Częstochowa, and Betar in Hrubieszow).[39] Under the leadership of Peretz Lasker, Betar managed to transfer many of its members from the closed Warsaw ghetto to the movement's farm near Hrubieszow, where in the summer and fall of 1941, Betar members worked, listened to lectures, and engaged in military training.[40] The underground press of the youth movements also served as a key source of information on events throughout Poland, conveying information gathered by intrepid movement members otherwise denied to the ghetto inhabitants. Access to information about the scope of the Nazi annihilation of the Jews of

Eastern Europe after the summer 1941 played a key role in the formation of the resistance groups in the Warsaw ghetto.

The Bund was also responsible for organizing a wide range of activities in Warsaw, reaching a broader cross-section of the Jewish public than the pioneering Zionist youth movements. While the party's veteran leadership left Warsaw at the start of the war, young members of the Tsukunft youth movement assumed a leadership role, led by Abrasha Blum (1905–43), who had come to Warsaw from Vilna in 1929. More than anyone else, Blum was responsible for maintaining the Bund's work in Warsaw and preventing the complete disintegration of the party. Like the Zionist parties, the Bund established an underground network that offered both educational and political activities to teenagers and youth in the Warsaw ghetto. Thanks to its prewar political leadership and its connections with Polish political parties, the Bund was in much closer contact with the Polish underground, with the Polish government-in-exile, and with political leaders in London and New York. As the news of atrocities perpetrated in Lithuania and Poland began to spread at the beginning of 1942, the Bund drafted detailed reports authored by Leon Feiner (the Bund's principal liaison with the Polish underground) which, with the assistance of the Polish underground, were sent to London in May 1942. These reports played a pivotal role in spreading awareness of the Final Solution and included details on the use of gassing vans at Chelmno (although they underestimated the number of Jews murdered at the time—seven hundred thousand).[41]

The Bund's underground work in the Warsaw ghetto was supported in large measure by money transferred from the Jewish Labor Committee in New York to the Polish government-in-exile in London and then to Warsaw. (JDC, while technically prohibited from sending money to occupied Poland following the American entry into the war in December 1941, also organized relief through the ŻSS and employed IOUs: prosperous Jews in the ghetto with nowhere to stash their technically illegal funds were promised reimbursement for loans to the JDC, if they survived the war).[42]

The leaders of the pioneering youth movements who had returned to occupied Poland from Vilna after the start of the war (in the case of Hashomar Hatzair—Tosia Altman, Josef Kaplan, Mordecai Anielewicz, and Shmuel Breslaw) sought to maintain contact both with the movement in Vilna and the leadership in Palestine and the HeHalutz office in Geneva. Female members of the underground, like Tosia Altman, Frumka Plotnicka, and Chajke Grossman, played a key role traveling to the various movement branches in the *Generalgouvernement* and Galicia to assist in organizing the movement and sharing information between parts of occupied Poland. Feigele Peltel (later known as Vladka Meed) would become the most well known of the female couriers for the Bund after the war. These women risked their lives to smuggle material and information, as well as people, in and out of ghettos, using prevailing gender stereotypes, which kept women out of positions of leadership in other domains and made women (not circumcised) less likely to arouse suspicion, to engage in extremely dangerous activities essential to the underground.[43]

These youth movement leaders in turn became the leaders of the ghetto resistance and took the initiative in determining political and social action underground. Before the war, the Zionist youth movements were largely dependent on *shlichim* (emissaries) from Palestine in determining policy formation. During the war, however, largely cut off from the outside world and far more independent and autonomous than before, the youth movements functioned as a source of information from the outside world, emerging as an alternative leadership organization to the *Judenrat*. The youth movement leaders, because they were indeed younger than the other political leaders, were not confronted with the impossibly difficult task of serving on the *Judenrat*. Nonetheless, the youth movements quickly became highly critical of the *Judenrat* and Jewish police, often making them the first targets of both their political and physical attacks in the ghetto underground. The youth movements were some of the first to assess the early Jewish massacres as part of a comprehensive program, and were thus instrumental in the early organization of resistance.[44] The mobility of the youth movement leadership also enabled them to publicize the first news of atrocities in Lithuania, as Tosia Altman's return from Vilna accomplished in late 1941.[45]

After the German invasion of the Soviet Union in June 1941, contact between Warsaw and the movement leadership in Palestine became increasingly difficult. In the case of Hashomer Hatzair, after receiving reports of systematic slaughters of Jews taking place to the east, Tosia Altman traveled to Vilna in December 1941, entering the Vilna ghetto on Christmas Eve, together with Haika Grossman. While Altman argued to the movement members there that the movement should focus its efforts on saving the activist core of the movement located in Warsaw, Abba Kovner, leader of Hashomer Hatzair in Vilna, argued that the Nazi slaughter of the Jews in Lithuania and Poland was not local in nature, but part of an overall systematic plan bent on the total extermination of the Jews of Europe. As Ziva Shalev describes, Tosia Altman was told that a decision had been taken among the leadership of the various youth movements in Vilna that the Jews should not go to their deaths without a fight ("Let us not go like sheep to the slaughter," in the words of the manifesto composed by Abba Kovner). Shalev speculates that Altman may have even delivered the Vilna underground's manifesto to the Hashomer Hatzair members in the Warsaw ghetto.[46]

In Warsaw, the leadership of the Jewish public—both the alternate leadership of the youth movements and the official *Judenrat* leadership—initially met the reports of systematic extermination skeptically. Still, Hashomer Hatzair began to focus its efforts increasingly on organizing armed resistance. The timing of this realization and the subsequent decision to organize armed resistance would be a point of contention between the various movements during and after the war.

At the time, individual movements, including Hashomer Hatzair, the Bund, and Betar, began to come to the realization that the reports of murder throughout Poland pointed to the systematic nature of the extermination, necessitating a form of resistance that exceeded what they had so far engaged in and would require the acquisition of arms.[47] Nonetheless, each movement continued to function independently in its efforts to organize resistance. The underground reports of the Jewish National Committee and the Bund written in the year after the revolt would differ in their assessments of whether the decision to engage in armed revolt was taken before or after the large-scale deportations from Warsaw to Treblinka in the summer of 1942.

The Shift to Armed Resistance

At this point, the youth movements and the Bund began to change the focus of their activities—from maintaining an underground organization directing educational and cultural activities for youth in the ghetto to raise morale—to a concerted effort to prepare for armed resistance in the ghetto. The three main branches of the underground—the socialist-Zionist youth, Betar and the Revisionist Zionists, and the Bund—each worked to organize in the ghetto, usually separately. Efforts to acquire arms during this period were largely unsuccessful due to the inability to establish contacts with the Polish underground. Decisions over how and when to organize armed resistance would become a point of contention in reports drafted by the various movements after the revolt. Nonetheless, as Havi Dreifuss argues in her study of the Warsaw ghetto, it is important not to overestimate the impact of the underground movements on Jewish life in the ghetto before 1943. Even though the Jewish press in the ghetto published over three thousand pages of material printed by the various underground political parties, after two-and-a-half years of occupation, Jewish society underwent a certain process of atomization and began to disintegrate. Even though there is no doubt the ghetto was home to broad-based cultural, social, and religious activities, these were limited to specific groups, and their influence on the general public was limited. Just as there was no leadership in the ghetto that was accepted by the general public, underground groups and political organizations were seen to be taking care of their own, not the broader Jewish public.[48] This point is crucial for our subsequent analysis of the relationship between the underground and the broader Jewish public during the revolt: Were the ghetto fighters fighting for themselves or on behalf of the Jewish masses?

Meanwhile, as the cumulative process of extreme hunger, daily terror, and continued oppression led to the polarization and atomization of Jewish Warsaw, in the spring of 1942 the Germans had begun to implement the so-called Final Solution in the *Generalgouvernement* within the framework of Operation Reinhard, sending transports of Jews from the ghettos of Poland to the newly constructed killing centers at Belzec (where killing began in March 1942), Sobibor (May 1942), and Treblinka (July 1942). In his diary, Chaim Kaplan began to report the rumors that hinted at the systematic Nazi policy of extermination:

> It is reported that the Führer has decided to rid Europe of our whole people by simply having them shot to death. . . . You just take thousands of people to the outskirts of a city and shoot to kill; that is all. . . . In Vilna 40,000 Jews were shot to death. . . . Had [Hitler] not stated that if war erupted in Europe, the Jewish race would be annihilated? This process has begun and will continue until the end is achieved. (February 2, 1942)
>
> I was told by an acquaintance of mine who has seen the official documents that thousands of Jews have been killed by poison gas. It was an experiment to test its effectiveness. (February 23, 1942)[49]

By spring 1942, the details described by Kaplan in his diary became more specific as he included more detailed rumors regarding transports by rail cars and the execution of Lublin Jews. In June 1942 the news grew even worse and hinted at a more systematic slaughter of the Jews of the *Generalgouvernement*:

> A catastrophe will befall us at the hands of the Nazis and they will wreak their vengeance on us for their final downfall. The process of physical destruction of Polish Jewry has already begun. . . . Not a day goes by that the Nazis do not conduct a slaughter. . . . The rumors that reach us from the provincial towns are worse than the tidings of Job. (June 16, 1942)
>
> Every day Polish Jewry is being brought to slaughter. It is estimated . . . that three-quarters of a million Polish Jews have already passed from this earth. . . . Some of them are

> sent to a labor camp, where they survive for a month at the outside. . . . Some are shot; some are burned; some are poisoned with lethal gas; some are electrocuted. (June 25, 1942)
>
> It has been decreed and decided in Nazi ruling circles to bring systematic physical destruction upon the Jews of the General Government. . . . The killing of thousands of people has turned into a business that employs many hands. After the souls expire, they strip the corpses. Their clothing, shirts, and shoes are not wasted, but are collected in piles upon piles and turned over for disinfection, mending, and repairs. Hundreds of Jews are employed in these tasks. (July 10, 1942)[50]

Kaplan recorded the sense of bewilderment and confusion on the part of the ghetto's population as the liquidation approached, along with the dashed hopes of survival and the terror of deportation: "*There is an instinctive feeling that some terrible catastrophe is drawing near for the Warsaw ghetto, though no one can determine its time or details*" (June 20, 1942). Despite a brief moment of optimism that the deportation would be delayed, the announcement of the "resettlement" was devastating for Kaplan: "*I haven't the strength to hold a pen in my hand. I'm broken, shattered. . . . A whole community of 400,000 people condemned to exile*" (July 22, 1942).[51]

On July 22, 1942, the Great Deportation from the Warsaw ghetto to Treblinka began, as German SS and police authorities initiated the process that led to the deportation of approximately 275–300,000 Jews from the ghetto by September 12, 1942. Adam Czerniakow, chairman of the Warsaw ghetto *Judenrat*, decided to commit suicide on July 23, 1942, rather than comply with the deportation order, writing in his final note, "They are demanding that I kill the children of my people with my own hands. There is nothing for me to do but die."[52] Marek Edelman and Antek Zuckerman, both leaders of the ŻOB, later suggested that Czerniakow should not have died alone with the knowledge that "deportation to the East" actually meant death in the gas chambers; instead, they wished that he had called upon Jews in that moment to defend themselves.

Even so, the newly formed underground struggled to convince the leadership in the ghetto that the time was right for resistance. Many believed the Germans, hoping that after several thousand Jews were seized for deportation, the remainder of the population would be allowed to live. Better to sacrifice the few to save the many.

Chaim Kaplan's final diary entries captured the destruction of Jewish Warsaw:

> 30 July 1942
>
> The seventh day of the expulsion. Living funerals pass before the windows of my apartment—cattle trucks or coal wagons full of candidates for expulsion and exile, carrying small bundles under their arms.
>
> Their cries and shrieks and wails, which rent the very heavens and filled the whole area with noise, have already stopped. Most of the deportees seem resigned to their fate.

Kaplan evidently made his final entry a day or two before his own deportation to Treblinka; it read: "When my end comes—what will happen to the diary?" Chaim Kaplan and his wife are believed to have perished in Treblinka death camp.[53]

Rachel Auerbach, who had worked with Ringelblum in compiling materials for the Oneg Shabbes archive, was an eyewitness to the destruction of the ghetto. Writing on the Aryan side of Warsaw in November 1943, Auerbach wrote her own *Yizkor* prayer, recalling the Jewish prayer for the dead recited four times a year on Jewish holidays. She compared the deportations to a deluge, "that's how the Jewish masses flow to their destruction at the time of the deportations. Sinking as helplessly in the deluge of destruction . . . a yielding to the inevitable; a gravitation toward mass death that is no less substantial than the gravitation towards life. Sometimes the two antipodes follow each other in the same being. Who can render the stages of the dying of a people?" Auerbach's *Yizkor* which went on to list all of the different types deported to their horrible deaths from the ghetto, children, boys, girls, young men, workers, *halutzim* (Zionist pioneers), students, pious Jews, artisans, mothers, fathers, grandfathers, grandmothers, petty thieves, street vendors, bagel sellers, ghetto peddlers, ghetto smugglers, and more. Too many to list and too many to be remembered by name. "At the end of the prayer in which everyone inserts the names of members of his family there is a passage recited for those who have no one to remember them and who, at various times, have died violent deaths because they were Jews. And it is people like those who are now in the majority."[54]

Jewish masses sinking helplessly in the deluge of destruction—this was the image of Jewish Warsaw Auerbach could not erase from her mind. For those who had lived through the trauma of the deluge, the Warsaw ghetto of mid-September 1942 bore no resemblance to the ghetto of July. Dreifuss estimates approximately fifty-five thousand Jews were left in the ghetto after the deportation of three hundred thousand Jews to Treblinka (thirty-six thousand registered officially, under twenty thousand "illegals"). Of children and the elderly, 99 percent had been murdered; out of fifty-five thousand children in the ghetto before the deportations, only 250 remained.[55] The ghetto was divided into three main districts at the end of September 1942 (distinguished in later reports of the fighting): the central ghetto, the area of the brushmakers shops, and the workshops area.

In the fall of 1942, as reports regarding the deportations to Treblinka and Auschwitz, and the liquidation of Jewish communities throughout Poland, filtered into the ghetto, the various underground organizations struggled to create a unified armed resistance group.[56] Putting prewar political divisions aside, the left-wing and centrist Zionist youth movements (including Hashomer Hatzair, HeHalutz, Gordonia, Left Poalei Zion, Poalei Zion Z.S., and the General Zionists) joined together with the Communists to form a broad-based public political group, called the Jewish National Committee and an expanded ŻOB.[57] The newly formed group resolved to meet any renewed attempt at mass deportation with armed resistance. Even the Bund agreed to join the ŻOB after lengthy discussions, resolving to coordinate its activities with the Jewish National Committee and the Jewish Coordinating Committee with limited political cooperation (thus not betraying its political principles opposing Zionism). The ŻOB combat units would be organized around political parties and youth groups. Despite complex negotiations to include the Revisionists, in the end the Revisionist Zionists and Betar maintained their own separate independent armed organization, the Jewish Military Union (Żydowski Związek Wojskowy, or ŻZW).[58]

The command of the ŻOB included Mordecai Anielewicz (Hashomer Hatzair); Yitzhak Zuckerman (Dror HeHalutz), deputy commander; Marek Edelman (Bund), intelligence chief; Yochanan Morgenstern (Poalei Zion Z.S.), finances; Hirsch Berlinski (Left Poalei Zion), planning; and Michael Rosenfeld (Communist). Arie (Jurek) Wilner represented the ŻOB before the military forces in the Polish underground and Dr. Adolf Berman represented the Jewish National Committee before Polish civilian institutions.[59] By late September 1942, forced laborers working in the shops composed the ghetto population of approximately 55,000; the ŻOB counted an estimated six hundred members, but by this point had acquired almost the full support of the remaining ghetto population who both understood the nature of Nazi policy and came to respect the leadership of the youth movements and fighting organizations.[60] The underground worked to purge traitors from the ghetto and put up posters warning the surviving population of the murderous intentions of the Germans. As knowledge of the true nature of Treblinka became widespread, some began to seek ways to remove family members to the Aryan side of Warsaw, while others began to build hiding places and bunkers inside the ghetto.[61] In the words of Ringelblum, from this point forward "a paradoxical situation arose." While the adult generation continued to worry about survival, about the possibility of continuing life,

> the youth—the best, the most beautiful, the noblest element that the Jewish people possessed—spoke and thought only about an honorable death. They did not think about surviving the war, they did not arrange "Aryan" Papers, they did not get apartments on the other side. Their only worry was about the most honorable death, the kind of death that a two-thousand-year-old people deserves.[62]

In conjunction with the six-month anniversary of the Great Deportation, the ŻOB planned a retaliation against the Jewish police for January 22, 1943, calling on the remaining Jews of Warsaw:

> Jewish masses, the hour is drawing near. You must be prepared to resist, not give yourselves up to slaughter like sheep. Not a single Jew should go to the railroad cars. Those who are unable to put up active resistance should resist passively, meaning go into hiding. . . . Our motto should be: *All are ready to die as human beings.*[63]

At the same time, the ŻZW issued a parallel call for resistance:

> *We are rising up for war!*
>
> *We are rising in the name of the war for the lives of the helpless masses whom we seek to save, whom we must arouse to action! It is not for ourselves alone that we wish to fight. We will be entitled to save ourselves only when we have completed our duty! As long as the life of a Jew is still in danger, even one, single, life, we have to be ready to fight!!!!*
>
> *Our watchword is:*
> *Not even one more Jew is to find his end in Treblinka!*
> *Out with the traitors to the people!*
> *War for life or death on the conqueror to our last breath!*
> *Be prepared to act!*
> *Be ready!*[64]

Before either the ŻOB or the ŻZW could act on their plans for January 22, 1943, however, SS and police units launched a new *Aktion* seeking to round up approximately eighty-five hundred Jews. Following a January 9, 1943, visit by Reichsführer SS Heinrich Himmler to the ghetto, where he was surprised to learn that nearly forty thousand Jews had been kept alive as workers in the ghetto, he ordered the total liquidation of the ghetto by February 14, 1943, with the remaining Jews and production facilities transferred to a concentration camp in the Lublin district.[65] On the first day of the round-up, on January 18, 1943, German forces managed to capture approximately three thousand Jews for deportation to Treblinka, catching the ŻOB and ŻZW largely off guard. Among those killed on the first day of the round-up was Yitzhak Giterman, the JDC director and the main organizer of self-help in the ghetto, killed as he ran from apartment to apartment in his housing block on Muranowska Street to warn Jews of the *Aktion*.[66] On the second day of the round-up, the ŻOB, under the leadership of Anielewicz, did manage to mount several attacks against German soldiers, in some cases embedding themselves with Jews being marched to the *Umschlagplatz* for deportation. Anielewicz led a group of Hashomer Hatzair fighters in battle; Yitzhak Zuckerman led a group from Dror and Gordonia that included Zivia Lubetkin and Tuvia Borzykowski; and Marek Edelman, led a group from the Bund. Tosia Altman, who had been instrumental as an underground courier for Hashomer Hatzair, was caught in the round-up but managed to escape at the *Umschlagplatz* with the aid of a Jewish policeman. Although the January revolt did not succeed in preventing the deportation of approximately five thousand Jews, it did teach the ŻOB several important lessons: 1) German soldiers would flee when shot upon by Jewish fighters; 2) the tactic of ambush was more successful than open street fighting, which had cost the ŻOB some of its top fighters in the January days of battle; 3) the January round-ups were an indication that the Germans intended to act upon the final liquidation of the ghetto (leading ghetto inhabitants to construct hundreds of bunkers underneath buildings. The ŻOB built its main command bunker at Mila 18, which would serve as headquarters for the April revolt); 4) inhabitants would support the ŻOB in its efforts to engage in armed resistance against the Germans, having learned from the previous summer that deportation likely meant death.[67]

Following the January uprising, a period of relative quiet ensued, as German officials debated the proper course of action, with some arguing for complete liquidation of the ghetto and others lobbying for the continued use or transfer of the workers in the armaments, leather, and textile factories in Warsaw to other parts of the *Generalgouvernement*. It is unclear to what extent the January uprising influenced German policy in their approach to liquidating the ghetto, although clearly the final liquidation was delayed beyond Himmler's original February 14, 1943, deadline. The remaining Jews in the ghetto had been convinced that the time had come for armed resistance as the course of last resort, refusing to believe German assurances that transfer to labor camps at Trawniki or Poniatow would enable them to survive until the end of the war.[68] The remaining population also devoted itself to preparing bunkers in the ghetto, described by Gutman as a type of "bunker mania." In his memoirs, Dr. Mordechai Lensky writes of the period, "one can say without exaggeration that the entire population, from the young to the old, was engaged in preparing hiding places. . . . No one thought of willingly going to Treblinka. The survivors prepared everything necessary for remaining in hiding for months."[69] Havi Dreifuss emphasizes that one of the lessons learned from witnesses to the January resistance was that armed resistance was not the only way to "fight back." Some realized that it would be even better to engage in passive resistance and go into hiding.[70]

Following the January uprising, the ŻOB focused on applying the lessons of January in preparation for the next *Aktion*. It was clear to the ŻOB that they lacked sufficient weaponry and they thus focused on acquiring funds to purchase arms, while also working to purge any dangerous collaborators from their midst.[71]

The leadership of the ŻOB worked together with the Jewish National Committee in the months between the January 1943 resistance and the April 19, 1943, revolt to try to secure arms and support for the Jewish fighting organization. Before the April revolt, Mordecai Anielewicz crossed from the ghetto to the Aryan side of Warsaw to attend a meeting with Adolf Berman and Leon Feiner[72] to demand further arms and support for the ŻOB. Adolf Berman, who had already met Anielewicz in the ghetto, would later describe the meeting, in which "Anielewicz issued a scathing attack against the Polish government-in-exile in London, and against the AK [Armia Krajowa, Polish Home Army] commander's indifference to the fighting Ghetto," making a plea for arms and ammunition.[73]

How Did Information on the Revolt Emerge from the Ghetto?

Despite the frustration expressed by Anielewicz and the ŻOB with the lack of support from the Polish underground, the connection between the ŻOB inside the ghetto and Yitzhak Zuckerman (ŻOB) and Berman (JNC) outside the ghetto would continue during the uprising, playing a crucial role in the spread of information from inside the ghetto to the outside as the events unfolded. Once the revolt began on April 19, Berman and Zuckerman played a central role in affecting the manner in which the revolt would be understood and interpreted in the outside world. The nature of their interactions with the ŻOB inside the ghetto influenced the narrative of the uprising as they drafted reports relayed by actors outside that incorporated the voices of participants inside the ghetto.

In reviewing the sources of information available for events inside the ghetto, several types of sources are clear, including: information provided by inhabitants of the ghetto themselves, during and after the uprising; notices provided by eyewitnesses from the Jewish underground and Jewish National Committee outside the ghetto; reports of the Polish underground sent to the Polish government-in-exile; reports of non-Jewish Polish eyewitnesses outside the ghetto; German accounts of the revolt, in particular the report of Jurgen Stroop; diaries and testimonies provided by surviving ghetto fighters written in hiding after the uprising; and diaries and testimonies of Jewish noncombatants who survived the revolt inside the ghetto collected after the war.

According to historian Dariusz Stola, reports sent from occupied Warsaw traveled to the Polish government-in-exile in two primary ways: either as dispatches sent via radio and secret transmitters from Poland, or longer messages passed by secret couriers. Members of the Polish government-in-exile radioed secret messages via hidden transmitters in Poland to both the civilian and military branches of the government-in-exile in London.[74] The coded messages, which were brief and often superficial in nature (for both technical and security reasons), usually took several days to sometimes several weeks to decipher in London. Anything longer and more detailed needed to be written in code, microfilmed, and then sent with secret couriers who traveled on routes via Hungary, Slovakia, Romania, Turkey, or Germany, France, Portugal, and Switzerland, sometimes never making it out of occupied Europe. This meant that the initial reports of the Warsaw Ghetto Uprising, delivered via radio and secret transmitters, would be brief and sketchy; longer, more detailed reports would take six months to more than a year to emerge from occupied Poland. While the ŻOB would be the critical organization responsible for combat in the ghetto, the Jewish National Committee played the most prominent role in spreading information about the uprising outside the ghetto.[75]

As new research by Havi Dreifuss explains, the formation of a hierarchical structure for the Jewish National Committee and the ŻOB was largely foreign to the youth movement members of the ŻOB, who saw this largely as acceding to the demands of the Polish government-in-exile—a means to try to secure arms and support from the Polish underground.[76] Leaders of the youth movements generally represented the members of the fighting underground, while older communal and political activists came to lead the Jewish National Committee and the underground of the Jewish Labor Bund. One of these was Adolf Berman, a psychologist and left-wing Zionist activist, who had continued his work as director of CENTOS (*Centralne Towarzystwo Opieki nad Sierotami*, the Central Association for the Care of Orphans) with the outbreak of World War II. During the war, he continued leading the efforts of Left Poalei Zion in Warsaw, supported the creation of a Jewish fighting organization, and was among the founders of the antifascist bloc formed in March 1942, and was soon joined by Hashomer Hatzair, He-Halutz, Dror, and the Poalei Zion Z.S.[77] Among the aims of the bloc were an attempt to organize "joint forces for a political and propaganda war against Fascism" and the organization of combat divisions, which came to be known as the bloc's military division.[78] Following the arrest and murder of the leading figure in the battalion, Andrzej Szmidt (Pinkus Kartin), by the Gestapo, however, the bloc had largely ceased to exist by June 1942.[79] From September 1942, Berman lived on the Aryan side of Warsaw, representing the Jewish National Committee and serving as secretary of Zegota, the Polish Council for Aid to Jews.[80] The Jewish

National Committee, organized in October 1942, was supposed to be the "political face" of the ŻOB and represent the ŻOB in negotiations with the Polish underground and by extension maintain relations with the Polish government-in-exile; the Bund would not join the Jewish National Committee but did join the ŻOB and cooperated with the JNC through the Coordinating Committee. After the uprising, the JNC remained the major Jewish underground organization in the *Generalgouvernement*.[81]

When the uprising broke out on April 19, 1943, Yitzhak Zuckerman was on the Aryan side (having been sent by the ŻOB on an unsuccessful mission to try to secure arms from the Polish underground after the arrest and capture of Arie Wilner on the Aryan side of Warsaw on March 6, 1943). After Wilner's arrest and subsequent torture by the Gestapo, he was liberated from the Pawiak prison by the ŻOB and returned to the ghetto. Zuckerman was dispatched to the Aryan side of Warsaw two weeks before the revolt. Dreifuss argues that the decision to send Zuckerman to attempt to secure arms from the Polish underground led to a reorganization of the ŻOB command structure, with Marek Edelman placed in command of the brushmakers area, Eliezer Geller in charge of the shops, Israel Kanal replacing Anielewicz as commander of the central ghetto, and Anielewicz promoted then to commander of the ŻOB as a whole.[82] Tosia Altman, the Hashomer Hatzair underground courier, had entered the ghetto in order to spend Passover with her comrades on the inside (the first seder was Monday night, April 19, 1943).

The final liquidation of the ghetto began on Passover eve, April 19, 1943 (14 Nisan 5703). Approximately two thousand German soldiers (including SS troops, German police, and army soldiers), commanded by SS Senior Colonel Ferdinand Von Sammern-Frankenegg, entered the ghetto early that morning. While the German forces were surprised by the size of the Jewish resistance, the ŻOB and the Jewish fighters were prepared for the German liquidation. The day before, the ghetto had begun to receive reports that German forces were massing outside the ghetto. Accordingly, Jews began to gather in their bunkers that night and ŻOB fighters prepared to encounter the German forces in their combat units, mobilized by 2:15 a.m.[83]

As the uprising unfolded, Zuckerman could only watch helplessly on the Aryan side, trying to send a message to his comrades, including his girlfriend and future spouse, Zivia Lubetkin. At the start of the uprising, he was able to send a message that conveyed his distress at not being able to join them in the struggle: "I am standing before the Ghetto walls and I see the flames rising from its fires. Meanwhile I can't help with anything. Be strong! I am sorry that I am not with you."[84] After the first day of fighting in the ghetto, Anielewicz managed to send a letter to Zuckerman (which would become known as the "last letter of the Warsaw Ghetto Uprising's commander") via the Jewish cemetery. Berman asked Zuckerman to translate the letter from Hebrew to Yiddish (Berman did not read Hebrew) so he could show it to the Polish underground to convince them to offer assistance to the Jewish fighters.[85] While Israel Gutman cites Anielewicz's last letter as one of the primary sources of information from inside the ghetto (and the letter has been reproduced and reprinted in books, monuments, and museums around the world) as Dreifuss notes, Zuckerman's translation removed "two sections that were of a personal and military nature,"[86] and the Yiddish letter that Berman received (the Hebrew original was lost) was, in turn, "significantly different from the letter that Berman would eventually deliver to the Polish underground."

> Shalom, Yitzhak.
>
> I don't know what to write you about. I will forego personal details this time. I have only one way to express my feelings and those of my comrades: What we have lived through here is beyond description. All we know is that what has happened has surpassed our most daring expectations. Twice the Germans fled from the Ghetto. One of our groups held onto its position for 40 minutes; the second—more than six hours. The mine we laid in the brushmakers' area exploded. From our side we have thus far lost only one casualty: Yechiel met a hero's death, a soldier killed at his machine gun.
>
> When we began to receive news yesterday that members of the PPR attacked the Germans and that the radio station SWIAT broadcast

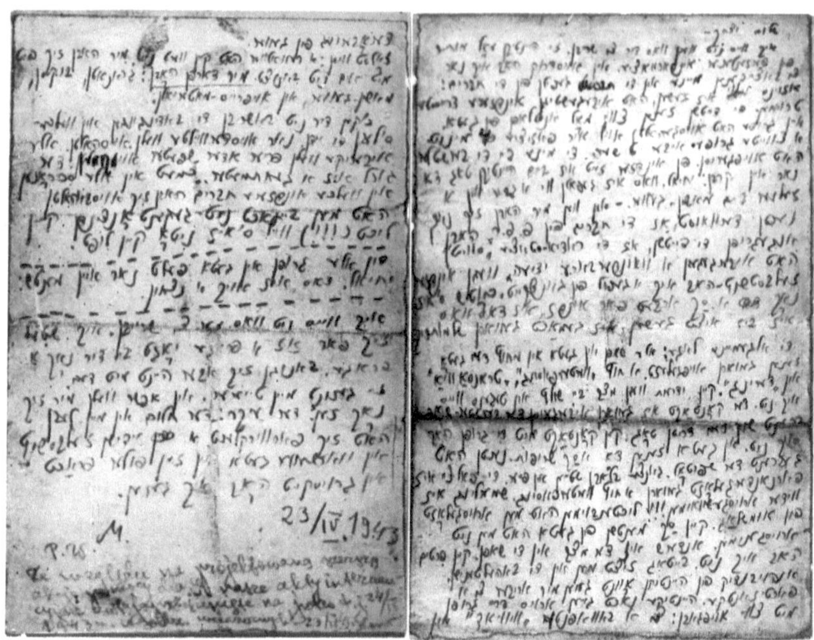

The last letter of Mordecai Anielewicz, commander of the Warsaw Ghetto Uprising, written to his second-in-command, Yitzhak Zuckerman, on April 23, 1943, during the uprising. (Ghetto Fighters House Archives, catalog number 1038)

a wonderful report about our self-defense—I experienced a feeling of contentment. Great work still remains before us, but all we have accomplished until now has been worthwhile.

As for the general situation:

All the workshops in the ghetto and outside of it have been closed, except for the *Verterpasung*, *Transavia*, and *Doering*. I do not know what is happening in the Többens and Schultz area. We have lost contact.

[Here Anielewicz expands on conditions in the various workshop areas on fire.]

Beginning with tonight we are adopting the tactic of partisan warfare. Tonight three fighting units will go out into the combat area.

They will have two tasks: armed reconnaissance and the capture of weapons. You should know, the pistol has no value to us, we cannot use it. We need: grenades, rifles, machine guns and explosives.

> It is impossible to describe the conditions under which the Jews in the Ghetto are living today. Only a few will survive. All others will perish sooner or later. Their fate is sealed. In practically all the bunkers where thousands of Jews are hiding it is impossible to light a candle for the lack of air!
>
> From all of the groups in the ghetto we have only lost one person: Yechiel. This alone is a victory. I do not know what else to write here. I can only imagine, that one question leads to another, but I will suffice with what I have written until now.
>
> Be well, dear friend. Maybe we will see each other some day. The main thing: the dream of my life was realized. I have been privileged to witness Jewish Self-Defense in the Ghetto in all of its greatness and majesty.[87]

Berman apparently decided to edit the document in a way that he thought would better serve the interests of the remnants of Polish Jewry. Dreifuss explains the multiple ways in which Berman would modify the letter from Anielewicz in order to make it seem more appropriate as a message from a military commander sent to the Polish underground, including military language changes, political changes, stylistic changes, changes to the dating of the letter (written on April 20, 1943, not April 23, 1943!), and more.[88] Berman was keen to modify Anielewicz's last letter in order to enhance the ŻOB commander's stature before the Polish underground. Other changes noted by Dreifuss included Berman's removal of references to the Polish Workers Party (PPR), praised in the first draft, because Berman was aware that the Polish government-in-exile had disavowed the PPR (composed largely of members of the prewar Communist party).[89]

Such changes may not seem major, but they do emphasize a number of key themes: the significance of Jewish self-defense; the motivating factor of revenge; the importance of presenting an image of a professional fighting force to the outside world, especially to the representatives of the Polish government-in-exile, from whom the Jews still hoped against hope to receive aid; and the trope of Jewish heroes led by a military commander in the form of Anielewicz. While the ghetto fighters presented their struggle in military terms (as did much of the newspaper coverage presented in the next chapter)—both at the time and in subsequent testimonies—the tendency to do so overlooked the experiences of most of the ghetto population buried in bunkers and diminished the immense power disparity between the ŻOB and the German Army.[90] Ghetto fighters and the Jewish National Committee had a clear interest in exaggerating the military capabilities of the Jewish Fighting Organization if they were to have any chance of securing additional support from the Polish underground in the way of arms and material support, and their testimonies must be read in light of this. This research also suggests how important it is to read the subsequent ŻOB and Bund reports critically as well, because presumably these reports underwent a similar process of editing before being shared with the world. The tendency to present the commander of the ŻOB in a military light (Anielewicz had not served in the Polish army nor received any formal military training) is noteworthy, for as will be seen in the following chapters, newspaper coverage abroad described the events in the ghetto in military terms—as a "battle" and as armed conflict, which it was, but certainly not in a traditional military sense as a confrontation between two relatively equal forces on a battlefield.

How then did this image of a military confrontation make its way to the outside world? Communication between the ghetto and the Aryan side continued after April 19, and after Anielewicz's "last letter" of April 20 (dated April 23, 1943, by Berman). During the uprising, Dreifuss notes, the only way the ŻOB was able to maintain contact with the Aryan side was through telephone messages (they could no longer pass secret messages through the Jewish cemetery and Jewish workers were no longer sent outside the ghetto to work). Tosia Altman was made responsible for making phone calls to the Aryan side, which she made to Frania Beatus, Zuckerman's courier on the Aryan side.[91] The Bund also managed to use the telephone to pass messages: Abrasha Blum, one of the Bund's leaders, was twice able to reach Leon (Mikolaj) Feiner, the Bund representative on the Aryan side, and deliver him short messages. As Vladka Meed, underground courier for the Bund, would recall in her memoir:

> That evening [April 19] Mikolaj [Feiner] briefly summarized the situation for us. On the night of April 19, he said,

he had been awakened by a telephone call from Abrasha Blum in the ghetto.

"Active resistance has begun," Abrasha told him. "All the groups of the Fighting Organization are participating in the struggle. It's all very well organized and disciplined. We are now engaged in a battle near the brush factory. For the time being there have been only a few casualties. There are more casualties among the Germans."

According to Meed, a second phone call came on the night of April 22: "'Michał Klepfisz is dead. He fell in the fighting. We are short of ammunition. We need arms'. The conversation (was) interrupted by the telephone central office. It was the last phone call from Abrasha Blum."[92]

Other phone calls from inside the ghetto to the Aryan side also made it through, including calls from Tosia Altman focused on the need for additional arms and a message sent from the ghetto on April 22 (published by Adolf Berman after the war).

We are healthy. Have you sent us a food package [weapons]? Remember the eggs [grenades] and sweets [bullets], and what is most important, the aunt [guns]. We need the aunt here. You don't have to send sausages [pistols]. We're wondering how we can see you. Maybe we will see each other yet. T. [Tuvia [Tadek] Szajngut, one of the fighters on the Aryan side] should go to the cemetery to pray for the souls of the dead [an attempt to contact the Ghetto through the cemetery].[93]

A third message, attributed to Anielewicz by Berman was sent on April 26 and made it clear that the fighting organization had already suffered tremendous losses and that the "last days are growing nearer":

Today is the eighth day in which we stand in a battle for our lives. The Warsaw Ghetto, one of the last ghettos in existence, was suddenly besieged by a regular German army that began exterminating the remaining Jews. In the first days, the Germans were forced to retreat, leaving behind many of their dead. Afterwards, when they brought reinforcements of tanks, armored cars, canons and even airplanes, they initiated a formal siege and began systematically burning down houses. The number of our people who were slain by gunshot, of men, women and children who burned to death, is immense. Our last days are growing ever nearer. But so long as we have bullets we will continue to fight and defend ourselves. We rejected the German ultimatum that we surrender, because the enemy does not know mercy, and we—we have no choice. In our last days, we demand of you: remember how we were betrayed. The revenge for our holy spilled blood will come! Send help to those who would be saved from the enemy in the last hour, so that the struggle will be carried on. 26.4 [1943].[94]

Havi Dreifuss speculates that the first two messages may have been composed by Anielewicz or at least with his assistance, but the third message may have been composed by Tosia Altman. Either way, the April 26 message made it clear to the recipients in the Jewish underground within occupied Poland that the days of the ghetto fighters in Warsaw were numbered; the reference to "betrayal" may also convey the bitterness at being abandoned by the Polish underground.[95]

It is also clear that Zegota, the Council for Aid to Jews, was actively working to convey information on what was transpiring in the Warsaw ghetto, as was "Wacław," a.k.a. Henryk Woliński, head of the Jewish affairs desk of the Polish underground Armia Krajowa (AK). "Wacław" (Woliński) would later head the AK's Jewish affairs department and continued to support Jewish resistance activities in Warsaw throughout the war. According to Gutman, Zegota reached an agreement with Feiner and Berman "on transmitting messages and cables abroad through the communications channels of the Polish underground." Thanks to this agreement, at the beginning of 1943 "regular reports and appeals for help from the Jews of Poland began to reach the Jewish representatives in the London-based Polish government-in-exile and Jewish leaders and parties in the United States and Palestine."[96]

The information bulletins drafted by the Jewish National Committee on the Aryan side of Warsaw, along with any messages received from the ŻOB inside the ghetto, were included in a parcel of documents sent to London by Wacław on April 30, 1943. Also included were situation reports drafted by the Bund and the JNC detailing events in Warsaw during the first week of the uprising.[97] Ignacy (Isaac) Schwartzbart, a member of the Polish National Council in London, received the messages from the Polish underground and communicated information to the Jewish Agency executive (chaired by David Ben-Gurion, the quasi-governmental body of the Zionist organization in Mandatory Palestine) with the assistance of the Polish consul in Tel Aviv, Henrik Rosmarin.[98]

The Jews fighting in the ghetto were well aware of the significance of the events they had initiated as they took part in them, described by Anielewicz as "beyond description . . . what has happened has surpassed our most daring expectations." As I have noted, notices detailing events in the ghetto, which would later serve as sources for historians writing the history of the revolt, were written with a Polish audience in mind, in hopes of spurring the Polish underground to offer greater assistance and join the fight. But they were not just calls for support but also declarations that the battle waged in the ghetto was a battle for revenge against the oppressor and a battle for freedom on behalf of humanity. The ghetto fighters and the underground, aware that they "may perish in the struggle" understood that they would become symbols of freedom. They also understood that the documentation of their struggle in the ghetto would form a critical part of the historical record of the Jewish struggle in the war. Fighting for their "three lines in history" (to borrow Dolek Libeskind's term) every communiqué, every declaration, every report issued from the ghetto—and after the uprising, every testimony smuggled out of Warsaw—took on a significance that transcended the physical time and space of Warsaw as it entered the realm of History. But the exchange of information between the

Jews of occupied Warsaw and Poland did not begin just in the aftermath of the revolt; it continued fitfully throughout the war as information trickled out of Warsaw before, during, and after the uprising. The atmosphere in which these messages were shaped, however, would also affect the way the history of the uprising was recorded and interpreted: as a struggle for Polish freedom, as Zionist revolt against Nazi oppression, as the struggle of the Jewish masses united in a fight for freedom, or all of the above.

These messages, which would be relayed in subsequent communications both by the Polish underground and by underground radio, played a crucial part in relaying the news of the uprising to the outside world. Cables sent by the Polish underground, along with those relayed by the Jewish National Committee and the Bund figured prominently in the newspaper reports abroad that were published in late April and early May 1943. The second cable, which was dated April 28 and signed by Leon Feiner[99] and Adolf Berman was the first to reach London and reported worldwide on May 24, 1943. Leon Feiner, who had served as one of Jan Karski's underground guides to the Warsaw ghetto, described the first ten days of the revolt in the report.[100]

> In this 10th day of the heroic battle the SS and the Wehrmacht are laying siege to the Warsaw ghetto. They are incessantly bombarding the 40,000 Jews with the use of artillery, flamethrowers, and incendiary bombs dropped from airplanes. They are blowing up apartment buildings with mines—the ghetto is in flames. Clouds of smoke shroud the city. Women and children perish as the enemy murders en masse. The Jewish fighters battle fiercely and the result has been heavy losses for the enemy. German war-related factories are in flames. . . . Immediate, effective help can be given out by the Allied might. On behalf of the millions of Jews already killed, and the name of those now being burned and massacred, and the name of those fighting heroically and all of us who are doomed to death, let the mighty revenge of the allies on the blood thirsty enemy be

Dr. Leon Feiner, a key activist of the Bund and a leader in the ŻOB, the Jewish Fighting Organization, in the Warsaw ghetto. (Ghetto Fighters House Archives, catalog number 1248)

> visited now and not in the distant future—revenge in the generally accepted meaning. May our closest allies at long last become aware of the scope of their responsibility in the face of the unprecedented Nazi crime against an entire people whose tragic epilogue is now being played out. Let the heroic effort of the desperate people of the ghetto, unique in history, finally arouse the world to deeds commensurate with the greatness of the moment.[101]

As events transpired in the ghetto, Berman and Zuckerman kept a daily record of events from their vantage points on the Aryan side, which would later be identified as "notices published by the Jewish National Committee."[102] These reports, later described by Zuckerman as "propaganda communiqués," need to be read cautiously from a historical perspective. As he described the process in his posthumously published memoir, *Surplus of Memory*:

> Afterward, almost every day, we issued propaganda communiqués in which *Dichtung und Wahrheit* (fiction and truth) were intermingled. Historians tend to think that everything written in a document is the truth; but I can't prove it isn't so. Sometimes, we "fabricated" things, and they weren't precise; and I would add that this wasn't so important to me in that period. For example, it didn't occur to me then to treat the names I wrote there as if they were real names, as Kermish, Blumenthal, Trunk, Friedman, and Mark do; because that wasn't the function of the documents we were issuing. At that moment I wasn't thinking of historical precision. It was an appeal to the Poles designed to stir their feelings of sympathy for our struggle; and it didn't matter how that battle occurred or how we were defending our lives. It was not an official bulletin of the Israeli Ministry of Defense. And sometimes the Ministry of Defense isn't so precise either. We didn't have newspapers then, we didn't have radio, and

> we wanted to create a sympathetic public opinion. We conveyed them to the Polish underground and they took care of publishing them. They were typed up in Polish (Berman did that). Things were collected from all kinds of sources and I always knew they weren't terribly precise. And if I had it to do all over again, I would probably shape the material again in the same form.[103]

Zuckerman also acknowledged that certain political considerations may have influenced the writing of subsequent reports sent by the Jewish National Committee and the ŻOB. For example, describing a report he would send to London at the end of 1943: "What I wrote in the Jewish Fighting Organization report sent to London at the end of 1943, that the Bloc was founded by the initiative of Po'alei Zion Left, is nonsense. The truth is that I didn't want to delay sending the report to London by debates with Berman, so I decided to give in."[104] Zuckerman also elaborated elsewhere in his memoir on the need to downplay Communist involvement in the establishment of the ŻOB, due to concerns about the response of the anti-Communist underground. Later generations of historians would debate whether reports and communiqués drafted by Zuckerman were indeed reliable sources, although Israel Gutman and Havi Dreifuss have argued persuasively that his reports were in fact accurate assessments based on the information he had available at the time.[105]

With Zuckerman's caution in mind, therefore, we can read the notices of the Jewish National Committee as an account of the battles taking place in the ghetto, written by him, the ŻOB deputy commander on the Aryan side, and Berman, the head of the Jewish National Committee. Zuckerman, desperate to know what was happening to his dear comrades in the ghetto, and desperate to partake in the fighting, was left to report on events with an eye to encouraging the Polish underground to assist in any way they could. As Dreifuss's research also demonstrates, however, Berman was also well aware of the manner in which his audience (the Polish underground) would interpret the reports, and was likely interested in emphasizing the military potential of the Jewish fighting force in the ghetto. Such an approach would have thus also focused primarily on the relatively small number of ŻOB fighters in the ghetto, while largely ignoring the experiences of the forty thousand Jews hiding in bunkers and apartments in the ghetto.

The first seven notices issued by the Jewish National Committee and the Bund together, while combining Zuckerman's *dichtung und wahrheit*, also conveyed (in real time) the essential components of the Jewish narrative of the revolt, from the perspective of eyewitnesses like Berman, Zuckerman, and Feiner, while incorporating information received from inside the ghetto via telephone and telegram.[106]

To summarize the key points in the developing narrative that would shape the historiography of the revolt:

- "ghetto was encircled by German troops and the Polish police, and German tanks and armor[ed vehicles] entered it. The ŻOB displays resistance." (Notice #1, April 19)
- "On Monday, April 19, the battle between the Jewish fighters and SS and German gendarme forces continued in the afternoon. The Germans are forced to proceed house by house. In the streets the piles of casualties grow higher." (Notice #2, April 20)
- "the ghetto comes under heavy shelling, heard from a distance of dozens of kilometers. Streetcars and pedestrian traffic on the streets bordering the ghetto come to a halt. At No. 2 Muranowska Street, Jewish fighters fly the Polish flag and the blue-and-white [Zionist] flag." (Notice #3, April 20)
- "over 100 German dead and wounded. Weapons were taken from dozens of Germans. Several tanks were set ablaze." (Notice #3, April 20)
- "the Jewish fighters threw Molotov cocktails at the tanks entering the ghetto. Jewish fighters, women among them, engaged in combat in Zamenhof, Mila, and Niska streets. Powerful blazes raged in the ghetto." At 21:00 a telegram

arrives from ŻOB headquarters: "Our people are fighting superbly. Morale is outstanding. Our losses are relatively few. We will fight as long as we have breath in our bodies." (Notice #4, April 21)

- "the Germans have employed the tactic of setting fire to the ghetto. Thousands of women and children were burned alive in their homes. Desperate cries for help burst from the houses. People [engulfed] in flames appear at the windows of buildings." (Notice #5, April 22)
- "According to estimates, German losses for the three first days of fighting amount to approximately 200 killed and 400 wounded." (Notice #5, April 22)
- "The heavy bombardment has not dampened the spirit of resistance. Fighters are setting fire to German factories and warehouses, and shooting at the tank crews." (Notice #5, April 22)
- "Resistance continues. One of the ŻOB's commanders has fallen: 'Michael' of the Bund, the engineer [Michael] Klepfisch." (Notice #5, April 23)
- "Leaflets of the Polish underground organizations have appeared in the streets of Warsaw, protesting the Germans' barbarity and expressing esteem and respect for the courage of the ghetto fighters." (Notice #5, April 25)
- "The weakening of resistance of the fighting ghetto stems from the dwindling supply of ammunition along with buildings set on fire by incendiary bombs and flamethrowers, driving people out of bunkers and exposing them to German rifle and tank fire. At night the inhabitants try to escape from the [ghetto's] quarters that are on fire, to less dangerous areas, and the fighters are continuing their attacks." (Notice #6, April 28)
- "In the large Schultz factory, workers and fighters are offering armed resistance to its liquidation. In heavy combat, thirty Germans fell, and three fighters. On April 28, SS and

> Wehrmacht troops were brought to the Schultz factory as major reinforcements. The fighting continues, the Germans torch buildings, and giant fires rage." (Notice #7, April 29)

It seems that these were the seven notices delivered as part of the parcel sent from Warsaw to London on April 30, 1943 (and reported on May 24, 1943). The reports conveyed the broad outlines of the progress of the revolt: German attempts to liquidate the ghetto were initially repelled; the Jewish fighting organization employed guerrilla tactics that forced the Germans to proceed in house-to-house fighting sustaining high numbers of casualties; Jewish fighters, including women, fought superbly and morale was high; primary losses among the Jewish population were sustained by "civilians," whose experiences are described as distinct from "fighters"; the Germans shifted tactics to begin burning down houses and apartment blocs; dwindling supplies of ammunition led to a weakening of the resistance; the Polish underground held the Jewish efforts in high esteem; Többens and Schultz were forced to dismantle their factories. Interestingly, only one ghetto fighter was mentioned by name in these reports: One of the ŻOB's commanders has fallen: "'Michael' of the Bund, the engineer [Michael] Kleppfisch."

Within occupied Poland, too, the last message received from Anielewicz (or perhaps composed with his assistance) on April 26, 1943, was also distributed by the Jewish National Committee and the Bund as part of a desperate plea for assistance to the Polish underground:

> Eight days already the Warsaw Ghetto has borne the fire of struggle against the murderous occupier. For more than a week, the Jewish Combat Organization has led a heroic war in the name of the honor and glory of the Jewish public. The Ghetto bleeds [to death]. Thousands of people have been murdered by the Hitlerist oppressors or have been burned alive by the horrible fires. Nevertheless, the Ghetto continues to struggle. The Jewish fighters do not lay down their weapons, they fight to their last breath.

> The Warsaw Ghetto's tragic, heroic war has inspired respect and admiration among the entire informed [enlightened] Polish public. But these signs of support for the embattled Ghetto have yet to be expressed practically by Poland's secret military authorities.
>
> Despite receiving a number of messages [that have promised] to intervene and take action to provide large-scale military assistance, this support has not yet materialized. Despite repeated queries by the ŻOB headquarters that we have put before to the relevant parties (two ŻOB telegrams, a letter written by the Jewish Combat Organization's commander and so on), no help with ammunition or other combat equipment of any kind has reached the embattled Ghetto.
>
> We are coming to you now, in the last moments, [as] the Ghetto fires continue to burn, [as] the nightly battles thunder, we urgently ask you for an immediate supply of military equipment and ammunition to the fighters.[107]

By the tenth day of the uprising, it was clear to some members of the ŻOB (who rejected the idea of certain death and symbolic sacrifice in the ghetto), that a way out of the ghetto should be found for those remaining fighters who wanted to escape. Once they managed to escape via the sewers under the burning ghetto and find shelter on the Aryan side of Warsaw, they would work to insert their voices into the narrative of the great battle.

2

News about the Destruction of European Jewry and the Uprising during WWII

It took months for the Great Deportation from Jewish Warsaw to be fully reported in the press, but news of the revolt was conveyed almost immediately. News coverage in the Jewish and non-Jewish press in the summer of 1942 focused on the progress of the war effort, detailing German advances toward Stalingrad in Russia and the British defense of Egypt in North Africa. Information on the liquidation of the Warsaw ghetto began to trickle out in the weeks after the Great Deportation began, although it was difficult for observers in the free world to piece all the information together or corroborate the shocking information included in the reports. This chapter will examine how news of the revolt was reported in New York, London, and the Yishuv in Palestine, and how existing political frameworks shaped subsequent interpretations of the uprising. Through an examination of the ways in which the Warsaw Ghetto Uprising was reported in April and May of 1943 and subsequently interpreted and commemorated in the first year after the revolt, we can begin to understand how and why the event was transformed into the defining symbol of Jewish resistance, Jewish sacrifice, and Jewish martyrdom during and after World War II.

The Jewish Telegraphic Agency (JTA), which had been founded in 1917 to provide world Jewry with news from the European war fronts, proved indispensable during the Second World War. By 1925, more than four hundred newspapers (Jewish and general) subscribed to the JTA cable service, creating a certain informational uniformity in the Jewish press, which was still segmented by ideological differences. During World War II, JTA would break numerous stories concerning the fate of European Jewry.[1] Reporting on the Great Deportation from Warsaw pieced together information emerging from occupied Poland. On July 28, 1942, the English-language version of the JTA bulletin reported, "Hundreds of Jewish women, children and aged men in the Warsaw ghetto were massacred last week by Gestapo agents in a pogrom that lasted for several days and may still be going on," according to information that reached the Polish government-in-exile in London. However, the exact number of Jewish victims was unknown, as was the duration of the "pogrom." JTA also reported that "at the same time thousands of able-bodied Jewish men were seized and sent to occupied Russian territory for forced labor at constructing fortifications behind the Nazi lines," according to Polish sources.[2] On August 17, 1942, JTA reported that the "mass-expulsion of Jews from the Warsaw ghetto 'to an unknown destination in the east' was begun by the Nazis last week" and that Dr. Adam Czerniakow, president of the Jewish Council in the Warsaw ghetto, committed suicide, rather than acquiesce to an order that he "submit a list of 100,000 Jews to be deported."[3] By September 9, 1942, JTA in Geneva published a story with the headline "Deportation of 300,000 Jews from Warsaw Ghetto Reported," although their destination was not known. Some four months after the deportations from Warsaw began, on December 3, 1942, the American Jewish Committee, American Jewish Congress, B'nai B'rith, and other leading U.S. Jewish organizations issued a proclamation that declared: "The greatest calamity in Jewish history since the destruction of the Temple has befallen all Jewish communities in the European lands occupied by the enemy. His [Hitler's] deliberate and Satanic purpose to destroy Jewish life wherever his power reaches has now been exposed to the world."[4] Jewish organizations understood that the Jewish world had not seen an event of such magnitude in two thousand years, but how did ordinary Jews in the free world understand, interpret, and explain such events at the time? How might this context have conditioned responses to the Warsaw Ghetto Uprising at the time it took place?

The timing of the revolt by the remaining inhabitants of the Warsaw ghetto was critical: it coincided with their own awareness of the mass destruction of European Jewry and anger at the apathy of the surrounding world, coupled with an intense feeling of powerlessness to rouse the conscience of the so-called civilized world and stop the destruction. As we will see, there was already a transition, outside of Poland, to memorialization of the destroyed Jewish communities of Europe. World Jewry, also increasingly aware that the Jews of Europe had been abandoned, likewise concluded that the isolated Jews of Europe would need to resort to taking matters into their own hands. Not that Jews in the free world did not care deeply about events in occupied Europe or respond with pride to news of the revolt. On the contrary, even though the movements in Europe were forced to make decisions on their own without guidance from outside, the leaders in the Yishuv and America still identified with their movements' affiliates and, from the moment that news of the uprising began to spread, sought to determine the role their members may have played in the resistance and whether they might be able to take credit for it.[5]

The Jewish Press during World War II

In analyzing the responses of world Jewry to events in Europe more generally, and to news of the uprising specifically, it is important therefore to also provide a framework for understanding how news traveled from occupied Europe abroad during the war, and the role played by the Jewish press in this process before and during the war. Several studies have focused specifically on the question of journalism and the Holocaust, including the works of Yosef Gorny, Deborah Lipstadt, and Laurel Leff.[6] Gorny examines the press within the framework of a "transnational community," arguing the global Jewish press brought Jews of diverse ideological backgrounds together by reporting events of concern to Jews, which, during the Second World War, shared a common focus on occupied Europe (in addition to reporting local news in the United States, Palestine, Great Britain, and elsewhere). According to Gorny, this press was foremost a vehicle for disseminating ideologies. In Palestine, *Ha'aretz* (daily circulation of 11,000) expressed the liberal general Zionist approach, *Davar* (15,000 daily circulation) carried the message of socialist Zionism as the influential daily paper of the General Federation of Jewish Workers, edited by Zalman Rubashov and Berl Katznelson, and smaller papers like *Hatzofe* (national religious Zionism) and *Hamashkif* (Revisionist Zionism) also circulated. In the United States, the largest and most significant newspaper was the *Forverts*. Launched in 1897 and led by editor Abraham Cahan, the *Forward* became one of America's premier dailies, with a circulation of 275,000 in the 1930s, renowned as a fighter for social justice, trade unionism, moderate democratic socialism, democracy, and Jewish rights.[7] Other significant papers in the United States included *Der Tog* (liberal general Zionist; 55,000 copies), *Der Morgn Zhurnal* (Mizrahi religious Zionism; 55,000), *Morgn Frayhayt* (American Communist Party, 12,000 copies), and the Poalei Zion newspapers *Idishe Kempfer* and *Jewish Frontier*. In New York, the German-Jewish newspaper *Aufbau*, founded in 1924 and published as a weekly since 1939 under chief editor Manfred George, was the most influential paper among German-Jewish exiles. And, of course, Jewish Americans got their news from other large dailies and small-town newspapers. In Great Britain, the main paper was *The Jewish Chronicle*, which adopted a general Zionist perspective. The Jewish press, especially in the United States, created a space for Jews to both express and negotiate their identities, reflecting a type of cultural pluralism rather than melting pot.[8] During the war, it was common for the American Jewish papers to focus on the heroism of Jewish soldiers; for example, in its coverage of the heroism of two American Jewish GIs in October 1942, the *Forverts* noted:

> every people is proud of its heroes, but pride among the Jews is special for a profound psychological reason: The Jews are a people of martyrs (*a martirer folk*) subject to the derision and contempt of antisemites of various ilk, who disparage its contribution to the society in which it lives.

> Now, however, given the actions of these two men, even the greatest of antisemites would not dare belittle the Jews' heroism. (*Forverts*, October 2, 1942)[9]

The Jewish Press in the USSR and *Davar* in the Yishuv also included features on Jewish heroism, often intended to confront the canard that Jews were a cowardly people. Nonetheless, given the string of horrific news reaching the Jewish world in 1942 and 1943, it is not hard to understand why Jewish readers might have believed such stereotypes regarding Jewish powerlessness.

Beginning in the summer of 1941 with the invasion of the USSR and the deployment of the Einsatzgruppen, German forces transitioned to the mass murder of European Jewry. The majority of Jewish victims were murdered between spring 1942 and the end of 1943 as the killing centers became fully operational.[10] Just as the German war machine began to suffer setbacks on the military front (at Stalingrad and in North Africa) "the chronology of Hitler's victory on the military front was the opposite of his victory on the Jewish front."[11]

By the spring of 1943, therefore, when the Warsaw Ghetto Uprising took place, the time for the rescue of most of European Jewry had passed. But Warsaw represented a dramatic breakthrough in terms of contact and communication, in that the "Jew-Zone," in the heart of the destructive abyss, managed to break through the Nazi shroud of secrecy and make its calls heard by the rest of the world.[12] This means the context of the events is extremely important for understanding how Jews perceived and interpreted news of the Warsaw Ghetto Uprising: How powerless were Jews in fact to stop the Nazi extermination of European Jewry? How much did Jews around the world know and understand about the Final Solution and how did this knowledge influence interpretations of the uprising?[13]

Reporting the Destruction of European Jewry

The final liquidation of the Warsaw ghetto and the revolt that broke out on April 19, 1943, did not take place in a news vacuum. In fact, by the end of

1942, the Nazi plans for extermination became known, although as Laurel Leff has demonstrated, news coverage in the American media varied considerably, especially when it came to the *New York Times* and mainstream press. On August 29, 1942, Rabbi Stephen Wise, President of the World Jewish Congress (WJC), received a copy of a telegram sent from Gerhart Riegner, the WJC representative in Switzerland, that explained Riegner had "received alarming report that in Fuhrer's headquarters plan discussed and under consideration all Jews in countries occupied or controlled Germany number 3–1/2 to 4 million should after deportation and concentration in East at one blow exterminated to resolve once for all Jewish question in Europe."[14] Despite Riegner's alarming telegram, Rabbi Wise did not publicize the report, yielding to a request by the U.S. State Department to wait until the shocking news could be confirmed.[15] Thus while the SS and its auxiliaries deported nearly three hundred thousand Jews from Warsaw to the Treblinka killing center from July 22 to September 12, 1942, and another three hundred thousand Jews from Czestochowa and the Radom district of the *Generalgouvernement* between September 22 and November 5, news that the State Department had confirmed a German plan to kill all the Jews finally appeared in *The New York Times* only on November 25, 1942 (on page 10).[16]

Coverage in the general press differed significantly from coverage in the Jewish press. In *The New York Times*, a November 25, 1942 story by London bureau chief James MacDonald reported on the latest Polish government-in-exile report, quoting Polish officials to the effect that only forty thousand ration cards had been printed for Jews in Warsaw ghetto in October 1942 (down from 433,000 in March). "The story also reported that Jews were being loaded into freight cars so crowded that they died of suffocation or from starvation and thirst." According to *Times* sources: "Wherever the trains arrive half the people are dead. Those surviving are sent to special camps at Treblinka, Belzec, and Sobibor. Once there the so-called settlers are mass-murdered." On page 10 of the same day's *New York Times* a story by the reporter in Jerusalem for the first time mentioned Auschwitz as an extermination center ("Polish Christian workers have confirmed reports that concrete buildings being used by Germans as chambers to put thousands of Jews to death"). A third November 25, 1942 story (also printed on page 10) came from the Associated Press in Washington: "Rabbi Wise learned through sources confirmed by the State Department that about half the estimated 4,000,000 Jews in Nazi-occupied Europe had been slain in an extermination campaign," quoting Wise as saying he had awaited confirmation since Labor Day. "'The State Department finally made available today the documents which have confirmed the stories and rumors of Jewish extermination in all Hitler-ruled Europe', Dr. Wise said." In contrast, other newspapers detailed the shocking reports from Poland on the first page: the *New York Herald Tribune* ran State Department confirmation on page 1; the left-wing *PM* was one of the only newspapers to run a series of stories based on the extermination news and call for an activist rescue policy.[17]

In the Jewish press, the devastating news received the attention it deserved. In the Yishuv, on Thursday, November 26, 1942, the banner headline atop the front page of *Davar* read: *Nikmat Dam Yeled Katan Od Lo Bara Ha-Satan* (Satan has not yet created a fitting revenge for the blood of a small child). The next day's paper called for three days of mourning in the Yishuv to mark the destruction (*hurban*) of European Jewry. On Sunday, November 29, 1942, all rabbis of the Yishuv would lead days of prayer accompanied by shofar blasts and rending of garments. Days of mourning would last until the beginning of Hanukkah (December 3, 1942) as Jews in the Yishuv were called upon to avoid excessive enjoyment. *Davar* also reported on efforts in New York to organize labor unions to apply pressure by all means possible to allied governments to stop the slaughter of European Jewry. The front page of *Davar* on Thursday December 3, 1942, detailed the cries of anger and mourning that had spread throughout Palestine, in services held in Jerusalem, Haifa, Tel Aviv, Petah Tikva, Rehovot, Netanya, and elsewhere. David Remez called upon the Yishuv to rouse the world out of its silence to move to action—but in truth there was little the Yishuv could do. As Dina Porat's groundbreaking study, *The Blue and Yellow Stars of David*, details, the vast disparity between the might of the German machinery of destruction and a Yishuv community with meager resources constrained by British policy, meant that the general attitude of the Yishuv leadership was both one of helplessness and despair. Even so, the Jewish Agency executive had proposed three days of protest and calls to action from November 30 to December 2, 1942, and newspapers reported one hundred thousand people participated in memorial services on those days.[18] The November 23, 1942, statement of the Jewish Agency executive about the systematic murder taking place in Europe and the extermination of millions of Jews along with the three days of mourning became "a watershed in the Yishuv's consciousness. It was a dividing line between the first three years of the war, during which the Yishuv was unaware of what was happening in Europe, and the three subsequent years."[19]

The depths of Jewish despair were indeed felt globally as Jewish organizations in the United States (including the American Jewish Committee, American Jewish Congress, B'nai B'rith, and other leading Jewish organizations) proclaimed the "Greatest Calamity in Jewish History," marking the beginning of Hanukkah with a declaration stating that "nearly two million Jews have already cruelly been done to death and the remaining millions live in the shadow of impending doom. In the hour of their unspeakable grief and travail, the Jews of America in the spirit of an ancient and invincible faith turn once again to Him who has been the Guide and Guardian of Israel throughout all generations." On December 3, 1942, JTA printed a report from the Jewish Labor Committee received from the Catholic underground movement in Poland: "The Jews in the Warsaw ghetto, isolated from the rest of the world, are all condemned to death. There is no hope for them. No one can aid them. Nazi patrols are shooting Jews at sight in the streets of the ghetto. The sidewalks are littered with corpses of murdered Jews."[20]

On December 8, 1942 Rabbi Stephen Wise (American Jewish Congress), Adolph Held (Jewish Labor Committee), Henry Monsky (B'nai Brith), and Rabbi Rosenberg (Agudath Israel) were granted an audience with President Roosevelt where they presented him with an appeal to "institute action" against the Nazi massacres. The appeal, made jointly with, as well, the American Jewish Committee, the Synagogue Council of America, and the Union of Orthodox Rabbis of the United States, stated clearly the "news of Hitler's edict calling for the extermination of all Jews in the subjugated lands." Two million Jewish men, women, and children had already been murdered, while five million more lived under the "threat of a similar doom." Detailing the record of the Nazis' heinous crimes "without parallel in history," the organizations turned to Roosevelt to hold Hitler and the Nazis accountable for their crimes:

> In this hour of deepest anguish and despair we turn to you, Mr. President. You are the symbol of humanity's will to fight for freedom. . . . We ask you once again to warn the Nazis that they will be held to strict accountability for their crimes. We ask you to employ every available means to bring solemn protest and warning to the peoples of the Axis countries so that they may be deterred from acting as the instruments of the monstrous designs of their mad leaders.[21]

In the moment of the "greatest calamity in Jewish history," American Jews had to hope that the creation of an American commission to review Nazi crimes might strike fear in the hearts of the enemies of civilization. A subsequent report by Adolph Held provided details on the meeting, quoting Roosevelt at length, including his explanation that, "it is not in the best interest of the Allied cause to make it appear that the entire German people are murderers or are in agreement with what Hitler is doing."[22] Roosevelt still hoped some components of the German people would rise "against the whole Hitler system." Still, on December 17, 1942, close to four months after the Riegner telegram, the Allied nations, including the governments of the United Kingdom and the United States, issued a press release stating explicitly that the German authorities were engaging in mass murder of the European Jews, and that those responsible for this "bestial policy of cold-blooded extermination" would "not escape retribution."[23] American Jewish organizations hailed the declaration of the United States government and Allied nations on Nazi massacres in Europe, even though JTA cited a *New York Post* editorial that argued "It is not good enough because it will not stop the extermination," and one in the *New York Times* that noted, "the most tragic aspect of the situation is the world's helplessness to stop the horror while the war is going on."

In London, Szmuel Zygielbojm, the Bundist leader and member of the National Council of the Polish government-in-exile in London, drafted a telegram to Prime Minister Winston Churchill, conveying the desperation of the remaining Jews in Warsaw who had witnessed the mass slaughter of Polish Jewry. They "beg you to find means to save those few Polish Jews who still may have survived."[24] Despite such public pleas to those in power, these appeals seemed to fall on deaf ears and no help arrived as the Nazis implemented the Final Solution. We now know that SS chief Heinrich Himmler had issued a general order on July 19, 1942, after a two-day visit to Auschwitz, that by December 31, 1942, SS and police authorities "resettle" all Jews residing in the *Generalgouvernement*, either to killing centers or in closed camps located in the major cities of Warsaw, Kraków, Czestochowa, Radom, and Lublin.[25] In Himmler's order, he explained the ideological justification behind this series of cleansing actions "necessary for the separation of races and peoples demanded by the new organization of Europe and the security and cleanness of the German Reich and of its sphere of interest."[26] In his monumental study of the extermination, Saul Friedlander notes that "by early 1943 the information about mass extermination of the Jews was so widespread in the Reich (even if the 'technical details' were mostly not precise) as to have probably reached a majority of the population. A recurring rumor mentioned the gassing of Jews in tunnels somewhere on the way to the East."[27]

Such a context, both the growing general awareness of the Nazis' plans for total annihilation of European Jewry and the awareness among Jews still living in occupied Europe, obviously influenced the way in which the Warsaw Ghetto Uprising was interpreted and understood. Much has been written about the choice to engage in armed resistance as a decision taken by Jews who understood that while death was almost a certainty, what remained within their control was "how they would die."[28] The scholarly literature has focused on a collective sense of despair, helplessness, and desperation in the Jewish world as news of the total destruction spread. To this must be added the beginning of a transition from despair to grief and mourning over the death of European Jewry, individually and collectively.

Even so, most events in occupied Europe were not reported abroad. Thus, for example, the January 18, 1943 ("first revolt"), in the Warsaw ghetto, which would be cited prominently in all testimonies of ghetto fighters on the origins of the April 1943 uprising, was not reported in the press. In fact, on February 5, 1943, the JTA reported that the "Nazis Make Warsaw 'Judenrein,' Deport Remaining Jews from Ghetto":

> Not a single Jew remains in the Warsaw ghetto, the report received here today from Poland stated. The several thousand Jewish artisans there who were permitted to remain after the mass-deportation of hundreds of thousands of Jews, because they were considered "valuable" to German war industries, were all deported from the city in the middle of last month.[29]

In the Yishuv, news of the January 1943 uprising had spread to the Zionist leadership, although it did not seem to be picked up by the press. At the annual Tel Hai commemoration (held on 11th of Adar to mark the death of the Zionist national hero Joseph Trumpeldor, who died defending the Tel Hai settlement on March 1, 1920) on February 16, 1943, David Ben-Gurion conveyed the news of the January uprising in Warsaw, drawing a connection between Tel Hai and the Warsaw ghetto, between "combatant Zionism in Palestine and the Jewish uprising in Poland," noting the Warsaw fighters "have learned the lore of the new death decreed to us by the defenders of Tel Hai and Sejera—heroic death."[30] According to historian Idith Zertal, "this single sentence in fact embodied the ambivalence with which the community in Palestine and, later, the Jewish state related to the ghetto uprisings, as well as the whole spectrum of Jewish armed struggle during the Holocaust: appropriation and exclusion, deference and arrogance."[31] While "heroic Palestinian Zionism" taught the ghetto fighters how to fight and to die, Zertal notes, Ben-Gurion still made a division between "us and them, Eretz Israel and the Diaspora."[32]

The Jewish press also reported in late January and early February 1943 on the German defeat at Stalingrad and the Red Army's counteroffensive, including victories in Bilogorod, Kursk, Volchansk, Novochirkask, Rostov, and elsewhere. In the Yishuv, the 17th of Adar or February 22, 1943, was declared a day of mourning with a general assembly at the Jewish Agency including the ultra-Orthodox Agudath Israel, a labor stoppage of two hours from 11am to 1pm devoted to lectures by teachers on the seriousness of the moment, and cessations of leisure activities, including closure of cinema and theaters. On the same front page, a story detailed how, in Poland, "the slaughter continued."[33]

At the same time, during the early months of 1943, another story of remarkable self-sacrifice began to circulate, first in the United States, and then in the Yishuv. On January 8, 1943, the *New York Times* published a letter purportedly received from Warsaw, "93 Choose Suicide before Nazi Shame: Jewish Teacher and Students in Warsaw School Foil Plan to Force Prostitution." Jews across the religious and political spectrum reacted to this story, seen as a remarkable and classic example of *Kiddush Hashem* (sanctification of God's name). The letter, dated August 11, 1942, was purportedly received at the offices of the American Beth Jacob Committee in New York, and related a plan by ninety-three Jewish girls and young women to choose mass suicide instead of forced prostitution. The author of the letter, a young disciple of Sarah Schenirer (founder of the Beth Jacob movement, a network of Agudes Israel schools created to combat the acculturation of Orthodox Jewish women in Poland) declared: "It is good to live for God, but it is also good to die for Him. . . . All of us have poison. When the soldiers come we shall drink it. . . . We have no fear."[34] The Yishuv was also captivated by the story (reported in *Davar* on February 17, 1943)—in Petah Tikvah and Tel Aviv, streets were renamed after "the Ninety-Three."[35] Even though it was later debunked as untrue, in early 1943 the story was embraced around the Jewish world as a paragon of Jewish female valor, the ninety-three maidens choosing suicide and *Kiddush Hashem* rather than being defiled by Nazi soldiers in a brothel. The case is instructive, for it reveals how easily fake news could spread at the time and also shows how eager the Jewish public was to hear stories of Jewish martyrdom as heroism.

Jews abroad entered 1943 with the news that European Jewry was undergoing "complete annihilation" and yet felt largely powerless to stop it. Newspaper headlines covered the progress of the war effort in Europe and announced the "greatest calamity in Jewish history" was unfolding.[36] In the United States, Britain, the Soviet Union, and Palestine the major obstacle to expression was not how to convey something that had never been described before; instead the primary challenge was "how to combat the apathy and matter-of-factness of one's fellow countrymen and women." As Roskies and Diamant note, by the end of 1942, without actual written materials from occupied Europe, Jews in the United States developed elaborate protest pageants in an attempt to commemorate the destruction and break through the apathy with calls to rescue the surviving remnant and avenge the slaughter.[37]

Both screaming headlines and memorial pageants like one performed in New York, *We Will Never Die*, marked the transition from calls for rescue to calls for commemoration by Jewish communities in the United States.[38] In order to break through the apathy of allied countries and fellow citizens going about their everyday lives, Jewish communities in the United States organized mass protest rallies in an attempt to capture the attention of the public and of political leaders to make one last desperate call for rescue. At the same time, growing awareness of the destruction that had already been accomplished turned such rallies into large-scale memorial ceremonies.

Speaking at the "Stop Hitler Now" protest rally held at Madison Square Garden on March 1, 1943, before an audience of twenty thousand (with another fifty thousand crowded in the streets listening on loudspeakers) gathered to pressure the United States to aid European Jewry, Dr. Chaim Weizmann, president of the World Zionist Organization, noted that scholars of the future would be overwhelmed both by the monstrosity of the Nazi crimes and the troubling apathy of the civilized world in "the face of this immense systematic carnage of human beings whose sole guilt was membership in the people who gave the commandments of the moral law to mankind."[39] Weizmann joined Stephen S. Wise, Mayor LaGuardia, Governor Dewey, and other leaders in decrying both the Nazi crimes and the shocking apathy of the world.[40]

One week later, Ben Hecht's *We Will Never Die: A Memorial Dedicated to the 2,000,000 Jewish Dead of Europe*, opened in New York, including music by German-Jewish refugee composer Kurt Weil. The production employed the expertise of theatrical producer Billy Rose, playwright and director Moss Hart, and actors Edward G. Robinson, Paul Muni, and Sylvia Sydney. The show played for over one hundred thousand American Jews (and some non-Jews, too) from its opening in Madison Square Garden on March 9, 1943, until the last updated performance at the Hollywood Bowl on July 21, 1943. *We Will Never Die* sought to give the millions of Jewish dead a voice: six Jews, "two men, a rabbi, two women and a child" emerged out of giant Tablets of the Law to represent the "six million Jews, in German-held lands," of whom the "Germans have said that none shall remain." The six symbolic voices, each coming from a different point in Europe, asked the audience to "remember us." As they moved off stage, a choir recited the *Kaddish*, while, as some scholars have suggested, the pageant in which it was embedded marked the beginning of a secular liturgy to commemorate the Holocaust.[41]

At the same time, as the protest pageant played to tens of thousands of Americans, Jews in the Yishuv read in the press and in other publications the last letters from members of Zionist youth movements in Europe. Bracha Habas, a prominent journalist, author, and editor of multiple collections for a broad audience, collected and published 250 letters from youth movement members in a volume titled *Mikhtavim min hageta'ot* (Letters from the ghettos).[42] Included in the Habas collection was a letter from Tosia Altman, prewar Hashomer Hatzair activist and wartime underground courier (who had by 1943 already become a household name in the Yishuv). Tosia Altman's last letter was anything but a battle cry for freedom, instead expressing the bitterness of a Jew in occupied Europe who felt abandoned by the rest of the Jewish world:

> I think you'll agree with me [she wrote to her unidentified addressee in a kibbutz] that one shouldn't draw strength from a poisoned well. I am trying to control myself not to vent the bitterness that has accumulated against you

> and your friends for having forgotten us so utterly. I blame you that you didn't help me with a few words at least. But today I don't want to settle my accounts with you. It was the recognition and certainty that we will never see each other again that impelled me to write. . . . Israel is vanishing before my eyes and I wring my hands and I cannot help him. Have you ever tried to smash a wall with your head?[43]

Letter writers, particularly in Zionist circles, wrote in code employing their knowledge of Hebrew language to convey hidden messages, referring to the beloved homeland as "Moledet" and expressing longing for marriage with the land (Aliyah). As historian Emil Kerenji notes, such letters pointed to the "ironic predicament of Polish Jewry in late 1942," who felt overwhelmingly isolated in Warsaw and the remaining ghettos of the *Generalgouvernement*, yet "maintained a feeling of connectedness to their fellow Jews in the free world."[44] Such letters, written in coded language, conveyed the despair of the remaining population in Poland, but also took time to decipher. Thus letters that hinted at decisions to engage in resistance, or perhaps resolutions to die fighting in a united front between Zionist and non-Zionist parties, only became clear with the passage of time and events.[45] In his *Warsaw Ghetto Rising* published in late 1944, Melech Neustadt included one such letter, received in March 1943, by way of explaining the difficulty of comprehending the news sent in coded language at the time:

> WE WANT TO INFORM YOU ABOUT A HAPPY EVENT WITHIN THE FAMILY. DESPITE THE DISTRESSING TIMES, OUR DEAR AMI HAS DECIDED TO MARRY MISS HARIGEVICZ. THEY HAVE NOT YET FIXED THE DATE OF THE WEDDING BUT IT WILL BE QUITE SOON. IF DARKA CHILLUF OR MEILECH HACALSKA WANT TO SEND WISHES, THEY MUST HURRY. THE MARRIAGE CEREMONY WILL PROBABLY BE CELEBRATED AMONG A LIMITED CIRCLE IN THE HOME OF AUNT HAGANSKA. REGARDS

TO YOU AND ALL OUR RELATIVES, ESPECIALLY FROM THE YOUNG COUPLE.

As Neustadt would explain in the 1944 publication, only later, once events had made the meaning of the coded words clear, did the recipients in the Yishuv come to understand the message:

> Our interpretation, now confirmed, was as follows: Firstly, all internal disputes as to the necessity of resistance had ceased; hence the emphasis on "Ami" (my people) "has decided." Secondly, they knew they were facing certain death from the beginning of the fighting, yet they were determined nonetheless upon resistance by force of arms. This was the meaning of "to marry Miss Harigevicz" (from the Hebrew *Hariga*—killing). Thirdly, they expected fighting to break out any day, and in fact we now learn that the deportation of the 40,000 Jews who still remained in Warsaw was due to take place in the middle of March, 1943. It was on the night of the 14th–15th March that the "Jewish Fighting Organisation" put up posters on the Ghetto walls calling upon the Jews not to permit themselves to be driven out and to resist deportation by force of arms. The Nazis wished to avoid a clash of arms and on the 20th of March they circulated leaflets intended to pacify the Jewish workers by explaining that the "Jewish Fighting Organisation" was only trying to incite them. Fourthly, if help could be given, it must immediately be done. Fifthly, they realised that only limited numbers could take part in the actual fighting units. That was our interpretation of the phrase.[46]

At the time, however, Jews in the Yishuv and in America did not know what was to come. Simultaneous with the outbreak of fighting in the Warsaw ghetto on April 19, 1943, the other major news item that captured the attention of the world Jewish press was the ill-fated Bermuda Conference, convened in response to urgent demands to rescue what was left of European Jewry. On January 20, 1943, the British Foreign Office, in response to public pressure from Parliament, humanitarian organizations, and the Church, proposed British and American consultation to come up with a possible solution to the crisis; the result was the Anglo-American Conference on Refugees, held in Bermuda April 19–30. Consultations at the conference, which would ultimately prove completely ineffective, attracted a good deal of attention in the Jewish press in late April.

The organizers of the Bermuda Conference did not invite Jewish organizations to attend, reinforcing a sense of powerlessness and impotence on the part of world Jewry to make a dent in the apathy of the world. Much of the time at Bermuda was spent debating whether it was even appropriate to refer to the Jews as the Nazis' primary victims. Both Dr. Harold W. Dodds, head of the American delegation, and Richard K. Law, head of the British delegation, indicated "that the solution of the refugee problem lies in an Allied victory." Aid to refugees would be considered secondary to military efforts and "no plan [would] be considered by the delegates which can be construed in any way as tending to retard the war effort."[47] Law suggested reviving the Evian Conference (the July 1938 conference of thirty-two countries convened to discuss the German-Jewish refugee crisis) as an outcome of the conference (and indeed, when the report of the Bermuda Conference was published seven months later on December 10, 1943, the only positive suggestion was to restart the Evian Committee—too late to engage in any effective rescue efforts for most of European Jewry, with the notable exception of the War Refugee Board in 1944, which would ultimately play a crucial role in the rescue of tens of thousands of Jews). Unable to participate at the conference itself, the majority of American Jewish organizations, represented together by the Joint Emergency Committee for European Jewish Affairs, made the text of their appeals sent to the Bermuda Conference public through the press, conveying the "anguish of the Jewish community of this country over the failure of the United Nations to act until now to rescue the Jews of Europe." Despite authenticated knowledge for six months regarding the murder of three million Jews and broad calls for support, "no action has as yet been taken. In the meantime it is reported that thousands of Jews continue to be murdered daily. . . . Unless action is undertaken immediately, there may soon be no Jews left alive in Europe."[48] As the labor Zionist publication the *Jewish Frontier* noted in an editorial in May 1943, titled "The Gentlemen at Bermuda," "Hitler has won another victory at Bermuda . . . the so-called Refugee Conference has made a mockery, not only of the agony of millions of helpless human beings, but of the great cause of liberation to which the democratic world is committed, and which alone makes the horror of our time understandable and endurable."[49]

Likewise, on April 19, 1943, the front page of *Davar*, which reported on the opening of the Bermuda conference that day, included a banner headline in bold print: "BERMUDA TODAY: SAVE THOSE BEING LED TO SLAUGHTER!" In a poem in the same edition of the newspaper, Natan Alterman contemplated the "Pesach of the Diaspora," likening the sacrificial offering of the Paschal lamb to the sacrifice of the diaspora Jewry in Europe.

Pesach of the Diaspora

And the smoking and destroyed nation
Which is trodden to dust by the threshing sledge
Is singing its song in a beautiful voice
On the sanctified eve when the Holiday begins.

In towns bloodied from sorrows
Which cover its eyes with the shadow of death,
The nation sits tonight in white clothes,
In grandeur of immortality.

And the whip hit him and boiled his blood
The officers of the region spat in his face
But straight stood the candles of his ancient Holiday,
And illuminated his face as it would light up a king's.

And the swords of his haters are drawn as is the custom
And between him and them there is only one step,
How much silence and how much awe and festivity,
Our history put in you, the eve of Pesach!

The night of Spain and the evil plots of the monks in their cells,
A night of a luminous moon and a sinking silence
A sacred night and a night of blood libels
And the night of "pour your wrath" and an angel at the door.

In the towns of hatred, in the towns of sorrows
Where the road from them—the valley of death,
A nation sits at its Festival in white clothes,
In a silence of Holiday and immortality.

And the eyes of his orphans shine like candles of light
And his daughters in white and in plaited braids,
Father, look at your nation, it is pure, it is pure!
Pure like gold he is already refined, heaven is its witness.

Because it was thrown to the dogs who seek its skin,
And there is no saviour and comforter for it,
And there is no Holiday like its Holiday and there is no song like its song
As it sings to you tonight.

To its fallen and broken roofed houses
The Shechina looks in and bites her lips,
Because it's a Holiday she can't cry! Because it's a Holiday! Because it's a Holiday!
And the daughter in white smiles to the candles.

Consolation, consolation the daughter still will behold!
And the nation when it rises from its mourning—will still have strength!

And this night, this Pesach sacrifice,
The world will not forget! It will not be able to forget!

Natan A.

Alterman describes the Jewish people as a nation "smoking and destroyed . . . trodden to dust by the threshing sledge," who may be remembered in the future, through that "Passover sacrifice" which the nation and the world will not forget.[50] Nonetheless, though largely destroyed, Alterman invokes the language of the prophet Isaiah, *Nachamu, Nachamu Ami*—"comfort, comfort, my people"—read on the first Shabbat after Tisha b'Av, after the three weeks of mourning for the tragedy of the destruction of the Temple in Jerusalem.

As the Jewish press reported on the deliberations at the Bermuda Conference, it is safe to say that the rather limited scope of the discussions and the self-imposed boundaries on the delegates only contributed to a sense that world Jewry was largely powerless and that democracy had failed in its obligation to protect the Jewish minority.[51] If we add to this the complete sense of helplessness and despair that someone like Zygielbojm in London may have felt knowing that his friends in Warsaw still believed that if he managed to reach the proper ears in London or Washington, someone would intervene to help, the depth of the feelings of abandonment for Jews both inside and outside occupied Europe is clear.

Reporting the Revolt in April and May 1943

When news did begin to spread throughout the world of the remarkable, unexpected, and surprising turn of events inside the ghetto, however, the actual coverage varied depending on the political orientation and audience of the publication.[52] This wide-ranging tone in reactions to the revolt makes clear the importance of distinguishing between types of coverage: the Jewish Telegraphic Agency, which faced growing difficulties during the war both reporting the news, and then having its stories picked up; the general press, like the *New York Times* and other mainstream news sources, which consistently underreported Jewish atrocities; and the rest of the Jewish press, which was segmented according to political ideologies.[53]

The Jewish Telegraphic Agency report of April 23, 1943, delivered the news of the Warsaw ghetto revolt with the headline "Nazis Start Mass-Execution of Warsaw Jews on Passover; Victims Broadcast S.O.S.," detailing the massacre of the last thirty-five thousand Jews in Warsaw and quoting the secret Polish radio station SWIAT and its frantic appeal from occupied Poland: "Death sentence has been proclaimed on the last 35,000 Jews in the Warsaw ghetto. Gun salvoes are echoing in the streets of Warsaw. Women and children are defending themselves with bare hands. Save us." At this point the broadcast was suddenly cut off.[54] The story was picked up by almost all of the Jewish press, having managed to travel from Warsaw to the outside world via various wartime channels. Reports were issued by the Polish underground, the Jewish underground, by German military channels, through underground radio, as well as through the "rumor mill."[55] In the case of the Warsaw Ghetto Uprising, the Polish underground first cabled London about the uprising on April 20, 1943, the day after it broke out.[56] Stefan Korbonski (chief of directorate of civil resistance) cabled London that the Germans had entered the ghetto on the previous day and a dramatic battle had begun: "The Jews are defending themselves; we can hear shots and grenade explosions," the cable read. "The Germans have used bombs and armored cars. They have losses." Korbonski sent a second cable on the following day detailing continued fighting in the ghetto, shots, fires, and explosions. According to historian Joshua Zimmerman, the cables reached Ignacy Schwartzbart[57] of the Polish national council in London on April 23, 1943, and on the same day the uprising was reported in the international press for the first time. The cable from Warsaw reported:

> The liquidations of the central ghetto in Warsaw began at 4:00 AM on April 19. Cordons of German and Polish police, a strong unit of gendarme and SS, as well as armored vehicles and tanks have surrounded the ghetto. . . . The Jewish Combat Organization has mounted strong resistance. Continuous fighting has been taking place for three days with huge explosions going off on the streets that shake the whole of Warsaw. The effect of the explosions is that the

> ghetto is engulfed in a cloud of smoke and numerous fires. Today—the 21st—the fighting continues.[58]

Jewish leaders in Warsaw also managed to send at least five cables to representatives of the Polish government in London. Moreover, the Jewish National Committee and the Coordinating Committee wrote the daily communiqués on the Aryan side of Warsaw, detailing events as they transpired in the ghetto.[59]

The first cable was sent by a joint representation of the Bund and the Jewish National Committee via delegate Jankowski's office and was addressed to Zygielbojm and Schwartzbart. The cable began by informing London that the Germans had entered the ghetto the day before. "The ghetto offers heroic resistance, there is great excitement all over." The Polish people outside the ghetto "watch the struggle with admiration and open sympathy for the ghetto fighters." The cable then called for immediate revenge and asked for the international Red Cross to visit ghettos and death camps. However, the cable never reached London and only the last paragraph came through on May 4.

Later testimonies of ghetto fighters also detailed various means by which news could flow from the ghetto and its environs to the outside world. Sounds of gunfire, tank battles, bombardments, and then the flames and smoke of the final liquidation made it clear to all of Warsaw's residents that a great battle was underway. For those Jews trapped in the ghetto, however, there were still other means of communication. As surviving ghetto fighters like Zivia Lubetkin and Vladka Meed would note, telephones within the ghetto still worked in the first week of the uprising. The messages detailed in the previous chapter reveal underground fighters were also able to pass messages through the sewer system or smuggling routes through the Jewish cemetery. Even so, such information would prove fitful and incomplete. Furthermore, coded messages would take time to be deciphered and were often misunderstood or misinterpreted.

How did newspapers translate this information for diverse Jewish audiences? The Jewish press reported what was known as information traveled from Warsaw to London to New York and the Yishuv, although such reporting would be interpreted and filtered ideologically. For the *Forverts*, for example, the extermination was *the story* and attracted a great deal of attention.[60] The *Forverts* made the beginning of the uprising its cover story on April 23: "NAZIS SLAUGHTER LAST JEWS OF WARSAW, SECRET RADIO REPORTS THE NAZIS LEADING THE LAST 35,000 JEWS TO THE SLAUGHTER (*shkhiteh*)." The *Forverts*, like JTA, also cited the secret radio report, and the article also noted the Nazi massacre began just as Jews around the world "mark(ed) the festival of freedom." And then again on April 25, 1943, the *Forverts* reported that Jews were still fighting:

> Those who are currently mounting the resistance, are the healthiest and *most militant* Jews, who remain in Warsaw, after the Nazis had carried out the great mass murder and deportation last fall. The weapons with which the Jews are fighting, were provided by the Polish Underground movement, which also sent trained commanders for this last battle. [*sic*][61]

Initial reporting in the newspaper of the Israel workers movement, *Davar*, edited by one of the leaders of Labor Zionism, Berl Katznelson, paralleled reports in *Forverts*, while also emphasizing the continued connection between underground Zionist activists in Poland and the movement in Geneva and the Yishuv.[62] The headlines described the fighting Jews of Warsaw as both the *She'erit Hapletah* (surviving remnant) of the Jewish Diaspora and as the rebels *(Mitmardim)* fighting the Nazis. Like *Forverts*, *Davar* reporting mistakenly assumed trained officers from the Polish underground had been sent to the ghetto to help "manage the Jewish defense there" (*Davar*, April 27).

On April 30, 1943, *Davar* included a message "from well-known leaders of the Zionist movement in Poland" that had been reported by the Jewish Telegraphic Agency, which asked for arms and indicated that

> the Jews who still remain in the Warsaw ghetto are putting up a vigorous fight against the Nazis "for the sake of Jewish

> honor and the little that has been left." It appeals for urgent aid to enable the Jews to acquire arms for themselves and food for their children and concludes with greetings to the Jewish people the world over and to the international labor movement.

The message concluded with sharp criticism, clearly born out of intense feelings of abandonment by the Jews in the democratic countries, especially the Jews of America, charging them with indifference. "While we are being exterminated, they indulge in olympic calmness," the message read.[63]

News of the fighting in Warsaw spread rapidly through occupied Europe, too.

By April 22, the news had spread to Vilna and throughout the ghetto; Herman Kruk wrote in his April 30 diary entry:

> "Warszawskie Getto Kona!' [The Warsaw Ghetto is Dying]. . . ." Yesterday *Swit* [SWIAT] once again sounded the alarm to the world, and once again the radio announcer repeated, as if he wanted the world to remember, the Warsaw Ghetto is bleeding to death. The Warsaw Ghetto is dying! Warsaw Jews are defending themselves like heroes. For 13 days now, the Germans have had to fight with the ghetto for every threshold. Jews do not let themselves be taken and are fighting like lions . . . the Warsaw Ghetto is dying! . . . And my own sister and children? . . . I am ashamed of my silence.[64]

In Germany, even Josef Goebbels, Reich Minister of Propaganda took note, recording his reaction to the revolt in his journal on May 1:

> Reports from the occupied territories do not bring anything sensationally new. Noteworthy though is the exceptionally sharp fighting in Warsaw between our police and even Wehrmacht units and the rebelling Jews. The Jews have

> managed to organize defense of the ghetto. The fighting there is very hard; it goes so far that the Jewish command issues daily reports. This whole fun will probably not last long. One sees though what one may expect from the Jews when they manage to set their hands on weapons. Unfortunately they have in part also good German, mainly machine guns. God knows how they got them.[65]

While there was little that Jews abroad could do to support the revolt as it transpired, on May 2, 1943, approximately two weeks into the revolt, *Davar* reported on a special new tax issued by the labor movement in the Yishuv to support the defense of Warsaw: "TO ENCOURAGE THE REVOLT (*mered*) AND THE DEFENDERS IN THE GHETTOS."[66]

And on May 5, 1943, *Davar* reported on a "telegraphic cry for help from the underground in Poland" received by Szmuel Zygielbojm in London. With no more than 10 percent of the prewar Polish Jewish population alive, the report said, "the time for statements and declarations has passed—what is needed now is immediate rescue work."[67]

Reports from the Polish underground about the revolt also reached the Jewish antifascist committee in the far reaches of the Soviet Union. A May 10, 1943, story reported in the JTA, dateline Kyubeshev (now Samara, in southwestern Russia, the wartime capital of the USSR) reported that the flags of Britain, Poland, and Russia were flying proudly above the Warsaw ghetto. (The Jewish National Committee's communiqué of April 21, 1943 had cited only two flags, the Polish and the Zionist flags, flying above no. 2 Muranowska Street.)

> From the highest buildings in the ghetto, the embattled Jews flew the flags of Poland, Great Britain and the Soviet Union, the report reveals. Bands of Jewish insurgents stormed the infamous Paviak prison and released scores of political prisoners. Fierce battles broke out in the ruined Nalevki district and on Muranov Square when the Germans threw artillery, tanks and bombers against the Jews.

The report concluded that "on April 18, SS detachments broke into the ghetto and were met by machine gun fire and hand grenades, supplied to the Jews by members of the 'National Guards', the Polish underground army. (It is not known whether the battle in the ghetto still continues.)"[68]

While the Jewish press reported the dramatic events in Warsaw along with mistakenly noting an armed revolt in Bialystok (this revolt actually began on August 15, 1943), *Forverts* continued to report on the Bermuda Conference and the course of fighting in North Africa, where thirty thousand Jews in Tunis had been freed by the Allied advance (as reported on May 9, 1943).

As coverage in the Jewish press continued to highlight the revolt, along with news on other fronts of the war effort, by Monday, May 10, the *Forverts* added a new trope in its coverage of Warsaw, reporting on "The Jewish Heroes of Warsaw." The cover story that day detailed how "Open uprising broke out on the 18th of April in the Warsaw Ghetto when Nazis entered to drag Jews to the slaughter.–Jews met the murderers with machine guns and hand grenades. . . . Nazis forced to bring canons, tanks, and aeroplanes to suppress the uprising.—Paid dearly for the murders of Jews." Citing the May 10, 1943, JTA report, the *Forverts* offered greater detail on the "heroic uprising in Warsaw conveyed to Soviet press by Polish underground reports here," explaining the Jews did not fight alone but that the Nazis were also attacked from behind by the Polish underground.

By Wednesday, May 12, however, the *Forverts* reported on page 9 about the liquidation of the ghetto. Citing a JTA report from London on the same day: "The Jewish ghetto in Warsaw is already completely 'liquidated' by the Nazis, despite the heroic resistance of the Jewish people, said a broadcast of the secret Polish radio, SWIAT, which was heard here Monday night. The radio announcer simultaneously appealed to the Poles in the Warsaw region, that they should give support to Jews who had escaped from the ghetto" and offer assistance and hiding places to Jews from the ghetto.

Other Jewish newspapers in New York also began to pick up on the trope of heroism. Samuel Margoshes, editor of *Der Tog*, noted his suspicions of "Nazi propaganda as a pretext for Nazi atrocities," initially dismissing the possibility that unarmed Jews might rise up against the "greatest military

די אידישע העלדען פון ווארשע

אפענער אויפשטאנד האט אויסגעבראכען דעם 18טען אפריל אין ווארשעווער געטא ווען נאצים זיינען געקומען שלעפען אידען צו דער שחיטה. — אידען האבען די מערדער באגעגענט מיט מאשין־ביקען און האנט־גראנאטען. — האבען זיך אריינגעריסען אין טורמע און באפרייט געפאנגענע. — נאצים געצוואונגען צו ברענגען קאנאנען, טענקס און עראפלאנען צו אונטערדריקען אויפשטאנד. — האבען טייער באצאהלט פאר רציחות אויף אידען.

Forverts headline, Monday, May 10, 1943, the Jewish heroes of Warsaw.

machine the world has ever seen. . . . However, I see now that I was mistaken. There was an upsurge of Jewish resistance in the Warsaw ghetto, and it was one of the miracles of our age."[69]

As reports indicated that the fighting in Warsaw was winding down, and the Jewish press began its search for the uprising's Jewish heroes, coverage shifted to a new focus: the death of the Bund representative to the Polish government-in-exile in London, Szmuel Zygielbojm.[70] On May 14, the *Forverts* reported that Zygielbojm had killed himself after learning of the murder of his wife and daughter in the Warsaw ghetto. The *New York Times* included an obituary of Zygielbojm on May 15. The text of Zygielbojm's final telegram to Emanuel Nowogrodsky (secretary of the American Representation of the Bund in New York) made clear, however, that his suicide was not just in response to news of the death of his family. Zygielbojm had acted out of a sense of obligation to all of the Jews of Poland, whom he had left behind in 1940, and as a protest against the inaction of the democratic nations of the world. As he wrote in his final telegram, "perhaps my death will cause what I didn't succeed while alive that concreet [*sic*] action should be taken at last to save the less then 300 thousend Jews who remained by now in Poland out of 3 millions and a half."[71]

Speculation in the press soon turned to explaining why Zygielbojm had chosen to take his own life. Set against the backdrop of the Warsaw Ghetto Uprising, which Jews in the free world believed was still underway, the question of whether his suicide was an act of helplessness and despair or a heroic effort to arouse the conscience of the world took on great significance, and was subject to interpretation in different segments of the Jewish press, which also scrutinized his last letters, which had been made available.

Zygielbojm's last letter would be printed in the *Forverts* on June 3, and in the *New York Times* on June 4. In contrast to the glowing tributes to Zygielbojm in the Jewish socialist press, coverage in the Labor Zionist press was muted and even critical of Zygielbojm's choice to commit suicide, comparing it to that of the head of the Warsaw Judenrat, Adam Czerniakow, who had taken his own life at the start of the Great Deportation.[72] The Zygielbojm suicide, while capturing attention in the general and Jewish press in New York, London, Palestine, and around the world, also signified the dramatic conclusion to the end of Warsaw Jewry, which was taken to symbolize the tragic ending of Polish Jewry. In fact, just as the Warsaw Uprising symbolized the last desperate act of the Jews of Poland driven to revolt as a final "deed," the suicide of Zygielbojm, representative of Polish Jewry (and indeed Warsaw Jewry) to the free world, would be conflated with the final liquidation of the ghetto. As can be seen in the responses in *Davar* and the *Forward*, however, the choice made by Zygielbojm to commit suicide would also be interpreted through a political lens: for Bundists in New York, his life and death would be commemorated and celebrated; for Zionists in the Yishuv, his example was one to be disparaged and forgotten.

By the end of May 1943, further details on the dramatic fighting in the ghetto began to emerge. On May 24, JTA reported that Ignacy Schwartzbart delivered to the British parliament secret reports he and Szmuel Zygielbojm had received from the Jewish National Committee in Warsaw. These two cables, dated April 28 and May 13, would be reported extensively in the Jewish press, adding further detail to the dramatic saga of the revolt, and clarifying that the Jewish fighters in the ghetto had received little support from the non-Jewish population of Warsaw, despite appeals. Many of the Jews in the ghetto had been burned alive by Nazi flamethrowers, but the messages indicated "about 1,000 Nazis have been killed. Particularly stiff resistance was put up by several thousand Jews who barricaded themselves in the underground storehouses of the ghetto."[73]

On June 1, JTA offered further details on the two cables that had reached London the week before. The April 28 report was not only an appeal to the conscience of the world for support. It also began to fill in crucial details on the "heroic fighting," identifying the existence of a "Jewish fighting organization (which) shows great ingenuity and courage" and offering a name: Michał Klepfisz, identified as "an engineer, [and] one of the pillars of the determined resistance," who had "died like a hero."[74] The contents of the April 28 cable were also reported in the *Forverts* on May 24, with a headline declaring "Warsaw Jews send a report from Ghetto Battle." The headline further announced, "Heroic Jewish fighters send a report from Warsaw in the middle of the battle with the Nazis. Reports of murders and horrible revenge." The Yiddish paper referenced Klepfisz as the "leader of [the] Jewish fighters," who had fallen "in battle," and reported that "the Polish people are amazed by the heroic spirit of the Jewish resistance, while the Nazis are wild with embarrassment and rage."[75] The second appeal, which was sent on the 11th of May, read thus: "The heroic resistance of the Warsaw Ghetto continues. Several strongly defended points remain. The Jewish fighting organization demonstrates great fighting ability and courage. The leader of the Jewish 'Bund' Klepfisz, who is one of the leaders of the uprising, fell in the battles like a hero."[76]

The *Forward* published an article on Saturday, May 29, 1943, offering further detail on who the actual leaders of the revolt had been, indicating "200 Jews Lead the Battle in the Warsaw Ghetto":

> The 200 Jews led thousands of young people, older men, women, and children—radicals, Orthodox, and other groups—in battle against the Nazis. People battled with weapons, which were smuggled through the underground movement. . . . In

> the last few days various reports about the Jewish "revolt" [*oyfshtand*] in Warsaw have begun to emerge. It is impossible to discover the truth, but it is clear that a great, bloody battle has taken place.

In Palestine, news coverage also offered greater details on the end of the revolt, while interpreting its conclusion in slightly different terms. *Davar* also reported the name of Klepfisz as leader of the revolt on May 24, while the *Palestine Post* of May 25 reported that "the Jewish fighting organizations earned the admiration of the Polish workers' association." Here, however, the article introduced a new historical parallel to one last desperate stand of overmatched and isolated Jews: Masada.

> As the epic struggle of the Warsaw ghetto, recalling the saga of Massada of old, neared its inevitable end, remnants of provincial Jewish centres were also wiped out. What amounts to a final appeal received in London by underground channels declared:
>
> > *In the name of millions of Jews, already murdered, in the name of the burned and massacred, in the name of those fighting heroically and of all of us condemned to death, we appeal to the world for help. Yet the free world, the world of justice, remains apathetic. It is amazing. We expect help for the survivors who are saving themselves.*

In *Davar*, a May 28, 1943, editorial (likely written by Berl Katznelson) interpreted the revolt through a distinctly socialist Zionist lens:

> The latest chapter of the defense by the Jews of Warsaw was described by British radio as "one of the most tragic and heroic chapters of the war." Foreigners were amazed by the majesty of this battle, a battle of the chained against their jailors, of the doomed against their executioners. . . . For us

> this conclusion is not surprising. From all of the development of European Jewry in the last generations does this battle emerge. It is the finale of the struggle of generations of Polish Jews to integrate and blend the magnificence of Jewish originality into the pride of human uprising.

While specific details on the identities of most of the fighters was lacking, Katznelson explained that the ghetto uprising had been nourished

> by the spirit of the great loyalty and the great national creative endeavor that hovered over the great city. . . . the world will surely be even more surprised if it realizes that the heroism of Warsaw is not the last link in the chain of *Jewish defense and martyrdom*; if it understands that generations of Jews trained themselves to take this stand until the generation that was put to the historical test—and passed it—came along. The world now knows that the defenders of the ghettos left behind a great testament and that fulfillers of this testament will be found wherever Jews respond.[77]

While Katznelson saw the revolt as an evocation of the Jewish national spirit, a spirit that did not die in Warsaw but would be carried on by the fulfillers of this testament, Zygielbojm's suicide continued to evoke differing responses among Zionists and Bundists.

On Thursday, June 3, 1943, the text of Zygielbojm's letter was reported in the *Forverts*, and the *New York Times* devoted a lengthier article to the story, including a full reprinting of Zygielbojm's last letter to the Polish president, Wladyslaw Raczkiewicz, and prime minister, General Wladyslaw Sikorski:[78]

> I cannot continue to live and to be silent while the remnants of Polish Jewry, whose representative I am, are being murdered. My comrades in the Warsaw ghetto fell with arms in their hands in the last heroic battle. I was not permitted to

> fall like them, together with them, but I belong with them, to their mass grave.
>
> By my death, I wish to give expression to my most profound protest against the inaction in which the world watches and permits the destruction of the Jewish people.[79]

Davar also carried the text of Zygielbojm's letter on June 3, 1943. The *Jewish Frontier*, a Labor Zionist monthly, edited by Marie Syrkin,[80] published an editorial on Zygielbojm's *Last Stand* in its June 1943 edition.[81]

The Last Stand (Editorial)

> Zygielbojm had to leave the grimacing illusion of a civilized world in which the conventions of humanity prevailed. There was a real world from which he had shortly come and to which he was allied, the grim world of the ghetto where the assassin raged, gassing and choking efficiently, systematically so many thousand per day. Zygielbojm could not divorce himself from that reality; he could not make his peace with the ghostly world of occasional speeches, averted faces and closed doors . . . If Zygielbojm had not killed himself, few would so much as have known of the strange request which issued from the 30,000 Jews who were all that remains of the hundreds of thousands once shut up in the Warsaw ghetto.
>
> But something glorious happened in the Warsaw ghetto which Zygielbojm did not live to witness. *The 30,000 made a last stand. They did not let themselves be led to slaughter.* [My emphasis.] They knew what fate awaited them, and they died fighting. We do not know the details of that fierce and hopeless struggle, foredoomed from the beginning; we only know that the German murderers were forced to bring up tanks and artillery before they could complete their carnage. The Jews, furnished with arms smuggled to them by the Polish underground, fought fiercely—man, woman and child—barricading themselves and their houses. According to information from the Polish government, nearly 1,000 Nazis were killed or wounded before the last of Warsaw Jewry was murdered.
>
> A heroic, somber battle in which the victory is surely not to the thugs who completed their planned assassination! The Warsaw ghetto has been

"liquidated." Leaders of Polish Jewry are dead by their own hand. And the world which looks on passively is, in its way, dead too.

June, 1943

The Transition to Commemoration

As the Jewish world transitioned from reporting the revolt to commemorating the event, several key questions would emerge that would influence the manner in which the uprising would be interpreted: Who were the leaders of the revolt, Bundists, Zionists, or others? Was it a popular revolt of all of the surviving Jews in the Warsaw ghetto, a revolt led by the solidarity of the working classes, or a battle led by an elite cadre of armed fighters inspired by the pioneering spirit of the *halutzim*?

At the same time, as news of deaths and names of heroes began to emerge (Klepfisz, the Bundist engineer, remained the name most cited as one of the leaders of the revolt), and as Jews around the world began to take stock of the meaning of the "heroic, last stand" of the Warsaw Jews, who "would not be led like sheep to the slaughter," memorial services were organized. In the Yishuv, Zivia Lubetkin and Tosia Altman were eulogized in June after it was believed they had both died in the uprising (Zivia, it was later discovered, had in fact survived; Tosia died in a fire two weeks after the end of the uprising).[82] On June 1, 1943, *Davar* reported their deaths among the "heads of the Zionist socialist underground in Poland" and announced memorial services for them and Josef Kaplan (Kaplan had been killed in September 1942) sponsored by Hashomer Hatzair.

> Zivia and Tosia. The Nazi murderer can no longer do anything to you. Now we can reveal to all, near and far, what you meant to us in the recent years. And what you meant to our devastated people in Poland and to all for whom a Jewish heart beats in their chest. Zivia—was the center of the activity in Poland in most recent period. She was not

just the address—she was also its leader and the spirit of action of our movement.

The story noted that the two were almost always linked in their underground and defense work. For ten days, the newspaper noted, they had held onto the information that the two had fallen in battle. Hoping there had been some kind of a mistake, the newspaper held off on publishing the information, until it became clear (mistakenly) that the information was correct.

On June 4, 1943, *Davar* carried an article describing how Hashomer Hatzair had united with the memory of the defenders of the Warsaw ghetto. At a meeting of the Kibbutz Ha'Artzi HaShomer Hatzair at Mitzpe Yam (which would later be relocated to the Negev and renamed Kibbutz Yad Mordecai after Anielewicz), the "hearts of the movement" were united with the images of the two defenders of the ghetto—Tosia and Zivia—as well as the memory of Josef Kaplan, a member of the central leadership of Hashomer Hatzair. "Those there who were burned in the flame (*shalhevet*) of defense on the honor of Israel and those here who descended to the depths of the sea, guided us with their lives" said Meir Ya'ari in words of opening. "To the great deeds of the bravery there and the best of our defense here the world responds in Bermuda. . . . We will surround them with a ring of love. In our uniting with their memory we sense what is the glory of man which raises our movement. In their actions they have bequeathed upon us faith until the end."[83]

Ya'akov Amit, a leader of Hashomer Hatzair from Lithuania, spoke of the moral, symbolic, and educational meaning of Tosia and Zivia's actions. "Tosia and Zivia represent in themselves the collective ideal of a generation of pioneers in the horrible test which fate had brought upon them. Tosia and Zivia and thousands like them have cast upon us a mission (*shlichut*) and have planted within us the strength to carry out this mission." Amit, uncertain that the Jewish people possessed the ability to absorb the lessons of their heroic example, called on the movement: "Do not forget! Do not allow the Jews to forget!"

And Azriel Schwartz (editor of the poetry collection *Plucked Leaves: Poems of Nations at War*, 1943) sought to correct premature comparisons

צביה לובטקין וטוסיה (טובה) אלטמן

מראשי המחתרת הציונית הסוציאליסטית בפולין

שטוקהולם, 28 במאי (טלגרפית). קבלנו ידיעות מ־27 ומ־30 באפריל, מודיעים על מותם של טוסיה וצביה, הן ורבים מבני משפחותיהן, בקרב ההתגוננות בוארשה.

טוסיה אלטמן

צביה לובטקין

Davar, June 1, 1943. Zivia Lubetkin and Tosia (Tova) Altman, "Among the leaders of the Zionist Socialist Underground in Poland."

of Warsaw to Masada. "There are those who seek to compare Warsaw to Masada, however, inasmuch as Masada fought opposite a destroyed Jerusalem (today) Warsaw fights opposite a Jerusalem that is rising and being built. We also could have been the last ones. We were saved by a miracle. We have remained the first to redemption and the heavy and growing responsibility falls upon us—we have been made the bearers of the banner of Israeli hope."[84]

On June 6, 1943, HeHalutz and Kibbutz HaMeuchad held a memorial service at Kibbutz Yagur to remember the "ghetto fighters (who) saved the honor of the Jewish people," singling out specifically Zivia Lubetkin (of the Dror youth movement) and Tosia Altman (Hashomer Hatzair). The speakers who eulogized them noted that the "ghetto rebels saved the honor of Israel and created with their lives one of the tales of greatest heroism of our time. . . . [O]n this new Masada generations will be built." The two women, described by Reuters as the two "Joans of Arc" were rapidly transformed into symbols of loss and suffering, as well as models of incredible self-sacrifice in a manner that was clearly gendered.[85] Zivia Lubetkin and Tosia Altman came to stand in for the death and suffering of millions of Jews in a way that male fighters did not; while Mordecai Anielewicz and Yitzhak Zuckerman would eventually become known as the leaders of the revolt in Zionist circles, Zivia came to represent the sacrifice of the Jewish people and their resurrection.[86]

Natan Alterman wrote a poem in Zivia's honor, published in *Davar*, called "A Hebrew Maiden," in which he described the deceased heroine as one "who lived in the expansive house of death, *yearning to become a homemaker*" (*Davar*, June 4, 1943). Zivia, the Hebrew maiden, was described by Alterman as one who could be found in the home of the deceased Jewish nation, "ready and available for any task." Alterman concluded his tribute to Lubetkin: "young maiden, the chronicles of history look to you, to remember you and to preserve your appearance."

On June 14, the Jewish National Council in Palestine organized a "Day of Protest against Allies' Indifference to Jewish Tragedy," proclaiming that day "a day of solidarity with the heroic stand taken by the Jews in the Warsaw ghetto as well as an expression of protest on the part of the Palestine Jews against the indifference of the Allied Nations to the unprecedented Jewish tragedy."[87] The Zionist leadership issued a remarkable statement that expressed admiration for those leading the fight in Poland, and a complete identification between the Zionist struggle in the ghettos of Poland and the struggle for national liberation in Palestine.[88]

> Today the Yishuv will demonstrate, the avant-garde of the nation fighting for its redemption, its identification with the enslaved and depressed diaspora . . . in the countries of

occupied Europe in the hands of the Nazis, with the diaspora in Poland standing in the last remnants of its strength on its soul and on the honor of Israel. . . . today the Yishuv will . . . demand that Allies fighting against the evil Nazis rescue the "surviving remnant" of the Diaspora in Europe, the heroes on the Jewish front that has risen in Poland. . . .

The Jewish front that has been established through their heroism in the streets of the Warsaw ghetto and in the ghettos of other cities unites and joins with the fronts of our battles against the Nazi evil, one shoulder together with the Allied Nations, with the front in the war for the building of the homeland for establishment and for freedom.

Jerusalem, 11th Sivan 1943 (signed by the "Zionist leadership")

Beyond an expression of pride in the actions of the Zionist underground and the call for rescue issued by the leadership, one can read here, too, admiration for the Zionist heroes who had joined the fight against the Nazis, a fight Jews in the Yishuv had been unable to join but whose time "too will come." In expressing pride in the Zionist leaders of the resistance in Poland, this fight became the fight of the Zionist movement in the Yishuv, too. Heeding the call of the leadership, hundreds of thousands in the Yishuv would sign a declaration calling for rescue and join a general strike in solidarity with European Jewry.[89]

As Jewish leaders in the United States, the Yishuv, and England began the search for the names of heroes from the uprising, the community also began the process of commemorating the event, some two months after it took place, in the midst of a fierce war.

On June 3, 1943, JTA reported that London's *Evening Standard* proposed making April 19 of every year a so-called Jewish Day:

April 19, the day when human valor converted the Warsaw ghetto into a fortress of freedom should be an honored day among men cherishing mercy and tolerance. . . . Jews are

> fighting today on all fronts for the cause of humanity, and the Jew will be among the proud participants of common victory.[90]

Two weeks later, on June 19, 1943, the Jewish Labor Committee organized a mass meeting in New York to commemorate the Jewish heroes of the Warsaw ghetto. The Saturday evening meeting at Carnegie Hall celebrated the heroes and honored Szmuel Zygielbojm, featuring such speakers as the Polish ambassador; Dr. Stephen S. Wise, president of the American Jewish Committee; and Adolph Held, chairman of the Jewish Labor Committee along with leaders of the American labor movement.[91] Lucy Dawidowicz (née Shildkret) recalled the service in her memoirs:

> We went and we wept, yet there was pride in what the Polish Jews had done. For the first time anywhere during the German occupation of Europe, a civilian population had taken up arms against their German oppressors. Not just any civilian population, but the most oppressed, the most helpless, the most desperate. In the next weeks, Bundist and Zionist underground reports from Warsaw reaching the West gave details of the fighting and listed the names of the dead and the few survivors. . . . *The events of the Warsaw ghetto burned into my consciousness. . . . The Warsaw ghetto became a constant part of my internal life. I used to imagine myself there, test myself as to how I would have behaved. Would I have had the courage to fight? Would I have had the stamina against despair?*[92]

Writing in the Labor Zionist publication *The Jewish Frontier* in July 1943, Marie Syrkin also expressed a desire to know the identities of the heroes, "who were able to fight back instead of letting themselves be herded helplessly into sealed trains or lethal chambers."

> We do not know the names of the heroes, and we cannot pin medals on their breasts—even posthumously. But here

> and there a figure emerges. We all know the names of Adam Czerniakow, and of Zygielbojm who killed himself in London in protest against the indifference of the world. To these names we can now add that of Zivia Lubetkin, "The Mother." Zivia, "The Mother," (*die mame*) was not old, nor did she have children of her own. She lost her life, at the age of 28, as a leader of the ghetto's final battle. *Young as she was, she was the "mother," by virtue of strength and solicitude, of the crushed, the abandoned, the helpless. . . .*
>
> There is another circumstance that we must note. The defenders raised a flag to fly from the Ghetto wall. It was the Jewish flag—the Star of Zion. . . .
>
> . . . *The badge of shame became a banner, and the strength which transformed it, the strength of Zivia and her comrades, came from the most ancient as well as the newest source of Jewish strength—Zion.* In their last moment, the Jews of the Warsaw ghetto were not alone. They had lost the present, but they raised the flag which made them one with the past and with the future.[93]

In the summer of 1943, most Jews in the free world felt that a remarkable outbreak of glorious Jewish resistance had taken place, and that the lives and deaths of the Jewish heroes and martyrs needed to be celebrated and commemorated. In fact, from a historiographical standpoint, there was a lack of context, which, while understandable, may help to explain why for many years the distinction between Jewish resistance and Jewish passivity was so prominent: the centrality of the Warsaw Ghetto Uprising as a focal point of Jewish celebration and commemoration obscured other aspects of *amidah* and other ways of defining resistance.[94]

Reports in the Jewish press offered tantalizing details on the uprising from scattered sources, including an August 16, 1943, story in JTA citing the Polish underground newspaper *Polska*, "disclosing that the Jews in the Warsaw ghetto used German guns and were dressed in German military uniforms and helmets when they waged their heroic resistance against the

Nazi 'liquidation' of the ghetto" and that the Jewish fighters "were assisted by firemen, air-raid wardens and nurses."[95] On Friday, August 20, 1943, *Forverts* published a report citing a declaration by Stephen S. Wise of the American Jewish Committee that four million Jews in Europe had been murdered since the beginning of Nazi killing operations in 1942. A related article cited reports that only one hundred thousand Jews remained alive in Poland. Nonetheless, "the surviving Jews continued to fight" in various places in Poland, in a message reportedly received by Ignacy Schwartzbart in London on August 10.[96]

In August 1943, the World Jewish Congress published *Lest We Forget: The Massacre of the Warsaw Ghetto*, one year after the Great Deportation, which decimated the largest Jewish population center in Europe. Founded in 1936 by Stephen Wise and Nahum Goldmann, the WJC sought to represent Jewish interests internationally, with headquarters first in Paris, then Geneva, and finally in New York after 1940. The WJC, notably in the case of the Riegner telegram, played a critical role in raising public awareness of the Nazis' program of extermination and lobbied allied governments to organize rescue and relief.[97] *Lest We Forget* focused primarily on what was termed the "massacre of the Warsaw ghetto," and included very detailed information on the process of the round-ups in Warsaw, the deportations of July–September 1942, and the physical layout of Treblinka.[98] Describing the functioning of the Treblinka camp, the report explained: "When the execution chambers are filled to the brim, the doors are sealed and the slow strangulation of live persons by the steam issuing from the numerous vents in the pipes begins. In the beginning, stifled cries penetrate to the outside, gradually they quiet down, and 15 minutes later the execution is complete."[99] Describing the nature of the Jewish response to Nazi terror, the authors wrote "the majority of the Jews submitted passively to the German terror; large transports of Jews departed daily for Treblinka. After a few days the battle ceased. The fate of the remnants in the ghetto is undecided."[100]

As historian Zohar Segev suggests in his study of the World Jewish Congress, in the report on the Warsaw ghetto we can begin to see a clear distinction made by outside observers in the Jewish world in regard to

Jewish behavior in occupied Poland: passivity vs. resistance. The passivity of the Jews murdered in Treblinka was juxtaposed to the active choice to resist undertaken by the heroes of the Warsaw ghetto.[101] The authors of the WJC report acknowledged that at the time of their writing, the reports on the uprising were mainly based on the observations of Polish witnesses and bystanders. Even so, they wrote with admiration for the "Jewish fighting organization [which] led the defense in the ghetto. Their forces were small, they did not have much ammunition. Nevertheless they fought for four weeks with more effort than the Germans in this tragic struggle."[102] Isaac (Ignacy) Schwartzbart wrote the report on the revolt in the ghetto on the basis of information he had received in London; the report would be reprinted in *The Black Book of Polish Jewry* (1943) with the title "The Battle of the Warsaw Ghetto." Initially, Schwartzbart wrote, the administrators of the workshops sought to convince the Jews to go passively, of their own accord. By the spring of 1943, however, "The Germans recognized the danger of keeping tens of thousands of determined young men and women in an enclosed part of Warsaw. When they realized that their efforts to clear the ghetto with the consent of the Jews had failed, they decided to liquidate the ghetto by force."

While the report focused primarily on what was termed the "massacre of the Warsaw ghetto,"[103] it concluded with praise for the heroes of the uprising, noting that despite "hundreds of burned and ruined houses,"

> *The ghosts of the heroes of the ghetto battle will forever honor the streets Nalewki, Nowolipie, Nowolipki, Franciszkańska, Karmelicka, Miła, Niska, Plac Muranowski, Smocza, Gęsia,* et al. *But persistent reports in the press in spring and summer* 1943 *indicate that not only their spirit but also their successors survive and carry on the fight there. The curtain may not yet have been rung down.*

In October 1943, the American Federation for Polish Jews published *The Black Book of Polish Jews: An Account of the Martyrdom of Polish Jewry under the Nazi Occupation*,[104] reprinting nearly verbatim the reports on Treblinka and the battle of the Warsaw ghetto included in the WJC publication *Lest We Forget.* Jacob Apenszlak's foreword explained that the book, as the "first complete account of the most monstrous persecution in human history is intended to fill the glaring gap in contemporary war literature which has not yet told the detailed story of the great martyrologies of modern times."[105]

Likewise, the *American Jewish Yearbook* (*AJYB*) for 1943, published by the American Jewish Committee in September 1943, included some further detail on the uprising in Warsaw.[106] The section on eastern and southern Europe, written by Moses Z. Frank, covered occupied Poland. He summarized reports conveyed by Zygielblojm in London on the deportations of July–September 1942 that reduced the ghetto's population by three hundred thousand.[107] Frank's section on the uprising also cited the January 1943 "first revolt," detailed in cables received by the Bund in February 1943.

> But it appears that a full-scale organized resistance did not get under way until sometime in April and that it continued well into May. As far as can be gathered from reports, the fight between the Jews and the Germans ended in the complete eradication of the Warsaw ghetto and other ghettos. It was a daring, if futile thing for the Jews to undertake against the overwhelming superiority of the enemy. But even from the garbled and clouded reports received so far, we can piece together a heroic story that will forever light up the dark and sordid tale of the Nazi-built Warsaw ghetto. Jews and Poles together fought off the Nazis for days and accounted for over a thousand of them. Warehouses and factories, (800 according to SWIT, the secret Polish radio) were put to the torch by the defenders, who were assisted by Polish underground squads. If, after achieving their "victory," the Nazis proceeded to liquidate the ghetto, it must have caused ironical laughter somewhere—but it was not the Nazis who laughed.

The *AJYB* report also noted Zygielbojm's suicide, along with the deaths of well-known figures in Warsaw and "some of the heroic leaders of the ghetto uprising," specifically mentioning Zivia Lubetkin and Tosia Altman, who "met their death in the battle of Warsaw."

> Thus the period under review, from the summer of 1942 to the summer of 1943, marks the year of the worst massacre of the Jewish people. The extent of the slaughter was epitomized by a message from underground Poland, according to Stockholm sources on February 5, which said: "Doctor Harigah visited the Lwow Jewish community during . . . January and remained there for several days, after which he proceeded to the neighboring Jewish communities." *Harigah* is a Hebrew word; it means slaughter. (309–10)

In November 1943, JTA published a story citing an eyewitness purported to have escaped from the ghetto (operating under the pseudonym Edward Warshawski) who offered even greater details on the uprising. "Strange as it may seem," the escaped Jew said, "there was a great wave of optimism among the Jews in the Warsaw ghetto during the battle that raged there. The Warsaw Jews, aware of the fact that they would eventually be crushed by the superior military force of the Germans, were nevertheless imbued with the spirit that the Jewish people will live long after the Germans are defeated in this war. Intense cultural activity and a wonderful revival of religious feelings marked Jewish life in the ghetto despite the fact that conditions became worse for them with every day."[108]

Beyond newspaper coverage and rallies, we can also see how over the course of 1943, news about the uprising began to be interpreted in broader public settings. At the same time, the politicization and mythologization—indeed fictionalization—of the heroism of the uprising began to enable diverse audiences to imagine themselves in the same situation. In October 1943, a few days before Yom Kippur, NBC radio broadcast *The Battle of the Warsaw Ghetto*, a play written by Morton Wishengrad as part of the Eternal Light series.[109] The play, which was part of an American Jewish Committee series that confronted anti-Semitism, started with a cantor chanting *El male rahamim*, the traditional Ashkenazi memorial prayer. "Hear him with reverence," the announcer instructed. "In the Ghetto, thirty-five thousand stood their ground against an army of the Third Reich—and twenty-five thousand fell. They sleep in their common graves but they have vindicated their birthright . . . for they have made an offering by fire and atonement unto the Lord and they have earned their sleep." As historian Jeffrey Shandler notes, this historic broadcast was the first mainstream dramatic representation of the uprising, six months after the battle and in the midst of the High Holidays. The response was so overwhelming that the program was aired again for Hanukkah in December 1943.

In the radio play, Wishengrad situated the heroic struggle within a religious framework, making use of ritual music, biblical language, and imagery. An unnamed voice likened the victims of the Warsaw ghetto to the "scapegoats of the centuries" and recalled descriptions from Leviticus of the ritual release of scapegoats into the wilderness: "But for them in the Warsaw Ghetto there was no wilderness . . . only the abyss." In advance of Yom Kippur, the play made it clear who the new scapegoat offering this year would be. The protagonist, Isaac Davidson, one of the fictional ghetto fighters in the play, explained that after the Great Deportation:

> we no longer asked for rescue and for mercy—we asked for weapons. Through the Polish Underground which carried our appeals we asked the people of England, Russia, and the United States for weapons. And there was silence. You did not answer. . . . We waited for weapons that did not come. Five hundred thousand waited. Three hundred thousand waited. One hundred thousand waited. And finally thirty-five thousand waited who did not know where to look—but the answer came from under their feet—from the sewer under the Warsaw Ghetto.[110]

Isaac relates how dynamite, rifles, and grenades were smuggled through the sewers by the Polish underground to the Jews in the ghetto until April 19, 1943, when thirty-five thousand Jewish men, women, and children stood ready to greet a detachment of storm troopers in light tanks. After wiping out the entire detachment, the Jewish fighters battled SS troops, as "flags of the United Nations . . . floated over the roofs of the Ghetto" and Jewish engineers blew up eight thousand factories producing material for Germany. Isaac recounted the battle of the few against the many as a modern-day Hanukkah. "The entire ghetto was in flames," but the Jews continued to fight, "after thirty-seven days. A few Jews with guns fighting a Nazi army for thirty-seven days."

In the radio play, as the cantor chants one final *El male rahamim* prayer the voice of the narrator provides a final instruction to the listener:

> Hear him with reverence. For he sings a prayer for the dead—twenty-five thousand dead. It is no ordinary prayer and they are not ordinary dead. . . . They were Jews with guns! Understand that—and hear him with reverence as he chants the prayer. For on the page of their agony they wrote a sentence that shall be an atonement, and it is this: Give me grace and give me dignity and teach me to die; and let my prison be a fortress and my wailing wall a stockade, for I have been to Egypt and I am not departed.[111]

The Battle of the Warsaw Ghetto would be rebroadcast annually as part of the Eternal Light Series on NBC radio, usually on the April 19 anniversary of the uprising, with the script unchanged. Three performances in 1943 elicited ten thousand letters. The War Department sent transcripts of the show to be played on Armed Forces Radio around the world.[112]

In the radio drama, Wishengrad highlighted the heroism of the ghetto fighters, who did not despair in the aftermath of the Great Deportation but resolved to fight back, despite their perceived abandonment by the nations of the world. Without access to information regarding the origins of the Jewish underground or the names of the heroes who led the fighting, Wishengrad provided listeners with the tools to imagine themselves as if "I have been to Egypt and I am not departed." The themes combine religious tropes of sacrifice (*azazel*), resistance (the few against the many), remembrance (Egypt), persistence (Rabbi Tarfon), and resilience. Religious tropes, but not just of prayer: "They were Jews with guns!" While Wishengrad and his audience did not yet know the details of how the uprising was organized or who its leaders were, the symbolic value of the dramatic events needed to be commemorated, beginning the process of mythologizing the event and casting it in distinctly religious terms.

The *We Will Never Die* pageant was also updated by Ben Hecht to include a section on the Warsaw Ghetto Uprising.[113] Between the time of the original performance of the pageant in New York City in March 1943 and its subsequent July 23 reenactment at the Hollywood Bowl, new music for "The Battle of Warsaw" and the song "Battle Hymn of the Ghetto" were added by the film composer Franz Waxman, who conducted the Los Angeles Philharmonic at the West Coast performance.[114] While the Germans destroyed the last remaining Jews in the Warsaw ghetto, the "Battle Hymn of the Ghetto" declared that today in the ghetto the song of the Jewish ghosts remained; a voice calls out to the "herrenvolk," the "swine-hearted Germans," "What is it you hear in the ghetto today?"

"The Song of the Spirit that drifts from every one of the stones you conquered. The song of the brave Jews of Warsaw that will outlive your victories." The audio of "The Battle Hymn of the Ghetto" concludes with the Jews of Warsaw, "the scum of human chattel . . . who rise in fearless battle" singing "Though we die, we die in battle NOT beneath the tyrant heel." Echoing the Internationale, the updated pageant imagined the Jews of Warsaw refusing to die under the tyrant's heel, joining in a universal fight for freedom.[115]

The Politics of Memory

While artists, writers, and composers sought to channel the symbolic power of the ghetto revolt to dramatize its significance for audiences, debate began over its political meaning, and the search for the heroes who had organized the revolt, along with the sources of their inspiration, took on added weight. Jewish leaders in New York, London, and the Yishuv played a key role in both interpreting the events for a broader Jewish audience eager to learn the identities of the "Jewish heroes of Warsaw" and shaping the collective memory of the event for a Jewish public trying to imagine what it would have been like to take part in the ghetto revolt.

In New York, the Jewish Labor Bund and the Jewish Labor Committee seized on news of the uprising, and the leading role played by Michał Klepfisz, to highlight the heroism of its members in leading the resistance. Jacob Pat, who had arrived from Poland before the start of the war, became secretary general of the Jewish Labor Committee and would play a prominent role in organizing many of the large-scale demonstrations in New York in the year after the revolt. The American Representation of the Bund in Poland, which had been formed in November 1939 and included on its presidium Emanuel Nowogrodzki, Shloime Mendelsohn, and Szmuel Zygielbojm, began to focus increasingly on "information and propaganda activities" through the vehicle of the party newspaper, *Unzer Tsayt* [Our time].[116] In addition to reporting on events of Jewish interest in the United States, Great Britain, Palestine, Poland, the Soviet Union, and other countries, the Representation also used *Unzer Tsayt* as a platform to broadcast its ideology and to play an important role in the Representation's propaganda campaign on behalf of the Jewish Labor Committee's fundraising efforts.[117]

The September 1943 edition of *Unzer Tsayt* thus included a profile of Michał Klepfisz, identified as "the soul of the revolt":

> The outside world does not know yet who were the heroes of the revolt, its inspiration and leaders. Still one name is known—Engineer Klepfisz. About him the secret underground Polish radio station Swiat declared: "the leader of the Bund, engineer Klepfisz, who was the soul of the revolt, fell in the battles like a hero." Who was this man . . . who took revenge for the annihilation of a people? The armed revolt in the Warsaw Ghetto is one of the greatest wonders of this present war—who was one of the magicians of this miracle?

J. S. Hertz, author of the profile, provided biographical details on Klepfisz, aged 30, born on April 17, 1913. His father Yakov descended from the great

Warsaw Hasidic family Klepfisz and had been a Hasid in his younger years before becoming a Bundist. Both Yakov and his wife, Miriam, were teachers and active in the communal work of the Bund and Michał was raised in a Bundist environment, active in Zukunft from a young age, as well as in the sport club Morgenstern and the student group Ringen. When the war broke out he escaped to L'vov, where he worked in a Soviet airplane factory as an engineer. When he learned about the fate of Henryk Ehrlich and Viktor Alter, the two most prominent leaders of the Bund in prewar Poland, who were arrested by Soviet authorities in October 1939, he decided to return to the German zone, eventually returning to Warsaw. As Hertz describes, living through the mass deportations and witnessing the murder of four hundred thousand Jews in Warsaw "did not kill the spirit of the Jewish workers underground to support the honor of the Jewish people."

> Michał Klepfisz was among them. His character and his military knowledge made him the ideal leader of this wondrous ghetto revolt, which will be both in terrible and in good times, for oppressed and for free people, a symbol of hope and pride.
>
> "Fallen in the battles as a hero"—thus did the underground voice declare from Poland. A tragic ending for a great famous epoch of Jewish life. With his young blood has Klepfisz sealed this period . . . be remembered for eternity.

As Jewish political leaders began to interpret the significance of the uprising based on information they had at their disposal, the surviving ghetto fighters in the Jewish Workers Underground and the Jewish National Committee in Warsaw worked to document the history of the revolt in the months after it had been crushed. However, the reports written by the Bund and the Jewish National Committee would not be received in London, New York, and the Yishuv until February 1944.

In January 1944, at the YIVO (the Yiddish Scientific Institute, which had been forced to relocate from Vilna to New York in 1940) annual conference held at 55 West 123rd Street in Manhattan, Shloime Mendelsohn delivered a speech entitled "The Battle of the Warsaw Ghetto" (published by YIVO that spring)[118] based on the sources of information currently available: underground reports, the Polish underground press, reports of the representative of the Polish government that were sent to the Polish government-in-exile in London, eyewitness accounts (including the account of the "underground delegate sometimes Klonowski, sometimes Warszawski" who left Warsaw in September 1942 and Poland in March 1943 and whose descriptions of the battle are based only in stories he heard). As Mendelsohn noted, there were as yet no details available by fighters who participated in the revolt. This would suggest that the underground reports of the Bund, composed in June and November 1943, had not yet been received by Mendelsohn, and were thus not integrated into his January 1944 lecture.

Mendelsohn, who had been one of the Bund's leaders in Warsaw before the war broke out and had escaped to Vilna and then Stockholm,[119] explained to his audience that "it is as yet impossible to give a complete picture of the resistance in the Warsaw Ghetto and the struggles that took place in the streets of Białystok, Nieśwież, and Krynki. The material is as yet too scarce. In the present war, and in Jewish history, this resistance is an event of such scope and magnitude that each fact is important, each detail significant. It is therefore necessary to collect whatever information is available, so as to have at least a partial picture of what occurred in the Ghettos in the year 1943."[120] Mendelsohn provided an overview of what was known at the time, attempting to summarize the factors that led to the revolt in April 1943, highlighting the efforts of the "working class and the intelligentsia" to convince the masses of the necessity of revolt. In the midst of the Great Deportation of July and August 1942, the "idea of revolt was born." But without arms, little could be done.

After the January 1943 revolt, which "lasted almost eight days and was conducted mainly by the Fighter Organization without the participation of the general population," the underground had three months to plan for a larger uprising. During this time, Mendelsohn reported, the underground organized, prepared spiritually and politically, armed a large portion of the population, and dug tunnels outside the ghetto walls.

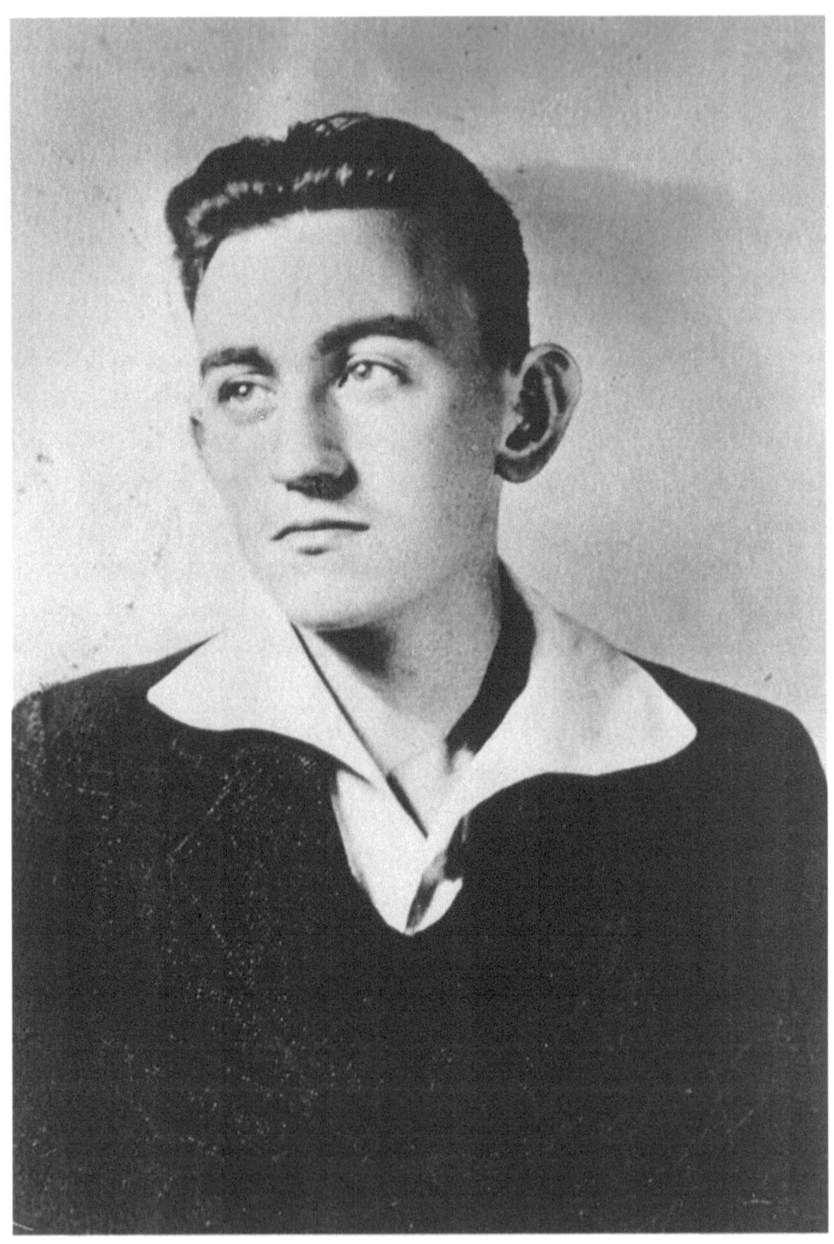

Portrait of Michał Klepfisz, member of the Jewish underground in the Warsaw ghetto. (United States Holocaust Memorial Museum, courtesy of Rose Klepfisz, photo archives no. 90330)

> [A]ll this demanded extraordinary discipline, an unimaginable will, tremendous self-sacrifice and sublime revolutionary strength. Human dignity, Jewish pride and revolutionary tradition must have combined to organize and plan a war which everyone knew would be lost. Is this not an act that our rational minds are incapable of comprehending?[121]

Noting that the ghetto had ceased to believe the lies of the Germans, Mendelsohn argued the "slave house became transformed into a palace of glorious heroism."

From a Bundist perspective, understanding the revolt as a popular uprising rather than a resistance operation led by a narrow cadre of elite fighters was critical:

> The armed resistance started on April 19th had become a people's war in the truest sense of the word. All sections of the Jewish population of 40,000 partook in the struggle; some with gun in hand, some by service work, others by bringing medical aid to the wounded. That is the vital characteristic and the historic significance of the revolt. It was prepared by an underground Coordination Committee (of the General Jewish Workers Alliance and the Jewish National Committee) and carried through heroically by the Jewish people at large.[122]

According to Mendelsohn, the appeal to the surrounding Polish population

> leaves no doubt that the fighters thought not only of dying with dignity but also of arousing the conscience of the world. . . . [T]hey believed that the heroic fight would force the Allies to act against Hitler's headsmen and thus prevent further slaughters. . . . [W]ith the great pain of humiliation, we must admit that the call to the world remained unheard.

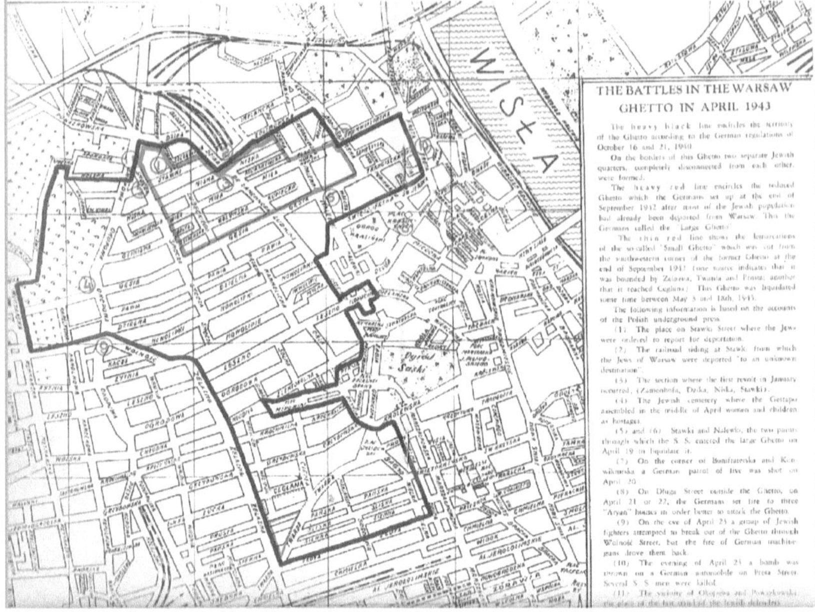

Map of the Warsaw ghetto, with main battles identified. (Published in *The Battle of the Warsaw Ghetto*, YIVO, Spring 1944)

Finally, at the conclusion of his lecture, Mendelsohn spoke of the Jewish Fighting Organization that "led the struggle." Even so, Mendelsohn highlighted the role of young workers, including specifically the only fighter mentioned by name: Michał Klepfisz, identified as a "pillar of the resistance," who was "trained for struggle in the prewar Jewish labor movement."

> The first report on the Ghetto revolt broadcast by the Polish underground radio station *Swit* on April 22, mentioned the name of Michael Klepfish who fell in battle and characterized him as "the pillar of the resistance." This young engineer, 28 years old, was trained for struggle in the prewar Jewish labor movement. We have no knowledge of any other names of the heroes who fell in the Ghetto battle, of those unknown soldiers from all sections of the Jewish population. . . . Let us hope that we shall succeed in obtaining as many names as possible of those who died in order

> that the Jewish people in Poland might live. The memory of each of them is sacred to us.*
>
> *As this pamphlet goes to press, the first list of persons who fell in the Ghetto battle was received in New York. It contains 222 names.

In her memoirs, Dawidowicz recalled hearing Mendelsohn reading his speech at YIVO annual conference in January 1944:

> [I]n the crowded hall you heard only Mendelsohn's voice, punctuated by occasional sharp gasps among the audience, quick intakes of breath. The atmosphere was heavy with grief. When he finished, the hall was hushed. No one applauded. Spontaneously everyone rose to honor the fallen Jews of the Warsaw ghetto. Then someone said: "Let's recite Kaddish." From the other end of the room, a man began to intone the Jewish prayer for the dead. Everyone joined in, amid a surge of sobbing.[123]

Thus, we can see in Mendelsohn's dutiful accounting the significance of context (YIVO), audience (New York City), and the sources of information that had reached New York by January 1944.

Conclusion

It is clear that even before the identities of the heroes had been confirmed, as reports began to emerge from Warsaw, shared by the Jewish Workers Underground, the ŻOB, and the Jewish National Committee identifying the leaders of the revolt and names of the fighters, their identities were received, interpreted, and analyzed in a framework that was already quite contested and heavily weighted with meaning and significance, and that built on preexisting political and religious frameworks within which such information was processed and incorporated. At the same time, the heroic saga of the revolt was mythologized in a manner that captured the attention of Jews (and others) around the world, allowing them to imagine what it might have been like to be *there*, engaged in the struggle against the Nazi oppressor. Surely the Jewish heroes of Warsaw were motivated by a desire to engage in self-defense—not to save their own lives, but to save their own dignity. But were they motivated by a Zionist connection to the Land of Israel that inspired their revolt against Diaspora oppression? Or did they rise up in defense of Poland, and the ideals of democracy, the universal brotherhood of man, and the rights of the working class to resist totalitarianism? Or were the fighters united by a drive to take revenge and kill Nazis? In any case, it is clear that the revolt was too powerful a symbol to not be seized upon by Jews from across the ideological spectrum well before the war was over. The timing of the uprising, coinciding with—and pushing—the transition to memorialization and mourning for what had befallen an entire people, also solidified the event as a date to remember both the heroes and the martyrs of Warsaw particularly and of European Jewry more broadly.

3

The Surviving Ghetto Fighters Write the First Draft of a History of the Revolt

As Jewish communities abroad sought to imagine what it must have been like to be inside the ghetto as the revolt took place, members of the Jewish Fighting Organization were also concerned with telling their story during and after the revolt. During the revolt, the primary motivation for the underground communiqués may have been to secure support from the Polish underground, which, while not entirely absent, certainly disappointed the ŻOB, who felt abandoned in their desperate struggle. The fact that members of the ŻOB managed to survive and escape the burning ghetto through the sewers played a crucial role in ensuring their story would be told. After May 1943, the surviving ghetto fighters and activists on the Jewish National Committee engaged in a frenzy of activity: to organize relief work, to rescue those Jews who could still be saved, and at the same time, to draft reports of the uprising, first writing reports in June 1943 that would not reach London and then the rest of the world until February 1944.

Even though the surviving members of the Bund and the Zionist youth groups reached out to their own separate organizations for support in the year after the revolt, what is striking in these accounts is the degree to which the fraternal nature of the collaboration between members of the ŻOB—a solidarity forged in the heat of battle—continued in the period after the uprising and in hiding on the Aryan side. If we consider, therefore, that the members of the ŻOB—and the Jewish National Committee and the Bund—lived together in hiding and simultaneously drafted their reports of the uprising, there is a disconnect between their professions of unity and solidarity and the interpretations of the political groups in New York and Tel Aviv that would highlight only the work of their own movement members. Despite such differences, however, these reports solidified certain aspects of the narrative, including the distinction between combatants and civilians and a decision to engage in armed resistance that was driven by a desire for vengeance and the quest to preserve human dignity.

Organizing the Remnants of the ŻOB in Warsaw

By the tenth day of the revolt, it became clear to some members of the ŻOB (who rejected the idea of certain death and symbolic sacrifice in the ghetto), that a way out of the ghetto should be found for those remaining fighters who wanted to escape. Simcha (Kazik) Rotem (Ratheizer) escaped from the ghetto via the tunnel dug by members of Betar and the ŻZW in Muranów Square and connected with Yitzhak (Antek) Zuckerman outside the ghetto, only to discover he had no plan to rescue the Jews who remained in the ghetto. After one week outside the ghetto, Kazik managed to sneak back into the ghetto via the sewers with Polish sewage workers as guides, where on May 8, he discovered other members of the Jewish underground who had also decided to use the network of tunnels designed to remove waste from the city as a means of escape.

> At this point something impossible happened, so impossible that it's difficult to believe that it actually happened, but it's a fact. I started to hear murmuring in the sewer, but I wasn't sure and I didn't know who it was—maybe it was the Germans. The whole thing occurred in a matter of seconds, and suddenly inside the sewer we met up with ten Jews I

> knew, among them—the first one I saw—was Pnina Greenspan.[1] You can imagine such a meeting, suddenly, inside the sewer—joy and elation! In the meantime I had almost lost the sewer workers because they didn't want to wait anymore. They had already understood what was going on, so we had to do things very, very quickly.[2]

In a postwar testimony, Zivia Lubetkin, part of the group that managed to escape from the sewers with the assistance of Kazik, recalled the experience as she and Marek Edelman led a group (some of whom had escaped from ŻOB command bunker at Mila 18) out of the ghetto.[3]

> The sewer was an abyss of darkness. I felt the water splash around me as I jumped and then resume its flow. I was overcome by a dreadful nausea there in the cold, filthy water. I felt that nothing—not even freedom—was worth this.
>
> Very few could come with us. The aged and the children would only die on such a trip. They did not even ask to go along. Sixty people crawled through the narrow sewer, bent almost in half, the filthy water reaching up to their knees. Each held a candle. We half-walked, half-crawled like this for twenty hours, one behind the other, without stopping, without food or drink, in that terrible cavern. Hunger and thirst weakened us. Part of our group were the eighteen who had survived the catastrophe at Mila No. 18 and who had not yet recovered from the effects of the gas. Some of them were unable to walk and we dragged them through the water by their hands and feet.
>
> One crawls through the sewer, and always there is the agonizing thought: how shall we explain, when we meet our comrades again, why we did not remain, why we are alive at all? All of us were poisoned by the thought of those we had left behind, and this robbed us of all possible joy in our good fortune.

The surviving ghetto fighters who had managed to sneak out of the sewers with Kazik and Zivia Lubetkin gathered initially in the Lomianki Forest not far from Warsaw. Zivia Lubetkin, Tosia Altman, Marek Edelman, Hirsch Berlinski, Israel Kanal and Tuvia Borzykowski were among the initial leaders of this group; Yitzhak Zuckerman would join them in the forest after a few days.[4] Most of the surviving fighters eventually left the forest near Warsaw (where the danger of capture was too great) and moved to partisan camps in the Wyszków Forest near the Bug River.[5] On May 17, Tuvia Borzykowski returned to Warsaw; two days later, on May 19, Zivia Lubetkin and Marek Edelman moved to an apartment on Komitatowa 4 where Yitzhak Zuckerman and Kazik were living. Tosia Altman, Hela Schiffer, and Eliezer Geller were housed in a celluloid factory on November 11 Street (11 Listopada Street); on May 24 the factory caught fire and Tosia and another member of group were turned over to the Gestapo; badly burned, Tosia was soon tortured to death and died from her wounds.[6]

In his postwar testimony, Tuvia Borzykowski related that he first heard of the tragedy on May 24, 1943: "Yitzhak enters. He does not look his usual gay self; for a long while he paces the room saying nothing. Eventually Zivia gets him to tell us what is the trouble. In a trembling voice, in short, broken sentences, he tells her that the group which was hiding in the house on No. 10 11 Listopada Street is no longer alive . . . the tragedy occurred in the most unusual way. There was celluloid stored in the building which once housed a factory, someone lit a match, the celluloid caught fire and within seconds the entire house was in flames."[7]

The return to Warsaw after the revolt was clearly a devastating period for the surviving members of the ŻOB, all of them incredibly traumatized by what they had endured. As Bella Gutterman writes in her biography of Zivia Lubetkin, the return to safe houses on the Aryan side of Warsaw "was a difficult time for the survivors, and Zivia found it especially hard to overcome her depression. The destruction of the ghetto, the loss of close friends, and the sense of guilt and pangs of conscience over what she saw as a twofold desertion—first of her fellow fighters and second of her friends in the sewage canals—all added to the heavy loss of her comrades at Mila 18, from which pure chance had saved her."[8] Her concern for Yitzhak

Zuckerman, Gutterman notes, who spent his days on the streets meeting with various contacts, only exacerbated her distress to such an extent that she was unable to stem the frequent, uncharacteristic, tearful attacks she was subjected to, even in the presence of friends. As Zuckerman later recalled on one day when he returned home late and she feared he had been caught, "I never saw a person as miserable as Zivia. Nothing could stop her tears. She was sure everything was over and that I was dead . . . she broke down and couldn't restrain herself."[9]

In the apartment on Komitatowa 4, Zivia and Antek drafted a telegram to the leaders of the Yishuv to inform them of the end of the Warsaw ghetto fighting. The June 15, 1943, letter to Yitzhak Tabenkin of HeHalutz and Meir Ya'ari of Hashomer Hatzair offered an initial description of uprising and emphasized the central role played by members of HeHalutz and Hashomer Hatzair in the struggle. In the letter they listed among the fallen: Mordechai Anielewicz, Berl Brojda [Broyde], Chana [Plotnicka], Tosia [Altman], Lea[h Perlstein], and Miriam [Heinsdorf]. They informed Tabenkin and Ya'ari that a few fighters had crossed over to the "Aryan" side at the end of the battles and that ŻOB members had also engaged in resistance in Czestochowa and Bialystok. "In Lvov and Bedzin, murderous Aktions are now being conducted. Frumka [Plotnicka] is now in Bedzin, Mordechai Tenen[baum—Tamaroff] in Bialystok, and [Abba] Kovner in Vilna." The writers called for monetary help and asked for assistance in finding possible ways out, demanded vengeance "in the name of three million Polish Jews," and requested that the Jews of Belgium, the Netherlands, and France be informed that their traveling to Poland means death. (It is not clear when this letter was received by Tabenkin and Ya'ari).[10]

On June 22, 1943, Isaac Schwartzbart, representative of the World Jewish Congress in London, also relayed information he had received from Zuckerman and Lubetkin in Warsaw to Yitzhak Tabenkin and Meir Ya'ari via the Jewish Agency for Palestine in Jerusalem regarding the deaths of hundreds of Hechalutz and Hashomer fighters in the form of a telegram.

> For Tabenkin and Jaari Received Yesterday Message from Cywia and Icchak Dated June 22nd Sad News

> Stop Hundreds from Hechaluz and Haschomer Fell Fighting Stop Frumka and Mordechai Living You Will Receive after Few Days Full Message from Andrzejewski[11]

Lubetkin's biographer, Bella Gutterman, suggests that "after the fighting in the ghetto, Zivia and her comrades developed insights and conclusions that resulted from the experiences and what they had seen that 'raised second thoughts as to the ghetto uprising, joining the partisans, and rescue,'"[12] Devastated by the tragic loss of their friends, Zivia and her comrades "changed their view and no longer saw the Uprising inside the ghetto as an option for the few remaining Jews in the ghettos to take action." Zivia advised fighters in Częstochowa to give up on the idea of revolt and escape to forests where they could join the partisans.[13] Ruzhka Korczak, a leader in the Vilna underground, would also relate that Zivia and Tosia had sent a message to Vilna, ordering them "not to carry out the revolt because the casualties in Warsaw had been too heavy."[14] At the same time, Zivia and Yitzhak rejected attempts by the Yishuv to rescue them as the last witnesses of the uprising. Instead, Antek and Zivia began to work more closely with Jews living under Aryan aliases in Warsaw and the activists of the Jewish National Council and the Coordinating Committee (Adolf Berman, Batya Temkin Berman, and Bund member Leon Feiner). After the safe house at Komitatowa 4 was exposed, the group had to move to Pańska 5 where Luba Gavisser was already living under an Aryan identity;[15] then Zivia moved to another apartment at Twarda 23 with Tuvia Borzykowski, Leyzer Levin, and others. Eventually, Gutterman notes, Zivia moved back to Pańska 5, where the group worked on recording the history of the uprising and creating an archive of the Jewish Fighting Organization.

In her postwar memoir, Vladka Meed described the "clandestine lodgings" the surviving ghetto fighters and underground members had secured, such as the apartment at Leszno 18, which "had been converted into a hideout for Zivia Lubetkin, Antek, and Marek Edelman, the surviving members of the military command of the ghetto's Fighting Organization. It also served as a coordinating center for other surviving ghetto fighters,

Jewish partisan groups, and the fighting organizations active in various concentration camps throughout Poland."[16] She also noted the importance of the house on Miodowa 24, which was an important meeting place for couriers on the Aryan side, who came "from different social strata and belonged to diverse political groups. Nevertheless, together they formed a close-knit group, almost a family, each looking after the other."[17]

Bernard Goldstein,[18] one of the prewar leaders of the Bund active in acquiring arms for the revolt from the Aryan side in April 1943, described the situation in Warsaw after the revolt:

> After the ghetto had been destroyed, we faced one urgent task: organizing help for those who were left on the Aryan side, providing them with apartments, hiding places, documents, and food. We began to get word of the liquidation of other ghettos, and of uprisings in labor camps and ghettos. We were asked for help, for weapons. Such requests came from the camps in Trawniki, Poniatow, Skarzhisko, Plaszow, Belzhitz, and others.
>
> Around Warsaw, hiding in the woods and in the open countryside, were possibly twenty thousand uprooted homeless wanderers. We estimated that the Bund alone was helping about three thousand of them. Until the outbreak of the Warsaw uprising, the organized help of all Jewish groups and organizations had reached about eight or nine thousand people. Generally each political party or group took care of its own members and periphery, but some centralization of the relief work was achieved through the Jewish Coordinating Committee, comprised of the leaders of all the Jewish groups, and through the Council for Aid to Jews [Zegota] in which all the Polish underground parties were represented.[19]

Although each party took care of its own, it is clear that the camaraderie born out of the shared struggle in the ghetto continued in the period afterward, as surviving members of the ŻOB lived together and supported one another. Goldstein also described the hideout at Leszno 18, secured through the assistance of Marisha Feinmesser, Maria Savitzka, and her brother Gentiles to hide the commanders of the organization (Antek, Zivia, and Marek Edelman) after the safety of the apartment at Panska had been compromised. This was the same hideout described by Zuckerman, where the archive of the ŻOB had been kept (before it was destroyed in the Warsaw Uprising of August 1944):

> It was a cheery, spacious apartment of three rooms, with a blind wall facing the Evangelical church. Parallel to this wall we built a second solid wall, providing a hiding place large enough to accommodate as many as ten people. Such a major construction operation required large quantities of building material, as well as a great deal of hammering and the removal of debris; it was difficult to do secretly. The work was carried on under the pretext that Marisha was putting in a bathroom in honor of her marriage and her new position in life. The wall was built by our wonderful comrades Chaim Ellenbogen, Simcha Roteiser [Kazik], and Shwentochovsky, a Polish electrical worker who housed some of the partisan comrades in his own apartment.
>
> Shwentochovsky used his electrical skill to set up a clever signal system at the apartment entrance. On the door he installed a well-concealed pinpoint, wired to the bell. If the pinpoint was pressed with a coin or other piece of metal the bell rang, indicating that a friend was coming and that we had no need to hide behind the double wall. Strangers had to knock because there was no door bell. Whenever we heard a knock, we rushed behind the wall.
>
> The comrades from Panska, Marek, Antek, and Zivia, moved into this apartment. Later Rifke Rosenstein and I moved in, too. We felt wonderfully secure with our hiding place behind the solidly constructed double wall. It was

entered by lifting a board in the wardrobe wall. Marisha or Maria would buy food across the street at 13 Leshno in a store owned by a Gentile friend of Marisha's. She herself kept some Jewish children and knew the secret of our apartment. Only those of us who had Aryan faces, Antek Zuckerman and myself, were permitted to leave the apartment. Zivia, Rifke, and Marek were not allowed to show themselves on the street at any time. Marek's Jewish face, his black hair, and his dark eyes had been a handicap in getting him moved into the apartment. Shwentochovsky belonged to the volunteer fire squad of the city electrical works and had managed to smuggle out an additional uniform. He and Marek arrived dressed as firemen. . . .

> Behind the security of the double wall we kept some of our more important documents, sums of money belonging to the party and to the fighting organization, and a store of guns, ammunition, and hand grenades. The cost of buying, rebuilding and maintaining the apartment was borne by both organizations, the Bund and the Jewish fighting organization.[20]

As Bernard Goldstein of the Bund would detail in his memoir, the connection between the surviving members of the underground movements in Warsaw and their comrades abroad played a crucial role in maintaining the morale of the survivors.

> Through the official channels of the government-in-exile we were also able to send reports to our comrades abroad, to the representatives of the Bund in the United States, and to the Jewish Labor Committee. With their help, during 1943 and 1944, our contacts abroad were better organized and functioned fairly regularly. We were able to tell the world about the battles in the ghetto, about the situation of the rescued handful, about the crematoriums and the gas chambers.[21]

Both the Jewish Workers Underground and the Jewish National Committee maintained contact with their respective movements in the free world (the Bund in London and New York; the World Jewish Congress, the Jewish Agency, and representatives of the Zionist political parties and youth movements in Geneva, London, and Tel Aviv).[22]

Like the surviving members of the ŻOB, Adolf Berman also maintained contact with Zionist leaders in the Yishuv, in London, and in Geneva, sending letters to Ya'akov Zrubavel (Left Poalei Zion), Isaac Schwartzbart, and Alfred Silberschein, all dated July 31, 1943.[23] In his letter to Schwartzbart in London, Berman, writing on behalf of the Jewish National Committee, acknowledged receipt of telegrams from Schwartzbart in May and June, as well as $10,000 earmarked for the General Zionist organization and Poalei Zion Z.S. He also noted that an initial payment of $10,000 from the Jewish Agency was used to "fund active rescue, assistance activities, and objectives of the ŻOB whose squads were fighting in the outlying cities of Czestochowa, Bedzin, Bialystok, and others." Berman estimated some three hundred thousand Jews remained in Poland (in ghettos, camps, in hiding on the "Aryan" side, and in forests), and the expense of rescuing each amounted to thousands of zlotys. "Thousands are dying every day, and recently the Zionist activist Menachem Kirschenbaum and his family were murdered" (despite their holding Paraguayan citizenship).[24]

In the letter to Zerubavel, Berman replied to the telegram they received in May, but noted they still had not received the information and urgent aid that had been promised them. Berman related to his correspondents that "Antoni" (code name for Nathan Buksbaum, one of the leaders of Left Poalei Zion in Poland) "went to the foreign nationals' camp near Hannover" (this camp, connected to the Hotel Polski affair, turned out to be a German deception; all those who volunteered to be transferred there were sent on October 21, 1943, to their deaths in extermination camps). Writing to Dr. Abraham Silberschein of the WJC in Geneva, Berman, on behalf of the Jewish National Committee, expressed confidence in the means of rescue being used by the addressee and his comrades, and notified Silberschein of the deaths of Gitterman, Neustadt, and Bornstein, three of the four members of the AJDC (American Joint Distribution Committee, or the "Joint") in Poland.[25] He sounded an alert about what was going on in the Vittel and Hannover camps, and expressed his suspicion of liquidations, alerting his correspondents that the Gestapo was rounding up individuals with foreign passports.

As Berman's letter to Schwartzbart noted, the money received by the JNC from the Jewish Agency was used to fund relief work, rescue, and continued activities of the ŻOB. According to the estimates of Joseph Kermish, the intensive work undertaken by the Jewish National Committee and the Bund in the aftermath of the Jewish revolt in Warsaw funded up to one hundred thousand zlotys per month of relief work to aid the estimated twenty thousand Jews surviving in Warsaw and its environs.[26] In her memoirs, Zivia Lubetkin related that

> the Jewish underground, the Jewish fighting organization, the Jewish national committee, the Bund . . . were in constant contact with the world Jewish organizations. The Polish Underground, which was connected with the Polish government-in-exile in London, transferred secretly money and letters to and from London. The moneys were used to acquire arms and for broad-based, but modest relief work, to Jews in hiding. We estimated that in Warsaw and its environs approx. 20,000 Jews were in hiding, passing as Aryans or hiding in Polish homes. Some 12,000 of them, who were in need of financial help, medical assistance, apartments, forged documents, found us and asked us for help. With the assistance of Jewish representatives was established the "Jewish Help Committee." (This group included the Polish underground and Polish parties and was supported by the Polish government in exile).[27]

Vladka Meed also noted the importance of funds arriving from abroad (in the case of the Bund, from the Jewish Labor Committee in America), which helped finance their underground work to shelter the surviving Jews of Warsaw:

> Funds eventually began to reach us through the same underground channels. First mainly from the Jewish Labor Committee in the United States. Subsequently from other Jewish organizations and to some extent from the Polish government in exile as well. The money reached the Coordinating Committee in American dollars which were exchanged for zlotys on the black market.
>
> The primary objectives of the Coordinating Committee were to supply material aid for Jews hidden in the Aryan sector, provide them with the necessary documents, finding hiding places, aid for the children, establish contacts with inmates of slave labor camps, with Jewish partisans and with friends abroad. And to keep constant touch with the Polish underground. In Warsaw alone and nearby areas we ministered to some 12,000 persons.[28]

While working to organize relief and rescue those Jews who could still be saved, the surviving ghetto fighters and the Jewish National Committee set out to draft reports of the uprising, first writing reports in June 1943 that would only reach London, New York, and the Yishuv in February 1944.[29] Even though the surviving members of the Bund and the Zionist youth groups reached out to their own separate organizations for support in the year after the revolt, what is striking in these accounts is the degree to which the fraternal nature of the collaboration between members of the ŻOB—a solidarity forged in the heat of battle—continued in the period after the uprising and in hiding on the Aryan side.

Leon Feiner, chairman of the Bund's Central Committee, described the spirit this way:

> The participants in the uprising were ideologues who swam in different currents. An exemplary fraternity of arms exists among Bundists, halutzim (Zionist pioneers), members of Hashomer Hatzair, and others. It is a steadfast spirit . . . an *esprit de guerre*, a spirit of sacrifice, courage, revenge, and

> dignity. The battles . . . are not only manifestations of the wish to avenge the unpunished murder of an entire people, not only a way against the deprivation of rights, but a manifestation of the will to atone with dignity for having been ensnared by the Nazis' deceits . . . to fight for dignity and to fight uncompromisingly against fascism, on behalf of a new world.[30]

All the same, this also makes clear that those writing the reports were aware of the audience among fellow party members that would be reading their reports, and the impact they might have. Bernard Goldstein described the exchange of information as a source of "great joy" that sustained members of the Bund as they tried to survive in hiding:

> I remember our great joy in July 1944 when the Polish government forwarded to us a microfilm which contained articles from *Unser Tsait*, the New York Bund magazine, and other documents . . . Our joy was boundless. The microfilm was a direct, almost a personal greeting from our comrades in America. We felt bound to them across the years of blood and suffering which divided us. Using a photographic enlarger, we transcribed all the documents, duplicated them on our machine, and distributed them among the comrades in the hiding places. This contact with America did much to raise our morale. It reminded us that we had friends. It gave us the feeling that if this wonderful miracle of communication could be accomplished, all was not yet lost.[31]

Through the reports of the Bund and the Jewish National Committee there was an exchange of information going on *during* the war; that is, the first draft of history was being shaped by reports that emanated from the war zone and were received, interpreted, publicized, and politicized in New York, London, and Tel Aviv. While the reports may have described the unity and fraternity of the fighting organizations, this did not deter the recipients—in the Zionist movement and the Bund—from emphasizing the leading role played by their own movements in the uprising. At the same time, as Zuckerman and others noted subsequently, political considerations also influenced the drafting of the reports. The involvement or participation of certain segments of the underground, notably the Communists and the Revisionist ŻZW, were barely mentioned.[32] Such reports were also printed and published in Poland; Zegota also worked to distribute underground publications on Jewish subjects, which included the bulletin "Before the Eyes of the World" (*Na oczach świata*), which dealt with the armed struggle of Warsaw Jewry and was published by the Armia Krajowa (Home Army). As a precautionary measure, the place and date of publication were listed as "Zamość 1932." Maria Kann (a Catholic Polish woman) wrote and assembled the material, which included a series of documents and reports by Polish and Jewish eyewitnesses and observers, as well as an evaluation of the Warsaw Ghetto Uprising in the chapter "In the Steps of Bar Kochba."[33]

The first reports of the uprising to be received in New York and Tel Aviv at the beginning of 1944 still carried the themes of political unity and fraternity that reigned in the ghetto as it was taking place; by the end of 1944, however, perhaps as a result of political interpretations by movement members in New York and Tel Aviv, the partisan acrimony between the Bundists and Zionists began to influence the narrative.

"The Battle of the Warsaw Ghetto": The Reports of the Bund and the Jewish National Committee

The "Battle of the Warsaw Ghetto" report from the Jewish Workers Underground reached the American Representation of the Bund in New York (via London) in February 1944. Two separate reports (report A and report B) were written by the underground—the first dated June 22, 1943, and the second from November 15, 1943; the reports were later reprinted as appendices to Marek Edelman's *The Ghetto Fights*, published in 1945 and cited extensively in *Ghetto in Flames*, published by the Bund in New York in 1944.[34]

The authors of the first report, dated June 22, 1943, attempted to provide a description of "the historic events that occurred in the Warsaw Ghetto," noting that lack of space prevented them from offering the precision and esteem that "even the smallest detail deserves." Even so, it would be impossible for someone who was not there to appreciate the magnitude of what had just transpired in Warsaw:

> Unfortunately the lack of space makes it impossible for us to describe the events in full, giving an idea of their magnitude and color, nor can we give the sequence of the events in a manner that pays the full tribute due to the dignity of those events. This will be done one day—and it should be. . . . Here only a few fragmentary remarks.—What was going on in April and May in Warsaw, that Jewish-German war, that as it has been named the Battle of Ghettograd—this really does surpass any analogy from the history, either of our own or of any other nation. Various were the stages of this war, its forms and methods, imposed by the peculiar set of circumstances; and on their background were performed various defensive-offensive acts of the partisan warfare. The unforgettable, deeply moving images of the ghetto, enwrapped in the clouds of smoke, lit by the enormous glow of blazing fires, this staccato clatter of machine guns, the roar of howitzers, the pandemonium of the heavy artillery—exploding mines, crashing buildings—and these people of ours living amidst the inferno. . . . It seems that there is no master of pen, brush or sound, who could represent in full the Great Event which was happening before our eyes, neither could he express what we all experienced in those terrible, tragic and yet great days.[35]

The report noted that the battles, which began on April 19 and lasted about one month, were directed by the Jewish Fighters' Organization, which was the "backbone of the entire battle" and was the "armed organ of the

Co-ordinating Committee of the General Jewish Workers Union 'Bund' of Poland and the Jewish National Committee." Noting that neither the Revisionists nor the Agudah belonged to the Jewish Armed Resistance Organization, the Bund's report explained that while the Revisionists mustered a small "organisation for vengeance" of their own, it ceased to exist after the second day of the Battle. Workers and youth formed the majority in the Jewish Armed Resistance Organization. The youngest was Lusiek, thirteen years of age, a member of the Bund youth group, Skif; the oldest was forty. Highlighting the *esprit de guerre* of the various ideological streams, the report continued: "All the members of the resistance organisation were idealists, adherents of various political trends. *Their fraternity in battle (Bundists, Chalucym, Shomrim and others) was exemplary*" (my emphasis).

The report also noted that the general population had shifted its attitude to the idea of resisting the Nazis. The fighters were not just motivated by despair; "many a fighter had ample opportunity to rescue himself by leaving the ghetto." Instead the resistance was a response of the Jewish public to Nazi oppression:

> the fighters were full of a noble sense of duty, a soldier's duty, of a powerful desire to carry on the fight for honour, for human dignity. They were anxious to take revenge on Fascism, on the enemy of their people, on the enemy of mankind. The precautions of the Germans bordered on cowardice. The prolonged heroic resistance of the Ghetto banished the legend of the invincibility of the German Army, showed the Polish nation its vast possibilities in resisting the Nazis and strengthened its self-reliance. The "Jewish-German War" lent strength to the splendid spirit of resistance against the Germans, with which the Polish Underground had already been marked.

The Bund's report also highlighted the action's effect on the Polish underground, who (answering the ŻOB's manifesto calling for armed resistance) "immediately responded with messages of solidarity and admiration. . . . The capital city of Poland, as well as the entire country, seethed with excitement because of the Battle of the Ghetto."[36]

Painting a picture of complete destruction, the report indicated several thousand Jews "killed, burnt alive, suffocated by gas" and twenty-five thousand deported to Trawniki, Majdanek, and Lublin. "The Warsaw Ghetto is now one big cemetery. Somewhere in the catacombs hundreds and perhaps thousands of those who survived the battle are still living in agony." While the September 1939 bombardment destroyed seventy-five thousand homes, the present battle had destroyed over a hundred thousand.

> As for German casualties: more than one thousand were killed or wounded and tremendous material losses were suffered by German war production enterprises that were set on fire and destroyed by the Jewish Armed Resistance Organisation.
>
> The casualties suffered by the Resistance Organisation were comparatively small, but many of its best members, including its commander-in-chief M. Ordche—Hashomer, Engineer Klepfisz, Armament Chief and Berek, both members of the Central Committee of the Bund, fell in the fight.

In the report, M. Ordche is identified as "commander-in-chief" of the resistance organization—this referred to Mordche (or Mordecai Anielewicz), but recipients in New York or London would not have known his identity at the time. According to the Bund's report, once the fighting had come to an end, the various detachments of the Jewish fighting organization (approximately two hundred surviving members, according to the report) struggled to "reach the outlets of this Hell." The first messenger to bring news of the desperate struggle was "[Zalman] Frydrych, a member of the Bund, who was prominent in our pre-war athletic organisation, Jutrznia. A former soldier in the Polish Army, he was a man of unusual bravery and courage."[37]

> Not long after he accomplished his mission, he together with a detachment of fighters of the Resistance Organisation,

> was captured by the enemy outside the Ghetto and shot. He made his last journey through subterranean channels to reach us, well aware of the importance of his task, and accomplished it against tremendous odds and under unusually dramatic circumstances.
>
> These members of the Resistance Organisation who remained alive tried to get out of the Ghetto through underground channels and passages. It was a fantastic undertaking, accompanied by untold difficulties and danger.
>
> Several detachments numbering some seventy people in all, managed to reach the forest under sensational circumstances. Several other detachments were caught by the Nazis, either at the outposts of the Ghetto or already outside of the Ghetto, but they died fighting until their last round of ammunition.
>
> The remaining members of the Resistance Organisation, some sixty of them, did not manage to reach the outposts of the Ghetto and probably died in the underground channels, surrounded by the Germans.

Concluding its account with the sober statement that "the Warsaw Ghetto . . . has officially ceased to exist," the Bund's report also indicated that the revolt in Warsaw had inspired acts of resistance elsewhere in Poland and that the only remaining ghettos were now in Zagłębie Dąbrowskie, Łódź, Białystok, Vilna, Radom, and a few smaller ghettos—but "All these sooner or later will share the fate of others already liquidated."

The Bund report explained that its coordination with the Jewish National Committee—(with "Zionist organizations and their youth groups")—for armed resistance was limited to the "fighting sector of the active resistance in Warsaw." The Coordinating Commission outside the ghetto had one representative each from the Bund and the JNC, to obtain arms and supplies, possibly from outside. The authors explained "our outstanding contribution was supplying the Jewish Fighters' Organisation with explosives and the production of ammunition for active resistance here in the ghetto. In this respect the services of Comrade Michał Klepfisz an engineer, were invaluable. He was killed in the last battle." Finally, the report tried to provide a sense of the daily terror the surviving Jews continued to be subjected to, and fear of arrest and death, a double conspiracy of being Jews in the political underground, "100 times harder than Tsarist times . . . we live under the pressure of the terror. People perish daily" as victims of blackmail, denunciation, and Gestapo informants. As Bundists, the authors of the report also felt a need to explain why, under the circumstances, they had deviated from a broader sense of obligation to the Polish public and the working classes to a more specific focus on the Jewish community and "an almost exclusive preoccupation with the Jewish sector . . . we still do not forget the position taken as a whole: the situation of whole Poland and all peoples in their fight for freedom and we understand clearly what is the world fighting for and what goal it tends." The report was signed Warsaw, June 22, 1943.

The second report from the Jewish Workers Underground Movement (named report B), dated November 15, 1943, but also received in London and New York in February 1944, included even greater detail on the fighting, as well as the names of some of the leaders of the revolt. The November report summarized the incidents of rebellion that had followed the Warsaw revolt, including Białystok ("strongly influenced by the Bund"), Treblinka, where the "revolting Jews slaughtered the entire 30-men Nazi guard unit that had patrolled the camp" and two hundred Jews fled, smaller rebellions in Tarnow, Będzin, Czenstachow, and Borislaw, as well as the Sobibor rebellion, which "culminated in the successful escape of a large number of Jews from that camp." The report then detailed the history of the organization of the Jewish Fighters Organization in Warsaw. The report dated the first meeting of political parties to organize armed resistance as taking place in January 1942, but "The participants did not know each other well enough at that time and most of them were afraid lest information about the creation of such an organisation would reach the Germans and give them an excuse to further persecutions." At the same time, the report noted, working together with the Polish Socialist Organization (RPPS), members of the Bund began to organize their own self-defense organization, identifying

Abram Fajner, Zalman Frydrych, Szmul Kostrynski, Lejbel Szpichlerz, and Marek [Edelman] as "officers of the self-defence detachments."

> The members of our self-defence organisation received their military schooling from instructors of the PS (Polish Socialists). The most active members of the self-defence organisation were former members of our Skif and Zukunft (youth organisations of the Jewish Labour Movement before the outbreak of the war).
>
> The names of the following persons, who are known to you, will give you an idea of the elements who joined our self-defence organisation: Jurek Blones,[38] Janek Bilak, Gąbrys Fryszdorf, Jankiel Gruszka, Natan Liebskiend, David Peltz, Weiwel Rosowski, Szperling, Pola Lifszyc (intelligence), Cywia Waks (intelligence) and others.

Over the course of 1942, the report notes, the Bund continued to lead underground efforts and warn the Jewish population of Warsaw of the dangers confronting them:

> Our *Weker* (the clandestine newspaper of the Jewish Underground Labour Movement) kept urging the Jewish population to resist. However, the Jewish police, together with the Jewish hirelings of the Gestapo as well as some of the elements close to the Kahal (Board of the Jewish Community) went out of their way to prevent an uprising of the Jews.
>
> After 22 July 1942, while the deportation of the Jews of Warsaw was being brutally carried out, a second conference of all Jewish political parties took place. Not being able to convince them, even at that time, to wage armed resistance, we issued an appeal of our own to the Jews of Warsaw revealing the truth about the dreadful fate that was being prepared for them by the Nazis and calling for armed resistance.

The report noted that Jews refused to heed warnings, fearful of resistance leading to collective retribution. (The report also did not include mention of the March 1942 meeting described by Zuckerman, when, he alleged, the other parties determined armed resistance was premature.) This account was directly contradicted by the reporting of the Jewish National Committee, which highlighted July 28, 1942, as the date when representatives of the leftist Zionist groups, HeHalutz, and other political leaders "demanded decisive action."[39] The report of the Jewish Workers Underground does not mention such a meeting, instead indicating "we utilised this time to rebuild our own Resistance Organisation. We simultaneously again tried to contact the representatives of the ZKN (Jewish National Committee) in an effort to establish a mutual resistance organisation. At the end of October 1942, a Co-ordinating Committee was appointed consisting of one representative of the ZKN and one of the Bund (Jewish Labour Movement of Poland). Our representative A. Blum died a soldier's death."[40]

The Bund's report cites the early efforts of ŻOB in eliminating opposition, highlighting the assassination of Lejkin of the Jewish police, before turning to the events of January 1943. While later accounts would specifically identify the bravery of Mordecai Anielewicz in distinguishing himself in the fighting of January 18, 1943, he was not identified by name here.

> During the first armed battle against the Germans, the legend of an invincible German, holding the life and death of hundreds of thousands of Jews in his hands, vanished. Our fighters concentrated in five spots, mainly waged guerrilla warfare against the Germans. Nevertheless several more important battles took place.
>
> The biggest battle broke out on the corner of Zamenhofa and Stawki Streets. The Germans totally surprised by the armed resistance of the Jews, stopped the deportation after two days. This unexpected success greatly increased the prestige and the role of the ŻOB.
>
> The authority of the ŻOB (Jewish Armed Resistance Organisation), after the January battles, grew steadily from

> day to day. At that time, the ŻOB governed the entire life of the Ghetto. For example, at the request of the ŻOB, the Jewish Community Council contributed one million zlotys towards the sole purpose of buying weapons. This amount was paid in cash within a period of three days.

The report summarized the uprising in April 1943, which lasted almost seven weeks, in great detail. The report focused on the collective enterprise of the fighting organization in resisting the liquidation, excluding the names of any specific ghetto fighters (who would be identified at the end of the report in a separate section). Instead, the report focused on outlining the major engagements in the course of the fighting, from the first week of direct conflict with German forces to the period after day ten of the revolt, when the Germans changed tactics and began burning the ghetto down.

> Being unable to perform their planned deportation of the Warsaw Jews by means of lies and false promises, the Germans finally resolved to deport the remaining Jews forcibly.
>
> On 19 April 1943 at two o'clock in the morning, the Germans surrounded the Ghetto walls with many guards (every 25 meters) consisting of German, Ukrainian, and Latvian Fascist soldiers. Carefully, in singles, in twos and threes, the German soldiers entered the Ghetto.
>
> But this time we were prepared. At four o'clock, before dawn, all our resistance groups were mobilised and at their assigned positions. They were prepared to meet the hated enemy. The number of armed resistance detachments were: eight in the centre of the Ghetto, five in the territory of the brush factories and seven in the vicinity of the big Schultz and Többens factories.
>
> At six o'clock in the morning, on 19 April 1943, 2000 armed SS men along with tanks and cannons, three trucks

loaded with ammunition and an ambulance entered the Central Ghetto. The entire German deportation staff followed the SS army.

Among the members of this deportation staff were the following officers of the Gestapo and SS: Michalsen, Handke, Hoffle, Mireczko, Bareczko, Brand and Mende.

There were no Jews to be seen anywhere, all of them were hidden in subterranean, previously prepared trenches and holes of all sorts. Only the members of the ŻOB remained on the surface and were on the alert. Our fighters were concentrated to defend three strategic points, barring entry into the main street of the Ghetto.

The first armed battle took place on Nalewki Street where two resistance units, behind barricades, defended the street. The battle there lasted six hours and brought about the first defeat of the Germans. The Germans retreated, leaving behind many of their soldiers who had been killed.

Simultaneously the main battle raged on the corner of Zamenhofa and Mila Streets.[41] Our fighters, after building barricades to shut off the four corners of those streets, daringly attacked the main German detachment, which had entered the Ghetto. After the first salvos from machine-guns and hand-grenades were successfully aimed at the compact ranks of SS men, the entire street was deserted. The green uniforms of the Germans were no longer to be seen anywhere. They took shelter in nearby stores and gates and exchanged some shots with the defenders of the Ghetto.

After a cessation of fifteen minutes, tanks appeared. They came quite close to the spot where our fighters were gathered. After a while, incendiary bombs, calmly and carefully aimed, set the first tank on fire. The flames spread with unexpected swiftness and soon there was an explosion. The tank was lost. The other tank immediately left, together with the panic-stricken Germans.

Their retreat was covered with renewed gunfire and grenades. The German casualties numbered 200, killed and wounded. We lost only one soldier. After two hours, the Germans brought cannons, which were placed outside of the Ghetto, and successfully bombed the spot of their previous defeat. They took our defence strongholds, and freed the entrance into the Ghetto.

Suddenly, from the windows of the other side, Zamenhofa 29, grenades were thrown. This was the second attack against the Germans, which was being carried out on the same place by one of our resistance groups that had deliberately not participated in the previous battle, lest its whereabouts should be discovered.

Fifty Germans were killed, our group escaped without any casualties. At five in the afternoon, there were no longer any Germans in the Ghetto. They left the Ghetto in order to gather somewhere on a deserted territory nearby. Our temporary success had been a result of the suddenness and quickness of our resistance, performed from well-disguised spots.

The second day of the Battle of the Warsaw Ghetto, 20 April 1943, began with a large concentration of SS detachments, along with artillery, on the territory between the Ghetto and the Aryan districts (Plac Krasinskich).

However, they had not yet dared enter the populated Ghetto streets. At about three o'clock in the afternoon, a detachment of 300 SS men arrived near the gate to the district of the brush factories. They stopped for a little while, but this brief pause was sufficient for our fighters to cut an electric wire, which caused a mine explosion under the very feet of the SS men. The Germans ran away, leaving 80 to 100 killed and wounded. Only after two hours did they come back.

After the previous costly experience, they were now more careful and alert. Thirty SS men entered the gate to this

> district. Our fighters, hidden in selected spots, waited for them. Grenades and incendiary bombs met the Germans. Only two of the 30 SS men escaped. Those who were not hit by grenades burned alive.
>
> But now the Germans brought their artillery into the battle. The district was shelled from all four sides. In the meantime, two high officers from the SS came into this district. They appealed to our fighters to put down their arms and proposed a fifteen minute truce.
>
> Our fighters replied with more gunfire. From the other side of the district, somewhere near Franciszkanska Street, a second detachment of SS men tried to reach our fighters. Met by several well-aimed shots, this detachment gave up also and turned back. Once more the entire district was clean of Germans. That was the second complete victory for our fighters.

The report detailed the shift in German tactics as large conflagrations burnt down the ghetto building by building, killing fighters and residents in hiding indiscriminately. Concluding the account of the revolt:

> All in all our offensive and defensive battles lasted ten days. Our meager ammunition was already disappearing, the bits that were left were used exclusively for self-defense and guard duty.
>
> According to our accounts the Germans suffered about 1200 casualties killed and wounded. Sporadic fights, waged by our fighters against the Nazis, took place long after the Battle of the Warsaw Ghetto was over. They occurred primarily at night. The Germans burned the Ghetto systematically. After two weeks the entire Ghetto, as well as the previously decimated districts ceased to exist.
>
> Lack of water and food rendered impossible the life of those who still fought. The Germans then commenced

> burning down buildings. They hoped to destroy, together with the houses, the remaining dug-outs and nests of our fighters and to break their will to fight. The Germans used gas bombs.
>
> During this final period of the last struggle against the Germans who invaded and seized our dug-outs, one after another, or suffocated the fighters by means of gas bombs, the majority of the ghetto defenders died.
>
> A large number of the officers in charge of the Jewish Armed Resistance Organisation gathered in a special dug-out and committed suicide in order to escape from the clutches of the Germans. Only a small fraction of them was able to escape through the city's sewers and reach the Aryan districts.
>
> The four resistance groups that still remained in the Ghetto waged guerrilla warfare against the Germans for a month, all of the members of these four groups perished.

While the first part of the report summarized the efforts of the fighting organization and did not distinguish between the Bund and the ŻOB, the report concluded by focusing specifically on the identities of members of the Workers Underground, i.e., the Bund, who had joined the fighting. Even so, it highlighted the closeness of Bundists and Zionists in the fighting organization, "as members of a close family," united by a "mutual aim."

> Our Party was a member of the Jewish Armed Resistance Organisation for more than six months—from October 1942 until May 1943. We joined hands with all Jewish Zionist underground organisations. Our comrades lived and worked with the others just as members of a close family. A mutual aim united us.
>
> During this entire period of over half a year, there were no quarrels or struggles, which are common among adherents of different ideologies. All overworked themselves in

organising the mutual defence of our dignity. All fought equally in this historic life and death struggle.

There was no difference between the members of our Party and the others in regard to sacrificing themselves or performing their soldiers duty until the very last. However, we are reporting here primarily about our own members.

At the beginning of the battle, in January 1943, we possessed four well-organised resistance detachments of our own. The officers in charge of them were: Jurek Blones, Welwel Rozowski, Lejwik Granzalz and Dawid Hochberg.

Our comrade X[42] led the entire resistance of the brush factories' territory. Our comrades who had been active before the January 1943 battles, were on the Coordinating Committee and the General Staff of the mutual Jewish Armed Resistance Organisation.

The following of our comrades were members of the Auxiliary Committee of the ŻOB, located in the Aryan districts of Warsaw: Frydrych, S. Fund, Celemenski, Wladka-Peltel-Fajga. Michał Klepfisz led and organised the entire production of hand-grenades and incendiary bombs in the Aryan districts, as well as in the Ghetto.

The majority of all our fighters was killed in action, either in the Battle of the Warsaw Ghetto or immediately after reaching the Aryan districts through the sewers. Jurek Blones, who led our resistance group in the district of the brush factories was one of the most brilliant and gallant fighters.

Twice during the battle he rescued his detachment from sure death by alone engaging an entire detachment of attacking Germans. Mejlach Perelman, on his beat around the Ghetto walls, though wounded by three German shells, nevertheless for a long time covered the escape of his comrades, when he could no longer stand on his feet, he turned his gun over to one of his comrades, knowing how precious weapons were.

We took him to the backyard, near the dug-outs of his group, but he could not walk in. He was too weak, we carried him upstairs and put him in a certain room. When our man who was on duty called on him and wanted to help him, Perelman did not permit him to stay, "Take the rest of my weapons," he said. "I cannot use them any more, but you will need them." On the following day, the Germans set fire to the building he was in and he was burned alive.[43]

Tobcia Dawidowicz, a liaison officer of our resistance group in the Schultz and Többens territory, though wounded in the leg, nevertheless successfully led her group towards the sewers in order to help them escape. Not wanting to become a burden to her comrades, she remained in the Ghetto after all her comrades had entered the sewers.

Dawid Hochberg was an officer in charge of a resistance detachment in the Central Ghetto. When the Germans discovered the dug-out of his comrades, he handed his gun over to one of them and barricaded the entrance into the dug-out with his own body. It took the Germans 15 minutes to remove his body from the small entrance. In the meantime, the fighters of his group, along with other Jews that were hidden in the cave, escaped through another exit.

We can relate many other stories such as these about our fighters who struggled and died as heroes. Those comrades who functioned as collaborators with the ŻOB during the Battle of the Warsaw Ghetto also died. They were: Luzer Klog, Grylak, Kiersz, Bluma Klog, Renia Pizyc and many others.

The Jewish Armed Resistance Organisation continues activities even now, after the Battle of the Warsaw Ghetto, establishing new contacts and maintaining old ones. Our representative is still on the General Staff of this organisation and in the Coordinating Committee which supervises its work.

It is clear from the reports of the American Representation of the Bund in New York that they received this information and quickly worked to disseminate the names of the Bundist heroes within the movement. Thus, for example, in the March 15, 1944, bulletin of the Bund *Yedies* of (Bulletin #53) the group shared a list of names based on letters and documents received by the American Representation of the Bund in Poland, from February 15 to March 15, 1944. "We do not yet have the names," they wrote, "of the thousands of Bundists and Zukunftists who fell in the armed uprising against the fascist enemy in Warsaw, Bialystok, Zaglembie, Tarnow and several other cities." Nonetheless, they wanted to share the names of thirty-one "fallen heroes" that had come into its possession, including Blones, Dawidowicz, Eiger, Frydrych, Klepfisz, Perlman, and Rozovski. The list concluded with a call to "honor their memories!"

As will be discussed below, the reports of the Jewish Workers Underground would also be incorporated into Bundist accounts of the uprising, published later in 1944 both in the newspaper *Unzer Tsayt* and publications like *Geto in Flamen* (Ghetto in Flames).

The Reports of the Jewish National Committee

At the same time, the Jewish National Committee and the remnants of the Jewish Fighting Organization drafted reports that were sent to London and then conveyed from there to Tel Aviv. The authors of these letters and reports—both Yitzhak Zuckerman and Zivia Lubetkin, as well as Adolf Berman and David Guzik on behalf of the Jewish National Committee—wrote specifically for their intended recipients—in this case the Zionist leadership, which, like the Bund, emphasized the role of their own organizations' members, while also highlighting the collaboration between the Bund and the Jewish National Committee in the fighting of the ŻOB. All the same, as will be seen, these reports were read and interpreted in a partisan environment and suggested a different chronology for the organization of resistance efforts and the evolution of the ŻOB in the ghetto.[44]

Following the initial letters sent to leaders in the Yishuv in June and July 1943, another series of letters between Zivia Lubetkin and Antek

Zuckerman and the movement leadership and Jewish Agency were exchanged dating from November 1943 and March 1944.[45] The relationship between the youth movements and the movement leadership in the Yishuv had clearly become strained by the prolonged isolation of the movements in occupied Poland during the war and the perception that the leadership (Ya'ari for Hashomer Hatzair and Tabenkin for HeHalutz) did not sufficiently care about the fate of the movement members in occupied Europe. As historian Avihu Ronen notes:

> In the middle of 1943, after the arrival of reports about the Warsaw Ghetto uprising, the leaders of the two kibbutz movements, Tabenkin and Ya'ari, gave much more thought to their comrades in occupied Poland than they had earlier in the war. In fact, from August 1940 to early 1943, for almost two-and-a-half years, hardly any contact between the pioneering movements in Poland and movement headquarters in the Yishuv had taken place. After intensive correspondence to the beginning of the war with the pioneering movements' centers in Poland, which had moved to Vilna, and once members of the Hashomer Hatzair and HeHalutz leaderships emigrated to Palestine, there were only tenuous communication through the offices of Nathan Schwalb, head of the HeHalutz center in Geneva.[46]

The combination of the shocking news in November and December of 1942 of the extent of the catastrophe and then the reports of resistance in early 1943, followed by the revolt in April 1943, led Tabenkin and Ya'ari to seize upon the news and view events as an expression of their movements' work.[47] In a series of letters written to the movement leaders in November 1943 and again in March 1944, Antek and Zivia attempted to both relay news and reestablish connection with the movement center. Writing to Tabenkin, Ya'ari, and Eliyahu Dobkin (head of the Jewish Agency immigration department) on November 15, 1943,[48] Antek and Zivia attempted to convey the enormity of the destruction. Echoing the words of the Jewish Workers

Underground report (perhaps written by Marek Edelman), they describe a disaster that "those who live in London or Tel Aviv cannot conjure up, even in the sickest of their imaginations," together with the heroism of those who had chosen to take up arms in the name of HeHalutz and labor Zionist youth movements.

> At the time of writing this letter, we don't know if we will ever see each other again. From among three and a half million Jews who were in Poland, today there remain barely 200,000. By the time you receive this letter, it's possible there will be half [of that]. Only recently, that is to say, in the past week, the Trawniki, Poniatowa, and Lublin camps were liquidated. Nearly 40,000 Jews were exterminated. The remainder of the camps are on the verge of liquidation. Every day, hundreds of Jews in hiding on the "Aryan" side are killed after the iniquitous [literally: "sons of Belial"] turn them over to the Germans. It is difficult to describe and difficult to believe that such things occur. Those who live in London or Tel Aviv cannot conjure them up, even in the sickest of their imaginations. All centers of Jewish life have been erased from the earth. Their inhabitants have found their deaths in the shower rooms of Treblinka, Sobibor, Belzec, and Auschwitz.
>
> In order that these may be remembered, those who fought with weapons in their hands against the enemy, I write about the last days of "Hehalutz", the youth movements of Dror, Hashomer Hatzair, Akiva, Gordonia. *The history of Hehalutz–is in some sense the history of the Jewish Fighting Organization* [my emphasis]. At the beginning of the liquidation operation, there still existed hundreds of concentrations of Jewish youth in Jewish towns, 5 kibbutzim in Warsaw, 3 kibbutzim in Czenstachow, 2 in Bialystok and Vilna, Zarki, Ostrowitz, Benzin, agricultural haksharot. These kibbutzim were the nucleus of resistance against the

> Nazi oppressor. . . . While in the first Aktion (July–August 1942) there was no resistance palpably present, by the second Aktion (January 1943) and the ghetto's liquidation (April 1943), the heroic deeds of the ŻOB were etched in the blood of its members and commanders—and so too in Bialystok, Vilna, and Czestochowa. Emissaries went out from Warsaw to organize resistance cells in other places, and fell in the line of duty.[49]

In the letter, Lubetkin requested that the memory of the resistance fighters be commemorated and she made a direct connection between HeHalutz (and its associated Zionist youth movements) and the history of the Jewish Fighting Organization (ŻOB). Not only in Warsaw, but in multiple locations where Zionist youth were concentrated, resistance to the Nazi occupation grew—for example, in the *hakhsharot* (Zionist pioneering training centers) in Częstochowa, Białystok, Vilna, Zarki, Ostrowiec [Swietokrzyski], Hrubieszow, and Będzin. While in the first *Aktion* (July–August 1942) there was no resistance palpably present, by the second *Aktion* (January 1943) and the ghetto's liquidation (April 1943), the heroic deeds of the ŻOB were etched in the blood of its members and commanders—and so too in outlying regions. Emissaries went out from Warsaw to organize resistance cells in other places, and fell in the line of duty. Lubetkin named a list of activists who fell, and asked that they be remembered. She noted the cooperation of ŻOB members with the Coordinating Committee of Jewish social organizations and institutions, and emphasized their part in resistance and aid activity. By identifying the kibbutz groups in the ghettos as the nucleus of the resistance and explaining that the "history of Hehalutz . . . is the history of the Fighting Organization," she also made clear that without the Zionist youth movements there would have been no resistance. The solidarity of the youth, who remained unified in their kibbutzim in the ghettos, made resistance possible, she said. The list of fighters to remember—from Białystok, Będzin, Vohlin, Vilna, Częstochowa, Krakow, Auschwitz, and including twenty-four fighters from Warsaw—consisted of HeHalutz and Hashomer Hatzair movement members who had perished, names such as Plotnicka, Kaplan, Anielewicz, Braude, Breslaw, Altman, and Vilner that would become a prominent part of historical accounts of the revolt. (Abba Kovner was the only fighter from Vilna listed; she would not have known he was, in fact, alive.) She concludes with the exhortation, "THE LIST IS NOT COMPLETE, REMEMBER THEM!"

Finally, detailing efforts to still smuggle Jews out of Europe via Hungary (and inquiring into the fate of a group which traveled that route in 1942), Lubetkin concluded her letter with the message that "[our] spirit is not broken . . . we are sure that you would do everything in order to save us if you had the power to do so, but you are powerless. It is easier for us to die knowing that there is a free world, that the Land of Israel will become a homeland for the Jewish people." She updated them regarding the fate of Eliezer Geller and sent regards to her sister Ahuva Lubetkin (in Ben Shemen) and Sara Cukierman (in Ramat Hakovesh).[50]

Meanwhile, the Jewish National Committee, "residing in Warsaw outside the boundaries of the Ghetto," drafted a letter to Isaac Schwartzbart in London on November 15, 1943 (received in London February 13, 1944—some 3 months later)—signed by "Dr. A. Berman (Borowski), Icchak Cukierman [Yitzhak Zuckerman], and D. Kaftor [Guzik]."

> Dear Dr. Schwarzbart,
>
> We write to you in the blood which tens of thousands of Jewish martyrs are again shedding. We in Poland are now going through the epilogue of our terrible tragedy. The Hitlerite barbarians facing their defeat are murdering the few remnants of the Jewish population.

Summarizing the most recent exterminations of inmates at the Trawniki camp on November 3, 1943, and camps in Lublin as well as Galicia and L'vov's Janowska Street, the authors explained to Schwarzbart "we have no doubts that during the next days or weeks all Jewish centres which still remain, all camps and the few ghettoes will be exterminated. . . . We are making desperate efforts to save, at the last moment, from the camps—the individuals whose value is greatest for our social and cultural patrimony. But these undertakings are extremely costly and difficult. We are concerned that in the near future out of 3.5 millions of the Jewish population in Poland, only a small quantity of people, some tens of thousands, will survive, hiding outside the camps and the Ghettoes in the Aryan quarters or in the forests, leading literally the life of cavemen."

> In the last moment before death, the remnants of Polish Jewry appeal for help to the whole world.
>
> We know that you are with us with the whole heart and your whole soul, that you are deeply affected by our martyrdom which is unparalleled in history. We also know that you are helpless. But may those factors who could have helped us [*sic*] know that we are thinking of them.
>
> The blood shed by 3 million Polish Jews will be avenged, not only on the Hitlerite beasts but on those who, in their indifference and obstinace [*sic*] but uttered words and did not act to save a people condemned to exgermination [*sic*] by the Hitlerite murderers. Nobody among us, the last Mohicans of an extinguished people, will forget it or pardon it.
>
> May this, perhaps our last voice from the abyss, reach the ears of the whole world.
>
> We desire that the Jewish people and the whole world shall know that our youth has valiantly defended the life and the dignity of our people. After the heroic epic of the Warsaw Ghetto, we witnessed during the last months the beautiful, splendid fight of the Jews in Bialystok. This fight took place at the end of August. . . .
>
> In the fourth day of the "action," the armed fight started. Heavy fighting took place in several streets. The Germans used in the "action," as in the Warsaw, armoured cars and field artillery. . . . [Summary of fighting in Bialystok.] "The heroic fight in Bialystok will pass into history together with the defense of the Warsaw Ghetto."[51]

Berman, Zuckerman, and Guzik also summarized for Schwartzbart other cases of resistance, including the dramatic camp uprisings in Treblinka and Sobibor, as well as

> actions of armed resistance (in) Czenstochow, in Bendzin, in Wilno, in Tarnow and other small centres. The final liquidation of the ghetto in Tarnow took place during September 1–3, 1943. Jews were loaded into trucks (150 people in each) filled with carbide and chalk. The trucks were then sealed, soaked with water, and the Jews sent down to death. All the children from the Ghetto were collected in one building. The children were told they were going to a hostel. The building was then hermetically sealed and blown up. In the course of the liquidation the Jews started to defend themselves. The Germans used hand-grenades and broke the resistance of the Jewish fighters.

According to Berman, Zuckerman, and Guzik (of the JDC), the Jewish National Committee was composed of parties and youth movements affiliated with Zionist politics, including "General Zionist, Poale Zion Right, Poale Zion Left, Hechalutz, Hashomer Hazair, Dror, Akiba, and Gordonia" (the Revisionists were not mentioned) and headed by themselves but the authors, echoing the report of the Jewish Workers' Underground, explained to Schwartzbart that the fighting in the ghettos of occupied Poland transcended party divisions:

> Fighters belonging to almost all ideological movements took part in brotherly ranks in the fights in the above-mentioned towns, youth of Hechalutz and Hashomer, of the Poalei Zion and of the Bund. *They were united by a fight not for life but to the death, by the fight for the honour and dignity of the Jewish people* [my emphasis]. We endeavoured through our Jewish Fighting Organisation to organize with all our forces this fight to assist and sustain them.

The authors summarized for Schwartzbart their efforts to secure the release of leaders and scholars from camps, as well to provide "considerable financial assistance" and documents to Jews hiding in the Aryan quarters.

> We are a small group of leaders who remain alive, and who in spite of towering difficulties and dangers, undertook the task of social service for the remnants of the tortured Jewish population. We are resolved to perform our task despite all difficulties and hindrances—until the end. . . .
>
> Representatives of all the above mentioned organisations form with them the Jewish National Committee, To the closes [*sic*] collaborators belong among others: Dr. Emanuel Ryngielblum, Cywja Lubetkin, Advocate Gottesman from Cracow, Joseph Sack, Lejzor Lewin, Szloma Grajek, Szymon Rathauser, Pola Elster, Hersz Berlinski, Basia Temkin-Bermanowa. [many unable to go out because of non-Aryan appearance] . . .
>
> An atmosphere of harmonious brotherly collaboration reigns in the Jewish National Committee. The J.N.C. is with contact with the Bund and coordinates its actions with it. The J.N.C. form together the Jewish Coordination Committee. Like the Jewish national Committee, the Jewish Coordination Committee is not a political body not a political representation. The task of the Jewish Coordination Committee is to coordinate the action of defence and assistance. . . .[52]
>
> The J.N.C. is engaged, in addition to its defence and relief actions, in collecting reports, documents and all materials for the future recording of our martyrdom which is unparalleled in history. This work is directed on our behalf by the historian Dr. Emanuel Ryngielblum in collaboration with Hersz Wasser, the author Rachela Auerbach and others. . . .
>
> . . . Your cables and letter give to us all in our difficult life a few moments of joy. We do not feel that we are isolated, Your letters dispatched in the 21st July (the letters of

> Dr. Schwartzbart to Warsaw and Cracow, the letter from Berl, the letter from the Committee for Rescue of Jews in occupied Europe) have all been received your cables of the 27th September and the 4th October 1943. . . .
>
> The advocate Gottesman from Cracow is in Warsaw working with us. He sends to you and to all the General Zionists his warmest greetings.
>
> Kaftor [Guzik] sends his greetings to all of you and to his colleagues in the Joint Distribution Committee. He is astonished that they give no sign of life.
>
> Convey our hearty greetings to Berl Locker and to all those who collaborate with you.
>
> The Jewish Fighting Organisation in Poland are sending fighting greetings to all Jewish soldiers who are fighting for their liberation against Hitlerism and Fascism for their liberation, on all fronts of the world.
>
> Signed The Jewish National Committee Warsaw November 15, 1943
>
> Dr. A Berman (Borowski), Icchak Cukierman, D. Kaftor

As Zuckerman detailed in *Surplus of Memory*, "The Jewish Coordinating Committee (ŻKK) in Warsaw consisted of A. Berman, Leon Feiner, David Guzhik, and me. We would meet every other week or ten days. Normally I would meet with Berman every day or every other day, and we also had constant contact through couriers."[53]

The report also included a list of 244 fighters who fell in defense of the Warsaw ghetto along with party affiliation. (It is not clear to me at what point this list was alphabetized and translated into English.) Among them, the first two were the most prominent members of Hashomer Hatzair, Mordecai Anielewicz and Tosia Altman. Also appearing was Michał Klepfisz (as Dror, instead of Bund?), Dolek Libeskind (from Krakow?), and Tobcia Dawidowicz (Dror, instead of Bund?).

In addition to detailing the names and affiliations of the fighters, the report provided specific details on the history of the fighting organization, so it would not be forgotten by history. The tone of this report does not suggest partisan infighting; to the contrary, "an atmosphere of harmonious brotherly collaboration reigns in the Jewish National Committee." It does voice displeasure that they suffer from lack of contact and assistance from the outside world. That which has been received, financial or otherwise, is simply too late. Nonetheless, the report describes an atmosphere of harmonious collaboration between the movements, with the fighters united "by a fight not for life but to the death, by the fight for the honor and dignity of the Jewish people."

Despite the difficulties of communication during the war and under German occupation, contact and correspondence had been established and the Jewish National Committee and Jewish Fighting Organization received letters of support from Berl Lokier and Nachum Goldmann, on behalf of the Jewish Agency and the World Jewish Congress.[54] Indeed, as noted in the letter of the Jewish National Committee, such contact in the form of cables and letters "give to us all in our difficult life a few moments of joy. We do not feel that we are isolated." Furthermore, the Jewish National Committee and the Bund depended on large sums of money (fifty thousand zlotys to rescue one individual from a camp; ten thousand zlotys to resettle someone in hiding on the Aryan side). This correspondence indicated that despite their almost total isolation, the surviving members of the underground believed communication was possible, as was the transfer of large sums of money.[55]

Lokier, one of the leading figures of Poalei Zion and the Jewish Agency representative in London, wrote back to his correspondents in Warsaw, in response to their November 15, 1943, letter. His February 19, 1944, letter expressed his sorrow but also pride in the Jewish resistance, and praised the daring efforts of the JNC and ŻOB "to collect the material necessary to document in the future the history of the suffering and heroism of the Jewish people" (Yiddish *Layden un heroism*; Hebrew *sevel ve-gevurah*). He specifically noted the list of heroes as a "document of pride that will be preserved for generations." He described the hardships in Mandatory Palestine where there are "no lack of difficulties," work taking place in the Negev, and the participation of Jews fighting the foe in Africa and Italy.

List of those who fell in the defence of the Warsaw Ghetto 

The organisation to which each of them belonged is designated by the following innitials: A-Akiba, B-Bund, D-Dror, G-Gordonia HH-Hashomer hazair, HZ-Hanoar hazioni, L-Left, PL-Poale Zion Left PR-Polae Zion Right

1. Anielewicz Mordchaj HH
2. Altman Tosia HH
3. Alexandrowicz Jakob HH
4. Asz Eliezer HZ
5. Aresztaj Zacharjasz D
6. Altemnberg Estera D
7. Alterman Szloma D
8. Arbuz chaiim HH
9. Bresler Szmul HH
10. Blones Mejlech A
11. Berman Franka L
12. Baum Mosze HZ
13. Blones Icchak HZ
14. Brojdo Berl G
15. Bigelman Menachem D
16. Blausztaj Icchak D
17. Bartmesser Nute D
18. Baran Dwara D
19. Blones Jurek B
20. Blones Guta B
21. Blones Lusiek B
22. Brylantsztej Stasiek B
23. Brzezinska Zocha L
24. Blank Marek G
23. Baczynski Szlama HH
24. Chadasz Icchak HH
25. Chmielnicki Nachum B
26. Cukier Nesia D
27. Cygiel Mosze D
28. Chrzanowicz Icchak D
29. Cebularz Tosia L
30. Dolek Libeskind A
31. Drenger Symek A
32. Drajer Abraham D
33. Drezno Abraham D
34. Dobuchno Szaul D
55. Dawidowicz Tauba D
56. Dunski Sewek B
57. Dembinski Icchak L
58. Dembinska Dorka L
59. Djament Abraham, PL
60. Elek HH
61. Edelsztej Zwi D
62. Erlichman Sujka G
63. Einsdorf Miriam HH
64. Eiger Abram B
63. Fajner Abram B
64. Finkielsztej Majorek D
65. Fass Jozef L
66. Frenkiel Toba, HH
67. Farber Jozef, HH
68. Finkielsztej Motek, D
69. Furmanowich Pessia, D
70. Folman Marek, D
71. Futerman Ignac, D.
72. Finkielsztej Cyla, B
73. Fajgenblat Jakob
74. Blum Abrm (Abrasza), B
75. Finkielsztejn Abram, D.
76. Fidelrajd Symcha, PR
77. Fidelrajd Pola PR.
78. Goldsztajn Icchak, B.
79. Granatsztej Sara, D.
80. Gutrajman kuba L
81. Gold Wulf, L.
82. Grauman Chana, HH
83. Gutterman, D.
84. Grynbaum Icchak, D.
85. Gutsztadt Cypora, D.
86. Gutman Henach, D.
87. Gerszuni Gedalja, D.
88. Grauzalc Leib, B.
89. Gryszpan Jurek, L.
90. Gertner Israel, B.

"List of those who fell in the defense of the Warsaw Ghetto," page one of three. (Jewish National Committee, Ghetto Fighters House Archives, catalog no. 10450)

He remarked on the activities of the *Jad ha-Hacala* (Hebrew in Polish transcription: literally "hand of rescue") on behalf of European Jewry, their efforts in the matter of the Jewish Agency, the Workers' Union, and the work of Melech (Neustadt) in Constantinople (Istanbul), and the activities of Anszel (Reiss) in London. Despite these efforts, however, Lokier expressed the guilty feelings on the part of the Yishuv in Mandatory Palestine for not having done enough. Noting that the "White Paper" (Britain's blockade on Jewish migration to Palestine) was not yet dead, Lokier concluded with the hope for a better situation in Mandatory Palestine.[56]

At the same time, Nachum Goldmann sent a letter greeting his brethren in the name of the World Jewish Congress, expressing solidarity with the suffering, courage, and struggle of his addressees. While "he and his brethren" admitted their guilt for not providing adequate help, he promised yet to send all the necessary assistance to effect the rescue, requesting from his addressees not to doubt the bonds of brotherhood.

> Nachum Goldmann (London, March 7, 1944)
>
> To those who are in Poland I pass along brotherly blessings in the name of World Jewish Congress. We know your suffering, about your heroism, about your war. We know that we are guilty of not doing enough to assist you and your complaints are justified. We promise you at the last minute to send all the help, which we believe, will aid your circumstances. We believe that soon you will receive the fruits of our efforts. Be strong and do not doubt the bonds of our brotherhood.
>
> Nachum Goldmann[57]

Even though sporadic messages arrived, the funding received by the Jewish National Committee and Zegota and the Bund underground in Warsaw was even more important. According to historian Daniel Blatman, by the end of 1943, the Jewish Labor Committee had raised $81,000 and relayed that sum to London to transfer to Leon Feiner as Bund representative on the Zegota council; between January and November 1944, Emanuel Szerer and Lucjan

Blit sent another $83,000 on behalf of the JLC from London. (Feiner became aware that not all the funds had been received in Warsaw, as Polish officials were helping themselves to some of what was transferred for relief work.)[58] As important as this connection to the outside world was, the knowledge that a line of correspondence did exist between Warsaw and London, facilitated with the assistance of the Polish underground and the Polish government-in-exile, also reinforced the sense of abandonment by other colleagues whose letters had not been sent or received. Zivia Lubetkin and Yitzhak Zuckerman expressed their frustration at not having heard back from Tabenkin and Ya'ari in a letter sent on March 8, 1944, as they noted their last contact from Schwartzbart was four months earlier. While it is not clear when the letters from Lokier and Goldmann were received in Warsaw, it is clear that there was an expectation of correspondence from the Yishuv, via London, as indicated in the extreme disappointment at the lack of contact from their youth movement leaders. Zivia and Yitzhak wrote to Tabenkin and Ya'ari in March 1944:

> We are stunned by your silence. We only received a reply from Szwarcbard [Schwarzbart] to our telegrams to you [pl.]. For four months already, we've had no news from him either. The situation of the Jews remaining alive is catastrophic. We are unable to provide the material assistance required by the Jews who are still in the camps. For these few camps, we haven't the power to organize effective defense.
>
> The majority of the Jews in hiding on the "Aryan" side are unable to benefit from our assistance due to the poverty of the funds we command. We require at least 40,000 dollars per month. We have not yet received the 15,000 pounds sterling that were promised to us in the written notification sent by Scwarzbard. Please send money as quickly as possible. Don't leave us abandoned to the mercies of fate. [Signed]: Cywja, Icchak[59]

Two days later, Yitzhak and Zivia sent a follow-up letter to Tabenkin and Ya'ari, further detailing their frustration at the lack of contact.

During the past four months, we have sent you a number of letters and telegrams in which we described in detail the conditions under which we work and live. Meanwhile we have received no reply. We don't understand the reason for this persistent silence.

During the past quarter of a year, the number of Jews in Poland has progressively lessened. The "work camps" in Trawniki, Poniatowa, Majdanek, and Lublin have been liquidated. All the Jews were killed on the spot. Those Jews armed with weapons supplied by the ŻOB put up resistance and were burned alive in the barracks. In Lvov, the last legal Jews were starved. A not-large group of fighters won a heroic battle against the guards and escaped to the forests. In Bedzin, the liquidation of the camp is ongoing. In January, news was received of the liquidation of the last hermetically sealed ghetto in Lodz. Nearly 50,000 Jews are still living in the remaining camps, the majority being concentrated in Plaszow, Krakow, Skarzysko, Starachowice, and Bedzin. Infectious diseases and hunger spread very quickly. The Germans put the sick to death immediately. The final liquidation of Polish Jewry is going to take place very soon. In the lands of Poland, in the camps, in Lodz, and in the "Aryan" areas, some 150,000 Jews are living at present. Their situation is entirely hopeless.

For the continuation of our work, much money is needed in order to (a) organize armed resistance in the existing camps, and (b) offer material assistance to the Jews in the camps and those in hiding on the "Aryan" side. To our regret, assistance from you does not arrive frequently and is limited in scope. We require at least 40,000 dollars per month. As victory approaches, our situation becomes tragic. We are claiming assistance from you—and without casting any doubt on your good will—which surely you can grant us.

A while ago, the He-Chaluts group in Zaglebie succeeded in reaching Hungary via Slovakia. To the best of our knowledge, the chalutsim [i.e., Zionist pioneers] succeeded in reaching Mandatory Palestine via Turkey. Do you know how they are? Is it within your power to make contact with us via Hungary? A liaison person came to us from the "Jewish Committee" in Hungary, who was ready to transfer us there. It's clear that we are remaining in Poland. Our desire is (a) to rescue the Jewish children who remain alive, and (b) to organize the civic activists and the youth who have survived. Do you know something about this committee? Can you help us also in this matter?

We know that the fate of the Land of Israel [i.e., Mandatory Palestine] is now on the agenda. If our voice still has any significance, know that we are with you. Let us hope that the spilled blood of millions will not have been in vain. With a fraternal handclasp,

Yours, Icchak, Cywja[60]

On April 19, 1944, marking the first anniversary of the uprising, Zivia, Yitzhak, and Tuvia Borzykowski sent a letter to Labor Zionist leaders and HeHalutz/Hashomer Hatzair in the Yishuv:

Letter to Dobkin, Tabenkin, Ya'ari, Berl (Katznelson?), Tel Aviv (ca. April 19, 1944)[61]

Dear friends! One year has passed from the days of heroic resistance of the Warsaw ghetto. Together with the entire world, even we in the underground, celebrated the anniversary and consecrated the day. Almost everyone has fallen. From all of our large families no one remains except individuals in certain locations. . . . [Lists fights in Warsaw, Bialystok, Krakow, Tarnow, Czenstachow, Bedzin, etc.]

Sixty of the fighters in Warsaw were our members. Out of the general number of 22 divisions—all the 11 largest ones were Halutzim. The commander of the Jewish fighting organization was our member Mordechai Anielewicz . . . on 17 August will be one year since the battles in Bialystok whose severity were no less than the battles in Warsaw. At their head stood M. (Trump) [Tennenboim, code name Trump(eldor)]. There were rumors that he was brought by the Germans to a concentration camp in Lublin but these rumors are not true. If there will remain in future generations the echoes of the Jewish fighting organization, we believe that also the Polish Hehalutz will not be forgotten. We do not exaggerate: in the days of destruction and death Hehalutz marched at the front of the

Jewish masses in Poland and was the arm and the brains of all activities. In the terrible moments it fulfilled its role in the defense of its people, we were witnesses to this. *The number of our friends who remain alive dwindles from day to day* [my emphasis]. Verman went to the street but did not return. Jacob Faigenblat and Guta Kabinetkofsky were caught by the Gestapo. They fell in battle with weapons in the hand. In the Czenstachow district our partisan division was dismantled and only individuals were saved. In some of the camps can be found small groups of our friends members (Czenstachow and Skarzysko). Recently we established contact with Strachowice, a place where a small gathering of our people with K. Z. A few times we sent money to Lwow, but the connection is minimal. We know that in Vilna is A.K. [Abba Kovner]. We have had no success establishing contact with him. A. M. and Y.K. [Yitzhak Katznelson] are with groups of our friends and left a year ago with foreign passport, to a camp in Bergen near H. But we have no news from them. We are very concerned about their fates. We try to help them! Until today we continue to work in the ŻOB to provide arms to groups of Jews and to fulfill the rescue work. One of our members stands at the head of the fighting organization. We do not want to list now the hundreds of our members who distinguished themselves in battle and all of those who continue to work tirelessly to for fill [*sic*] their obligation to our movement and to the people. We want to just remember the mother P. who works with us: her three children she sacrificed on the altar of our honor, her oldest son who fell in partisan battle with the Germans in Czenstachow, her youngest son Marek who excelled in the defense of the ghetto Czenstachow and afterwards fell in underground work. Her only daughter H. 17 years old who participated in the revolt in Krakow and is now located in the concentration camp in Auschwitz. Today, with pride the mother continues her activity with us and brings assistance to hundreds of Jews living dangerously underground. And we want to recall one more: our poet Y. K. who in the days of the second liquidation and in the first defense of the Warsaw ghetto (18–21 January 1943) refused to go into hiding in together with his son D. (His wife and young children were taken in the first liquidation), he participated in the battles of our division together with us defended our honor. One year ago he went out with D. to the camp for foreigners in Vittel. We have no news from him. They took care of him. Details on our lives and our work you will find in the general letters and in the reports to be sent. *Write to us about your lives. Until now we have received no letters. In these moments of tragedy great national tragedy which has no precedent . . . for us cut off from the homeland, and hiding with a little faith and hope, with evidence of the blood battle of humanity, our work and blood have been spilled but we want to know that it is not wasted.*

In the name of those who remain alive we send to you greetings of life to the Yishuv, to the labor federation, to the kibbutz movement, and to all our brothers and sisters. Our fighters send greetings to all the Jewish soldiers fighting on every front against our common enemy.

Despite everything, we have not forgotten.

Yours, Zivia, Yitzhak, and Tuvia B.

This letter, sent one year after the Warsaw ghetto revolt by Zivia, Antek, and Tuvia Borzykowski is striking. On the one hand, they emphasized the leading role played by HeHalutz in leading the resistance: "If there will remain in future generations the echoes of the Jewish fighting organization, we believe that also the Polish Hehalutz will not be forgotten. We do not exaggerate: in the days of destruction and death Hehalutz marched at the front of the Jewish masses in Poland and was the arm and the brains of all activities. In the terrible moments it fulfilled its role in the defense of its people, we were witnesses to this." The names of heroic figures—Anielewicz, Katznelson, Kovner, and others—are included or alluded to, while the authors highlighted the continuing struggle and dedication of the Jews who remained dedicated to saving the last remnants of Polish Jewry. The image of P., the mother from Częstochowa who sacrificed her three children for the honor of the Jewish people, for the defense of the Jewish masses, and yet continued to aid in the underground work of the ŻOB was an incredibly powerful symbol. And yet, the undertone of abandonment and isolation remained for the writers, cut off from the homeland, desperate to receive some word from the Yishuv, to know that their struggle had not been in vain.

In the days, weeks, and months after the revolt, the surviving ghetto fighters worked to ensure their story would be known in the outside world. As the surviving members of the fighting organization, they emphasized the role of their own movement members in the struggle, which focused on armed resistance and not the experiences of the Jewish masses who concealed themselves in the subterranean bunkers of Warsaw. As they marked the first anniversary of the revolt in Warsaw, Jewish communities in New York, London, and the Yishuv also planned major commemorations to mark "the days of heroic resistance."

4

The First Anniversary of the Revolt

ABROAD, A BATTLE FOR credit was brewing among the groups associated with the uprising, as we will see in the next chapter. Despite this, the remaining members of the Jewish Fighting Organization struggling to stay alive in hiding on the Aryan side of Warsaw hoped that on April 19, 1944, Jews around the world would join them in commemorating the first anniversary of the revolt, consecrating the day by holding memorial services.[1] This chapter will examine the ways in which, by the first anniversary of the revolt, the Warsaw Ghetto Uprising was seized upon by Jewish communities around the world as evidence that Jews had joined the struggle against fascism and was utilized as a prism for memorializing the destruction of European Jewry. In the United States, Jewish leaders could present it as part of the Jewish contribution to the Allied war effort, as the outcry of the oppressed who refused to submit to fascism and instead joined the fight to defeat Nazism. The Jewish Labor Committee celebrated the heroism of the workers who joined the Polish nation in the struggle against German oppression. Jewish religious leaders marked April 19 as a day of sorrow and mourning, when the heroism of the ghetto fighters could be remembered together with the suffering of the Jewish martyrs. The timing of the revolt was critical, as Jews eagerly sought hope amidst despair and heroes to whom they could connect. Within a year of the uprising, Jewish communities in New York, London, and the Yishuv had transformed the anniversary of the revolt into the focal point of Jewish commemorations of the destruction of European Jewry, albeit in crucially differing ways that reflected divergent worldviews. As the heroes of the revolt were mythologized, the Bund and the Zionist movement grappled for credit.

The First Anniversary in New York

In advance of the first anniversary, the U.S. State Department issued a message declaring:

> No finer page has been written in the long history of the Jews than the battle waged by unarmed men, women and children against the brutal Nazi murderers . . . the heroic defenders of the Warsaw ghetto have strengthened the spirit of free peoples resolved upon the extinction of Nazi tyranny and the liberation of all oppressed peoples.[2]

The *Daily Worker* (a Communist daily published in New York with a circulation of thirty-five thousand), included tributes offered by American leaders, including one by Harold Ickes, Secretary of the Interior and one of President Roosevelt's longest-serving cabinet secretaries, which read, in part: "Jews through the centuries have fought for the democratic way of life, and the magnificent gesture of Warsaw a year ago is but a token of the fight that must be carried on until every vestige of Hitlerism has been eradicated."[3]

For a broad swath of the American Jewish community—Reform, Conservative, and Orthodox—who felt largely powerless to formulate an effective response to Nazism and the devastating news of the destruction of European Jewry, the one-year anniversary of the Warsaw Ghetto Uprising presented an opportunity, as it did for Communists, Bundists, Zionists, the American Jewish Committee, and other organizations, to focus their collective commemorative energy. The Jewish Telegraphic Agency announced in advance that "the first anniversary of the heroic resistance of the Jews in the Warsaw ghetto, which the Germans were not able to suppress for more than a month, will be commemorated tomorrow by Jews throughout the United States with memorial meetings, a fifteen-minute work stoppage, and the issuance of a proclamation by the American Jewish Conference to the democratic world pleading for the rescue of those Jews who can still be saved." Likewise, the Synagogue Council of America (an umbrella body bridging the three primary Jewish denominations) proclaimed April 19, 1944 to be a day of prayer and sorrow, calling all rabbis to "convoke special services on April 19 to honor and mourn the heroes and martyrs of the ghettoes who sacrificed their lives in the cause of the United Nations and for the glory of Israel, and to dedicate themselves to the effort of rescuing the survivors."[4] Special prayers were to be recited in advance of a two-minute moment of silence at 11:00 a.m., while another prayer for private gatherings would be recited during a fifteen-minute work stoppage at work, home, or in the factory. Among the purposes to be served by marking the day through such prayer and reflection, the council suggested, was "to honor the heroes and martyrs of the ghettos who have given their lives for the ideals of the United Nations and for the glory of the Jewish people." Furthermore, it was hoped that such actions might speed the rescue of those who survived, while mobilizing the strength to aid in the victory of the United Nations, allied in the struggle to defeat the Axis powers. The letter was signed by Dr. Israel Goldstein, rabbi of Congregation B'nai Jeshurun in New York, head of the Zionist Organization of America and later the American Jewish Congress.[5]

Judge Joseph M. Proskauer, president of the American Jewish Committee, issued a statement emphasizing that the Jews of Warsaw fought not only as Jews, but as Poles loyal to their homeland.

> in all the heroism of this world-wide war, no single act compares with the valor of the starving, downtrodden Jews of the Warsaw Ghetto. April 19, 1943, is a date that will long be remembered in Jewish annals. It commemorates the day when thirty-five thousand Jews—men, women and children—rose in righteous wrath against the despoiler.

> Thirty-five thousand Warsaw Jews, the remnant of the greatest Jewish community in continental Europe, entered into a suicide pact. Though resistance was futile, though it spelled inevitable death, these heroic Jews chose to die fighting. They chose to sacrifice their lives upon the altar of the battle against totalitarianism. . . . Those Jews of the Warsaw Ghetto fought and died for their homes, for the land of their nativity. Although theirs had not always been the happiest lot, although Poland was all too often susceptible to anti-Semitic hate, these Jews fought to the death an aggressor who had ravished their land. Those Jews fought and died in the Warsaw Ghetto, fought as Poles just as their brothers in the United States, Great Britain, Russia and Jews of all other nationalities are fighting side by side with their Christian brothers against the Axis Powers. The battle of the Warsaw Jews, their hopeless battle, must ever be an inspiration to us all. It is appropriate that we who live commemorate their valor on the anniversary of their battle to the death. It is fitting that the traditional Hebrew prayer for the dead, El Mole Rachamin, be said for those who died (so) that freedom may live.[6]

A booklet of special prayers and devotions was prepared by the Committee for Intercession of the Synagogue Council of America. The booklet was sent to religious leaders of American Jewry for use in the synagogue and the home, along with special prayers to be recited.[7] Among the prayers was one to be recited before a moment of silence:

> My God, my God, why hast Thou forsaken me?
> Why hidest Thou Thyself in times of trouble?
> Oh my God, I call by day, but Thou answerest not and at night, but I find no relief.
> Oh Lord God of Israel, turn from Thy wrath, and hold back this evil against Thy people.

Have compassion on us, Oh Lord, in thine abundant mercy, and deliver us not into the power of the tyrants.

Arise, Oh God, plead thine own cause, for thy sake are we killed all the day, are we treated as sheep at the slaughter.

For lo, Thine enemies are in an uproar, and they that hate Thee have lifted up their head. They have called, "Come, let us blot out their existence, that the name of Israel may be no more."

As a father hath compassion upon his children, so have Thou compassion for us, Oh Lord.

Our anguish is locked up within us, and we are silent. In our hearts we sanctify the memory of the slain who are silenced forever. May our silence be felt to the ends of the earth. May it stir the souls of men, and reach up to Thee, O God of Mercy.

Amen.

Services were to be concluded with solicitations for the work of the United Jewish Appeal, "which is engaged in the work of rescue and relief of the victims of Nazi aggression." It is important to note that in a religious sense, the trope of "sheep to the slaughter" was a point to be celebrated: Jews were willing to show their devotion to God and died to sanctify the name of *Hashem*. The ghetto fighters would invert this trope, arguing against the passivity of those Jews who allowed themselves to die passively, led like sheep to the slaughter.[8]

The *Jewish Daily Forward* on April 19, 1944, called on Jews in New York to mark the day of memory for the heroes and martyrs. Noting that the ghetto fighters had written a "chapter of light in the human struggle for freedom" against the Nazi barbarians, the *Forward* called upon readers to participate in the 11:30 a.m. march to City Hall and the evening program at Carnegie Hall featuring a speech by Jacob Pat of the Jewish Labor Committee, as well as remarks by other notables, including the Yiddish writer H. Leivick.

In his remarks at Carnegie Hall, Leivick reflected on the meaning of the revolt in Warsaw, for Jews in America, and indeed for the entire world. The revolt had surely transformed those who lived at the time, filling them with wonder, with fear, and with guilt and shame. Leivick stood in awe of the heroism of the fighters, a defiance that also filled him with guilt and anger—for it symbolized the inability of Jews around the world to respond to calls of their brothers for aid, and the indifference of the world to that same cry for help. And it filled him with guilt before the millions of "silent, submissive, and lost" Jews, "slaughtered like sheep."

> We do not know what to call the Jewish uprising against the Germans in the ghetto: resistance, a revolt, or some loftier name. Whatever name we give it, the simple fact itself will transcend our words and fill us with wonder and fear, with prayer, with an upsurge of rebellion—and with the consciousness of guilt. Our own lives have been transfigured, and must be understood anew and justified in a new way. . . . Let us call that expression a miracle, the miracle of heroism, of the heroism which lay in the depths of our people's spirit, and its faith, its Torah, its culture, its literature and its movements of liberation.[9]

For Leivick, the revolt not only signified guilt, and shame, and anger—for American Jews, he argued, it "consecrated our names, too" exalting them and uniting them again for the Jewish bond of freedom, justice, and proud national culture. For American Jews who had been separated from the wellspring of Jewish national culture and peoplehood in Europe, the Warsaw Ghetto Uprising was a reminder of the strength and power the Jewish people might still possess. A separate article on the front page of the *Forward* that day also reprinted the "last cry of the Jews in the ghetto to the Polish people in Warsaw."

In a letter to all workers in greater New York, Jacob Pat called on the working classes to observe the date of the uprising with a work stoppage "to honor the memory of the courageous dead and to mobilize all forces to aid and rescue the living."

> Mass shootings, torture, gas chambers, murder trucks, starvation—the whole gamut of Nazi bestiality had slaughtered 3,000,000 Polish Jews. Some 50,000 remained in the Warsaw Ghetto while the world looked on expecting their life blood to be squeezed out drop by drop. Instead the tortured and starving picked what weapons lay at hand, turned every yard, house and cellar into a fortress, put the torch to what they could not defend and sold their lives to avenge their relatives, friends and coreligionists to raise an inspiring story on behalf of the ideals of freedom, decency, and humanity.[10]

On April 19, 1944, over thirty thousand Jews gathered in New York City before the steps of City Hall to hear speeches by Mayor La Guardia and prominent Jewish leaders. The headline in the next day's *Forverts* read, "Hundreds of Thousands of Jews in New York Honored the Jewish Heroes and Martyrs of Poland," with the continuation, "with sorrowful demonstrations, marches to City Hall, with the participation of the Mayor."[11]

The *New York Times*, in an editorial devoted to the first anniversary of the revolt, termed the Battle of the Warsaw Ghetto "an example of courage that history can scarcely match," noting "All faiths and creeds thrill at the heroic story."

> What is important is that they, the most helpless and hopeless of all Hitler's victims, defied the tyrant's wrath and set for the rest of us an example of courage that history can scarcely match. The whole human race owes them a debt of gratitude for the inspiration their self-sacrifice gives to the cause of freedom.
>
> They did not die in vain, those Jewish martyrs. When the war entered its blackest phase, the flaming spirit of their

JEWISH LABOR COMMITTEE

APRIL 19, 1944—FIRST ANNIVERSARY OF THE REVOLT OF THE GHETTOS

•

Brothers and Sisters:

We have ceased work to commemorate a most tragic and unprecedented event. Today is the first anniversary of that fateful April 19, 1943 when the persecuted, hungry, and enslaved Jews of the Warsaw ghetto had seized weapons and ammunition and launched a most heroic battle against the Nazi murderers.

We mourn for the millions of Jews who perished in the ghettos. Our hearts and our thoughts burn with aroused indignation and hatred for the Nazi butchers. We pledge ourselves to struggle unceasingly against the Hitler hordes until victory comes, as come it must.

Hitler's brutal reign over Germany started with his anti-Jewish pogroms. Soon he turned to the extermination of the labor movement. His strongest and most effective weapons consisted of race hatred, bigotry, and dissention among nations, as well as among peoples. His vicious power grew daily until he finally threw the whole world into the bloodiest conflagration in the history of mankind.

But those upon whom the barbaric Nazi wrath has fallen most heavily, have been the Jews of Europe. Nearly four million Jews were killed. Some were tortured to death; others suffocated in gas chambers.

From June to October 1942, approximately 300,000 Jews were killed by the Nazis in the single city of Warsaw, which was the biggest Jewish center in Europe. Only 40,000 remained alive. Those surviving were busily and self-sacrificingly engaged in mapping a courageous stand against the Nazi oppressors. The fighting underground organizations consisted of all Jewish labor groups, and other Jews who managed to escape death. The non-Jewish underground organization of Polish labor joined hands and helped their Jewish brothers in the common struggle for survival.

On the 19th of April the Jews of the ghetto took to the streets and opened fire. It was a most inspiring battle, lasting more than a month — 30 days and 30 nights in succession.

When the Jewish ghetto fighters began their insurrection they knew they could not rely on, or hope for, aid from the outside world. Their battle was a glorious symbol of man's resistance to tyranny and slavery. Instead of submission, they chose resistance, and gave a most inspiring account of themselves.

Today, on the first anniversary of that amazing struggle, we salute the memory of the ghetto heroes. We pledge ourselves to avenge the crimes against the Jewish people and other victims of Nazi savagery. We urge, and we request, that the United Nations exert all their power and influence to rescue and aid the remaining Jews. We solemnly vow to do everything to win the war and a peace based on freedom, equality, and justice to all.

Jewish Labor Committee proclamation, April 19, 1944 (JLC Archives, Tamiment).

Commemoration of the first anniversary of the Warsaw Ghetto Uprising, New York City, 1944. (YIVO Photo Archives). Isaac Rubinstein, former chief rabbi of Vilna, speaking; New York City mayor Fiorello LaGuardia to his left.

הונדערטער טויזענטער אידען אין ניו יארק עהרען
די אידישע העלדען און מארטירער פון פוילען

גרויס געוויין אין ווארשעווער שוהל און אויף די גאסען; די פאלקס - פארזאמלונג אין קארנעגיע האל

"Hundreds of Thousands of Jews in New York Honor the Jewish Heroes and Martyrs of Poland." *Jewish Daily Forward*, April 19, 1944.

> Polish ghetto shone as a pillar of light in the darkness to all who struggled toward the dawn of a better day for all mankind. With Lidice, Warsaw will be a beacon for humanity for centuries to come.[12]

Among those pictured behind Mayor LaGuardia and Rabbi Rubenstein on the steps of City Hall were the poet Julian Tuwim and the artist Arthur Szyk. Julian Tuwim, a Polish exile, wrote the manifesto *We Polish Jews* in New York in April 1944. Anticipating both the fragments of the ghetto walls and the monument that would be created by Natan Rapaport in Warsaw (dedicated on the fifth anniversary of the revolt), Tuwim called for a "new monument (to) be added to the national shrine" that would honor the heroes of the Jewish people alongside their martyrs:

> I believe in a future Poland in which [the Star of David painted on the Warsaw ghetto fighters' armbands] will become the highest order bestowed upon the bravest among Polish officers and soldiers. They will wear it proudly upon their breast next to the old Virtuti Militari. . . .
>
> . . . And there shall be in Warsaw and in every other Polish city some fragment of the ghetto left standing and preserved in its present form in all its horror of ruin and destruction. We shall surround that monument to the ignominy of our foes and to the glory of our tortured heroes with chains wrought from captured Hitler's guns, and every day we shall twine fresh live flowers into its iron links, so that the memory of the massacred people shall remain forever fresh in the minds of the generations to come, and also as a sign of our undying sorrow for them.[13]

The Polish-Jewish artist Arthur Szyk, had traveled from England to Canada in July 1940, before arriving in New York in December. Szyk almost single-handedly led an artistic effort to convince the American public to support the war effort and created *The Repulsed Attack* to commemorate the first anniversary of the revolt. The image in *Our Journal*, published by the American Council of Warsaw Jews on April 30, 1944, also appeared in numerous other publications. The cover page of *Our Journal* in English noted that the volume was published to "remember the heroic struggle of our brothers in Warsaw (a city that no longer has any Jews)." And indeed, Szyk's illustration depicted only male fighters, triumphant over the fallen SS, wearing the star of David as a mark of pride, not a badge of shame. While Szyk did not depict any female fighters (by then the names of Tosia Altman, Zivia Lubetkin, Tobcia Dawidowicz, and others had been reported in various places), he did represent the revolt as a popular uprising, reflecting a cross-section of the Jewish population, young and old, religious and secular, middle class and working class among the fighters.

The First Anniversary in London

In London, Isaac Schwartzbart called for April 19, 1944, to be commemorated in order to arouse British Jewry to continue relief work and "enlighten the British public opinion on the fact that the heroic battles of the Jews in Poland, in Warsaw and in other Polish towns, were acts of Jewish self-defence and armed actions to assist the cause of the United Nations." Schwarztbart proposed a memorial service and sermon by Chief Rabbi Dr. Joseph Hertz, speeches by prominent British personalities and Polish Jews, the observance at 12 p.m. by Jews nationwide of two minutes of silence, dedicated articles in the Jewish press, and more.[14]

Members of the Polish government-in-exile attended the Warsaw Ghetto Memorial, along with representatives of the Polish High Command, the Jewish Agency, and the Board of Deputies of British Jewry. A message from the Polish premier Stanisław Mikołajczyk was read, stressing that Poles and Jews were united in a common struggle.[15] In his sermon at the Nelson Street Synagogue, which hosted the national day of mourning, Rabbi Szpetman declared:

> we assembled here not as the representatives of the parties of groups to which we belong, but as Jews who came to

דער העלדישער קאמף פון אונזערע ברידער אין דער ווארשעווער געטא געגן די נאצי־בארבארן.
געמאלן פון בערימטען פויליש־אידישן קינסטלער **ארטור שיק**.

Arthur Szyk, *The Repulsed Attack*, in *Our Journal*, the publication of the American Council of Warsaw Jews, April 30, 1944. Also printed in *Forverts* and numerous other publications. (From the collection of Gregg and Michelle Philipson)

> mourn their fallen brethren. Even our old lamentations would not be adequate to describe our present-day tragedy. We have lost the greatest and most vital and creative Jewish centre, the source of our strength and the pride of our youth. Even the Shechinah is bitterly mourning at the greatest of calamities. We shall never forget those who perished at the hands of the foe and those who fell in desperate battle against him. God will pay our enemies in the way they deserve. His judgment will surely come.[16]

Noting the coincidence of the day of mourning taking place during the counting of the *omer* between Passover and Shavuot, B. Margulies, chairman of the Federation of Polish Jews, asked: "we remember our fallen brethren in the days of the Sephirah, days of mourning. But who could count today the number of our victims?" Isaac Schwartzbart, representing the National Council of Poland, took the day of mourning as a call to continue working for the Jewish future: "Our tears at the great tragedy must at the same time be a source of new strength to go on living and working. Letters from the Ghetto of Warsaw show that our heroes died in battle with the hope that a free world will come to exist after the war and that the Jewish people will be redeemed in Eretz Israel. We must work for this aim and thus honour our heroes."

Anshel Reiss, representing the Jewish Agency for Palestine, echoed the call to work for a Jewish future in the Land of Israel, while also drawing a stark distinction between the deaths of those fighters who died for the cause of the war effort and those who died a meaningless death, and rebuking those who had not done enough to rescue the Jews of Europe:

> Our enemies try to exterminate the Jews of Europe. At the same time our friends are not active enough in their efforts to stop the mass murder. I can still see before my eyes those good and devoted Jews, workers for our cause, like Rabbi Nissenbaum,[17] as well as so many younger men and women, who perished at the hands of our enemies. They

> died a meaningless death without bringing use to the Allied cause, with the shining exception of the heroes who fought in the ghettoes. They took up arms as soon as they could secure them and fought to the last. Our duty to their memory will not be done unless we devote ourselves to work for the cause of freedom and for the redemption of the Jewish people—the two great causes for which our martyrs have given their lives.

Speaking on behalf of the Polish Minister of Information, Prof. Kot, Dr. Witold Czerwinski noted again the heroism of Michał Klepfisz, as leader of the fighters, while also pointing to the battle as a harbinger of postwar cooperation between Jews and Poles in the building of a "new and just prosperity" in Poland:

> I take this occasion to state once more how profound is the appreciation of the Polish people and the Polish government of the heroic defense of the Warsaw Ghetto. The Polish National Council has expressed its feelings in a recent resolution, and the President of the Republic bestowed the highest Polish military decoration, the 'Virtuti Militari' on Michel Klepfisz, the gallant leader of the fighters of the Warsaw Ghetto, whose bravery and valour rank with that of the Maccabeans.
>
> The battle of the Warsaw Ghetto will remain in the annals of this war as one of the outstanding feats of heroism. The brotherhood in arms of the Jewish and Polish people in Warsaw will tend to tighten their co-operation in the fight against the common enemy in Poland and on all the military fronts, and also in the building, when peace is won, of a new and just prosperity.

A memorial publication, *Remember the Warsaw Ghetto*, also included a brief summary of the details of the battle, "led and conducted by the Jewish

Fighting Organization with the help of the Polish Underground," and a two-page list of the names of "those who fell in defence of the ghetto," featuring a photo of Michał Klepfisz. The alphabetical list of names of fighters replicated the one sent to London by the Jewish National Committee in November 1943. The publication concluded with a page that featured an excerpt from the last letter of Szmuel Zygielbojm.

One month later, at a "service of Mourning and Prayer for the Martyrs of the Warsaw Ghetto" held at Bevis Marks Synagogue in London on May 22, 1944, the Chief Rabbi of England, Rabbi Joseph Hertz, delivered a sermon entitled "The Battle of Warsaw."

> We are assembled in this venerable House of Worship to call to mind, with poignant sorrow and sacred pride, the lightning-flashes of deathless glory that a year ago

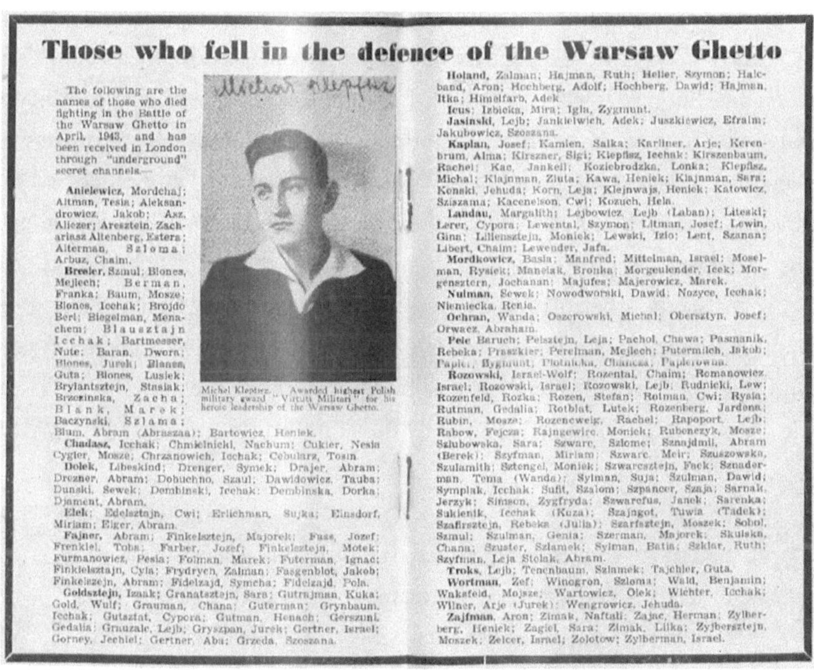

Those who fell in the defence of the Warsaw Ghetto

The following are the names of those who died fighting in the Battle of the Warsaw Ghetto in April, 1943, and has been received in London through "underground" secret channels.—

Anielewicz, Mordchaj; Altman, Tesia; Aleksandrowicz, Jakob; Axz, Aliezer; Aresztein, Zachariasz Altenberg, Estera; Alterman, Szloma; Arbuz, Chaim.

Bresler, Szmul; Blones, Mejlech; Berman, Franka; Baum, Mosze; Blones, Icchak; Brojdo Berl; Biegelman, Menachem; Blausztajn Icchak; Bartmesser, Nute; Baran, Dwora; Blones, Jurek; Blanes, Guta; Blones, Lusiek; Brylantsztejn, Stasiak; Brzezinska, Zacha; Blank, Marek; Baczynski, Szlama; Blum, Abram (Abraszaa); Bartowicz, Heniek.

Chadasz, Icchak; Chmielnicki, Nachum; Cukier, Nesia Cygler, Mosze; Chrzanowich, Icchak; Cebularz, Tosia.

Dolek, Libeskind; Drenger, Symek; Drajer, Abram; Drezner, Abram; Dobuchno, Szaul; Dawidowicz, Tauba; Dunski, Sewek; Dembinski, Icchak; Dembinska, Dorka; Djament, Abram.

Elek; Edelsztajn, Cwi; Erlichman, Sujka; Einsdorf, Miriam; Elger, Abram.

Fajner, Abram; Finkelsztejn, Majorek; Fuss, Jozef; Frenkiel, Toba; Farber, Jozef; Finkelsztejn, Motek; Furmanowicz, Pesia; Folman, Marek; Futerman, Ignac; Finkielsztajn, Cyla; Frydrych, Zalman; Fasgenblot, Jakob; Finkelszejn, Abram; Fidelzajd, Symcha; Fidelzajd, Pola.

Goldsztejn, Izaak; Granatsztejn, Sara; Gutrajman, Kuka; Gold, Wulf; Grauman, Chana; Guterman; Grynbaum, Icchak; Gutsztat, Cypora; Gutman, Henach; Gerszuni, Gedalia; Grauzalc, Lejb; Gryszpan, Jurek; Gertner, Israel; Gorney, Jechiel; Gertner, Aba; Grzeda, Szoszana.

Holand, Zalman; Hajman, Ruth; Heller, Szymon; Halcband, Aron; Hochberg, Adolf; Hochberg, Dawid; Hajman, Itka; Himelfarb, Adek.

Icus; Izbicka, Mira; Igla, Zygmunt.

Jasinski, Lejb; Jankielwich, Adek; Juszkiewicz, Efraim; Jakubowicz, Szoszana.

Kaplan, Josef; Kamien, Salka; Karliner, Arje; Kerenbrum, Alma; Kirszner, Sigi; Klepfisz, Icchak; Kirszenbaum, Rachel; Kac, Jankell; Koziebrodzka, Lonka; Klepfisz, Michal; Klajnman, Ziuta; Kawa, Heniek; Klajnman, Sara; Konski, Jehuda; Korn, Leja; Klejnwajs, Heniek; Katowicz, Sziszama; Kacenelson, Cwi; Kozuch, Hela.

Landau, Margalith; Lejbowicz, Lejb (Laban); Liteski; Lerer, Cypora; Lewental, Szymon; Litman, Josef; Lewin, Ginn; Lilienszteijn, Moniek; Lewski, Izio; Lent, Szanan; Libert, Chaim; Lewender, Jafa.

Mordkowicz, Basia; Manfred; Mittelman, Israel; Moselman, Rysiek; Maneiak, Bronka; Morgeulender, Icek; Morgensztern, Jochanan; Majufes; Majerowicz, Marek.

Nulman, Sewek; Nowodworski, Dawid; Nozyce, Icchak; Niemiecka, Renia.

Ochran, Wanda; Oszerowski, Michal; Obersztyn, Josef; Orwacz, Abraham.

Pelc Baruch; Pelsztejn, Leja; Pachol, Chawa; Pasmanik, Rebeka; Praszkier; Perelman, Mejlech; Putermilch, Jakob; Papler; Sygmunt; Plotnicka, Chancza; Paplerowna.

Rozowski, Israel-Wolf; Rozental, Chaim; Romanowicz Israel; Rozowski, Israel; Rozowski, Lejb; Rudnicki, Lew; Rozenfeld, Rozka; Rozen, Stefan; Rolman, Cwi; Rysia; Rutman, Gedalia; Rotblat, Lutek; Rozenberg, Jardena; Rubin, Mosze; Rozencweig, Rachel; Rapoport, Lejb; Rabow, Fejcza; Rajngewirc, Moniek; Rubenczyk, Mosze; Szlubowska, Sara; Szwarc, Szlome; Sznajdmil, Abram (Berek); Szyfman, Miriam; Szwarc, Meir; Szuszowska, Szulamith; Sztengel, Moniek; Szwarcsztejn, Fack; Sznaderman, Tema (Wanda); Sylman, Suja; Szulman, Dawid; Symplak, Icchak; Sufit, Szalom; Szpancer, Szaja; Sarnak, Jerzyk; Simson, Zygfryda; Szwarcfus, Janek; Sarenka; Sukienik, Icchak (Kuza); Szajngot, Tuwia (Tadek); Szafirsztejn, Rebeka (Julia); Szarfsztejn, Moszek; Sobol, Szmul; Szulman, Genia; Szerman, Majorek; Skulska, Chana; Szuster, Szlamek; Sylman, Batia; Szklar, Ruth; Szyfman, Leja Stolak, Abram.

Troks, Lejb; Tenenbaum, Szlamek; Tajchler, Guta.

Wortman, Zef; Winogron, Szloma; Wald, Benjamin; Waksfeld, Mojsze; Wartowicz, Olek; Wichter, Icchak; Wilner, Arje (Jurek); Wengrowicz, Jehuda.

Zajfman, Aron; Zimak, Naftali; Zajac, Herman; Zylberberg, Heniek; Zagiel, Sara; Zimak, Lilka; Zyjbersztejn, Moszek; Zelcer, Israel; Zolotow; Zylberman, Israel.

Michel Klepfisz. Awarded highest Polish military award "Virtuti Militari" for his heroic leadership of the Warsaw Ghetto.

"Those who fell in defence of the Warsaw Ghetto." *Remember the Warsaw Ghetto*, issued by the Federation of Polish Jews in Great Britain (London: Narod Press, 1944). (United States Holocaust Memorial Museum Library)

> illumined the terrible darkness which enveloped the last days of the Warsaw Jewish community. It is a story that would require the pen of a Prophet, and should be written in letters of fire; and as for Israel's martyrdom of to-day, only a *paytan*—one of those great elegiac poets of the Middle Ages who gave voice to the storm of sighs and torrents of tears that accompanied the massacres of which they were eyewitnesses—could depict its horror and woe. One who is neither Prophet nor paytan, must confine himself to a bald statement of heart-breaking facts.[18]

Rabbi Hertz narrated the historical facts about the destruction of Polish Jewry known at the time, while consigning the acts of deathless glory that defined the end of the ghetto to the sphere of liturgical writing and prophecy. Nonetheless, despite his attempt to confine himself to the facts, Hertz could not restrain himself, venturing an account that celebrated the glory of Warsaw Jewry's now legendary exploits. He explained in his sermon that when the "largest Jewish Kehillah in Europe had been reduced to 40,000 souls, who by now knew full well the doom that awaited them. . . . The unexpected happened. This remnant of Warsaw Jewry, starved and enfeebled by physical and mental suffering that had passed the limit of human endurance, resolved to fight their fiendish murderers to the last drop of blood. . . . Soon the whole ghetto turned into a fortress, and every house into a citadel." Recounting the heroic deeds of women, young girls, and defenders who managed to kill one thousand of the enemy in the last six weeks of the ghetto, Rabbi Hertz tried to draw the appropriate parallels from Jewish history:

> For staggering courage, this Battle of Warsaw is unsurpassed in the whole history of heroism. It is an epic struggle that recalls the glories of the Maccabees and the amazing self-slaughter at Masada. Like them, the men and women who in our day fearlessly defied the fury of the inhuman oppressor, died for the honour of their people. And they died in the

> hope that a free world would emerge from this war; a world in which, even for the Jew, there would be freedom from fear, freedom to live. Their dying was a Kiddush Hashem; a sublime proclamation for all time, "magnified and glorified be God's great Name," *Yisgaddal v'yiskaddash shemeh rabbo.*[19]

Rabbi Hertz concluded his sermon with a call to Anglo Jewry not to remain silent, and the hope that the remembrance of the "immortal heroes and heroines of Warsaw, and our mourning for the millions of our brethren from the Atlantic to the Volga, from Norway to Crete . . . rouse in men of goodwill everywhere a new pity, a new justice and new humanity." Finally, he prayed that from the calamity would emerge a "new loyalty to the ideals of our Sacred Faith," along with submission to God's inscrutable will.[20]

The First Anniversary in the Yishuv

While Jews in New York and London marked the first anniversary with large-scale mass demonstrations that included the broader non-Jewish public and linked the heroism of the ghetto fighters with the suffering of Jewish martyrs, commemorations of the first anniversary in the Yishuv were more muted. As Dina Porat has detailed in her study of the Zionist leadership's response to the Shoah during the war, the Yishuv was ambivalent about how to respond to the first anniversary of the revolt. What was the meaning of the uprising? Should it be celebrated as an example of *Kiddush Hashem*, collective martyrdom? Uncertainty over the details and identities of the heroes made it difficult to celebrate the revolt even if, as Porat suggests, over the course of 1943 "the Yishuv's attitude changed, from disdain for the Diaspora's passivity—and the emergence of corruption and deterioration in the ghetto's public life, to a steadily growing admiration for demonstrations of human and moral heroism, not necessarily for armed resistance."[21]

Coverage in the Yishuv press focused on descriptions of the impressive demonstrations in New York and on what was known regarding the uprising, but little appeared on commemorations in the Yishuv itself and no calls to mark a widespread day of remembrance. Instead the anniversary was marked with a "Day of Outcry for the Rescue of the Survivors [She'erit ha-Peletah]." As in New York, work ceased, and fasting and public rallies took place. On April 21, an article in *Davar* noted commemorations in the United States to mark the "day of the Warsaw Ghetto Heroes," citing proclamations by President Roosevelt that "all people who support freedom in the world will forever remember the heroic war of the Warsaw ghetto fighters."

> A large procession before the city hall (in New York) included over 15,000 demonstrators, among them 5,000 Jews from Poland, and with them rabbis, artists and writers of all kinds. At the head of the procession marched Rabbi Rubinstein from Vilna, a former member of the Polish senate, the mayor La Guardia received the procession with warm heartfelt remarks and highlighted the heroic actions of the ghetto fighters. All of the synagogues in America were full as people participated in reciting "Yizkor" prayers.[22]

An additional short article noted that on the same evening (April 19) a large gathering took place at Carnegie Hall where speakers demanded that all possible must be done to save the surviving remnant (*She'erit Hapletah*). Among the demands enumerated were that all Jews be granted refuge from Nazi oppression, that the gates of Israel be opened, and the neutral countries be supported in their efforts to rescue Jews. *Davar* noted that among the speakers were Stephen Wise, Nahum Goldmann, Arieh Tartakower, and Israel Goldstein (although no speakers from the Jewish Labor Committee or Bund were listed). The *Palestine Post* marked the one-year anniversary by publishing an account of the revolt based on the compilation of reports published by the World Jewish Congress (noted above as "The Massacre in the Warsaw Ghetto"). The front page highlighted the large gatherings and work stoppages taking place in New York and also noted the "Jewish Labor Committee is to launch a campaign to raise $250,000 for Jews in occupied Poland. A Ghetto Exhibition of documents and pictures showing Nazi persecution of Jews is also to be held."[23] In its front-page article on the fighting in the ghetto one year earlier, the newspaper reported that "arms were smuggled into the Ghetto by the Polish Underground army, and a second source of supply was a munition production plant organized by the engineer Michał Klepfish, who was killed in the battle. The fighters were mainly young men and women led and organized by the Jewish Workers Union ('Bund') which has become the backbone of the resistance movement. Arms were also captured from German stores."[24]

The General Zionist newspaper *HaBoker*, in Tel Aviv, included a similar report on what was known about the uprising one year earlier, echoing the coverage in the *Palestine Post* and also noting that a "portion of the arms in the ghetto were supplied by a special factory organized by Michał Klepfisz." An article in *Davar* on April 21, 1944, by Dr. Joseph Kruk discussed the "holy day" one year after the revolt.

> They knew that they had sentenced themselves to death. The wild Nazi beasts would kill them without mercy. But they decided to pay a dear price for their lives: the Germans would understand what the meaning of Jewish bravery was: ancient Masada in the new Warsaw. . . . The Jewish fighters of the Warsaw Ghetto have not stopped to live among us. They will live among us not only one day a year, on the day of memory, when they died. Instead, they will enter deeply into our hearts and souls. We will not forget them for eternity. . . . We have all been orphaned. We have lost the best and bravest among us. But we have also become their inheritors. . . . It is upon us to save the remnant and to take revenge on the murderers. Cursed be the man who will forget this.
>
> The dead will live amongst the living![25]

While linking the fighters in Warsaw with the Jewish heroes of ancient Masada (who also chose to "sentence themselves to death"), Kruk, a Poalei Zion activist from Częstochowa, Poland, also suggested that the surviving

Jews could be the inheritors of their heroism who would thus live on forever. In honor of the first anniversary of the revolt, the Jewish National Council in Palestine decided to observe a "year of mourning" as "sign of mourning for the residents of the Warsaw Ghetto who perished during the epic battle with the Germans."[26] Nonetheless, Zionist leaders in the Yishuv were divided over whether the example of the ghetto fighters in Warsaw would be one to uphold as a model for Zionist youth as a whole to learn from—this consensus would only emerge after the war.

On May 16, 1944, writing in *Davar* one year after the fall of the Warsaw ghetto, Yitzhak Gruenbaum (General Zionist leader, delegate to the Sejm in Poland, and head of the Rescue Committee of the Jewish Agency executive) summarized what was known about the revolt, indicating that most details had not yet reached the Yishuv.[27]

> A full year has passed from the day when the remnants of Jewish Warsaw raised the miracle of revolt against Nazi Germany, which was occupied with the complete destruction of Polish Jewry and the Jews of Europe deported there from other lands. . . .
>
> When the news reached us about the Warsaw Ghetto Revolt, it was as if a heavy stone had been removed from our hearts, which weighed on us all the time. We could not understand why the Jews of Poland, who knew how to fight for their honor in the most recent period, went to their deaths like a lamb led to the slaughter. Were the German hangmen able to murder their spirits when they led their bodies to the slaughter? And here the revolt in the Warsaw Ghetto broke out, and here news began to arrive of other battles. The Jewish front had opened in Poland, the battlefront of the Jewish people in the valley of death.
>
> They tell: in one of the large houses in one of the streets of the Warsaw Ghetto gathered the surviving heroes and among them they carried a flag. The Nazis were forced to conquer one floor after another. The defenders retreated

> from the bottom floor to the top and continued the battle until the last fighter. And then, the flag bearer, a young pioneer, gathered the Zionist flag and flung himself from the top floor to the ground and was crushed. The symbol of Warsaw and Polish Jewry which sacrificed its soul with the name of Zion on its lips.
>
> And our prayer, that their suffering and their deaths, the deaths of heroes, will be a symbol and a sign that the days of the redemption of the Jewish people in its own land will soon be upon us.[28]

"The symbol of Warsaw and Polish Jewry . . . sacrificed its soul with the name of Zion on its lips": the symbolic significance of the revolt. Why had the Jews of Poland gone like sheep to the slaughter? They had not gone passively to their deaths, it turned out, but the source of the courage to resist, to fight back, according to Gruenbaum, was Zion. One year later, describing news of the revolt as a "stone removed from (the) heart" of the Yishuv, Gruenbaum captured the meaning bestowed on the event, even before exact details of what had transpired were known—young fighters, bearing the Zionist flag, had restored the pride of a shattered people. But crucially for Gruenbaum and perhaps the Yishuv as a whole, the symbol and sign of the redemption of the Jewish people was a young pioneer who gathered himself in the Zionist flag and jumped from the top floor of the building to his death—a heroic, symbolic death, a dead hero who sacrificed himself for the cause of Zion and the Jewish people.

How do we account for this discrepancy between commemorations in America and the Yishuv on the first anniversary of the revolt? In the United States, Jewish leaders could present the revolt in the Warsaw ghetto as part of the Jewish contribution to the Allied war effort, as the outcry of the oppressed who refused to perish under the heel of fascism and would join the allied cause to defeat Nazism. The Jewish Labor Committee celebrated the heroism of the workers who joined the Polish nation in the struggle against German oppression. Jewish religious leaders marked April 19 as a day of sorrow and mourning, where the heroism of the ghetto fighters could be remembered together with the suffering of the Jewish martyrs. The timing of the revolt was critical as Jews eagerly sought hope amidst the despair, a light in the darkness, and heroes to whom they could connect—but who were the heroes and what was the political ideology that animated their actions? It is clear that within a year of the uprising, the revolt had been transformed into the focal point of Jewish commemorations of the destruction of European Jewry, providing the ideal prism through which to remember not only the heroes and martyrs of Warsaw but more broadly of Europe as a whole.

While Jews in the free world desperately sought to imagine what it must have been like to participate in this glorious uprising, the lack of a complete picture did not prevent them from marking the date. As the heroes of the revolt were mythologized, the Bund and the Zionist movement continued to grapple over credit for the revolt. And while it was the name of Michał Klepfisz that had become known as the most prominent leader of the revolt in the first year after the event, this would soon change, as new reports drafted by the underground in Warsaw reached London and the Yishuv. Nonetheless, it is clear that even before the identities of the heroes had been confirmed, as reports began to emerge from Warsaw, shared by the Jewish Workers Underground, the Jewish Fighting Organization and the Jewish National Committee identifying the leaders of the revolt and names of the fighters, their identities were received, interpreted, and analyzed in a framework that was already quite contested and heavily weighted with meaning and significance, and that built on pre-existing political frameworks within which to incorporate such information. At the same time, the heroic saga of the revolt was mythologized in a manner that captured the attention of Jews around the world, allowing them to imagine what it might have been like to be *there*, engaged in the struggle against the Nazi oppressor. Surely the Jewish heroes of Warsaw were motivated by a desire to engage in self-defense not to save lives, but to save their own dignity. But were they motivated by a Zionist connection to the Land of Israel that inspired their revolt against Diaspora oppression? Or did they rise up in defense of Poland, and the ideals of democracy, the universal brotherhood of man, and the rights of the working class to resist totalitarianism? Or were the fighters united by a drive to take revenge and kill Nazis? Regardless, it is clear that the revolt was too powerful a symbol not to be seized upon by Jews from across the ideological spectrum well before the war was over. The timing of the uprising, coinciding with the transition to memorialization and mourning, also solidified the event as a date to remember both the heroes and the martyrs of Warsaw, and of European Jewry more broadly.

Geto in Flamen (Ghetto in Flames)

For the Jewish Labor Bund, the revolt signified a miraculous coming together of the Jewish people, who had discovered strength in unity. In 1944, the American representation of the General Jewish Workers Union in Poland (the Bund) published *Geto in Flamen* (Ghetto in Flames), a volume including chapters providing background history on "the Jewish-German war," the "underground Bund," and "the miracle of Uprising"; a chapter on Szmuel Zygielbojm; portraits of the ghetto heroes; messages delivered by luminaries at the first anniversary of the uprising (Einstein, Eleanor Roosevelt, LaGuardia, Lehman, and more); as well as poetry and stories.[29] The volume, perhaps the first anthology to be published in the United States dedicated specifically to the uprising, highlighted a distinctly Bundist perspective, featuring the Jewish Workers Underground reports noted above, as well as essays and background by prominent figures in the Bund and Jewish Labor Committee (including Hodes, Hertz, Pat, Nowogrodzki, and Mendelson). From the Bundist perspective, the revolt was a popular uprising, the reflection of a spirit that emanated from a broad swath of the surviving population in Warsaw, and a continuation of the Jewish workers' struggle throughout the war.

Leyvik Hodes, a Bundist activist who had reached New York in 1940 following his escape from Kovno, was one of the editors of the volume and wrote the chapter "The Jewish-German War."[30] As he noted, it was still "too early to write the history of the Jewish-German war; there will still come people who observed the great heroism and can help write the history." Nonetheless, Hodes detailed what information had reached New York, primarily through reports of the Jewish Workers Underground in Poland. He explained that the uprising did not emerge from nowhere but was instead the continuation of "years of struggle and through the spirit of resistance in general, which pulsed in the Jewish quarters since the first days of the Hitlerist occupation. This was the continuation of the heroic participation of Warsaw in the September 1939 [*sic*], in which the Jewish workers, under the leadership of the 'Bund' played a largely conspicuous (noteworthy) role," inspired especially by the "unforgettable" Szmuel Zygielbojm.[31] Why had resistance not developed earlier? Hodes explained to his readers that the murderous activities first began in Soviet-occupation areas conquered by the Germans in the summer of 1941. Citing a Bund report of August 31, 1942, he noted that the deportation of the Jewish population of Warsaw in the summer of 1942 prevented the outbreak of armed uprising then. Nonetheless, "all Jewish institutions besides the Judenrat engaged in passive resistance." Hodes listed the three primary factors that "paralyzed the will to resist": the deception of the Germans, the tactic of collective responsibility, and the complete isolation of the Jews in the ghetto and their abandonment by the world. Based on reports of the Bund from June 22 and November 15, 1943, Hodes detailed conferences between members of the Coordinating Committee and the Jewish Fighting Organization with members of the Polish military underground (with one member of Bund and one member of the Jewish National Committee representing the Jewish underground). Hodes explained that one of the means to acquire arms was through the black market purchase of weapons sold by Germans to Poles ("using money sent by the Jewish Workers Committee in New York for underground work"). The second method was through self-manufacture, especially explosive materials manufactured by the Bund's own Michał Klepfisz (pictured in the book), who according to the report of June 22, 1943, stood at the top of this effort "under the eyes of thousands of angels of death, preparing dynamite, bombs and hand grenades for the battle, for which they were prepared to give their lives . . . which would become known around the world!" Hodes' account detailed the first uprising in January 1943 (based on the June 22 report) and offered a description of the April uprising in great detail. Describing the "armed brotherhood" in the ghetto, Hodes noted for his readers:

> In order to have a full picture of the Warsaw uprising it remains for us to describe several factors. The Jewish fighting organization was—as it is written in the report of the underground Bund—in every sense of the word a "fighting brotherhood" from broad segments of Jewish society. In brotherhood did the Jews fight side by side, shoulder by shoulder, *bundists*, *shomrim*, and *halutzim*. And all were fundamentally inspired by the same revolutionary flame to participate in the unique human desire to have revenge, to beat fascism and the number one enemy of the Jewish people. . . . To take part in the struggle for their holy right to live and die there, where their parents and grandparents lived and died. It is in Warsaw that was created the unity of the highest deeds, the one and only form of unity, which is both human and national, productive and creative.

His account described the "folk character of the uprising" which reflected the effort of the broader Jewish population.

> To be sure the Jewish fighting organization included adults, those with military training and physical capabilities which meant that for many reasons they numbered only several thousand people. However the uprising never would have taken place without the support of the entire people who were driven by the same initiative as the active fighters. Each all the more so understood well, that—whether he belonged to the fighting organization or not—he would be carried in the same mass as the followers of the uprising and would later be the same victim of the German bestiality. People therefore believed that although the fighting organization numbered only several thousand, the call to "fall with honor!" captured the spirit of the entire Jewish people.
>
> In this way the uprising quickly became a general people's uprising. The report of the Bund emphasized "the

> participation of the entire people" and in this way differed greatly in the support between 1942 and 1943.

Furthermore, Hodes noted, the revolt was *not* the course of last resort, a last struggle of a caged people: "the uprising was in no way an act of desperation. Many of the fighters could have personally saved themselves. But for them physical salvation and life would have meant nothing without spiritual salvation." In this sense, the fighters were motivated not only by a need to save the spirit of Jewish people, but even more broadly, reflected and was motivated by "the inner drive of the fighters and the more so to struggle for their freedom and human rights. But it was among other things also directed to the people of Poland outside the ghettos and to the wider world." Hodes interpreted the declaration made by the Jewish fighting organization sent to Poles on the area inside of the city calling on "Poles, citizens, soldiers of freedom" to "avenge the crimes of Oświęcim, Treblinka, Belzec and Majdanek" as part of broader struggle on behalf of the Polish people: "Long live the brotherhood of struggle and the blood of the fighting Poland. Long live freedom. Death to the murderers and hang man. Long live the fight for life and death to the occupiers!" Concluding the chapter with the new symbol of "ghetto-grad" (compared to Stalingrad), Hodes explained how the uprising became an important symbol to the broader Jewish and Polish public in occupied Poland who began to fight at Treblinka, Trawniki, Będzin, and Częstochowa: "Ghettograd became a bright shining point to which all Jews could lift their eyes."

Other chapters in the volume described the underground work of the Bund and paid tribute to the heroes who were no longer alive: Szmuel Zygielbojm (who had killed himself in London), Lozer Klug (died in 1943), Abrasha Blum (shot in June 1943 after surviving the armed revolt), Sonia Nowogrodski (killed in Treblinka in 1942), and a few other members in hiding or now in the Polish army. Jacob Pat, the leader of the Jewish Labor Committee in New York, dedicated his chapter, "The Miracle of Revolt (Uprising)," to explaining how the "revolt and the resistance was a miracle that illuminated the darkness," intending "to better understand the miracle, to take a deeper look within it."

> The miracle of resistance began a long time before, that is, in the days of 1939, when the deceased Arthur Zygielbojm, had at a peoples meeting on Grzybowska street, called on the Jews of Warsaw not to go into the ghetto, to oppose the Nazi decree [which would only lead to catastrophe]. . . . Then began the resistance. The following months, weeks, and days in the Warsaw Ghetto can be reckoned as one long daily resistance of the Warsaw Jews.
>
> The Resistance was expressed in the creation of House Committees, which were formed by the residents. It was expressed in the underground fighting organization. It was expressed in the underground publications, in the pages of the illegal newspapers, in the meetings in the Warsaw cemetery, in the establishment of the people's kitchens, in the organization of self-help.
>
> The spirit of resistance was expressed in various new legal and illegal institutions, which were created. Emissaries went forth from Warsaw into the Polish provinces to bring greetings and support. Resistance was even expressed in a Jewish theater in the Warsaw Ghetto.
>
> There could of course be no possibility of developing armed resistance, of organizing armed groups, of developing plans for a revolt until July 1942—until the great deportations began which were signaled by the suicide of the chairperson of the Judenrat, Czerniakow.

Echoing Hodes, Pat depicted the resistance as the creation of the broader Jewish public, emanating from the spiritual defiance of the people and the broader categories of *amidah* demonstrated by the will to maintain Jewish dignity and life in the ghetto. Explaining that armed resistance did not develop earlier for two main reasons, lack of arms and fear of collective retribution, Pat described the "by now well known" January 1943 first encounter between the SS and the Jewish Fighting Organization which "until then did not exist but was created in fire." Pat explained that the revolt was led by the Jewish National Committee and the Bund but *was also a general people's revolt representing the will of the Jewish public*, people of different backgrounds and ideologies united in a struggle against oppression:

> We have information about the establishment from the reports of the underground Bund and reports from the Jewish National Committee. The Jewish fighting organization was composed of the Coordinating Committee, which existed, represented by the General Jewish Labor Bund and the Jewish National Committee. Which means, that the most important Jewish groups in the ghetto, the tips of the groups, reached an agreement about an armed revolt, both about their organization and leadership. In reports can be seen that the majority in the fighting organization were a working class element of youth. The youngest were 13 years of age and the oldest—40 years. The blood, which flowed in the ghetto, unified all. In the report of the Bund it stated: "All participants in the revolt were Jewish people from various directions. This was an exemplary fraternal struggle of Bundists, Chalutzim, Shomrim, and Others." The declaration speaks clearly and starkly about the organization of the resistance, about its character and composition, and about the support of the people that nothing needs be added—people of ideology, and people of different strands, in a fraternal struggle.

Pat noted that the Warsaw uprising was not unique; indeed "Uprisings took place, as we already know, in ghetto after ghetto, concentration camps, places of suffering. Each Uprising shines brilliantly in the darkness of our night. The history of each Uprising, when it will be written, if it will be written, will itself be an epic poem, but here I will just recall two uprisings." Pat goes on to discuss Bialystok and Treblinka, the most wondrous of all uprisings. "The heroes in the ghettoes were not just the great inheritors of generations and periods, but also the beginning of a new heroism." As we have noted, the death of Szmuel Zygielbojm (also known as Comrade Arthur) and the uprising were merged both chronologically and symbolically for the Jewish Labor Bund. While Zionist leaders in the Yishuv may have been critical of Zygielbojm's choice to engage in *Kiddush Hashem* there was no such critique in Bundist circles; on the contrary, Comrade Arthur's heroic deed was celebrated and fused with the heroism of the Warsaw ghetto fighters. A chapter in *Geto in Flamen* by Emanuel Nowogrodski, "Zygielbojm, Pages from a Life," provided a portrait of the life of the Bundist leader, while another chapter, "My Journey through the Nazi Hell," included excerpts authored by Zygielbojm himself describing his experiences in Nazi Poland. Finally, Shloime Mendelsohn, who had delivered the memorable lecture at YIVO in January 1944 that detailed what was known about the uprising for a large crowd mesmerized by the heroism he detailed (as recalled by Lucy Dawidowicz) explained Zygielbojm's suicide thusly in the volume:

> The suicide of Comrade Szmuel Zygielbojm (Arthur) shook the Jewish and likewise the non-Jewish world. Arthur's deed is inscribed in the Jewish history. Future historians will not know the chapter of "Jewish life, death, and struggle in Nazi Poland," without knowing the name of Szmuel Zygielbojm. And because he performed this act while holding a most important position, to which he represented the Jewish labor movement—the Bund—is Arthur's tragic call and protest to the world simultaneously an act of heroic Jewish worker-hood. Not only was Arthur a child of the Bund, not only did Arthur forge his character in the Bund, not only did he learn his drive to struggle in the Bund—but in his final moments of his life did he in an extraordinary manner demonstrate the absolute unity of the Bund with the destiny of the Jewish masses. The emissary not only thought of himself as the mouth of the silent and bloodied Jews, but he also felt truly, that he was physically a part of the same masses. When they were

> murdered and died, it was impossible for him to continue living.

The remainder of *Geto in Flamen*, beyond detailing Zygielbojm's final letter, highlighted the names of the young heroes of "Ghetto-Grad," as a chapter by H. S. Kazdan has it. Included among the new pantheon of Bundist heroes were Zalman Friedrich, who the underground reports describes as a "true hero who during the battles and in the underground movement demonstrated unusual heroism, self-sacrifice, and died with weapons in the hand"; Nokhem Khmielnitsky and Volf Rozovsky; Tobcia Dawidowicz—"very social, beloved by all children, always with a beautiful smile on the lips. Belonged to SKIF to which she dedicated her life"; and Jurek Blones, also a member of Skif, who helped save Jewish homes while they burned on Mila Street.

In his chapter, "The Ghetto Heroes," S. Hertz identified specifically the names of the Bundists included in the list of 230 ghetto fighters sent out by the Jewish National Committee.

> It is difficult to know who were all of the heroes of the ghetto battles. In the last report of the underground Bund, in which were depicted the great uprising of the Warsaw ghetto it said: it is impossible to give the names of all of the fallen Bundists, so great were their numbers. Here we present the names of a few who played an especially important role in preparing and leading the uprising. To these come the names of Bundists, and young Bundists we find in a list which the Zionists sent from Poland.
>
> The Engineer Michał Klepfisz.
>
> His name, in connection with the armed revolt in the Warsaw Ghetto, was the first to become known. Already on 11 May 1943, when small camps of ghetto fighters had already staged the revolt, the Polish underground radio station SWIAT declared: "The heroic resistance of the Warsaw ghetto continues on. A few strongly defended

> points continue. . . . The leader of the Jewish Bund, engineer Klepfisz, who was the soul of the revolt, fell in the battles, like a hero."

In addition to Klepfisz, who was the "soul of the revolt" because he was the one who prepared the arms and explosives, Hertz specifically identified the Bundist fighters Abrasha Blum, Lozer Klug, Moshe Koifman, Avram Berek Sznajdmil, Henekh Rus, Zalman Friedrich, Volf Rozovsky, Abram Fajner, Miriam Shifman, and Toibe Dawidowicz, and added the names of twenty-four other fighters, "our comrades who we know about who fell in the battles of the Warsaw ghetto. The friends are well known to us but unfortunately we have no information about their role in the underground movement during the fighting in the ghetto."

The volume concluded with a list of messages sent to the monthly publication of the American Bund, *Ghetto Speaks*, on the anniversary of the uprising, including notes from such prominent figures as: Eleanor Roosevelt, Albert Einstein, Governor Dewey, Wendell Wilkie, Mayor LaGuardia, Herbert Lehman, and many others.

Even with the names of the Bundist heroes identified, what seemed most important to the Bund was the idea that the revolt in the ghetto signified the power of Jewish unity and Jewish peoplehood. The identities of the fighters were certainly important to members of the movement, but for a broader audience, the idea that a broad cross-section of the Jewish public, religious and secular, Zionist and socialist, workers and pioneers, could unite in common struggle against the enemy, was the most powerful message of all. This was also the theme that a Yiddish playwright seized upon in dramatizing the "miracle of the ghetto," continuing the process of immortalizing the heroism of the Warsaw ghetto in this other dramatic sense.

Der Nes in Geto (The Miracle of the Warsaw Ghetto)

H. Leivick wrote the new theatrical production *Der Nes in Geto* (*The Miracle of the Warsaw Ghetto*) and staged it under the direction of Jacob Ben-Ami of the New Jewish Folk Theater in New York.[32] Like the radio play of Wishegrad, the Leivick play recounted the bravery of one family and its neighbors, featuring as its central character a student who at first argued against armed violence but finally became convinced that it was necessary to fight when his sweetheart was killed on an underground mission. The souvenir program for the play, which featured an illustrated cover by Arthur Szyk,[33] included a few words from Leivick highlighting the importance for him of staging a drama on the uprising as soon as possible, even as the war continued.

> While the events are so extraordinary we all stand before a question: should we try now, at this time, to produce on the stage the drama of Jewish heroism, or should we wait until a later time, when the events will be removed from us by an appropriate distance? Our answer must be: we must not wait. We Jews in America must as early as possible show the experiences of our folk-heroism, of our people's tragic *glory*. But this must be done with tact, with belief, with love for our people. We must however *achieve* a part of the holiness and bravery which our brothers demonstrated in the hour of their wondrous uprising in the Warsaw Ghetto.

Six months after he had addressed the crowd at Carnegie Hall in conjunction with the first anniversary of the revolt, Leivick's newest play sought to channel the guilt, shame, and anger of American Jews into a united feeling of pride in Jewish national culture and peoplehood and a renewed dedication to celebrate the heroism of the Jewish people.

Szyk's heroic image of Jewish men and children engaged in battle against an unseen enemy captured the themes of the play and Leivick's call for Jews in America to "show the experiences of our folk-heroism, of our people's tragic *glory*." The historical specificity of the Szyk image was secondary, as in this case the scene chosen for the cover had in fact been created almost ten years earlier to dramatize another episode of Jewish heroism. The one-armed hero in the center of the cover was none other than Josef

Trumpeldor, who had died in Palestine defending Tel Hai in 1920, becoming a Zionist hero. As he died he was supposed to have said, "No matter, it is good to die for our country."

The play opened in October 1944. In it, a diverse group of characters representing a broad cross-section of Jewish society—a Zionist, a Bundist, a Hasidic rabbi (Reb Itzik), a fighter from the Land of Israel named Joseph, the daughter of a convert, and others—unite to become the backbone of the struggle against the Nazis.[34]

The first act opens on Passover eve, as the remaining Jews, trapped in the ghetto, prepare for the holiday while waiting for the arrival of weapons with which to fight the Nazis. The first scene is set in a basement synagogue, where two young Jews, Yudel and Leibush, stand, immersed in prayer, as if in a dream. The stage directions indicate that above the Holy Ark, a large banner proclaims: "Gevald Yidn, Zayt Zikh Nisht Meya'esh!" (Woe Jews, do not despair!)[35] As the characters in the small *shtibel* (little prayer house) prepare for the first night of Passover, likening their present imprisonment in the ghetto to slavery in Egypt, one character named Isaac asks: "Why is this night different from all other nights? On all other nights we let ourselves be led like calves into the gas chambers. But on this Passover night we will not let that happen. We will shoot. With what will we shoot, ha? With what? Now this is a *kashya* [a question]."[36] The play charts the transformation of Jews traditionally unprepared for combat, who come to realize that the only path is armed struggle. Israel, who initially adopts a passive stance, eventually embraces armed resistance after his girlfriend, Rachel, dies in the second act on an underground mission to obtain arms outside the ghetto (after the Polish underground fails to deliver needed weapons). In the third act, Israel returns to the ghetto with dynamite, which he uses to blow up a German tank on a suicide mission, declaring to the other fighters, "I know that even in your fear you are wonder-Jews, yes, wonder-Jews. I have brought a little dynamite. And a few grenades. And I know now, that with one grenade it is possible to destroy a whole tank." Israel comes to represent the transformation of the Jews in the ghetto, who discover the inner strength they possess. Before exploding himself along with the tank, Israel proclaims to those assembled around him, "The wicked one may be stronger than us, but not his wickedness. Tanks will continue to come—let them come. We will confront them. For what do we need dynamite? With our hearts will we destroy the tanks. A Jew is stronger than tanks."[37]

After the death of Israel, who sacrifices himself in the name of the Jewish struggle against wickedness, the remaining characters, led by Reb Itzik holding a Torah scroll, swear an oath never to surrender:

> By the living Torah we take an oath to further sanctify God's name; to continue our war with the Nazi, may his name be blotted out, may his memory, like the memory of Amalek, be erased from the face of the earth. The blood of our holy ones will never be silent. And man will never find peace, as long as there are those who live without freedom, as long as the Jews are not saved. We all swear to not surrender to the enemy until our final breath. Amen.[38]

The play concludes with this final prayer, signifying the Jewish conversion to a resolute militancy, with all characters holding their guns aloft.

Leivick's play clearly resonated with a broad Jewish audience, as it would play for twenty weeks in New York before traveling to Milwaukee, Chicago, and Montreal over the next year. For Leivick, the idea that Jews could discover the inner strength to transform a history of Jewish passivity into a determination to struggle against oppression was "the miracle in the ghetto." The specific political identity of the heroes—from the most traditional to the most secular, from Zionist to Bundist—made the more general transformation of the Jewish people more significant than the names and identities of the actual heroes of the ghetto.

While historians have generally seen the politicization of the revolt occurring after the war with the first encounter of the survivors with their new homes, the polemics of 1944 between the Bund's *Geto in Flamen* and the Labor Zionist's publication *The Warsaw Ghetto Rising*, which would appear later in 1944, makes clear that within one year of the revolt, the battle for credit in Jewish public opinion meant the Warsaw Ghetto Uprising was too great a symbol to relinquish to the political enemy. The brotherhood of

The Miracle of the Warsaw Ghetto at the New Jewish Folk Theatre. (American Jewish Historical Society, Theater and Film Poster Collection of Abram Kanof, P–978)

the fighters did not extend to New York and Tel Aviv. Beyond emerging disagreements over who played a leading role in the revolt, one of the key questions that would divide Zionist and Bundist accounts of the uprising were questions of historical interpretation: Was the revolt a popular revolt or a Zionist revolt? A reflection of the Polish-Jewish will to fight back or the bold stroke of a small cadre of the Zionist avant-garde who sensed the need to overthrow the yoke of Nazi oppression because of their connection to the Land of Israel?

For surviving members of Zionist groups still trapped in Warsaw, the construal of the revolt by Bundists abroad as a popular uprising led by a Bundist hero and explosives expert was not a symbolic or historical interpretation they were willing to accept.

5

Crafting a Zionist Narrative of the Revolt

By the first anniversary of the Warsaw Ghetto Uprising, a narrative of the revolt had begun to take shape in the popular imagination of the Jewish public in the free world. The event was seen as a popular uprising led by workers, pioneers, and even religious Jews, who realized the need to take up arms in defense of Jewish dignity and in support of the allied war effort against Nazism. The leading figure, awarded the Polish medal of honor, was Michał Klepfisz, a member of the Jewish Labor Bund who specialized in the manufacture of explosives.

Just a year after the revolt, Zionist leaders in the Yishuv were still unsure how to incorporate the uprising into the collective identity of the new "state in the making." While Jewish groups in America organized impressive demonstrations and rallies commemorating the first anniversary of the revolt, the more ambivalent response of the Yishuv reflected an uncertainty over how to understand it. As Yitzhak Gruenbaum noted on the first yahrtzeit of the liquidation of the ghetto, "We could not understand why the Jews of Poland, who knew how to fight for their honor in the most recent period, went to their deaths like a lamb led to the slaughter. Were the German hangmen able to murder their spirits when they led their bodies to the slaughter?" While the news of the revolt restored pride in the ability of Polish Jews to fight back, opening a "battlefront of the Jewish people in the valley of death," knowing the identities of the Jewish heroes of Warsaw would be crucial to facilitating a Zionist embrace of the event.

But to what extent was this image of the revolt crafted by political leaders in New York and London? What was the relationship between historical documentation and political interpretation? A little over one year after the revolt had been finally crushed by SS general Jurgen Stroop, the Jewish National Committee in Warsaw succeeded in sending a trove of 120 pages on microfilm (including a detailed history of the Jewish Fighting Organization, accounts of surviving fighters, and other documentation) that would enable the Zionist movement finally to take credit for leading the revolt, detailing the role played by Zionist groups and the leadership of Mordecai Anielewicz as commander of the ŻOB.

As Melech Neustadt would note a year after the event (in *The Warsaw Ghetto Rising*), most of the initial accounts in the free world "were based on smuggled letters and reports which could only hint at what occurred. Naturally many of those accounts were filled out by conjecture and imagination." Over the course of 1943, therefore, once the uprising had been suppressed and once the surviving ghetto fighters had managed to find shelter on the Aryan side of Warsaw, Yitzhak Zuckerman, Adolf Berman (of the JNC), Marek Edelman, Leon Feiner (of the Bund), and others worked to establish connections with the outside world, secure funding to continue their relief and rescue work, and, at the same time, write the first draft of the history of the revolt and convey it to the outside world. The initial reports sent out by the Jewish National Committee and the Jewish Workers Underground and the Bund emphasized the fraternal nature of the collaboration between members of the ŻOB—a solidarity forged in the heat of battle—which continued in the period after the uprising and in hiding on the Aryan side. These groups dedicated themselves to recording the history of the resistance and revolt in its immediate aftermath, to ensure that their chapter in history would be recorded.

What sources did they use to write this history? While the archive of the ŻOB was destroyed in the Polish Uprising of August 1944, the Jewish National Committee managed to send out several early testimonies from Warsaw on May 24, 1944, including the reports of Shalom Grayek, Kazik

(Simche Rathoyzer), Tuvia Borzykowski, and a piece called "Silhouettes of Fighters," by Hersh Wasser, among other documents, in addition to the ŻOB report written by Yitzhak Zuckerman. These testimonies, drafted by members of Zionist youth movements, played a crucial role in the Yishuv's embrace of the event. This chapter will examine the ways in which memory of the uprising was mobilized by the Zionist movement (often in direct opposition to the Jewish Labor Bund and in response to the early testimonies), even as it debated how best to incorporate the doomed struggle of Warsaw's Jews into the Zionist narrative. These materials would play a critical role in how the history of the revolt would be written for years to come, and in many respects, have shaped the historiography of the Warsaw Ghetto Uprising, both in terms of the history and development of the ŻOB, and in the role played by the eyewitness testimony of fighters in the ghetto.

The May 24, 1944, Parcel

As Jews across the world marked the first anniversary of the revolt, the surviving members of the ŻOB and the Jewish National Committee worked feverishly to document what had transpired one year before. Over the course of several months, members of the Jewish National Committee worked to collect testimonies, write reports on the history of the ŻOB, and send letters to contacts in New York, London, and Tel Aviv. Although many messages written in Warsaw never made it to Jews in the free world, the surviving members of the underground were aware that the parcel of over 120 pages, dated May 24, 1944, had special significance. Adolf Berman described the process of typing all 120 pages in a letter to David Guzik of the JDC.[1]

> Berman to Guzik, May 26, 1944
>
> Dear Mr. Jan [code name for Guzik],
>
> This week we accomplished a great task: a large shipment to L[ondon]. I worked on this day and night for a period of ten days, May 15–25.

> This [past] week I went to sleep every night at 4 AM. I had to write, edit, and collect material at the greatest possible speed, but in the end an impressive parcel was sent: a typed, ten-page summary letter with 18 addenda attached—in total, 120 typed pages. If this parcel will arrive at L[ondon], this will have tremendous significance!! I am sending copies of the main, joint letter to [you] via Mr. Jozef, along with a line about other documents. As [you] will see, we added your name [among the signatures] on the main letter, and noted your work and [that of] the Joint [AJDC; American Jewish Joint Distribution Committee] also in the other material.

The materials received in London in 1944 from the remaining survivors of the ghetto were written in an atmosphere of uncertainty—the authors' personal survival seemed unlikely, as arrest and capture by the Gestapo took place daily and they were valuable targets. Even so, the drive to document and testify to the Jewish heroism upended the usual priority to survive at all costs.

Among the microfilmed documents sent on May 24 was a letter of fraternal greetings sent to the Histadrut—the Jewish Labor Federation in Palestine—from Adolf Berman, Yitzhak Zuckerman, Zivia Lubetkin, and Josef Sack, which they sent through "seas of blood and through mountains of dead bodies." Although few of them remained alive, and unsure whether they would survive, they wanted the workers movement in the Yishuv to understand "that the Jewish workers in Poland completely fulfilled their obligation. They fought with weapons in their hands for the honor of the Jewish people and fell in unparalleled struggle. They were encouraged by the belief in the future of a Jewish socialist working Land of Israel."[2] The parcel of 120 pages would have the utmost significance in shaping the narrative of the Warsaw Ghetto Uprising that would be embraced in the Yishuv, where the leadership still expressed ambivalence over how to incorporate the event into a Zionist worldview. The contents allowed the Yishuv to celebrate the uprising as a sign of Zionism's resilience under the most oppressive conditions—in the shape of its young heroic fighters in the Warsaw ghetto.

A microfilm reel smuggled by the Jewish underground out of Warsaw to London on May 24, 1944. The original inscription on the box read "NKZ [ZKN, the Polish acronym for the JNC, spelled backward], III [March]." (Ghetto Fighters House Archive, photo no. 1175)

What were the documents sent to New York and Tel Aviv and how did these shape the first draft of history of the revolt? The determination of the surviving members of the ŻOB to establish contact with London, Istanbul, Geneva, and the Yishuv indicated a drive to record their version of events, both in contrast to what would be reported by the Germans (as in the Stroop report), in case they did not survive, and to ensure that accurate details would be recorded for posterity. At the same time, it is also clear that the author(s) of the ŻOB reports and other testimonies were already quite aware and quite sensitive to a second battle: the battle for credit. Therefore, the narratives that emerge from the ghetto, crafted by the surviving fighters and eyewitnesses, were written both as an accounting of the glorious epic of Jewish heroism and to provide details for an audience in the free Jewish world hungry for the narrative arc of the saga, the climax of which had erupted across time and space into their consciousness. To what extent did the reports emerging from Warsaw actually alter the interpretations of those who received them? Or did these reports only serve to confirm what they already knew and understood?

The trove of material—letters, reports, surveys, diaries, testimonies, and poems—was collected, edited, written, and typed over the course of several months by JNC activists and the Bund in Warsaw, working jointly under the Coordinating Committee, an effort headed by Adolf (Abraham) Berman and Emanuel Ringelblum. Batya Temkin-Berman, who took part in the project, also described it in her diary.[3] All 120 pages were copied onto a microfilm reel, which was smuggled to London with the help of the Polish Council to Aid Jews (RPZ—*Rada Pomocy Żydom*, or Zegota) by the office of the empowered representative of the Polish government-in-exile. Witold Bienkowski, head of the Jewish section in the representative's office, was the liaison.[4]

In his *Warsaw Ghetto Rising*, published in 1944 in Tel Aviv, Melekh Neustadt (Noy) listed the sources of information that came into the possession of I. Schwartzbart and A. Reiss in London in 1944 through the May 24 parcel, helping to fill out the picture of what had actually transpired in Warsaw in April–May 1943 (interestingly, Neustadt did not mention the Bundist representative in London, Emanuel Szerer, in his account, who presumably also received a copy of the materials); these sources included "a series of accurate and detailed reports written by the surviving initiators, leaders, and fighters of the rebellion themselves," including:

> an itemized report from the Jewish National Committee in Poland;
>
> an account of the establishment of the Jewish Fighting Organization with full details as to the stages of its development and of the Battle of the Warsaw Ghetto in the months of April and May, 1943;
>
> a report of the department of the National Committee operating in the "Aryan" part of Warsaw;

diaries kept by a number of the fighters reporting in complete detail on the course of the fighting in various sections of the front;[5]

letters from the headquarters of the Poalei Zion–Z.S. and Left Poalei Zion parties in Poland, as well as of the "Hechalutz" movement and its affiliated youth organizations;

a special letter of greeting addressed to the "Histadrut" (General Federation of Jewish Labour in Palestine);

a letter to his friends from one of the leaders of the General Zionist Group "B";

a description by a boy of 13 of the life of the Jewish children in Warsaw during that fateful period;[6]

a letter describing the great efforts of the Jews to continue their cultural life even in the Ghetto [Ringelblum's "last letter"];

an account by an eyewitness who had spent a year in the death camp of Treblinka;

a description of the liquidation of the concentration camp at Poniatov;

poems written in the Ghetto which reflect the mental and spiritual state of the Fighters of the Ghetto;

and a considerable quantity of other material.

Special thanks were due, Neustadt said, to the members of the Jewish National Committee, "if any of its members or of the participants in the battle are still alive to receive them," for disclosing, "beyond a shadow of doubt, the social forces which initiated, prepared and conducted the rising,—a feature which has unfortunately been ignored hitherto in both Jewish and non-Jewish circles. We prefer to believe that this omission was not intentional but was due merely to the absence of adequate and reliable information."[7]

While there is not adequate space in this chapter to analyze all of these documents separately, it is quite clear that in the first year after the uprising in Warsaw, the members of the Jewish National Committee and the surviving members of the Jewish Fighting Organization, were extremely active in compiling the materials that would become the essential components of the first draft of the history of the uprising that would be written. Taken together, the sources compiled would be rapidly interpreted and reprinted in America, London, and the Yishuv, albeit in different contexts for different audiences.

Included in the package were the last words of prominent Jewish activists who had managed to survive the uprising but would not survive the year that followed—including perhaps most notably, the historian, social welfare activist, and ghetto archivist Emanuel Ringelblum, who, as noted by Adolf Berman, was arrested by the Gestapo on March 7, 1944, and killed one week after the final draft of the letter was written.

Ringelblum had been caught in the ghetto during the uprising and deported to the Trawniki labor camp near Lublin; after three months in the camp Berman had helped to organize his escape with the assistance of the underground.[8] Since then, with his wife, Yehudis, and son, Uri, Ringelblum had been living in hiding in a bunker nicknamed Krysia, built under a greenhouse behind Grojecka 81. The family was part of a group of forty Jews who lived in hiding in the bunker from November 1943 until their discovery and capture by the Gestapo on March 7, 1944. As historian Sam Kassow notes, in his time in the Krysia, Ringelblum worked on four major projects: a study of Polish-Jewish relations during the war and a study on the Jewish intelligentsia (both of which were later published) as well as an essay on Trawniki (lost) and a study on Jewish resistance (never completed).[9] Ringelblum immersed himself in these projects, emerging from the Krysia from time to time to meet and consult with Berman or Guzik.[10]

Ringelblum also wrote a short biographical profile of Mordecai Anielewicz, whom he described as "a young man, approximately 24 years old, average height, narrow face, long hair, with a sympathetic appearance." Ringelblum first met him at the start of the war when he came to borrow a book, expressing an interest in Jewish history, and especially in matters related to Jewish economic history. Ringelblum would have occasion to lecture periodically in seminars organized by Hashomer Hatzair in the ghetto, and described Anielewicz's unique devotion to other members of the movement, obtaining food for the communal kitchen and risking life and limb to save those in danger. Describing his final days and death in the revolt in Warsaw, Ringelblum concluded his tribute:

> Mordecai fell together with the best of his comrades from the fighting organization. The workers' movement will remember that Mordecai Anielewicz was one of those who from the first moment dedicated his life to the service of the Jewish people, honoring and standing up for the world revolution and the first workers' state in the world.[11]

The last letter from Emanuel Ringelblum and A. Berman written in March 1944 and received in London and New York in May, went through several drafts, and emphasized the leading role played by the Zionist groups in the uprising, most likely in response to an awareness that Bundist groups abroad were trying to take credit for the revolt.[12] Titled "To Live with Honor and Die with Honor,"[13] the letter was addressed to YIVO, the Jewish Scientific Institute, to the Jewish PEN Club, to Sholem Asch, H. Leivik, I. Opatoshu, and Dr. Raphael Mahler, most of whom were connected with Yiddish socialist circles in New York.

> Dear Friends,
>
> We are writing to you at a time when ninety-five percent of the Jews of Poland have already perished in gruesome sufferings, in the gas-chambers of the slaughterhouses of Treblinka, of Sobibor, of Chelmno and Oswiecim [Auschwitz], or were murdered in the countless "liquidation-actions" in Ghettos and camps. The fate of the tiny remnant of Jews who still suffer and expire in some of the concentration camps has also been sealed, and they too will die in the gas chambers and from the Nazi murderers' bullets.
>
> At the very moment when the Jews of Poland fell under the fearsome yoke of Hitlerism, the unceasing social activity of wide-spread, mutual self-aid began whose motto was support and struggle. With the considerable and active support of the JOINT, a large network of welfare

> institutions was established, which was directed by the Z.T.O.S., the Jewish Social Welfare Association, the CENTOS, Center for the Welfare of Orphans and Children, and TOZ, the Society for Preservation and Health of the Jewish Population. Significant activity was developed also by the ORT, the Association for Spreading Vocational Education Among Jews.
>
> Tens of thousands of Jews, adults and children alike, managed to stay alive for a prolonged time only thanks to the support of these institutions and the ramified network of House-Committees, which cooperated with them [. . .] The motto of Jewish communal leadership was "to Live with Honor and to Die with Honor."

Ringelblum and Berman described various aspects of underground work and cultural activity for their addressees, individuals and organizations devoted to the preservation of Eastern European Jewish culture, explaining "they kept alive the banner of culture and struggle against barbarity to their last breath." However, when the deportations from the ghetto began, those involved in underground work and cultural activity shifted their focus to armed struggle:

> The period when the murderous deportation actions started, the idea of putting up a fight took the place of self-help. *Heading the struggle was our heroic youth of all orientations with those faithful to Eretz Israel in the forefront* [my emphasis]. The superb epos of armed Jewish resistance in Poland began,—the heroic resistance of the Warsaw Ghetto, the magnificent fighting in Białystok, the destruction wrought by Jews in the slaughterhouses of Treblinka and Sobibor, the battles at Tarnow, Bedzin, Czestochowa, and other localities. Jews demonstrated to the world their ability to give armed battle, to die with dignity in battle with the mortal enemy of the Jewish people and of all humanity.
>
> This is all we wish to tell you, dear friends. We, the survivors, aren't many . . .
>
> Dr. Emanuel Ringelblum, Dr. A Berman
> Warsaw, March 1, 1944

In a postscript, Berman explained that this letter would indeed be the last word from Dr. Emanuel Ringelblum:

> The letter was written in March 1, 1944. One week later, on March 7, the Gestapo discovered the underground hideout in the Jewish Quarter, in which Dr. E. Ringelblum was hiding. He, together with his wife, Jehudith, and his son, Uriah, and thirty-five others, mostly intelligentsia, underwent terrible torture at the hands of the Germans and were shot in the ruins of Warsaw. Thus ended in martyrdom, the life of a noted historian, an enthusiastic communal worker and one passionately devoted to present-day Jewish culture.

In the collection of Adolf Berman housed at the Ghetto Fighters House Archive is an earlier version of the letter, written by Ringelblum in January 1944. While most of the letter is largely similar to the later version sent in the May 1944 shipment, highlighting the underground work in the ghetto and all of the efforts in the arena of social welfare work, one crucial paragraph seems to have been revised, specifically in discussing the origins of armed resistance.

The January 1944 version reads:

> When the period of the murderous liquidation "Aktionen" began, the concept of mutual self-help gave way to that of struggle [against the foe]. *This struggle was carried out first and foremost by courageous youngsters from all the youth movements and an organized part of the proletariat* [my emphasis]. The glorious act of armed Jewish struggle in Poland began. A courageous defense of the Warsaw ghetto, the fine battle for Białystok, the destruction of the killing sites in Treblinka and in Sobibor by the Jewish forces of the struggle, battles in Tarnow, Będzin, Nowogrodek, Częstochowa, and more. The Jews showed the world that it is within their ability to

> fight when armed and to die with honor in combat with the mortal enemy of the Jewish people and of all humanity.

As we have seen elsewhere, Adolf Berman revised and edited such sources for political reasons, and there is no reason to doubt that in this case, perhaps as Kassow suggests, in response to a distinct feeling that the Bund abroad was trying to take credit for the revolt, he felt it necessary to state in no uncertain terms that "those faithful to Eretz Israel" stood at the forefront of the armed struggle. But again, as Havi Dreifuss's research on the last letter of Anielewicz also demonstrates, we must appreciate the role that the Jewish National Committee and (perhaps also the surviving members of the ŻOB) played in shaping the Zionist narrative of the revolt for an intended audience abroad, but especially in the Yishuv.[14] Rather than emphasize the notion of fraternal cooperation and and *esprit de guerre* manifested in a struggle "carried out first and foremost by courageous youngsters from all the youth movements and an organized part of the proletariat" Berman (and perhaps Ringelblum?) felt it important to state in no uncertain terms that it was Zionist youth who led the struggle (with "those faithful to Eretz Israel in the forefront").

In this sense, the work of the surviving members of the Jewish Fighting Organization hiding on the Aryan side of Warsaw would be crucial in making this Zionist identification with the revolt possible. Despite their frustration over the "persistent silence" and the urgent need for funding to continue their relief work for the survivors in Poland, at the same time, over the spring of 1944, the ŻOB wrote up an account of its efforts, included in the parcel.[15] Taken together with the report of the Jewish Workers Underground received in February 1944, this was one of the first attempts to write the history of the resistance in the ghetto, one year after the revolt was crushed.

The authors of the report were aware that the reports of the Bund had been interpreted and utilized in a partisan spirit abroad, and were thus quite keen to correct the historical record. In a letter included in the parcel, the Jewish National Committee members in Warsaw voiced their frustration with the way in which the Bund had managed to "take credit and almost complete responsibility for the battles in the Warsaw ghetto."[16]

A few words on internal relations and relations between the organizations. Our connections with the Polish underground movements continue to be close and warm. The atmosphere in the Jewish national committee—is an atmosphere of harmonious cooperation and friendship. Relations with the Bund are regular and friendly. We maintain an active cooperation and the committee for assistance to the Jews in the Jewish fighting organization for collaboration of activities. *For the sake of truth we wish to address a few points regarding news from abroad which we have received, that the Bund abroad seeks to take credit and almost complete responsibility for the battles in the Warsaw ghetto. They take for themselves the decisive responsibility and in the name of historical truth you must uproot this false legend.* The battle in the Warsaw Ghetto, as well as the other ghettos and in the camps was organized and carried out by our movements and first of all by the movements affiliated with the Labor movement in the land of Israel: Hehalutz, Dror, Hashomer Hatzair, Poalei Zion Smol, and Poalei Zion right. These movements led the battles, contributed the largest number of fighters, and sacrificed the greatest share of blood. The commander of the Jewish fighting organization was our heroic comrade Mordechai Anielewicz, the commander of Hashomer Hatzair. In the central command we had 4 members and the Bund had one. Out of the 22 fighting units of the Jewish fighting organization our movements—eighteen, the Bund—four.

In the general number of fighters the Bund did not have more than 18%. The divisions of the Bund in the framework of the Jewish fighting organization fought bravely, although all of the groups fought in a manner that was particularly extraordinary. However, it was not them that determined the atmosphere and the character of the battles. Even now at the head of the Jewish fighting organization stand our members.

> We appreciate very much the bestowing of the medal *virtuti militar* to Michal Klepfish, member of the Bund.[17] *The fighter Klepfish fought heroically, but he was not but one of the hundreds of heroic fighters.* If the intention was to bestow symbolically the medal to the Jewish fighting organization to all of the heroic fighters—we are convinced that it would have been appropriate to bestow the medal to the commander of the Jewish fighting organization.
>
> The fact also pains us (and perhaps the mistake is ours) that the Bund claims the monopoly abroad amongst the activity of the labor movement, and especially in England and the United States, that is dominated by the Jewish Labor Committee in America. Do the movements of Poalei Zion right and left not continue in *hasbara* [propaganda work/public diplomacy] amongst the workers movement? *The workers movements around the world should know that the organizers and leaders of the Warsaw Ghetto Uprising—was the workers movement on behalf of the working land of Israel, that the hundreds of fighters fought and died with the idea that their deaths should be one of the foundations of a socialist future for the masses of Jews in the land of Israel.* [My emphasis throughout.]

This gives context to the project undertaken by the Jewish National Committee to correct what they saw as a perversion of the historical record by the Jewish Labor Bund abroad. The history of the ŻOB, the testimonies, and the accompanying letters sent as part of the May 24 package were thus part of an effort to correct a perceived error in the historical narrative of the uprising that had begun to take shape around the world, or in the words of the Jewish National Committee, to "uproot a false legend" that the Bund led the revolt.

At a 1951 meeting of surviving ghetto fighters in Israel, historian Joseph Kermish asked the group how they wrote the ŻOB report that would be sent in May 1944. The group explained that Antek (Zuckerman) wrote the report, with edits by Adolf Berman and Josef Sack.[18] They used original sources collected in the ghetto, but most were destroyed during the Polish Uprising at Leszno 18. In one revealing exchange, Kermish asked the group about the use of sources to write the report:

> ZUCKERMAN: there is no doubt, that this document was written on a documentary basis. There were announcements, letters received from the camps, numbers, information on the situation of the organization for aid in Warsaw, and all of this information was used for the writing of this report. It is possible, that certain things which we knew then, were shown to be incorrect afterwards. . . .
>
> KAZIK: as far as I remember, this document was written in Panska 5, in the month of June 1943, approximately. (Antek: much later!) it is possible it was later. Anyway, in 1943. Of this I am sure. It was written on the basis of documents, as Yitzhak [Zuckerman] already pointed out, with the assistance of testimonies of people who were alive, included among them Zivia and Marek Edelman. I do not know who translated this material. Apparently, Dr. Sack. This can be seen as reliable, as Dr. Sack is also a professor of the Polish language.
>
> ZIVIA LUBETKIN: if you are asking today about sources, then you are interested in documents, testimonies. So we had some very important sources: people who remained alive. Yitzhak composed this document, but at the time of the battles he was on the Aryan side. The people who participated in all of the activities then, those at least who remained alive, wrote afterwards, everyone about his portion. For example, about the brush makers wrote Kazik, about the Tobbens shops wrote Stephan [Grayek], Tuvia wrote about the group that I was also part of—about Miła. But these were things that were not in history, but events that took place then which had just happened to us.[19]

As Simha Rotem explained in the preface to his memoirs, Yitzhak Zuckerman already began to collate testimonies of surviving ghetto fighters as the remnants of the ŻOB sheltered in safe houses on the Aryan side in late 1943–44.

> In the spring of 1944 a small group of Jewish Fighting Organization (ŻOB) members gathered in an apartment hideout on the Aryan side of Warsaw, at Panska Street 5, to record our experiences during the war since 1939. Some had been in permanent hiding in the apartment; others, who had come from the "outside," were surviving leaders of the organization and former Jewish leaders in Poland. At that time—between the Warsaw Ghetto Uprising (April-May 1943) and the Polish Uprising (August 1944)—one of the most important activities of the ŻOB was documentation. Its leaders had a strong sense of history and felt they were the *last remaining Jews* [my emphasis]. Hence they assumed the responsibility to preserve, and to tell the story of Polish Jewry in the days of destruction and revolt. Many accounts were written in that ŻOB apartment; Yitzhak Zuckerman, alias "Antek" was the group's life force, devoted to collating the accounts.[20]

Kazik, who described himself as "not interested in history," did not want to record his account but Zuckerman "kept after me to write my memoirs as a fighter. So in the spring of 1944, I sat down at Panska 5 and wrote, in Polish, a kind of retrospective diary. I normally spoke Polish, although at home we also spoke Yiddish." When Kazik arrived in Palestine in 1946, Melech Neustadt showed him a Hebrew translation of the account to be included in Neustadt's book *Destruction and Uprising of the Jews of Warsaw*.[21]

The Establishment and Development of the Jewish Fighting Organization: The May 24, 1944, Report

While written by Zuckerman (with editing by Adolf Berman and Josef Sack), the history of the Jewish Fighting Organization sent to London and then Tel Aviv in May 1944 was a collective enterprise.[22] When compared with the report of the Jewish Workers Underground from the same time (and bearing in mind that surviving Bundists and Zionist ghetto fighters were *living together* in hiding in Warsaw) there are several points of deviation that require emphasis here. First, Zuckerman's account clearly focuses on the role of HeHalutz in first assessing the scope of the Nazi's Final Solution and then responding to this knowledge by establishing the Jewish Fighting Organization. The key dates of emphasis in the narrative of resistance are also significant as they establish a timeline in the decision-making process to organize armed resistance, as well as identifying the early initiators of the resistance movement:

- October/November 1941: an emissary from HeHalutz traveled to the East and came back with news of mass killings
- In the second half of March 1942 HeHalutz convened meeting with Poalei Zion Z.S., Left Poalei Zion, and Bund where HeHalutz relayed reports and assessed operations under threat of general extermination; Hashomer Hatzair was not there; Bund felt it was too early to organize resistance
- July 22, 1942: beginning of deportations
- July 28, 1942: Hashomer Hatzair, Dror, and Akiva establish ŻOB under HeHalutz auspices
- September 3, 1942: the ŻOB loses Josef Kaplan and Shmuel Breslaw
- January 18, 1943: liquidation actions and fighting of Anielewicz
- March 14, 1943: propaganda campaign on ghetto walls
- April 18, 1943: beginning of final liquidation action
- May 8, 1943: end of command bunker

The report opens by declaring its intent to help its readers "understand the struggle of the Jewish public which began on the same day the Germans began the murder of the Jews—to which we responded in defense, with the establishment of the Jewish Fighting Organization." It highlights the decision to engage in armed resistance, a decision taken upon learning of mass killing. Zuckerman's report thus begins with the invasion of the "territory east of Lvov" in 1941 and the beginning of mass shootings in late 1941 in Vilna and the surrounding region. Unlike the Bund's report, Zuckerman devotes attention to the manner in which information flowed into the *Generalgouvernement* regarding the liquidation actions, highlighting the role of representatives of HeHalutz in Vilna who understood that the annihilation of Jews in the East was the beginning of a general liquidation, as well as reports from Frumka Plotnicka in the Vohlin region and reports of murders in Chelmno that began to reach them in Warsaw.

While some believed that Warsaw "was in the heart of Europe" and would be spared, the report indicated that representatives of HeHalutz began to organize resistance groups. The first critical step in organizing the resistance was the late March 1942 meeting when "Hehalutz convened, after appropriate preparations, initial consultations of the political parties, in which participated Leyzer Levin, Shalom Grayek—Poalei Zion, ZS; Melekh Faynkind, Hersh Berlinski—Left Poalei Zion; Orzech, Abrasha Blum—Bund; and Yitzhak Zuckerman, representative of Hehalutz."[23] With new information indicating "the beginning of an operation aimed at complete annihilation of the Jews of Poland," the representative of Hehalutz recommended the following concrete proposals:

a) Establishment of a general Jewish fighting organization
b) Joint representation of all the Jewish political parties and the youth movements before the Polish military authorities (underground armies)
c) Establishment of an apparatus in the Aryan residential district whose responsibilities would include acquisition of arms and to organize workshops to create arms in the ghetto

The report indicated, however, that while Poalei Zion Z.S. and Left Poalei Zion supported the plan, the Bund declared it was too early to speak of a general Jewish fighting organization, and "the meeting did not bring any positive outcomes."[24] In his memoir, *Surplus of Memory*, Zuckerman goes into much greater detail regarding his recollections of that meeting.[25] At the time, a detailed report of the same meeting was delivered by Eliyahu Gutkowski to the Ringelblum Archive, now located at Jewish Historical Institute in Warsaw. "Eliyahu Gutkowski wrote down what I said, and that's preserved in his handwriting, which only I could decipher, since he recorded things only in outline form. That was right after I came from the meeting and everything was fresh in my memory. Zivia and Mordechai Tennenbaum and Eliyahu Gutkowski were in the room. That was in my underground apartment where I lived after I ran away from Dzielna."[26] As Zuckerman would later recall in his memoirs,

> My first appeal didn't turn out well since, without the Bund, He-Halutz meant nothing to the Polish parties. If there had been different leaders of the Bund, they might have been persuaded to join us. So we tried to initiate something with Poalei Zion ZS . . . but to know what Poalei Zion ZS thought of the subject we posed, all you had to was look at the representatives they sent to the meeting (Morgenstern and Sack didn't show up; they sent second class reps, Grayek and Levin; even Poalei Zion Left didn't send Ringelblum and Sagan but instead sent Berlinski). The Bund actually sent two people (Orzech and Blum) they respected highly.

Even so, Zuckerman would explain later, Orzech felt that the Jewish underground should wait for the Poles to join the fight.[27]

Despite the reluctance of the Bund to organize a combined resistance force in the ghetto, Zuckerman's May 1944 report detailed the formation of the antifascist bloc in the ghetto in March 1942, whose aims were to organize joint political activity and create antifascist fighting groups and a mutual aid committee for victims of fascism.[28] The group also began to publish a joint newspaper (*Der Ruf*). The first fighting groups were also established under auspices of the antifascist bloc, led by Yosef Kaplan (Hashomer Hatzair), Mordecai Tennenbaum (HeHalutz), Fiszelson (Poalei Zion Z.S.), and Hirsh Lent (Left Poalei Zion). Hundreds of young members of the youth movements and workers joined the fighting groups. According to the report, however, despite extensive reporting on the mass murders in the underground press, the Jews of Warsaw refused to believe that such a mass annihilation was possible: "The Jewish underground press carried extensive reports about these mass murders. But Warsaw did not believe. Simple common sense refused to accept the possibility of the mass destruction of tens and hundreds of thousands of Jews." Jews refused to believe, accused the underground of "panic mongering," in the belief that even if true for Ponary and Chelmno, such things would never happen in Warsaw.[29] At the same time, the report noted that "by means of murder, oppression, hunger; by means of ghettos and deportations, the Jewish masses were being prepared for inaction. . . . Hundreds of thousands of Jews went without resistance. If one does not believe in death, why should one offer resistance? Indeed many volunteered for 'resettlement'."

> On Wednesday July 22 the liquidation of the Warsaw ghetto began. Communal council convened to consider appropriate measures. . . . Opinions were divided. The representatives of the leftist Zionist groups, of Hehalutz, as well as several other political leaders, demanded decisive action. The majority, however, was for waiting. How long? Until the situation became clarified.
>
> On July 28, 1942, a meeting was held of He-Halutz and its youth-movement branches: Ha-Shomer Ha-Za'ir, Dror, and Akiva. It was decided to set up the Jewish Fighting Organization YKA (*Yidishe-Kamf-Organizatsie*). The organization signed proclamations which it issued in the Polish language with the initials ŻOB: *Zydowska Organizacja Bojowa*–Jewish Fighting Organization. The members of the Command were: Breslaw, Cukierman, Zivia Lubetkin,

> Mordecai Tenenbaum and Josef Kaplan. A delegation was sent to the Aryan side [i.e., outside the ghetto], to the Poles: Tosia Altman, Plotnicka, Leah Perlstein and Arie-Jurek Wilner, in order to make contact with the Polish Underground and to obtain weapons for the ghetto.

A combat organization was created, but the total arsenal of the entire ghetto was one pistol![30] The first three decisions undertaken by the new fighting organization (as it awaited arms from the Aryan side) included issuing a proclamation that "resettlement meant Treblinka and that Treblinka meant death," forging German "life cards" for factory work, and actively opposing the Jewish police as executors of German orders, including condemning commandant of Jewish police Josef Szerynski to death. "To our amazement and bitterness this proclamation did not, at the time, find acceptance. People were still incredulous. The Jews were being led to their death, and the Jewish postal service in the ghetto was active" (bringing "greetings" from the deported Jews). In the meantime, the ŻOB fired its "first shot," with Israel Kanal seriously wounding Josef Szerynski. On September 3, 1942, however, comrades Josef Kaplan and Shmuel Breslaw were tragically lost, captured by the Gestapo, along with any arms the ŻOB had managed to procure.[31]

The ŻOB report detailed how the liquidation in the ghetto continued and the newly formed ŻOB struggled to organize an effective response: "One felt ashamed to be alive! Many comrades argued that the ghetto ought to be set on fire, that one ought to attack the Germans with bare fists and die." During the January 18, 1943 liquidation action, "some of the armed units in the Central Ghetto under the command of Mordecai Anielewicz deliberately allowed themselves to be seized together with a few hundred other Jews . . . after an hour's battle, the entire group perished with the exception of the commander, who miraculously got away."[32]

It also added details left out of previous accounts of the January 18, 1943 revolt. According to the ŻOB report,

> other groups under the command of Yitzhak Zuckerman, Eliezer Geller and Arieh Vilner fought a partisan war inside

> the houses, in Zamenhof 56, Muranowska 44, Miła 34, 41, and 63 and in Stawki attacked passing German groups. In particular Zechariah Artstein, Benjamin Wald, and Hanoch Gutman distinguished themselves with their heroism [three commanders of the Dror groups]. Only one fighter fell in our groups—Meir Finkelstein. . . . The Germans were panic stricken to enter buildings; on the third day they stopped the liquidation action. In the area of the workshops Israel Kanal fought heroically as head of a small group of fighters. As a result we obtained several dozen rifles and guns.[33]

The ŻOB report distinguishes between the armed resistance organized by the fighting organization and the "passive resistance" of the Jewish population who now chose to go into hiding, jump from trains, and escape from certain death at Treblinka.

> The passive resistance of the civilian populace as well as the combat of the ŻOB units forced the Germans to discontinue the liquidation action in Warsaw. The populace hid in shelters; when caught, they broke the sides of the freight cars and jumped off the trains running at full speed. A few Jews even managed to escape from Treblinka. The repercussion of the shooting and exploding hand grenades electrified the population. *Everywhere all the fighters were greeted as saviors* [my emphasis]. The population supported them as best they could: bakers made gifts of bread, leatherworkers made holsters. The combat organization grew in numbers and strength from day to day.

To raise funds for the fighting organization, the report explained, taxes were levied on "wealthier elements of the Jewish population" and the Jewish Council paid one million zlotys. The report highlighted the predominance of pioneering Zionist youth in the twenty-two fighting groups of the ŻOB, including "11 units of the youth groups within the Hehalutz organization (Dror—5, Hashomer Hatzair—4, Akiva—1, Gordonia—1); of the rest: Bund—4, right labor Zionists—1, left labor Zionists—1, Hanoar Hazioni—1 and the left-wing trade unions—4. The Jewish National Committee therefore had 18 groups." The report also listed the names of the commanders of each group, explaining that nine of the groups were billeted in the Central Ghetto, eight in the area of the Többens Schultz Workshops, and five in the brushworks ghetto. Zuckerman's report also described how "for weeks we dug tunnels all the way to the gates of the ghetto where the German sentries were posted and we laid mines."[34] In February 1943 the Nazis began a propaganda campaign centered around factory owners Többens and Hallmann to convince Jews that resettlement efforts would relocate workers to Poniatowa and Trawniki where they would remain through the war.[35] In response, the report noted, on March 14, 1943, ŻOB posted proclamations calling for resistance to German decrees; on March 20, Többens posted placards in response to ŻOB. "But the German propaganda bore no fruit. No one believed it."

The final section of Zuckerman's report detailed the events that would become known as the Warsaw Ghetto Uprising. "The night of April 18 the final act of the tragedy of the Warsaw ghetto began. It was intended as a birthday gift for the Fuhrer."

> The ŻOB rose to fight. At 2:00 a.m. the Germans posted patrols, 25 meters apart, composed of Germans, Letts, and Ukrainians, around the walls of the ghetto. . . .
>
> By 4:00 a.m. all combat groups at assigned positions . . . at 6:00 a.m. 2,000 heavily armed SS men entered the Central Ghetto, with tanks, rapid fire guns, three trailers loaded with ammunition, and ambulances. The Jewish populace was nowhere to be seen; all were hidden in underground bunkers or other hiding places. Only ŻOB was on the alert above ground. The fighters were located at three ghetto key points, which controlled access to the main ghetto streets. . . .
>
> . . . The first engagement at Nalewki was won by the fighters . . . the main onslaught at corner of Zamenhof

> and Miła, soldiers fled for hiding . . . a tank was destroyed with incendiary bottles . . . the Germans lost 200 killed or wounded, only one fighter lost. . . .[36]
>
> . . . At Zamenhof 29 a group of hidden fighters showered the Germans with grenades.
>
> On the 2nd day of fighting a group of 300 SS men approached the gate of the brushworks area, they stopped long enough for a mine to be exploded under their feet, leaving 80–100 dead and wounded . . . by the end of the second day Germans began to set fire to buildings in the ghetto . . . by the end of the first week, outright siege of the ghetto began, flamethrowers spread death among the populace. Planes cruising overhead dropped explosives and incendiary bombs. Fighters forced the Germans to fight for every street, for every house. The situation nevertheless became increasingly intolerable. The pavement became a sticky tar, wells filled with rubble, food stores destroyed and ammunition ran out; fighters dressed as Germans attacked by surprise.[37]

In Zuckerman's account of the April conflict, few fighters are mentioned by name (in the January 1943 encounter he mentions himself, Geller, Vilner, Artstein, Wald, Gutman, and Meir Finkelstein, as well as Israel Kanal). Likewise, in the description of the explosives from the second day of the revolt Klepfisz is not mentioned by name. In concluding the account of the revolt, the report details the decision by the surviving fighters to pursue a way out of the ghetto once it became clear the struggle was futile.

> The ŻOB command decided to send a delegation to the Aryan side to connect with Zuckerman; on the night of May 8 Simcha Rathauser returned to ghetto but it was too late.
>
> . . . On May 8 Germans surrounded the main bunker of combat organization and closed all five entries, Aryeh

> Wilner addressed all fighters and summoned all to commit suicide . . . Lutek Rotblat was first shooting his mother then himself . . . Mordecai Anielewicz, commandant of the Combat Organization also died here.
>
> Approximately 80 people were rescued, most of whom later perished in the forests or Aryan side; the groups of Josef Farber and Zechariah Artstein continued fighting for weeks after.

The conclusion of the report described the subsequent "liquidation and defense of the ghettos in Czenstachow, Będzin, Białystok, and other cities." Using military language, the report describes the battles in Białystok, which lasted for eight days, while also highlighting the revolts in the two death camps Sobibor and Treblinka. After the war, Zuckerman would also emphasize that the examples of armed resistance in Warsaw, Częstochowa, Będzin, Białystok, Sobibor, and Treblinka were all connected through the work of the ŻOB.[38]

The ŻOB report, in response to concerns that the Bund abroad was claiming too much credit, sought to emphatically demonstrate that members of HeHalutz were the first to call for armed resistance, organized the fighting organization, and composed a disproportionately large portion of the fighting groups (eleven out of twenty-two groups belonged to HeHalutz; eighteen out of the twenty-two were Zionist groups affiliated with the Jewish National Committee). Furthermore, Mordecai Anielewicz was clearly identified as commandant of the fighting organization, and other leading figures in the fighting organization affiliated with HeHalutz and Zionist movements were also singled out by name (in contrast, members of Bundist groups were not mentioned).

In addition to the report on the history and development of the ŻOB written by Zuckerman, the Jewish National Committee also included in the May 24 package a series of individual testimonies written by surviving ghetto fighters who had participated in the uprising, as well as portraits of fallen fighters composed by Hirsch Wasser.[39] As Zivia Lubetkin would point out in the 1951 meeting with Kermish, the most valuable source available for the writing of the ŻOB report were the testimonies of the eyewitnesses, the participants in the battles who documented what they had experienced. Zuckerman and Berman were on the Aryan side; they could only compile and reconstruct the narrative of the revolt second hand, on the basis of what they heard from those who witnessed different aspects of the conflict, from their own subjective vantage point. The combination of these "living sources" makes it possible to compare the process of shaping collective memory while preserving individual memory.

The report on the ŻOB was thus a collective project, based on individual accounts by ghetto fighters with different vantage points, collected, analyzed, and collated by Zuckerman, Berman, and others, and finally typed by Berman for delivery from Warsaw. In reading the individual testimonies included in the same parcel (as well as those that would be provided by surviving ghetto fighters later), several key questions must guide the analysis of these texts: How do the individual testimonies included in the May 24 parcel differ from the ŻOB report? How do they explain the choice to engage in resistance? Do they identify party affiliation of fighters or emphasize the camaraderie born of shared struggle? How do the surviving ghetto fighters define heroism (and how do they characterize the choice of most Jews in the ghetto to go into hiding underground)? How do they explain the choice to resist? Do they present resistance as heroism? As a break with Jewish passivity? Do their testimonies offer a dry account of events as they transpired or do they dramatize?

The three testimonies of surviving ghetto fighters included in the May 1944 shipment belonged to Kazik, Stefan Grayek, and Tuvia Borzykowski, each of whom covered a different aspect of the event in their respective testimonies. Kazik (Simcha Rotem [Ratheiser]), who would lead the surviving fighters out of the ghetto through the sewers, had been a member of Hanoar Hazioni before the war. Born in 1924, the eldest of four children, he lost his brother Israel and an additional five family members with the destruction of their house in a German aerial bombing in which he was also injured. When the ghetto was sealed, his parents sent him to family relatives in a village called Klwów, near Radom, where he remained for three months. In 1942, he returned to the ghetto and joined up with the ŻOB.[40]

Kazik's testimony is a very matter-of-fact accounting of what happened that attempts to detail the timing of events. He does not mention party affiliation or backgrounds; in most cases, other fighters, regardless of movement, are mentioned only by first name—supporting the notion of *esprit de guerre* and camaraderie of the underground and battle.[41] The "dry" nature of Kazik's account is noteworthy, especially as he, like the other surviving ghetto fighters, had endured the most horrific of circumstances, trauma that, as he would later say in Lanzmann's *Shoah*, could not be put into words: "human language cannot really convey the horror we had to confront in the ghetto; in addition to fighting the Germans we also had to fight hunger, thirst, and disease; streets destroyed, needed to climb over piles of bodies."[42]

Photo taken ca. 1943 on the Aryan side of Warsaw. Kazik on left, with Stefanem Szwarskim (a Pole whose aunt sheltered Kazik after the uprising; Szwarskim was murdered by Gestapo searching for Kazik). Yitzhak Zuckerman is in the background. (Ghetto Fighters House Archives, catalog no. 20939)

Kazik does not mention the ghetto population in any detail; he only refers to encounters between ghetto fighters and Germans. In subsequent interviews elsewhere, Kazik would also include much more detail.[43] Kazik's testimony included in the May 24, 1944, shipment begins with the "defense of the brushmakers' area." Reinforcing the disparity between the size of the Jewish units and the German army, Kazik's account emphasizes both the hopelessness of the military struggle and the Jewish determination to exact some measure of revenge on their oppressors:

> On the first day, April 18 [1943] at midnight, we were suddenly awakened by the alarm bell at the observation post. We all leaped up. [lists the fighters who were with him]. . . .
>
> At 4 in the morning, we saw at the Nalewki Passage a line of Nazis marching to the Central Ghetto. They walked and walked endlessly. There were a few thousand of them. They were followed by a procession of tanks, armored vehicles, light cannons, and a few hundred Waffen SS on motorcycles. "They're going as to war," I said to my companion at the post, Zippora [Lerer]; and suddenly I felt how very weak we were. What were we and what was our strength against an armed and well-equipped army, against tanks and armored vehicles, while we had only pistols and, at most grenades? But our spirit didn't flag. Here we were waiting to settle accounts with our executioners at last.[44]

Describing the third day of the revolt (April 20, first day of Passover 1943; Kazik dates the evening of April 18 as the first day of the revolt), Kazik recalls the approach of a unit of about three hundred Germans into his area of the ghetto, when a mine prepared by Michał Klepfisz (cited by name by Kazik) went off in the street: "Suddenly there's a tremendous explosion. I see bodies flying, arms and legs cut off. Eighty to a hundred killed are lying in the streets. The rest of the Germans retreat in a panic."[45] By the end of the third day the nature of the conflict had changed; no longer able to encounter the enemy directly, the ghetto fighters now endured bullets, grenades, and flames dispatched by an enemy they could not see, could no longer engage:

> Cannons roar. Machine guns and mortars rumble. Bullets rain down. All of us are standing at our positions, and the enemy isn't there. We're in despair, there's nobody to fight against. The Germans have taken up positions outside the walls and pour a hail of bullets and grenades down on us. Suddenly, flames surrounded our house . . . [forced to retreat] we discover the body of our comrade, Michał Klepfisz, who had been hit by submachine gun bullets.[46]

By the tenth day it was clear to the ŻOB that there was simply no way to continue to engage the enemy from within the ghetto.

> On the tenth day after the aktsia [liquidation action], the Ghetto is burned. Everywhere—sooty bodies. In the streets, in the courtyards, and in the cellars, people are burned alive. Because of this dreadful situation and the inability to continue the war because of (1) lack of equipment, (2), a lack of food and water, and (3) the impossibility of engaging the enemy in battle—since he is not within the Ghetto but is destroying the Ghetto from outside—we are forced to accept the idea of getting our people out to the forest to continue with our war. . . .
>
> On April 29 [Thursday], the command staff, which included Mordechai (Anielewicz), Zivia Lubetkin, Marek (Edelman), Michal (Rosenfeld) and Berlinski (Hirsh), decided to send Zygmunt (Fryderych) and me to make contact with the commander of the Jewish Fighting Organization on the Aryan side, Antek.[47]

Kazik's description in the testimony makes it clear that the leadership (composed of members of multiple political parties) decided not to fight until the death, but to continue the fighting outside the ghetto, to seek engagement with the enemy, and not to commit an act of collective suicide or martyrdom. After a week outside the ghetto seeking to organize some kind of rescue plan, Kazik returned on May 8, accompanied by Ryszek and two sewer workers (who had to be coaxed to lead them to the ghetto through the sewer with brandy, beer, and his gun, "drunk as hell"). Kazik tried to find the surviving fighters but was unable to find anyone in the ghetto to return with him, and he descended back into the sewers to return to the Aryan side. "I consider why I am returning. Suddenly I felt good among those ruins and those bodies that were so dear to me. I want to take revenge and perish. But I don't give into my weakness. Duty called me to go back."[48]

As alluded to in chapter 3 above, in the sewers Kazik ran into ten fighters in a side channel (these were Shlomek Shuster, Guta, Eliezer, and Yurek Blonas, Abrasha Blum, Abraham Stolak, Bronka Manalek, Janek Bielak, Faygele Goldstein, and Pnina Papier—mainly a group of Bundists from Franciszkanska 22 who left on the night of May 8). As he described in the testimony:

> On the way, I talk with Shlomek Shuster and learn these details from him: The shelter at Miła 18 was discovered only on May 8, during the day. Most of our companions committed suicide at the last minute. I understand the act well: hungry, broken, and exhausted, a hopeless situation, without any help.

Kazik concluded his testimony with a description of the rescue of the group from the sewer and the manhole on Prosta Street. While the group was supposed to emerge at 5:00 a.m., a delay in bringing trucks to the spot delayed their exit from the sewers until close to 10:00 a.m. Kazik, together with Kostek, Jurek, Ryszek, and Wacek, surrounded the manhole with trucks to obscure it from the view of a German-Ukrainian sentry post at the corner of Zelaszna Street, the post of the small ghetto.

> We open the manhole cover. They begin coming out of the cistern. I don't recognize anyone, even though I knew them all, for these weren't people but exhausted ghosts, barely

tottering on their feet. A crowd of people gathered around, looked on, and said, "The cats are coming out."

As soon as Kazik noticed no one else was coming out, he gave the order to "close the manhole cover and go. In the truck I find out that 15 people are left in the sewer who were in a side sewer." Kazik decided that the truck would deliver those who had emerged from the sewer to the (Lomianki) woods, while Ryszek, Wacek, and Jurek were sent back to recover the remaining group from the sewer in Warsaw. When they didn't return that evening Kazik returned to Warsaw. Near Bank Square he noticed a group of people gathered and discovered Ryszek and Jurek killed. He concluded his testimony:

> Later I learned that they had reached Warsaw and gone to Prosta Street, to the cistern. But a post of gendarmes was already standing there. A woman who recognized them turned them in, testifying that they had participated in bringing out the people. Those who were left in the sewer came out of the cistern and fought the gendarmes. A skirmish erupted and they were all annihilated.[49]

Thus, Kazik framed his testimony with the beginning and the end of the revolt from his first-person perspective, beginning on the first day, April 18 at midnight, and ending with the rescue of the last group from the sewer (and the failed rescue of the last fifteen) on May 10. Not having been in the ghetto for the first year of its existence, he does not mention this period. Nor does he seem overly concerned with party politics.

Kazik's testimony would be included in Melech Neustadt's *Hurbn un Oyfshtand*.[50] Neustadt would describe Kazik as "one of the young fighters, who distinguished himself with great bravery." In the conclusion to his later memoir, however, Kazik notes: "a harsh and disappointing reality awaited me in Eretz Israel."

> My meeting with Melekh Neustadt, one of the first people I met here, concerned the fighters of the Warsaw Ghetto.

The monument at 51 Prosta Street in Warsaw (dedicated in 2010) commemorating the escape from the sewers led by Kazik. (Photo by author)

> I was interrogated about everyone who had been killed, but I was never asked, even remotely, about those who had survived.
>
> In almost every meeting with people in Eretz Israel, the question came up, "How did you survive?" It was asked again and again, and not always in the most delicate way. I had the feeling that I was guilty for surviving. This was why, even after I learned Hebrew, I didn't talk very much. I avoided exposing my past. I preferred not to talk about myself and where I had spent the war years.

The second testimony included in the May 24 shipment was the report of Tuvia Borzykowski. His testimony, "In the Central Ghetto," was an excerpt from his diary describing the battles in the ghetto between April 19 and 24, and was originally written in Polish. This was an abbreviated version of a longer manuscript; while the original manuscript was lost, Borzykowski's testimony would be translated into Hebrew and was also published by Neustadt in 1946 in the collection *Hurbn un Oyfshtand* (*Hurban U-Mered shel Yehudei Varsha*).[51]

Borzykowski was born in Lodz in 1911 and raised in Radomsk (his pen name in Dror underground publications was "Radomski"). He was summoned to Warsaw in 1940 to engage in educational work and joined the ŻOB in summer 1942 after the deportations. One of the last to crawl out of the sewers, he remained in Poland after the war to engage in education work with survivors (he spoke at the 1947 commemoration in Warsaw and immigrated to Israel in 1949, where he joined Kibbutz Lochamei HaGetaot). His testimony would later be published in Yiddish in Poland in 1949 as *Tsvishn Falendike Vent* (*Between Tumbling Walls*).[52] He died in 1959 after a prolonged illness.

Unlike Kazik, Tuvia's testimony includes more rhetorical flourishes and he notes the emotional responses of other fighters.

> April 19, 1943, Passover eve. A beautiful spring day. The boys find themselves in their position [and he notes surprise

Kennort Krakau
Kreish. Distrikt Krakau
Kennummer 654036
Gültig bis 29 Juli 1948
Name Borzykowski
Vorname Tadeusz
Geboren am 14. 5. 1910.
Geburtsort Warschau.
Distrikt Warschau
Land
Beruf erlernter
ausgeübter
Religion röm.-kath.-rzym.-kat.
Besondere Kennzeichen keine - nie ma
Borzykowski Tadeusz
Krakau, den 29 Juli 1943.

A forged Aryan identity card for Tuvia Borzykowski, member of the Jewish Fighting Organization (ŻOB) in the Warsaw ghetto. (Ghetto Fighters House Archives, catalog no. 1623)

that the day of reckoning should be such a beautiful day] and were very sad that nature should laugh at them in such a cruel way.[53] Thought that our final battle would take place under black skies dark as lead with hurricane and storms. At approximately 6 in the morning came running to the commander of the group Joseph with black eyes bulging and hair flying in the wind. He brought a command from the general commander to start the attack. The Germans were already near our position on the corner of Nalewki and Gesia. We heard the order: fire! The tremendous sound of bullets and grenades flying above the heads of the Germans. Explosions all around echoing all over the ghetto. Our battle for our three positions was at its peak. The couriers for the commanders were running from position to position. . . . The commander informs us the Germans have left 40 plus dead in the battlefield.

On our side there were no casualties. It is difficult to describe the happiness in our platoon. We all knew that a real war awaited us and despite the many casualties on the German side we knew we would eventually fall in battle.

> Our happiness in the face of death emanated from the sight of the dead Germans scattered in the street.[54]

Tuvia continues by describing the hunger and exhaustion of his group after not sleeping all night. They sleep and play games trying to pass the time. Suddenly one of the lookouts bursts in and reports the Germans are advancing with tanks from the triangle (Gesia, Nalewki, and Franziskanska). Behind a barricade, the Germans began to shoot at the ŻOB's position.

> After thirty minutes of firing we saw to our joy that again dozens of dead and wounded Germans lay in the street. On our side there were no casualties. The Germans shot blindly because they were afraid to come out from behind the barricade. We shot precisely on target. We attempted not to waste bullets. The first day of battle ended with our victory.[55]

While the next day's battles were more difficult, Tuvia again describes a victory in street battles and on the roofs of buildings for the ghetto fighters, again ending in the flight of German soldiers from the ghetto. With the shift in German tactics to even more destructive warfare—basically burning everything in sight—the ŻOB also shifted tactics, organizing into smaller groups of fighters and avoiding all direct confrontations, with the bunker at Miła 29 becoming the base of operations.

> The spirit of the fighters did not break. Everyone requested the most dangerous and most difficult task for himself. This bunker was well supplied and even contained a radio. In the moments of silence we heard news from the world. We heard about the defense in the ghetto, and we felt a connection with the world.[56] One minute after the news on the ghetto, they played music and we understood that we were alone and in a hopeless situation. On Shabbat, the 24th of April, flames began to enter

> our shelter, and we had no choice but to escape outside immediately. We had to run onto the street in the clear day with a group of civilians also inside the bunker and cross the street. A group of 40 fighters, led by Pawel and Lutek, advanced in front of the civilians. We thought battle was unavoidable but luckily we did not encounter any Germans and made it to Miła 9. There the situation was horrific. Three courtyards filled with refugees from burned houses. Great tumult with the noise of women crying![57]

Borzykowski's testimony concludes on April 24, providing a detailed snapshot of the first five days of the revolt. Like Kazik, his account does not specify party affiliation, although he does reference the relationship between the fighters and the civilians in the ghetto, who took shelter in the bunkers together.

The report of Stefan (Shalom) Grajek, about the battles in the Többens-Schulz workshops, was the third eyewitness report included in the May 24, 1944, shipment. Grajek's report is reproduced in Neustadt, *Hurbn un Oyfshtand*, 264–71 and in *Sefer Milhamot* [excerpted], 171–73. Born in Warsaw in 1916 and an activist in Poalei Zion, during the April 1943 uprising Grajek was in a combat unit commanded by Eliezer Geller in the Többens-Schultz workshops area. He succeeded in getting to the Aryan side of the city, where he made contact with Yitzhak Zuckerman. On April 28, 1943, forty fighters left the burning ghetto through a tunnel which had been dug at Grajek's initiative, to a shelter he had prepared on the Aryan side of Warsaw. (According to Moshe Arens, this departure was through the ŻZW headquarters tunnel in Többens-Schulz area. This tunnel connected to the sewer system.) After the revolt, Grajek became responsible for setting up hiding places on the Aryan side for members of the underground. Grajek later took part in the Polish Uprising of August 1944. He was caught by the Germans but managed to survive. After the war, he was active in smuggling immigrants to Mandate Palestine in the frameworks of the Bricha (the semiorganized clandestine movement of escape from Poland) and Ha'apalah (the immigration movement designed to break the British blockade and conquer the shores of Palestine after the war). He himself immigrated to Israel in 1949.

Grajek's testimony offered a third eyewitness perspective of a participant in the uprising, in this case, from the vantage point of a fighter who could speak to the conflict in the area of Többens-Schultz workshops (Kazik was in the brushmakers area; Tuvia Borzykowski in the central ghetto—in fact in subsequent publications these testimonies were titled in this way). Grajek, who had been active in Poalei Zion Z.S. before the war offered a detailed description of the locations of the various fighting groups in the area of the Többens-Schultz workshops, as well as some perspective on how things sounded and looked from their part of the ghetto as they heard the beginning of the battles in the central ghetto. "The whole night of April 19 we heard great noise. People could not sleep. Automobiles driving by, military marching, regular noises of shooting. What was happening?"

Stefan Grajek (right) taking Tuvia Borzykowski through the streets of the Aryan side of Warsaw to a hiding place, after his previous place was discovered. Photographed shortly after the suppression of the Warsaw Ghetto Uprising. (Ghetto Fighters House Archives, catalog no. 2848)

> With the dawn a horrifying picture appeared on the street. The walls of the ghetto were surrounded by gendarmes. The guards were reinforced with SS Men—there was no way out of the ghetto, all exit permits were canceled. People were running on the streets like crazy. We attempted to communicate with the Central Ghetto. The phone was not working. We could see nothing but the ghetto surrounded by guards and guns prepared to fire. From a distance we heard the sounds of shots and explosions. At this time a liquidation action was taking place at the central ghetto. The German managers of the workshops, those who provided the "power of bread," came to our place and contended that the deportation action would not affect the productive elements and was only directed against the "wild ones" in the ghetto. But no one took their words seriously. Our first task was to organize our five in groups and take up combat positions. The fighting group in our workshop, at Leszno St., #76, under the command of Eliezer Geller, took up a position next to the windows on the third floor. Through the rooftop we maintain a connection with the group of David Nowodworski on the Nowolipe 67, and with the group of Heniek Kava at Leszno 74, factories of Tobbens. Lilith (Regina Puden) was the courier who maintained a connection between the groups.

Grajek described the layouts of the various positions of fighters associated with the ŻOB in the area of the workshops, including groups at Nowolipe 41, Smocza 6/8, Leszno 36, Nowolipe 31, Nowolipe 66. He also noted the ability of his group in the area of the workshop to maintain telephone contact with the ŻOB fighters in the Central Ghetto at the beginning of the revolt as they "heard about their great victories in the first battles." The next morning, the commander of the area gave an order to start the battle.

> At approximately 10 a.m. began our first attack. At the same time a group of gendarmes marched on Leszno street

> in the direction of the ghetto. When they got close to the guard post on the corner of Leszno and Zelazna, the group at Leszno 76 (Eliezer Geller, Aharon Chmielnjcki, Yaakov Putermilch, Iziv Levski) opened fire on them. Two large explosions, thrown with success, blew up the group. The Germans ran away and left more than 10 killed in the street. The group at Nowolipe 67 had already left several weeks before a mine under the guard post next to Smocza Street. When the German platoon reached the spot the fighters connected the mine to an electric wire. How great was their dejection however when the mine did not explode. The young men were angry, the women cried, there was no electricity. Out of great anger therefore the group threw bombs. The result was better than expected; two large explosions led to many German casualties.

Grajek explained that in this way the Germans came to understand that they were in danger even in the "productive" parts of the ghetto. The fighters used times of quiet to establish connections with the other groups through couriers. Grajek's group also guarded the shelters of the civilian population (noting the efforts of the fighting groups to protect Jewish civilians in the ghetto and marveling at their ability to instill fear in the German enemy).

> In the following days the Germans began to enter houses. How great was the happiness of the fighters, when they saw through the window SS men being punished for refusing to obey the orders of their officers. Day and night the ghetto burned. The fire and smoke forced the fighters to uproot from place to place. Only rarely were they able to find an appropriate base of operations.
>
> At the time of the final battles we inflicted losses upon the enemy but we also began to sustain heavy losses. The hunger and hopelessness led us to find a way to try to cross to the Aryan side. After many attempts, which took several days, I

> received an order from the commander to cross to the Aryan side to establish connection with Antek. That same night [according to Neustadt this was April 29] we moved 40 men through the sewer system [according to Neustadt this was at Leszno 56]. But the path through the canals was discovered. The remainder of the groups who tried to find a way through the chains of guards of the Germans were killed in street battles. For a long time we listened to the echoes of shots in the ghetto and we know that our groups continue to fight the Germans from all sides.

In addition to the three first-hand accounts by Kazik, Borzykowski, and Grayek, the May 24 shipment included what Neustadt would label "a description by a boy of 13 of the life of the Jewish children in Warsaw during that fateful period."[58] Finally, it included "Silhouettes of Fighters," written by Hersh Wasser about the deceased fighters Abram Diamant, Sha'anan Lent, and Abram Eiger, and their heroic deaths in the ghetto uprising in the first week of May.[59] Hersh Wasser was the secretary of the underground Oneg Shabbes archive, who, together with Rachel Auerbach, was one of only two of the primary activists to survive and help recover the archive after the war.[60] Wasser had been an important activist of Left Poalei Zion in Lodz before the war and director of the Borochov Library in Lodz; he headed the *landsmannschaft* department of the Oneg Shabbes during the war and served as Left Poalei Zion representative to the ŻOB. During the uprising, Kassow writes, Wasser was put on a train to Treblinka but managed to escape. He and his wife, Luba, found a hideout in the northern part of Warsaw, which they shared with Hirsch Berlinski, commander of the Left Poalei Zion fighting groups in the uprising, along with Pola Elster and Eliyahu Erlich. After their hideout was discovered, Wasser survived the shootout with the Germans but the rest were killed; it was largely thanks to Wasser that the Oneg Shabbes archive was discovered after the war.[61]

Wasser described Diamant as an "old warrior": "a worker aged 42, tall, with broad shoulders, with a soft, yet focused look full of strength, generous, courageous." His wife and daughter were taken to Treblinka in the first day of deportations on July 22, 1942.

> But Abraham Diamant did not break—instead his gaze grew more stern and his hands balled into fists. He became a zealous partisan of active warfare against the Hitlerite beast. From the first moment of the organization of fighting battalions Avraham Diamant was connected to them body and soul. As a corporal in the Polish Army, a brave and talented fighter, he again took into his hands a rifle. He did not ask for praise. The fighters of the ghetto would say that the struggle of the fighting Jews, and even their deaths was not wasted. The struggle of the soldiers of the ghetto was part of the war of the forces of freedom against fascism. Their struggle sent a message for a better future to Jews the world over. The ghetto fighters would be the builders of tomorrow.

As described by Wasser, on his first day of fighting, April 20, 1943, Diamant took up his position on Świętojerska 32 and on this day he killed seven Germans and silenced a nest of informers. As a veteran of the Polish Army, Diamant likely had firearms training most of the other fighters did not possess, and put this training to good use in the conflict. On the first of May he fought in the ruins of the house on Franciszkańska 30, where a battalion of ŻOB fighters guarded the entrance to a bunker housing civilians. Wasser described a hellish firefight, which would also be recorded in the diary of the battalion commander Hirsch Berlinski after the uprising.[62]

> The Germans found our bunker. Germans are in our bunker, someone reports from the first entrance. Z. Stolak runs to that entrance with a few fighters. They shoot salvos, Germans respond with grenades. The dugout-entry is blocked with debris, the command is given to slip through the other dugout and give battle in the yard. Among the first three out is Diamant. We fight tooth to tooth, eye to

eye; two Germans are wounded, a third escapes. We—Jelen, Diamant, Abramek—take up positions among the debris, our purpose being not to let the Germans break through to the second entrance. This is partly achieved, most of the fighters are out in the yard and the battle goes on. As Diamant is hit, his hand grabs close to the heart, he struggles to hand me his gun, fails, falls down into the burning cellar with his rifle, disappears in the smoke and flames.

When we were burying our dead in the evening, his body was missing in that common grave. Only his body was missing. His name survives. It shall remain as a symbol of a fighting spirit and readiness for sacrifice.

A companion in battle.[63]

Wasser also described the young partisan, Sha'anan Lent, aged 16, who fell on May 3, 1943, "and will also remain in the hearts of the fighters as a symbol of the Jewish youth come to life" and Abram Eiger, a Dror fighter who died as he cursed the Germans, delivering "a prophetic speech in the face of the Germans" before "a rain of fiery lead fell on the young hero."[64]

Unlike the testimonies provided by the surviving ghetto fighters, Wasser's "Silhouettes of Fighters" detailed the exploits of fallen warriors. These two types of sources—the words of the living witnesses and the profiles of those who fell in defense of Jewish Warsaw—would set up a painful dichotomy between those who died a heroic death and those who somehow lived to tell the tale, obligated by the survival to detail the heroic struggle of those who would not survive. As Kazik would also note in his later memoirs, this dichotomy set up a challenge for survivors in their encounter with Israeli society after the war: How and why had they managed to survive? Why did they not die heroically fighting in the ghetto? It would become easier to tell the tales of those who died than to recount one's own exploits during the war.

"Explode this False Legend": *The Warsaw Ghetto Rising*

The shipment of documents from Warsaw to London and then to the Yishuv would play a central role in shaping a Zionist narrative of the revolt, one that would allow the Zionist movement to see the Warsaw Ghetto Uprising as a tale of Zionist heroism, more than one year after the events had transpired.

In his *Warsaw Ghetto Rising*, published in 1944 in Tel Aviv, Melekh Neustadt listed the sources of information that came into the possession of Zionist representatives in London in 1944, helping to fill out the picture of what had actually transpired in Warsaw in April and May 1943; these sources included "a series of accurate and detailed reports written by the surviving initiators, leaders, and fighters of the rebellion themselves," as well as a number of testimonies written at first and second hand. Neustadt, who had been so active compiling information sent to the Yishuv by the Jewish National Committee (and would be the author-editor of the document collection *Hurbn un Oyfshtand* [Destruction and revolt in the Warsaw ghetto] published in 1946) published *The Warsaw Ghetto Rising: As Told by the Insurgents* in large part as a response to the Bundist claims of credit for the revolt and the publication of the Jewish Labor Underground's reports by the Bund.[65]

Neustadt was a Mapai party leader and member of the Zionist Actions Committee. Born in Radomysl in Galicia in 1896, he settled in Palestine in 1926 and became active in the Histadrut (Federation of Labor). In 1942, Neustadt had gone to Istanbul on behalf of the Histadrut to try to contact members of HeHalutz in occupied Europe.[66] Much to his surprise he discovered in the summer of 1942 that it was indeed possible to still contact the movement in occupied Europe and urged the Histadrut and World Jewish Congress to open offices in Istanbul in June 1942. By the end of the summer of 1942, however, reports soon spread regarding the physical extermination of Polish Jewry—it was too late. Even so, Neustadt worked into 1943 to try to organize rescue out of the Istanbul office.[67] After the revolts, Neustadt tried to convince the surviving ghetto fighters to leave occupied Poland, to survive as the last remaining eyewitnesses to what had transpired, but the activists refused to leave.[68]

Melekh Neustadt (Noy), cover of *The Warsaw Ghetto Rising* (1944).

Until now, Neustadt explained, "smuggled letters and reports could only hint at what had occurred" but the arrival in May 1944 of such a quantity of detailed information from the actual participants in the uprising would enable him to write a factual accounting of "the social forces which initiated, prepared and conducted the rising,—a feature which has unfortunately been ignored hitherto in both Jewish and non-Jewish circles." Neustadt explained the need to set the record straight in response to complaints emanating from the Jewish National Committee that a distorted picture of the uprising, mistakenly emphasizing the role of the Bund, was being presented abroad.[69] Even so, Neustadt indicated that as leaders in the Yishuv attempted to decipher the actual chain of events leading the revolt:

> The truth of the matter is that we have felt all along that injustice is being done to our comrades of the Palestine Labour movement. We had in our possession indubitable evidence of the active and often the guiding role played by the Zionist-Socialist groups in the organisation of the Jewish Underground in the face of Nazi oppression, and particularly in the building up and carrying into effect of the resistance movement in the Warsaw Ghetto. We have, however, hitherto refrained from drawing attention to this aspect of the matter, nor have we reacted in any way to certain reports which have not merely failed to credit our comrades with their organising and directing part in the rising, but in many cases have not even mentioned them at all. They endeavoured, with a measure of success, to create the impression that others had done this work.[70]

Neustadt argued that while Zionist leaders in the Yishuv had refrained from politicizing the revolt, Bundists abroad had in fact erroneously taken credit for the events, and it was only in response to complaints emanating from the surviving ghetto fighters and the Jewish National Committee themselves that he now felt obligated to set the record straight.

> The latest report of the Jewish National Committee in Poland, written at the end of May, 1944, after emphasizing the harmonious and brotherly collaboration in the Jewish National Committee, and stressing the satisfactory, correct and even friendly, relations with the "Bund," goes on to say: *"From information reaching us from abroad we have the impression that the 'Bund' abroad are endeavouring to place the battle of the Ghetto in Warsaw to their own credit by ascribing to themselves the predominant, if not the exclusive role. In the name of historical truth you must explode this false legend and undeserved merit. The battles in the Ghetto of Warsaw, like those in the other ghettos and concentration camps, were initiated, organised and conducted by our organisations, in the first place by pro-Palestinian organisations of workers and youth: 'Hechalutz', 'Dror' 'Freiheit' and 'Hehalutz Hazair'—(the youth of Poale Zion-Z.S.), 'Hashomer Hazair', Poale Zion—Z.S. and Left Poale Zion. These organisations took the leading part in the battles, they supplied the largest number of fighters, and offered the greatest sacrifice of blood."*[71] (My emphasis.)

Neustadt was also critical of Bundist efforts to claim itself as "sole representative" of the Jewish labor movement in Poland and "to create the impression that the 'Bund' is identical with the Jewish Workers' Underground movement in Poland." He also took the Bund to task for writing about the activities of the so-called Bund in Poland, using again and again the expression "the Jewish Workers' Underground Movement" to create the impression that the Bund and the Jewish Underground were one and the same thing. Neustadt specifically cited Shloime Mendelson's speech at the forty-third convention of the Workers' Circle in the United States, where Mendelson made the statement that "underground activity is being carried on chiefly by the 'Bund', which has taken the leading part in the organisation of the movement of resistance." The Bund, Neustadt charged, continued to "pervert the facts of this sacred and wonderful event," even selecting only the names of the Bundists from the list of 223 Jewish fighters killed in the uprising.

The Bund, he stressed: "published a report in the American press in March 1944 to the effect that 'a new list has been received of 36 members of the "Bund" who were killed in the Warsaw Ghetto rising.' They gave the names of these members without even mentioning the other 187 slain of whom 150 were members of the Zionist-Socialist movement." Noting that the Revisionists and Aguda also complained that none of their members appeared on the list, Neustadt explained that "if our comrades in Warsaw had listed their names we would have added them, too."[72]

Echoing the report of May 1944 received from the Jewish National Committee, Neustadt also sought to explain the "tragic illusion"—why Jews offered no resistance against the deportations from the very beginning. Neustadt distinguished between the broader Jewish public, which continued to believe in the tragic illusion of survival, thus being paralyzed into passivity, and the members of Zionist groups, who were the first to report on massacres in the East and then urge Jews to prepare active resistance. As Neustadt writes: "To the credit of our movement it should be recorded that we have never harboured such illusions. Even at that time it had already been decided to raise the first fighting units out of the ranks of the Palestine Labour Organisations." Again relying on the report of the Jewish National Committee from May 1944, Neustadt noted that it was HeHalutz which in March 1942 arranged a conference of all Jewish political parties based on the news emanating from the East, in order to form "a general Jewish fighting force," but the Bund determined such efforts were too early, preventing the formation of such a force before the deportations.

Explaining further the "passivity of the Jewish population" who were deceived by Nazi orders and clung to the belief that escape was still possible, Neustadt blamed the Bund for also supporting this position. He pointed to the Bund's August 31, 1942, report, when there were still 150,000 Jews left in the city, which even then counseled restraint: "those who have decided on active resistance face the tragic question as to whether they are entitled to bring certain death upon others who might otherwise still have a faint chance of escape."[73]

Here again, Neustadt highlights a critical difference of opinion: Was the revolt a people's revolt or the enterprise of just a few fighting units? If the masses continued to believe in the possibility of survival and the Bund also believed that active resistance meant "certain death," then, Neustadt speculated, it was not the entire forty thousand remaining residents that took part in the fighting "but only a number of fighting units among them." These fighters had been trained and were ready for battle, but (citing the report) "it was not fighters we lacked—but arms!" In July they had only one revolver, and in August 1942, five revolvers and eight hand grenades. Thus, Neustadt concludes, the organization of the revolt and of the ŻOB took place before arms were sent to them (by Polish military authorities, not as a result of assistance from the Polish underground) and "it was only at the end of 1942 or at the beginning of 1943 that they received a large consignment of arms sent to them by the Polish military authorities—revolvers, hand grenades and explosives." While the Bund reported in *Unzer Tsayt* in June 1943 that "groups of the Polish Underground hastened to the aid of the Jewish fighters. . . . Polish blood mixed with that of the Jewish heroes," according to Neustadt, "this is in no way corroborated by the reports which we received from Warsaw." For Neustadt this is a crucial point: the revolt was organized, conceived, and orchestrated by Zionist groups without the assistance of the Polish underground. It was a Zionist revolt in execution and in meaning, a revolt against the oppression of Nazis and not in defense of the Polish homeland. The appeal to the Polish Underground issued during the fighting went unheeded, as he saw it. Furthermore, despite rumors at the time of assistance from "Russian parachutists" or of British, Polish, and Soviet flags flying in the ghetto, there was simply no corroboration of such outside aid.

In describing the reports included in the May 24 parcel, Neustadt implies their reliability by drawing attention to their admirable restraint and objectivity. He also regrets what might have been different had more assistance, arms, and training arrived before the revolt:

> It is difficult to shake off the disturbing and terrible thought, upon reading the reports and factual description of the fighting, that matters might have been entirely different if our comrades had been provided with sufficient arms,

> help and training in good time. In their description of the fighting they use no superlatives. They make no attempt to cast a heroic glamour over anyone. They simply state the dry facts. "On such and such a date, at such and such an hour, and such and such a place, fighting took place. We fired so many shots, threw so many bombs; the Nazis suffered so many casualties and we so many." Here were our boys and girls, young, inexperienced, inadequately armed, ill-fed and exhausted, causing hundreds of casualties among the enemy, and destroying powerful tanks with home-made bombs. They were absurdly outnumbered, one of our youngsters to many of the enemy.[74]

He also celebrates the choice of the ghetto fighters to die by their own hands rather than fall to the Germans, noting specifically the act of Lutek Rotblat, who shot his mother, then himself. Lamenting the late decision to organize resistance, Neustadt notes: "Reading all these records, one is tormented by the reflection that if these fighters had acted when there were still a million Jews in Poland, when they could have raised a powerful underground army of hundreds of thousands, if then they had received arms, encouragement, help, and training, how different things might have been!"

Finally, Neustadt set out to demonstrate that Zionist groups played the leading role in the revolt and dominated the Jewish Fighting Organization numerically and militarily. On a statistical level, the composition of the Jewish Fighting Organization, according to the report received from Poland, highlighted the predominance of Zionist youth among the twenty-two fighting units that had taken part in the battle. "The composition of the fighting forces shows of what valuable and loyal elements our movement in Poland was made up, something we failed to appreciate in its proper light before the war." Again, Neustadt reiterates, it was simply not possible that the will to resist and the heroism of the fighters sprang from a "deeply rooted Bundist consciousness that only the soil of Poland was the true home of Polish Jewry." Only those who were "true to Zion" until the last moment led the revolt. Nonetheless, "The 'Bund' is now trying to convince the world that the heroism displayed by the Ghetto fighters sprang from the deeply-rooted Bundist consciousness that only the soil of Poland was the true home of Polish Jewry." Citing a July 1943 article by Emanuel Sherer (the Bund representative in London), which claimed that even "the non-Bundists who participated in the fight, even those opposed to this principle of ours, had been attracted by this deeply rooted emotion, the very 'Bundist' feeling, that Poland is the home of the Polish Jews and that nothing, not even the Nazi highly equipped barbarity, can banish us from *our homes*, from *our country*," Neustadt responded: "In this there is a suggestion that those who did not have such a feeling could not fight at all and the implication that the 'Bund' initiated the rising and represented the bulk of the Ghetto fighters. It is also a slur on those whose hearts remained true to Zion until the last moment." Citing the letter addressed to Berl Locker, Anshel Reiss, and himself in November 1943 from Poalei Zion Z.S. in Poland: "To the extent that any credit is due to us at all it is because in spite of everything we have preserved the ideological and moral strength which guided our actions. That is not tribute to us but a tribute to the value with which our flesh and blood are imbued. It is thanks to these values that the Palestine Labour movement was able to initiate and organize the Ghetto rising." Quoting from the May 24 report of the Jewish National Committee, Neustadt reinforced this point: "Let the world Labour Organisations in all countries know that the pro-Palestine Labour movement organized and conducted the battle of Warsaw, and that hundreds of fighters fought and died with the thought that death would form one of the foundations of the socialist future for the Jewish masses in Palestine."[75]

Neustadt criticized the Bund for taking credit for leading the uprising when it was clear that no more than 18 percent of the fighters in the Jewish Fighting Organization were Bundists. He quoted a letter from the headquarters of the Bund in Poland written in May 1944: "the boasting of certain elements with deeds which were not theirs for purely political reasons is so grotesque, and at the same time, in the light of our tragedy, so macabre, that any controversy on this subject would seem a disparagement of the greatness and dignity of the cause." He disputed the Bundist claim that Michał Klepfisz was in fact the leader of the uprising and sought to set the record straight with previously unknown information:

> This also led to a regrettable error when the name of Michael Klepfisz, a member of the "Bund," a brave and loyal fighter who lost his life in the Ghetto fighting, was publicized as the central figure of the rising. The real leader was in fact Mordechai Anilewitz, a member of "Hashomer Hazair." His second in command was Isaac Z., one of the heads of the Hechalutz movement in Poland. *The Executive Council of the Histadrut received a telegram in the 23rd of May 1943, from one of its representatives in a neutral country (the telegram was held up for ten days by the Censorship) giving the names of several comrades who had fallen in the Ghetto fighting. One passage read: "Mordechai was the father of the Defence." As we did not know which Mordechai was meant, (Mordechai Tennenbaum who had been appointed commander of the rising in Białystok was also in Warsaw) we did not publish this news but asked for further details. In the meantime a telegram from the Polish Telegraphic Agency was published on the 26th of May 1943 announcing: "the heroic death of Engineer Klepfish, a member of the 'Bund' and one of the central figures of the armed resistance movement." On the basis of this "Bund" circles broadcast as a fact that he had headed the rising. We assumed that our comrades had made a slip in reporting the facts.*[76] (My emphasis.)

While acknowledging how important Klepfisz was, as an engineer, in the manufacture of homemade weapons in the ghetto, Neustadt was able to now concretely advance the fact that the M. Ordche referred to in the Bundist report was none other than Mordecai Anielewicz, previously unknown outside Poland, who would become known as the leader of the Warsaw Ghetto Uprising.

One final point in Neustadt's analysis bears mention. As will be recalled from the discussion of correspondence between the surviving ghetto fighters and the Yishuv, the letters of Zuckerman and Lubetkin expressed resentment over the lack of contact from the Yishuv and betrayed a sense of abandonment and detachment from the Zionist home. How then to defend the claim that it was the connection with Zion that inspired the revolt? While highlighting the degree of contact between the Yishuv and the fighting organization, Neustadt also explained the confusing nature of such correspondence which, written in code, only made complete sense with the benefit of hindsight (for example, the letters that noted the desire of "dear Ami" to marry "Miss Harigevicz" at a marriage ceremony to be "celebrated among a limited circle in the home of Aunt Haganaska"). He noted that as representative of the Executive Committee of the Histadrut he continued his efforts to rescue prominent members of the Jewish underground, including Emanuel Ringelblum, but by the time a list of nineteen members to be rescued reached Warsaw, only three remained alive (presumably Ringelblum, Zuckerman, and Lubetkin). "They did not accept our proposal as they considered it their duty to serve their people until the end. Since then we have learned that one of the three, Dr. Emanuel Ringelblum, a young historian, and a member of the Left Poale Zion, is no longer alive."

Over the next two years, Neustadt would painstakingly transcribe, annotate, and footnote the materials received in the May 1944 shipment for the 1946 publication of *Hurbn un Oyfshtand* (Destruction and revolt).

While historians have generally seen the politicization of the revolt as occurring after the war, with the first encounter of the survivors with their new homes (i.e., New York and Israel), the polemics of 1944 between the Bundist interpretations advanced in publications like *Ghetto in Flames* and the Labor Zionist arguments of *The Warsaw Ghetto Rising* make clear that within one year of the revolt, the Warsaw Ghetto Uprising was too great a symbol to relinquish to the political enemy in the battle for Jewish public opinion. The brotherhood of the fighters did not extend to New York and Tel Aviv. Beyond emerging disagreements over who played a leading role in the revolt, key to the division between Zionist and Bundist accounts were questions of historical interpretation: Was the revolt a popular revolt or a Zionist revolt? a reflection of the Polish-Jewish will to fight back or of the zeal of a small cadre of the Zionist avant-garde? More fundamentally, how was armed resistance framed in the political sphere after the revolt? And what role did the surviving ghetto fighters themselves play in shaping the ways in which resistance would be understood and interpreted in the aftermath of the Warsaw Ghetto Uprising?

6

The Place of the Warsaw Ghetto Uprising among the Surviving Population in Europe

Starting in the summer of 1944, the Red Army began to liberate eastern portions of Poland and the Baltic states from Nazi occupation; Warsaw would not be liberated until January 1945. In the aftermath of the war, as survivors struggled to come to terms with the devastation around them, they also quickly turned to preparing for their postwar lives. The surviving members of the Jewish Fighting Organization played a key role in arguing that the wartime struggle continued, primarily as part of the struggle to create the Jewish state. In the displaced persons camps, the ghetto fighters would occupy a central place of honor. Commemorations of the uprising in the DP camps and in postwar Poland emphasized the symbolic meaning of the event for the broader surviving population and soon came to be linked with the postwar struggle for the creation of the Jewish state.

The Liberation of Warsaw

As individual Jews began to emerge from their hiding places or from the Nazi camps, they tried to organize the remnants of the destroyed Jewish community. The city of Lublin, in southeastern Poland, became one of the first centers for

Survivors of the Jewish underground pose atop the ruins of the Mila 18 bunker in the former ghetto, ca. July 1945. Among those pictured is Simcha Rotem (Rathajzer, a.k.a. Kazik) (left). (United States Holocaust Memorial Museum, courtesy of Leah Hammerstein Silverstein, photo no. 17920)

Jewish political reorganization following its liberation on July 23, 1944.[1] The Polish Uprising in Warsaw began on August 1, 1944, and lasted sixty days, until it was brutally suppressed at the beginning of October. It was launched by the Polish Home Army (Armia Krajowa), the largest Polish resistance organization, based on orders from the London-based Polish government-in-exile. Their goal was to take control of Warsaw from the Germans before the Soviet army reached the city, as the Red Army appeared on the other side of the Wisła River not far from Warsaw. Approximately twenty-three thousand young Polish fighters launched the uprising on August 1. On August 4 the rebels freed hundreds of Greek and Hungarian Jews imprisoned at the Gęsiówka concentration camp on Gęsia Street, Jews who had been brought from Auschwitz to clear rubble from the destroyed ghetto, specifically because they could not speak Polish. The newly freed prisoners immediately joined the uprising. Other Jews joined the insurgents, often fighting and dying under assumed identities that concealed their Jewish origins. Antisemitism within the Armia Krajowa made it risky for Jews to reveal their Jewishness, even as they joined Poles in the fight for national liberation.[2] Nonetheless, Jewish fighters still joined in. Among the fighters was Samuel Willenberg, who fought with the army in September 1939 and was a participant in the revolt at Treblinka. Willenberg joined the AK battalion "Ruczaj" during the August 1944 revolt, as did Adina Blady-Szwajger, a pediatrician in the Warsaw ghetto who had aided the ŻOB in the 1943 revolt, and joined the Polish army in setting up a field hospital during the later action. Dr. Blady-Szwajger recalled the beginning of the revolt:

> At five o'clock I heard shots. I ran out onto the stairs. I will never forget that moment. Somebody was running down the stairs—a Polish officer!! In the uniform of Carpathian Brigade! Everybody cried and I cried with them. There was a commotion in the basement. I went downstairs. They were organizing a field hospital. I went up to the commander, a Major "Pobog" whose surname I don't remember. I introduced myself and said who I was and I was immediately accepted as one of the hospital staff.[3]

Jewish children in Warsaw at the time served as liaisons, delivering supplies and information to fighting groups. Members of the Jewish Fighting Organization (ŻOB) who had survived the ghetto uprising also took part in the fighting. Yitzhak Zuckerman, who had become "commander" of what remained of the ŻOB after the death of Anielewicz, led a battalion of Jewish fighters that included Edelman, Lubetkin, and other fighters, an autonomous platoon within the Armia Ludowa ("the People's Army," composed of Communist fighters).[4]

The Jewish National Committee published leaflets, one of which (issued on August 22, 1944, under the title "A Voice from the Depths") linked the continued struggle against Hitler and Nazism with the creation of a Jewish state in the Land of Israel:

> And so, Hitler has not attained his objective. And he shall not be able to attain it. The Jewish people lives! Out

> of 17 million, over 5 million have been exterminated. But the Jewish people of 12 million fights with greater determination and force for its existence and for its better future. The Jewish masses throughout the world share our tragedy with us; they suffer together with us, and are doing all they can to arouse the whole world concerning our situation and coming to our help. They are fighting with great energy and enthusiasm in order to re-establish Jewish life anew and to bring about an economic and social resurrection.
>
> Only one, sole historic compensation can be considered after the flood of Jewish blood that has been spilled: an independent, democratic Jewish State in which the tortured Jewish people will have an unrestricted opportunity for development and productive existence.[5]

The Jewish Telegraphic Agency also detailed the role played by Jews in the August 1944 uprising, citing testimony delivered by a representative of the Polish Socialist Party, who reported that two hundred thousand Jews remained alive in Poland.[6] Two weeks later, another report of the Jewish Telegraphic Agency, headlined: "Jewish Youths Fighting Germans in Warsaw Streets Call for Urgent Help from London," cited Dr. Emanuel Szerer, the Bundist representative on the Polish National Council, who had received a message from the Jewish underground movement in occupied Poland, dated August 18, telling of the participation of Jewish youth in the battle against the Germans which was now raging in the city of Warsaw.[7] The message concluded with a plea for help:

> For eighteen days . . . the people of Warsaw have been waging an unequal fight against the barbarian invader. The surviving Jewish youth is fighting together with the whole of Warsaw. We fight against the enemy for the common Polish cause. Do your best to ensure immediate and effective help.

The report also noted that

> the contribution of the Polish Jews to the Polish fight for freedom was emphasized in a message issued by the delegate of the Polish Government-in-Exile in occupied Poland, made public here today. The message was addressed to the coördinating committee of the Jewish underground in Poland, composed of members of the Jewish Socialist Bund and of the Zionist organization. A similar message was also sent to the Jewish coordinating committee by the Polish Underground Council to Assist Jews.

Finally, the Polish National Council also proposed renaming the streets of the Warsaw ghetto after fallen Jewish heroes as soon as Warsaw was liberated from the Germans. (Eventually, only one street would be renamed: after Mordecai Anielewicz.)

The surviving ghetto fighters would also make much of the experience of joining in the August 1944 struggle and the camaraderie that carried over from 1943 as the Bundist and Zionist members of the ŻOB fought together in a unit in Warsaw's Old Town. Vladka Meed described the efforts of the surviving members of the ŻOB and the Coordinating Committee to enlist Jewish participation in the Polish Uprising:

> In general Jews enlisted in the *P.A.L.* (Democratic Socialists) and *Armia Ludowa* combat groups, not primarily because these Jews were socialists or communists, but because the *Armia Krajowa* was filled with anti-semitic agitators. Even while fighting the Nazis, the Jewish insurgents in the Armia Krajowa units suffered persecution from their Polish comrades. The Poles assigned them to the most dangerous missions and the most difficult tasks—and on occasion shot them in the back. Jews naturally chose to enlist in those groups where they felt they would be welcome.[8]

On August 5, the German troops, heavily reinforced, began a counterattack and soon put the city center under siege. On September 14, Polish army units that had parachuted into Warsaw took control of the right bank of the Vistula River; they also managed to transfer several battalions to the left bank, suffering heavy casualties. Despite their efforts, though, they could not help the rebels. The city center fell to the Germans on October 2, signaling the end of the Polish Uprising in Warsaw. In all, about 16–20,000 Polish fighters were either killed or went missing and 7,000 were wounded. Approximately 150,000 civilians were also killed, including several thousand Jews who had hidden with Poles in Warsaw after the ghetto was liquidated in May 1943. About 16,000 German soldiers were killed or went missing and 9,000 were wounded. Most of Warsaw's surviving civilians were deported by the Germans to nearby camps, and 65,000 were soon transferred to concentration camps. About 100,000 were taken to do forced labor in the Reich, while the rest were spread out over the *Generalgouvernement*.[9]

Yitzhak Zuckerman and Zivia Lubetkin found shelter with a Polish doctor, Stanislaw Switala, who offered them refuge in his hospital, along with Tuvia Borzykowski and several other members of the ŻOB.[10] Other Jewish fighters, like Bernard Goldstein, passed up opportunities to blend in with Poles in prisioner of war camps, choosing instead to remain hiding in a bunker until liberation.[11]

Soviet troops liberated Warsaw on January 17, 1945, after failing to intervene as the Germans crushed the revolt, revealing a completely devastated Warsaw. Only 174,000 people were left in the city and, according to Polish data, approximately 11,500 of the survivors were Jews.[12] Zuckerman later recalled that after liberation, he finally wept:

> For me, January 17, the day the Soviet forces entered Warsaw, was one of the saddest days of my life. I wanted to weep, and not tears of joy. This was the first time I wanted to weep. Apparently that was a human weakness. . . . Zivia had never seen me cry because I had never cried. Our comrades hadn't seen me in a state of depression. I had to live, to hold

> out; but on January 17, everything was shaken. Of course, other days followed: going out to the towns, searching. It's not easy to be the last of the Mohicans![13]

Zuckerman and Zivia soon reconnected with Adolf Berman and set about the work of "assembling the remnants." After connecting with the newly formed branch of the Jewish Central Committee in the Praga suburb of Warsaw, Zuckerman, Lubetkin, and Adolf and Basya Berman traveled to Lublin where they met Jews who had survived in other parts of Eastern Europe, including Abba Kovner, Mordechai Rosman, Leib Lewidovski, and Yosef Sklar.[14]

Throughout 1944 and the beginning of 1945, the surviving members of the ŻOB and Jewish National Committee continued to maintain contact with the Jewish Agency, the Joint Distribution Committee (JDC), and others, explaining the dire situation that continued to confront the Jews who had managed to remain alive in Poland. Likewise, the JDC, the Jewish Labor Committee, and others struggled to distribute funding to what remained of Polish Jewry. Despite the cooperation between members of the Jewish National Committee, the ŻOB, and the Bund in Poland, disputes over allocation of resources sent from abroad persisted.[15] In a letter sent by Adolf Berman on March 7, 1945, to Yitzhak Gruenbaum, a member of the Jewish Agency's Joint Rescue Committee, Berman provided details on the fate of movement activists and requested that Gruenbaum expedite the transfer of funds for much needed work in Poland. Fifty thousand Jews had been registered since liberation and the previous shipment of funds sent from the Yishuv had been quickly distributed. Berman explained to Gruenbaum that he was now serving (since the liberation) as a delegate to the KRN (State National Council) and was chosen as vice chairman of the Central Committee of the Jews in Poland, established in October 1944. Among the activists of the ŻOB and the Jewish National Committee, Berman reported the following "alive and active": Yitzhak Zuckerman, Zivia Lubetkin, (David) Daniel Guzik, Hirsch Wasser, (Batya) Basia Berman, Josef Sak, Stefan (Shalom) Grajek, and others.[16] He added that since April 1944 none of the promised funds from overseas had been received by the

Rescue Committee, nor did an expected infusion of cash from the Joint arrive. He asked that the matter be dealt with.[17]

Organizing the Surviving Population in Poland

The relief work undertaken by the Jewish National Committee, the surviving members of the ŻOB, and the Coordinating Committee would quickly be translated into leadership of the surviving remnant in the newly liberated areas of Poland. Access to resources proved vital in organizing the surviving Jewish public, as did wartime credit built up by leaders of the resistance. At the same time, liberated Jews first searched for family and friends, looking for news of who had survived and how others—most—had perished. From the beginning, it was altogether unclear what sort of Jewish population existed in the wake of the war in Poland.[18] Reports emerging from Lublin by January 1945 did not paint a promising portrait of the Jewish situation. The Jewish population continued to be ravaged by disease and malnutrition and the public kitchens could not provide sufficient food to satisfy the minimum needs of the hungry and the needy. Jews had considerable difficulties regaining possession of lost property, both individually and communally. While many Jewish orphans were wandering the streets of Lublin, the Jewish orphanage there continued to be occupied by Polish institutions. Surviving Jews faced continuing violence and hostility from the local population, suffering both physical and verbal attacks, as well as vandalism to their homes and shops.[19] An estimated 10–12 percent of the Jewish population in Poland in 1945 was between the ages of 15 and 20.[20]

The first recourse for many young Jewish survivors in Poland was to turn to the local Jewish committees that had been formed, seeking solutions to their most pressing needs, including food, shelter, health, and security, before they could turn to the larger questions of how and where to continue their lives. Beginning in the summer of 1944 in eastern Poland, Jewish survivors rapidly organized a system of communal and political organizations.[21] The new Communist-dominated government allowed a number of Jewish political parties and organizations to operate freely. Almost all prewar parties were reconstructed and legally recognized by the Polish government, including the Bund (and its youth organization, Tsukunft); Marxist Zionist parties like Left Poalei Zion (youth group: Borochov Youth), and youth movements like Hashomer Hatzair; non-Marxist socialist and bourgeois Zionist groups like Poalei Zion Z.S., Dror, Ichud, and Hitachdut; and the religious Zionist Mizrachi. Of the major prewar parties only the ultraorthodox Agudas Yisroel and right-wing Revisionist Zionists were not officially recognized.[22] As many of the liberated Jews began to turn to the Jewish committees for assistance, the ability of vying political groups to provide for survivors would go a long way toward securing a crucial base for political support and success.[23] Bundist, Communist, and Zionist groups jostled for control of the Jewish committees in liberated cities, struggling to secure access to resources provided for the Jewish community of survivors.[24]

The first convention of the Central Committee of Polish Jews (CKZP), headed by Emil Sommerstein, a prewar Zionist activist and Zionist deputy to the Sejm, was held on November 29, 1944, in Lublin.[25] From the outset, although dominated by a Zionist majority, the CKZP leadership consisted of people belonging to prewar political parties or underground organizations set up during the war, including Communists and Bundists, as well as members of the Jewish Fighting Organization and former partisans.[26] While the Zionists rejected any potential for a viable future in Poland and advocated emigration, the Bund charged the Zionists with being indifferent to the needs of the Jewish community, alleging that the Zionists manipulated the desperation of the Jewish refugees for their own ends.[27] The Bund was committed to fighting together with the Polish working class in Poland's postwar redevelopment and accused Zionist leaders of attempting to create a state of panic in order to encourage emigration. In January 1945, the surviving leaders of the Bund in Poland—Leon Feiner, Salo Fiszgrund, and Bernard Goldstein—also came to Lublin to organize. Having participated in the Polish government-in-exile during the war, the postwar situation, and the growing realization that Poland would fall under the Soviet sphere of influence, left the Bund in a bind. Would the Bund maintain its alliance with the nationalist government-in-exile, or would they seek to form an alliance with pro-Soviet forces in order to guarantee protection of the Jewish population in Poland into the future? While they had not forgotten the persecution of the Bund in the Soviet Union (and the murders of Henryk Ehrlich and Viktor Alter, interwar leaders of the Bund in Poland executed on Stalin's orders in the USSR), Bundist leaders ultimately calculated that the only hope for a Bundist future in Poland would rest in a rapprochement with the Soviets.[28]

Any measure of wartime détente between the Zionists and Bundists soon gave way to intense postwar political competition over leadership of the Jewish public, especially in organizing what remained of Jewish youth. Political calculations notwithstanding, support on the ground would be determined by the ability of the various Jewish groups to provide services. Through children's homes and kibbutzim, the political parties competed for children—both those who had survived in Poland and later those returning from the Soviet Union. Zionist youth movements parlayed their wartime leadership in the resistance into a claim for postwar leadership of the Jewish public, arguing they were best equipped to lead the surviving population into the future (and out of Poland, with the Bricha, the semiorganized clandestine movement of escape and repatriation). For the political parties vying for control of the committees, Jewish youth formed a vital constituency, not only because of the number of youths who had survived, but as the future of their movements. For the youth who turned to the committees, ideological debates over the Jewish future were largely beside the point. Their allegiance would be determined by the ability of political groups to provide for their basic needs and, as it became increasingly clear that Poland remained unsafe for Jews after the war, the ability to offer a promise of departure. Some Bundists also made the decision that remaining in Poland would be impossible, and many chose to depart, making their way to the displaced persons (DP) camps in Germany and Austria, and eventually to destinations in America, Australia, Argentina, and elsewhere.[29]

Crucially, wartime involvement in the resistance, with the Warsaw Ghetto Uprising the symbol of greatest distinction, would be useful in recruiting young survivors into both the Bund and Zionist groups. But would wartime resistance be understood by survivors to have been part of the struggle to build a free and democratic Poland or part of the struggle to build a Jewish state?

The Postwar Organization of the Youth Movement and Bricha

When Zuckerman and Lubetkin arrived in Lublin on January 20, 1945, they discovered there was a general consensus on the need for the Zionist solution by this budding leadership, and agreement was reached on the official formation of a Bricha movement, with a coordinating committee led by the partisans Mordechai Rosman, Nisan Resnik, and ŻOB veteran fighter Stefan Grajek.[30] While the members of this initial group in Lublin were split over the need for immediate or gradual departure, those who remained in Lublin and later in Warsaw focused their efforts on the organization of the Jewish people for departure from Poland.

Abba Kovner, who had been the leader of the Jewish underground in Vilna and then fought with partisans, argued that any effort to reestablish Jewish institutions on the accursed European soil would be a betrayal of the Jewish dead.[31] While Zuckerman agreed with Kovner over the need for departure from Poland, he rejected immediate departure and Kovner's ideas for revenge. (Ultimately, Kovner would form a revenge group of fifty like-minded survivors, who tried to organize a mass operation meant to poison six million Germans. It is possible the failure to organize a revolt in the Vilna ghetto may have motivated Kovner's desire for postwar revenge; Zuckerman, Lubetkin, and others had indeed already seen "German blood flowing in the streets.") Instead, Antek argued that youth movement activists could not desert the Jewish public and needed to remain behind in order to assist in organization. Kovner, Kempner, Lidovsky, and Lubetkin left with a group in March 1945 to explore a path of possible departure via Romania; Zuckerman and (later, after her return from Romania) Lubetkin stayed behind to begin organizing what was left of the Jewish public. Kazik, who was able to find his parents in Grodzisk after liberation, also traveled to Romania in the spring of 1945, before returning to Poland to help organize groups for departure, eventually leading a group from Czechoslovakia to Hungary. Kazik would join Kovner's revenge group, participating in a failed attempt to poison the bread supply at a prison camp for SS-officers near Dachau.[32]

Shalom Cholawski, a wartime leader of the underground in Niezwicz and leader of the uprising there, who later fled to the forest and joined the partisans as part of the Zhukov partisan unit, was one of the founders of the Pachach (PHH—Partisans, Soldiers, and Pioneers) movement with Yitzhak Zuckerman after the war.[33] Part of their success in recruiting new members, he later argued, derived from the fact that the partisans and ghetto fighters "embodied the powerful yearning for battle and revenge: they were determined to continue the struggle."[34] As Zuckerman suggested, the leadership role of HeHalutz in the resistance left them in the best position to lead Jewish youth in Poland following the war. While the Jewish people as a whole may have been ill-prepared to confront the challenge, it was the movements affiliated with the labor Zionist groups who took the lead in the resistance and thus needed to take the lead in organizing what remained of Jewish youth in Eastern Europe, to lead them to the Land of Israel. Zuckerman understood that after the war, young survivors still needed leadership and guidance for the future. While Kovner and his followers were focused on channeling rage into revenge, Zuckerman sought to channel this energy into organizing the people and creating a Jewish state, while also memorializing the fallen members of the Jewish underground.

Marking the Second Anniversary of the Revolt

On April 19, 1945, surviving members of the ŻOB in Warsaw set up the first memorial stone at the bunker at Mila 18.[35]

Marking the second anniversary of the Warsaw Ghetto Uprising in Poland in April 1945, the president of the Polish provisional government, Edward Osuba-Morawski, acknowledged the struggle in the Warsaw ghetto as part of the struggle of the Polish nation. "The insurrection in the Warsaw Ghetto was a fitting reply to the massacre of over 3,000,000 Polish Jews by the Germans," President Edward Osuba-Morawski said in a statement broadcast over the Lublin radio on the occasion of the second

An assembly in Warsaw on the second anniversary of the ghetto uprising. In the photo: Yitzhak Zuckerman (center, in the black coat) and Tuvia Borzykowski (seventh from the left). In the foreground are wreaths and a placard in Polish: "Honor to the heroes who fell in battle." The Judenrat building appears in the background. Photographed on April 19, 1945. (Ghetto Fighters House Archives, catalog no. 20940)

anniversary of the revolt. Declaring that "Polish democracy acknowledges the ghetto battle as part of its own struggle," Morawski said that "today there is no room for racialism and anti-Semitism in Poland." In a statement sent from London to Poland on the occasion of the anniversary, the Bundist leader Emanuel Szerer likewise linked the role played by Jews in the revolt to a new commitment of the Polish republic to rebuild a democratic and free future: "that a guarantee that Jews and non-Jews, in the future, will live in freedom, equality, and justice in Poland will simply be a repayment of democracy's debt to the Jews for the battle in Warsaw and other contributions."[36] In Palestine, the Hebrew press carried editorials marking the anniversary of the ghetto revolt on April 19, 1945.[37]

In New York, the American Federation of Polish Jews organized a mass meeting at the Hotel Commodore, where two thousand people marked the second anniversary of the uprising with a mass recitation of the Kaddish prayer.[38] New York Governor Thomas E. Dewey paid tribute to the "tens of thousands of Polish Jews who died as martyrs in a desperate resistance against the Nazi oppressors. I join in the fervent prayer." Governor Dewey's message said, "of the American Jews of Polish background that the Jewish culture of Poland may be revived and brought to now flower in a Polish nation devoted to liberty and personal freedom in a world at peace." Herbert C. Pell, former American representative on the United Nations War Crimes Commission, voiced a tribute to the late President Roosevelt (who had passed away on April 12, 1945) and a pledge of support from President Truman.

At Carnegie Hall, the American League for a Free Palestine (led by Peter Bergson, a.k.a. Hillel Cook) held a "Never Back to the Ghetto Rally." The Jewish Labor Committee scheduled a photographic and documentary exhibition at the Vanderbilt Gallery, "Heroes and Martyrs of the Ghettos," running April 19 to May 25, with opening ceremonies to be addressed by Governor Dewey. It was billed as the "first exhibition to deal with Jewish resistance against the Nazis."[39]

An outline for the exhibit explained the goals:

> To display dramatically the story of Jewish persecution under Nazism, with particular emphasis on the murdered Jews of the Warsaw Ghetto, and their heroic resistance. [. . .] It will be the aim of the exhibit to impress on the American public at large the brutality and the ruthlessness with which the Nazis have undertaken to exterminate the Jews; the heroism with which the Jews have attempted to resist; the necessity for prompt and effective aid to those Jews who still survive.[40]

The exhibition was aimed at a broad public audience and began by demonstrating the place of Jewish culture in modern life and "Jewish contributions to Human culture" in the fields of philosophy, religion, literature, language, art, science, commerce, and labor. A second section on Jewish culture in twentieth-century Europe sought to "stress the fact that Jews in Europe lived a typical community life, participated in typical cultural and vocational pursuits, and accept(ed) full community responsibilities." For the designers of the exhibit, it seemed important to communicate that Jewish people had not only made important contributions to the modern world but were a "typical" people who had become part of the societies in which they live.

The Jewish Labor Committee also wanted to use the exhibit to demonstrate that the threat of Nazism was directed not only against the Jews but was "anti-Catholic, anti-Christian, anti-Semitic, and for paganism." Nazis were "against other people," including anti-French, anti-Negro, anti-Russian, anti-American, anti-British, anti-Polish, "for the Herrenvolk," and above all, antidemocratic and fascist. Ultimately, the exhibit aimed to make the case that the Jewish heroes of the ghetto contributed to the worldwide struggle against fascism, thus bolstering the place of Jews in American society.[41]

In order to maximize the impact of the exhibition the Jewish Labor Committee organized an informal writers committee to consult on it, sending invitations to prominent writers and publishers from Time-Life Magazine and Alfred A. Knopf to consult on "how best to spotlight this most unusual undertaking on a national scale."[42] Paul Muni (born Meshulem Meir Weisenfreund, a star of the Yiddish theater in New York and Academy Award winner in 1937 for his role as Louis Pasteur), performed at the opening of the exhibition, reading the last manifesto of the ŻOB, as well as excerpts from the last letter of Szmuel Zygielbojm.[43] It is noteworthy that the title of the exhibition, "Heroes and Martyrs" (with an exhibit catalogue graced by a sketched image of a gaunt man presumably dying in the ghetto) reinforced a dichotomy of Jewish behavior that would persist long after the war.

The Context of Liberation

One week before the April 19, 1945, exhibit, American forces from the Sixth Armored Division, Third Army, liberated the Buchenwald concentration camp on April 11, 1945, where they found more than twenty-one thousand people, exhausted, emaciated, many near death. The following day, General Eisenhower visited Ohrdruf, a subcamp of Buchenwald and the first camp liberated by U.S. troops. When the soldiers of the Fourth Armored Division entered the camp, they discovered piles of bodies, some covered with lime, and others partially incinerated on pyres. In a subsequent cable to General George C. Marshall, the head of the Joint Chiefs of Staff in Washington, Eisenhower described his trip to Ohrdruf, "*the most interesting—although horrible—sight that I encountered during the trip was a visit to a German internment camp near Gotha. The things I saw beggar description.*"[44] General Eisenhower was not only disturbed by the Nazi crimes he had discovered at Ohrdruf but was also determined that the world must know what happened in the concentration camps. On April 19, he again cabled Marshall, this time with a request to bring members of Congress and journalists to the newly liberated camps so that they could bring the horrible truth about Nazi atrocities to the American public.[45] That same day, Marshall received permission from the secretary of war, Henry Lewis Stimson, and President Harry S. Truman for these delegations to visit the liberated camps. Ohrdruf made a powerful impression on General George S. Patton as well. He described it as "one of the most appalling sights that I have ever seen." Ten days later, on April 29, American forces liberated Dachau about ten miles northwest of Munich. Over sixty thousand prisoners were found at the camp, in addition to piles of bodies brought to the camp at the end of the war.

On May 8, 1945, headlines in the general and Jewish press declared the end of the war in Europe. The Jewish Telegraphic Agency bulletin for May 8 declared "Jews throughout the World Greet V-E Day, Rejoice at Final Destruction of Nazism."[46] In the Yishuv, spontaneous demonstrations took place in the streets, while synagogue services recited special prayers issued by the chief rabbinate. Dr. John Slawson, vice president of the American Jewish Committee, declared that "the remnants of the Jews of Europe and the free Jewish communities everywhere share the joy of free men," but warned "this victory will not be complete if humanity does not learn the most significant lesson of the struggle—the setting of one group against another, one nationality against another, must lead to strife and world conflagrations." Dr. Israel Goldstein, president of the Zionist Organization of America, expressed hope that V-E day would "open the eyes of the world to the reality and scope of the Jewish problem and to an understanding that the solution of this problem is an inextricable part of a world charter for a just peace."[47] For Jewish communities around the world, the end of the war meant coming to terms with the destruction of a civilization, amidst questions of who, if anyone, had survived, and discussions over how to memorialize the catastrophe.

In the pages of *Davar* on May 25, Mordecai Shenhavi laid out his vision for *Yad Vashem Legolah Hanihrevet* in order to memorialize the "Millions with neither a grave nor a gravestone (a monument). . . . For these millions of holy brethren, we are obligated to create an eternal memorial." Shenhavi's goal was to "build an everlasting memorial—a teacher and guide for future generations . . . (to) preserve the memory of each individual victim and allow every Jew to consecrate the memory of the victims dear to him." A central part of Shenhavi's vision included erecting a monument to Jewish heroism:

> The Warsaw Revolt—the symbol of the heroism of our brothers and sisters in the horrible war; our part in the underground armies; the heroism of the individual—will all these remain only legends and stories told by heart? We will erect a monument for the bravery of Israel, a monument which will carry for the future the will of the people to live and exist.

As such, the only appropriate date for commemoration was a "Warsaw Ghetto Day":

> A "Warsaw Ghetto Day" shall be declared as a day of remembrance and a celebration of heroism. On that day the Yishuv and delegations from all Diaspora countries shall participate in mass pilgrimages to the Hall of Remembrance. Mass graves in the countries of [our] suffering and the Jewish cemeteries shall also be sites of pilgrimage on that day. Memorial services shall be held at the Monument

> to the Unknown Victim—and there shall be one symbol that unites the entire nation in memory of that bitter era and the lesson that the ghetto fighters taught us. . . . [Remembrance Day] shall enhance the memory of the fallen until it becomes an enduring bond between the Jewish people and its destiny, and it shall serve as an important foundation on our people's path to building its country.[48]

Shenhavi emphasized that Yad Vashem—the conceptual idea for a memorial—needed to be in the Land of Israel, "the center of the national revival. . . . This everlasting memorial can and should be built only in the place where the Jewish national pulse is felt. Only Eretz Israel knows how to host and safeguard this national asset."[49]

As the scholar Mooli Brog notes, after Shenhavi's plan was laid out, the General Zionist Council, convening in London in August 1945, decided to appoint the Jewish National Council, the main executive institution of the Yishuv, to the task of commemorating the Holocaust in Palestine. The conference resolved that the memorial should be designed in such a way as to stress "the location of its hub—Jerusalem. The project, which will expand to the entire country, will include memorial forests and schools for child survivors."[50]

Already in 1942, Mordechai Shenhavi had begun to imagine what such a memorial, situated in the Land of Israel, might look like. Shenhavi, a founder of the socialist-Zionist Hashomer Hatzair youth movement and a member of Kibbutz Mishmar Ha'emek, envisioned a national memorial site in Palestine for Jewish victims. As Brog has argued, Shenhavi's plans for Yad Vashem lay dormant for several years as the Yishuv focused on other matters deemed more pressing than commemoration—amid concerns over finances, the security situation in Palestine, and a general ambivalence over memorializing the destroyed Diaspora. After two years without discussion of his plans, however, the Jewish National Fund leaders came back to Shenhavi's proposal in February 1945, likely in response to a report about a new commemoration plan on the agenda of the World Jewish Congress in the United States.[51] The WJC plan, drafted by Baruch

Zuckerman and Jacob Helman, called on the World Jewish Congress, the Jewish Agency, and Jewish religious institutions to declare a permanent day of mourning and "to make pilgrimages to the memorial on that day. The most appropriate day is the Jewish date that corresponds to April 19, 1943," the day when the Warsaw Ghetto Uprising began.[52] As other ideas began to emerge about appropriate memorialization of the victims of the Shoah in the Land of Israel, Shenhavi hastened to renew interest in his ideas. Leaders of the Jewish National Fund and Keren Hayesod, the fundraising arm of the Zionist movement, also argued that such a memorial should only be located in Israel in a manifesto aimed at the American Jewish community:

> for a special project of thanksgiving, a project of rescue, building, resurrection, and redemption! . . . Jews who have miraculously survived the horrors of physical and spiritual annihilation—only if they mobilize at this historic moment for a creative, redemptive enterprise will they justify the miracle that they have experienced. . . . Eretz Israel is ready. By order of [Divine] Providence, it was miraculously spared from the inferno so that it could fulfill its historical role: to rebuild the battered Jewish people. It stands strong. It awaits the grand act of all the Jewish masses wherever they are.[53]

While Shenhavi envisioned the memorial project being a center of moral support for the nation and all diaspora Jewry, for the Zionist members of the Jewish Fighting Organization the revolt continued to be clear evidence of the need for the creation of the Jewish state. Two parallel processes had begun to crystallize: 1) The memory of the Warsaw Ghetto Uprising would prove useful in mobilizing surviving Jews in the struggle for the creation of a Jewish state and 2) the Jewish national home would be deemed the only appropriate place to commemorate and celebrate the heroism of the Jewish fighters.

HeHalutz, the Bricha, and the Organization of Surviving Jewish Youth

As leaders in the Yishuv came to see the Warsaw Ghetto Uprising as the symbolic focus for postwar commemorations of the destruction of European Jewry, activists from the Jewish underground came to see the leadership role played by their movement members as a recruiting tool to enlist surviving Jews in the Bricha. Yitzhak Zuckerman, writing in June 1945 to friends and members of the movement in Romania, explained that only HeHalutz, which had maintained a sense of solidarity embedded in their link to the Land of Israel before and during the war, could lead the Jewish youth in postwar Poland.[54] In his immediate postwar testimonies, Zuckerman and (later Lubetkin) argued that only those imbued with the Diaspora-negating Zionist ideology had the courage to resist (this betrayed a consistent inability to recognize the contributions of other resistance movements—notably the Bund and the Revisionists—in his reporting on the revolt). As he wrote in his June 1945 letter to members of HeHalutz:

> A large portion of our people became extinct before our eyes. Why were so many millions made extinct? Because we were so many. And why were we so many? Because we are a rotten people [a *paskudne folk*], a people who slept at the time we needed to work, worked in the time we needed to fight, and who did not have a sense for this small thing, which exists in the blood of every *sheygetzel*—the instinct to defend its own land.[55]

While acknowledging that had the Germans reached Palestine, the result would have been the same (mass death of Jews) he also noted the difference between how Jews in the Land of Israel would have responded where not only five hundred but hundreds of thousands would have fought. And who led the ghetto revolts?

> Who fought? Who led the battles? Out of 22 fighting groups in the Warsaw ghetto only one of the groups was

> made up of civilians (of the Noar Tzioni) and the remaining were 21 groups from the labor movements; and of these 21 labor groups and youth 75% of these were ours! And who were the leaders, this you know. Already in the January revolt, in the Warsaw ghetto, only Hehalutz fought. Who stood to defend our honor in Kraków? Our movement and the wonderful people of Akiva, who during the war were connected by thousands of threads to us and to the Halutz, and the Jewish movement of the PPR. Besides them no one else! Who defended Czenstachow, Bialystok? And who organized the different fighting organizations and the different camps? . . . In a word: did our movement stand up to the historic test? It stood! Was our education correct? It was correct! To know to work in a time of peace and to know to fight in a time of war. And what are the conclusions?[56]

For Zuckerman, HeHalutz, animated by a powerful Zionist ideology and a connection to the land of Israel, inspired the resistance and stood up to the historic test in a way the Polish Jewish masses could not. He concluded his letter to the movement members by discussing the importance of unity among the movements to work together to educate the youth.

> In sum, did He-Halutz disappoint? Absolutely not! And the conclusion is that no other force has the power to exalt and raise the youth except He-Halutz. Instead of fading, we should reinforce its strength. The way of He-Halutz is the way of all Jewish youth. We want a working nation and a working youth; that is our lesson and our ambition. . . . Our destiny here is to work and to fight. Our destiny is to be connected with the building and fighting portion of the settlement and the land—with the Histadrut.[57]

For Zuckerman, HeHalutz was no longer the province of only the "elite" youth in the Jewish community; now, "the way of He-Halutz (was) the way of all Jewish youth." Determined to continue on in Poland in order to organize what was left of Polish Jewry, and especially Jewish youth in Poland, Zuckerman was convinced that the leadership role of the pioneering Zionist youth movements during the war made them the natural leaders of surviving Polish Jewry. Zuckerman was also convinced that the surviving youth could play a vital role in the struggle to create a Jewish state.

Zuckerman realized the need to work on the ground, organize kibbutzim, and provide aid, thus tending to the needs of the Jewish population on an immediate level, and not just on an ideological basis. This choice to focus on the majority of Jewish youth and not just the elite would entail a significant shift in the approach of Zionist movements after the war, not only in the numbers who joined but in the perceived ideological "quality" of the new membership as well. The movements viewed the kibbutzim as a method of enlisting followers and expanding the ranks of the Zionist parties, but the youth who joined the kibbutzim tended to stay because of the psychological support they derived from the communal structure, which proved highly therapeutic for many of the survivors. In the kibbutzim, youth learned Jewish history, Hebrew, movement folksongs, principles of socialism, and more. The communal setting created a sense of family and emphasized the positive potential of a Jewish future, despite the dark Jewish past. Just as importantly, the identification of the youth movements and the individual kibbutz groups with the wartime resistance of the heroic ghetto fighters substituted the individual experiences of the young members for a part in the collective and heroic struggle of the Jewish people in a larger cause—providing meaning to their lives in the aftermath of destruction.

The impressive ability of the pioneering youth movements to assert control over the Zionist movement in Poland by the end of 1945 augured well for their ability to seize control of the *She'erit Hapletah* (surviving remnant) in postwar Europe.[58] It was this growth in kibbutz membership that enabled Yitzhak Zuckerman, attending the first Zionist conference to be held since the end of the war, to proclaim in London in August 1945:

> Friends! Poland can provide one thousand chalutzim [pioneers] each month. The Jewish youth is completely oriented

> towards aliyah. 1500 Jewish youths are located today in kibbutzei-hakhsharah, and thousands more will join: it is not only that they are preparing themselves for aliyah to Eretz Yisrael, but that they strive to make aliyah with all their might, and *they will go up*.[59]

The growth in membership in the kibbutzim of the youth movements suggests that their organization, access to resources, emergence as a gathering place for youth, and promise of departure all enabled them to organize Jewish youth after the war more successfully than any other organization. The Jewish youth found them to be welcoming homes that could provide them with the camaraderie, education, and above all, warmth that they sought after the war.

Two sources provided the majority of funding for the kibbutzim of the youth movements and Bricha after the war: local Jewish committees and the American Jewish Joint Distribution Committee (JDC). Yitzhak Zuckerman and others were highly successful in obtaining funds for kibbutzim from local committees.[60] As Zuckerman noted later, he took advantage of his position on the Central Committee of Polish Jews to secure funds for the HeHalutz activities.[61] He was also successful in tapping connections in the JDC as a source for Bricha funding. Zuckerman leveraged his close wartime relationship with the JDC representative in Warsaw, David Guzik (who had helped finance the Warsaw Ghetto Uprising and worked with the Jewish National Committee after the revolt), to continue JDC support for his efforts after Guzik reestablished the JDC office in Warsaw after the war.[62] As Zuckerman recalled in his memoirs, his early connections with the Joint were vital not only in securing money for Dror, but in assisting the Joint in establishing connections in Poland. Zuckerman's networking enabled him to obtain funding not only for his own movement (Dror), for Hehalutz in general, but also to make requests on behalf of the Jewish Agency for Palestine as needed—all through his close connections to Guzik and Joe Schwartz, director of European operations for the JDC.[63]

According to Yochanan Cohen, one of the emissaries from the Yishuv and among the first to arrive in Poland to assist with organizing immigration activities, most of the responsibility for funding the Bricha fell on the broad shoulders of the JDC.[64] Thus, access to resources, wartime leadership, a compelling and practical solution to the postwar displacement of the surviving population, and a growing demand for departure from Poland all worked to place the surviving ghetto fighters, Zuckerman in particular, in a leading role among the surviving population in Poland, especially among those who gravitated toward the Bricha. It should come as no surprise then, that memory of the Warsaw Ghetto Uprising, in particular, and resistance in general, would play a central unifying role among the surviving population. The centrality of wartime resistance was not the exclusive province of the Zionist movements, however; on the contrary, Bundist leaders also sought to highlight their wartime role in the resistance to recruit followers afterward. Nonetheless, the Bricha was in many respects a continuation of the wartime activity of the Jewish underground, and in particular of the Jewish Fighting Organization, led in the postwar period by Yitzhak Zuckerman. For the youth movements, the wartime struggle against Nazi oppression would be translated into a postwar struggle for the creation of the Jewish state.

Over the course of 1945 and 1946, the movement would continue to grow, with some 110,000 Polish Jews choosing to depart Poland with the Bricha even before the Kielce pogrom of July 1946; of these, some 33,600 were youth organized in kibbutzim.[65] Regardless of what their rationale was for joining the kibbutzim, these groups formed the backbone of the Bricha and assisted in pushing the problem of Jewish refugees to the center of British and American governmental attention. Continued antisemitism in Poland after the war convinced many surviving Jews to seek a secure future elsewhere.

In addition to organizing children and youth in kibbutz groups, partisans who emerged from the forests or returned from the Soviet Union also joined the newly formed organization of Partisans, Soldiers, and Pioneers (Pachach). According to Shalom Cholawski, a member of Hashomer Hatzair and the driving force in organizing Pachach, the organization was able to channel the survivors' drive for revenge into the struggle for the creation of the state.[66] Yitzhak Zuckerman encouraged Cholawski to establish the pioneers and partisans group.[67] As 1945 progressed and more Jews returned from the Soviet Union, Jewish veterans of the Polish Army and the Red Army joined the partisans and pioneers. The members of Pachach—numbering in the thousands—offered guidance and encouragement to the *She'erit Hapletah* in Poland and the camps in Germany, Austria, and Italy as they embarked on what was technically an illegal trek to Eretz Israel. Cholawski argues that the partisans and ghetto fighters inspired the youth movements, occupying a vital place in the survivors' inner world and in public life as well based in large part on the moral authority they had accrued through resistance activities during the war. Pachach headquarters were in Lodz, and the main branches were set up in Lodz, Kraków, Walbrzych, Lublin, Bytom, Białystok, and Liegnitz.[68] In February 1946, the group held its first conference in Lodz; a manifesto directed at the Jewish soldiers of Poland was published in the movement newspaper, *Nasza Walka* (Our struggle):

> 16,000 Jews fought in the ranks of the Polish army. . . . Must the Jewish fighting force, which only yesterday executed heroic deeds, today disintegrate into thousands of fragmentary units in the new reality? We are united by yesterday's combat, today's pain, and faith in tomorrow.[69]

Pachach worked to collect the testimonies of partisans and ghetto fighters, publishing some of the accounts of armed Jewish resistance in the pages of its journal *Farn Folk*, distributed in the Jewish DP camps after the war. Many of these accounts would be translated into English and subsequently published in the first postwar histories of the resistance (such as Marie Syrkin's *Blessed Is the Match*, to be discussed in chapter 8) making *Farn Folk* an important source for early research on resistance.[70]

In the months after liberation, the surviving partisans and ghetto fighters rose to positions of prominence in leading what remained of European Jewry. At the special conference of the World Jewish Congress, meeting in London on August 19–23, 1945, Adolf Berman, Stefan Grajek, and Yitzhak Zuckerman were among the delegates representing Polish Jewry.

As the report of the conference summarized, resistance leaders from Belgium, France, Italy, and Poland related how "in the most perilous of circumstances the Jews fought for liberty and freedom not only for themselves but for civilization and democratic humanity at large."[71]

> But the speakers did not come merely to mourn their Jewish dead, massacred by the satanic carnage of Hitlerism. Every resistance leader re-affirmed the faith of their Jewish communities in a Jewish National Home in Palestine and in the ideals of democracy and progressive civilization for which they fought, and for which the Jewish people sacrificed six million martyrs.

The summary of the resistance leaders' presentations emphasized that the destruction of European Jewry, the "sacrifice of six million martyrs" would not be completely without meaning—for the continued faith of those same leaders in the creation of a Jewish state, and in defending the ideals of democracy and progress, could provide some hope for the future. Dr. Stephen S. Wise was inspired by the heroism of the resistance leaders, who reminded him of the Jewish heroes of old:

> Listening to these epic stories of Jewish resistance, [I have] seen a vision of Jewish unity, Jewish solidarity and Jewish survival . . . reaffirming my faith in the oneness of the Jewish people which, from Modin in the times of the Maccabees to Warsaw in our own day, was forever the people of Resistance always in the forefront of the struggle for Liberty and Freedom.

Nearly three months later, on November 11, 1945 (Armistice Day), a conference of Jewish fighters gathered ("for the first time in history") in Paris, including "soldiers from the Jewish Brigade, American Jewish soldiers, partisans from Lithuania, Poland, and Russia." The proceedings of the conference were reprinted in *Unzer Veg* (Our way), the central organ of the Liberated

Jews in Germany, which noted the participation of Dr. Blumovicz, a former partisan leader in Belarus, who came from the DP camps in Germany. Ben-Gurion, speaking on behalf of the Jewish Agency for Palestine, greeted "Jewish soldiers and fighters" and celebrated the example of the fighters:

> In the last war we saw a new occurrence—not just soldiers in uniforms—but "Resistance"—the resistance of underground people. . . . But this is a new phenomenon only in European history—but not for the Jewish people. The entire history of our people is an incessant resistance between not wanting to forego our national and religious ideals and the universal ideals of mankind; the resistance of a small people against a large, antagonistic world.

Linking the struggle of the resistance during the war with the continued struggle to build the Jewish state, Ben-Gurion argued that Jews now needed to stand up against the British in order to see the establishment of that state. "This is the commandment of a million fighting Jewish soldiers, and six million murdered, and generations of Jews who have been victims. Jewish independence—and a Jewish state!" (The transcript noted "long-lasting, stormy applause.") Grabowski, speaking on behalf of the Jewish Brigade, also greeted the Jewish fighters gathered at the conference. "We were once perceived as cowards, as deserters from the military. But in the last world war the Jews informed the world, that they are the first to go into battle. . . . Jews must fight for their own home: a Jewish home, a Jewish state!" The conference then adopted resolutions to call for a worldwide organization of Jewish fighters—"Brit Lochamim Yehudim"—which would support the creation of a free Jewish land of Israel.[72]

Organizing the Surviving Remnant in Postwar Germany

The representatives of the Central Committee of Liberated Jews came to the Conference of Jewish Fighters from the displaced persons camps of postwar Germany, where the majority of the Jewish population, perhaps some thirty-five out of fifty thousand liberated in Germany, was in the American zone of occupation in Germany, many of them around Munich. While a small population of surviving Jews had been liberated from concentration camps in Germany, the arrival of large number of displaced persons traveling in kibbutz groups with the Bricha dramatically reshaped the demography of the surviving population there. The Jewish survivors in Germany organized quickly amongst themselves to represent the needs of the surviving Jewish population in the summer of 1945, with the Central Committee of Liberated Jews forming in the American zone under the leadership of Samuel Gringauz and Zalman Grinberg, and the Central Committee of Liberated Jews in the British zone under the leadership of Josef Rosensaft. Complaints of continuing deprivation and poor organization of recovery coming from Jewish chaplains and the people themselves eventually prompted American officials to take a greater interest in the problem of the displaced persons. President Truman dispatched Earl Harrison to survey conditions, and in his scathing report back to Truman, Harrison concluded that we are "treating the Jews as the Nazis treated them except that we do not exterminate them." He proposed that Jews be separated in their own camps—until then they had been forced to live with other national groups and former collaborators—and, to resolve their refugee status, he proposed that one hundred thousand immigration certificates to Palestine be granted immediately. Following Harrison's report, American authorities, under the leadership of General Eisenhower, worked to ameliorate conditions for Jewish displaced persons, moving Jews to separate camps and agreeing to the appointment of an Adviser for Jewish Affairs.

While the American Jewish Joint Distribution Committee did not gain access to the survivors until the beginning of August 1945, its first demographic studies in the American zone of Germany indicated a surviving population of Jews with almost no children under age five, and a disproportionate number between the ages of fifteen to thirty.[73] The big influx of Bricha groups in the summer of 1946 "brought a fresh human element," with repatriates from the Soviet Union, Poland, and elsewhere in Eastern Europe.[74] The arrival of Bricha groups led to a noticeable shift in the displaced persons population, with increasing numbers of children and young people, although 68.1 percent were between the ages of eighteen and forty-four.[75] By the end of 1946 the Jewish displaced persons population in the American zone of Germany had swollen to over 145,000. This constituted a 356 percent increase over the nearly 40,000 Jews in the zone to begin the year.[76]

While still living in a transitional situation, hoping for the possibility of emigration, displaced persons succeeded in creating a vibrant and dynamic community in hundreds of DP camps and communities across Germany, Italy, and Austria. With the assistance of representatives from the United Nations Relief and Rehabilitation Administration, the Joint, the Jewish Agency, and other organizations, schools were established throughout the camps. The largest camps, including Landsberg, Feldafing, and Föhrenwald in the American zone of Germany, and Bergen-Belsen in the British zone, boasted a vibrant social and cultural life, with a flourishing press, theater life, active Zionist youth movements, athletic clubs, historical commissions, and yeshivot testifying to the rebirth of Orthodox Judaism. Displaced persons took an active role in representing their own political interests: political parties (mostly Zionist in nature, with the exception of the Orthodox Agudat Israel) administered camp committees and met at annual congresses of the *She'erit Hapletah*. The Zionist youth movements, with the assistance of emissaries from Palestine, created a network of at least forty agricultural training farms throughout Germany on the estates of former Nazis and German farmers, demonstrating their ardent desire for immigration to Palestine and performing an act of symbolic revenge against the Germans.

In the DP camps of postwar Germany, where Zionism quickly became the overarching political ideology, the ghetto fighters also came to assume a central presence in the collective memory and self-identification of the surviving remnant. The practice of lionizing the heroes of the ghetto revolts was commonplace; the Hashomer Hatzair youth movement, for example, renamed its kibbutzim after the movement's fighters who had perished, calling them the "Ghetto Fighters Kibbutzim": Mordecai Anielewicz, Chaviva

Reik, Yosef Kaplan, Tosia Altman, Aryeh Vilner, and Zvi Brandes.[77] (This was a decision taken at the first Hashomer Hatzair movement conference in postwar Germany at Biberach on December 10, 1945.)[78] The identification of the kibbutzim and the youth movements with the resistance played a key role in fostering new identities for the survivors. And by linking the identity of the individual kibbutzim with the heroism of wartime fighters, the movement cemented the identification of Hashomer Hatzair with the ghetto resistance in the minds of the young survivors.

Leaders of the Jewish displaced persons spoke about the important function that Warsaw could play in organizing the Jewish public after the war. Within this society as a whole, political leaders and the historical commissions also attempted to elevate the place of the ghetto fighters, as the revolt "enjoyed an uncomplicated place of honor" within the collective memory of the *She'erit Hapletah*.[79] As noted by historian Ze'ev Mankowitz, the valor of "the ghetto fighters, the dedication of the underground movements and the heroism of the partisans" was marked at every opportunity, perhaps, he suggests, as a means of lightening the burden of victimhood and "the torment of helplessness."[80] For the surviving population in postwar Germany, which boasted a wide range of wartime experiences and prewar places of origin, it was by no means self-evident that the Warsaw Ghetto Uprising would indeed become the central focal point of wartime remembrance. On the contrary, with such a wide range of wartime experiences, any number of events could have served as an organizing principle for commemorative activities for this diverse population of liberated Jews. And yet Warsaw emerged as the focal point.

As historian Laura Jockusch has observed, the historical commissions in the DP camps, and the publication projects of historians like Israel Kaplan in *Fun Letsten Hurbn*, which encouraged survivors to offer testimonies and write their own histories, published a large number of these "by men, women, adolescents, and children from various regions in Eastern Europe, especially Lithuania, Byelorussia, Galicia, and the Ukraine, reflecting a broadly eastern European Jewish experience of Nazi occupation." Despite presenting a wide range of wartime experiences, including the testimonies of Jews who survived in ghettos, concentration and forced labor camps, as well as extermination camps, and of Jews who survived hiding in forests, bunkers, on the Aryan side of segregated cities, or fighting with the partisans, Jockusch notes that "*Fun Letsten Hurbn*'s comprehensive treatment of the past did not resonate with a readership affiliated with Zionist parties and youth movements and eager for laudatory works on ghetto uprising and resistance movements."[81]

The first anniversary of the revolt marked in the DP camps—that is on April 19, 1946—highlighted the centrality of the event in the developing ethos and collective identity of the *She'erit Hapletah* and also pointed to some explanations for how and why the Warsaw Ghetto Uprising became a central focal point for commemoration among the diverse population of survivors. *Unzer Veg*, the weekly newspaper of the Central Committee of Liberated Jews in Bavaria, offered extensive coverage of the memorial services dedicated to the third anniversary of the revolt, including a flag on the cover page with the Hebrew initials *Zayin, Mem, Vav* for *Zakhor Mered Varshe*—Remember the Warsaw Revolt, 1943/6.

As coverage in the paper detailed, in honor of the third anniversary of the uprising, the Federation of Polish Jews in Bavaria held a "Mourning academy dedicated to the Warsaw Ghetto Uprising" on the evening of Thursday April 18 at the Prince Regenten Theater in Munich, where, "hearing of the battles in the streets of ghetto, the audience in the hall was electrified." Rabbi Abraham Klausner, who had been so influential in helping to organize the *She'erit Hapletah* and was considered by the survivors to be an "honorary DP,"[82] explained that "the rebels were an example, representing the unity of the people, and served as front fighters for the Jewish state in the land of Israel. Through the building of our homeland with united powers will we be able to continue the struggle which surely did not end in the resistance of the Warsaw Ghetto."[83]

The editor of *Unzer Veg*, Levi Shalitan, drew a parallel between Masada and Warsaw, while Dr. Zalman Grinberg spoke about the spiritual, physical resistance in the ghettos and camps, describing the "uprising in Warsaw (as) the expression of the resistance will of the six million killed Jews in Europe." Vladka Meed (Feigele Peltel) also spoke at the "mourning academy," offering the testimony of a participant in the uprising with details

Unzer Veg, April 19, 1946 (vol. 29).

on how it came to pass. In her remarks that evening, however, Vladka also reflected on the motivations and the meaning of the revolt. "Revenge and hate, struggle for humanity, to save the honor of a desperate people, this united all those who would no longer remain slaves. . . . The leaders of the underground fighting organization was a general command of all the underground groups in the ghetto, for whom the primary concern was acquisition of weapons," she explained.[84]

As the historian Ze'ev Mankowitz explained, by the first anniversary of the Warsaw Ghetto Uprising to be commemorated in the DP camps, the centrality of the revolt in the collective ethos of the surviving remnant was unquestioned. "Warsaw was an accessible model because the fighters were perceived as representative of East European Jewry as a whole. . . . The revolt, therefore, expressed and symbolized what masses of Jews wished to do but were unable to attain."[85] Although most of the surviving population had not been able to participate in the resistance, the ghetto fighters fought and died for the Jewish future, successfully rescuing Jewish honor and in this way managed to preserve the future of their people. For the *She'erit Hapletah*, therefore, marking the heroism of the ghetto fighters also meant recalling that their heroic actions would serve as "a wellspring of spiritual strength and national will for both the survivors and future generations."[86]

Despite the presence of fighters from other movements in the DP camps, the lessons of the revolt were understood to support the Zionist position. Why had revolt been possible in Warsaw, according to this political viewpoint? Because what remained of the Jewish masses of Poland had been concentrated in Warsaw in the ghetto; the surviving members of the Zionist elite finally managed to pull off the revolt once they had risen to the dominant position of the surviving Jewish population, suggesting that only if the Jewish people would be concentrated in their state would they be able to realize their full historical strength. Even in the aftermath of such destruction, this political viewpoint turned the concentration of a Zionist elite in the ghetto into a positive development: it had resulted in the revolt, demonstrating the potential of Zionism to overturn thousands of years of historical oppression.

Speaking approximately ten days after the third anniversary of the revolt, at a "mourning academy" organized in honor of the third anniversary in Feldafing DP camp on April 27, 1946, Levi Shalitan would further emphasize the centrality of Warsaw to the future identity of the surviving remnant: "a people cannot live off Treblinkas and Majdaneks—only thanks to Warsaw can this people live on. . . . That which you and I did not know, Warsaw did know!"[87] The coverage in *Dos Fraye Wort* noted that the audience heard with great interest all of the speeches. Following an artistic presentation by a drama group, the academy concluded with the singing of "Hatikvah" (the future Israeli national anthem).

Dos Fraye Wort included remarks by Moshe Shertok (later Sharett) in honor of the third anniversary of the revolt. Shertok characterized the Warsaw heroes as "holy": a "holy matter of the heroic demonstration of Jewish bravery, which we experienced in our generation, were the ghetto fighters. The struggle of these unknown heroes, men and women alone and weak, small in number and unarmed, a small little holy David(s) against the strong force of Goliath(s) [*klejner hajleke dowidlech kegn a sztarke macht fun goliasn*] without any connection with the outside world, without any hope."[88]

The emphasis on Warsaw as a central organizing principle of the collective DP identity was not universal, however. Dissenting voices argued against the creation of a cult of heroism, the fear being that the memory of the uprising was already being perverted in the service of the Zionist movement to recruit young followers.[89] Nonetheless, such concerns of political manipulation of the memory of the ghetto fighters were a minority viewpoint in the DP camps, as the Zionist political consensus coalesced around the largely unquestioned place of honor occupied by the ghetto fighters.

The May 10, 1946, cover page of *Unzer Veg* highlighted the centrality of the ghetto fighters as a source of pride for the survivors. Noting the remarkable heroism of the Jewish fighters in the armies and the Jewish Brigade, *Unzer Veg* called on its readers to "pick up on these holy examples of Jewish honor to ensure that that eternal strength of the people of Israel lives on!" Dr. Abrasha Blumovicz, the partisan leader and a member of the executive committee of the Central Committee of Liberated Jews, linked the wartime resistance to the struggle for the creation of the Jewish state.[90]

For international observers tasked with finding a solution to the Jewish refugee problem after the war, the symbol of the Warsaw Ghetto Uprising also proved powerful in justifying the need for a political solution to the problem of Jewish statelessness. Six months after the Harrison report, on February 11, 1946, the Anglo-American Committee of Inquiry visited the Warsaw ghetto as part of their tour of Poland and the DP camps in Germany to assess the best solution to the Jewish refugee crisis after the war.

According to the Jewish Telegraphic Agency, they "toured the ruins of the Warsaw Ghetto, and viewed huge open graves containing the carbonized bodies of martyred Jews." As JTA reported, the visiting members of the AACI wept before the mass Jewish graves, which they "suggested [must] be preserved intact as evidence that the Jews suffered terrible sacrifices in the battle to destroy Nazism. The people in England and America, they said, had no conception of the heroism and sufferings which the Jews endured." After meeting with representatives of the Polish government, including the foreign minister Wincenty Raymowski and Jacob Berman (brother of Adolph Berman and an adviser to Prime Minister Osóbka-Morawski), the subcommittee, led by Sir John Singleton, met with Dr. Emil Sommerstein, chairman of the Central Jewish Committee, who explained that most of the Jews of Poland would choose to emigrate from the country because they could see no future there and "feel they are alone." Sommerstein explained to the committee members that "the only solution for the problem of the Jews is creation of their own state in Palestine." JTA concluded its report noting that "the Anglo-American probers will shortly leave for Lodz where the 'League for Working Palestine' plans to organize a street demonstration of all Jews in the city to indicate their desire to go to Palestine."[91]

On the third anniversary of the revolt, the Jewish community of Poland also marked the occasion with solemn tributes to the ghetto fighters. As noted in JTA coverage, "At meetings and religious services throughout the country today, the surviving Jews of Poland paid tribute to the 40,000 who were killed in the Battle of the Warsaw Ghetto, which began April 19, 1943."[92] At a ceremony on the site of the ghetto, "a mass of ruins covering the bodies of tens of thousands of Jews," Dr. Emil Sommerstein, president of the Central Jewish Committee, laid a wreath amidst the debris, on the "symbolic graves of the fallen Jewish heroes."[93] A memorial stone featuring a red circular tablet was laid in the ghetto to commemorate the fallen heroes, with writing in Hebrew, Yiddish, and Polish: "the fallen were exemplars of the heroic struggle for the honor and freedom of the Jewish people, for a free Poland, for the freedom of mankind." The tripartite declaration memorialized the fighters in their struggle as Jews, as Poles, and as human beings.

Dr. Adolf Berman opened the ceremony in the name of the Central Committee of Polish Jews by noting that on "these days, on the third anniversary, on the rubble of honor and freedom of the Jewish people thrown in the struggle against the greatest enemy of humanity, have Polish Jewry laid the cornerstone for a memorial for the ghetto fighters, who will for generations stand as a testimony to the greatest heroic deeds, the extraordinary martyrology and willingness to sacrifice which were brought on the altar of the holiest ideals of humanity." Yitzhak Zuckerman spoke as "one of the commandants of the Jewish Fighting Organization":

> our youth began to organize earlier . . . overcoming obstacles, blood, by collecting one pistol and another pistol did we build to April 19! Through fires and shots, through great sacrifices in the time of the first liquidation actions, through the January battle of 1943, was made the way to the last struggle.
>
> Who were the fighters? Halutzim, Bundists, Members of the [Communist] PPR, Poalei Zion, children of the Folks-Masses. They represented the best traditions of the most recent generations.
>
> This was a conscious path to the last unparalleled struggle—and death.
>
> Warsaw was the beginning of our struggle. Our call was heard in other ghettos. Białystok, Częstochowa, Będzin, Vilna. The echoes were heard in Treblinka and Bełżec, and represented the most dreadful struggle in human history. The

> echo was heard in the forests of Poland, Belarus, Ukraine, Lithuania, and inspired the Jewish partisans who led a merciless struggle against the enemy. The uprising inspired Jewish soldiers all over the world, the brothers in the Red Army, the Polish Army, and the armies of all countries.[94]

Other speakers representing the Polish government also spoke, while Salo Fiszgrund, representing the Bund, recalled the contributions of the Jewish working classes in the ghetto uprising, also noting differences in commemorations in New York, Moscow, Tel Aviv and elsewhere (his remarks were not reproduced in full).

In the pages of the Bundist publication, the *Folktsaytung* in April 1946, the movement noted its dedication to ensure that those bodies which still could be recovered from the rubble might be accorded the dignified funerals they deserved. The Bund was committed to recovering the bodies of its fallen heroes, so they could receive a proper burial.

> The Central Committee of the Bund in Poland has decided to make all strenuous efforts in order to exhume the bodies of our comrades—Zalman Frydrych, Jurek Blones, Gute Blones, Feigele Goldstein, Gabrish Fryshdorf, and Lusiek Blones, the martyrs in the struggle with the brown fascists, to bring them to proper burial in the Jewish cemetery in Warsaw. (Special thanks to our comrades who knew the exact spot where their bodies were located). The funeral took place on Friday, January 11, 1946.[95]

Among those participating in the ceremony at the cemetery were Bundists, members of Tsukunft, and other "sympathetic parties." Among the speakers were Henryk (Salo) Fishgrund (who noted the leading roles of Abrasha Blum and Michał Klepfisz) and Marek Edelman:

> For the first time, said comrade Marek Edelman, in Jewish history, the first time in Jewish Warsaw, did Jewish workers and

> the broader Jewish public organize a revolt against the brown bestial dark forces whose goal was to eradicate the Jewish people.
>
> The six martyrs, concluded Comrade Marek, fulfilled that which they set out to accomplish . . . but we must continue in the same way, to struggle for the ideals for which our six martyrs perished.

Also present at the ceremony was Jacob Pat, representative of the Jewish Labor Committee, who stood in awe of what the ghetto fighters had accomplished and brought greetings from the American Jewish community, who honored the Jewish masses of Poland, but whose inaction and passivity during the war was regrettable. The ceremony concluded with the singing of the Bundist Oath (*di shvue*), the Internationale, and other songs of the workers movement.[96]

At the same time, political divisions emerged among the movements in postwar Europe, often fomented by emissaries from the movements sent from the Yishuv, meaning that any wartime unity between Dror, Hashomer Hatzair, HeHalutz, Revisionists, the Bund, and other groups disappeared. Instead, a kind of competitive heroism of wartime ghetto fighters played a large role in fostering this postwar division as young movement members identified with their movements' heroes. The history of their leadership in wartime resistance became a core part of each movement's educational framework in the postwar period.

In the DP camps, the youth of Hashomer Hatzair learned about the wartime heroism of the movement in leading wartime resistance. Volume two (April 1946) of the movement's newspaper dedicated to the three-year anniversary of the Warsaw Ghetto Uprising claimed "our movement was among the first to make the call for rebellion."[97] The cover was graced by a drawing of the ruins of the ghetto, and the first page profiled Mordecai Anielewicz, including a selection from his last will and testament to the world: "How happy am I that I am one of the first Jewish fighters in the ghetto." The volume also included part of Abba Kovner's appeal to the Jews of the Vilna ghetto "not to go like sheep to the slaughter," as well as the hymn of the United Partisans Organization (Fareynigte Partizaner Organizatsye), "Zog Nit Keyn Mol."[98] Articles by ghetto fighters Ruzhka Korzcak, Abba Kovner, and Chaya Klinger detailed their wartime activity in the resistance. Later editions of the newspaper continued this emphasis with profiles of other resistance leaders after whom Hashomer Hatzair kibbutzim were named, including Yosef Kaplan and Tosia Altman (volumes 3 and 4), as well as leaders like Frumka Plotnicka and Abba Kovner.

Likewise, the Dror movement emphasized the leading role of its members in wartime resistance as a recruiting tool, a way to maintain morale, and as a justification for its place as a leader of postwar Jewish society. Unlike Hashomer Hatzair, which had lost its main resistance leaders in the Warsaw ghetto (Anielewicz, Altman, Kaplan, and Breslaw, among others) the merged Dror/HeHalutz movements could boast two of the most well-known leaders of the Warsaw Ghetto Uprising, Yitzhak Zuckerman and Zivia Lubetkin, who played an active role in organizing surviving youth after the war. As part of its educational efforts in the DP camps, they published a volume, *Warsaw Ghetto Uprising*, along with Poalei Zion Z.S. in Landsberg, which included Zuckerman's May 1944 ŻOB report, a testimony from "Zivia"—the lesson of the Warsaw uprising, "The People Did Not Believe"—excerpts from the Borzykowski and Grajek testimonies, and a poem by Yitzhak Katznelson, "With the Halutzim."[99]

The Pachach movement, which by December 1946 counted forty-five hundred members in Bavaria, two thousand in Austria, and a thousand in Italy, estimated that of its members in Bavaria, 40 percent were partisans and ghetto fighters while 60 percent had been front-line soldiers (70 percent Polish Army veterans; 30 percent Red Army veterans). The movement also counted three hundred children, 20–25 percent women, 65–70 percent war wounded. Three thousand of the partisans emerged from the forests, many of whom had been the organizers of ghetto revolts. The movement counted thirty-two branches and six kibbutzim. Its members were also engaged in various forms of vocational training.[100] The Pachach movement publications also highlighted the central role its members had played in leading the resistance. For example, the April 4, 1947, edition of the Pachach bulletin in Germany was dedicated to the fourth anniversary of the

השומר
הצעיר

מוקדש למרד גיטו ורשה.

השחרור שאחר לבא..

מס. 2

הוצאת „השומר - הצעיר" בגרמניה

מינכן אפריל 1946

Cover page from the publication *Hashomer Hatzair*, issued by the Hashomer Hatzair socialist-Zionist youth movement in Germany, April 1946. The issue is dedicated to the commemoration of the Warsaw Ghetto Uprising. (United States Holocaust Memorial Museum Photo Archives, no. 05947)

-16-

דער ערשטער אויפרוף

אנגעשריבן דורך אבא קאוונער
ארויסגעגעבן דורך פאר. פארטיז. ארג.

לאמיר נישט גיין ווי שאף צו דער שחיטה!

יידישע יוגנט גלויב נישט די פארפירער פון די אכציק טויזנט יידן אין ירושלים־דליטא איז געבליבן נאר צוואנציק טויזנט. פאר אונ־זערע אויגן האט מען אוועקגעריסן די עלטערן, ברידער און שוועסטער. ווו זענען די הונדערטער מענער, געכאפטע אויף ארבעט דורך דער שטאטישער פאליציי? ווו זענען די נאקעטע פרויען און קינדער, ארויסגעפירטע אין גרויליקער נאכט פון דער פראוואקאציע? ווו זענען די יידן געכאפטע אין יום-כיפור? און ווו זענען אונזערע ברידער פון דער צווייטער געטא? וועמען מען האט ארויסגעפירט

Second page from the publication Hashomer Hatzair, issued by the Hashomer Hatzair socialist-Zionist youth movement in Germany. The page includes Abba Kovner's call to resistance in Vilna including the phrase: "Let us not go like sheep to the slaughter." (United States Holocaust Memorial Museum Photo Archives, no. 05937) (United States Holocaust Memorial Museum Photo Archives, no. 05937)

Yitzhak Zuckerman delivers a speech at a Pachach political meeting in the Zeilsheim displaced persons' camp. (United States Holocaust Memorial Museum Archives, courtesy of Alice Lev, no. 89638)

Warsaw Ghetto Uprising.[101] While most previous volumes of the newspaper dealt with movement education, Labor Zionist education, information about Zionist congresses, materials for kibbutzim and *madrichim* (youth movements leaders), and news in the movement, the April edition included extensive focus on the uprising, with a factual survey written by Melech Neustadt.

Likewise, when the Hashomer Hatzair movement was renamed Hashomer Hatzair Be-Ha'apalah (literally, Hashomer Hatzair conquers the shores of Palestine) in Germany in 1947, it is clear that the movement saw its leadership in the wartime struggle against Nazism as justifying its postwar leadership of the *She'erit Hapletah* in the struggle against the British blockade—the new form of underground resistance. Regardless of what members' experiences had been in the war, whether in the forests, in hiding, in the Soviet Union, in concentration and labor camps, or in the ghettos for that matter, they now adopted the collective heroic identity provided by membership in the group and continued the heroic legacy of wartime resistance through participation in the struggle to create the Jewish state. In this way, the postwar activities of the youth—as pioneers, as *ma'apilim* (conquerors of the shore), and as soldiers defending the Jewish people—continued the wartime resistance of their new heroes.

The centrality of this transformation was perhaps given clearest expression in the film *Von Horvot bis zum Heimland* (*From Ruins to Homeland*), with a script written by the noted Yiddish author, Chaim Grade, produced and directed by Yitzhak Goskind. The film, which was created by the Hashomer Hatzair youth movement, most likely in late 1947, included a reenactment of the Warsaw Ghetto Uprising and made a direct link between the revolt in Warsaw and the struggle to realize the creation of the Jewish state.[102]

The film opens with a scene of young men in Hashomer Hatzair uniforms marching up a hill carrying torches as part of commemoration of the Warsaw Ghetto Uprising. As one of the young *chanichim* (movement members) sings to the group, the narrator (Naftali Radenbloom) explains that Hashomer Hatzair members in Poland can be seen visiting the grave of their brothers in Warsaw, while one member tells the story of the last days of the ghetto. In what must be one of the earliest postwar dramatic recreations of the liquidation and uprising in the ghetto, the film intersperses actual footage of the ghetto with reenactments of young Jewish fighters battling the Nazi foe. Viewers are taken into the ghetto, where they see a sign over a wooden fence warning of the danger of epidemics; a uniformed German; a shot of the brick wall dividing the ghetto from Aryan Warsaw; and scenes of Jews hurrying along crowded streets and over the wooden bridge over Chlodna Street that connected the two parts of the ghetto.

The film introduces the idea of resistance through a reenacted scene of a man reading a Yiddish-language leaflet about the resistance in the ghetto and a close-up of a ŻOB poster plastered on a wall: LONG LIVE FREEDOM! LONG LIVE ARMED RESISTANCE! The narrator notes that Jews died with honor, and we see footage of youths at a postwar commemoration ceremony, interspersed with footage purporting to show the German assault on the ghetto during the uprising. Explosions and automatic weapons light up the night. As German soldiers use flamethrowers to set buildings on fire, reenactments feature a male Jewish fighter tossing a hand grenade out a window at passing German troops and a female fighter stabbing a German soldier in the back. The reenactment of the uprising concludes with destruction: destroyed buildings in the ghetto and a shot of the renamed M. Anielwicza street completely destroyed, with the street sign standing in piles of rubble.[103]

The film symbolically connects the struggle in the Warsaw ghetto to the work of the postwar Zionist youth movements whose members now march through the ghetto, as "the inheritors of the ghetto heroes . . . of the bequest of the fallen . . . they will be able to march into the future proudly, not only as the descendants of martyrs but also of brave heroes." Showing Jewish youth marching with flags and signs in Polish, Hebrew, and Yiddish, while others play drums, the film roots itself in the postwar commemorations of the ghetto uprising while transitioning to the postwar struggle for the creation of the State of Israel. The film highlights the agricultural work of a kibbutz group in Germany preparing for their lives in Israel, dreaming of working the Negev, dreaming of the land of Israel and the holy eternal city of the forefathers (Jerusalem), the new city of Tel Aviv, and more, while others engage in vocational training to prepare for their future lives. *Ma'apilim* are shown approaching the shores of Palestine on an immigrant ship (perhaps *Exodus 1947)* before being intercepted by the British blockade and forcibly loaded onto another ship surrounded by barbed wire. At the Poppendorf DP camp, British military police armed with batons guard the camp, and one boy holds a hat with "Exodus" written on it. Linking the postwar struggle to conquer the shores of the Land of Israel and break the British blockade with the wartime resistance, the film concludes with close-ups of a maquette of the Warsaw ghetto monument (not yet completed) and people posing as if they are reenacting the scene in the monument. After a close-up of the monument, the film concludes with a cut to a young hero (ghetto fighter) lifting an older man and announces: "The future generations will not know of the shame of the ghetto."

Conclusion

After the brutal suppression of the Warsaw uprising, the city was completely destroyed. The ghetto fighters who managed to survive until liberation in January 1945 made their way to Lublin, where they began to participate in organizing the surviving remnant of Polish Jewry. Ghetto fighters played a leading role in forming the Bricha, parlaying their wartime role in leading the resistance into a postwar claim to lead the surviving Jewish population as the Bricha brought a hundred thousand Jews to the DP camps. As the Yishuv in Palestine embraced the leading role of Zionist youth in the revolt in Warsaw, the surviving members of the Jewish Fighting Organization argued that the wartime struggle continued as part of the struggle to create the Jewish state. In the DP camps, the ghetto fighters occupied an uncomplicated place of honor. Commemorations of the Warsaw Ghetto Uprising in the DP camps and in postwar Poland emphasized the symbolic meaning of the event, which preceded the factual basis for understanding what actually happened. In this way, the revolt in Warsaw was linked with struggle to create a Jewish state. This was especially clear in films like *Von Horvot bis zum Heimland*, produced in postwar Germany, where both literally and symbolically, the members of the youth movements took up the mantle of the Warsaw Ghetto Uprising to carry on the struggle for creation of the Jewish state.

7

The First Published Testimonies of the Surviving Ghetto Fighters

The symbolic power of the revolt would be mobilized politically in the service of the Zionist movement in the effort to create the Jewish state. Surviving youth in the DP camps were taught to carry the legacy of the ghetto fighters into the struggle to build the Jewish homeland. For political purposes, symbols and heroes—the legends of the ghetto fighters, the names of the fallen, the figure of Anielewicz rising above all—would be critical in this process. But as this book has already demonstrated, politicization of the revolt did not occur only in Tel Aviv and New York; it took place in Warsaw, too, and in the reading of the words of those who emerged from Warsaw. The revolt in Warsaw already became the focal point of Jewish commemorations in the first years after the uprising. Broad segments of the Jewish public around the world were eager to hear the testimonies of the "Jewish heroes of Warsaw," the first witnesses to emerge from the destroyed city who could attest to this "most glorious page in the annals of Jewish history."

In the case of the Warsaw Ghetto Uprising, multiple testimonies recorded by surviving ghetto fighters from different backgrounds and different political parties detail unique aspects of the events of April and May 1943 that would ultimately be combined to write a collective history of the uprising. It was not the only event in the history of the Holocaust where multiple survivor testimonies would be collected and recorded after the event by survivors: for example, the escape from Sobibor on October 14, 1943, in which an estimated fifty-eight Jews managed to survive until the end of the war, would be the subject of individual and collective testimonies by all of the surviving escapees (see for example the collection of postwar testimonies housed at the Jewish Historical Institute in Warsaw). Likewise, Christopher Browning has demonstrated in his study of survivor testimonies from the Starachowice forced labor camp the value of aggregating and comparing survivor testimonies to write a history based on the collective memory of a place and an event.[1] In this sense, the testimonies of the survivors of the Warsaw Ghetto Uprising—recorded in the immediate aftermath of the revolt and then, in some cases, multiple times over the course of many years after the war, sometimes together, sometimes translated into various languages—presents a fascinating opportunity to examine the interaction between memory, testimony, politics, and history.

While these testimonies were received and published in the free world already in 1944, we know they were not the first testimonies from occupied Europe to be shared publicly during the war: for example, the aforementioned *Letters from the Ghettoes*, compiled by Bracha Habas, appeared in the Yishuv in 1943. Likewise, portions of Jan Karski's *Story of a Secret State* appeared earlier in 1944 (selections were published in *Colliers* in January 1944). Selections from the Diary of Mary Watten (Berg) were also published in American newspapers in 1944 after her arrival in the United States in March 1944.[2] So even though the testimonies of the surviving ghetto fighters were not the first to emerge from occupied Europe, the dramatic nature of the revolt had already seized the imagination of the Jewish and non-Jewish public around the world, with commemorations observed as early as April 19, 1944, which meant that tremendous value would be associated with the testimonies that would emerge from the ghetto both during and after the war.[3]

In the first year after the war, the testimonies of three surviving ghetto fighters, Marek Edelman, Zivia Lubetkin, and Vladka Meed (Feigele Peltel) would play a critical role in satisfying public interest in the dramatic event and further entrenching certain narrative aspects of the history of the revolt. At the same time, these testimonies were written and delivered with specific audiences in mind: Marek Edelman's *The Ghetto Fights*, written in Warsaw and commissioned by the Bund in New York; Zivia Lubetkin's account, delivered at the party conference of HaKibbutz HaMeuchad (the United Kibbutz movement) at Kibbutz Yagur on June 8, 1946; and Vladka Meed's serialized account, written for the *Jewish Daily Forward* in New York for an American Jewish audience in the summer and fall of 1946. How did these testimonies serve to entrench the Warsaw Ghetto Uprising as the paradigmatic example of Jewish resistance during the war? Did these testimonies challenge the notion that Jews allowed themselves to be led "like sheep to the slaughter" or did they reinforce this image of wartime Jewish passivity? Who were the heroes of the revolt according to these testimonies? Did the heroes die a heroic death or did they live to tell the tale? Can the testimonies of the ghetto fighters help us to understand how they viewed their actions? Was it self-evident that this event would become the focal point for Jewish memory of the Shoah? Did their testimonies change with the encounter with Israel and America? Or had they been shaped by prewar and wartime experiences? How might preconceived frameworks of understanding the revolt in Israel and America have shaped the reception of their testimonies? Did the surviving ghetto fighters feel like their audiences could actually understand them? Were they speaking the same "language"? Could they bridge the gap in understanding between "here and there"?

By 1945, the surviving ghetto fighters from Warsaw began to disperse to new homes—the majority of the Zionist members of ŻOB traveled to the Yishuv, many already in the summer of 1945. Zivia Lubetkin would arrive in late May 1946, while Zuckerman would settle there in 1947, where the married couple established Kibbutz Lochamei HaGetaot near Akko in April 1949. Vladka Meed traveled to New York in late May 1946; Marek Edelman, dedicated to the reconstruction of Poland, remained in Poland until his death in 2009.

It would be a mistake to simply read these testimonies as strict historical accounts by eyewitnesses and participants in the revolt; we must also read these texts as accounts of very traumatized individuals. In these first encounters with Jews in the free world, could they actually convey what they had just experienced, what it was like to "be there"? While the temptation is to read such texts purely for their narration of the events leading to the revolt and the details of the uprising itself, as Amos Goldberg's research argues, the examination of Jewish experiences in the Shoah should not look only for reaction, resistance, and *amidah*, but should instead focus on the fundamental transformation and degradation of the individual human being under the occupation, a transformation that can chart the process of social or anthropological death that precedes biological death.[4] In this sense, historians should be careful not to simply read such testimonies merely as wartime records of events, but should pay attention to the experience of the writer, of the impact of sustained trauma on the individual and how this might be reflected in the text, in the manner in which events that are "indescribable" are, nonetheless, recorded. Even the testimonies of the ghetto fighters—Edelman, Zivia, Antek, and Vladka—who supposedly rose above it—can be read through the lens of the trauma they must have experienced. How do their testimonies describe the effects of sustained degradation and trauma on the Jewish population of Warsaw? Does this provide insight into the acquiescence, on the part of so many, to deportation orders? For a reading audience devastated by news of the destruction of European Jewry, testimonies of fighters would have been a welcome change of subject. If Jews around the world were eager to know what it was like to "be there," but (as Antek and Zivia noted in their letter to leaders of the Yishuv) "those who live in London or Tel Aviv cannot conjure [the lived experience] up, even in the sickest of their imaginations," how did testimonies seek to bridge this divide? Was it possible to convey the trauma? Likewise—did gender matter? Did male and female fighters remember the revolt differently?

Such considerations mattered little to recipients of such testimonies during and after the war—readers and audiences who, as demonstrated in previous chapters, were far more concerned with establishing the identities of the "Jewish heroes" and claiming credit for one political party or another. Still, if we bear this gap in comprehension in mind, we can appreciate this

Marek Edelman, ca. 1945. (United States Holocaust Memorial Museum, courtesy of Benjamin Miedzyrzecki Meed, photo archives no. 02333)

disconnect between the fighters and witnesses who lived through the events, and the audiences in the free world, who would never fully understand, because they were not there.

Marek Edelman's testimony, *The Ghetto Fights (Getto Walczy)* was first published by the Bund in Warsaw in the summer of 1945 (in Polish).[5]

Edelman was born in Homel (in present-day Belarus) in 1919 and lost both parents before he reached his teens. His father died in 1924 and his mother, Zipporah, active in the Bundist women's organization YAF (*Yiddishe Arbeter Froy*—Jewish Women's Workers Association), passed away in 1934 when he was fifteen. As Luba Blum (wife of Abrasha) explained in her review of the memoir, Marek was raised with socialism in his "mother's milk." As a fifteen-year-old orphan he came under the influence and supervision of his teacher and the principal of his Yiddish school, Sonia Nowogrodzki (whose choice to join the Jewish masses in deportation to Treblinka was described in his account). He was twenty when the Germans invaded Poland in September 1939 and he began working as a messenger in the hospital, which afforded him the opportunity to recruit underground members and gain access to needed supplies. Edelman joined the ghetto's Jewish Fighting Organization (ŻOB) in November 1942 and at the beginning of the uprising on April 19, 1943, Edelman and his unit were in charge of defending the brushmakers area of the ghetto. After the ŻOB forces began to withdraw to the central ghetto, Edelman and his group joined the fighters centered at 30 Franciszkanska Street. He connected with Zivia Lubetkin after the collapse of the Mila 18 command bunker and was part of the group led through the sewers by Kazik on May 9–10, emerging from the manhole on Prosta Street and fleeing in the truck to Lomianki Forest. Edelman later joined other members of the ŻOB who took part in the Polish Uprising of August 1944.

Edelman's testimonial is written in a restrained, matter-of-fact tone. He brought the initial publication to the well-known Polish writer Zofia Nałkowska, who called it not only a "shocking historical document but a dramatic work of great literary value." Nałkowska translated the book into English and it was published by the American Representation of the General Jewish Workers' Union of Poland in New York in 1946. The book would be translated into various languages over the years, although it is important to note that while the testimony would be translated into Yiddish and English immediately after the war, it took until 2001 to be translated into Hebrew—and it was not mentioned in Melech Neustadt's 1946 publication. Despite his relationship before, during, and after the revolt with the surviving Zionist members of the ŻOB (including Yitzhak Zuckerman and Zivia Lubetkin), Marek's story would be almost completely written out of the Israeli narrative of the uprising.[6] Edelman chose to stay in Poland after World War II, and became a cardiologist, eventually becoming the most prominent ghetto fighter to remain in Poland, a symbol of the Jewish struggle alongside Polish fighters in 1944, and in the 1980s a prominent supporter of the Solidarity movement.[7]

In her foreword to the memoir, the writer Zofia Nałkowska described Edelman's account as an authentic document about "perseverance and moral strength" able to achieve something few masterpieces could achieve:

> It gives in serious, purposeful, reticent words a record, simple and unostentatious, of a common martyrdom, of its entire involved course. It is also an authentic document about perseverance and moral strength kept intact during the greatest tragedy in the history of mankind.[8]

Edelman's narrative, while self-described as having "no literary value," is in fact a searing account of the period from September 1939 to May 1943, written with incredible insight, analysis, moving detail, and a deep understanding of human behavior. Edelman emphasized the Bund's determination to continue its political and social activities in the atmosphere of terror and fear from the beginning of the occupation, while acknowledging the paralyzing effect of oppression and dehumanization that led to passivity and apathy. He focuses on the origins of resistance in the ghetto, the determination to oppose Germans at all times, and the great difficulty in convincing the ghetto population of the need for resistance. He barely mentions his own role and generally refers to himself in the third person. He pays special attention to the fear and starvation that prevented the population from believing deportation to the East meant mass slaughter, even after the return of Zygmunt Frydrych with his eyewitness warning from a deportation train bound for Treblinka. Edelman repeats the phrase "The Ghetto does not believe" several times, underlining the difficulty of the ŻOB in convincing the ghetto population of the death sentence and need for resistance. At the same time, he provides important background on the dehumanization experienced by the Jewish population, offering context on how and why it was so difficult to convince the population of the need to resist, including the degree to which atomization divided the ghetto.

> The instinct for self-preservation finally drove the people into a state of mind permitting them to disregard the safety of others in order to save their own necks. True, nobody as yet believed that the deportation meant death. But the Germans had already succeeded in dividing the Jewish population into two distinct groups—those already condemned to die and those who still hoped to remain alive. Afterwards, step by step, the Germans will succeed in pitting these two groups against one another and cause some Jews to lead others to certain death in order to save their own skin.[9]

He also indicts Judenrat leader Adam Czerniakow, who Edelman believed should have convinced the ghetto inhabitants not to board the deportation trains instead of committing suicide (a view he continued to maintain forty years later, as he explained to the Polish journalist Hanna Krall: "that wasn't right: one should die with a bang. At that time this bang was most needed—one should die only after having called other people into struggle."[10]) Even at the end of the deportation period, in September 1942, he pointed out, surviving Jews continued to be divided by German policies, fighting over precious slips of numbered paper that could guarantee life. "Some fought for the piece of paper loudly, shrilly attempting to prove their right to live. Others, tearfully resigned, meekly awaited their fate."[11] Throughout his testimony, Edelman offers insights into the thinking of the Jewish masses, including vignettes to attempt to describe the scenes at the Umschlagplatz, to communicate the indescribable.

> No words of any human language are strong enough to describe the "Umschlag" now, when no help from anywhere or anybody can be expected. The sick, adults as well

> as children, previously brought here from the hospital, lie deserted in the cold halls. They relieve themselves right where they lie, and remain in the stinking slime of excrement and urine. Nurses search the crowd for their fathers and mothers and, having found them, inject longed for deathly morphine into their veins, their own eyes gleaming wildly. One doctor compassionately pours a cyanide solution into the feverish mouths of strange, sick children. To offer one's cyanide to somebody else is a really heroic sacrifice, for cyanide is now the most precious, the most irreplaceable thing. It brings a quiet, peaceful death, it saves from the horror of the cars.
>
> Thus the Germans deported 60,000 people within two days.[12]

Edelman's description of offering one's cyanide to someone else as a "really heroic sacrifice" is remarkable—first because it suggests that true heroism, in his eyes, is to furnish another the most peaceful way to die, to save someone from the horror of the train cars (let alone the gas chambers at Treblinka). Heroism does not mean killing Nazis, it means choosing the circumstances of one's own death, or more accurately, compassionately choosing the circumstances of another's death. In one of his vignettes, Edelman offers personal recollections that detail the fighting that led to the death of the Bundist hero, Michał Klepfisz:

> In one of the attics we are suddenly surrounded. Nearby, in the same attic, are the Germans and it is impossible to reach the stairs. In the dark corners of the attic we cannot even see one another. We do not notice Sewek Dunski and Junghajzer who crawl up the stairs from below, reach the attic, get behind the Germans, and throw a grenade. We do not even pause to consider how it happens that Michał Klepfisz jumps straight onto the German machine-gun firing from behind the chimney. We only see the cleared path. After the Germans have been thrown out, several hours

later, we find Michał's body perforated like a sieve from two machine-gun rounds.

The brush-makers' area could not be taken.[13]

Edelman would later explain fighting in the ghetto uprising as choosing "how to live life with the moments before we died"—the primary motivation in this context being to die honorably. References to revenge as a motivation, while prominent in Lubetkin and Zuckerman's accounts, do not feature prominently in Edelman's narrative. Edelman concludes his account on May 10, 1943, noting that the history of the Warsaw Jews had come to an end. Those who did not perish carried the memories of the fighters whose blood had soaked into the pavement of Warsaw, and in passing the memory onto his readers in Poland and America, he had now conveyed the obligation of memory—to keep the memory of the fighters alive—forever.

While the first half of his account distinguishes between the underground, and specifically the Bund, determined to organize resistance and

Yitzhak Zuckerman, Stefan Grajek, and Marek Edelman visiting the area of the ruined Warsaw ghetto. (Ghetto Fighters House Archive, no. 984)

defy the Nazis at all costs, and the general population *who refused to believe*, the period after the deportations is a turning point. Then the general population began to see the value of resistance, especially after January 1943, when they came to realize that German plans could be frustrated. Edelman is typically humble—he has the talents of a great writer—and his account conveys great emotional depth and narrative power. He focuses on the Bund's role in organizing the resistance and specifically singles out Bundist activists for his audience—but he is also willing to address the role of Hashomer and HeHalutz and the process whereby the ŻOB was formed and Anielewicz became its commander.

Zivia Lubetkin in the Yishuv

While Edelman first wrote his testimony in Polish and in Poland, where he would remain for the rest of his life, Zivia Lubetkin's 1946 testimony in Hebrew focused primarily on the role of HeHalutz in accounts intended for audiences in the Yishuv. In their immediate postwar testimonies, both Zuckerman and Lubetkin argued that it was the link to the Land of Israel that gave them the courage to resist. Zuckerman believed that only those imbued with the Diaspora-negating Zionist ideology had the courage to resist (this betrayed a consistent inability to recognize the contributions of other resistance movements in his reporting on the revolt—notably the Bund and the Revisionists). As noted in the previous chapter, writing to the Yishuv in June 1945, Zuckerman argued clearly that HeHalutz stood at the forefront of resistance, leading the ghetto revolts.[14] For Zuckerman, HeHalutz, animated by a powerful Zionist ideology and a connection to the Land of Israel, inspired the resistance and met the historic test as the Polish Jewish masses could not.

Meanwhile, Zivia Lubetkin arrived in the Yishuv at the end of May 1946, where she provided her extraordinary firsthand testimony to members of the Labor Movement, the Haganah, and the Palmach. Female fighters like Zivia Lubetkin and Tosia Altman came to stand in for the death and suffering of millions of Jews in a way that male fighters (like Antek) did not; even in life, Zivia continued to represent the sacrifice of the Jewish people and their rebirth.[15] She was greeted in Israel as a "comrade, a soldier, and a military leader" and was received as the "face of the heroic battles that are unparalleled in history."[16] On arrival in Haifa she wrote to Yitzhak Zuckerman that the reactions of the movement members caused her great emotional distress. Given that she had been mourned as dead in June 1943, her arrival in the Yishuv was marked like the arrival of "someone who had been resurrected."[17] She was depicted as a "daughter of the Yishuv" and her pioneering and heroic spirit were an extension of her connection to the Yishuv. While she hoped to reunite with her sister Ahuva, it became clear that the reunion with the movement and the Kibbutz HaMeuchad took precedence. Sharon Geva notes that Zivia was overwhelmed by the very public nature of the encounters, that her colleagues there could not understand the "real her," and she missed Yitzhak.[18]

On her first night in Israel (when she was deprived of that reunion with her sister) she met with movement members and then had a late-night meeting with Yitzhak Sadeh and members of the Palmach (literally "strike force," the offensive assault companies of the Haganah).[19] Years later, the Israel Defense Force (IDF) Chief of Staff, David (Dado) Elazar would describe the Palmach meeting with Zivia on the sands of Caesarea that night: "When Zivia . . . told the story of the Warsaw Ghetto, we felt certain that we belonged to the same group of fighters, sons of the same nation, fighting the same war."[20] The next day she met the leader of the Dror movement, Yitzhak Tabenkin, who was well aware of the anger Zivia and Yitzhak had expressed in their letters at the sense of abandonment they experienced; Tabenkin made it clear to Zivia that her message would have to be a positive one, one that could help in the Dror movement's efforts to recruit emissaries for their important work (this was soon after the split between Hashomer Hatzair and Kibbutz HaMeuchad, as well as the split of Dror from Mapai).[21] She also traveled to Tel Aviv to meet with leaders of the Yishuv at the Histadrut building in Tel Aviv.

Zivia also endeavored to meet with the leaders of Hashomer Hatzair (despite the split from Dror and the tension with Meir Ya'ari, who believed Antek seized too much credit for the resistance for himself). Gutterman notes that Lubetkin felt an obligation to "go to them" to commemorate the

Hashomer Hatzair movement members who fell fighting in the ghetto. "Fate had it that not one of your members who took part in the Warsaw Ghetto Uprising is still alive, and I therefore see it as a sacred mission to myself to divulge to you whatever I know about them so that their part in the ghetto fighting and the uprising shall never be forgotten . . . the struggle in the ghetto and in the camps was the creation of two movements—yours and ours."[22]

At her testimony at Kibbutz Yagur on June 8 (almost exactly three years after she was eulogized there in 1943), at least three thousand were in attendance to hear Zivia describe the destruction of Warsaw for eight straight hours.[23] While other survivors had already reached Israel and shared testimonies on the Shoah, leaders of the Yishuv like Eliyahu Dobkin and Yitzhak Tabenkin often believed they were hearing exaggerated reports.[24] Perhaps by June 1946, one year after end of war, the Yishuv was prepared to believe, which is why her testimony set off such a shockwave.[25]

Tabenkin introduced her with words of praise, which also included a key message: "Have we not turned over a new page in the history of Israel? Have we not created a new and different type of Jew? . . . Jews were now forced to be strong to overcome weakness."[26] Tabenkin, in introducing her remarks, identified her actions with those of the movement as a whole; echoing Zuckerman's rhetorical questions from one year earlier—did we pass the test? Did our movement display the same passivity of those who went to Treblinka? Her words and actions proved the movement had rebelled and survived. Speaking for eight hours in perfect Hebrew, her testimony had an impact—it stood alone and was immediately reprinted and circulated far and wide (as *Aharonim al ha Homah* [The last ones on the wall]).[27]

Lubetkin's testimony differs from Edelman's in a number of crucial respects. The dramatic nature of the event and the air of expectation that greeted her words must be appreciated; likewise, there is a noticeable shift in tone from the letters she and Zuckerman sent to the Yishuv in 1944. Whereas those letters expressed a sense of solidarity with their future compatriots, after her arrival in May 1946, Lubetkin wrote to Zuckerman that she felt a disconnect from the people she had met in Yishuv, who could not really understand her. Thus Zivia opened her much anticipated and

Zivia Lubetkin speaking at a conference of Kibbutz HaMeuchad at Kibbutz Yagur, 1946. (Ghetto Fighters House Archive, no. 21078)

Delegates at the conference of Kibbutz HaMeuchad, 1946, listen to Zivia address the crowd at Kibbutz Yagur. She can be seen in the distance, in the center of the photo. Ghetto Fighters House Archive, no. 21081.

emotional remarks with an acknowledgement of the mixed emotions she too felt at this incredible moment. On the one hand, she had been dreaming of this moment for twelve years, but for her, this great anticipation and excitement was tempered by what she had just endured in the previous six years:

> Dear friends! Different feelings are swirling inside of me in this meeting with you. For 12 years I have dreamt about this meeting with you. Many of you, certainly, remember still what the encounter with the land was like for you, with comrades, with the kibbutz, with the home. And you can certainly not imagine what this encounter is like for me, when on top of everything I have endured six years like these. They almost would not have been imaginable, that

> someone from among us would have the honor to one day encounter you. And nonetheless—it is difficult and very sad.[28]

While the people in the land seemed happy and carefree, she still had the misery and the overcrowding of the ghettos right before her eyes. In her remarks, Zivia sought to overcome the disconnect she felt between the festive air of life in the Yishuv (the Shavuot holiday was celebrated in the kibbutzim the week before) and the horrors of life under the German occupation by describing her first encounter with the German occupation in January 1940 after her return from Soviet-occupied L'vov. Although first overwhelmed by the sight of Jews wearing the armbands, people dying of hunger, and Jewish police enforcing German regulations, over years of destruction and death, "there was almost no feeling of hope, they stopped feeling, they stopped being disgusted." Speaking directly to her audience, she explained "and perhaps the only thing which sustained us still in life was you: the land, the Yishuv, the workers movement, the kibbutz, the home. . . . It was only thanks to you that we stayed alive."

Despite this sense of connection to the Yishuv, she realized that in delivering her remarks and in painting a picture of what life was like over there, she would be attempting to bridge a chasm separating one world from the other. She decided to "speak simply" and enable her audience to "complete the picture." Still she acknowledged the two paramount questions at the forefront of movement members' curiosity: "How could this thing happen, that an entire people, millions of Jews went to the slaughter? What was the destiny of our movement and its members?"[29]

Like Edelman, Zivia also sought to explain to her audience where the movement drew the strength to resist and why it took so long for resistance to develop. She divided the six years of the war into two periods: before the liquidation (of the ghetto) and after the liquidation. While the deportations marked a psychological turning point, when it became clear that eradication of the Jews of Poland was the Germans' ultimate goal, she explained how the first period under the Germans began a process of spiritual destruction, which paved the way for a later physical annihilation.

While Jews perceived this as two periods, only with the benefit of hindsight could she know that this was "from the first day of the conquest of Poland, a satanic plan that from the first day until the last day was conducted just as the Germans know how to conduct it—in exact, complete, order."

Like Edelman, Lubetkin's description of the early period emphasizes the process of dehumanization, which she labels "spiritual destruction, erasing the human image," crucial preparation for the subsequent physical annihilation. She outlines the edicts imposed on the Jewish population, ordered to wear a Jewish star, "forbidden to ride on the train, forbidden to engage in commerce, forbidden to hold money, forbidden to hold apartments, forbidden to breathe, forbidden to live. The thing was done step by step."

> And in response to the edicts there was even a feeling among the Jews: "We will still show them, our enemies! They will not defeat us!" We also had this feeling amongst ourselves: many would fall at the hands of the Germans, from hunger, from disease,—but the vast majority will remain. Our task therefore was to protect, that the *she'erit hapletah*, in particular the youth—would be complete spiritually and physically, so that after the war it would be able to fulfill its responsibilities.[30]

As good movement members, they had been focused on protecting and cultivating the Jewish youth, especially in a period where no other form of Jewish leadership could be trusted and all members of the Judenrat, without exception, were seen as "traitors."

Even so, Zivia admitted that she came to regret the movement's exclusive focus on the Jewish youth, believing they should have worked with the broader Jewish public from the beginning. Nonetheless, the work in the early period, which was heavily influenced by the leadership of Yitzhak Katznelson and focused on maintaining connections with Israel, on training of kibbutz groups, and on communication work to overcome barriers and isolation imposed by the Germans, would be crucial in the later emergence of resistance. As Zivia explained: "There was no city in Poland where you could not trace a revolt to the existence of a kibbutz."

Unable to join together with the Bund, she said, HeHalutz, the Left Zionists, and the Communists formed an antifascist bloc to work together with the PPR (Polish Workers Party) and the Polish Armia Ludowa. Even so, the group was unorganized and without arms when the Germans began the first deportation action. Zivia explained to the audience what she meant by *akcjia* (liquidation action), the ways in which the Jewish public was deceived by letters from family members "working in Białystok," and the role played by the Judenrat and the Jewish police, who would even turn over their parents, their children, and their spouses. Like Edelman, she was quite critical of Adam Czerniakow, who chose suicide rather than informing the Jewish public that deportation to the East meant death. While critical of the Judenrat and the Jewish police and their role in the liquidation, Zivia also explained how the German policies successfully divided the Jewish population by atomizing Jewish society ("every Jew thought to save his own soul"), thereby preventing unified action. "After the Germans poisoned the soul and removed the human image, then came the extreme hunger. So is it any wonder the Jews went where they were told to?"[31] Eventually the underground managed to convene a meeting of proletarian parties; the Bund sent an emissary to Treblinka, who reported back that Treblinka means death; the Bund also began to prepare for defense. At the time, they still believed that they would receive arms from the Polish underground and the Polska Partia Socjalistyczna (Polish Socialist Party), but nothing came.

Zivia's description of the period of the Great Deportation focuses less (compared to Marek Edelman) on the suffering of the Jewish masses and more on the challenges that confronted the underground in acquiring arms and organizing resistance. For those who managed to survive the deportations, however, the experience imprinted a resolve to save Jewish honor and to choose the manner of their deaths—not only as individuals, but as a collective. Embarrassed to have survived the deportation and witness the death of hundreds of thousands of Jews, Zivia described a general sense "that there was no point to this kind of life . . . it would be better to commit suicide fighting. We would go outside, to the street. We still had two guns and ten liters of gas for starting fires. We would kill as many Germans as we could, and then they would kill us. This was a general consensus." But there was one member of their group (perhaps Zuckerman—she does not give a name) who said something different, that they were not only responsible for their own lives and deaths, but should "do something that would be more than the death of individuals, something that would also save the honor and lives of all those who had managed to survive the killing."[32]

The other lesson learned by the underground after the deportations, Zivia explained, was that they could rely only on themselves, not on outside groups and not on the Jewish establishment. They resolved to try to connect with all of the other parties, including Zionists, Bundists, and Revisionists, and also formed the Jewish National Committee. After "difficult negotiations" with the Bund they managed to form an expanded ŻOB, although they were unsuccessful in convincing the Bund to cooperate in other towns; the Bund wanted to work together only in Warsaw and did not want permanent cooperation. While the Communists joined forces with them, they felt it would be better to escape to the forest and fight from there, in order to engage in revenge actions. Still, out of a sense of obligation to the wider Jewish public, the Communists decided they could not abandon what remained of the Jewish population in the ghetto.

The motivations for armed resistance spelled out by Zivia here are noteworthy: to take revenge, to rescue the dignity of the Jewish people, to fight as Jews, to stand by the Jewish community, to save their honor—above all, "to do something Jewish," not merely as part of the general war. While Bundists like Edelman tried to connect with the Polish underground and the Home Army (of Poland), the Zionist youth felt isolated and alone, determined to wage their struggle on behalf of the Jewish nation.

In Zivia's account, the January 1943 revolt also emerges as a major turning point, because it showed the underground they had the power to foil German plans, taught them valuable lessons about how to confront the Germans, and raised the standing of the resistance before the Jewish public. Even so, she explained, the timing of the January 1943 *akcjia* surprised them when it began. More Jews had been herded to the Umschlagplatz for deportation, where thousands of Jews would be crowded for days without food and water, beaten by Jewish police, waiting for transports. The group headed by Anielewicz, which had mingled in with some of the civilians being transported to the Umschlagplatz, attacked the Germans and called on the Jews to disperse, but as Zivia explains this approach was not effective; most of the people in the transport were so caught off guard and unsure what to do that they still ran toward the Umschlagplatz and the entire resistance unit was killed except for Anielewicz and one female fighter. The second (and more effective approach, it turned out) was to hide in buildings and ambush Germans by surprise, which proved a better tactic than face-to-face combat.

Beyond restoring Jewish honor, however, another powerful force motivated the Jewish fighters: Revenge. Among Zivia's group waiting to ambush the Germans was Zechariah Artstein, a member of Freiheit, from Pruszków, whose parents had died in the ghetto and who had witnessed all levels of human degradation in a work camp. He was determined to exact revenge and was the first to exit the room they were in and fire: "we killed dozens of Germans and our group of forty managed to gain weapons in this way and only lost one man in the fight. . . . *We did not know what to do. We had killed Germans, acquired weapons, and even stayed alive. This was some kind of miracle, something unforgettable*" (my emphasis).

Following this successful, even miraculous encounter during the January revolt, she also noted a significant change in attitude on the part of the Jewish population: "we also reached a bunker of Jews and for the first time were welcomed with open arms; a rabbi even blessed us, saying we had saved Jewish honor; finally we had received some level of appreciation from the Jewish population and this gave some small pleasure."[33] Like Edelman, Zivia also sought to convey the significance of the January revolt from a psychological standpoint—the degraded and humiliated Jews in the Warsaw ghetto had learned that they could kill Germans and live to see another day, that the Germans did not want to risk lives in clearing the ghetto. "All sorts of legends began to spread about Jews with tanks, Jews pouring burning water, *Jews telling Germans they refused to go with necks outstretched.*" The January action also raised the stature of the ŻOB in the eyes of the

Poles, which proved critical in acquisition of arms. With the end of the *akcjia*, Jews began to prepare to defend and protect themselves. "The January Revolt taught us, the fighting organization, how to prepare for the battle that faced us." Between January and April, the ŻOB began to prepare a military strategy: they learned the importance of preparing fighters in units, dividing into divisions in specific sections so they would not be surprised by the entry of the Germans.

One can imagine the impact of Zivia explaining military strategy to her audience at Kibbutz Yagur (or for that matter to members of the Palmach the week before) who may have trained for military engagements but had as yet seen limited action. Improved relations with the Polish underground led to a shipment of fifty guns and fifty grenades, along with explosives to prepare land mines (Zivia made no mention of Michał Klepfisz and his role in fashioning explosives for the ŻOB). In the period between the two revolts the underground became the government in the ghetto, "even the Judenrat would not act without consulting the underground." The arrest of Aryeh Wilner, captured on the Aryan side trying to acquire arms, was a major setback for the underground. Interestingly, Zivia does not mention here that her partner and future husband, Yitzhak Zuckerman, was designated as Wilner's replacement on the Aryan side to acquire arms.

After what must have been several hours of speaking, Zivia finally reached what was the climax of her testimony: the April revolt. It is worth noting that she dedicated almost the same amount of time to the January revolt as she did to the April revolt. The level of detail in Edelman's testimony is lacking in Zivia's testimony about April, although she does expand on a few key episodes: the first days of the revolt, the end of the command bunker at Mila 18, and the escape through the sewers. As the news came through on April 18 that on the next day (the eve of Passover, April 19) the *akcjia* would begin, Zivia recalled passing through the whole ghetto to spread the news, and passing a difficult, sleepless night. And while the entire ghetto had come to support the cause of revolt, Zivia still made a clear distinction between the "elderly" who "we told to hide themselves in bunkers," and the youth, "to arm themselves." She explained to her audience that while in

January only members of HeHalutz participated in the fighting, by April "all of the parties entered the ŻOB including the socialist-Zionist parties, the Bund, the Communists, and of course the Halutz youth." Distinguishing between the fighters of the ŻOB and the rest of the ghetto population, she suggested "if only had we had more arms and material of a better quality (we had guns, grenades, some sten guns, Molotov cocktails), thousands, not just hundreds, would have joined in the fighting."

As Zivia describes the first day of the revolt, a number of differences from Edelman's testimony are noteworthy. First, she contradicts Edelman's assertion that the Bund participated in the fighting in January 1943, stating that only HeHalutz fought in January, and she makes clear that the revolt was the work of hundreds of fighters, not thousands: lack of access to arms made the difference and prevented the revolt from becoming a mass popular revolt. As the German Army (tanks, armored personnel carriers, infantry) entered the ghetto "as if marching to the battle front," Zivia described the planting of land mines where Germans had to pass on the main roads used to enter the ghetto, electric mines under the ground, which could be timed to explode (but again makes no mention of Michał Klepfisz or his role in manufacturing explosives). Likewise, she says that Klepfisz died but does not elaborate on his "heroic death" in the way Edelman does. Zivia recalls exploding mines, seeing "the arms and legs of hundreds of Germans fly in the air. I will not forget this sight for the rest of my life. . . . One young woman in my group, Tamar, laughed and said: 'this time we will not go like sheep to the slaughter, and if we are killed it will cost them dearly'."

> And truly . . . this army, which had conquered all of Europe, and not just Europe, retreated from the ghetto. We ourselves could not understand how this had happened. From among us two comrades died, who *fell by chance [my emphasis]*—Klepfisz from the Bund and Ze'ev. And the Germans retreated leaving behind hundreds of wounded. This repeated itself for three days, and the Germans were not able to enter the ghetto.[34]

Afterward the Germans switched to different tactics; instead of marching into the ghetto as whole units, they snuck in one at a time, which made the task of defending the ghetto even more difficult. Then, as Zivia explained, the Germans began to bomb from the air and the whole ghetto caught fire: "we were not fighting the Germans now, we were fighting the fire." After the first few days of fighting, the fighters found themselves in a situation they had not prepared for: "our physical strength diminished—we did not plan to stay alive, did not have enough food, and we did not prepare a retreat strategy because we did not think we would stay alive." The fighters ran out of ammunition—of bombs and grenades—and started to search for ways out of the ghetto. They had no contact with the outside; once the ghetto started burning the phones stopped working. Escape from the ghetto also seemed hopeless: they tried to sneak groups out of the ghetto but all were killed in encounters with the Germans. Soon they started to look for ways to sneak through the sewers, the challenges of which Zivia attempted to explain to her audience, of navigating subterranean passageways to escape from the ghetto, mentioning the role of Simcha Ratheizer in seeking a path through. As the situation grew more dire, the Germans began to search for Jews hiding in the bunkers, pointed out by collaborators or those forced to identify openings to bunkers at gunpoint. This also led to the discovery and death at the main ŻOB command bunker at Mila 18.

> In our bunker, of the Jewish Fighting Organization, which we entered in the days of the battles, sat 120 people of the best of the fighters and among them—Mordecai Anielewicz, Tosia, Vilner, Berl Broide, Nadia Zucker, Tuvia Borzykowski, and other comrades. I also sat there, and just by chance, one day before the beginning of the end of this bunker, I left to go to the same spot where we found the entrance to the sewers. I had a friend there and with his help I wanted to convince the Jews to remove our group from there. I went there with another friend of ours who is alive and today in Israel and his name is Haim.[35] By then it was dark and the

> group we were with told us to wait and that we would look for the group the next day.

By the next day, when Zivia returned to look for the bunker, they could not find the entrance they had left the day before. The bunker, which had multiple hidden entrances on three sides, had become unrecognizable. After some searching, Zivia managed to find thirty people who had been sheltering there and were still alive. From these, they heard what had happened in the final moments. While they had developed a number of plans in case the bunker was found by the Germans, they hadn't reckoned on poison gas being pumped into it.[36]

As Zivia related in her testimony:

> Aryeh Vilner called out: "Suicide!" and so began a series of suicides. One asked a comrade to shoot him but this did not happen in the bunker. No one killed his comrade.[37] A small group managed to sneak through the basement to escape the bunker, but for most of the people they did not have the strength to go, and only a few were saved.
>
> Thus Tosia was also saved. We found them half poisoned and exhausted and they barely resembled humans, and we moved to a place from where the day before we had sent the group to the Aryan side. We met up with our friends and through the sewage canals we exited the ghetto.

After two days and two nights in the sewers they emerged on May 10. (Zivia explained that another group, including Zechariah Artstein, Gutman, Yosef Farber, and others who had stayed in the ghetto to fight for another week, emerged from the ghetto a week later and were killed by the Germans; she makes no mention of those left behind in the sewers described in Kazik's account.) "In the forest we met those who left before us, including Grayek from the movement and Eliezer Geller from Tobbens Shultz. . . . We stayed together, a group of 60 fighters. And among us was also Tosia. At the time when you mourned me and Tosia in Israel, Tosia was still alive." This statement is one of several instances in the testimony where Zivia speaks directly to her audience, referencing the connection between the Yishuv and the fighters trapped in Poland, reinforcing the power of her testimony, as one who has literally returned from the dead.

Noting the many names of fighters and activists she could not detail in her testimony, the remainder of Zivia's public testimony that day at Kibbutz Yagur detailed the efforts to establish a relief committee, which used money provided through the Polish government-in-exile to assist twelve thousand Jews hiding on the Aryan side and the Jewish part in the failed Polish Uprising in Warsaw, until they were finally liberated. After detailing the organization of the resistance and the uprising in Warsaw, as well as others aspects of wartime experience and the work that remained to rescue the remnants of European Jewry, she concluded her testimony with two observations, answering questions she was sure her audience must have. The first question: "How did it happen that an entire people went like this, necks outstretched, to the massacre?" Defending the behavior of the Jewish people, she answered: "I doubt that any other nation would respond differently under these circumstances of terrible isolation in the entire world, against a machinery of destruction so organized by the Germans." "If we had not been members of the movement, if we had not absorbed from our childhood the values which you gave to us. . . . We were able to make the stand that we made in the ghetto because we were a movement, collective, because everyone of us knew that he was not alone."[38]

It was the connection to the movement, the feeling of belonging to a collective, that sustained the ghetto fighters and became the source of their strength. Zivia distinguished herself from the broader Jewish public who "did not know what to do." Those who belonged to the movement, who had been raised and educated by the values of the movement, knew what to do. While the broader Jewish public was lost and confused, Zivia argued, "Because of the values on which we were raised and educated from them we always found the way. This was the strength which enabled us to live, and in fact this is the force which strengthens today the lives of the survivors." She rejected the celebration of individual heroes (of Yitzhak or Zivia, of Mordecai or Frumka) and elevated the ideals of the movement.

A true Zionist would have known how to behave. This point is crucial: it reinforced the Zionist worldview and simplified the complexities of wartime behavior. Those who allowed themselves to be led like sheep to the slaughter had not been raised on the ideals of the movement.

Zivia concluded her testimony by discussing the two emotions that motivated the surviving members of the movement after liberation: revenge and a desire to reconnect with Israel. Crucially, in the immediate aftermath of the war they channeled the drive to reconnect with the movement that had raised them and with the Land of Israel into gathering the surviving youth and immediately organizing kibbutzim that would come to form the backbone of the Bricha. In this way, the drive to resistance was fused with the struggle to create the state as the surviving members of HeHalutz worked to show the surviving youth in Poland, "a path, show them a way, some real solution. And we knew that if we did not organize them they would scatter and never reach Israel and be lost to the pioneering movement."[39]

Zivia's story was subsequently serialized in the publications of the workers' movement. *Davar Hashavua* and *Commentary* (in English) reprinted Zivia's description of the final days of the uprising and her escape from the ghetto through the Warsaw sewers. People who heard Zivia speak that day at the conference described it as a transformative experience. The poet Haim Guri described it as a "sublime and terrible occasion . . . it came as a knife to the heart."[40]

In analyzing Lubetkin's testimony from June 8, 1946, it is clear she worked to speak directly to her audience and she was clearly oriented to the party congress of Dror and Kibbutz HaMeuchad at Yagur. The influence of Tabenkin and his "guidance" also need to be taken into account, as is the fact that she spoke without notes (except, apparently, for a prewritten opening statement) for hours in a row. Hence it is not surprising that she would leave out details; Edelman's testimony by comparison is in a published pamphlet that would have been edited and revised.

Later Lubetkin and Zuckerman would be the driving force behind the creation of Kibbutz Lochamei HaGetaot (four kilometers north of Acre), with the groundbreaking ceremony taking place on the sixth anniversary of the Warsaw Ghetto Uprising. There, Zuckerman in particular would embark on a series of projects to write the history of Jewish resistance during the war.

Through their testimonies, surviving ghetto fighters gave meaning to the actions of comrades who had defended the honor of the Jewish people through their sacrifice, while also trying to explain how it was that other kin could be marched like "sheep to the slaughter." The testimonies of Lubetkin and Zuckerman suggest that their ability to act and act bravely came from their connection to the Land of Israel and the movement's ideology and education. Nonetheless, the dichotomies and imagery that became standard in the aftermath minimized the complexity of wartime Jewish behavior. And that effect was the more tenacious, given the outsized influence of the surviving ghetto fighters themselves in shaping the historiography of resistance and the debates that would dominate the field. Still, as ghetto fighters like Lubetkin would detail the heroic efforts of the resistance, they struggled with their place in the broader history of the Jewish people. Were the sheep they disparaged part of their flock? Or were they an obstacle to the revolt? Did resistance signify the choice of a minority of Zionist heroes or was it a true Jewish response? As "the last ones on the wall" (the title of Zivia's published speech at Yagur), they carried the burden of survival and a responsibility to the dead, whose sacrifice they could never fully redeem.

Vladka Tells Her Story

In the same week that Zivia Lubetkin arrived in the Yishuv at the end of May 1946, Vladka Meed arrived in New York and introduced herself to an American audience. Vladka's testimony was published in a series of articles she wrote for the *Forverts (in Yiddish)* over the course of approximately six months in 1946.

Vladka Meed (nee Feigele Peltel) was born in Warsaw in 1921. From an early age, Vladka was involved in Bund youth organizations (Skif and Tsukunft) and was educated at secular Yiddish schools sponsored by the Bund. After the German occupation of Warsaw, she used her Polish appearance to provide food and income for her family, standing in breadlines instead of her father and selling her mother's wares on the streets of the more

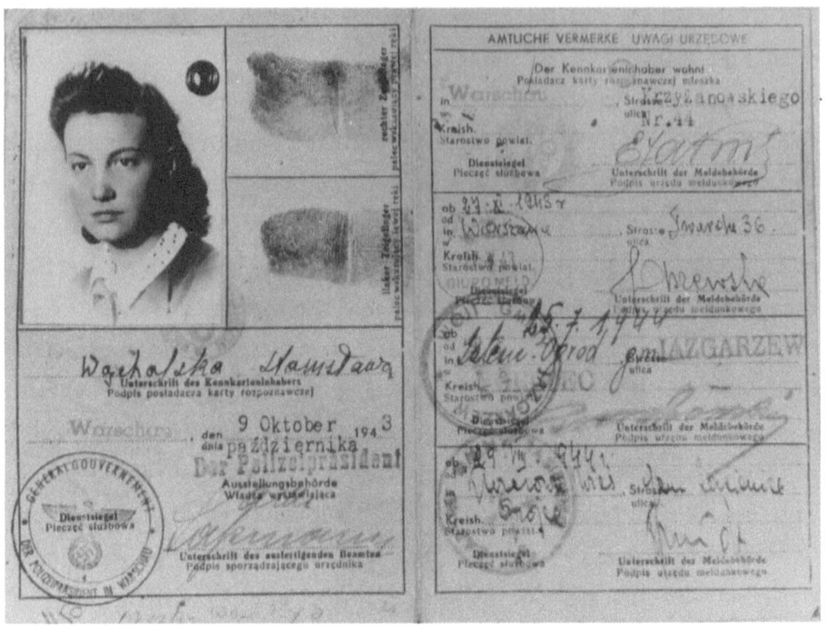

False identification card issued in name of Stanislawa Wachalska, used by Vladka Meed (Feigele Peltel) while serving as a courier for the Jewish underground in Warsaw. (United States Holocaust Memorial Museum, photo archives, no. 02325)

affluent Warsaw neighborhoods to provide for her family. In the fall of 1940, when the ghetto was created, the Peltel family was forced to relocate to a small one-room apartment. Vladka's father died from pneumonia in 1941 and in August 1942 her mother, brother, and sister were rounded-up and deported to Treblinka. At that time Vladka was working in the Többens factory in the ghetto and living in its adjacent dormitory. When not working in the factory, she devoted her energies to organizing children's groups for the Bund underground. In the fall of 1942, she joined the newly created Jewish Coordinating Committee. Because of her Polish appearance, the underground smuggled her out of the ghetto in December 1942 to work as a courier for the Coordinating Committee on the Aryan side. She specifically worked to obtain arms for the ŻOB and to find hiding places for Jewish women and children. She also assisted Jews already in hiding with money, food, clothing, documentation, medical care, and shelter. During the revolt, Vladka worked to find shelter for the surviving fighters who managed to escape the ghetto.

After the revolt was crushed, Vladka was arrested, along with Abrasha Blum, and both were jailed at the local precinct house. Her adoptive Polish mother, Anna Wachalska (Vladka used the false identity of Stanislawa Wachalska), helped rescue her through a bribe offered to the police, but help arrived too late to save Blum, who had been turned over to the Gestapo. Following a period of hiding in the countryside, Vladka returned to her duties as a courier for the underground. Not long after moving to the Aryan side, she met up with Benjamin Miedzyrzecki, who would eventually become her husband. Together Vladka and Benjamin participated in the Polish Uprising of August 1944 and joined the evacuation of the Polish population after the revolt was suppressed by the Germans.

Shortly after liberation, Benjamin and Vladka were married in a Jewish ceremony in Warsaw. They soon moved to Lodz, where Benjamin opened a leather goods store. Continued antisemitism after the war made it clear that it would be impossible for the couple to remain in Poland, and they left Poland for the United States in February 1946. They were arrested by British police, however, at the border between Germany and Belgium and imprisoned in Aachen. A British rabbi serving in the area helped secure their release but they were in such poor health that they had to be taken to a convalescent home in Garmisch-Partenkirchen in the Bavarian Alps. After their recuperation they moved to an apartment in Munich (in the previous chapter, Vladka's testimony at an April 1946 "mourning academy" in Munich is detailed). In Munich, a United Nations Relief and Rehabilitation Administration official approached Benjamin and asked him to put together a list of fifty Jewish survivors to be sponsored by an international relief committee affiliated with the Jewish Labor Committee, to immigrate to the United States. The group sailed from Bremerhaven on May 24 on board the SS Marine Flasher.

Just weeks before she journeyed to America, a short testimony by Vladka was also published in the DP camp newspaper, *Unzer Veg*, on the third anniversary of the Warsaw Revolt, April 19, 1946. On June 1, approximately one week after her arrival in New York, Vladka was introduced to the readers of the *Forverts* as a "heroine from the Warsaw Ghetto." Borekh Shefner, a journalist active with the Bund in interwar Poland, interviewed Vladka for the article, introducing the "24 year old heroine" to the newspaper's readers.[41] Shefner began by asking Vladka if she was ever afraid. At first she answers: "no. And the answer is so simple and without pose, that it is simply all."

> But wait, she now remembers. One time she was indeed a little frightened. . . . This was right before the Warsaw uprising when she was on a specially dangerous mission: she was sent to purchase weapons from criminals in the Polish underworld about whom was known they had already exposed members of the underground movement. But the Bund gave her the task to acquire weapons for any price . . . and she did.

Shefner writes that when Hitler started the war Vladka was only seventeen years old. But Vladka's war against Hitler had begun much earlier—when she was a Jewish working child in Warsaw and joined the Bund's child organization Skif, as one of "the leaders of the Jewish socialist youth movement . . . and when the war began in September 1939 she immersed herself with all her soul in the work to help organize the Jewish underground movement in Poland."

She saw her mother and brother and sister taken away to be deported to Treblinka.

Shefner's profile highlighted the "singular emotion" that enabled Vladka to draw strength for the most difficult moments: "As one draws water from a deep well—the feeling of revenge against the Germans. Each day and each hour and each minute and each second awake and asleep—REVENGE." After Vladka escaped from the ghetto, Shefner writes, "on this night ended the story of Feigele Peltel and began the legend of 'Vladka'."[42]

Shefner's introduction of Vladka as a "heroine of the Warsaw Ghetto" presents her as a superhero, motivated by a drive to avenge the loss of her family in her war against the Germans. This celebration of individual

וולאַדקע׳ — אַ העלדין, פון וואַרשעווער געטאָ

איהר אמת׳ער נאָמען איז
פייגעלע פעלטעל.—פינף
יאָהר איז זי געווען פאַר־
שטעלט ווי א פוילישע
מיידעל אונטער׳ן נאָמען
וולאַדקע. — די העלדישע
אַרבייט וואָס זי האָט אין
די יאָהרען דורכגעפיהרט
אין דעם קאַמף געגען די
נאַצים און צו ברענגען
הילף צו די אידען אין די
לאַגערען. — זי איז איצט
אין אַמעריקע. — א גע־
שפּרעך מיט איהר.

פון ב. שעפנער

Vladka—a Heroine of the Warsaw Ghetto, *Forverts*, June 1, 1946.

heroism stood in stark contrast to the reception accorded to members of movements nourished on the ideals of collectivism and self-sacrifice.

Vladka began writing weekly installments for the *Forverts* on June 29, 1946, which would be published regularly for the next five months, until November 16. The series would subsequently be edited and published as her memoir, *On Both Sides of the Ghetto Wall*, first published in Yiddish.[43]

Years later, in an interview with the sociologist William Helmreich, Vladka recalled the emotions that she grappled with while writing her account:

> WH: How did you come to write the book?
> VM: At first I wrote for the *Forverts*. The people suggested I should write it as a book. It was very hard. I would cry and want to stop because what happened became very vivid in front of my eyes. I didn't concentrate so much on my personal life because my personal life was not so important. It

was like a little drop, not even a drop, a speck in the lives of all the others who perished.

WH: But it's an answer to those historians who deny resistance?

VM: Yes, it is an answer; today people look at it differently. To go on with life was not so easy in the ghetto. And it was, in a way, resistance. The survivors achieved quite a bit and the children also achieved. Life and how to live is the resistance. The desire to live is also very strong.[44]

While Helmreich saw Vladka's testimony as a response to those who would deny the fact of Jewish resistance, Meed's response is enlightening: she is not focused on armed resistance; just continuing to live, to reject the German death sentence, she says, is resistance. Looking back in a 2001 interview with Rochelle Saidel on the writing of the memoir, Meed said she would approach the book differently if she were to write it again, with the "same thoughts but different feelings." "At that time I thought, 'who would be interested in people's feelings from a world destroyed?'" she explained. "I limited myself in expressing feelings, I survived. I should cry? Here in the [United] States I learned that the individual means a lot and people are very interested in personal things, everyday life." If she were to write her book again, she said, "I would write with more emotional input, but I considered my feelings not important compared to what took place."[45]

In Vladka's own self-analysis her book reads more as a narrative of events in Warsaw than a memoir; it explains how things changed when the deportations started and offers objective descriptions rather than meditating on the situation. Her story is told in a matter-of-fact way, opposed as she is to the idea of using "literary language" regarding the Holocaust.

Because Vladka's testimony was presented in a serialized form, its tone was more episodic, with less of a narrative arc than the testimonies of Edelman and Lubetkin. Even when the testimony was published in 1948 as *Fun Beyde Zaytn Geto Moyer*, Vladka maintained the episodic format, as the week-by-week episodes were presented as separate chapters. For this reason, too, Vladka seems to have less of a central theme than Edelman (who clearly seeks to demonstrate the difficulty in convincing the ghetto to fight back and who focuses on the central role played by the Bund in organizing the revolt) or Lubetkin (who also focuses on the evolution of armed resistance in the ghetto and, in her case, the central role played by Zionist youth). Vladka's is, as she notes in later years, an objective, dry account. She presents herself as an outside observer whose key role was mainly to witness the heroic deeds of others. Even so, one emotion does seep through: an angry disbelief that the world could stand silent as these monstrous crimes occurred.

In the June 29, 1946, edition of *Forverts*, Vladka's first article in the series begins in August 1942 with a recollection of "the week when the Germans sent 110,000 Warsaw Jews to Treblinka."[46] Unlike Edelman and Lubetkin, Vladka does not provide the context of the period from the outbreak of the war with its steady dehumanization of the Jewish public. On the contrary, she begins with the decimation of Jewish Warsaw, focusing on the Great Deportation. "August 1942. The extermination of the Warsaw Ghetto continued. *Akcjies* continued nonstop in the streets, in the shops, in the home. No papers or connections helped anymore." The first escapees from Treblinka arrived in the ghetto, describing horrible things. It was hard to believe, Vladka recalled, that these things could have happened to her mother, her brother, her sister.

> I was now alone. My entire family had been taken away. My father had died in the ghetto. All were gone. My heart no longer trembled when an *akcjia* came, I had nothing left to fear. . . . In quiet moments, I regretted not having been sent away with them, that I could not help calm my mother, extend a hand to my sister, lift my little brother's spirits with a smile.
>
> Where are they now?!

In the version published as *On Both Sides of the Wall*, Vladka began her memoir on July 22 with the start of the liquidation action and described the capture of her family in greater detail. There the same passage was slightly revised, adding more details on her emotions and state of mind:

> I was alone now—my mother, brother, and sister had gone to some dreadful unknown. My heart no longer jumped as much during a roundup as it had before. There was very little left to fear now.
>
> A few people fortunate enough to escape from Treblinka had returned to the ghetto with their stories of their gruesome experiences. I refused to believe that my loved ones could be dead. Better not think about it, I told myself; they must be alive somewhere. I often felt sorry that I had not gone with them. Why should I be subjected to the constant anguish, the constant fear of deportation, when there was no way out anyway? I was depressed and apathetic, going mechanically through the days.
>
> It was as if my heart had been turned to stone, as if my will to live had dissolved. Had it not been for my friends, I would have been trapped more than once. They did not desert me in my time of need.[47]

In the second installment of Vladka's recollections, published in the *Forverts* on July 6, the headline read: "Vladka describes the plan to leave the ghetto and pass as a Polish *shikse.*" She tells that Abrasha Blum, "the spirit of the entire Bund's work," summoned her and explained the importance of the new task that unites everyone: resistance.

> [We] must be prepared to fight. We must initiate contact with the area inside. Create weapons. Remove women and children who cannot fight as far from the ghetto as possible.
>
> I sit with eyes wide open and absorb the words. Finally now is the time. How often had we thought and dreamed about this moment. Now we stood before an established fact. Our only dream, to take revenge on the Germans. Revenge for my mother, for my sister, for my brother. . . . All the Jews with no difference in beliefs and ideologies we are joined together in one great mission—revenge!

> The faces of the members assembled begin to shine. In their eyes flickered a spark, a flame. No one moved. People began to discuss the question of how to organize the groups.[48]

Vladka was designated to cross to the other side because she could pass as a Christian. While most of her testimony is devoid of emotion and does not delve deeply into the political motivations of the various parties in the ghetto, Vladka does single out here the central driving force that led the Bundists and the Zionists to unite: "our only dream, to take revenge on the Germans." The thought of avenging the death of her mother, brother, and sister animates Vladka, too: "Of course I want to! I answered with excitement—but how? No one must know about this, answered Abrasha, in a few days you will receive instructions." Vladka told no one and waited. And then one night, another Jewish hero appeared, calling her to action:

> 10 o'clock at night. I was at home. Someone knocked. I opened the door. A tall man stood in the door and asked for me. I did not know who it was. In the Corridor it was dark and there was no light. I invited the man to come into the room. And there, I wonder! It was Michał Klepfisz! Tall, with bare head, in a dark coat, he smiled, the heroic pillar of the ghetto uprising. . . .
>
> I peppered him with questions and he told me to prepare myself to leave. I asked him to stay but it was late and I had to run to meet with Blum.[49]

In Vladka's account, Klepfisz appears again, identified for an American audience who would have been familiar with his reputation as the "heroic pillar of the ghetto uprising."

Subsequent installments of her account included descriptions of smuggling arms into the ghetto, the struggle against Polish blackmailers, the January 1943 revolt, efforts to save Jewish children, preparations for the revolt, and the revolt itself. As a member of the Bund, Vladka's recollections would of course focus more on her experiences and encounters with other members of the Bundist underground and highlight the movement's activities in the resistance. The first draft of her account published in the *Forward* in 1946 still focused on the fraternity and collaboration between various members of the underground, united by the drive to avenge the killings of loved ones and comrades. By the time her memoir was published in 1948 by the Workmen's Circle, it is clear some minor editing had taken place.

For example, on September 21, 1946, Vladka described the April 1943 revolt for readers of the *Forverts*:

> I do not know if I can describe in my words to provide a picture of what happened behind the sealed ghetto walls and on the Aryan side in the days of the ghetto uprising.
>
> I will try to tell in a manner that is as simple and clear as possible, what I alone saw on the Aryan side and later heard from my friends, the ghetto fighters.
>
> All preparations of the Jewish underground movement—from the fighting organization in ghetto and outside the ghetto [*its supporters outside the ghetto* in the book version] were in full burn [full speed].
>
> *All the political divisions in the fighting organization were almost completely gone in this feverish time.* [This sentence appears in *Forverts* but not in the book.]
>
> None of our illegal organizations knew exactly when the final Jewish *akcjia* would take place. People thought perhaps late April or May so were ready for fighting at any minute.[50]

In the *Forverts* version, Vladka also described the role of "Comrade Mikolai (Dr. Leo Feiner), representative of the Coordinating Committee, together with Antek (Yitzhak Zuckerman), representative of the Fighting Organization on the Aryan side, and their efforts to come to an understanding with the Polish Underground movement" to aid with the resistance. In the book version, however, Antek no longer appears. Instead, the sentence reads "Comrade (chaver) Mikolai (Dr. Leo Feiner), representative of the coordinating committee, was to reach an understanding with the Polish underground movement."[51]

While Edelman and Lubetkin offered recollections as direct participants in the historic battles in the ghetto, Vladka's perspective was as an observer outside the ghetto, waiting for updates that came through brief telephone calls from inside the ghetto to Mikolai (Leon Feiner). Recalling the first days of the revolt, Vladka cites a call from Abrasha Blum with a brief update on the fighting:

> That was all. No appeals for help, no cries of despair. Just a simple terse communiqué from the battlefront.
>
> The third night of April 22/23rd, at the same time, came a second telephone call. "Today was a bad day. Michał Klepfish fell in battle. We are short of ammunition. We need arms." The conversation was interrupted by the telephone central office. There were no more calls from Abrasha Blum. What more was there to add? These words spoken in the middle of the fight in the burning ghetto, spoke for themselves. Michał Klepfish had fallen. On 17 April two days before the ghetto uprising on the day of his birthday, Michał succeeded in purchasing a revolver. He managed to smuggle it into the ghetto on the same day. Now he was no longer among the living. He was not the first and not the last to fall.[52]

Lamenting their inability to help the fighters in the ghetto and the lack of support from the Polish underground, Vladka says, "all of our plans on the Aryan side seem to come to nothing. . . . Bitter and depressed we wandered on the Polish streets and sought to establish contact with the ghetto. Still alone. Even now when the whole Polish underground was inspired by the ghetto struggle, we received no significant help. The ghetto was alone in its struggle, and we on the Aryan side, are alone in our helplessness."

Vladka describes managing to get closer to the ghetto, to Świętojerska 21, the house of the Dubiels. She managed to get past a German sentry by convincing him she was going to visit her mother. From the house of these Polish friends she was able to see some of the battles, the fires, the shootings raging in the ghetto. Returning to her dwelling she observed even more atrocities. Still she wrote:

> The ghetto fought above all. On the 5th day of the uprising the Coordinating Committee on the Aryan Side issued a declaration in the name of the fighting ghetto. The declaration was written in Polish. The appeal stressed the heroism and determination of the fighters, the ferocity of the struggle. Each house in the ghetto is a fortress against the Germans. The Jewish insurgents (*oyf-shtanders*) send their fervent greetings to all who struggle against Nazism. The declaration read: "We will avenge the crimes of Dachau, Treblinka, and Auschwitz. The struggle continues for our freedom and yours." Signed: Jewish Fighting Organization. The poster was printed in Żoliborz street. Shooting in the ghetto continued.[53]

Describing how the ghetto was alone in its struggle, as no help from the Polish underground was forthcoming, but all around those outside of the ghetto stood in wonder and amazement, Vladka asked, "Why was the world silent?"

> This was happening in the heart of a city with thousands of people. Helpless men, women, and children were being burned alive—and the world was silent.
>
> Where was the conscience of the world?[54]

On the eleventh day of the revolt, she met with the two ghetto fighters Zygmunt (Zalman Frydrych of the Bund) and Kazik (Simcha Rotem; a.k.a. S. Ratheizer, of Zion-Dror). Both had left the ghetto to bring help for their fighting comrades.[55]

On September 28, Vladka's account included a description of the heroic death of Melech Perlman (a fighter in the central ghetto, shot and wounded on a night mission in the ghetto, who sacrificed himself so that his comrades might escape) and concluded with a description of Kazik leading the group out via the sewers. In *Forverts*, there is no mention of Mordecai Anielewicz; in the book version, the account is even more detailed and includes a copy of Mordecai Anielewicz's last letter.[56] "In fire and smoke was the Warsaw ghetto destroyed."

Vladka continued her account in the October 12 issue with a next chapter on Abrasha Blum. Vladka concluded her series on November 16, 1946 with some final thoughts and vignettes, which surely came straight from the heart. Unlike Zivia, who reinforced her connection to the Land of Israel, to the movement, to the cause that sustained her in her time of struggle, Vladka emphasized her feelings of abandonment, alienation, and indeed her anger at the silence of American Jewry.

November 16, 1946

> Now, when the time comes for me to write the last of the series of articles I do not know with what to end. Various feelings and memories come to me. Perhaps I should deal in the last lines with the holy sorrow, which we have been left with from my fallen ghetto comrades, or perhaps I should end with the cry, the strong scream against all around, against the world, which stood silently and passively in the time of our destruction.
>
> Even now. At this moment of concluding, come to mind certain moments of quiet and heroic outstanding actions. . . .
>
> In these articles I have described moments of underground struggle against Nazism with which I had personal contact or directly participated in. That which I described is only a small part of the general struggle against the Nazi regime and I have tried to create an impression, that Jewish heroism was not only reflected in the revolt and the uprising by itself. But no. From the very beginning of the Nazi occupation, in

> each corner of ghetto life the Jews undertook a quiet self-sacrificing stubborn struggle against the occupier.

Her concluding paragraphs depict April 19 as the culmination of a long process of resistance that began long before the armed revolt.

> 19 April, the outbreak of the Warsaw ghetto revolt, what is the culmination point of a long chain of quiet heroic acts of the Jewish people in the time of the Nazi regime. And together with the heroic ghetto revolt will this struggle find its way into Jewish history as one of the truest heroic chapters.
>
> But even then, when one is occupied with all the memories of that heroic struggle, a question burns in the mind and the heart which cannot be ignored and demands an answer; a question which comes to all of those who remain.
>
> Where were you, Jews in the free lands in these horrible times? Why were you silent?
>
> No, this is not any question. This is a reproach.
>
> The world knew about it as underground messengers and messages were sent, reports in newspapers and radio reports. Even when people did not want to believe this was enough to awaken the consciousness of the world.

Vladka writes that the silence of the world reinforced the helplessness and isolation of the Jews, thereby enabling the Nazi plan of annihilation. Surely, her readers would respond that horrible things happen in wartime . . . but still, she rebuked them for their silence.

> Our one hope was to hear your screaming protests, the burning protest for those who were close to a horrible death. And now in the present day, when the small remnant of Jews struggles to continue its existence, the question remains: have you fulfilled your obligation to them?

Subsequently her published memoir would be lauded by reviewers Philip Friedman and Koppel Pinson as:

> A second outstanding work is the volume of memoirs by Wladke, "On Both Sides of the Ghetto Wall." This book captivates the reader by its utter simplicity and freshness of approach. The author, whose real name is Feigele Peltel, was 17 years old when the war started and a member of the youth group, "Zukunft." She put herself at the disposal of the underground organization of the Jewish Workers' Bund as soon as the Germans occupied Poland. Because of her "Aryan" appearance, her courage and readiness for self-sacrifice, she was appointed to the dangerous post of liaison officer under the name "Wladke." She carried out perilous missions to maintain contact with the "Ayran" section of Warsaw and with Jewish ghettos and labor camps in the provinces. Her description of these journeys are most absorbing and full of deep sympathy. At the same time, they are free of the false pathos and literary exaggerations which characterize so much of the memoir literature of this kind. Her diary covers the period between July 22, 1942 and liberation at the beginning of 1945.[57]

Following her arrival in New York, Vladka was busy as a self-described freelance writer and lecturer and soon became probably the most prominent voice of Holocaust memory in New York, hosting a radio show on WEVD. In the years that followed, Meed continued to lecture on the Holocaust, and, together with her husband was extremely active in Holocaust education and memorialization. As vice president of the Jewish Labor Committee, she for many years ran the Yiddish Cultural and Welfare Department and was responsible for a filmstrip and an exhibit on the Warsaw Ghetto Uprising. For about ten years she was the Jewish Labor Committee's Yiddish-language commentator on a weekly program on WEVD, the Yiddish radio station in New York.

The rebuke with which Vladka ended her series, a rebuke for the silence of world Jewry and specifically American Jewry, is absent in subsequent published versions of the testimony, but the reproach was always there: "Where were you, Jews in the free lands in these horrible times? Why were you silent?" Instead of an invocation of Jewish heroism, instead of a confirmation of the Zionist worldview, she makes an assignation of guilt. How would American Jews respond to this reproach? It is understandable that Jews in the Yishuv would interpret Warsaw in terms of the struggle to build the state and as a confirmation of the Zionist worldview. For Jews in America, where no monuments would be built to the actual ghetto fighters, could the abstract idea that Jews had fought back, that Jews had taken up arms in the defense of freedom, overcome guilt for their own silence during the Holocaust? Unlike Lubetkin's account, which could be used in service of building a Zionist future, the accounts of Marek Edelman and Vladka Meed may have rested uneasily with Jews living in Poland or America.

8

Literary and Artistic Representations before the Fifth Anniversary of the Revolt

As the surviving ghetto fighters made their way to their new homes in Israel, in America, and, for Marek Edelman, in a rebuilding and increasingly communist Poland, they would find that their individual threads of the historical record would be incorporated into collective memory projects in their new homelands. Within five years of the revolt, however, the specifics of their individual memories would matter less than the symbolic significance of the revolt: What did the uprising mean for the future of the Jewish people? How might it be used in the service of social and political agendas after the war? How did these agendas frame the ways in which the revolt would be remembered?

By 1948, the most important issue before the Jewish people was the creation of the State of Israel; the Warsaw Ghetto Uprising was too powerful a symbol not to be used to advance this cause. While ample historical evidence on the revolt had emerged by 1948, Jewish communities in Israel and America worked to incorporate the Holocaust, and specifically, the Warsaw Ghetto Uprising, into a collective memory that supported (and did not challenge) preexisting worldviews and could be utilized in envisioning a Jewish future. How were the Jewish people supposed to make sense of the massive calamity, the destruction of an entire civilization? The history of the uprising came to be interpreted either as part of the struggle against fascism and totalitarianism in defense of democracy or as justification for the creation of the Jewish state. The contribution of the heroes and martyrs of Warsaw was also understood in this way, as a sacrifice for a greater cause, as a step on the path to rebirth of the Jewish people. The two poles of Jewish behavior, of heroes and martyrs, of ghetto fighters vs. sheep to the slaughter, of Warsaw vs. Treblinka, also seem to have been enshrined within the frameworks for understanding the event, regardless of ideological viewpoint. This duality would be evidenced in various Jewish cultural arenas engaged in shaping collective memory after the war.

As scholars of collective memory have argued, societies "remember" through the collective language of literature, monuments, memorials, and art. As Yael Zerubavel argues in her study of Israeli national tradition, memory is shaped in negotiation between the present and the past, between

> available historical records and current social and political agendas. And in the process of referring back to these records, it shifts its interpretation, selectively emphasizing, suppressing, and elaborating different aspects of that record. History and memory, therefore, do not operate in totally detached, opposite directions. Their relationships are underlined by conflict as well as interdependence, and this ambiguity provides the commemoration with the creative tension that makes it such a fascinating subject of study.[1]

Thus, according to Zerubavel, history and memory are in a constant fluid relationship, operating not in a linear direction, with history shaping memory, but functioning in a dynamic, interdependent manner. One of the questions this study seeks to answer, however, is to what extent do the individual memories of participants and witnesses to an event actually shape the collective memory of the event? Does collective memory take shape before individual memories are incorporated into a society's understanding of an event? Writers, poets, artists, journalists, and others play a crucial role in producing collective memory—helping a society understand what its members are supposed to "remember" from an event they did not experience. The process of memory-making continues to develop and is constantly re-forming, depending on the social and political needs of a particular moment.

While Maurice Halbwachs's notion of collective memory suggests a type of framework of memory in which individuals understand and contextualize their own memories in relation to and through collective memory, how do we account for the possibility of the simultaneous creation of individual memory, collective memory, and historical memory?[2] In the case of the Warsaw Ghetto Uprising, what is the relationship between the contributions of the historical actors (i.e., the testimonies of ghetto fighters); the creation of a collected history of the event (e.g., Yitzhak Zuckerman's efforts to create a collective report and other documentary collection projects) and the work of historians to historicize the event soon afterward; and the perceptions of individuals outside Warsaw who remember hearing about it and soon formed a "memory" based on imagining what it may have been like to be in the ghetto as it erupted in revolt? Do such perceptions change over time? To what extent are they encoded by the "social frameworks of memory"? How much does one's position in society influence one's perception or memory of an event?

Early representations of the uprising in postwar literature, including travelogues, short stories, theatrical productions, and novels, played a role in the process of fictionalizing and mythologizing the event in early postwar memory of the Holocaust. Jews around the world projected diverse religious, political, and historical interpretations onto the last battle of Warsaw's Jews, making the dramatic framework of the event sufficiently flexible as to absorb a broad range of Jewish responses to the Holocaust. Even as historical research on the uprising developed, many of the social frameworks that influenced the shaping of memory were already in place, exercising a powerful influence on the ways in which the revolt would be collectively "remembered."

The Ruins of Warsaw

During the war, Jews in Israel and America tried to imagine what it must have been like to be among the heroic fighters engaged in the last battle of the Warsaw ghetto. In the aftermath of the war, a series of visitors—correspondents, writers, and political leaders—visited Poland and Warsaw, writing travelogues that attempted to capture the sights and sounds of a destroyed civilization for Jewish audiences abroad. In this genre of postwar reportage, Poland quickly became the focus, with the destroyed city of Warsaw becoming an allegory for the destruction of European Jewry.[3]

For the visitors to the ruins of postwar Poland, the remains of the ghetto were of course a required destination, although what remained of the Jewish section of Warsaw was nearly impossible to navigate. The scholar Jack Kugelmass tells how the author S. L. Shneiderman made use of a guidebook that had been issued by a professional society for blind workers in Warsaw and navigated the ruins of the former ghetto using the diary of a ghetto fighter, Heniek Robenlicht. As Shneiderman recounted for his readers, walking over the rubble of a destroyed street in the ghetto, pieces of metal in the charred remains of the ghetto now seemed like trophies commemorating the heroic struggle:

> In front of me lay a four-sided piece of metal with a large engraved number "23" and the name Nowolipki. I apparently found myself standing next to the house where I had lived. I picked up the piece of metal and held onto it like a trophy. The metal, which must have been in place while the ghetto was in flames, had the color of ash, but the letters and the number that would at night be lit by the lantern above the house, remained legible.[4]

Jacob (Yakov) Pat traveled to Poland for two months in 1946, sent by the Jewish Labor Committee to distribute aid to the surviving Jewish communities there. In his travelogue, *Ash un Fayer: Iber di Hurves fun Poylen (Ashes and Fire: On the Ruins of Poland)* Pat detailed his travels (his sixty days in Poland) for an American reading audience, writing both to describe the destruction of Polish Jewry and to inspire support for the "remnant of Israel" that he found in Poland—help for the homeless, the children, the youth; help for Jewish culture, for the working people "rescued from the ovens," striving to build a productive life; help for the tens of thousands of Jews who returned from Soviet Russia.[5]

As the English language reviewer Hal Lehrman described the book in his highly positive review in *Commentary*:

> For his two-month tour of post-liberation Poland, the Yiddish writer Jacob Pat came equipped with a nimbler pencil than most, a larger notebook, a greater capacity for patient listening, and a sure instinct for selecting the human essentials from each saga of inhumanity. *Ashes and Fire* will endure as a documentary monument to the murdered Jews of Poland and to those who emerged alive, "every one of them a miracle of survival." Fortified in English by a

Ruins of the Warsaw ghetto, July 1945. (United States Holocaust Memorial Museum, courtesy of Israel Gutman, photo archives no. 07243)

Cover of Jacob Pat's *Ash un Fayer: Iber di Hurves fun Poylen* [Ashes and fire: On the ruins of Poland], with illustration by Chaim Gross. (Courtesy Renee and Chaim Gross Foundation, New York)

distinguished translation, the book deserves to endure also as a classic in the universal literature of martyrdom.[6]

While Pat sought to detail all aspects of what he witnessed in Poland over those sixty days—his encounters in Oświęcim, his birthplace of Białystok, Lublin, Częstochowa, Tarnów, and Treblinka (among other places)—he framed his wrenching account beginning and ending in the ruins of the destroyed Warsaw ghetto. In Lehrman's review this aspect stood out as well, for "*Ashes and Fire* confirms with fresh detail the already well-authenticated fact that the Jews of the Warsaw Ghetto and the partisan forests merit a chapter all their own in the epic of hopeless resistance which the world has been writing since Thermopylae."[7]

On his tour of the Warsaw ghetto, Pat was accompanied by Marek Edelman, who described the ghetto as the burial place of the Jewish people, site of "the greatest Jewish *akedah*." His first main chapter begins in Warsaw, where he visits what remains of the ghetto to see the greatest grave of the Jewish people. What does he see there? "A sea of destruction . . . a horrible memorial to generations and generations. No more Nalewki, no more Muranów, no more Dzika . . . no more Miła and Karmelicka . . . nothing is there."[8]

> I was on the field of a wasteland, what was once called Plac Krasińskich . . . with my guide, the captain of the ghetto fighters, the great grandson of the Vilna Gaon, Marek Edelman, "Here was the beginning of the ghetto battle"—he showed me a second destroyed vista . . . "here we planted mines, where the Germans entered." . . .
>
> . . . We were by the doors of the former brush makers shop of the German slave factory, about which one will still write one of the most dramatic "*velt megiles*." Here began the decisive ghetto fight. Here did Jewish young heroes kill 300 Germans; here did Jewish children give their lives into the heavens above, like angels—as a Mama tells her children—thrown like stars into the heavens in the night. . . .

> I walk on and on, and stop before another high mountain of rubble. Inside lies the body of Michał Klepfisz, one of the Ghetto heroes whose name is even now being woven into Jewish legend, whose aged grandmother, when taken to Treblinka, took with her only a pair of slippers and a pair of Sabbath candles.

Continuing his description of the destroyed city, Pat tries to imagine for his readers the dramatic events that transpired under the remains of the burned-out city:

> We were on the former Wałowa Street. All lay in ruins. When Wałowa burned and on the crossing raged a fiery battle war with the Nazis, forty Jewish ghetto heroes stood their ground here in the fight for hours between burning and falling houses—approximately thirty heroes fell dead here. The mountain of destruction and misfortune—the *mountain* of stones and iron—is so large and tall, that the dead still lie beneath it.—Here was Gęsia Street, here was a hospital, the legendary Jewish doctor—Heller-Broide—was here until the last man died. In the ghetto struggle did she also fall here.
>
> I am on the corner of Zamenhof-Gęsia Street. Two structures stand here one facing the other. In one building was once a military prison, and later stood there the main Nazi offices in the ghetto. In the opposite house stood the secret headquarters of the underground Jewish fighting organization. For many months the Jews worked in fear of discovery by the Nazi headquarters. When the days of the ghetto revolt began, the *building* of the Jewish heroes *rose up* over the building of the Nazi headquarters. Later, when Warsaw was liberated from the Nazis, the memorial to the ghetto fighters was placed in the same spot.

Marek Edelman points out where the Mila 18 bunker was among the ruins of the Warsaw ghetto. Behind him stands Jacob Pat, a delegate of the American Jewish Labor Committee (formerly of Białystok). (United States Holocaust Memorial Museum, photo archives no. 02345)

With Edelman as his guide through the ruins of a destroyed civilization, Pat attempts to convey for the reader the depth of his heartbreak, the degree to which he has been shattered by this experience.

The subsequent chapters detail Pat's two-month journey across a destroyed Poland. In concluding his travelogue, however, Pat brings his readers back to Warsaw. Still Pat feels he cannot do justice to the magnitude of the heroic struggle mounted by the ghetto fighters. As one who was not there but has only heard it described second hand, he does not feel adequate to detail it in all its glory and awe-inspiring greatness:

> Should I make a final accounting?—I will not do this, I will leave this to the readers, they can alone make their own reckoning. Today I want to write about why I have almost not written about the uprising in the ghetto.
>
> The greatness and the holiness of the Jewish heroism in the ghettos is so powerful, that I did not feel I could be its describer. Not being one of the rebels, not having the privilege to stand in the flames of the burning ghetto of Warsaw, not being in the fighting ghetto of Białystok, not being a fighting brother in the ghetto of Częstochowa, of Krakow, of Będzin, hearing the account of the only survivor: "You cannot understand us, because you were not here," I did not try to describe it. Only here and there did I recount one time and another time their stories. Each time I felt, that this is the *holy of holies* of 6 million dead Jews who died '*al kiddush hashem*' and only the Cohen Gadol [high priest] may enter there, a simple *Israelite* may not enter there.

Pat concludes his travelogue with the account of the heroic battle in the Warsaw ghetto, although he expresses a sense of trepidation, as one unworthy of describing the holiness of Jewish heroism, of depicting the *holy of holies* of six million dead. The allusion to the destroyed Temple in Jerusalem is not coincidental. As has been seen, the destruction of European Jewry was referred to as a *hurban*, akin to the destruction of the First and Second Temples in Jerusalem. The events that had transpired in Warsaw had transcended time and space and been elevated onto a metaphysical, even divine plane. For a secular Jewish socialist like Pat, active in the Jewish Labor Committee, guided through the ghetto by Marek Edelman of the Bund, there was no other way to describe what had taken place in the ghetto.

The inside cover of Pat's account included a photo of the destroyed Tłomackie (Wielka or Great) Synagogue in Warsaw, and he framed his account by concluding with a reflection on the two menorahs that remained standing amidst the destroyed synagogue: "the two menorahs," which miraculously he writes, "remained standing. They remained standing as a symbol." The menorah would be lit again, he concludes.

For readers of postwar descriptions, the ruins of the ghetto symbolized the destruction of European Jewry as a whole, while also becoming a figurative setting for assessments of the meaning of the destruction. Journalistic accounts of travels to the ruins of Jewish life in Europe were accompanied by imagined narratives of suffering and heroism. Pat expressed trepidation about telling the story of the revolt, as one who was not worthy. Other writers, however, did not hesitate to situate their accounts of Jewish heroism in the ruins of the ghetto, interpreting the meaning of the revolt in historical, political, and even theological terms. What could be learned from the example of the Warsaw Ghetto Uprising about Jewish behavior

Ruins of the Tlomackie Synagogue, Warsaw, with two menorahs among the ruins. (United States Holocaust Memorial Museum photo archives, no. 15871)

during the war? What did it mean to die *al Kiddush Hashem* in the Warsaw ghetto? Could the Jewish religion remain unchanged? Could Jews still believe in a God who would preside over such a calamity? As Pat detailed the ruins of Warsaw, it is not surprising that other writers, like Zvi Kolitz, would want to imagine what it must have been like to be inside that ghetto and how the experience of fighting back against the Nazis, changed the nature of the Jewish relationship with God.

"Yosl Rakover Talks to God"

The short story "Yosl Rakover Talks to God," written by Zvi Kolitz for *Di Yiddishe Tsaytung* in Buenos Aires and published on September 25, 1946, for a special issue in conjunction with Yom Kippur, imagined the last confessions of a fictional Hasidic fighter in the Warsaw ghetto. The story, which would come to be separated from Kolitz's byline, was subsequently published erroneously in the 1950s as an authentic document recovered from the ruins of the ghetto.[9] For Jewish readers already conditioned to reading imagined accounts of the last battle of Warsaw's Jews, it is unsurprising that the line between fact and fiction could become so easily blurred.

For Kolitz, the fictionalized setting of the Warsaw Ghetto was the ideal place to situate such a dramatic encounter, as the ruins of the ghetto became the stand-in for both commemorations and reflections on the meaning of the destruction of European Jewry. In September 1946, not long before the story was published, the first part of the Ringelblum *Oneg Shabbes* archive was unearthed in Warsaw. For Jewish readers who wanted to believe in the authenticity of the text, the angry encounter between a Jew who remained proud to be a Jew but whose relationship with God had been transformed had tremendous resonance after the war.

Kolitz was born in 1919 in Alytus, a small town in Lithuania (located between Grodno and Kovno); he left Lithuania with his mother and siblings in 1936 (studying in Florence for several years), before eventually reaching Jerusalem in 1940 where he joined the Revisionist movement and became involved in organizing the Irgun.[10] After a brief imprisonment by the British in Palestine, Kolitz attended the World Zionist Congress in

Basel in 1946 before traveling to Buenos Aires, where he was invited to write the story by *Di Yiddishe Tsaytung*. In an interview with Paul Baade years later, Kolitz explained that in his mind the struggle of the Jews in the Warsaw ghetto recalled Jacob's wrestling with the angel on the banks of the Jabbok, which "reached a new climax in the Warsaw Ghetto."[11] For Kolitz, the struggle of the Jewish people in the ghetto symbolized the dramatic transformation of the people who had wrestled with God and emerged forever changed. In the aftermath of the war, the creation of the State of Israel would reflect this permanent change.

In the story, Yosl Rakover rejects the notion that he must wait for a miracle, for God's intervention in history. On the contrary, for Kolitz, the Warsaw Ghetto Uprising represents the turning point in Jewish history when the Jewish relationship with God is transformed; no longer satisfied with waiting for a God who has "veiled his face in indifference," Yosl resolves to take action on his own by killing the Nazi aggressors, an action driven by the need for vengeance:

> Vengeance is holy, for it is mentioned between two names of God, as it is written: "A God of vengeance is the Lord!" Now I understand it. Now I feel it, and now I know why my heart rejoices when I remember how for thousands of years we have called upon our God: "God of Vengeance!" El Nekamot Adonoi.

By imagining his ghetto fighter as a pious Hasidic man who has lost all of his family, Kolitz transcends political difference between members of the fighting underground, seizing instead upon the motivation of vengeance, which did in fact unite a broad range of fighters. Unlike the fighters in the Jewish Fighting Organization who joined together, however, Yosl Rakover stands alone before his God and his enemies. He has chosen to continue to believe in God, despite God's best efforts to make him stop believing. At the same time, he has learned from the example of a God of vengeance to relish the opportunity to die taking revenge on Nazi soldiers for the death of his family and people. In this, Kolitz captures a major theme common to the testimonies of the ghetto fighters from all movements: the satisfaction of taking revenge, of seeing Nazi blood flowing in the streets. "Yes, I speak of vengeance. Only rarely have we seen true vengeance, but when we have experienced it, it was so comforting, and so sweet, such deep solace and intense happiness, that to me it was as if a new life had opened up."

Kolitz also articulates a proud defense of Jewish distinctiveness in general, and a specifically Zionist conclusion to the experience of such oppression in the war. For Kolitz, the only possible conclusion to the destruction of the ghetto as it symbolizes the extermination of European Jewry is continued pride in being a member of the Jewish people. Being Jewish, he explains, "is an art":

> I believe that to be a Jew is to be a fighter, an eternal swimmer against the roiling, evil current of humanity. The Jew is a hero, a martyr, a saint. You, our enemies, say that we are bad? I believe we are better than you, finer. But even if we were worse—I'd like to have seen how you would have looked in our place.

For Kolitz and for Rakover—the relationship has changed. Jews as actors in history must no longer be the blind supplicants of God. The Jewish God is a God of vengeance and the fighters in the Warsaw ghetto are the agents of his vengeance. By making his ghetto fighter a Hasidic man taking vengeance on the enemy, Kolitz argues that dying to sanctify God's name (*al Kiddush Hashem*) means taking vengeance in the name of God. Perhaps readers who wanted to believe this story was true also preferred to imagine a new type of glorious and heroic Jewish death.

Yitzhak Zuckerman Arrives in the Yishuv

While Yosl Rakover represented an imagined ghetto fighter, Yitzhak Zuckerman was a first-hand observer who joined the fight indirectly, but was determined to tell the world the story of the ghetto fighters. Zuckerman reached Palestine on April 29, 1947 (Antek and Zivia had been married by a rabbi in Basel, Switzerland, shortly after the Zionist congress in December 1946; Zivia gave birth to their first child in September 1947).[12] Zuckerman would subsequently work on the publication of the *Book of the Ghetto Wars* and other projects dedicated to telling the story of the ghetto fighters.

Zuckerman's arrival in the Yishuv was covered in various newspapers at the time. As the *Palestine Post* reported on April 30, 1947:

> Our correspondent in Haifa reports: yesterday in the morning, Yitzhak Zuckerman (Antek), commander of the Jewish fighting organization and one of the heads of the revolt in Warsaw, arrived on the ship Corinthia. On the deck of the boat, Zuckerman told our correspondent: "I have come to plant roots. I am going out to Yagur as a member of the kibbutz and a member of the Kibbutz HaMeuchad." He asked to pass regards to all his friends and acquaintances.[13]

Davar also reported on the reception that greeted Zuckerman after his arrival, noting his deep connection to the Land of Israel.

> Zuckerman responded: in the days of our great isolation and loneliness, when all was dark around us, what remained with us was the solitary belief in you—in the Yishuv, in the land of Israel, in the Jewish worker and the future of the nation. Now, two years after the liberation, after the many wanderings, the remnants of the Diaspora believe in you and wait for your help.
>
> I speak quietly—he added—but a great cry screams from within me of the masses who did not manage to reach the gates of Haifa. I can speak in the name of the hundreds of thousands who are in Bavaria and in Austria, France and Italy, who are on the roads or who have remained in Poland: YOU ARE THE LAST HOPE. If you do not extend your hands quickly and with great strength, they will be lost.

> From the Yishuv and from the workers movement we are waiting for assistance. For emissaries, for a great migration (aliyah). Only this will be the rescue . . . what we have done one year, two years ago, it is difficult to do now. There are young people there, children. They are suffering, not from hunger but from the extended waiting and they hope that the Yishuv and the movement will do all in their power to bring the She'erit Hapletah. They have done all they can for their part. They have moved themselves, walked the paths, relocated until they reached the final station. Woe to us if we do not save them now!
>
> Y. Zuckerman left yesterday for his home—to Yagur.[14]

Just over one week later, Zuckerman delivered his testimony to a meeting with the Kibbutz HaMeuchad leadership on May 9–10, 1947. What troubled Zuckerman, like the ghetto fighters who delivered testimonies before him, was the question of why the Jews had not rebelled earlier. Echoing the testimonies of both Edelman and Lubetkin before him, Zuckerman explained that Jews were passive because they could not imagine what would befall them. Using the first-person plural, in this case, he linked himself with the fate of the murdered Jewish people:

> Who could understand at the first minute that from the blue and white arm band with the Magen David, from the "*shande band*" stretched a long straight line to Treblinka. . . . We grew accustomed to everything. In 1939 we did not understand, did not believe, out of a lack of knowledge and a desire not to see. The Jewish public did not want to see. If we had seen, if we had understood, if we could have turned back the wheels of history to the year of 1939, we should have said: revolt immediately!

Zuckerman reflected on the manner in which the Jewish public (in which he seemed to include himself) did not struggle to alter its own destiny, allowing their history to be written for them: "We accepted the good and the bad. We blessed life as it was, as it was given to us, as the conqueror gave it to us."[15] Zuckerman lamented the late decision to revolt—but of course, he could only lament this with the benefit of hindsight. What would later be defined as "spiritual resistance," the Jewish ability to stand up against, to continue life in the ghettos in the most extreme of circumstances, came to be seen as an obstacle to organizing armed resistance by Zuckerman. At the same time, Zuckerman identified obstacles to armed resistance in the ghetto:

> And we were blocked by a wall of obstacles to our organizing of resistance. There were large blockages and obstacles in the ghetto. There were strands and different groups holding opposing viewpoints. There were opponents spewing evil and idealistic opponents pure hearted and just.
>
> There was a part that collaborated with the Germans: there was the police, there was the Jewish Council, there was an institution that was called by the name *Channastika*.
>
> From an objective viewpoint all of these institutions turned into institutions of treason, that were used and aided the hands of the Germans to deliver Jews to concentration camps, to death. . . .
>
> There were those who based their opposition to Jewish resistance or to Jewish struggle on general political grounds, on historic grounds, and on religious grounds.

In addition to those institutional obstacles to organizing resistance, Zuckerman also explained that the spiritual obstacle of "collective responsibility" also presented a barrier. The youth movements' focus on organizing educational activities for the younger generation in the earlier period of the ghetto delayed the shift to fighting the Nazi foe. And beyond spiritual and political obstacles, they faced "the objective barrier, the fact that we did not have weaponry and did not have military training."[16]

As will be noted in the next chapter, after his arrival in the Yishuv, Zuckerman and Lubetkin would work to establish Kibbutz Lohamei

Ha-Getaot, opened on the sixth anniversary of the revolt, which they saw as a "living monument."[17] The living heroes, like Zuckerman, Lubetkin, Carmi, Frimmer, Havka, and others had made their way to the Yishuv. For the most part, they joined kibbutzim (ninety-six became the founders of Kibbutz Lochamei HaGetaot near Akko in 1949) but the specifics of their own individual experiences became less important than the symbolic value of Jewish resistance—not as history, but as memory. But whose memory would be more powerful? That of the deceased fighters, the imaginary fighters, or the living fighters?

In the Yishuv, the arrival of the surviving ghetto fighters seemed to cement the identification of the revolt with the struggle for the creation of the state. This struggle helped to give the ghetto fighters a place in the newly created state, while also overshadowing the experiences of the majority of survivors, who were discouraged from sharing their "less heroic" tales of survival. At the same time, the fighters felt that the leaders of the Yishuv did not appreciate their sacrifice and preferred to sideline them and their experiences as part of a deeper ambivalence over integrating the history of the Shoah into Israeli history.[18]

Never to Forget, The Battle of the Warsaw Ghetto

The American Jewish community—Bundists, Communists, Zionists, mainstream American Jewish organizations, and others—had been divided by political ideologies that prevented an effective and organized communal response during the war.[19] After the war, all the movements tried to incorporate the memory of the Warsaw Ghetto Uprising into their worldview. One of the first literary treatments of the uprising in English, the illustrated, book-length poem *Never to Forget, The Battle of the Warsaw Ghetto* by Howard Fast and William Gropper, represented the Warsaw Ghetto Uprising as part of man's universal struggle for freedom, devoid of any specific Zionist references. The book was published in 1946 by the Book League of the Jewish People's Fraternal Order in New York, a section of the International Workers Order, a fraternal order and mutual benefit organization that grew out of a split between the Arbeter Ring and The Workmen's

Circle. The Jewish People's Fraternal Order was the largest section of the IWO, and the IWO's politics were "largely aligned" with those of the Communist Party. (The IWO was also responsible for Camp Kinderland and cemeteries, etc.)[20]

The author of *Never to Forget*, Howard Fast, was a novelist and later television writer who was the son of Jewish immigrants from Britain and the Ukraine. Fast, who spent World War II working with the United States Office of War Information, writing for Voice of America, joined the Communist Party USA in 1943.[21] The art was the work of William Gropper, a satirist and illustrator, who had already published a series of lithographs in 1943 soon after the revolt, titled *Your Brother's Blood Cries Out* (the title based on God's words to Cain in Genesis 4:10).[22] Most of Gropper's original lithographs reproduced in the 1946 publication depicted the subjugation of the Jews of Warsaw, the combatants fighting with meager weapons, overpowered by the SS troops looming over them, perhaps creating an image that would resonate with a universal call to aid the oppressed and powerless masses the world over.

Through poetry and art, Fast and Gropper turned the saga of the Warsaw ghetto into a universal struggle for freedom, "a song of my people that becomes a song of all people." *Never to Forget* presented the Warsaw Ghetto Uprising as part of the universal struggle of man against fascism; the blue Jewish flag would flutter alongside the red flag. Although Jews had perished in the Warsaw struggle, their weapons would be used in the cause of universal freedom until all men could live together in peace. The struggle of the Jewish people "becomes the song of all people." In the same way, Jewish suffering and the specifically Jewish mark of shame is understood to be borne in the "common name of humanity." More than anything else, the Jewish people died "for the cause of liberty."[23] While Yosl Rakover's intonation of the Shema prayer was presented by Kolitz, in his short story, as a proud declaration of Jewish national identity, Fast reinterpreted the traditional prayer "Hear O Israel, The Lord is our God, the Lord is One" to read:

> To the time we faced the Nazi in the streets of Warsaw,
> *Hear, oh Mankind, Men are brothers, Humanity is One.*

A Flag Is Born and *A Survivor from Warsaw*

As American Jews grappled with the questions of patriotism, Communism, and Zionism after the war, the blue Jewish flag would also be translated into dramatic representations of the Jewish struggle against oppression. Following the success of H. Leivick's *Der Nes in Geto* (*Miracle of the Warsaw Ghetto*) in 1944–45, *A Flag Is Born* opened on Broadway on September 4, 1946, starring well-known actors Paul Muni and Celia Adler alongside a young Marlon Brando.[24] The play was produced by the American League for a Free Palestine, the brainchild of Peter Bergson (a.k.a. Hillel Kook).[25] Written by Ben Hecht, directed by Luther Adler, and with music by Kurt Weill, the play was intended as propaganda to help mobilize American opinion for a Jewish homeland in Palestine. In 1943, Hecht and Weill had partnered to create the *We Will Never Die* pageant. *A Flag Is Born* linked the wartime suffering of the Jewish people with the need for a postwar solution to Jewish statelessness. The narrator emphasizes Jewish suffering during the war instead of Jewish heroism: "Of all the things that happened in that time—our time—the slaughter of the Jews of Europe was the only thing that counted forever in the annals of man. The proud oration of heroes and conquerors will be a footnote in history beside the great silence that watched the slaughter."

The play, set in a graveyard, features three characters—elderly Treblinka survivors Tevva and Zelda, who drag their tired and broken bodies searching for a path to Palestine, and Brando's David, an angry young concentration camp survivor.

As David leaves the graveyard of Europe for his new homeland, he offers a harsh indictment of Anglo-American Jewish silence, addressing his audience directly:

> Where were you—Jews? Where were you when the killing was going on? When the six million were burned and buried alive in the lime pits, where were you? Where was your voice crying out against the slaughter? We didn't hear any voice. There was no voice. You, Jews of America!

> You Jews of England! Strong Jews, rich Jews, high-up Jews; Jews of power and genius! Where was your cry of rage that could have filled the world and stopped the fires? Nowhere! Because you were ashamed to cry as Jews! A curse on your silence! That frightened silence of Jews that made the Germans laugh as they slaughtered.

In the play's finale, David delivers a fiery pro-Zionist speech, moves across a bridge into Palestine, and, as Edna Nahshon notes, "with the mixed sounds of 'Hatikvah' and gunfire in the background, raises Tevya's prayer shawl as a makeshift flag and marches off to war." According to Nahshon,

> *A Flag Is Born* was an unabashed propaganda piece. It focused on what one might call the "geopathological" state of the DPs (displaced persons) and emphasized the Zionist territorial solution, namely unrestricted immigration to Palestine and the Jews' right to restore and be restored in their land. The play's message went out loud and clear: Europe could not be home to the survivors of the Holocaust; the British announcement that survivors should go back to their places of origin was unacceptable; Palestine was the only option for Jewish resettlement; and the establishment of an independent "Hebrew" state there was imperative and non-negotiable.[26]

For American Jews, the play seemed to suggest, only support for Zionism could atone for the sin of silence during the war. Only through the symbolic transformation of Tevya's tallit into the Zionist banner could the deaths of millions of Jews find meaning after the war. *A Flag Is Born*, which ran in New York for 120 performances (three times as long as originally planned), then played in six North American cities, brought in more than $400,000 for the American League for a Free Palestine, the largest block of funds the league ever raised.[27]

Such symbolic transformations took place not only in the theater. Music also had the power to transform the meaning of traditional Jewish formulations for the new postwar context. In the summer and fall of 1946, a new hymn, labeled "The Warsaw Martyrs Hymn," began to circulate through the American Jewish press, first published in the Jewish National Fund's national magazine, *Land and Life*, in May 1946. "Ani Ma'amin" ("I Believe, I Believe") paraphrased the twelfth article of Maimonides' thirteen principles of faith, and expressed a continued hope for the ultimate coming of the Messiah. The melody for "I Believe, I Believe" or "The Warsaw Martyr's Hymn," was brought by Yossel Ostrovtzer to Palestine, according to the story related in *Land and Life*.[28] The hymn was described in the press as "rapidly spreading in the DP camps in Europe, in Palestine, and in many communities in the United States," revealing "the psychic conditions of the survivors [and] pointing up the healing quality of their hope for a Return to Zion." Over eight hundred years after Maimonides first articulated his faith in the ultimate coming of the Messiah, the elegiac hymn, emerging from the ruins of the Warsaw Ghetto, carried by a lone survivor to Palestine, was interpreted as a sign that the return to Zion had the power to heal the surviving remnant.

Soon afterward, Arnold Schoenberg composed *A Survivor from Warsaw*, a cantata, which, according to music scholar and historian Jeremy Eichler, "became the first major musical memorial to the Holocaust."[29] The text, written by Schoenberg in July 1947, depicts an inmate from the Warsaw Ghetto ("But I have no recollection how I got underground to live in the sewers of Warsaw for so long a time") now in a concentration camp, subjected to horrible beatings by SS guards. As the mostly unconscious prisoners are subjected to additional beatings and selected for the gas chambers, the group suddenly begins to sing the Shema in Hebrew:

> They began again, first slowly: one, two, three, four, became faster and faster, so fast that it finally sounded like a stampede of wild horses, and (all) of a sudden, in the middle of it, they began singing the Shema Yisrael.

Here again, as in Kolitz's short story and Fast's poem, the Shema prayer appears, sung by a group of prisoners destined for the gas chambers—used again by the composer to reflect the tension between a particular Jewish identity (Hear O Israel) and themes of universal and common suffering. The Albuquerque Civic Symphony Orchestra premiered the atonal musical memorial under the direction of Kurt Frederick on November 4, 1948. Eichler argues that as a musical memorial, *Survivor from Warsaw* was ahead of its time:

> *A Survivor from Warsaw* predated almost all of its sibling memorials, crystallizing and anticipating the range of aesthetic and ethical concerns that would define the study of postwar memory and representation for decades to come. It also constituted a uniquely personal memorial that may be read not only as a work of Holocaust art but also as a profoundly autobiographical document, one that sheds light on constellations of particularist identities often hidden beneath the "universalist" veil of one of the twentieth-century's most iconic musical figures.[30]

Contrasting with Fast and Gropper's literary treatment of the uprising, Hecht's propagandistic appeal to support the Irgun's struggle against the British, and Schoenberg's musical memorial to the suffering of Europe's Jews, Marie Syrkin's *Blessed Is the Match* was one of the first and arguably most influential early historical treatments of Jewish resistance in English. Syrkin had been active writing about resistance during the war in her role as one of the editors of the Labor Zionist *Jewish Frontier*, and afterward came out with *Blessed Is the Match*, published in 1947 by the *Jewish Publication Society of America*. The book underwent three additional printings in six months. Syrkin very clearly situated the Warsaw Ghetto Uprising within the context of the Zionist struggle for the creation of the state, especially important in 1947 when the book appeared.[31]

Marie Syrkin, *Blessed Is the Match*

Marie Syrkin was the only daughter of Nachman Syrkin, an early Socialist-Zionist thinker, and Bassya Osnos Syrkin, a feminist socialist Zionist activist. Born in Switzerland on March 23, 1899, Marie moved to the United States with her family in 1908, and in 1918 enrolled at Cornell University to pursue her literary studies.[32] In the 1930s, Syrkin became increasingly involved in Zionist activities and after her first trip to Palestine, in 1934, joined the staff of the *Jewish Frontier*. Syrkin reported on the increasing persecution of Jews in Europe, and in August of 1942, after learning of the Riegner cable sent from Gerhard Riegner to Rabbi Stephen Wise, president of the American Jewish Congress, wrote the first editorial in the American press to report that a systematic extermination of the Jews was already in progress.[33] Syrkin also wrote speeches for leading figures in the Zionist movement, including Chaim Weizmann and Golda Meyerson (later Meir); when the war was over, Syrkin traveled to Palestine and to the Jewish DP camps in the American zone of Germany to conduct research for her book on Jewish resistance. After the creation of the State of Israel, she traveled there to write a report on the exodus of Arab refugees from conquered Israeli territory that would become the basis for the Israeli government report to the United Nations on the matter.[34]

In the introductory pages, Syrkin explained that she could not write *Blessed Is the Match* as a chronological history of Jewish resistance during World War II because, she "shares the reader's reluctance to enter the ghetto gate." For Syrkin, it was easier to start her history with the parachutists from Palestine, working up the courage to confront the devastation of European Jewry in the camps and ghettos. Before introducing readers to the heroism of Hannah Senesh, however, Syrkin prefaces her history of the Jewish resistance with a story from Gan Dafna, a kibbutz near the border with Syria (upper Galilee)—perhaps not coincidentally the same kibbutz that Leon Uris would make the home of the fictional Ari Ben-Canaan of *Exodus*. At Gan Dafna, Syrkin meets former ghetto fighters who have since moved to the kibbutz to start their lives anew in the Land of Israel, introducing readers to Ud, the baby boy of two ghetto fighters from Warsaw, who named him "the ember plucked from the burning" Warsaw. Syrkin described spending an evening with Ud's parents:

> I asked about the heroes of the struggle—familiar names by now—Zivia, Frumke, Tosia, Yitzhak. The father rose. In the corner on a small table were some photographs. "This is Zivia," he said, "and this is Frumke." I had seen their pictures in the Jewish press, but these were the original photographs, smuggled out of Poland, precious pictures of comrades carried even in flight. I looked at the sensitive young faces, one living and one dead. The snapshots stood casually on the table, and one knew that they were viewed as the simple pictures of friends, not the portraits of already semi-legendary figures.[35]

Syrkin writes for an America audience which can identify with her perspective and can also understand the message she seeks to convey: the baby Ud symbolizes the new state; only here can he be reborn and here Ud, and the Jewish people, are fated to be. Syrkin also asks the ghetto fighters the questions that seem to be on the minds of Jews in the outside world, in Israel, America, and elsewhere:

> I asked the questions that tormented me, and they asked the questions that tormented them. For when I wondered why six million Jews had let themselves be led to the slaughter, they demanded, "Why did you let them be led?" And when I asked, "Did they not know where the train went?" they answered me at length, but they also returned the stern question, "Did *you* not know?"[36]

As Syrkin introduces readers to Ud, she also makes a historical leap: she argues that the fighters fought for Ud, that the fighters fought for the future of the Jewish people, but that they fought for the future of the Jewish people in the Land of Israel. While, as we have seen, this may have been the argument made by Antek and Zivia after their arrival in the Land of Israel, for others, the primary motivation at the time of the revolt was revenge and the defense of Jewish honor, not the question of where the Jewish future might be.

Syrkin begins her historical treatment of the "story of Jewish resistance" with the the parachutists from Palestine, and specifically, Hannah Senesh and her poem "Blessed Is the Match."

> *Blessed is the Match that is consumed in kindling flame.*
> *Blessed is the flame that burns in the secret fastness of the heart.*
> *Blessed is the heart with strength to stop its beating for honor's sake.*
> *Blessed is the match that is consumed in kindling flame.*[37]

As Syrkin explains, "The poem celebrates the self-immolation of the hero. There is no assurance that the ultimate issue will be life. There is only insistence on the sacrifice. That such a sentiment can be described as the national slogan of Palestine indicates the bitter lesson learned from the Nazi decade. The attempt to cling to life will surely result in death. The only hope lies in the readiness to die." For Syrkin, the willingness to sacrifice oneself—to die for honor—for the sake of the nation, this is the national slogan of Palestine and the heroic lesson of those who would sacrifice themselves for the cause of Jewish resistance so that Ud could be born in the Land of Israel. After telling the story of Senesh, Syrkin works her way back to the dramatic core of the story of Jewish resistance, "the ghetto battle." Again Syrkin reiterates the recurring question: Why did resistance come so late? "Why did the Warsaw ghetto fight back only when a mere 30,000 were left and over half a million had been massacred? Why was there an uprising in Treblinka only when a few hundred were left? How to explain this obedient pilgrimage to the extermination center in which six million human beings took part?"[38] Syrkin explains that Jews were unarmed, could not have known what was to come, isolated into ghettos where they were physically and psychically oppressed, and when news began to circulate of systematic extermination people refused to believe it could be true, promised by Nazis they could travel to Palestine, deceived into believing conditions in work camps were better: "human beings in this state of mind were easy prey for the Germans." Jews exhibited the "paradoxical faith of a people with a long history of persecution."[39] Just as they had survived other oppressors in the past, so too would they survive Hitler. When some tried to organize resistance, Syrkin explains, even on the trains, they were spat upon and told not to make trouble, manifesting a "sense of collective responsibility which enormously complicated the entire question of resistance. . . . It would be false, however, to leave the impression that passivity and a tragic readiness to be duped were the sole moods of the Jews in or outside the ghettos."[40]

The focus of Syrkin's history of the ghetto battles is the Warsaw Ghetto Uprising. In a chapter titled "The Struggle of the Spirit," she introduces readers to the struggle that preceded the armed revolt, including discussion of Ringelblum's last letter, forwarded to London in May 1944 (and from there to YIVO). Syrkin cites his letter at length to discuss activities in the Warsaw ghetto, including the intellectual life of the ghetto, YIKOR (the cultural organization), underground schools and library, the underground press, the secret Jewish archive, and the ghetto orchestra. "The slogan of this conscious, organized group in the ghetto was: 'To live with honor and die with honor.'"[41]

In describing the lead-up to armed resistance, Syrkin highlights the pioneering Zionist youth groups in a chapter subtitled "To Die with Honor," noting that as Zionist youth, they "received training which stressed the disregard of personal ease or safety for the sake of the group." Motivated by a sense of collective national responsibility by the suffering of the Jewish people, and trained with a collective ethos to sacrifice individual need for the "sake of the group," Syrkin makes clear that the Zionist youth were the obvious candidates for leadership of the underground. "As halutzim," she writes, they were "above average in courage and initiative. . . . It was therefore natural that, being young, idealistic, and consumed with a sense of responsibility for the fate of their people, they were in the forefront of those who strove to organize the Jewish communities for psychic and physical resistance." While Zionist groups were not the only factor in the Jewish underground ("as time went on, every political grouping in Jewish life joined in the organization of the resistance"), Zionist groups played a disproportionately large role. She also notes the tendency to focus on the identities of the "heroes," the names already known by members of the movements, "Zivia, Tosia, Hanka, Yitzhak Zukerman, Mordecai Anilewitz and others. But over and over again, some one would add: 'Yes, these were brave; but the bravest of all was—' and I would hear a fresh and unfamiliar name . . . the historian . . . might have to record a hundred or more names of leaders." Recalling the figure of Zivia, who she had already memorialized in June 1943 as the mother ("*die mame*"), Syrkin writes

> The most famous figure of all is Zivia Lubetkin. Of Zivia, too, I heard it said that her halo had been fashioned by the popular need to create a legendary figure—a kind of composite of all who fought and led. But one gets a notion of how central was Zivia Lubetkin's role from the fact that, in the entire underground correspondence of the period, Zivia's name was used as the code word for "Poland." . . .
>
> It is impossible to dismiss such avowals as "legends" or blind hero worship—particularly as the worshippers were themselves of no mean stature. This slight girl will remain in Jewish history, as well as in the code of the underground, as the symbol of resistance in the Warsaw ghetto.

Syrkin's chapter on the revolt itself parallels Zuckerman's report of the Jewish Fighting Organization, starting with the knowledge that mass exterminations had begun, which led the Jewish underground to try to organize. Syrkin criticizes the Bundists for "not realizing the situation was too desperate for political disputes." By labeling the socialists as "not nationalists," she seems to suggest they were incapable of putting the needs of the Jewish people as a whole above petty political disputes. In July 1942, she writes, the liquidation of the ghetto began. After the suicide of Czerniakow, HeHalutz demanded active resistance, but the majority wanted to wait and see. Finally, the Jewish Fighting Organization was formed. "At last unity was achieved; orthodox and atheist, communist, nationalist, assimilationist—representatives of all the various political trends which continued to flourish vigorously on the brink of the abyss—joined in the final conflict. Under the leadership of Mordecai Anilewitz, commander, and Yitzhak Zukerman, assistant commander, the Jewish Fighting Organization began the struggle." Syrkin describes the January 1943 battle and the attempted deceptions of Többens, before detailing (briefly) the April revolt in two pages. She describes April 19 as a "beautiful spring day," quoting Tuvia Borzykowski without naming him, and notes "the resistance put up by the ghetto fighters in the flaming ruin embarrassed the Germans." The death of Anielewicz marked the "formal end of the fighting" and she describes the escape through the sewers but does not mention Kazik, while Zuckerman is credited with making escape preparations. The remainder of the book unites the saga of Jewish resistance into one large category that includes the Jewish partisans in Vilna and Belarus as well as the resistance activities of Jews in Holland, France, the Maquis, and the efforts of rescuers who were also engaged in a form of resistance.

Syrkin concludes her story where she began: in Palestine, reinforcing the sense that resistance during the war was part of the larger struggle for the creation of the Jewish state. "Any discussion of Jewish resistance must include the *Haganah*, the 'illegal army' of Palestine, whose dissolution the British have demanded. For it is in the *Haganah* ('defense') that all the threads meet. The parachutists, the ghetto fighters, the conspirators who plotted salvation in Geneva and Istanbul and the partisans had been or were to become, a part of this strange soldiery whose mission was the bringing of life and whose greeting was *Shalom* ('peace')." It is not a coincidence that Syrkin concludes the book with *ha'apalah*, the movement of "illegal immigration" to conquer the shores of Palestine for those Jewish immigrants without *aliyah* certificates. For Syrkin, the *ma'apilim* "are the victorious heroes of a struggle, not the defeated who flee seeking mercy." The Ha'apalah, and the continuing fight to create the Jewish state, are an extension of the Jewish struggle for honor, for dignity, and self-sacrifice manifested in the heroic Jewish resistance during the war. When the book was first published in late August 1947, the dramatic saga of the *Exodus* had already reached its denouement, the passengers on the ship having been forcibly removed from the prison ship *Runnymede Park* in Hamburg.[42]

Reviewers like Meyer Levin (who would play a central role in the attempt to bring the diary of Anne Frank to the stage) celebrated the importance of the new book. Levin's review, published in *Commentary* in July 1947, emphasized Syrkin "has given us the first over-all picture of Jewish resistance in World War II, though we have had many reports and several books on various phases of the struggle before. For this reason, her book is important."[43] Levin also noted that Syrkin's account mentioned the role of the righteous Gentiles who saved Jews, along with the parachutists from Palestine, including the "brilliant Hungarian girl," Hannah Senesch (*sic*), "whose passion has already become a symbolic legend that inspires resistance in Palestine." In his review, Levin also emphasizes the Zionist conclusion reinforced by Syrkin, the centrality of the Jews of Palestine to the future of the Jewish people.

> The total picture emphasizes most strongly the role of Palestinian Jews, and this is where the emphasis belongs. Though numerically they represent perhaps one-twentieth of surviving Jewry, the Palestinians have already proven that they now carry the ark. Anyone who doubts or fails to understand the nature of our revival in Palestine needs only to compare what was done for European Jewry by Palestinians, to what was done by the rest of the world.
>
> We others gave money and moral encouragement, yes, but, as Miss Syrkin points out, the Palestinians could not differentiate between their lives and the total life of the people. They could not and they cannot rest until their people can live and rest.
>
> And even in the beleaguered ghettos, even in the maquis and in the woods of Poland, it is always the Hehalutz group or the young Zionist group that is first to devise and undertake resistance. They have the strongest sense of Jewish worth.[44]

Syrkin's emphasis on Zionist aspects of the revolt would prefigure subsequent treatments of the story that would reach an even broader audience, particularly in the form of John Hersey's *The Wall*, which would be published in 1950. Even though Syrkin's book was published by the Jewish Publication Society of America for a Jewish audience in English, the narrative focus of the story of Jewish resistance began to separate American Jews from a history they could not possibly fully understand. By essentially obscuring the Bundist account of the revolt and removing any reference to the revolt as part of democracy's fight for freedom, the central Zionist message in the revolt emphasized by Syrkin (and echoing Lubetkin and Zuckerman) made the case that only those with a connection to the Land of Israel would understand, that the revolt represented a casting off of the yoke of Jewish passivity, a rejection of "sheep to the slaughter" that American Jews, who remained in the Diaspora, may not be able to understand.

An April 1947 review of another book (Adah Auerbach's *Women in the Ghettos*) published in the Labor Zionist youth movement publication *Furrows* raised this point directly. The willingness of the Halutzim to die for their people would become a new source of strength, a new Torah on which the youth would be educated.

> The cry of the Ghetto was two-fold. In the first days of the Nazi occupation when the stark reality of mass extermination did not seem to be even a remote possibility, the call for rescue was raised—rescue from the stagnation of Ghetto life, from starvation and imprisonment. As the truth of their fate became increasingly clear and hope dwindled, the cry became—revenge! "Let us not be led like sheep to the slaughter—we shall die like men, like Jews."
>
> It is difficult to understand why, after a history of passive submission to pogroms, after centuries of silent *Kiddush hashem*, they should have suddenly found within themselves the almost inhuman moral strength to resist in the face of unavoidable death. "We knew," said one of the halutzot, "that our death would become a source of strength, a Torah on which the youth will be educated. About this we

> thought in the Ghettos and this became *our Torah*, which we repeated and studied, calmly and quietly." These words are the key to the resolution which fired the Polish *halutzim*. Here is a statement of youth, difficult for us to understand, which calmly decided its fate for the sake of posterity. Its reasonableness is too cruel and hard to be human. *Perhaps it stems from a feeling for* Am Yisrael *which American Jews can never fully realize* (my emphasis).[45]

The model of self-sacrifice, of embracing death while enacting revenge, was a Torah for the Jewish future, which only those who had a sense of responsibility for the collective future of the Jewish people could understand. In this Zionist reading of resistance, the choice to die fighting could be understood. Still, this developing historical framework within which the history and meaning of the Warsaw Ghetto Uprising (and more broadly the Holocaust itself) was understood, did pose a challenge for American Jews still invested in shaping their own collective memory of the war.

While historical treatments like Syrkin's created a narrative and a historical framework for understanding resistance, explaining its broader meaning and significance, Jewish communities also turned to the task of memorializing the Warsaw Ghetto Uprising through monuments, exhibitions, and memorials. Markers had been erected in the ruins of the Warsaw ghetto and efforts to memorialize the Shoah in the Yishuv through the creation of an appropriate monument had already commenced in 1945. But how would (or how could) American Jewish groups translate the meaning of the revolt into a monument?

An American Memorial?

On June 19, 1947, the committee for the American Memorial to Six Million Jews of Europe (an organization headed by Dr. Joseph Thon, president of the National Organization of Polish Jews; Arthur Szyk, well-known Jewish artist; and Adolph Lerner, author) announced that a "memorial to 6,000,000 murdered Jews of Europe will be erected in New York," to be designed by the internationally known sculptor Jo Davidson "already at work modeling the monument."[46] As noted in the announcement, the memorial would double as a "memorial to the 6,000,000 Jews exterminated by the Germans and to the fallen heroes of the Battle of the Warsaw Ghetto."

On October 19, 1947, fifteen thousand people attended a ceremony to lay the cornerstone for the memorial at a site selected on Riverside Drive and Eighty-Third Street in Manhattan. As reported in the *New York Times*, the ceremony included a symbolic burial of ashes from various extermination camps as well as speeches, memorial prayers, and musical selections. The fundraising materials by the committee declared that the memorial would "honor the heroes of the Warsaw ghetto, who, without outside aid, rose up against the might of the German army in an epic battle of 40 days and nights until nothing remained but ruin and smoke—to reaffirm those ideals of human liberty for which 6 million Jews sacrificed their lives."[47] According to James Young, the date for the dedication (three and a half years after the outbreak of the revolt) was not coincidental. Lerner (who had also been responsible for planning the Jewish Labor Committee's exhibit at the Vanderbilt Gallery in April 1945), would later report that "my decision to hold the dedication ceremony in September or October was chiefly influenced by the acute situation in Palestine where a bitter fight raged between the Jews and the English which caused the United Nations to put the Palestine question on the agenda before the assembly in October, 1947."[48]

The invitation to the opening event on October 19, 1947, invited participants "to be present at the solemn dedication at the site of the *American Memorial to the Heroes of the Battle of the Warsaw Ghetto*, Riverside Drive at 83rd Street, NYC, Sunday October 19, 1947, at 12:45pm."[49] The memorial would honor the heroes of the battle "who, without outside aid, rose up against the might of the German Army in an epic struggle of forty days and nights until nothing remained but ruins and smoke—and to perpetuate the memory of the six million Jews who fell in Freedom's battle against the Nazis . . . [the Memorial] will inspire the fulfillment of the world's obligation to those who survived the Nazi holocaust."

A fundraising pamphlet for the project included commentaries of major newspapers, including an editorial in the *New York Times* on the "memorial to the martyred."

> It is fitting that a memorial to the six million victims of the most tragic mass crime in history, the Nazi genocide of Jews, should rise in this land of liberty. It is gratifying that New York has been chosen for its site. The land, a little plot on Riverside Drive overlooking the peaceful Hudson, was dedicated in a solemn ceremony on Sunday as a hundred survivors of the Buchenwald and Dachau horror camps looked on.
>
> The monument itself will be a monolith. The sculptor, Jo Davidson, and his advisors have selected the forty-two day siege of the Warsaw Ghetto in 1943 to symbolize the general Jewish martyrdom. It is a good symbol. The 40,000 defenders of the ghetto, resisting the whole might of Hitler's Germany, fought without hope and only to inspire courage in others. None submitted. Some four hundred, later reduced to four survivors, escaped to carry on the fight elsewhere. At the end no one in the ghetto remained on his knees to beg for mercy. All men, women, and children, were dead.
>
> Amid tributes from many nations Mayor O'Dwyer laid the memorial cornerstone. May it prove an eternal foundation for the spread of good-will and understanding in our own land and among all people of the earth.[50]

At the dedication ceremony, Senator Robert F. Wagner directly evoked the struggle of Warsaw's Jews to anticipate the fight between the defenders of the Jewish state and the Arab threat. "The gallant spirit of the warriors of the Warsaw Ghetto who challenged the might of the German Army will be sufficient to repel the Arab attack. The Jews have throughout their long history known well the Valley of the Shadow of Death, and for them it holds no terrors. They have survived barbarism far worse than that with which the Arabs now threaten them."[51]

According to James Young, "the first proposed monument, designed by Davidson and architect Ely Jacques Kahn in 1948, consisted of a series of step-like blocks forming a pedestal, atop which stood a muscular heroic figure. With his arms swept back, his chest thrust forward defiantly, and sleeves rolled up, the bare-handed fighter towered over a rabbinical figure below, hands up as if beseeching the Almighty; another figure aided a fallen comrade, and yet another slumped dead against the front of the pedestal. Within months, however, and without much commentary, the New York City Arts Commission rejected the model and began the search for another."[52]

Among the subsequent proposals for the memorial, which was never built, was a design by the noted sculptor and artist Chaim Gross (1904–91). Gross (who also illustrated the cover of Jacob Pat's *Ash and Fire*), was born in Galicia to a Hasidic family but had largely avoided Jewish themes in his work for the first twenty-five years of his career after his arrival in New York in 1921. The destruction of European Jewry and the creation of the State of Israel led to a major shift in his art. He lost his brother, sister, brother-in-law, niece, and nephew in the Holocaust. In addition to these deeply felt personal losses, the horrors of the war and the annihilation of centuries of Jewish tradition and culture motivated a change in his art.[53] In 1949 he was one of five finalists in a competition at the Jewish Museum in New York City. His model incorporated branches of a menorah at various angles, with the figure of a woman atop the monument, arms stretched to the sky.

Another model, by Percival Goodman, was selected by the committee in 1950, but was eventually rejected by Parks Commissioner Robert Moses. In 1951, another sculpture by Erich Mendelsohn, a refugee from Nazi Germany, which would feature eighty-foot granite tablets of the Ten Commandments, became the focus of construction planning (although it too was never built after Mendelsohn died in 1953). As Hasia Diner notes, although the memorial was never built, some, like Rabbi Israel Taback, president of the Rabbinical Council of America, argued that history had already established a monument—the State of Israel.[54] Nonetheless, it is worth noting that it was evident to some who planned the memorial that the Warsaw Ghetto Uprising and the six million Jews martyred in the cause of human freedom were, if not quite synonymous, certainly worthy of being memorialized in the same place. Still, dueling political frameworks hampered the ability to agree on an appropriate memorial. The subsequent history of the memorial—which evolved from an initial effort to support the creation of the State of Israel, to something that evoked the shared Judeo-Christian ethos of the Ten Commandments, and eventually would result in the building of a Memorial Museum in Battery Park with a view of the Statue of Liberty—reflect the degree to which politics and context framed the literal shaping of memory.

As Hasia Diner's work has shown, the Warsaw Ghetto Uprising indeed became the "prism through which American Jews chose to remember the Holocaust." As a subject of historical and literary study, the Warsaw Ghetto Uprising dominated the "literature of the Jewish catastrophe" in the early years after the war. In a review of literature on the "Jewish Catastrophe" published in *Jewish Social Studies* in January 1950, Philip Friedman and Pinson make this point and introduce an important early treatment:

> The subject most frequently dealt with in the literature of the Jewish catastrophe is concerned with the Warsaw ghetto and the ghetto uprising. There are over 300 such items. Of these, the most valuable are the memoir literature and the collections of documents and source materials. The first serious study of the uprising in the Warsaw ghetto was by Dr. Josef Kermisz, published first in Polish and later in Yiddish translation. . . . The original Polish edition was published in Lodz in 1946. It has since, however, been superseded by fuller accounts based on more immediate experience.

Kermish's study included sections on the development of the resistance movement in Warsaw, preparations for the uprising and its ending, as well as a chapter on the attitude of the Polish population to the uprising. In his conclusion, Kermish argued "while they had not managed to rouse the conscience of the world to organize assistance which would never come, one goal of the uprising had been accomplished, it had saved the pride and honor of the Jewish people."[55] Kermish noted the significant moral impact of the revolt to the various ghettos and camps across the land, to raise the morale of the Jewish people, leading to revolts in Częstochowa, Będzin, Białystok, Treblinka, and Sobibor, as well as partisans fighting across Europe. Kermish concluded by predicting "The April Revolt, the first Jewish rebellion since the Bar Kochba revolt, will serve as a source of pride for Jews for generations of Jewish history."

Rachel Auerbach, The Jewish Revolt

Among those accounts that followed the early history by Kermish was one written by Rachel Auerbach, one of the last surviving contributors to the Oneg Shabbes archive, who would become a central figure in collecting survivor testimonies after the war. Auerbach, who had served as the director of a soup kitchen located at 40 Leszno Street in the Warsaw ghetto for three years, recorded her experiences in the ghetto at the request of Emanuel Ringelblum, although these did not figure into her account of the uprising published in 1948. Her ghetto diary and a study of hunger in the ghetto titled *Gets a teler esn: Monografie fun a folks kikh* (Grab a plate of food: Monograph of a folk-kitchen), were buried and later unearthed along with other material from the Ringelblum archives. After the liberation of Warsaw, Auerbach became active in documentation work, collecting testimonies and writing an early report on Treblinka for the Polish State Committee for the Investigation of Nazi War Crimes on Polish Soil (a fact-finding mission). Auerbach served as a member of the Central Jewish Historical Commission in Lodz, where she was an editor of the publication *Dos Naye Leben*. She also actively participated in the beginning of the publication of witness accounts in Yiddish and Polish, preparing a guide for the taking of testimony as well as a questionnaire concerning specific topics. Auerbach and Hersh Wasser managed to uncover the first half of the Ringelblum archives in December 1946, which included some of her ghetto writings. After moving to Israel in 1950, she continued collecting and publishing survivor testimonies and became the founder and director of the Department for the Collection of Witness Testimony at Yad Vashem in Jerusalem. She encouraged survivors to write personal memoirs and was active in the publication of the *Yizkor* books that focused on specific communities.[56]

While she had been involved in the work of documenting testimony during and after the war, and had been living on the Aryan side of Warsaw during the revolt, Auerbach's *Der Yiddisher Oyfshtand* omitted any specific references to the identities of the ghetto fighters, even though she relied on certain testimonies of ghetto fighters, including Edelman and Zuckerman. Why, in a historical treatment, did Auerbach avoid identifying the ghetto fighters by name?

Auerbach started her history of the Warsaw Ghetto Uprising by marking the fact that the date of the final liquidation had been timed to coincide with the beginning of Passover, "dates determined long before by Hitler's professors." Situating her history within the collective tradition of the Passover holiday, Auerbach created a framework of memory that employed the style of a modern Haggadah. "*Lomir geyn ke-seder*" she writes, let us follow the story in order. Auerbach emphasized "the armed brotherhood between

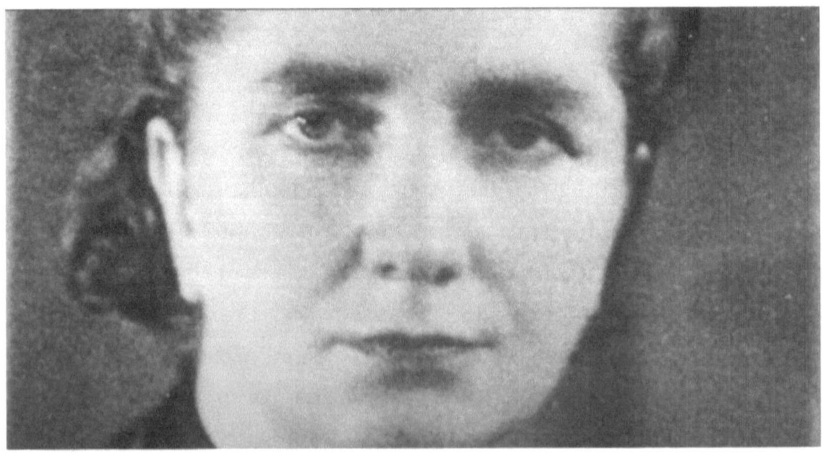

Rachel Auerbach.

the Jewish parties" as a source of strength, identifying national unity as the "secret and the foundation of the public's strength."

As the Germans approach the gates of the ghetto the cry goes out to the ghetto fighters:

> 12 o'clock at night—the fighting organization emerges from underground. The curfew is no longer in effect. With weapons in hand, in German helmets and uniforms, several patrols emerge into the ghetto. They stride over the streets, knocking, playing soldiers in the gates. People open their doors with fear, but they are recognized with an expression of surprise: Oh, Jewish children! Oh our youngsters. Oh, fighters! . . .
>
> They waken, warning. They call for a revolt to take place. On the walls of the ghetto hang already the manifest of uprising. The last call, to the last battle, ends with a declaration: fight . . . die . . . for the honor of the people!

She bases her narrative on the order of the Seder (except in this case, the Stroop report provides the narrative structure). And just as Moses is not mentioned in the Passover Haggadah, she does not refer to any of the heroes by name.

The Jewish people held their seders in the ghetto that Monday night—the first night of the revolt.

> Deep in bunkers, in desolate apartments, in which people sat . . . to the last moment did Jews sit by their set tables.
>
> The Haggadah says. . . .
>
> And they recalled the stories of Pharaoh in Egypt, mixed together with the actions of the evil Hitler.
>
> They told the story of Rabbi Eliezer, and Rabbi Yehoshua, and Rabbi Elazar ben Azariah, and Rabbi Akivah. . . .
>
> Like these wise men of Bnei Brak did the Warsaw Jews recall the miracles of the exodus from Egypt and spoke

> about the Uprising. The deeds of the young fighters—of Mila and of Zamenhof, of Nalewki and Smocza.
>
> The evil one must be annihilated, like Pharaoh with his solders.

The only ghetto fighter mentioned by name is Mordecai Anielewicz, in reporting on his death as commandant of the ŻOB on the night of May 8, 1943.

> Together with his military did Mordecai Anielewicz fall—the commandant of the Uprising. Fate had determined that it would be so.
>
> So that around his young heroic head would shine the same holy light. The halo of death.

Even so, the historical study devotes most attention to Jurgen Stroop, the destroyer of the ghetto. And she bases her data on Stroop's report, listing the size of his forces: soldiers, SS men, tanks, and armaments. Her study includes details from testimonies of ghetto fighters, including a description of the journey out of the ghetto by the surviving members of the ŻOB through the sewers, but she does not name them—no Kazik, no Lubetkin, no Edelman.

At the conclusion of her book, Auerbach includes a poem, titled "A Matzevah (A gravestone)" where she listed the names of the fighters, including references to biblical names, the names of prophets, Yiddish names, Polish names . . .

A Matzevah (A Gravestone)

> *Their names:*
> *Avraham, Yitzhak, Yakov,*
> *Sarah, Rivkah, Rachel, Leah.*
> *And a Reuven, with a Shimon, a Yosef, with a Benyomin.*
> *A Moshe with an Aaron, a Yehoshua,*
> *And a Michael and a Rafael and a Gabriel.*
> *And a David with a Shlomo, a Saul, as well as a Shmuel.*

And a Zecharyahu and Yechezkel, even a Yirmiyahu.

And a Yisroel with a Hanoch, with a Tuvia, a Menachem with a Simcha.

And a Meir and Eliezer, a Hananya with a Yochanan—like the Tannaim.

And a Tzvi Hersh and a Dov Ber, and Arieh Leib, a Wolf. . .

And a Miriam with a Deborah, with a Hannah, a Ruth.

A Shoshana and a Penina.

And a Necha, a Tema, a Zivia—

Like dear Mothers, of Old.

And a Fruma—like a firzogerin *(announcer).*

And a Taibeleh, a Feigeleh—from folk songs.

And because they were so young, so close to Mama's tenderness, they referred to one another with childish names. And because they grew up in Poland, they also called each other by Polish names.

There was a Lutek and an Edek.

A Yanek, a Mietek, a Sevek.

An Alek with a Tadek and even a Stashek.

An Antek, a Marek, and a Kazik.

And a Marisia and a Wandzia.

And a Stefia with a Ruzia.

And those, who had an old conspiracy. Tradition had, that they called one another with earnest names of the underground.

There was an originator Yuzef. And a fighter Ignatz, an Adam—written with Jewish letters.

And an Andrzei and a Pawel, an Aleksander.

And a Michael and a Zigmund—from the same delivery.

And a Leon with an—Adolf—from Germany.

And those who had a connection with the Land of Israel, were called with names great and fiery. With names from the desert, from the Tanakh.

And a Laban from a second city, from the same good kheder.

And a Yehuda was among the leaders. As once upon a time among the Hashmonaim.

And two Mordecais—from the same strong and flaming souls.
Let us praise the youth. Let us not mourn them. Let us love them, as if they all remained among us.
Let us keep them alive among us until our last breath.

Auerbach wants the memory of the fighters—both those whose names we know and those we do not know—to be embedded deep in the heart of the nation:

> We must honor the known and the unknown and the few who are famous—with exactly the same love—all the same.
>
> Our memorial for those who fell in battle, can only be a memorial—for unknown fighters. . . .
>
> The memorial tablets engraved—in the heart of the entire People.

Auerbach's gravestone for the fighters differed from a monument. How to capture the names of the known and the unknown? The famous and the anonymous? In drawing parallels to Passover, Auerbach mirrored the Haggadah's avoidance of hero worship, although she did want to be sure the names of the fighters were not forgotten. But how to memorialize them all? And to honor them all equally? Auerbach was aware of the historical tendency to engage in hero worship, a tendency that would be magnified in the creation of monuments to the ghetto fighters themselves, when heroic statues would be placed on pedestals.

The Monument to the Ghetto Heroes

By the fifth anniversary of the uprising, on April 19, 1948, its heroes would receive the monument envisioned by Julian Tuwim on the first anniversary, "a new monument (to) be added to the national shrine." The Rapaport monument, which today stands on the corners of Warsaw's Zamenhof and Anielewicz streets, the site of the former Judenrat offices, of the first battles in the ghetto, and now opposite the newly opened POLIN museum documenting a thousand years of Jewish history in Poland, has become the focal point for commemoration of the destruction and the revolt in Warsaw. American president Barack Obama visited the monument in 2011, and it is the site where Willy Brandt, chancellor of West Germany, fell to his knees in 1970. Likewise, in 1983, Pope John Paul II added an unscheduled stop at the monument during his visit to Warsaw.

Dedicated on the fifth anniversary, the monument, carved out of beautiful black labradorite stone against a background of granite blocks originally intended for a monument to Hitler, depicts the leader of the ŻOB, Mordecai Anielewicz, in its center. Inscribed in Hebrew, Yiddish, and Polish "To the Jewish people, its heroes and its martyrs," it literally enshrines in stone the paradigm of passivity and resistance, as the two sides of the monument symbolize the two types of Jewish responses to extreme persecution, with action that bursts forth in time and space on one side of the monument and a quiet resignation that recedes into the recesses on the other.

Born in Warsaw in 1911, Natan Rapoport was drawn to art and sculpture from a young age, although like many poor Jewish families in Warsaw, the Rapoports struggled to subsist on meager incomes. An active member of Hashomer Hatzair as a young man, Rapoport first studied art and sculpture in Warsaw, before later traveling to Rome and Paris in the 1930s. When war broke out, Rapoport fled east from Poland, eventually finding refuge in the USSR. From late 1943 until early 1945, Rapoport was in Novosibersk, where he was drafted into service on projects for the USSR, while continuing to work on a model for what would become his Warsaw Ghetto Monument. When the war came to an end, Rapoport returned with his family to Moscow and they were repatriated to Warsaw in early 1946. Having been urged by Ber Mark, editor of the Central Committee of Polish Jews (CKZP) bulletin *Dos Naye Leben*, to return to Warsaw, Rapoport approached the committee with a proposal to create a monument to the uprising and destruction of the Warsaw ghetto. Batia Donner, author of the definitive biography of Rapoport, notes that the sculptor participated in a tour of the destroyed ghetto led by Antek Zuckerman on August 19, 1946, together with other artists and writers, including Yisrael Barzilai and Avraham Sutzkever.[57] Barzilai, a prominent member of Hashomer Hatzair and Mapam, described Zuckerman's tour of the ghetto in *Al HaMishmar* (the Hashomer Hatzair movement newspaper):

> We descended to the ruins of the bunker and listened to Antek's quiet tale of simple things—how they lived in the ghetto, work conditions there, the first steps to organize battle divisions. He told us about Josef Kaplan and about Mordecai, about the first battle, about communication between the ghetto and the Aryan side, about connections between the fighting divisions.[58]

The CKZP formally decided on July 26, 1946, to turn to Rapoport to design the memorial to the ghetto fighters, with a special committee of Adolf Berman, Yitzhak Zuckerman, and Falk responsible for overseeing the process. Without a doubt, the political composition of the committee, along with the Hashomer Hatzair background of the artist, shaped the very specific political message of the iconic monument. As the historian James Young notes, the CKZP had already received a submission from a local Polish artist of two Hasidim hoeing potatoes, which they had rejected.[59] Rapoport presented the committee with a plaster monument that he had smuggled out of the USSR, and the design was accepted immediately. According to Young, Rapoport was adamant that the monument be placed on the site of the revolt, where Anielewicz had died in his bunker (as noted, the site had already been marked in April 1946 with a stone marker). Rapoport and the committee agreed to place the monument on a spot nearby. Funding was provided primarily by the American Jewish Joint Distribution Committee with an understanding that the CKZP would eventually reimburse the JDC.[60] Additional donations were solicited by the Jewish community in Warsaw.

While Rapoport and the CKZP had identified the ideal spot for the monument, the City of Warsaw Arts Committee hesitated to approve the proposed location of the monument as it was unclear where reconstruction of the destroyed capital would actually take place on the rubble of the ruined city.[61] Rapoport returned to Paris to work on the sculpture, showing his plan to other artists and former teachers. In an interview with James Young years later, Rapoport recalled the reactions of other artists to his plans, skeptical of their praise:

> "Could I have made a stone with a hole in it," he has asked, and said "Voila! The Greatness of the Jewish People? No, I needed to show the heroism, to illustrate it literally in figures everyone, not just artists, would respond to. This was to be a public monument after all. And what do human beings respond to? Faces, figures, the human form. I did not want to represent resistance in the abstract: it was not an abstract uprising. It was real."[62]

According to Young, Rapoport used human models from the Yishuv, kibbutzniks living in Paris after the war, to make, in his words: "a clearly national monument for the Jews, not a Polish monument. I wanted to show the Polish people who we really were."

Rapoport worked with Mark Leon Suzin, a survivor and architect based in Paris, to construct the base of the monument in Warsaw. Suzin and Rapoport traveled to Sweden in search of granite for the monument's retaining wall, and in one of the ironies of the monument's history, discovered there a huge cache of perfectly cut granite blocks, which had been ordered by the German sculptor Arno Breker during the war, destined for a monument in Berlin to commemorate Hitler's victory. Rapoport and Suzin requested that the granite, which was to be the background for the bronze relief, be sent directly to Warsaw. One month before the monument was unveiled in Warsaw, Parisian art critics had a chance to review it; among the accolades, one described it as "a living symbol of ghetto resistance, treated with breathtaking lyricism and grandeur."[63] Rapoport would call the unanimous acclaim from Parisian art critics "a victory in battle" itself.[64] The bronze was subsequently dismantled into three sections and transported by boat and truck from Paris to Warsaw, via Gdansk, at the end of March 1948. Rapoport completed final touches to the bronze and stone during the first two weeks of April.[65]

The unveiling of the monument was the main event in six days of programming to commemorate the fifth anniversary of the revolt, which included the opening of an exhibition at the Jewish Historical Institute dedicated to Jewish martyrdom during the war. Press reports detailed

> Thousands of Poles and Jews today attended ceremonies here marking the fifth anniversary of the uprising in the Warsaw ghetto in which over 40,000 Jews lost their lives. Among the participants in the ceremonies, which included the unveiling of a large memorial to the Jewish fighters and martyrs, some 3,000 delegates from communities in all parts of Poland, 200 delegates from Jewish communities outside the country and representatives of the Polish Government, the army and all political parties.[66]

Survivors of the ghetto battle and partisans who fought with the Polish and Soviet armies took part in the ceremonies, which were also attended by the Polish Premier Józef Cyrankiewicz, Minister for Justice Henryk Świątkowski, and Minister without Portfolio Władysław Baranowski. Świątkowski, addressed those gathered for the ceremonies to pay tribute "to the heroic deeds and battle of the Jews of Warsaw ghetto."[67]

Adolph Berman, speaking as a leader of the Jewish underground and as head of the Central Committee of Polish Jews linked the fight for the Warsaw ghetto to the struggle for a Jewish state, noting that those who fought in the ghetto would willingly offer their "blood as a contribution to the liberty and statehood of Palestine Jewry." At the same time, Berman presented the revolt as a central part of a broader opposition movement against Nazism led by the Polish Worker's Party, Marxist-Zionists, and young, progressive Jews. As Adolf Berman triumphantly proclaimed, "the armed brotherhood of the Polish and Jewish radical workers' movement was not a phrase, but a fact. . . . The uprising in the ghetto, the first massive, revolutionary rebellion in Poland during the occupation, undoubtedly became one of the sparks that triggered the Polish resistance movement."[68] Antek Zuckerman and Chaika Grossman arrived from Israel to speak at the ceremony, detailing the history of the battle in the ghetto. (The organizing committee sent invitations to a broad range of officials from the Jewish Agency, Histadrut, the kibbutz movements, and many more, but due to the security situation and increased military conflict in the Yishuv, most were unable to attend). A special choir of 250 orphaned Jewish children sang partisan hymns and battle songs.

The Jewish Telegraph Agency article also described the granite memorial:

> 50 feet high and 30 feet wide features four menorahs, one at each corner. The lights in the menorahs will burn eternally. The center piece, cast in bronze by the noted Jewish sculptor Prof Nathan Rappaport, depicts a group of ghetto fighters on one side, and a party of Jews being shipped to their deaths by the Nazis, on the other face. The monument, on the spot where the first contingent of some 2,000 Nazi troops entered the ghetto to suppress the uprising, cost 100,000,000 zlotys.[69]

On the same day, a "museum of Jewish martyrdom" was opened at the Jewish Historical Institute. "Authentic photographs and other graphic evidence portraying the life of the Jews of Poland in the various Nazi ghettos including torn and blood-stained Scrolls and prayer shawls, as well as drums, shoes and purses made of parchment ripped from the Torah fill the museum."

Additional speeches at the fifth anniversary dedication event included remarks by Rabbi Cahane and Rabbi Dreistmann, who recited the *Mourner's Kaddish.* Wary of conducting memorial services in front of a graven image, Rapoport's sculpture was covered by a white sheet while the rabbis recited prayers and Yoel Lazevnik read the megillah of dedication. Rapoport later recalled, "as we stood on the ruins of the ghetto, waiting for the ceremony to begin, pieces of paper from Jewish books burned by the Nazis began to fly through the air around us. A deep silence settled over the crowd. The seven branches of the menorahs on the monument burned seven flames. And then, as the rabbi recited his prayer, people began to quietly weep."[70]

General Kushko of the Polish Army bestowed the Grunewald Cross, second stage, posthumously upon Mordecai Anielewicz, as well as honors upon the partisans and ghetto fighters who fought with him. Sidney Silberman, a British member of Parliament, spoke in English: "it is alone a memorial to the heroic dead, it is a challenge and a warning to the living"; Dr. Abraham Levinson from Israel spoke (in Yiddish); as did Shmuel Mikunis, representative from the Communist Party in Israel.[71] A crowd of twenty thousand attended the dedication ceremony, including twelve thousand Holocaust survivors. Twenty-four countries were represented by a total of 133 delegations.[72]

As Young notes, the monument is an edifice that "literally supports the figures and meanings projected onto it." Metaphorically, Young argues, the monument recalls the ghetto wall that divided Warsaw's Jews from the rest of the city, while at the same time resembling a great tombstone (and indeed, the memorial is constantly adorned with wreaths, stones, pebbles, and *yahrtsayt* candles).[73] As a *matzevah*, or tombstone, Rapoport's monument has two sides that embed in stone the two types of death in the ghetto: on one side, Anielewicz and the fighters burst forth into time and space, making their mark on history; on the opposite side, in bas relief (the Jerusalem replica installed at Yad Vashem in 1976 displays the two side by side), the Jewish masses of three hundred thousand recede into history, marching passively to their deaths (like sheep to the slaughter). The group of seven ghetto fighters thrusts outward from the granite wall, a wall that evokes not only the walls of the ghetto but, as Young notes, was intended to evoke the Western Wall in Jerusalem. The monument is also framed by two menorahs that recall both the Temple in Jerusalem as well as the historical example of the Maccabees struggle.[74] The two menorahs also bring to mind the remaining menorahs from Tlomackie Synagogue (see bottom of page 357), highlighted by Jacob Pat in his travelogue, *Ash un Fayer*. Donner notes that Rapoport intended for the bronze side of the monument to be visible from a great distance (unlike the bas relief on the other side). Today the POLIN museum obstructs the view, and the monument must be approached more closely. Even so, the heroic side captures the visitor's attention first, before turning to the Jewish martyrs on the back.

Pomnik Bohaterów Getta, the Ghetto Heroes Monument, Warsaw. (Photo by author)

At the center of the seven bronze figures towering above the viewer stands Mordecai Anielewicz. Only Anielewicz looks forward, while the other figures gaze to either side, distracted by other threats. Anielewicz, the unquestioned leader, strides forward to confront the threat he must face, summoning the viewer to witness the scene before him. Anielewicz is a symbol of strength willing to sacrifice his life for the sake of freedom, but is also emaciated, with a bandage visible on his right arm. Even so he remains muscular, and his presence projects power, leadership, and command. In his left hand he holds a grenade, and he is flanked by two younger fighters—one holding a gun, the other a knife, while a much older, barefooted, bearded figure kneels at Anielewicz's feet, his disproportionately large hands grasping a boulder, ready to make use of it in the conflict. Beneath Anielewicz lies a fallen fighter, while above him a woman holds a child gazing into the skies above.[75] Flames seem to burn around them in the background.

While Anielewicz was unknown by the world in the first year after the revolt, by 1948 he had become the unquestioned symbol of Jewish heroism, representing the central figure upon which the foundation of a Jewish future would be rebuilt. (As noted, Rapaport himself had been a member of Hashomer Hatzair in his youth). Rapaport emphasized the youth of the heroic ghetto fighters, placing the oldest figure in the sculpture kneeling before Anielewicz. The only female figure is depicted as a symbol of motherhood, her bare breast exposed, holding not a weapon but a vulnerable baby, gazing above either in despair or in hope of salvation. Either way, Rapoport did not capture the role played by women in the revolt, in spite of the fact that their contribution was well known by then.

On the other side of the monument (today the POLIN Museum of the History of Polish Jews rises in the background) Rapoport created his tribute to the Jewish masses of Warsaw, over three hundred thousand of whom died in the ghetto and gas chambers of Treblinka.

Unlike the heroic fighters on the other side who burst forth into time and space, the bas-relief recedes into the stone. Compelled forward by a hidden force, the last march recalls the bas-relief inside the Arch of Titus in Rome, depicting the procession after the fall of Jerusalem. Here, the

Back of the Ghetto Fighters Monument, with POLIN Museum in the background. (Photo by author)

monument shows the Jews of fallen Warsaw resigned to their fate, women, children, and the elderly with their heads bowed, while a rabbinic figure wearing a tallit holds a Torah scroll in one hand while the other arm outstretched reaches out to God either for intervention or in accusation. Rapoport chose to portray mainly women, children, and the elderly on the deportation side. The majority of the figures are women (perhaps six out of nine); the first woman is in advanced stage of pregnancy with hands on her belly to protect a baby (who will most likely never be born). Next to her, a stooped grandmother, face covered by a veil, puts her hand on the shoulder of a young girl whose profile is visible. A young child holds the hand of an elderly woman—only he glances backward, offering a full facial depiction, engaging the viewer directly, perhaps asking an unspoken question. While the heroic fighter on the front of the monument gazes upward into the future, the wide eyes of the little boy are frozen in the present. Nazis are almost invisible in the background, seen behind the marching Jews as helmets and bayonets, perhaps because Rapoport wanted to avoid creating a monument that would glorify Nazi oppression. At the same time, however, the absence of any force compelling the "last march" of the Jews reinforces the contrast between those Jews marching passively to their deaths like "sheep to the slaughter" and the heroes on the front who chose to die fighting.

Conclusion

The Rapoport monument in Warsaw would come to be the defining symbol of the Warsaw Ghetto Uprising after its unveiling on the fifth anniversary of the revolt. As Hasia Diner notes, for years afterward, its image would grace American Jewish publications. It was fitting that the monument to the heroes of the uprising would be erected on the corner of the newly renamed Anielewicz Street. While no other street would be given the names of ghetto fighters as promised, the name of Anielewicz had become synonymous with the heroic resistance of the ghetto fighters. The two menorahs that Jacob Pat had noted as remaining from the Tlomackie Synagogue were now replaced by the two menorahs that framed Rapaport's monument. The eternal flame of Jewish life would not be extinguished. The obligation of the living would be to keep the memory of the dead alive until their last breaths.

By 1948, the Warsaw Ghetto Uprising was understood within preexisting interpretive frameworks and the heroes and martyrs of Warsaw were also viewed in this way: as sacrifices for a greater cause and midwives to the rebirth of the Jewish people. The two poles of Jewish behavior and experience—heroes and martyrs, ghetto fighters and sheep, Warsaw and Treblinka—also seem to have been enshrined within the frameworks for understanding the event, regardless of ideological viewpoint. In one case after another, we can see the duality set up: in Pat's *Ash un Fayer*, destruction and revolt; in Auerbach's history, a struggle to balance the names of the fighters with the anonymity of the masses; in Zvi Kolitz's story, the ruins of the ghetto become the site for a rejection of blind faith and passivity and a choice to become master of one's fate; in Marie Syrkin's history *Blessed Is the Match*, the ghetto fighters are valorized again for rejecting passivity; finally, in Rapaport's two-sided monument, the duality is enshrined in stone, becoming a new altar or "Eastern Wall" for pilgrims to memorialize the destruction, and affirm the defiant strength, of a civilization.

By April 19, 1948, however, the attention of the Jewish world had begun to shift to a much more pressing issue—the fighting in Palestine that would lead to the outbreak of war with the British withdrawal in May. The cover page of the *Forverts* that day focused on fighting between the Arab Legion and the Haganah around Jerusalem. The Hadassah convoy massacre, which took place on April 13, attracted much greater attention than the unveiling of the monument in Warsaw. As new chapters in the history of the Jewish people were being written, some feared the heroism of Warsaw would soon be forgotten. On April 20, the *Forverts* reported that the Bund had organized a small memorial service to be held at the Rand School on Fifteenth Street in honor of the anniversary—but each year the size of the crowd in attendance continued to decline.

9

Warsaw in Israel and America, 1948–53

Approximately one month after the dedication of the Ghetto Heroes Monument, on May 14, 1948, the day on which the British Mandate over Palestine expired, David Ben-Gurion proclaimed the creation of the State of Israel at the Tel Aviv Museum. The proclamation, which invoked the historic connection of the Jewish people to the Land of Israel, "the birthplace of the Jewish people," also addressed the most recent catastrophe, "another clear demonstration of the urgency of solving the problem of its homelessness by re-establishing in Eretz-Israel the Jewish State, which would open the gates of the homeland wide to every Jew and confer upon the Jewish people the status of a fully privileged member of the community of nations."[1] The new state was recognized that night by the United States and three days later by the USSR.

Five days later, on May 19, 1948, Egyptian forces attacked Kibbutz Yad Mordecai, where a force of approximately 110 men and boys from the kibbutz (small children had been evacuated the night before), along with Palmach members led by Alex Biber, the Haganah commander of Yad Mordecai, and Tuvia Reich, a Palmach captain, prepared to defend the kibbutz. Arrayed in two squads armed with light weapons, a medium machine gun, and a PIAT (projector infantry anti-tank weapon), the small force waited for the advancing Egyptian forces.[2] The Egyptian assault, aided by fighter bombers, mortars, tanks, and armored cars, took five days to conquer Yad Mordecai, which had been renamed by the Hashomer Hatzair movement after Mordecai Anielewicz in 1943. The Egyptians sustained four hundred casualties to Yad Mordecai's sixty-three: twenty-three dead and forty wounded. Importantly, the five days it took to conquer the kibbutz enabled the Givati Brigade to organize a defense that would halt the advance toward Tel Aviv.[3] Following the counterattack by the Israeli Defense Forces (IDF) in October 1948, Israel was able to retake the abandoned Jewish settlements, including Yad Mordecai on November 4, 1948.

The educational officer for the Givati Brigade at the time was none other than Abba Kovner, survivor of the Vilna ghetto and leader of the United Partisans Organization, who had tried unsuccessfully to organize revenge operations in Europe after the war. Between June 1948 and May 1949, Kovner wrote thirty battle missives distributed among the soldiers, distinguished by both their poetry and pathos, as well as their violent rhetoric.[4] As a veteran of battles in occupied Europe, Kovner, "through his gory battle missives . . . sought to cleanse the fighters of the guilt and shame of bloodshed and to give words to an unspoken trauma." In his poetic language, scholar Michal Arbell argues, Kovner made a direct link for the soldiers fighting the Egyptian enemy—at times equating the Egyptians with the Nazis, as in a poem from a missive published in July 1948. The poem urged Jewish soldiers to fight for "our homes, for the lives of our children," as "the souls of six million—the souls that did not get to see the day—call us from the ground: let the great revenge come—let the people of Israel be free, forever!"[5]

Beyond helping to create a symbolic link between the war in Europe and the war for a Jewish state, survivors of the Holocaust also played a disproportionately large role in the fighting in 1948.[6] The IDF also formed a special partisans platoon, attached to Givati Regiment 51, Company T, which included Kazik (Simcha Rotem), who served as the platoon's social commander.[7]

Once the war was over, commemorative events in the newly created state resumed, including the dedication of the Ghetto Fighters Kibbutz in the north on April 19, 1949 (located on the site of a previously occupied Arab village, A-Samaria, near Akko).[8] Although the actual cornerstone for the first blocks of living quarters for the new kibbutz was laid on February 10, 1949, the Kibbutz HaMeuchad movement decided that the actual settlement ceremony should take place on the sixth anniversary of the Warsaw Ghetto Uprising, next to photos from the Holocaust and the uprising. The manuscript from Yitzhak Katznelson's "Song of Lament" and pages from the diaries of the ghetto fighters were included in a special exhibition, in addition to photos. *Davar* announced the establishment of the kibbutz—"The Ghetto Fighters Settle in the Galilee on the Anniversary of the Warsaw Revolt" (*Davar*, April 19, 1949)—where, strung between "two cypress trees, hung a banner": "the desperate heroism of Israel has not yet ceased." The crowd of thousands, which included leaders of the revolt, partisans, leaders of the workers movement, staff from the Polish consulate, and representatives of Polish Jewry, as well as large numbers of residents from surrounding kibbutzim and many soldiers, heard speeches from prominent Yishuv leaders, former ghetto fighters, and musical performances concluding with the singing of the "Partisans Song," before the playing of "Hatikvah" on the flute.[9] The commemoration ceremony was also a dedication, which captured the transition from remembering the past to building for the future. Both symbolically and physically, those who struggled to create the state and establish new homes there continued the struggle commenced by the fighters in the Warsaw ghetto.

One year later, on April 19, 1950, the cornerstone was laid for the permanent building of the Ghetto Fighters House Museum, which would be funded by Kibbutz HaMeuchad (meaning that the Museum would focus primarily on the activity of the Dror movement, much to the chagrin of members of Hashomer Hatzair and other movements).[10] While the ghetto fighters affiliated with Kibbutz HaMeuchad established the Ghetto Fighters House, most Bundist fighters more typically moved to new homes in America and Australia (or in the case of Marek Edelman, remained in Poland). Rose Klepfisz, the widow of Michał Klepfisz, arrived in New York on April 11, 1949, with her daughter, Irka (Irene).[11] Eventually, Dr. Philip Friedman hired her to work as an archivist at YIVO, where she helped to compile the YIVO bibliography and "Guide to Jewish History under the

Nazi Impact." She would go on to become an archivist at YIVO and later the JDC. In April 1949, the Bund also published the volume *In Heldiszn Gerangl* (In Heroic Struggle), dedicated on the sixth anniversary of the Warsaw Ghetto Uprising, to document the Bund's role in the ghetto battles. The volume included excerpts from Marek Edelman's *The Ghetto Fights*, Meed's *On Both Sides of the Ghetto Wall*, and Bernard Goldstein's *Five Years in the Warsaw Ghetto*, as well as profiles by J. S. Hertz of Bundist heroes Abrasha Blum, Michał Klepfisz, Berek Shnajdmil, Moshe Kaufman, Henekh Rus, Zalman Frydyrych, Tobcia Dawidowicz, Mejlech Perlman, Lejb Gruzaltz, the Blones family, and many others.

While archivists and historians were working to document Jewish history under the Nazi impact, popular works of fiction would end up reaching a much broader audience in America. In 1950, John Hersey, already the recipient of a Pulitzer Prize for his novel *A Bell for Adano* and acclaimed for his reporting for the *New Yorker* on Hiroshima, made the Warsaw ghetto and the uprising the subject of his next novel, *The Wall.* Hersey's novel quickly became a Book-of-the-Month-Club selection and a *New York Times* bestseller.[12] Although Hersey included a disclaimer in the front matter noting the book was a work of fiction, many readers believed the novel to be true, and indeed his meticulous research and writing style made it seem like a work retelling actual events. Hersey's attention to historical detail resulted from three years of research conducted by Mark Nowogrodzki and Lucy S. Dawidowicz (the same who tried to imagine herself inside the ghetto at the memorial service at Carnegie Hall some two months after the revolt), who helped uncover and translate the Yiddish and Polish documents Hersey used to give his novel a feeling of historical authenticity. In making the novel more mainstream and appealing to a broader audience, Hersey also downplayed any references to socialist or communist Jewish groups who may have played a role in the revolt. Historian Nancy Sinkoff argues Hersey was concerned about Cold War anticommunism, and thus very carefully made sure his ghetto fighters were members of Hashomer Hatzair and not the Bund: "as he explained to Nowogrodzki: 'I settled on (the Zionist) Hashomer (Ha-tsa'ir and not the socialist Bund) for the central characters partly because Hashomer would be unfamiliar to most Americans readers and so would not summon an immediate hostile response, as the mere words Socialist and Communist are apt to do.'"[13] Those familiar with the history of the Warsaw Ghetto Uprising also objected to the fact that Hersey obscured the actual identities of Ringelblum, Anielewicz, Edelman, and others. Still, as Moses Leavitt of the JDC noted, that a non-Jewish writer had written such a popular book on an important Jewish topic seemed to mitigate these concerns. Reviews in the major Yiddish newspapers in New York generally expressed an appreciation for Hersey's careful attention to historical details.[14] What seemed to especially perturb Rachel Auerbach, nonetheless, was the fact that "Hersey's novel suited its American audience's view of the war," which underscored the triumph of universal good over universal evil and minimized specific Jewish suffering. For a popular audience, this meant downplaying Jewish rage and the desire for revenge, turning the tragedy of the Warsaw ghetto into a triumphant celebration of the forces of democracy and goodness over fascism and evil.[15]

This tendency to fictionalize history to fit the American context would continue, issuing in Leon Uris's popular *Mila 18* in 1961, and later in the popular TV mini-series *Holocaust* in 1978 (with the fictional character Moses Weiss fighting in the Warsaw ghetto), and a made-for-TV version of *The Wall* based on the Broadway play of the same name, broadcast on CBS in 1982. These creative renderings continued the trend established already during the war in the radio play *The Battle of the Warsaw Ghetto* and the show *Miracle in the Ghetto*. Despite the concerns of Rachel Auerbach about the obscuring of the historical record, the broad popularity of Hersey's novel indicated that what mattered more to American audiences, both Jewish and non-Jewish, were the universalizing moral lessons that could be drawn from the uprising, and more broadly from the Holocaust itself. For most Americans, the specific identities of the ghetto fighters were less important.

In Israel, on the other hand, the specific identities of the fighters mattered greatly, as did the political motivations that guided their actions. In 1951, Israel's Knesset passed legislation making Yom HaShoah vehaGevurah the 27th of Nisan—the same year the Ghetto Fighters House Museum was opened at Kibbutz Lochamei HaGeta'ot and a statue in memory of

Mordecai Anielewicz was unveiled at Kibbutz Yad Mordecai. The Jewish National Fund dedicated a "Martyrs' Forest" in the mountains outside Jerusalem, and the Ministry of Religious Affairs created the *genizah* (a storage area for holy books) on Mount Zion for Torah scrolls desecrated by the Nazis.[16] Prime Minister David Ben-Gurion spoke at the dedication ceremony, as did Zivia Lubetkin, who noted the appropriate symbolism of locating the forest in the hills on the path to Jerusalem.[17] In her remarks at the dedication of the Martyrs' Forest, Zivia Lubetkin recalled that

> Two things unified our brothers as they walked the final path, and this was in fact their epitaph: to take revenge and to remember, to remember not to forget. . . . And all of those who remain alive from the troubles of the Nazi period know and feel this. Bless the Jewish National Fund for establishing two monuments to the living and the silent: the Ghetto Fighters kibbutz in the north and here near Jerusalem—the Martyrs' Forest, a forest which will take root and remind all who pass of the horrors of the Holocaust and the destruction and the secret of bravery. On this day we will remember not only the horrors of the Shoah in the millions who were burned in the ovens and in the gas chambers, but we will also remember those who fought alone in battle. Without weapons, with no ground beneath their feet, no sky above their heads. Although they were not able to save the lives of millions, they were able to save their honor. And it is not coincidence, that this holy forest will be planted on the path to Jerusalem. Not only that the eyes of all those perished looked to Jerusalem, but also this generation that looked at the depths of destruction and was able to witness the establishment of Israel must remember that the path to independence leads along the path of the forest of the martyrs.

At the dedication of the Martyrs' Forest, Lubetkin emphasized the relationship between the heroes and the martyrs: although the heroes had not been able to save the lives of millions, they had saved their honor, and the honor of the Jewish people. For the heroes to be heroes, they needed the martyrs to have been sheep led to the slaughter—the two would exist in an enduring relationship with one another. While the voices of the martyrs had been silenced, the living monument in Israel would speak for them. The physical and spiritual rebirth of the Jewish state would give meaning to their deaths.

The statue of Mordecai Anielewicz was dedicated on the site of the destroyed (and soon to be rebuilt) Kibbutz Yad Mordecai on April 19, 1951. Nathan Rapoport, who had moved to Israel not long after the dedication of the Ghetto Heroes Monument in Warsaw, was commissioned to create it. While the kibbutz had been named after Mordecai Anielewicz in 1943, after its destruction in 1948 the leaders of the kibbutz insisted they would rebuild the new kibbutz around the statue that Rapoport would build. Symbolically, then, Kibbutz Yad Mordecai would rise again as a testament to the strength of Anielewicz. Rapoport's monument, twelve feet high, modeled after Michelangelo's *David*, showed a figure armed with a single hand grenade instead of David's stone for his sling. Anielewicz's David turned to face the Nazi Goliath. At Yad Mordecai, however, his backdrop would not be the ruins of the Warsaw ghetto—instead, the ruins of the kibbutz water tower destroyed by Egyptian shelling would become the backdrop and foundation for the young fighter, now transformed into a muscular and determined kibbutznik.[18] The fusion of the Warsaw Ghetto Uprising with the creation of the Jewish state was complete (at least for the Labor Zionist movements; the Revisionists would wait decades to have their stories restored to the narrative).

Isaac Schwartzbart titled his remarks prepared for the dedication of the statue, "The Lasting Significance of the Warsaw Ghetto Uprising."[19]

> On April 19, at the "Yad Mordecai" Kibbutz of Hashomer Hatzair in Israel, there will be unveiled a monument to Mordecai Anielewicz, the commander of the Warsaw Ghetto Uprising in 1943. Kibbutz Yad Mordecai lies at the entrance to the Negev wilderness which is gradually being transformed into fertile land for the Jewish people. The settlement

Monument to Mordecai Anielewicz next to the destroyed water tower at Kibbutz Yad Mordecai.

> is situated not far from famous Negbah, very near to the Mediterranean, and not far from Gaza, the strip of Israel land held by Egypt. More than 50 chalutzim fell in the battle of Yad Mordecai during the Arab-Jewish hostilities in 1948. And now a monument is about to be unveiled there which is to perpetuate the memory of the uprising of the remnant of the Jews in the Warsaw Ghetto, where *thousands of Jews, men and women, fell in the battle for the honor of the Jewish people and for the idea of freedom for all people as against the atrocious barbarism perpetrated by Nazi Germany in World War II* [my emphasis].
>
> Will the uprising of the Warsaw Ghetto find an eternal monument in the history of the Jewish people and in the hearts of generations, present and, to some, throughout the centuries? Today we can only wish so.

Schwartzbart referred directly to the process of shaping collective memory, of seizing upon a specific event that would "lend wings" to the vision and imagination of the Jewish people. In referencing other sites of Jewish heroism, including "Modin and Massada, the revolt of the Maccabees and uprising of Bar Cochba [which] have sunk deeply into the national consciousness of our people," becoming touchstones for the Zionist reading of Jewish national history, Schwartzbart hoped that the Warsaw Ghetto Uprising would also find its way into the hearts of generations of Jewish people. In his remarks, however, Schwartzbart also acknowledged an implicit divide between what he referred to as eastern and western Jewry—eastern Jewry imbued with a national consciousness that enabled it to recognize great moments in the struggle for Jewish freedom in its history, as opposed to western Jewry, imbued with a diaspora consciousness, focused on assimilation and emancipation, which perhaps prevented it from integrating the memory of the Warsaw ghetto into the "holy of holies" of Jewish history. For Schwartzbart, the memory of thousands of Jews, men and women, falling in battle for the honor of the Jewish people, was the singular event from the latest destruction to be imprinted on the Jewish national consciousness.

By 1951, the World Jewish Congress had seized upon the Warsaw Ghetto Uprising as the cornerstone of an effort to arouse the national consciousness of the Jewish people. As Zohar Segev has detailed in his study on the World Jewish Congress, this was consistent with a WJC effort to create "an ambience of nationalism among the Jews of the Diaspora in the wake of World War II."[20] The WJC emphasized that the fighters in the Warsaw ghetto did not die only for the Jewish people, but for all mankind in the battle against forces of evil that yet may rise again. This argument, that could channel Jewish nationalism into a more general sense of Jewish contributions to the struggle for democracy and freedom against totalitarianism (and as the Cold War developed, against Communism) found a receptive audience among Jews and non-Jews alike in the United States.

By 1953, on the tenth anniversary of the revolt, the place of Jewish heroism as reflected in the ghetto revolts was enshrined in law, when Israel's Knesset passed the "Martyrs and Heroes Remembrance Law" (or Yad Vashem Law). In Israel, the ghetto revolt served as an object lesson on the need to sacrifice the individual for the honor of the Jewish people. The Yad Vashem law, signed by Moshe Sharett, Ben-Zion Dinur, and Yitzhak

Ben-Zvi, stated this clearly, fulfilling Shenhavi's vision of a memorial authority in the Land of Israel that would commemorate "the heroic stand of the besieged and fighters of the ghettoes, who rose and kindled the flame of revolt to save the honour of their people."[21] As Ben-Zion Dinur had argued before the Knesset, Yad Vashem could play a central role in shaping the collective memory of the nation; as he expressed it: "The I of the nation only exists to the extent that it possesses a memory." *Davar* based its support for Yad Vashem on the fear that the "ghetto fighters struggle could be distorted by the rewriters of history in Poland and their fellow travelers in the country . . . who combine even the memory of sublime national heroism with their absurd, sycophantic refrain about the battle cry of the faithful of the revolution."[22] Likewise, by establishing Yom HaShoah vehaGevurah as the 27th day of the month of Nisan, exactly one week before the 5th of Iyar, Yom Ha'Atzmaut, Israel's Independence Day, the State of Israel created a new dynamic on the Jewish calendar, with history and memory progressing from destruction to rebirth, from Yom Hashoah to Yom Ha'Atzmaut. (On April 8, 1959, the Knesset officially passed the Martyrs' and Heroes' Remembrance Day Law, solidifying the resolution first passed in 1951.)

With the establishment of Yad Vashem, the process of instilling the revolt as the central focal point of Jewish memory and seizing it as part of the Zionist master narrative was complete. And what of Schwartzbart's hope that the Warsaw Ghetto Uprising would find its place in the "Holy of Holies" of Jewish history? Had the Jewish people in fact understood that "the spirit which animated the fighters of the Warsaw Ghetto Uprising (was) an integral, inseparable part of the eternal spirit which keeps our people alive and active, creative and optimistic despite all disillusionment and ever recurring suffering"? Did honoring the ghetto fighters obscure other aspects of Jewish experiences during the Shoah? For decades after the war, the focus on the Jewish heroes of Warsaw would overshadow the experiences of the vast majority of Jewish victims of the Shoah. In this sense, only Jews with a connection to the Land of Israel had the courage to fight back—and those who died did so to defend the ideals of freedom and democracy. The unity of the fighters was lost, the drive to seek revenge, the feelings of abandonment by the rest of the world—all of these messages, erased. On the tenth anniversary of the Warsaw Ghetto Uprising, Isaac Schwartzbart worried that the "eternal meaning and purpose of the Warsaw Ghetto Uprising" would only be realized if the coming generations felt the spirit that animated the fighters was the same spirit that kept the Jewish people alive despite "disillusionment and ever recurring suffering." The symbolic spirit that animated the fighters would be more important than the identities of the actual fighters themselves, just as political interpretations that reinforced the existing worldviews of Jews in Israel and America would matter more than the complexities of wartime behavior that led to the revolt. Historians would seek to record the names of heroes in the ghetto; memory only demanded that the Jewish people remember that those heroes had fought for Jewish honor and dignity.

One year later, on the eleventh anniversary of the revolt (in the context of the Kasztner Affair), the Hebrew poet Natan Alterman was among the first to raise the question of whether the heads of the Jewish councils throughout eastern Europe had in fact been justified in their efforts to *prevent* resistance. Perhaps the burden of the ghetto fighters needed to account for the fact that the entire ghetto was destroyed as a result of their actions. What responsibility did the fighters bear for the ultimate fate of the ghetto?[23] And what was the relationship between the fighters who died for the Jewish nation and the rest of those who died? Alterman's poem, published in *Davar* on the same day the newspaper covered the ceremony at the Martyrs' Forest announcing the beginning of work at Yad Vashem, sparked a debate over the actions of the ghetto fighters and the centrality of the revolt in Israeli memory of the Shoah.

Memorial Day—and the Rebels

And on Memorial Day the fighters and rebels said:
Don't set us on a bright pedestal to differentiate us
From the Diaspora. In remembrance we step down
To blend again in the dark with the House of Israel.
Said the fighters and rebels: This day is a true symbol,
Not a glorious barricade lost in flames, nor the image

Of a boy and girl thrusting to break through or die,
In the manner of pictures of ever-burning rebellion.
This is not history's quarry. Don't hoist battle flags here
As if they are the fulfillment, the honor, and the justice.
Said the fighters and the rebels: We are part of the nation,
Of its honor, heroism, and profoundly yearning weeping.

As the poem goes on, Alterman's nameless fighters and rebels give voice to questions raised by "Jewish fathers [read Jewish elders, or the *Judenrate*, in the ghetto] who said the underground will bring destruction (Shoah) on all of us." Those fighters who supposedly fought for the "honor of the nation" suddenly raise a troubling suggestion in Alterman's poem: "I fought and carried the banner of the miracle of the revolt . . . [but] the revolt is only one note in the tale, and was not a crossroads or the ultimate goal, and for its honor this nation will still yet compete with every other nation." Had the fighters joined the fight as individuals and not as representatives of the nation? Was the revolt in fact the historical turning point it had been made out to be? Alterman challenges the heroic interpretation of the fighters' actions to save the "honor of the nation," suggesting that both those Jewish elders and the Jewish boys and girls who walked to their final destination "leaving only one white sock in the archive as a stone of memory" deserve a share of the heroism and honor of the Jewish nation.

Despite the controversy raised by this poem, the Israeli public was not prepared for a debate over the historical interpretation of the revolt, let alone the role played by the young Zionist leaders of the underground and the complexities of Jewish behavior during the war. And the critique raised by Alterman was interpreted in a political sense anyway, as a challenge to the ghetto fighters specifically and the Zionist Left as a whole amidst the drama of the Kasztner Affair.[24] Nonetheless, even as the Warsaw Ghetto Uprising came to be understood by broad sections of the Jewish public as part of the struggle to create the Jewish state, it was still understood as the symbolic focal point for commemorations of the destruction of European Jewry as a whole. The event itself, not just the heroism of the ghetto fighters, was used as a symbolic counterpoint to the death of millions of Jews all over Europe.

Within ten years of the revolt, the main parameters for historical memory of the event had been well established. However, as this book demonstrates, the revolt itself, while described as a "revolution in Jewish history," was quickly assimilated into familiar cultural patterns of thought. From a Zionist perspective, the heroes and martyrs of the Warsaw ghetto and the duality of active heroism and passive martyrdom captured the ambivalence of memory. The heroism of the ghetto fighters provided a usable past in the struggle for the creation of the Jewish state; the martyrs and victims proved a more challenging narrative to swallow. As Levi Shalitan argued at a meeting to commemorate the revolt in 1946, "a people cannot live off Treblinkas and Majdaneks—only thanks to Warsaw can this people live on."[25]

The shaping of the collective memory of the Warsaw Ghetto Uprising took place *as the event transpired* and in its immediate aftermath. Jews around the world attempted to assimilate the event into a worldview that already made sense to them, which could provide meaning for meaningless death. For most Jews after the war, this would mean seeing it as part of the struggle for the creation of a Jewish state. In Israel, this would be perfectly represented at a place like Yad Mordecai, where the symbolic struggle of the ghetto fighters became the struggle of a Hashomer Hatzair kibbutz. And for the state as a whole, Yom HaShoah vehaGevurah fused the destruction of the Jewish masses with the heroism of the Jewish fighters, embedding collective memory of the struggle into the annual Jewish calendar. In America, the struggle of the ghetto fighters was folded into the universal struggle of humanity against the forces of darkness, a narrative of good vs. evil. The popularity of Hersey's *The Wall* gave early expression to this, as did subsequent fictionalizations in the American mass media. In the American context, too, the role of the Bund was minimized as it became more difficult to support a socialist or communist reading of the revolt. In Israel, the Labor Zionist parties became the primary lens for understanding how the revolt figured into the struggle to create the state, with the Revisionist Zionist role overlooked for decades and the role of the Bund still largely ignored.

For decades the focus on the revolt and on the ghetto fighters overshadowed the lives and deaths of the vast majority of Jews who remained in the ghetto. Despite early (and contemporaneous) accounts of the revolt as a mass popular uprising, such as Bundist leader Shloime Mendelsohn's description in a January 1944 lecture delivered at YIVO in New York as a "people's war in the truest sense of the word," in which "all sections of the Jewish population of 40,000 partook in the struggle,"[26] for decades the uprising has continued to be characterized as a military confrontation led by a few hundred determined young despite (not with the assistance of) the Jewish masses.

As this book argues, to understand this dynamic we must examine the role played by the ghetto fighters themselves in constructing the narrative of the revolt as it transpired and in its aftermath. The Jewish National Committee (Adolf Berman and Yitzhak Zuckerman, in particular) were keen to represent the uprising as a military encounter that could convince the Polish underground to support their efforts.[27] It would take more than a year for the name of Mordecai Anielewicz to become known in the broader Jewish world, and, by the end of 1944, the Zionist movement seized on the revolt as part of the armed struggle for the creation of the State of Israel.

Responses to the revolt in the first year after 1943 prefigured the differences between American and Israeli responses to the Holocaust in the decades after the war. In the United States, Jewish leaders could present the revolt in the Warsaw ghetto as part of the Jewish contribution to the Allied war effort, as the outcry of the oppressed who refused to perish under the heel of fascism and would join the allied cause to defeat Nazism. The Jewish Labor Committee celebrated the heroism of the workers who joined the Polish nation in the struggle against German oppression. Jewish religious leaders marked April 19 as a day of sorrow and mourning, where the heroism of the ghetto fighters could be remembered together with the suffering of the Jewish martyrs. Coming at a time when Jews eagerly sought hope amidst despair, it offered a light in the darkness, and heroes to connect to.

But who were the heroes? And more importantly, for some, what was the political ideology that animated their actions? It is clear that within a year of the uprising, the revolt had been transformed into the focal point of Jewish commemorations of the destruction of European Jewry, providing the ideal prism with which to remember the Jewish catastrophe in Europe as a whole. As the heroes of the revolt were mythologized, the Bund and the Zionist movement continued to grapple over credit for the revolt. And while it was the name of Michał Klepfisz that had become known as the most prominent leader of the revolt in the first year after the event, this would soon change, as new reports drafted by the underground in Warsaw reached London and the Yishuv. A little over one year after the revolt had been finally crushed, the Zionist movement would take charge of the narrative and take credit for leading the revolt, picking out ŻOB commander Mordecai Anielewicz as the true leader and worthiest to be lionized.

Nonetheless, it is clear that even before the identities of the heroes had been confirmed, as the first reports began to emerge from Warsaw, the identities of leaders and fighters were interpreted and analyzed in a framework that was already politically contested and heavily weighted with meaning and significance, and that built on preexisting political frameworks. At the same time, the heroic saga of the revolt was mythologized in a manner that captured the attention of Jews around the world, allowing them to imagine what it might have been like to be *there*, engaged in the struggle against the Nazi oppressor. Surely the Jewish heroes of Warsaw were motivated by a desire to engage in self-defense—not to save lives, but to save their own dignity. But were they motivated by a Zionist connection to the Land of Israel that inspired their revolt against Diaspora oppression? Or did they rise up in defense of Poland, and the ideals of democracy, the universal brotherhood of man, and the rights of the working class to resist totalitarianism? Or were the fighters united by a drive to take revenge and kill Nazis? It is clear that the revolt was too powerful a symbol to not be seized upon by Jews from across the ideological spectrum well before the war was over. The timing of the uprising, coinciding with the transition to memorialization and mourning of Jews throughout Europe, also solidified the event as a date to remember not only Warsaw but European Jewry more broadly. Nonetheless, to fully appreciate the significance of the revolt and why it became the central focal point of Jewish history and memory during and after the war, we must consider the experiences of all the Jews in the ghetto (and beyond), not just the few who were armed. As the field of Holocaust studies continues to grow and develop, we can only hope that future generations of historians will follow this approach, incorporating the volumes of source materials now broadly available in order to provide a more comprehensive and integrated picture of Jewish responses to German policies during the Holocaust.

On April 19, 2018, at noon, the noise of a siren echoed across Warsaw, and when it ended a ceremony to commemorate the seventy-fifth anniversary of the Warsaw Ghetto Uprising began in front of the Rapoport Ghetto Heroes Monument. The state-sanctioned ceremony, which included remarks by the president of Poland, Andrzej Duda, the Israeli ambassador, Anna Azari, and the president of the World Jewish Congress, Ronald Lauder, carried the shadow of Poland's February 2018 "Holocaust law," which had outlawed any speech that alleged Polish complicity in crimes against Jews during World War II. In his remarks at the ceremony, Duda emphasized that the fighters in the Warsaw ghetto were Polish citizens, that they had "flown both the Jewish blue-and-white flag, as well as the Polish red-and-white flag," over the walls of the ghetto during the revolt, that they received "rifles and machine guns" from the Polish underground, and that the news of the revolt that was broadcast by the BBC had been delivered by the Polish government-in-exile in London. The Warsaw Ghetto Uprising, according to Duda, was an "uprising of the people who decided to keep their dignity. . . . They perished for dignity, they perished for freedom but they perished for Poland because they were Polish citizens. . . . Poles and Jews deeply care about having one shared historical truth." Speaking on behalf of the World Jewish Congress, Ronald Lauder led a delegation of nearly a hundred Jewish community representatives from around the world to commemorate the anniversary. In his remarks standing in front of the monument, Lauder asked "where did they summon the courage to stand up to the Germans? Would any of us have been able to summon this courage?" Arguing that it goes against human reason to stand up to a much larger army in an impossible fight, Lauder said:

> Jewish fighters of Warsaw did it for the same reason that the Jews at Masada stood up to the Roman Legion 2000 years ago. Something deep inside them finally said enough, *maspik* . . . they refused to die like sheep. This handful of Polish Jews showed a courage that it is hard for most people to understand. What these brave young fighters did not know and what they could not know is what the effect their actions would have on future generations of Jews and all free people around the world.

Echoing the words of the Israeli ambassador, who noted that April 19, 2018 also coincided with Israel's Independence Day that year, Lauder also connected the uprising to the establishment of the Jewish state.

> Just 5 years after these brave young Polish Jews rose up against Nazi tyranny . . . the Jewish state of Israel rose from the ashes. The Jewish people lifted themselves up from what was essentially their grave to achieve their 2000 year old dream, to establish a modern Jewish state in their paternal homeland. And all of this within 5 years of the struggle here in Warsaw. *I believe that it was the heroism of the brave young Polish-Jews who stood up to the Nazis here that inspired the future young defenders of Israel who defeated armies many times their size.* We have seen this heroism and miracles throughout our history. From Moses and his successor Joshua to King David all the way down to Israeli commandos who stormed the airport at Entebbe to rescue innocent victims of terrorists in 1976. . . . In the end when they ran out of guns and ammunition and when they had no other alternative many of them committed suicide rather than be taken

> by the Germans. We are standing here on the modern-day Masada. . . . This is holy ground.[28]

It is not surprising that Lauder, standing in front of a monument that literally cast in stone the dichotomy between Jewish passivity and resistance, would draw a connection between the heroism of the Warsaw ghetto fighters and the creation of the State of Israel. Or that the President of the World Jewish Congress would note the history of Jewish bravery that stretched from Moses to Joshua to David, Masada, and Yoni Netanyahu, invoking the contrast between those who died fighting and those who allowed themselves to be led "like sheep to the slaughter." Such linkages have become commonplace in Jewish understandings of the meaning of the Warsaw Ghetto Uprising, and especially common when the Holocaust is invoked for political reasons.

What did Lauder not mention? These details were emphasized at a second memorial service held just two hours later—an unofficial ceremony held at Mila 18, the site of the command bunker of the Jewish Fighting Organization in the ghetto, where many of the leaders of the uprising were killed during the revolt. The ceremony organized by Jewish visitors from the United States and Canada provided a sharp counterpoint to the claims heard in President Duda's speech. Organized by the children of survivors from Warsaw and descendants of the ghetto fighters, including members of Hashomer Hatzair, Dror, the Bund, and the Workmen's Circle in New York, this ceremony featured readings in Yiddish and English from poetry written by Jewish socialists and socialist Zionists during the ghetto, as well as a reading from Vladka Meed's memoir, *On Both Sides of the Wall*. The passage read by Vladka Meed's son, Dr. Steven Meed, was an excerpt in which Vladka complained bitterly over the refusal of the Polish underground, the Home Army, to provide arms to the ghetto uprising. What few weapons they did receive, Vladka explained, came from another underground force, the People's Army, a Communist unit.[29] Even seventy-five years after the revolt, then, we can see that two frameworks of memory persist: "official" state-sanctioned memory at an event presided over by government officials, representatives of world Jewish organizations, and the ambassador of the Jewish state, who explain the meaning and message of the revolt, always in a political context. And then we have the countermemory, echoing the words of participants in the revolt, the words of those who witnessed the events in Warsaw as they took place, shaping another perspective, an alternate viewpoint at the site of the bunker, inside the ghetto. Seventy-five years afterward, history, meaning, and memory of the Warsaw Ghetto Uprising still remain open to interpretation, still in a dynamic relationship with one another.

Notes

Abbreviations used here to refer to archival material can be found in the Archives section of the Bibliography.

Introduction: Warsaw, A Place in Jewish History

1 The date was selected by the Knesset on April 12, 1951, and became law on August 19, 1953. The actual starting date of the uprising (14th of Nisan) was problematic as it was also the eve of Passover. Therefore, the 27th of Nisan, when the uprising was still taking place, was selected by the Knesset, to fall one week before Israel's Independence Day (on the 5th of Iyyar).

2 Gerhard Weinberg, "The Final Solution and the War in 1943," in *Revolt amid the Darkness*, ed. Alvin L. Rosenfeld (Washington DC: United States Holocaust Memorial Museum, 1993), 6.

3 Richard Kaplan, "The Myth of Jewish Passivity," in *Jewish Resistance against the Nazis*, ed. Patrick Henry (Washington DC: Catholic University Press, 2014). See also Nechama Tec, *Resistance: Jews and Christians Who Defied the Nazi Terror* (Oxford: Oxford University Press, 2013), 15.

4 Hilberg, "The Destruction of the European Jews: Precedents," in *The Holocaust: Origins, Implementation, Aftermath*, ed. Omer Bartov (New York: Routledge, 2000), 39–40.

5 Yael S. Feldman, "'Not as Sheep Led to Slaughter'? On Trauma, Selective Memory, and the Making of Historical Consciousness," *Jewish Social Studies: History, Culture, Society*, n.s., 19, no. 5 (2013): 159–69.

6 Rabbi Yisrael Rutman, "Like Sheep to the Slaughter," Aish HaTorah, accessed Oct. 29, 2014, http://www.aish.com/ho/i/48954636.html.

7 Haim Nahman Bialik, "City of Slaughter," in *The Complete Works of Hayyim Nachman Bialik*, ed. Israel Efros, trans. Abraham M. Klein (New York: Histadruth Ivrith of America, 1948), vol. 1, 129–34.

8 Feldman, "'Not as Sheep Led to Slaughter'?," 156, cites Ahad Ha'am's description of Kishinev victims in this way. Most recently, Steven Zipperstein, *Pogrom: Kishinev and the Tilt of History* (Liveright, 2018), examines the impact of the Kishinev pogrom on our understandings of twentieth-century Jewish history.

9 Feldman, "'Not as Sheep Led to Slaughter'?," 158. Feldman cites Zalman Rubashov, "Hake-Kishinev ya'asu et Yerushalayim?," *Kuntres ahedut ha-'avodah* 33 (Apr. 4, 1920): 6–8, which she points out is based on Genesis 34:31: *hakezonah ya'aseh et ahoteim* (should our sister be treated like a whore?).

10 Anita Shapira, *Land and Power: The Zionist Resort to Force* (Palo Alto CA: Stanford University Press, 1999), 176.

11 Haim Hazaz, *The Sermon*, in Robert Alter, ed., *Modern Hebrew Literature* (New York: Schocken, 1975), 275.

12 "Diary: Thoughts about Resistance and Its Consequences Are Evoked When News about Massacre Reach the Ghetto," in "Emanuel Ringelblum's Notes, Hitherto Unpublished," ed. Joseph Kermish, *Yad Vashem Studies* 7, Jerusalem 1968, 178–80.

13 Ringelblum, "Diary." See Oct. 15, 1942, entry.

14 Israel Gutman, *The Jews of Warsaw, 1939–1943: Ghetto, Underground, Revolt* (Bloomington: Indiana University Press, 1982), 291.

15 "Call to Resistance by the Jewish Fighting Organization in the Warsaw Ghetto, January 1943," *Archiwum Zydowskiego Instytutu Historycznego w Polsce* (Archives of the Jewish Historical Institute in Poland), ARII/333, cited in Gutman, *Jews of Warsaw*, 305. See also Joseph Kermish, ed., *Mered Geto Varshah be-Einei ha-Oyev* (Jerusalem: Yad Vashem, 1966), 589.

16 From a 1950 review of historiography by Friedman and Pinson, "Some Books on the Jewish Catastrophe," *Jewish Social Studies* 12, no. 1 (1950): 83–94. See also the dissertation of Mark Smith, "The Yiddish Historians and the Struggle for a Jewish History of the Holocaust," University of California at Los Angeles, 2016.

17 Philip Friedman, *Martyrs and Fighters: The Epic of the Warsaw Ghetto* (New York, 1954), 12.

18 Roni Stauber, *The Holocaust in Israeli Public Debate in the 1950s*.

19 Stauber, *Holocaust*, 169.

20 As Stauber points out, this may have reflected the debate over whether to stay in the ghetto or go to the forests amongst the underground movements in some of the larger ghettos.

21 Stauber, *Holocaust*, 174–75.

22 Hilberg, *The Destruction of the European Jews* (Chicago: Quadrangle Books, 1961), 324.

23 Hilberg, *Destruction of the European Jews*, 318.

24 Hilberg, *Destruction of the European Jews.*

25 Gideon Hausner, "Six Million Accusers," excerpt reprinted in Paul Mendes-Flohr and Jehuda Reinharz, eds., *The Jew in the Modern World*, 3rd ed. (New York: Oxford University Press, 2011), 788.

26 Hannah Arendt, "Eichmann in Jerusalem," part 1, *New Yorker*, February 16, 1963, https://www.newyorker.com/magazine/1963/02/16/eichmann-in-jerusalem-i.

27 Arendt, "Eichmann in Jerusalem."

28 "Greetings on Behalf of the State of Israel by His Excellency the Minister of Social Welfare, Dr. Yosef Burg," in *Jewish Resistance during the Holocaust, April 1968*, ed. Meir Grubsztein (Jerusalem: Yad Vashem, 1971), 15–16.

29 Mordecai Tenenbaum-Tamaroff, *Yediot* (Warsaw ghetto underground publication), June 9, 1942, cited by Yitzhak Zuckerman, "Twenty-Five Years after the Warsaw Ghetto Revolt," in *Jewish Resistance during the Holocaust*, 24.

30 Zuckerman, "Twenty Five Years after the Warsaw Ghetto Revolt," 27.

31 Lucy Dawidowicz, *The War against the Jews, 1933–1945* (New York: Holt, Rinehart, and Winston, 1975), 312.

32 Dawidowicz, *War against the Jews*, 313, 339–40.

33 Hilberg, *Destruction of the European Jews*, 14, and reprinted in "Destruction of the European Jews: Precedents," 39–40.

34 Gutman, *Jews of Warsaw*, ix.

35 Bauer, *Rethinking the Holocaust* (New Haven CT: Yale University Press, 2001), 120.

36 Bauer, *Rethinking the Holocaust*, 127.

37 Bauer, *Rethinking the Holocaust*, 141.

38 The German-Jewish theologian Emil Fackenheim argues that the Warsaw Ghetto Uprising was the ultimate Jewish response: "a decision by the

fighters to share the fate of the Jewish people, to affirm Jewish selfhood and self-respect (in defiance of Nazi decrees)." Rather than an act of self-loathing and suicide, Fackenheim explains, the revolt represented the highest affirmation, a "unique celebration of Jewish life." See "The Spectrum of Resistance during the Holocaust: An Essay in Description and Definition," *Modern Judaism* 2, no. 2 (1982): 113–30.

39 Israel Gutman, *Resistance: The Warsaw Ghetto Uprising* (New York: Houghton Mifflin, in association with USHMM, 1994), xx.

40 Gutman, *Resistance*, xi.

41 Dan Kurzman, *The Bravest Battle: The Twenty-Eight Days of the Warsaw Ghetto Uprising* (Da Capo Press, 1993), 17.

42 See for example, Dalia Ofer, "The Past That Does Not Pass: Israelis and Holocaust Memory," *Israeli Studies* 14, no. 1 (2009): 1–35; Ofer, "The Strength of Remembrance: Commemorating the Holocaust during the First Decade of Israel," *Jewish Social Studies* 6, no. 2 (2000): 24–55; Tom Segev, *The Seventh Million: The Israelis and the Holocaust* (New York: Hill and Wang, 1993); Roni Stauber, *The Holocaust in Israeli Public Debate in the 1950s: Ideology and Memory* (Portland OR: Valentine Mitchell, 2007); Idith Zertal, *Israel's Holocaust and the Politics of Nationhood* (Cambridge: Cambridge University Press, 2005). For an earlier example of the post-Zionist trend, see Shabtai B. Beit-Tzvi, *Hatzionut Hapost-Ugandit Bemashber Hashoah* [Post-Uganda Zionism in face of the Holocaust crisis] (Tel Aviv: S.B Beit-Zvi, 1977). Several more recent works have argued that the Labor Zionist master narrative excluded the Revisionist Zionist members of the Jewish Military Union from their rightful place in the history of the Warsaw Ghetto Uprising, including most notably Moshe Arens in *Flags Over the Ghetto: The Untold Story of the Warsaw Ghetto Uprising* (Jerusalem: Gefen Publishing House, 2011).

43 Yael Zerubavel, *Recovered Roots: Collective Memory and the Making of Israeli National Tradition* (Chicago: University of Chicago Press, 1995), 5.

44 See Zerubavel, *Recovered Roots*, 9. See also Zerubavel, "The Death of Memory and the Memory of Death: Masada and the Holocaust as Historical Metaphors," *Representations*, no. 45 (Winter 1994): 72–100.

45 Peter Novick, *The Holocaust in American Life* (New York: Houghton Mifflin, 1999).

46 Hasia Diner, *We Remember with Reverence and Love: American Jews and the Myth of Silence after the Holocaust* (New York: New York University Press, 2010), 74.

47 David Slucki, "A Community of Suffering: Jewish Holocaust Survivor Networks in Postwar America," *Jewish Social Studies: History, Culture, Society*, n.s., 22, no. 2 (2017): 116–45, also argues against the "myth of silence," highlighting the active role played by survivor organizations, especially the Katsetler Farband, in emphasizing Jewish resistance in the creation of a "community of memory" and focuses on the group's work in the early postwar period.

48 David Engel, "On Studying Jewish History in Light of the Holocaust," Maurice R. and Corrine P. Greenberg Inaugural Lecture (Washington DC: United States Holocaust Memorial Museum, April 16, 2002), 27. Engel argues that "historians of the Jews continue by and large to sequester the Holocaust not only rhetorically but in practice."

49 Friedlander, *The Years of Extermination: Nazi Germany and the Jews, 1939–1945* (New York: Harper Collins, 2007), xv.

50 Friedlander, *Years of Extermination*, 528.

51 Friedlander, *Years of Extermination*, 528.

52 Likewise, more encyclopedic approaches to the history of the ghetto as a whole, such as Barbara Engelking and Jacek Leociak, *The Warsaw Ghetto: A Guide to the Perished City* (New Haven CT: Yale University Press, 2009), provide a much broader "collection of studies on various issues connected with the sealed district." Going beyond the revolt itself, the guide reflects a broader historiographic appreciation for the life and death of Jewish Warsaw as a whole.

53 Havi Dreifuss, *Geto Varsha—Sof* [The Warsaw ghetto—the end, April 1942–June 1943] (Jerusalem: Yad Vashem, 2018), 11. Furthermore, the history of the Warsaw Ghetto Uprising has also been a central point in debates over Polish-Jewish relations during the war. As Joshua Zimmerman notes in *The Polish Underground and the Jews, 1939–1945* (New York: Cambridge University Press, 2015), "The Warsaw Ghetto Uprising is in

many ways the axis around which the problem of wartime Polish-Jewish relations is discussed."

Chapter 1. The Centrality of Warsaw

1 Antony Polonsky, "Warsaw," *YIVO Encyclopedia of Jews in Eastern Europe*, http://www.yivoencyclopedia.org/article.aspx/Warsaw.

2 Barbara Engelking and Jacek Leociak, *The Warsaw Ghetto: A Guide to the Perished City* (New Haven: Yale University Press, 2009), 15.

3 See in Meng, "Shattered Spaces: Jewish Sites in Germany and Poland after 1945," (Ph.D. diss., University of North Carolina, 2008), 1; statistics located in Gabriela Zalewska, *Ludność żydowska w Warszawie wokresie międzywojennym* (Warsaw: Wydawnictwo Naukowe PWN, 1996), 63.

4 See Polonsky, "Warsaw," and Blatman, "Bund," in *YIVO Encyclopedia of Jews in Eastern Europe*. For a more detailed discussion of interwar Polish Jewish politics, see Ezra Mendelsohn, *The Jews of East Central Europe between the World Wars* (Bloomington: Indiana University Press, 1983), 11–83.

5 For example, the May 21, 1942, Bund report, which was smuggled out of Warsaw by two Swedish businessmen, was a sign that Jews in Warsaw still believed they could communicate with the outside world; the ambivalent response and impact of the report is a different story. See discussion in Yehuda Bauer, "When Did They Know?" *Midstream* 24, no. 4 (1968): 51–58; Samuel Kassow, *Who Will Write Our History?: Emanuel Ringelblum, the Warsaw Ghetto, and the Oyneg Shabes Archive* (Bloomington: Indiana University Press, 2007), 298–99; David Engel, *In the Shadow of Auschwitz: The Polish Government-in-Exile and the Jews, 1939–1942* (Chapel Hill: University of North Carolina Press, 1987), 185–86; Dariusz Stola, "Early News of the Holocaust from Poland," *Holocaust and Genocide Studies* 11, no. 1 (1997): 6–9.

6 Cited in Garbarini, Kerenji, Lambertz, and Patt, *Jewish Responses to Persecution, 1938–1940* (Lanham MD: USHMM/AltaMira Press, 2011), 121. For the history of AJDC work in Europe during the Holocaust, see Yehuda Bauer, *American Jewry and the Holocaust: The American Jewish Joint*

Distribution Committee, 1939–1945 (Detroit: Wayne State University Press, 1981).

7 Engelking and Leociak, *Warsaw Ghetto*, 47–48.

8 Gutman, *Jews of Warsaw*, 121.

9 Kassow, *Who Will Write Our History?* 104–5.

10 In Levi Dror and Israel Rosenzweig, eds., *Sefer Hashomer Hatzair*, vol. 1, 1913–45 (Merhavia, Israel: Sifriat Poalim, 1956), 432. See in Israel Gutman, *Fighters among the Ruins: The Story of Jewish Heroism during World War II* (Washington DC: B'nai B'rith Books, 1988), 69–75. Also cited in Moshe Arens, "The Jewish Military Organization (ŻZW) in the Warsaw Ghetto," *Holocaust and Genocide Studies* 19 (2005): 205.

11 Raya Cohen, "'Against the Current': Hashomer Hatzair in the Warsaw Ghetto," *Jewish Social Studies* 7, no. 1 (2000): 67.

12 Arens, "Jewish Military Organization," 205; Gutman, *Fighters among the Ruins*, 70–71.

13 Yitzhak Zuckerman, *A Surplus of Memory: Chronicle of the Warsaw Ghetto Uprising* (Berkeley: University of California Press, 1993), 36–40; see also Arens, "Jewish Military Organization," 205.

14 Arens, "Jewish Military Organization,"; see also Haim Lazar's *Matsada shel Varsha* (Tel Aviv: Machon Jabotinsky, 1963). For a detailed history of the ŻZW, see Dariusz Libionka and Laurence Weinbaum, *Bohaterowie, hochsztaplerzy, opisywacze: wokół Żydowskiego Związku Wojskowego* [Heroes, hucksters, storytellers: The Jewish Military Organization] (Warsaw: Polish Center for Holocaust Research, 2011).

15 Kassow, *Who Will Write Our History?*, 106.

16 Kassow, *Who Will Write Our History?*, 106–7.

17 Friedlander, *Years of Extermination*, 38.

18 Szmuel Zygielbojm, "Kidnapping for Labor," no date (ca. December 1939), *Zygielbojm-bukh* (New York: Unzer Tsayt Farlag, 1947), 142–50 (translated from Yiddish). Also published in a slightly different translation, in David Engel, *The Holocaust: The Third Reich and the Jews* (New York: Longman, 2000), 105–6. See in Garbarini et al., *Jewish Responses to Persecution, 1938–1940*, 378–80. Zygielbojm (1895–1943) was a prominent Polish interwar Bundist. See also Daniel Blatman, "On a Mission against

All Odds: Szmuel Zygielbojm in London (April 1942–May 1943)," *Yad Vashem Studies* 20 (1990): 237–71.

19 Raul Hilberg, Stanislaw Staron, and Josef Kermisz, eds., *The Warsaw Diary of Adam Czerniakow: Prelude to Doom* (New York: Stein and Day, 1979), 140.

20 In Gutman, *Jews of Warsaw*, 50–51.

21 Engelking and Leociak, *Warsaw Ghetto*, 642; Chaim A. Kaplan, *Scroll of Agony: The Warsaw Diary of Chaim A. Kaplan* (Bloomington: Indiana University Press, 1999), 208.

22 Kaplan, *Scroll of Agony*, 220–24.

23 Gutman, *Jews of Warsaw*, 60–61. It is impossible to provide accurate numbers of Jewish refugees and ghetto inhabitants in Warsaw for this chaotic period. Gutman cites 130,000 Jewish refugees in Warsaw by April 1941, while Yehuda Bauer estimates the number of Jewish refugees in the city at 150,000 after September 1940: Gutman, *Jews of Warsaw*, 63; Bauer, *American Jewry and the Holocaust: The American Jewish Joint Distribution Committee, 1939–1945* (Detroit: Wayne State University Press, 1981), 69. Barbara Engelking and Jacek Leociak estimate the peak number of inhabitants of the Warsaw ghetto at 460,000 in March 1941 (15,000 more than Gutman's number for the same month), and quote Nazi documents that put the number as high as 490,000. Engelking and Leociak, *Warsaw Ghetto* 49. For a detailed discussion of the experiences of refugees in the ghetto, see Lea Preiss, *Displaced Persons at Home: Refugees in the Fabric of Jewish Life in Warsaw* (Jerusalem: Yad Vashem, 2015).

24 Gutman, *Jews of Warsaw*, 64.

25 Gutman, *Jews of Warsaw*, 85.

26 Gutman, *Jews of Warsaw*, 87. For a thorough analysis of the experiences of assimilated Jews in the ghetto, see Katarzyna Person, *Assimilated Jews in the Warsaw Ghetto* (Syracuse NY: Syracuse University Press, 2014). On Gancwajch specifically, see 67–68.

27 Gutman, *Jews of Warsaw*, 90–94.

28 For background on the work of the Joint in Warsaw, see Bauer, *American Jewry and the Holocaust*.

29 "Warsaw," in *The USHMM Encyclopedia of Camps and Ghettos*, vol. 2: Ghettos in German-Occupied Eastern Europe, ed. Martin Dean. For a

fascinating analysis of how the Joint functioned in Warsaw, utilizing funds accrued by a wealthy class of black-market operators who could not hold onto the cash for fear of violating German edicts (the JDC offered IOUs to be paid after the war), see Nathan Eck, "Legend of the Joint in the Ghetto," JDC Archives, New York Office, Country Files, Poland. Thanks to Linda Levi and Jeffrey Edelstein for this source.

30 Kassow, *Who Will Write Our History?*, 111–119.

31 Kassow, *Who Will Write Our History?, 1*21.

32 Gutman, *Jews of Warsaw*, 45–47; Friedländer, *Nazi Germany and the Jews*, vol. 2 (New York: Harper Collins, 2007), 148.

33 See "Thirteen Months of JDC work in Warsaw," United States Holocaust Memorial Museum Archives, RG-15.199M, American Jewish Joint Distribution Committee (Acc. 1999.A.0154 [ŻIH 210/6]); Bauer, *American Jewry*, 72–76; Kassow, *Who Will Write Our History?*, 114–15.

34 See Bauer, *American Jewry*, 73, on official JDC expenditures for 1940; on the crucial role of the AJDC for ghettos in Poland, see Trunk, *Judenrat: The Jewish Council in Eastern Europe under Nazi Occupation* (New York: Macmillan, 1972), 135–42.

35 For a thorough examination of Ringelblum's work in the Warsaw ghetto, see Kassow, *Who Will Write Our History?*.

36 For more on the work of Kaplan and Breslaw in the Oneg Shabbes, see Kassow, *Who Will Write Our History?*, 162–65.

37 Gutman, *Jews of Warsaw*, 135.

38 "Di yidishe yugnt in itstikn moment," in Dror underground newspaper, Tammuz [July-August] (1940): United States Holocaust Memorial Museum Archives, RG 15.079, Ring I-705 (Underground Archives of the Warsaw Ghetto, Ringelblum Archives). See Tuvia Borzykowski, *Between Tumbling Walls* (Tel Aviv: Ghetto Fighters' House and United Kibbutz Movement, 1976).

39 These farms were supported by JDC and Toporol (the society to encourage agriculture among the Jews); for more details see brief discussion in Gutman, *Jews of Warsaw*, 139–41. Further research is needed on this topic.

40 Arens, "The Jewish Military Organization in the Warsaw Ghetto," 212. The beginning of the roundups in the Lublin region in summer 1942 led

to closing of the farm, with most members either returning to the Warsaw ghetto or joining the partisans in the forests around Lublin.

41 Daniel Blatman, "Bund," *YIVO Encyclopedia of Jews in Eastern Europe*, http://www.yivoencyclopedia.org/article.aspx/Bund.

42 See in Catherine Collomp, "'Relief Is a Political Gesture': The Jewish Labor Committee's Interventions in War-Torn Poland, 1939–1945," *Transtlantica* (2014), https://transatlantica.revues.org/6942?lang=en. On JDC and IOUs, see Bauer, *American Jewry* and Eck, *The Legend of the Joint.*

43 For more on the role of women as couriers in occupied Poland and in the resistance more generally, see Dalia Ofer and Lenore Weitzman, eds., *Women in the Holocaust* (New Haven CT: Yale University Press, 1998), esp. Weitzman's article, "Living on the Aryan Side in Poland: Gender, Passing and the Nature of Resistance," 187–222; Nechama Tec, *Resilience and Courage: Women, Men, and the Holocaust* (New Haven CT: Yale University Press, 2003), 263–65.

44 See Israel Gutman, "The Youth Movement as an Alternative Leadership in Eastern Europe," in Cohen and Cochavi, eds., *Zionist Youth Movements during the Shoah* (New York: Peter Lang, 1995). On the Bund's leadership, see Daniel Blatman, *Lema'an Heruteinu ve-Herutchem: Ha-Bund be-Polin, 1939–1949* (Jerusalem: Yad Vashem, 1996).

45 Ziva Shalev, "Tosia Altman," in *Encyclopedia of Jewish Women*, Jewish Women's Archive, accessed Feb. 17, 2012, jwa.org/encyclopedia.

46 Shalev, "Tosia Altman."

47 Ringelblum (*Ktovim*, vol. 2, 147) described Hashomer Hatzair's acquisition of a first revolver at the end of 1941. Cited in Gutman, *Jews of Warsaw*, 165.

48 Dreifuss, *Geto Varsha—Sof: April 1942—Yuni 1943* [The Warsaw ghetto—the end: April 1942–June 1943]. (Jerusalem: Yad Vashem, 2018), 68–75.

49 Kaplan, *Scroll of Agony*, 296–99.

50 Kaplan, *Scroll of Agony*, 351, 370.

51 See as recorded in "The Terrible Choice: Some Contemporary Jewish Responses to the Holocaust, Chaim Kaplan," *JewishGen*, accessed

February 28, 2012, http://www.jewishgen.org/yizkor/terrible_choice/ter003.html; Kaplan, *Scroll of Agony*.

52 For a detailed account of the deportation, see Engelking and Leociak, 698–730. Havi Dreifuss, *Geto Varsha*, suggests it is possible there was another note that was not publicized, where Czerniakow advised the Jewish public to take his actions as a sign and draw their own conclusions. See Dreifuss, 150.

53 See Kaplan, *Scroll of Agony*; these passages also cited in "The Chaim Kaplan Diary," *Holocaust Education & Archive Research Team*, http://www.holocaustresearchproject.org/ghettos/chaimkaplan.html. Kaplan's war diary was discovered almost intact after the war on a farm outside Warsaw. Preserved in a kerosene can, the notebooks were legible and in good condition. The diary was published in Hebrew and in two English editions. The Hebrew edition was called *Megilat Yisurin Yoman Geto Varsha—Sept 1, 1939—August 4, 1942*.

54 See in Roskies, *The Literature of Destruction: Jewish Responses to Catastrophe (Philadelphia: The Jewish Publication Society, 1988)*, 461–64.

55 Dreifuss, *Geto Varsha*, 244–46.

56 On August 28, 1942, Gerhard Riegner of the World Jewish Congress office in Geneva sent his telegram outlining the Nazi intention to exterminate European Jewry to Stephen Wise and the U.S. State Department, but it took several months for the State Department to actually verify Riegner's alarming message.

57 Friedlander, *Years of Extermination*, 522.

58 Friedlander, *Years of Extermination*, 522; Arens, "Jewish Military Organization"; and Kassow, *Who Will Write Our History?*, 354.

59 Gutman, *Jews of Warsaw*, 291.

60 Gutman, *Jews of Warsaw*, 293.

61 Dreifuss, *Geto Varsha*, 310.

62 Ringelblum, *Ksovim* [Ktovim], vol. 2, 148–49, as cited in Kassow, *Who Will Write Our History?*, 371.

63 "Call to Resistance by the Jewish Fighting Organization in the Warsaw Ghetto," January 1943, *Archiwum Zydowskiego Instytutu Historycznego w Polsce* (Archives of the Jewish Historical Institute in Poland), ARII/333

(cited in Gutman, *Jews of Warsaw*, 305.) See also in Joseph Kermish, ed., *To Live with Honor and Die with Honor!: Selected Documents from the Warsaw Ghetto Underground Archives* (Jerusalem: Yad Vashem, 1986), 589.

64 "Call for Resistance," Archiwum Zydowskiego Instytutu Historycznego. See slightly different translation in Kermish, *To Live with Honor*, 590–91.

65 Gutman, *Jews of Warsaw*, 329.

66 Gutman, *Jews of Warsaw*, 309–10.

67 See "Warsaw," in *United States Holocaust Memorial Museum Encyclopedia of Camps and Ghettos*, and Gutman, *Jews of Warsaw*, 312, 316–17. Havi Dreifuss also argues that the January 1943 roundup reflected a clear tension between Nazi extermination policy and the needs of the SS for laborers; while Himmler desired a complete liquidation of the ghetto, the owners of the workshops still hoped to preserve some of their labor force. This tension, while not necessarily understood by the Jewish workers at the time, may have contributed to a sense that "survival through work" was still possible and may have led to a more destructive final liquidation action in April 1943.

68 Gutman, *Jews of Warsaw*, 334.

69 Gutman, *Jews of Warsaw*, 351.

70 Dreifuss, *Geto Varsha*, 333.

71 Gutman, *Jews of Warsaw*, 340.

72 Leon Feiner, a central activist of the Bund and a leader of the Jewish Fighting Organization (ŻOB) in the Warsaw ghetto was also known as "Mikolaj." Born in Krakow in 1886, he had served as chairman of the Bund Central Committee. Feiner was among the founders of the underground Zegota organization (code name for Rada Pomocy Zydom, the Polish Council for Aid to Jews) and served as its deputy chairman from January 1943 through July 1944 and then chairman in the last month before Warsaw's liberation from Nazi occupation in January 1945. He died a month later of cancer.

73 In Havi Dreifuss, "The Leadership of the Jewish Combat Organization during the Warsaw Ghetto Uprising: A Reassessment," *Holocaust and Genocide Studies* 31, no. 1 (2017): 36; Gutman, *Jews of Warsaw*, 358.

74 Dariusz Stola, "Early News of the Holocaust in Poland," *Holocaust and Genocide Studies* 7, no. 1 (1997): 3–4. According to Stola, the government's

delegate Ratajski, head of the Civilian Struggle Directorate Korbonski, and Home Army commander General Rowecki had "exclusive access to secret transmitters in occupied Poland." They sent messages to the civilian and the military branches of the government respectively: Ratajski and Korbonski to Interior Minister (and Deputy Prime Minister) Stanislaw Mikotajczyk; General Rowecki to the Supreme Commander (and Prime Minister) Gen. Wladyslaw Sikorski and his General Staff.

75 See Dreifuss, "Leadership of the Jewish Combat Organization."

76 Dreifuss, "Leadership of the Jewish Combat Organization," 32.

77 Gutman, *Jews of Warsaw*, 171.

78 Gutman, *Jews of Warsaw*, 172.

79 Gutman, *Jews of Warsaw*, 175.

80 See Natalia Aleksiun, "Adolf Abraham Berman," in *YIVO Encyclopedia of Jews in Eastern Europe*, http://www.yivoencyclopedia.org/article.aspx/Berman_Adolf_Abraham. See also Marci Shore, "Children of the Revolution: Communism, Zionism, and the Berman Brothers," *Jewish Social Studies*, n.s., 10, no. 3 (2004): 23–86. As Shore notes, some in the fighting underground (like Marek Edelman) were skeptical of Berman's pro-Soviet sympathies and of playing "both sides of the anti-Nazi underground." In September 1942, Berman and his wife Batya (herself an underground activist) moved to the Aryan side of the city, and he continued to function as spokesman for the Jewish National Committee and as secretary of the underground Zegota organization (the Polish Council for Aid to the Jews). He also kept a secret journal which was published as *Me'Yemei Hamachteret* [The underground period] (Tel Aviv: HeMenorah, 1970–71). In 1950, Berman immigrated to Israel, where he served in the country's second Knesset and was involved in activities of survivors' organizations. He died in 1978.

81 Kassow, *Who Will Write Our History?* See also Dreifuss, "Leadership of the Jewish Combat Organization," 24–60, 31.

82 See discussion in Gutman, *Jews of Warsaw*, 358, and in Dreifuss, *Geto Varsha*, 374.

83 See, for example, the reports of Borzykowski and Edelman; also in Gutman, *Jews of Warsaw*, 367–68.

84 Quoted in Dreifuss, "Leadership of the Jewish Combat Organization"; see Rufeisen-Schuepper, *Predah Me-Mila 18: Sipurah shel Kasharit (Farewell to Mila 18: The story of a courier)* (Tel Aviv: Lochamei HaGetaot, 1990), 108–9.

85 Dreifuss, "Leadership of the Jewish Combat Organization," 43.

86 The first part that was removed concerned Zivia Lubetkin, Zuckerman's girlfriend. Anielewicz wrote that he had not seen her since the uprising began, but that he knew that she was alive. The second part concerned the arms delivery that Zuckerman had unsuccessfully tried to pass to the fighters through the cemetery. In the Yiddish journal, preserved in the Ghetto Fighters' House Archives, these two parts are crossed out with hatch marks.

87 This translation based on Hebrew transcript reproduced in *Sefer Milhamot Ha-Getaot* (Tel Aviv: Hakibutz Hameuchad, 1954), 158. As Dreifuss explains, subsequent versions of the "final letter" include additions by Berman not part of the original letter.

88 Zuckerman and Basok also detailed this later in *Sefer Milhamot* (158) and explained the translation and publication history of the letter. "The letter was written in Hebrew to Y. Zuckerman and translated into Yiddish for the Coordinating Committee but without secret and identifying personal information. From Yiddish it was translated with changes into Polish for the underground radio station SWIAT. First published in the journal 'Na Oczach Swiata' [In the eyes of the world], the publication of the Catholic groups in the [Polish] Underground." In *Sefer Milhamot* Zuckerman reprinted the Yiddish version from the Berman archive; the original Hebrew version burned with the rest of the ŻOB archive at Leszno 18 during the Polish Uprising. In a conversation from February 26, 1981, Antek also explained what happened to the original letter (written in Hebrew, translated to Yiddish and then Polish, subsequently lost in the apartment on Leszno 18). See GFHA 2834. Because Dr. Berman had a copy of the Yiddish translation of the letter, this is the version that survived the war and became part of the Berman Archive now housed at the Ghetto Fighters House.

89 Dreifuss, "Leadership of the Jewish Combat Organization," argues that these changes helped shape a particular memory of the revolt, presenting

the ŻOB as a military organization with a clear command hierarchy and Anielewicz as supreme commander rather than a "union of ideological movements based on friendship and partnership."

90 Itamar Levin argues, for example, in *HaKrav HaAharon: Mered Geto Varsha: ha-sipur ha-amiti* [The Warsaw Ghetto Uprising: A new perspective] (Tel Aviv: Yediot Aharonot, 2009) that history of the Warsaw Ghetto Uprising is full of mistakes and oversights because it has been written by the surviving members of the youth movements and overlooks the experiences of those who did not survive, of the fighters who were not affiliated with any movements, including Jews who hid in the bunkers and those who hid on the Aryan side of Warsaw, and also of members of the Polish underground, the Wehrmacht, and the SS.

91 Dreifuss, "Leadership of the Jewish Combat Organization," 21. See Zuckerman testimony (second tape, 19:15), in Claude Lanzmann Shoah Collection, USHMMA, RG-60.5048.

92 Vladka Meed, *On Both Sides of the Wall: Memoirs from the Warsaw Ghetto* (New York: Holocaust Library, 1993), 141–42.

93 See in Dreifuss, "Leadership of the Jewish Combat Organization," 45. First published by Berman in his essay "Jews on the Aryan Side," in *Encyclopedia of Diasporas: Warsaw*, ed. Yitzhak Gruenbaum (Tel Aviv: Encylopedia of the Jewish Diaspora, 1952–53), 702; See also Adolf Avraham Berman, *Me'Yemei Hamachteret* (Tel Aviv: HaMenorah, 1970–71), 107.

94 Translation in Dreifuss, "Leadership of the Jewish Combat Organization," 45. For the original Yiddish version, see "Anielewicz's Letters," GFHA 9523, letter 1.

95 According to Dreifuss, recent research by Ronen Haran suggests that it was a message from Chajka Klinger, a Hashomer Hatzair member in Bedzin, sent to Nathan Schwalb of the HeHalutz office in Geneva, that conveyed the (erroneous) information on the death of Tosia Altman to the Yishuv. See Ronen Haran, "The Source of Reports on the Tragic Results of the Warsaw Ghetto Uprising in Palestine–Eretz Israel" [in Hebrew], MA term paper, Haifa University, 2013. Quoted in Dreifuss, "Leadership of the Jewish Combat Organization," 46.

96 Gutman, *Jews of Warsaw*, 356.

97 The Ghetto Fighters House Archive lists the following documents in the same collection: Attachment no. 1 (to Special Report no. 2, dated April 23, 1943), from the Coordinating Committee of Jewish Social Organizations and Institutions [Komisja Koordynacyjna Zydowskich Instytucji Spolecznych]; and the Bund: Announcement no. 4, Wednesday, April 21, 1943; two pages, typewritten, as well as a situation report issued by the Bund and the ZKN on the liquidation of the Warsaw ghetto, updated as of April 23, 24, and 25, 1943; and a letter written by Mordechai Anielewicz, commander of the ŻOB, to ŻOB deputy commander Yitzhak "Antek" Zuckerman, dated April 23, 1943, sent to London by Waclaw on April 30, 1943.

98 See in Dina Porat, *The Blue and Yellow Stars of David: The Zionist Leadership in Palestine and the Holocaust* (Cambridge: Harvard University Press, 1990), 8.

99 During the Nazi occupation of Poland, Feiner, even though he lived in the Aryan side of Warsaw under the assumed name Berezowski, was one of the central personalities of the Jewish underground in the city. He was the author of most of the communiqués of the Bund from Poland to the Western allies, in which he described Nazi terror and brutality.

100 See "Dr. Leon Feiner," GFHA, accessed August 1, 2020, http://www.infocenters.co.il/gfh/notebook_ext.asp?book=28967&lang=eng&site=gfh.

101 Reprinted in Władysław Bartoszewski and Zofia Lewin, eds., *Righteous among the Nations: How Poles Helped the Jews* (London: Earlscourt Publications, 1969), 730–31.

102 GFHA, 5984, part 2: Notices published by the Jewish National Committee [Zydowski Komitet Narodowy] and the Coordination Committee of Jewish Social Organizations [Komisja Koordynacyjna Zydowskich Instytucji Spolecznych] regarding the development of events in the Warsaw Ghetto Uprising in April 1943 (17 pages, printed, in Polish). These are published in Zuckerman and Basok, *Sefer Milhamot*, 178–85.

103 See Zuckerman, *Surplus of Memory*, 371. Zuckerman references prominent historians of Polish Jewry who would attempt to write histories of Jewish resistance in Poland, including Josef Kermish, Nachman Blumenthal,

Isaiah Trunk, Philip Friedman, and Ber Mark. *Dichtung und Wahrheit*, literally poetry and truth, is a reference to the memoir of the German writer, Goethe.

104 See, for example, Zuckerman, *Surplus of Memory*, 337.

105 See discussion in *Commemorating 70 Years Since the Warsaw Ghetto Uprising* (commemorative issue), *Yalkut Moreshet* 92–93 (9–10) (April 2013), in honor of the seventieth anniversary of the Warsaw Ghetto Uprising. Itamar Levin, "It Is Hard to Understand What He Saw by Himself," is especially critical of Zuckerman's tendency to put politics above historical accuracy, as a "man of the movement and not as concerned with historical details," while Havi Dreifuss, "Zuckerman: A Witness and a Source; A Leader and a Man," 117–32, argues that Antek was a public figure, not a historian. Historians need to read all of his testimonies carefully, but it is not fair to criticize his 1944 report. He was going off of data that was available to him.

106 GFHA, 5984, part 2, "Notices Published by the Jewish National Committee." English translation courtesy of GFHA.

107 See translation in Dreifuss, "The Leadership of the Jewish Combat Oraganization," 45. From "Reports and Announcements from the Żegota Council on the Condition of the Jews in the Warsaw Ghetto and the Provincial Towns of Occupied Poland during and after the Uprising" [in Hebrew], GFHA, 3169; printed copy, p. 25, handwritten copy, pp. 28–29.

Chapter 2. News about the Destruction of European Jewry and the Uprising during WWII

1 See Jonathan D. Sarna, "The American Jewish Press," in *The Oxford Handbook of Religion and the American News Media* (Oxford: Oxford University Press, 2012), 544.

2 "Women, Children, Aged Massacred in Warsaw Ghetto as Nazis Send Jews to Russian Front," Jewish Telegraphic Agency, July 28, 1942, https://www.jta.org/1942/07/28/archive/women-children-aged-massacred-in-warsaw-ghetto-as-nazis-send-jews-to-russian-front.

3 “Nazis Start Expulsion of Jews from Warsaw Ghetto; Community President Commits Suicide,” Jewish Telegraphic Agency, August 17, 1942, https://www.jta.org/1942/08/17/archive/nazis-start-expulsion-of-jews-from-warsaw-ghetto-community-president-commits-suicide.

4 “Greatest Calamity in Jewish History, Says Proclamation of Jewish Groups,” Jewish Telegraphic Agency, December 3, 1942, https://www.jta.org/1942/12/03/archive/greatest-calamity-in-jewish-history-says-proclamation-of-jewish-groups.

5 Avihu Ronen, in “The Cable That Vanished: Tabenkin and Ya’ari to the Last Surviving Ghetto Fighters,” *Yad Vashem Studies* 41:129–30, emphasizes that in many respects the Yishuv and the leaders of the youth movements had been largely disconnected from the youth movements in occupied Poland and Lithuania.

6 See Yosef Gorny, *The Jewish Press and the Holocaust, 1939–1945: Palestine, Britain, the United States, and the Soviet Union* (Cambridge: Cambridge University Press, 2011); Deborah Lipstadt, *Beyond Belief: The American Press and the Coming of the Holocaust* (New York: Free Press, 1986); Laurel Leff, *Buried by the* Times: *The Holocaust and America’s Most Important Newspaper (Cambridge: Cambridge University Press, 2005)*; Robert Moses Shapiro, ed., *Why Didn’t the Press Shout? American and International Journalism during the Holocaust (New York: Yeshiva University Press, 2003)*; Dina Porat and Mordechai Naor, eds., *Ha-itonut he-yehudit be-Eretz Yisrael nokhah ha-shoah 1939–1945* (Tel Aviv: Ministry of Defense, 2002).

7 *The Forward: History*, accessed September 15, 2017, http://forward.com/about-us/history/.

8 Gorny, *Jewish Press*, 6–7. See Horace Kallen, “Democracy vs. the Melting Pot,” *The Nation* (February 18, 1915). See also the work of Noam Pianko, *Jewish Peoplehood: An American Innovation* (New Brunswick NJ: Rutgers University Press, 2015).

9 In Gorny, *Jewish Press*, 7.

10 See Emil Kerenji, “The Peak of the Holocaust,” introduction to *Jewish Responses to Persecution*, vol. 4 (Lanham MD: Rowman and Littlefield, 2015), xxiv.

11 Roskies and Diamant, *Holocaust Literature: A History and Guide* (Waltham, MA: Brandeis University Press, 2013), 22.

12 For context on how knowledge of the Final Solution influenced Jewish responses in the Yishuv, see Dina Porat, *The Blue and Yellow Stars of David* and, in the United States, Alex Grobman, "What Did They Know? The American Jewish Press and the Holocaust, 1 September 1939–17 December 1942," in *America, American Jews, and the Holocaust*, ed. Jeffrey Gurock (New York: Routledge Press, 1998), 331–56. For an analysis of BBC coverage in England, see Jeremy D. Harris, "Broadcasting the Massacres: An Analysis of the BBC's Contemporary Coverage of the Holocaust," *Yad Vashem Studies* 25 (1996): 65–98. The terms "Jew-Zone" and "Free-Zone" are employed by Roskies and Diamant in their study *Holocaust Literature* to distinguish between works created in Nazi-dominated occupied Europe and works written in the free world.

13 As Dariusz Stola notes in his article "Early News of the Holocaust from Poland," *Holocaust and Genocide Studies* 7, no. 1 (1997): 1–27, Yehuda Bauer stressed the difference between having information and knowing of the Holocaust. Bauer, *The Holocaust in Historical Perspective* (Seattle: University of Washington Press, 1978), 18.

14 See "Riegner Telegram," Samuel Sidney Silverman to Stephen S. Wise, August 29, 1942. Jacob Rader Marcus Center of the AJA, accessed March 31, 2020, https://www.loc.gov/exhibits/haventohome/images/hh0171as.jpg.

15 See for example Friedlander, *Years of Extermination*, 461; David Wyman, *The Abandonment of the Jews: America and the Holocaust, 1941–1945* (New York: Pantheon Books, 1984), 42.

16 Leff, *Buried by the* Times, 156.

17 Leff, *Buried by the* Times, 156.

18 Jacob J. Schacter, "Holocaust Commemoration Tisha Be-Av: The Debate over Yom Ha-Shoa," *Tradition* 41, no. 2 (2008): 164–97.

19 Mooli Brog on Shenhavi, "In Blessed Memory of a Dream," *Yad Vashem Studies* 30 (2002): 297–336. See also in Porat, *Blue and Yellow Stars of David*, 51.

20 "Greatest Calamity in Jewish History, Says Proclamation of Jewish Groups," Jewish Telegraphic Agency, http://www.jta.org/1942/12/03/

archive/greatest-calamity-in-jewish-history-says-proclamation-of-jewish-groups.

21 "Report on Visit to the President," December 8, 1942, JLC, reel 31, folder 30.

22 "Report on Visit to the President."

23 "1942: Key Dates: December 17," in *Holocaust Encyclopedia*, United States Holocaust Memorial Museum, https://www.ushmm.org/wlc/en/article.php?ModuleId=10007765.

24 Papers of Shmuel Mordkhe Zygielbojm, YIVO Archives, RG 1454, folder 40: Zygielbojm's telegram to Winston Churchill, December 19, 1942 (received December 24, 1942).

25 Friedlander, *Years of Extermination*, 350.

26 Nuremberg doc. no. 5574; cited in Friedlander, *Years of Extermination*, 351.

27 Friedlander, *Years of Extermination*, 511, citing historian Peter Longerich, *"Davon haben wir nichts gewusst!" Die Deutschen und die Judenverfolgung 1933–1945* (Munich: Siedler, 2006), 236–37.

28 See Marek Edelman and Simcha Rotem's discussion with Berenbaum, "Some Clarifications on the Warsaw Ghetto Uprising," in Eric Sterling, ed., *Life in the Ghettos during the Holocaust*. According to Edelman: "resistance was not a choice to die with dignity but a choice of how to live life with the moments before we died" (22).

29 "Nazis Make Warsaw 'Judenrein', Deport Remaining Jews from Ghetto," Jewish Telegraphic Agency, February 5, 1943, https://www.jta.org/1943/02/05/archive/nazis-make-warsaw-judenrein-deport-remaining-jews-from-ghetto.

30 "The Tel Hai behest," 11 Adar 1943, quoted in "ba'maarakha" Tel Aviv 1957; in Zertal, *Israel's Holocaust and the Politics of Nationhood*, 25.

31 In Zertal, *Israel's Holocaust and the Politics of Nationhood*, 25.

32 Zertal, *Israel's Holocaust and the Politics of Nationhood*, 26.

33 *Davar*, Sunday, February 21, 1943, accessed, Jewish National Library, Tel Aviv University, http://www.jpress.nli.org.il/.

34 "93 Choose Suicide Before Nazi Shame," *The New York Times*, January 8, 1943, 8.

35 Judith Baumel and Jacob Schacter, "The Ninety-Three Bais Yakov Girls of Cracow," in Judith Tydor Baumel, *Double Jeopardy: Gender and the Holocaust* (Portland OR: Valentine Mitchell, 1998).

36 Roskies and Diamant, *Holocaust Literature*, 26.

37 Roskies and Diamant, *Holocaust Literature*, 30.

38 Roskies and Diamant, *Holocaust Literature*, 26.

39 Chaim Weizmann, "Deeds, Not Words," from "Address at Madison Square Garden Demonstration," March 1, 1943, *Furrows* 1, no. 5 (1943), published by Habonim Labor Zionist Youth.

40 *Furrows* 1, no. 5 (1943).

41 See Rafael Medoff, "'We Will Never Die': Shattering the Silence Surrounding the Holocaust," in *Holocaust Encyclopedia*, United States Holocaust Memorial Museum, http://www.ushmm.org/wlc/en/index.php?ModuleId=10007036. Cf. Eleanor Roosevelt response in April 14, 1943, column, "My Day," in Eleanor Roosevelt papers, accessed August 2, 2020, https://www2.gwu.edu/~erpapers/myday/displaydoc.cfm?_y=1943&_f=md056470.

42 Roskies and Diamant, *Holocaust Literature*, 38. On Habas, see *Encyclopedia of Jewish Women*, Jewish Women's Archive, accessed August 21, 2018, https://jwa.org/encyclopedia/article/habas-bracha.

43 See Ziva Shalev, *Tosyah: Tosyah Altman, meha-hanhagah ha-rashit shel ha-Shomer ha-tsair le-mifkedet ha-Irgun ha-Yehudi ha-lochem* (Tel Aviv: Moreshet, 1992), chap. 5; Bracha Habas, *Michtavim Min Ha-Getaot* (Tel Aviv: Am Oved, 1943), 41–43.

44 Document 1–7, letter from Warsaw ghetto, fall 1942, in Kerenji, *Jewish Responses to Persecution*, 24–25. Reprinted in Yitzhak Arad, Israel Gutman, and Abraham Margaliot, eds., *Documents on the Holocaust* (Jerusalem: Yad Vashem, 1981), 241–42.

45 In Melech Neustadt, *The Warsaw Ghetto Rising: As Told by the Insurgents* (Tel Aviv: World Union Poalei Zion-Hitachduth, 1944).

46 Neustadt, *Warsaw Ghetto Rising*, 37–38.

47 "Bermuda Conference Opened; Keynoters Say Solution Is Allied Victory," Jewish Telegraphic Agency, https://www.jta.org/1943/04/20/archive/bermuda-conference-opened-keynoters-say-solution-is-allied-victory.

48 "Bermuda Conference Closes; Decisions Remain Confidential; General Statement Issued," Jewish Telegraphic Agency, http://www.jta.org/1943/04/30/archive/bermuda-conference-closes-decisions-remain-confidential-general-statement-issued. The letter was signed by Stephen S. Wise, president of the American Jewish Congress; Joseph M. Proskauer, president of the American Jewish Committee; Henry Monsky, president of B'nai B'rith; Adolph Held, president of the Jewish Labor Committee; and Israel Goldstein, president of the Synagogue Council of America.

49 "The Gentlemen at Bermuda," *Jewish Frontier*, May 1943, in *Jewish Frontier Anthology, 1934–1944* (New York: Jewish Frontier Association, 1945), 378.

50 Alterman, "Pesach shel Galuyot," *Davar*, April 19, 1943, 2. See discussion in Hannan Hever, *Suddenly the Sight of War: Violence and Nationalism in Hebrew Poetry* (Stanford CA: Stanford University Press, 2016), 113. Special thanks to Nurit Patt for translation assistance.

51 Henry Friedlander, "Guilt for the Holocaust" in Jonathan Sarna, ed., *The American Jewish Experience*. (New York: Holmes & Meier, 1997). Friedlander also notes that the Nazis' sense that no one cared about the Jews may also have helped in the decision to accelerate the Final Solution.

52 Yosef Gorny, *Jewish Press*, 8.

53 See for example the works of Leff, *Buried By the* Times, and Deborah Lipstadt, *Beyond Belief: The American Press and the Coming of the Holocaust, 1939–1945* (New York: Free Press, 1986).

54 "Nazis Start Mass Execution of Warsaw Jews on Passover; Victims Broadcast S.O.S.," Jewish Telegraphic Agency, http://www.jta.org/1943/04/23/jewish-holidays/passover/nazis-start-mass-execution-of-warsaw-jews-on-passover-victims-broadcast-s-o-s.

55 On rumors, see Amos Goldberg, "The History of the Jews in the Ghettos," in Dan Stone, ed., *The Holocaust and Historical Methodology* (New York: Berghahn Books, 2012).

56 See Joshua Zimmerman, *The Polish Underground and the Jews, 1939–1945* (Cambridge: Cambridge University Press, 2015), 219.

57 Isaac Schwartzbart, 1888–1961, born in Poland, was elected to the Polish parliament in the interwar period as a member of the General Zionists

and fled first to Paris, then London at the beginning of the war. He was a member of the Polish government-in-exile from 1940 to 1945 and came to the United States in 1946. See Porat, *Blue and Yellow Stars of David*, 7.

58 Cable no. 639 from Warsaw, April 21, 1943 (signed by Sobolewski Mikolacczyk and Kalina Rowecki). Zimmerman, *Polish Underground and the Jews*, notes that Sikorski determined that Jewish uprising had no chance of success, thus Polish Home Army aid would be minimal; time was not right to start the general uprising: "a premature start to the general uprising would be tantamount to national suicide" (221).

59 Zimmerman, *Polish Underground and the Jews*, 226.

60 See Rebecca Margolis, "Review of the Yiddish Media," in Ruth Klein, ed., *Nazi Germany, Canadian Responses: Confronting Antisemitism in the Shadow of War* (Montreal: McGill-Queens University Press, 2012).

61 *Forverts*, April 25, 1943. My emphasis. The Yiddish word is *kemferisheste*. No trained commanders were sent by the Polish Underground to aid in the battle although the newspapers assumed this to be the case.

62 Berl Katznelson, 1887–1944, a leader of the Labor Zionist movement, central figure of the second *aliyah*, and editor of the Histadrut (General Federation of Jewish Labor) newspaper.

63 "Jews in Warsaw Ghetto Ask for Food and Arms to Continue Their Resistance to Nazis," Jewish Telegraphic Agency, http://www.jta.org/1943/04/30/archive/jews-in-warsaw-ghetto-ask-for-food-and-arms-to-continue-their-resistance-to-nazis; see also in *Davar*, April 30, 1943.

64 Herman Kruk diary, *The Last Days of the Jerusalem of Lithuania* (New Haven CT: Yale University Press, 2002), 524.

65 Goebbels diary, part 2, vol. 8, p. 196, in Friedlander, *Years of Extermination*, 525.

66 *Davar*, May 2, 1943.

67 *Davar*, May 5, 1943, "Telegraphic cry for help from the underground in Poland less than 10% of the prewar Jewish population remains in Poland."

68 "Embattled Warsaw Jews Fly Flags of Britain, Poland, Russia from Ghetto Buildings," Jewish Telegraphic Agency, http://www.jta.org/1943/05/10/archive/embattled-warsaw-jews-fly-flags-of-britain-poland-russia-from-ghetto-buildings.

69 *Der Tog*, May 14, 1943.

70 On Zygielbojm, see Daniel Blatman, "On a Mission against All Odds: Szmuel Zygielbojm in London (April 1942–May 1943)," *Yad Vashem Studies* 20 (1990): 237–71.

71 Zygielbojm Papers, YIVO Archives, RG 1454, Folder 47.

72 Gorny, *Jewish Press*, 13. A May 21, 1943, obituary by Herszl Berger in *Davar* described Zygielbojm disparagingly as a "second-rate politician, Bund apparatchik and a rigid fanatic."

73 "Members of British Parliament Receive Appeal for Assistance from Embattled Warsaw Jews," Jewish Telegraphic Agency, May 24, 1943, https://www.jta.org/1943/05/24/archive/members-of-british-parliament-receive-appeal-for-assistance-from-embattled-warsaw-jev.

74 "Jewish Council in Poland Sends Appeal to Jews of America; Describes Warsaw Fight," Jewish Telegraphic Agency, June 1, 1943, http://www.jta.org/1943/06/01/archive/jewish-council-in-poland-sends-appeal-to-jews-of-america-describes-warsaw-fight.

75 *Forverts*, May 24, 1943.

76 *Forverts*, May 24, 1943.

77 "Davar Hayom," *Davar*, May 28, 1943; see also in Gorny, *Jewish Press*, 11.

78 "Last Letter of Szmuel Zygielbojm." English translation: "Zygielbojm Letter to Polish President (May 11, 1943)," *Jewish Virtual Library*, https://www.jewishvirtuallibrary.org/jsource/Holocaust/zyglet.html.

79 Yad Vashem Archives, O-55.

80 On Syrkin's trajectory and legacy as a Zionist thinker, see Carole S. Kessner, "Marie Syrkin: An Exemplary Life," in *American Jewish Women and the Zionist Enterprise*, ed. Shulamit Reinharz and Mark A. Raider (Waltham MA: Brandeis University Press, 2005), 48–64. See in particular the November 1942 *Jewish Frontier* editorial regarding extermination of European Jewry.

81 Marie Syrkin, "The Last Stand," June 1943, *Jewish Frontier Anthology*, 389–91.

82 Zuckerman, in *Surplus of Memory*, 416: "I don't know the source of the information that reached Israel that Tosia and Zivia were killed. The two of them were alive at the time. The cable about their death came from Bedzin. You should know that Zivia's name was a common code word in foreign

correspondence, which stood for He-Halutz in Poland or our movement, Dror. Tosia Altman was a member of Hashomer Hatzair. The cable might have been meant to say that Jewish Warsaw no longer existed." As noted above, recent research by Ronen Haran, "Source of Reports," indicates the source of the mistaken information on Tosia to have been a telegram sent by Chajka Klinger from Poland to Natan Schwalb of Hehalutz on April 27, 1943. Quoted in Dreifuss, *Geto Varsha*, 46. See also in Avihu Ronen, "The Cable that Vanished," 129.

83 *Davar*, June 4, 1943, 1.

84 Hanan Hever, *Suddenly the Sight of War*, 36.

85 "Two Joans of Arc," June 7, 1943. Reuters called them the "heroines" of the ghetto.

86 See Orly Lubin, "Holocaust Testimony, National Memory" in *Extremities: Trauma, Testimony and Community*, ed. Nancy K. Miller and Jason Tougaw (Champaign: University of Illinois Press, 2002), 131–42.

87 "Day of Protest Against Allies' Indifference to Jewish Tragedy Proclaimed in Palestine," Jewish Telegraphic Agency, http://www.jta.org/1943/06/07/archive/day-of-protest-against-allies-indifference-to-jewish-tragedy-proclaimed-in-palestine.

88 "Mass Protest in Yishuv," *Davar*, June 15–16, 1943.

89 "Report on Hundreds of Thousands in the Yishuv Who Signed," *Davar*, June 16, 1943.

90 "London Paper Urges Observance of 'Jewish Day' to Mark Resistance in Warsaw Ghetto," Jewish Telegraphic Agency, http://www.jta.org/1943/06/03/archive/london-paper-urges-observance-of-jewish-day-to-mark-resistance-in-warsaw-ghetto.

91 "Mass Meeting in New York Will Commemorate Jewish Heroes of Warsaw Ghetto," Jewish Telegraphic Agency, http://www.jta.org/1943/06/16/archive/mass-meeting-in-new-york-will-commemorate-jewish-heroes-of-warsaw-ghetto.

92 Lucy S. Dawidowicz, *From That Place and Time: A Memoir, 1938–1947* (New York: Norton, 1989), my emphasis.

93 "The Flag in the Ghetto Wall" (July 1943), in *Jewish Frontier Anthology*, 381–88. Syrkin would later become known as the author of *Blessed Is the*

Match, one of the first postwar volumes on Jewish resistance written in English. My emphasis.

94 Yehuda Bauer, *Rethinking the Holocaust*, 120.

95 "Jewish Fighters in Warsaw Ghetto Were Dressed in German Uniforms to Confuse Nazis," Jewish Telegraphic Agency, August 16, 1943, http://www.jta.org/1943/08/16/archive/jewish-fighters-in-warsaw-ghetto-were-dressed-in-german-uniforms-to-confuse-nazis.

96 *Forverts*, August 20, 1943, 1, 8.

97 See Kerenji, *Jewish Responses to Persecution*, glossary.

98 Zohar Segev thinks it is mainly based on reports of the Polish government-in-exile but not based on information from Karski, who did not report on Treblinka. See description of report in *The World Jewish Congress during the Holocaust: Between Activism and Restraint* (Berlin: Walter de Gruyter, 2014), 28. Segev cites "document on Treblinka and Warsaw Ghetto" presented by WJC and a delegation of Polish Jewry, September 1943, AJA, 361 H294/2.

99 *Lest We Forget: The Massacre of the Warsaw Ghetto: A Compilation of Reports* (New York: World Jewish Congress, December 1943), 2nd printing, 9.

100 *Lest We Forget*, 35.

101 Z. Segev, *World Jewish Congress*, 30. He notes that the source was likely based on reports of a witness and not a participant to the events.

102 See in *Lest We Forget*. Segev notes: "Thus as early as 1943 a singular mix evolved containing criticism of the Jews' acceptance of their fate on the one hand, and glorification of Jewish resistance, particularly in the Warsaw Ghetto, on the other."

103 *Lest We Forget*. Treblinka report based on "official report submitted to the Polish government," reprinted in Jacob Apenszlak, ed., *The Black Book of Polish Jewry: An Account of the Martyrdom of Polish Jewry Under the Nazi Occupation* (New York: American Federation for Polish Jews, 1943), 141–47. See description of report in Z. Segev, *World Jewish Congress*, 28.

104 "Jacob Apenszlak, Former Editor of Leading Polish Jewish Newspaper, Dies in New York," Jewish Telegraphic Agency, http://www.jta.org/1950/03/30/archive/jacob-apensziak-former-editor-of-leading-polish-jewish-newspaper-dies-in-new-york. Before leaving Poland in 1939,

Mr. Apenszlak was the chief editor of *Nasz Przeglad* [Our review], the leading daily Polish-Jewish newspaper in Warsaw. In New York, he was associated with the American Federation of Polish Jews, the Institute for Jewish Affairs of the World Jewish Congress, the Jewish Agency for Palestine, and later the Israel Delegation.

105 Apenszlak, *Black Book of Polish Jewry*, viii.

106 *The American Jewish Yearbook, 5704 (September 30, 1943 to September 17, 1944)*, AJC Archives, http://www.ajcarchives.org/AJC_DATA/Files/1943_1944_2_Formatter.pdf. Harry Shneiderman's preface is dated September 2, 1943.

107 Harry Schneiderman and Morris T. Fine, eds., *American Jewish Yearbook, 1943*, volume 45 (Philadelphia: The Jewish Publication Society of America, 1943–5704), 306. The biography given there has: "Moses Z. Frank, LL.B., M.A., former editor, *Jewish Standard*, Toronto, and English section of *Toronto Hebrew Journal*; contributor to *Universal Jewish Encyclopedia* and Jewish periodicals in Hebrew and English." AJC Archives, http://www.ajcarchives.org/AJC_DATA/Files/1943_1944_7_Europe.pdf.

108 "Jews in Warsaw Ghetto Perished Confident of Jewish Future, Eye-witness Reports," Jewish Telegraphic Agency, http://www.jta.org/1943/11/02/archive/jews-in-warsaw-ghetto-perished-confident-of-jewish-future-eye-witness-reports.

109 Jeffrey Shandler, *Jews, God, and Videotape: Religion and Media in America* (New York: New York University Press, 2009), 76.

110 Morton Wishengrad, "The Battle of the Warsaw Ghetto," AJC Archives, http://www.ajcarchives.org/AJC_DATA/Files/RD2.PDF, 10.

111 Wishengrad, "The Battle of the Warsaw Ghetto," 14.

112 Shandler, *Jews, God, and Videotape*, 294n64.

113 Bret Werb, "*We Will Never Die: A Pageant to Save the Jews of Europe*," Orel Foundation, Articles and Essays, http://orelfoundation.org/index.php/journal/journalArticle/we_will_never_die_a_pageant_to_save_the_jews_of_europe/.

114 For Waxman's biography, see Waxman Papers, Special Collections Research Center, Syracuse University Library.

115 For the text, see Werb, *We Will Never Die*.

116 Daniel Blatman, *For Our Freedom and Yours: The Jewish Labour Bund in Poland 1939–1949*, trans. Naftali Greenwood (London: Vallentine Mitchell, 2003), 123–24, 128.

117 Saul Hankin, "'Brothers and Sisters of Work and Need': The Bundist Newspaper *Unzer Tsayt* and Its Role in New York City, 1941–1944," BA thesis, University of Michigan.

118 Shloime Mendelsohn, "The Battle of the Warsaw Ghetto," *YIVO Bleter*, Journal of the Yiddish Scientific Institute, 13 (Jan.–Feb. 1944). In his preface, Max Weinreich, research director of YIVO, noted that though the paper was delivered in Yiddish (at the eighteenth annual conference of the Yiddish Scientific Institute), "In view of the contemporary and historical interest of the subject, the Executive Board of the Institute resolved to issue this material in English translation and thus have its contents brought to the attention of American public opinion." Apparently an exhibit of Roman Vishniac photos of prewar Jewish life in Poland was on display at the same time.

119 Blatman, *For Our Freedom and Yours*, 27.

120 Mendelsohn, "Battle of the Warsaw Ghetto," *YIVO Bleter*, Journal of the Yiddish Scientific Institute, 13 (Jan.–Feb. 1944), 5.

121 Mendelsohn, *Battle of the Warsaw Ghetto*, 14.

122 It is important to note that this assessment of the revolt as a "mass popular uprising" confirms the recent research of Havi Dreifuss, who argues that historical accounts of the revolt need to consider the experiences of the thousands of Jews who resisted Nazi liquidation efforts, not just the exploits of a small band of armed fighters. See Dreifuss, *Geto Varsha*.

123 Dawidowicz, *From that Time and Place*, p. 11; also in Steven Rubin, ed., *Writing Our Lives: Autobiographies of American Jews, 1890–1990* (Philadelphia: The Jewish Publication Society, 1991), 232.

Chapter 3. The Surviving Ghetto Fighters Write the First Draft of a History of the Revolt

1 Pnina Grinshpan-Frimer was born in Nowy Dwor. With the outbreak of WWII she moved to Warsaw and joined the ranks of the ŻOB. During

the Warsaw ghetto uprising of April 1943 she fought in a combat unit of Left Poalei Zion. Upon the suppression of the uprising she was among the fighters who escaped via the sewers to the Aryan side of Warsaw and joined the partisans fighting the Germans in the Wyszkow Forest. During the Polish uprising in 1944 she was caught by the Germans, along with the fighters Dov Szniper and Janek Bilak. Pnina succeeded in disposing of her weapon; Janek Bilak's gun was found among his possessions and he was shot. After the liberation of Poland, Pnina emigrated to Mandate Palestine and married the fighter Chaim Frimer.

2 "I Thought I Was the Last Jew Alive: Conversations with Simha 'Kazik' Rotem, Survivor Who Took Part in the Warsaw Ghetto Uprising," Yad Vashem, accessed February 22, 2017, https://www.yadvashem.org/articles/interviews/kazik.html.

3 This excerpt comes from a testimony of Lubetkin's republished in *Commentary* magazine in May 1947. "The Last Days of the Warsaw Ghetto: A Survivor's Account of a Heroic Chapter in Jewish History," https://www.commentarymagazine.com/articles/the-last-days-of-the-warsaw-ghettoa-survivors-account-of-a-heroic-chapter-in-jewish-history/. See also as described in Zivia Lubetkin, *Biyemei Kilayon UMered* (Tel Aviv: Hakibbutz Hameuhad, 1989), 169 and Tuvia Borzykowski, *Between Tumbling Walls* (Tel Aviv: Ghetto Fighters' House and United Kibbutz Movement, 1976) 102–4. The testimony by Lubetkin at Yagur in 1946 (*Aharonim al ha-Homah* [The last ones on the wall]) contains a shorter description of this episode.

4 Simha Rotem, *Memoirs of a Warsaw Ghetto Fighter* (New Haven CT: Yale University Press, 1994), 60. See also in Bella Gutterman, *Fighting for Her People: Zivia Lubetkin, 1914–1978* (Jerusalem: Yad Vashem, 2014), 260.

5 Gutterman, *Fighting for Her People*, 261, notes this transfer facilitated by Armija Ludowa, but many were killed by Poles and Germans.

6 There are two versions of the story as to how the celluloid factory caught on fire. Zivia relates that Tosia had been accommodated in a safe house but returned to the factory for a meeting with other surviving fighters; according to Eliezer Geller, Tosia was living in the factory and the fire was started as she tried to heat ointment to heal her wounds. Geller escaped the factory

by jumping out of the loft but Tosia was badly burned and handed over to the Germans by Poles and subsequently tortured to death. Lubetkin, *Biyemei Kilayon UMered*, 178. See also description by Zuckerman in *Surplus of Memory*, 394–95 and by Hella Rufeisen-Schuepper, *Preidah Mi-Milah 18: Sipurah shel Kasharit* [Farewell Mila 18: The story of a courier] (Tel Aviv: Lochamei HaGetaot, 1990).

7 Tuvia Borzykowski, *Between Tumbling Walls*, 123–24.

8 Gutterman, *Fighting for Her People*, 267. See Kazik's description of this escape via the sewer in "I Thought I Was the Last Jew Alive: Conversations with Simha 'Kazik' Rotem, Survivor Who Took Part in the Warsaw Ghetto Uprising," Yad Vashem, accessed February 22, 2017, https://www.yadvashem.org/articles/interviews/kazik.html.

9 Zuckerman, *Surplus of Memory*, 429.

10 Letter written by Zivia [Lubetkin] and Yitzhak [Zuckerman], called Antek, to [Yitzhak] Tabenkin of the He-Chalutz movement and to [Meir] Ya'ari from the Ha-Shomer [ha-Tsa'ir] movement, in Tel Aviv (in Polish), GFH Archives 6070.

11 Telegram by Ignacy Schwartzbart, June 22, 1943, "To Jewish Agency Jerusalem. Frumka Plotnicka dies in August 1943 in Bedzin; Mordechai Tennenbaum in Bialystok in August 1943," Yad Vashem Archives M.2 895; GFH Archives 6070.

12 Gutterman, *Fighting for Her People*, 270.

13 For example, she told Rivka Glantz to escape and join the partisans (Lubetkin, *Biyemei Kilayon UMered*, 192).

14 In Porat, *Blue and Yellow Stars of David*, 242. The United Partisan Organization (*Fareinikte Partisaner Organizatzie*—FPO), formed in the Vilna ghetto in January 1942, never succeeded in initiating a revolt in Vilna. On July 15, 1943, the leader of the FPO, Itzhak Wittenberg, was arrested by the Jewish police; after being freed by his comrades in the FPO, he eventually turned himself in to avoid the liquidation of the entire ghetto. Without the support of the population of the ghetto, members of the FPO, led by Abba Kovner, eventually decided to take their fight to the surrounding forests following the final liquidation of the ghetto on September 23, 1943.

15 Gutterman, *Fighting for Her People*, 276–78.

16 Vladka Meed, *On Both Sides of the Wall: Memoirs from the Warsaw Ghetto* (New York: Holocaust Library, 1993), 187.

17 Meed, *On Both Sides of the Wall*, 187–88.

18 Bernard Goldstein, born in Siedlce, Poland, in 1889, was leader of the Bund prior to World War II. Goldstein helped smuggle in arms in preparation for the 1943 Warsaw ghetto uprising. As part of the ghetto underground, he organized manufactured fake documents for those marked for liquidation. Fleeing from the ghetto during the time of the uprising, he helped stage the Polish Uprising in Warsaw, which began on August 1, 1944. Following World War II, he immigrated to the United States, where he wrote his autobiography, *The Stars Bear Witness* (New York: Viking, 1949), reissued as *Five Years in the Warsaw Ghetto* (1959). He died in New York in 1959. "Bernard Goldstein," Guide to the YIVO Archives, accessed March 5, 2020, http://yivoarchives.org/index.php?p=collections/controlcard&id=33330.

19 Goldstein, *Stars Bear Witness*, 217–18.

20 Goldstein, *Stars Bear Witness*, 232–33. The hideout at Leszno 18 contained the secret archive of the ŻOB described by Zuckerman and others elsewhere—see for example, GFH Archives 2834. Zuckerman also describes a secret entrance to a bunker through the oven in the apartment.

21 Goldstein, *Stars Bear Witness*, 235.

22 For a discussion of the key role played by movement activists stationed in Geneva, see Raya Cohen, *Ben "sham" le-"khan": Sipurim shel edim la-hurban, Shvaits 1939–1942* (Tel Aviv: Sifriyat ha'apalah, 1999).

23 Four letters written by Berman to the Jewish leadership in London, Geneva, and Mandate Palestine, July 31, 1943, and May 12, 1944 (two pages, handwritten, in Polish), Adolf-Abraham Berman collection, GFH Archives 5814.

24 Four letters written by Berman to the Jewish leadership in London, Geneva, and Mandate Palestine, July 31, 1943, and May 12, 1944 (two pages, handwritten, in Polish), Adolf-Abraham Berman collection, GFH Archives 5814.

25 Yitzhak Gitterman was murdered in Warsaw in the *Aktion* of January 1943, Leib Neustadt was murdered in Warsaw's Pawiak prison, and Yitzhak

Bornstein, in Bedzin. For more on Silberschein, see Garbarini et al., eds., *Jewish Responses to Persecution*, volume 2 (Lanham MD: AltaMira Press, 2011). Born in L'vov in 1882, Silberschein had been involved in left-wing Zionist politics in interwar Poland, and was one of the founders of Jewish credit cooperatives in Galicia; during the war he organized relief efforts in Geneva, working with the World Jewish Congress to create RELICO. See Raya Cohen, *Ben "sham" le-"khan": Sipurim shel edim la-hurban, Shvaits 1939–1942* (Tel Aviv: Sifriyat ha'apalah, 1999)

26 Joseph Kermish, "Rescue Attempts during the Holocaust," *Proceedings of the Second Yad Vashem International Historical Conference*, ed. Yisrael Gutman and Efraim Zuroff (Jerusalem: Yad Vashem, 1977), 367–98.

27 Lubetkin, *Biyemei Kilayon UMered*, 181.

28 Meed, *On Both Sides of the Wall*, 182; Goldstein, *Stars Bear Witness*, 251. According to Catherine Collomp, citing a JLC report from 1944: "Reporting its activity for 1944, the JLC stated that it had sent 'large sums of money to the ghettos. This money was distributed for relief and rescue, for aid in the labor and concentration camps, for the underground movement and for the necessary preparations for resistance'." See her "Relief Is a Political Gesture: The Jewish Labor Committee's Interventions in War-Torn Poland, 1939–1945," *Transatlantica* 1 (2014), accessed March 5, 2020, http://transatlantica.revues.org/6942. See also "From Gas Chambers to a New Life," JLC Report, 1944, JLC Archives R2, B1, F8.

29 Zuckerman in *Surplus of Memory*, 408: "We were concerned with foreign contact. We all wrote letters, some of which were published by Neustadt (in 1946–47). Other letters were also written in the name of the Jewish National Committee."

30 See in Blatman, *For Our Freedom and Yours: The Jewish Labour Bund in Poland 1939–1949* (Portland OR: Valentine Mitchell, 2003), 117; from J. S. Hertz, *In di yorn fun Yiddishn Hurbn* (New York: Unzer Tsayt Farlag, 1948), 55–56.

31 Goldstein, *Stars Bear Witness*, 235.

32 The research of Dariusz Libionka and Laurence Weinbaum has detailed the systematic process of writing the Jewish Military Union (ŻZW) out of the historical record. See *Bohaterowie, Hochsztaplerzy, Opisywacze, Wokol*

Żydowskiego Związku Wojskowego [Heroes, hucksters, and storytellers: On the Jewish Military Union (ŻZW)] (Warsaw: Stowarzyszenie Centrum Badań nad Zagładą Żydow, 2011).

33 Joseph Kermish, "The Activities of the Council for Aid to Jews ('Zegota') in Occupied Poland," in Israel Gutman and Efraim Zuroff, eds., *Rescue Attempts during the Holocaust* (Jerusalem: Yad Vashem, 1974), 12. The report was published in Warsaw in December 1943.

34 Battle for the Warsaw Ghetto, "Report from the Jewish Workers Underground Movement," June 22, 1943, report A. Excerpts were reproduced in Marek Edelman, *The Ghetto Fights* (New York: American Representation of the General Jewish Workers Union of Poland, 1946) and *The Ghetto Fights* (London: Bookmarks, 1990). Several versions of the report from the Jewish Workers Underground movement dated June 22, 1943, exist and have been published in various sources: "The Ghetto Speaks," report of the American Representation of the General Jewish Workers' Union in Poland (1943); YIVO Archives; and WRB files. Excerpts also available at "Battle for the Warsaw Ghetto," Holocaust Education and Archive Research Team, http://www.holocaustresearchproject.org/revolt/warsawbattle.html.

35 "Council of the Rescue of the Jews in Poland," p. 508, WRB files, accessed February 3, 2017, http://www.fdrlibrary.marist.edu/_resources/images/wrb/wrb1436.pdf. "The Battle of Ghettograd" is a reference to the Battle of Stalingrad, which ended in February 1943 after five months of heavy fighting between German and Soviet forces.

36 Slight differences exist in the English translations of the report. For example, report A in the WRB files notes distinctions of Polish underground "according to the approach of different groups to the Jewish problem" and indicates the entire country "was electrified" by the battle.

37 Frydrych had also been active in gathering information on Treblinka before the uprising. Kazik recalled in a conversation with Michael Berenbaum that when the Great Deportation began on July 22, 1942, Frydrych was able to travel to the Malinka stop near Treblinka, utilizing connections through the Bund that he had with Polish railway workers, where he learned that thousands of Jews entered the camp daily, but none exited, nor

were there any signs of life in the camp. Berenbaum, "Clarifications on the Warsaw Ghetto Uprising," in Eric Sterling, ed., *Life in the Ghettos during the Holocaust* (Syracuse: Syracuse University Press, 2005), 19. Edelman in *The Ghetto Fights* recalls that after the beginning of the deportations, despite Frydrych's report, "even now the population stubbornly refused to believe the truth. They simply closed their eyes to the unpleasant facts and fought against them with all the means at their disposal."

38 Blones was born in Warsaw in 1924. He was fifteen years old at the outbreak of WWII, but despite his youth, he undertook underground missions of smuggling weapons into the ghetto. During the Warsaw Ghetto Uprising in April 1943, he commanded a combat squad in the brushmakers area. On May 8, he was among those who escaped from the ghetto via the sewers, but was sent back with Shlomo Shuster to help other fighters get out. This mission failed because the Germans had blocked the exits, and he was killed, together with his brother Eliezer and his sister Guta.

39 As detailed in chapter 5 of this book, the ŻOB report sent in May 1944 emphasized the July 28, 1942, conference called by HeHalutz and the youth groups associated with it: Hashomer Hatzair, Dror, and Akiva, where the groups decided to create the Zydowska Organizacja Bojowa, the Jewish Combat Organization, whose Polish-language appeals were signed with the initials ŻOB. The high command comprised Shmuel Breslaw, Zuckerman, Zivia Lubetkin, and Mordecai Tenenbaum. Tosia Altman, Frumka Plotnicka, Leah Perlstein, and Arieh Vilner (Jurek) were sent to the Aryan side to establish contact with the Polish underground movement and to obtain weapons for the ghetto.

40 Blum managed to survive the revolt and escaped to the forests. He returned to Warsaw but was soon caught and most likely killed by the Gestapo.

41 On the first day of combat, on April 19, 1943, Anielewicz and Israel Kanal were based in the ŻOB headquarters at 29 Mila St., in a building that overlooked the intersection of Mila Street and Zamenhof Street, which had been deemed a strategic location before the liquidation. Berl Braude (of Dror) also commanded a unit positioned there. One ŻOB member, named Yechiel (of Hashomer Hatzair) was killed. According to Chaim Frimer's testimony, it was Yechiel's commander, Mordechai

"Merdek" Growas, who shot and killed him to put him out of his misery. Unfortunately, his family name is unknown. See Aharon Carmi and Chaim Frimer, *Min Ha-Delekah Ha-Hi* (*From That Inferno)* (Tel Aviv: Kibbutz Lohamei HaGeta'ot, 1960–1961), 221.

42 Not identified here, this would have been Marek Edelman.

43 This episode is not without controversy. As Havi Dreifuss notes, other sources indicate that after Perlman was injured, Mordechai Anielewicz refused to let him into the bunker at Mila 18. Following this episode, the members of the Bund decided to leave Mila 18 and under the leadership of Leib Gruzalc, and they returned to the burned-out building on Mila 29. On 27 April they were located by the Germans and after Gruzalc and others were killed, the remnants made their way to Edelman and not back to the command bunker at Mila 18.

44 In his *Warsaw Ghetto Rising*, published in 1944 in Tel Aviv, Melekh Neustadt (Noy) listed the sources of information that came into the possession of I. Schwartzbart and A. Reiss in London in 1944, helping to fill out the picture of what had actually transpired in Warsaw in April–May 1943. These sources included "a series of accurate and detailed reports written by the surviving initiators, leaders, and fighters of the rebellion themselves."

45 See GFH Archives 6138.

46 Avihu Ronen, "The Cable That Vanished," *Yad Vashem Studies* 41, no. 2 (2013): 128; Ronen was also the son of Chajka Klinger and author of a study of her wartime and postwar experiences.

47 Ronen, "The Cable That Vanished."

48 Three letters written by Cywja [Zivia Lubetkin] and Icchak [Yitzhak Zuckerman] to [Yitzhak] Tabenkin, [Meir] Ya'ari, and [Eliyahu] Dobkin, Nov. 15, 1943, March 8, 1944, March 10, 1944 (six pages, handwritten, in Polish). (The latter two letters are to Tabenkin and Ya'ari only.). Adolf-Abraham Berman collection, GFH Archives 6138.

49 GFH Archives 6138.

50 GFH Archives 6138.

51 Report from the Jewish underground in the Warsaw ghetto, a list of underground fighters who fell in the Warsaw ghetto uprising. GFH Archives

2044. Reprinted in Melekh Neustadt, *Ḥurbn un oyfshtand fun di yidn in Varshe* (Tel Aviv: Executive Committee of the General Federation of Jewish Labour in Palestine, 169–81).

52 Noting contact with the Department for Jewish Affairs in the Armed Forces of Poland the report emphasized "the JNC has close and cordial relations with the representatives of the Fighting Underground of Poland," GFH Archives 2044, 5.

53 Zuckerman, *Surplus of Memory*, 426.

54 Letters of support, sent by Berl Lokier (February 1944) and Nachum Goldmann (March 1944) from London to the Jewish National Committee and the Jewish Fighting Organization, GFH Archives 5982.

55 See also the letter from Zuckerman and Lubetkin to members of HeHalutz in Slovakia, January 6, 1944, GFH Archives 4045. In the letter Antek and Zivia note the difficulties of getting survivors out of Poland and "huge" sums of money needed to smuggle individuals across the boundary ($100 a head—"these amounts will not enable a large scale exodus").

56 Two letters of encouragement and support, sent by Berl Lokier (February 19, 1944) and Nachum Goldmann (March 7, 1944) from London to the Jewish National Committee (Zydowski Komitet Narodowy) and the Jewish Fighting Organization (Zydowska Organizacja Bojowa) on behalf of the Jewish population of prestate Israel. Adolf Berman Collection, GFH Archives 5982.

57 GFH Archives 5982.

58 Blatman, *For Our Freedom and Yours*, 155–56.

59 Letter to Tabenkin and Ya'ari (Tel Aviv); dated March 8, 1943 [sic; intending 1944]. GFH Archives notes the year written in the source document is 1943; however, from the content of the text and a comparison with the letter of March 10 that particularly mentions the liquidation of the Trawniki and Poniatowa camps—which took place in the autumn of 1943—it appears that this letter was written on March 8, 1944. GFH Archives 6138, 2.

60 Letter to Tabenkin and Ya'ari (Tel Aviv), March 10, 1944, GFH Archives 6138.

61 Correspondence between members of the Jewish underground who found a hiding place on the Aryan side of Warsaw [in Hebrew], 1944, GFH Archives 1775.

Chapter 4. The First Anniversary of the Revolt

1 Letter to Dobkin, Tabenkin, Ya'ari, Berl (?), Tel Aviv (ca. April 19, 1944). Correspondence between members of the Jewish underground who found a hiding place on the Aryan side of Warsaw [in Hebrew], 1944, GFH Archives 1775.

2 "First Anniversary of Battle of Warsaw Ghetto Commemorated; State Dept. Lauds Heroes," Jewish Telegraphic Agency, http://www.jta.org/1944/04/13/archive/first-anniversary-of-battle-of-warsaw-ghetto-commemorated-state-dept-lauds-heroes.

3 *Daily Worker*, April 19, 1944, AJHS Archives SCA I-68.

4 AJHS Archives SCA I-68.

5 AJHS Archives SCA I-68.

6 "First Anniversary of Battle of Warsaw Ghetto Commemorated; State Dept. Lauds Heroes," Jewish Telegraphic Agency, https://www.jta.org/1944/04/13/archive/first-anniversary-of-battle-of-warsaw-ghetto-commemorated-state-dept-lauds-heroes.

7 AJHS Archives SCA I-68. The committee included Rabbis Milton Steinberg, Joseph Lookstein, and Max Maccoby, with Rabbi Ahron Opher as director.

8 I discussed this theme further in "We are fighting for three lines in history . . . it will not be said that our youth marched like sheep to the slaughter": "Writing about Resistance in the Immediate Aftermath of the Holocaust," a paper presented at the Beyond Camps and Forced Labour Conference, Imperial War Museum, London, 2015.

9 Speech of H. Leivick at Carnegie Hall, April 19, 1944, quoted in "The Battle of the Warsaw Ghetto, April 19–June 1, 1943" (New York: Farband Labor Zionist Order, n.d.), USHMM Library.

10 Jacob Pat, letter to workers of greater New York, April 19, 1944, JLC Archives, reel 32, folder 7.

11 *Forverts*, April 20, 1944.

12 "New York Newspapers Laud Jewish Bravery in Articles on the Battle of the Warsaw Ghetto," Jewish Telegraphic Agency, http://pdfs.jta.org/1944/1944-04-23_092.pdf.

13 Julian Tuwim, "We, Polish Jews" in *My, Zydzi polscy . . . We, Polish Jews*, ed. Ch. Shmeruk (Jerusalem: Magness Press, 1984), 19. See in Monika Adamczyk-Garbowska, "Patterns of Return: Survivors' Postwar Journeys to Poland," Ina Levine Annual Lecture, United States Holocaust Memorial Museum, February 15, 2007. (Washington DC: United States Holocaust Memorial Museum, Center for Advanced Holocaust Studies, 2007). As James Young notes, in the summer of 1943, the sculptor Natan Rapaport, who had fled from Warsaw at the start of the war and was in a forced labor camp in Novosibirsk in 1943, already submitted his first design for a Warsaw ghetto monument and memorial to the Soviet authorities in the summer of 1943, which was rejected as *too Jewish*. Young, "The Biography of a Memorial Icon," *Representations* 26, special issue: Memory and Counter-Memory (Spring 1989), 79–80.

14 Letter from I. Schwartzbart, proposal for first anniversary commemoration in London, GFH Archive 871.

15 "Members of Polish Government Attend Warsaw Ghetto Memorial in London," Jewish Telegraphic Agency, http://pdfs.jta.org/1944/1944-04-23_092.pdf.

16 "In Tribute to the Heroes," *Remember the Warsaw Ghetto* (Federation of Polish Jews in Great Britain, April 19, 1944), 13, USHMM Library.

17 Here Reiss refers to Rabbi Isaac Nissenbaum (1868–1942), a leader of Orthodox Jewry in Poland, noted for his religious Zionist activism. Nissenbaum died in 1942 in the Warsaw Ghetto.

18 "The Battle of Warsaw," The Chief Rabbi's Sermon, Bevis Marks, London, May 22, 1944, 2, USHMM Library.

19 "The Battle of Warsaw," 4.

20 "The Battle of Warsaw," 8.

21 Porat, *Blue and Yellow Stars of David*, 245.

22 *Davar*, April 21, 1944, 1.

23 *Palestine Post*, April 19, 1944, pp. 1 and 4.

24 *Palestine Post*, April 19, 1944, pp. 1 and 4.

25 Joseph Kruk, "The Holy Date: One Year after the Warsaw Revolt," *Davar*, April 21, 1944.

26 "Jews in Palestine Will Observe Year of Mourning for Heroes of Warsaw Ghetto," Jewish Telegraphc Agency, http://pdfs.jta.org/1944/1944-04-28_097.pdf.

27 Gruenbaum made *aliyah* in 1933; his son Eliezer was accused of being a kapo in Auschwitz—on this story, see Tuvia Frilling, *A Jewish Kapo in Auschwitz: History, Memory, and the Politics of Survival* (Waltham MA: Brandeis University Press, 2014).

28 Yitzhak Gruenbaum, "Yizkor LeMordei HaGeto Be-Varsha," *Davar*, May 16, 1944, 2.

29 *Geto in Flamen* [Ghetto in flames] (New York: American Representation of the General Jewish Workers' Union in Poland, 1944), Yiddish Book Center Digital Yiddish Library, accessed March 9, 2017, https://www.yiddishbookcenter.org/collections/yiddish-books/spb-nybc200540/geto-in-flamen-zamlbukh.

30 See "Leyvick Hodes," Yiddish Leksikon, accessed March 9, 2017, http://yleksikon.blogspot.com/2015/12/leyvik-leivick-hodes.html.

31 Leyvik Hodes, "The German-Jewish War," *Geto in Flamen*, 7–53.

32 Hasia Diner, *We Remember with Reverence and Love: American Jews and the Myth of Silence after the Holocaust, 1945–1962* (New York: NYU Press, 2010), 74. In October 1944 the New Jewish Folk Theater staged *Miracle of the Warsaw Ghetto* with music composed by Shalom Secunda and actor Sam Jaffee, offering English commentary to the play.

33 Souvenir program for the Yiddish Folks Theatre production of *Miracle of the Warsaw Ghetto*, 1944, Museum of the City of New York, Gift of Jacob Ben-Ami, 69.133.1, http://collections.mcny.org/C.aspx?VP3=SearchResult&VBID=24UAYWRP4QPIU.

34 See discussion in Baskind, *The Warsaw Ghetto in American Art and Culture* (Pittsburgh: Pennsylvania State University Press, 2018), 28–32.

35 H. Leivick, "Der Nes in Geto," *Nit Gedrukte Drames* [Unpublished works] (Buenos Aires: Congress for Jewish Culture, 1973), 217.

36 Leivick, "Der Nes in Geto," 224. See also in Baskind, *Warsaw Ghetto in American Art and Culture*, 29.

37 Leivick, "Der Nes in Geto," 318.

38 Leivick, "Der Nes in Geto," 320. See also excerpts from play in see in Shmuel Niger, *Kiddush Hashem*, 1948, 447–52.

Chapter 5. Crafting a Zionist Narrative of the Revolt

1 Part of a testy correspondence between Berman and Guzik about financial matters; see Letters from Guzik to Berman [in Polish], GFH Archives 5696.

2 Letter to Histadrut Labor Federation in Palestine, Signed Adolf, Zivia, Yitzhak, Josef, May 24, 1944, GFH Archives 5672, A1. Also published in Neustadt, *Ḥurbn un oyfshtand*, 263.

3 Published as Basia Temkin-Berman, *City within a City* (New York: IP Books & YIVO, 2012).

4 The documents were sent during 1944 to the U.S. and Palestine. The original inscription on the box read "NKZ [ZKN spelled backward], III [March]." The year 1944 was added later. Scans of the rest of the documents in the reel are also in file 5672 in the Collections Section of the GFH Archives.

5 In the 1946 publication of the transcribed sources, *Ḥurbn un oyfshṭand*, Neustadt included the following diaries sent to London on May 24, 1944: report of Shalom Grayek, 264–71; Kazik (Simche Rathoyzer), 272–85; Tuvia Borzykowski, 286–92. Neustadt also cites "Silhouettes of Fighters," written by Hersh Wasser and received in London on May 24, 1944, which includes profiles of Avraham Diamant, a 42 year old worker, "The Corporal" and a 16-year old young partisan, Sha'anan Lent, 286–300.

6 In Neustadt, *Ḥurbn un oyfstand*, 301–6, "Diary of a Boy."

7 Neustadt, *Warsaw Ghetto Rising*.

8 See Kassow, *Who Will Write Our History?*, 360–62.

9 Kassow, *Who Will Write Our History?*, 365.

10 A series of letters written from their hiding place by Emanuel and Yehudit (Jozia) Ringelblum and Marek Passenstein to Adolf and Batya Berman, GFH Archives 3162.

11 Emanuel Ringelblum [Adolf Berman?], "Essay in memory of Mordechai Anielewicz" [in Polish], GFHA 3172. See discussion in Kassow, *Who Will Write Our History?*, 370–72.

12 Kassow, *Who Will Write Our History?*, 385. See May 24, 1944, letter from JNC, including concerns about the Bund, GFHA 5867.

13 Excerpted in Kermish, *To Live with Honor and Die with Honor: Documents from the Warsaw Ghetto Underground Archives* (Jerusalem: Yad Vashem, 1986), 762. See also Ringelblum, "Little Stalingrad Defends Itself," in the same volume, 594, and in Neustadt, *Hurbn un Oyfshtand*, 307–15.

14 See Havi Dreifuss, "The Leadership of the Jewish Combat Organization during the Warsaw Ghetto Uprising: A Reassessment," *Holocaust and Genocide Studies* 31, no. 1 (2017).

15 The report, written by Yitzhak Zuckerman, can be found in the GFH Archives in Polish, Yiddish, and Hebrew, and forms the basis of Neustadt's report later in 1944. It was also reprinted in Neustadt's *Hurbn un Oyfshtand fun di Yidn in Varshe* (1946), in *Sefer Milhamot ha-Geta'ot* (edited by Zuckerman and Basok, in two parts, 1959) and excerpted in Lucy Dawidowicz's *Holocaust Reader*, and is cited extensively by Gutman in *Jews of Warsaw*.

16 Letter from the Jewish National Committee on May 24, 1944, GFHA 5867.

17 On the first anniversary of the ghetto uprising Klepfisz was posthumously awarded Poland's highest military honor, the Virtuti Militari medal, by the Polish government-in-exile in London. The medal is in the United States Holocaust Memorial Museum Collection, gift of Rose Klepfisz.

18 See 1951 document, "Meeting of ŻOB members, History of the Warsaw Ghetto Revolt" (Tel Aviv, Apartment of Aharon Carmi, December 12, 1951), GFH Archives 3643 and 1481. In attendance at meeting: Tuvia Borzykowski, Sarah Biderman, Shalom Grajek, Chmelnitski (Kutzik), Aharon Karmi, Zivia Lubetkin, Yakov Putermilch, Yitzhak Zuckerman, Kazik, Dr. Yosef Kermish.

19 See "Meeting of ŻOB members," GFH Archives 3643 and 1481.

20 Rotem, *Memoirs of a Warsaw Ghetto Fighter*, xi.

21 In Rotem, *Memoirs of a Ghetto Fighter*, 155–69. Includes English translation of account written in 1944 and published by Neustadt.

22 This report, the main part of which was written in Warsaw in March 1944, was sent to London on May 24. GFH Archives 5984 includes copies in

the original Polish as well as Hebrew and Yiddish translations. A full text of the report's original draft, in Hebrew translation, 10 pages, printed, is in collections file 2044 (originally entered as Holdings Registry file 10450). Also reprinted in Zuckerman and Basok, *Sefer Milhamot Ha-Getaot*, 101; Neustadt, *Ḥurbn un oyfshtand*, 128; and in English in Lucy Dawidowicz, ed., *A Holocaust Reader* (New York: Behrman House, 1976), 359–80.

23 Zuckerman explained later that Hashomer Hatzair didn't participate in the original meeting (*Surplus of Memory*, 171); "except for Kaplan they didn't know yet what I was driving at."

24 Also in Zuckerman and Basok, *Sefer Milhamot Ha-Getaot*, 102.

25 Zuckerman, *Surplus of Memory*, 170–75.

26 Zuckerman, *Surplus of Memory*, 171.

27 Zuckerman, *Surplus of Memory*, 172: "The words of the Bundist Orzech were painful. He said that Jews weren't the only ones being killed, so were Poles." In a footnote on the same page, translator and editor Barbara Harshav cites Zuckerman's *In Ghetto and Uprising* [in Hebrew] (Tel Aviv: Ghetto Fighter's House, 1985) in which Zuckerman further quoted Orzech: "'let's fight when the Poles do, and meanwhile—not!' The logical conclusion was that we had to adapt to the interests of the non-Jewish underground" (102).

28 Gutman, *The Jews of Warsaw*, 172. Zuckerman also listed the names of the representatives of the groups including Shachna Zagan (Left Poalei Zion), Yosef Levartovski (Jewish Communists), Josef Sack (Poalei Zion Z.S.), Zivia Lubetkin (HeHalutz and Dror), and Mordecai Anielewicz (Hashomer Hatzair). Lucy Dawidowicz writes that the antifascist bloc was probably initiated by the Communists who operated in German-occupied Poland under the name PPR (Polska Partja Robotnicza). The antifascist bloc collapsed in June after two PPR activists were caught by the Gestapo. In a letter of March 29, 1974, to Dawidowicz, Zuckerman confessed that for the sake of harmony he acceded to Adolf Berman's insistence that prominence be given to the antifascist committee in this report. Berman was then—in 1944—a top officer of the Coordinating Committee and of the Jewish National Committee. According to Dawidowicz, Zuckerman

himself did not then or later share Berman's evaluation of that group (Dawidowicz, *Holocaust Reader*, 362n21).

29 See translated in Dawidowicz, *Holocaust Reader*, 363. As Dreifuss argues in *Geto Varsha*, even though the Jewish underground had managed to publish various newspapers in the ghetto, its impact and readership was limited (63).

30 Yitzhak Zuckerman, "The Creation of the Jewish Fighting Organization in the Warsaw Ghetto," in Zuckerman and Basok, *Sefer Milhamot Ha-Getaot*, 104–5; also filed as "Report of the Jewish Fighting Organization," Yad Vashem Archives, O-25/96; and translated in Dawidowicz, *Holocaust Reader*, 364.

31 On September 3, 1942, the Germans arrested Josef Kaplan, a leader of Hashomer Hatzair and one of the founders of the Jewish Fighting Organization, at his workplace at the "Landau shop" and took him to the Pawiak prison. On hearing of the arrest, Breslav decided to go rescue Kaplan and headed out, armed with a switchblade knife. On the way, he was stopped by Germans on Gesia Street, and shot to death. On April 18, 1945, Shmuel Breslav was posthumously awarded the Virtuti Militari Cross, Fifth Class, by the Polish army High Command.

32 Translated in Dawidowicz, *Holocaust Reader*, 370.

33 Dawidowicz also records fifty German dead (but not in original report?), based on Zuckerman and Basok, *Sefer Milhamot Ha-Getaot*. Dawidowicz leaves out names of Zuckerman and other commanders in her excerpt.

34 This is also referenced in GFH Archive 5984 summary of report.

35 Dawidowicz, *Holocaust Reader*, 372–73. According to Dreifuss, *Geto Varsha*, 365, the posters put up by Többens ironically had the unintended consequence of elevating the status of the underground, whose impact until now was limited.

36 Dawidowicz, *Holocaust Reader*, 375. Note again the distinction between ŻOB and the ghetto population; later critics would complain that Antek focused exclusively on ŻOB and not unorganized groups of fighters, but this should not be surprising.

37 Dawidowicz, *Holocaust Reader*, 376.

38 The report was published by Habonim Dror under the title "They Rose in Arms: Defense of the Warsaw Ghetto," *Furrows* 3, no. 6 (April 1945).

39 GFH Archives 5672.

40 After the uprising, Kazik was in charge of leading the remaining ghetto fighters out of the ghetto via the sewers; afterward he organized hiding places for them in the forests and in the city until the end of the war. After the war, he joined Abba Kovner's revenge group, NAKAM.

41 Report also excerpted in Rotem, *Memoirs of a Warsaw Ghetto Fighter*, 155.

42 Complete transcript in text of Claude Lanzmann, *Shoah: The Complete Text of the Acclaimed Holocaust Film (New York: DaCapo Press, 1995)*, 197–200.

43 See the documentary film *The Last Fighters*, dir. Ronen Zaretzky (Jerusalem: Ruth Diskin Films, 2006), which follows Kazik back to the ghetto and includes detailed recollection of this episode.

44 Rotem, *Memoirs of a Warsaw Ghetto Fighter*, 156 (my emphasis).

45 In her translation of Rotem's memoir, Barbara Harshav notes that the mine was prepared by Klepfisz two months before the battle and planted by a Gordonia unit commanded by Eliezer Geller and a No'ar Tzioni unit commanded by Yakov Praszkar, and that Heniek Kleinweiss was especially outstanding at this work.

46 Rotem, *Memoirs of a Warsaw Ghetto Fighter*, 159.

47 Rotem, *Memoirs of a Warsaw Ghetto Fighter*, 162.

48 Rotem, *Memoirs of a Warsaw Ghetto Fighter*, 166.

49 Rotem, *Memoirs of a Warsaw Ghetto Fighter*, 169. He does not describe the incident with Zivia, Marek, and Shlomek in this testimony when the missing ghetto fighters were left behind in the sewer (in fact they are not mentioned by name); in his later memoir (*Memoirs of a Warsaw Ghetto Fighter*, 52–56) he describes the incident in greater detail and the anger of Zivia that he left fifteen fighters in the sewer.

50 Neustadt, *Hurbn un Oyfshtand*, 272–85.

51 "In the central ghetto"—an abbreviated excerpt from the diary Tuvia Borzykowski, GFH Archives 6081. For Tuvia Borzykowski's diary, see GFH Archives 1050. As Dreifuss notes, there are certain components from the diary not included in the subsequent testimony. For example, in his diary he would describe the efforts of ghetto fighters to enter bunkers and the negative responses of those in hiding who feared the fighters

endangered them unnecessarily. These descriptions were removed from the "Central Ghetto" testimony. See Dreifuss, *Geto Varsha*, 398n33.

52 The published version of Borzykowski's testimony, *Between Tumbling Walls* (Tel Aviv; Ghetto Fighters House, 1976) included the period in Warsaw after the revolt: Part 2—diary from the Aryan side (May 17, 1943–July 27, 1944); Part 3—August 1944 revolt; Part 4—In the abyss again, until January 1945 liberation. Also in Neustadt, *Hurbn un Oyfshtand*, 286–92. Neustadt explains that this testimony was included in the May 24, 1944, letter from Warsaw. The original handwritten testimony was lost. The Hebrew edition was translated by Moshe Basok and published in 1950 (*Bein Kirot Noflim*), and went through several printings, with English translations in 1972 and 1976.

53 In *Between Tumbling Walls*, 49: "Monday, April 19, 1943, the eve of Passover, was a beautiful day; the sun lights up the ghetto, penetrating all its dark corners with light. It was the day designated by the Germans for the final liquidation of the Warsaw ghetto. Having spent the night in expectation of tragic events to come, we regret it that the day of the killing of words such as was so beautiful. We felt that nature awakening from its winter sleep was also our enemy."

54 GFH Archives 6081, p. 1. In his account, Borzykowski also cites names of fighters like Yakov, Feivel "shooting from the window with an automatic rifle," Avraham, Moshe, the commander Zechariah who "was everywhere," "Zivia the Brave," and Rivka the "look out."

55 GFH Archives 6081, p. 2.

56 This is likely a reference to the broadcast of SWIAT on the uprising in the ghetto.

57 GFH Archives 6081, p. 4. Dreifuss notes that in the encounter with the Jews in the courtyard of Miła 9, civilians wanted to go with them but the fighters refused, said they were fighters on a mission. Carmi describes firing into the air to get civilians away from them. See Dreifuss, *Geto Varsha*, 433.

58 "Diary of a Boy," in Neustadt, *Ḥurbn un oyfstand*, 301–6; and in Zuckerman and Basok, *Sefer Milhamot Ha-Getaot*, 259–60. The diary was written in April 1944 (according to a footnote of Zuckerman and Basok). The

unnamed author described life in hiding on the Aryan side with another twelve-year-old boy. Eventually they were able to find shelter with the assistance of "Marisza" (Bracha Feinmesser).

59 "Figures of Fighters"—writings of Hirsch Wasser about the part played by Abram Diamant, Szanan [Sha'anan] Lent, and Abram Ajger in the Warsaw ghetto uprising, and on their heroic deaths (in 1943, on May 1, May 3, and May 1 respectively), Adolf-Abraham Berman collection, GFH Archives; also as "Portraits (Silhouettes of Fighters)" and "Soldiers without Weapons" in Neustadt, *Hurbn un Oyfshtand*, 293–306.

60 Kassow, *Who Will Write Our History?*, 1.

61 Kassow, *Who Will Write Our History?*, 150.

62 Hirsch Berlinski was an activist of the leftist Po'alei Zion party and one of the organizers of the Jewish Fighting Organization. During the uprising he commanded a detachment of Po'alei Zion fighters in the ghetto. On May 10, 1943, he escaped to the Aryan side of Warsaw through the sewage system and joined the Jewish Fighting Organization in the forests of Wyszkow. He participated in the Polish uprising and was killed on September 27, 1944, at age forty-eight.

63 Joseph Kermish, ed., *To Live with Honor and Die with Honor! Selected Documents from the Warsaw Ghetto Underground Archives "O.S"* [Oneg Shabbat] (Jerusalem: Yad Vashem, 1986), 604–6.

64 "Soldiers without Weapons"—a description of the resistance activities of the Jewish Fighting Organization [ŻOB] in the Warsaw Ghetto Uprising, GFH Archives 19874; also in Neustadt, *Hurbn un Oyfshtand*, 297.

65 *The Warsaw Ghetto Rising* (Tel Aviv: World Union Poale-Zion [Z.S.]—Hitachduth, February 1944; dated November 1944).

66 See in Porat, *The Blue and Yellow Stars of David*, 29.

67 Porat, *The Blue and Yellow Stars of David*, 29–30, 75.

68 See in Porat, *The Blue and Yellow Stars of David*, 241. Quoting Chaika Klinger of Bedzin, who arrived in Palestine in March 1944, she told the Histadrut executive that: "we received an order (a telegram sent by Tabenkin and Ya'ari ordering youth movement members to save themselves) not to organize any more defense—since those who were still alive were more important to the Yishuv as witnesses of what had happened

to the movement. It was hard for us to accept that kind of thinking. We felt that it was not permissible for us to remain alive because of what the comrades in Warsaw had done . . . nothing could justify us saving ourselves. We decided to prepare to defend ourselves," Histadrut meeting March 15, 1944, in Porat, *The Blue and Yellow Stars of David*, 242. For more background on Klinger see Avihu Ronen, *Condemned to Life: The Diaries and Life of Chaika Klinger* [in Hebrew] (Haifa: Haifa University Press, 2011).

69 Zuckerman, *Surplus of Memory*, 408–9, describes correspondence between the Jewish National Committee and the outside world in 1944.

70 Neustadt, *Warsaw Ghetto Rising*, 5.

71 Neustadt, *Warsaw Ghetto Rising*, 6–7.

72 Neustadt, *Warsaw Ghetto Rising*, 8–10. Moshe Arens points out that these testimonies and ŻOB report began the process of removing the ŻZW and the Revisionists from the historical record—and indeed, the emphasis in these sources is on the connection between the labor Zionists and the ŻOB. Arens points out that Stroop in his report focused on the fighting around Muranowski Square as the most intense of the revolt, in particular the "Battle of the Flags" (the Zionist and the Polish flag, which were raised by the ŻZW). See also Laurence Weinbaum, "Deconstructing Memory and History: The Jewish Military Union (ŻZW) and the Warsaw Ghetto Uprising," *Jewish Political Studies Review* 18, no. 1–2 (2006).

73 Neustadt, *Warsaw Ghetto Rising*, 15.

74 Neustadt, *Warsaw Ghetto Rising*, 20–21.

75 Neustadt, *Warsaw Ghetto Rising*, 28.

76 Neustadt, *Warsaw Ghetto Rising*, 29–30.

Chapter 6. The Place of the Warsaw Ghetto Uprising among the Surviving Population in Europe

1 For more on Lublin after liberation see Lucjan Dobroszycki, *Survivors of the Holocaust in Poland: A Portrait Based on Jewish Community Records 1944–1947* (M. E. Sharpe, 1994), 3–4; see also Bauer and Engel, cited below.

2 See "Jews in the Warsaw Uprising," Jewish Historical Institute, Warsaw, accessed November 21, 2017, https://www.jhi.pl/en/articles/jews-in-the-warsaw-uprising,28.

3 See Adina Blady Szwajger, *I Remember Nothing More: The Warsaw Children's Hospital and the Jewish Resistance* (New York: Pantheon, 1991), 167–69; see also Jewish Historical Institute, Warsaw, https://www.jhi.pl/en/articles/jews-in-the-warsaw-uprising,28.

4 In his memoir, *Surplus of Memory*, Zuckerman also detailed the experience of joining the Armia Ludowa, fighting mainly in the Old Town in the ill-fated revolt that would be brutally suppressed by the Germans (520–63). "Although I knew my place was in the ranks of the AL, I also carried on negotiations with the AK" (523). See also Rotem, *Memoirs of a Warsaw Ghetto Fighter*, 120.

5 Yitzhak Zuckerman read this leaflet at the Eichmann trial, session 25, May 3, 1961. Under questioning from the attorney general, he explained that the leaflet was drafted by Adolf Berman and written by the two of them. Nizkor Project, https://www.nizkor.org/session-025-08-eichmann-adolf/.

6 "Jews Battling Grimly on Streets of Warsaw; Only 200,000 Jews Survive in Poland," August 13, 1944, Jewish Telegraphic Agency, http://pdfs.jta.org/1944/1944-08-13_186.pdf.

7 "Jewish Youths Fighting in Warsaw Streets Call for Urgent Help from London," Daily News Bulletin, August 24, 1944, Jewish Telegraphic Agency, http://pdfs.jta.org/1944/1944-08-24_196.pdf.

8 Meed, *On Both Sides of the Wall*, 254. Eventually (as detailed in the next chapter), Vladka and her husband, Benjamin, realized that Polish antisemitism would make it impossible to remain in Poland and decided to make their way out of Poland to New York in June 1946.

9 See detailed account in Zimmerman, *Polish Underground and Jews*; statistics on p. 408. See "Group portrait of prisoners liberated from the Gesiowka concentration camp by the Zoska battalion of the Polish Home Army during the 1944 Warsaw Uprising," USHMM photo 98679.

10 See in Martin Gilbert, *The Righteous: The Unsung Heroes of the Holocaust* (Toronto: Key Porter, 2003), 152.

11 See in Zimmerman, *The Polish Underground and the Jews*, 410–11.

12 See "Warsaw," United States Holocaust Memorial Museum *Holocaust Encyclopedia*. While as many as 20,000 Jews may have been left in Warsaw after the ghetto revolt, it is not clear how many were killed in 1944 and how many actually managed to survive until the end of the war.

13 Zuckerman, *Surplus of Memory*, 557–58.

14 See in *Surplus of Memory*, 565–67.

15 See dispute between Jacob Pat and Joseph Hyman following complaint from Dr. Schwartzbard that $25,000 also be given to the Coordinating Committee for Labor Zionist groups in Poland: Letter from Jacob Pat to Joseph Hyman, January 2, 1945, JDC Archives, New York, 1945–54, File NY_AR45–54_00082_00678.

16 From the Adolf-Abraham Berman file, GFH Archives 5810.

17 From the Adolf-Abraham Berman file, GFH Archives 5810. Berman informed Gruenbaum that he had instructed people to search for Gruenbaum's son, Eliezer (see Tuvia Friling, *A Kapo in Auschwitz: History, Memory, and the Politics of Survival* [Waltham MA: Brandeis University Press, 2014]).

18 It is difficult to estimate the total number of Polish Jews who survived the Holocaust. The first official body representing Polish Jewry, the Central Committee of Polish Jews (CKZP) registered seventy thousand Jews on liberated Polish territory on June 5, 1945. See Natalia Aleksiun, "Where Was There a Future for Polish Jewry? Bundist and Zionist Polemics in Post–World War II Poland," in Jack Jacobs, ed., *Jewish Politics in Eastern Europe: The Bund at 100* (New York: New York University Press, 2001), 227. See also Morris Fine, ed., *American Jewish Year Book*, vol. 51 (Philadelphia: The Jewish Publication Society of America, 1950).

19 "The Situation of the Jews in Liberated Poland," report from Jerusalem, Jewish Agency, March 23, 1945, HAHP Archives (Gordonia/Maccabi Tzair Archives, 3/111). The document is a summary of reports from Lublin in January 1945.

20 David Engel, *Bein Shichrur Li-Verichah: Nitzulei HaShoah Be-Polin Ve-Hamavak al Hanhagatam, 1944–1946* (Tel Aviv: Amd Oved, 1996), 203–4 n221. On the basis of registrations from Jewish communities where the age

of registrants was noted, he concludes that it would seem that the proportion of youth to the general Jewish population was 10–12 percent.

21 Natalia Aleksiun, "Where Was There a Future for Polish Jewry? Bundist and Zionist Polemics in Post–World War II Poland," 228.

22 Aleksiun, "Where Was There a Future?"

23 See Engel, *Bein Shichrur Li-Verichah*, 73.

24 Engel, *Bein Shichrur Li-Verichah*, 73. See also Lucjan Dobroszycki, "Restoring Jewish Life in Postwar Poland," *Soviet Jewish Affairs* 3, no. 2 (1973): 58–72. Hana Shlomi, "*Hitargenut shel Sridei HaYehudim BePolin LeAchar Milchemet HaOlam HaShniyah, 1944–1950*," in Israel Bartal and Israel Gutman, eds., *Kiyum VaShever: Yehudei Polin LeDoroteihem* (Jerusalem: Shazar Center, 1997), and Natalia Aleksiun, "Where Was There a Future?"

25 David Engel, "The Reconstruction of Jewish Communal Institutions in Postwar Poland: The Origins of the Central Committee of Polish Jews, 1944–1945," *East European Politics and Societies* 10 (1996): 85–107. See also Dobroszycki, "Restoring Jewish Life," 4. The Sejm was the interwar Polish parliament.

26 From 1944–46, Zionists were the majority in the CKZP. By 1946, the CKZP consisted of thirteen Zionists (three Ichud, three Poalei Zion Z.S., three Left Poalei Zion, one Hashomer Hatzair S.Z., two HeHalutz, one Jewish Fighting Organization), four Bundists, six Communists, and two from Union of Jewish Partisans (PHH).

27 Aleksiun, "Where Was There A Future?," 229. Nonetheless, the Zionists themselves did not compose one unified camp. On the contrary, debates existed between the various Zionist groups, with disagreements over the shape and speed of Jewish departure from Poland, as well as the need for organizers required to effect this departure.

28 See in Blatman, *For Our Freedom and Yours*, 166–70.

29 For a detailed analysis of the Bund after 1945, see David Slucki, *The International Jewish Labor Bund after 1945: Toward a Global History* (New Brunswick NJ: Rutgers University Press, 2012).

30 Levi Arieh Sarid, *Be-Mivchan He-Anut*, 198–99; Engel, *Bein Shichrur Li-Verichah*, 69; Yehuda Bauer, *Flight and Rescue: Brichah* (New York: Random House, 1970), 25–29.

31 Kovner, "Reshita shel Ha-Bricha ke-tnuah Hamonit be-eduyotav shel Abba Kovner," *Yalkut Moreshet* 38 (1984); See discussion in Shalom Cholawski, "Partisans and Ghetto Fighters—An Active Element among *She'erit Hapletah*," in Israel Gutman, ed., *She'erit Hapletah, 1944–1948: Rehabilitation and Political Struggle* (Jerusalem: Yad Vashem, 1990), 250.

32 Rotem, *Memoirs of a Warsaw Ghetto Fighter*, 151–52. In his memoirs, Kazik indicates that he hoped to join Kovner in revenge activities in Germany. While this never materialized, he was able to reach Palestine in June 1946 after travel with Aliyah Bet on the ship *Biriya*, and being imprisoned at Atlit for a few weeks upon arrival. According to Dina Porat, *Vengeance and Retribution are Mine: The Yishuv, the Holocaust, and Abba Kovner's* Avengers [in Hebrew] (Haifa: Pardes, 2019), Kazik played a key role in a failed attempt to poison the bread supply at a prison camp near Dachau in April 1946. See also Simhah Rotem Holocaust Testimony, FVAHT Archives, HVT-3439.

33 "Shalom Cholawsky," Moreshet Archives, accessed March 9, 2020, http://www.moreshet.org/?CategoryID=368&ArticleID=729.

34 Shalom Cholawski, "Partisans and Ghetto Fighters," 249–50.

35 Zuckerman, *Surplus of Memory*, 676.

36 "Polish President Says Nation Acknowledges Debt to Heroes of Warsaw Ghetto Revolt," JTA Daily News Bulletin, April 22, 1945, 2, Jewish Telegraphic Agency, http://pdfs.jta.org/1945/1945-04-22_090.pdf.

37 "Polish President Says," Jewish Telegraphic Agency, http://pdfs.jta.org/1945/1945-04-22_090.pdf.

38 "Second Anniversary of Warsaw Ghetto Revolt Marked at Mass Meeting," JTA Daily News Bulletin, April 19, 1945, 3, Jewish Telegraphic Agency, http://pdfs.jta.org/1945/1945-04-19_088.pdf.

39 Organized by A. R. Lerner at Vanderbilt Museum. See in Janina Struk, *Photographing the Holocaust: Interpretations of the Evidence* (London: I. B. Tauris, 2004), 132. From Tamiment website guide to JLC Archives, accessed March 9, 2020, http://dlib.nyu.edu/findingaids/html/tamwag/wag_025_001/bioghist.html. See "Heroes and Martyrs of Europe's Ghettos," YIVO Archives RG 120 US F264. For more on the role of Peter Bergson and his group in raising American public consciousness of Jewish and

Zionist concerns both during and after WWII, see Judith Tydor Baumel, *The "Bergson Boys" and the Origins of Contemporary Zionist Militancy* (Syracuse: Syracuse University Press, 2005).

40 "Heroes and Martyrs," 692–694, JLC Archives reel 32, folder 13.

41 "Heroes and Martyrs," 694, JLC Archives reel 32, folder 13.

42 "Heroes and Martyrs," JLC Archives reel 32, folder 13.

43 "Heroes and Martyrs," 338–39, JLC Archives reel 32, folder 13. See also in Baskind, *Warsaw Ghetto in American Art and Culture*, 56.

44 Letter, DDE to George C. Marshall, April 15, 1945, Papers of Dwight David Eisenhower, The War Years 4, doc. 2418, Eisenhower Presidential Library and Museum, accessed May 30, 2018, https://www.dwightdeisenhower.com/187/Holocaust-Concentration-Camps.

45 See Cable, DDE to George C. Marshall, April 19, 1945, Papers of Dwight David Eisenhower, The War Years 4, doc. 2424, Eisenhower Presidential Library and Museum, accessed May 30, 2018, https://www.dwightdeisenhower.com/187/Holocaust-Concentration-Camps.

46 Jewish Telegraphic Agency, https://www.jta.org/1945/05/08/archive/jews-throughout-the-world-greet-v-e-day-rejoice-at-final-destruction-of-nazism.

47 Jewish Telegraphic Agency, https://www.jta.org/1945/05/08/archive/jews-throughout-the-world-greet-v-e-day-rejoice-at-final-destruction-of-nazism.

48 Mooli Brog, "In Blessed Memory of a Dream: Mordechai Shenhavi and Initial Holocaust Commemoration Ideas in Palestine, 1942–1945," *Yad Vashem Studies* 30 (2002): 297–336.

49 Shenhavi envisioned commemoration buildings, including a Hall of Remembrance, where all remembrance books and "special landmarks" would be placed, and recommended the inclusion of two additional memorial records: for immigrants who had perished en route and for resistance fighters. Brog, "In Blessed Memory of a Dream," 302.

50 Summary of resolutions pertaining to Yad Vashem, meeting in London, August 15, 1945, SZ Archives 14.3–95 (6). See Brog, "In Blessed Memory of a Dream," 297–336.

51 Discussed in Brog and also Eran Neuman, *Shoah Presence: Architectural Representations of the Holocaust* (London: Routledge, 2016) 72–73.

52 Quoted in Brog, "In Blessed Memory of a Dream." Brog notes the document was written in Yiddish; the English translation is based on a translation into Hebrew by Baruch Zuckerman himself, "The Yad Vashem Idea," *Gesher* 4, no. 2 (July 1958): 70–79. The Yiddish original is available under "Le-zikhroyn oylem," New York, February 3, 1945, Yad Vashem Archives, Administrative Archive, file 14.

53 Manifesto from executive organs of JNF and Keren Hayesod to American and Canadian Jewry, Central Zionist Archives, KKL5/12925. See in Brog, "In Blessed Memory of a Dream," 321.

54 Letter from Krakow to Romania, June 20, 1945, in Zuckerman, *Surplus of Memory*, 592–93; also in Zuckerman, *Yetziat Polin: 'al ha-Bricha ve-'al shikum ha-tnu'ah ha-halutsit* (Tel Aviv: Lochamei Hageta'ot, 1988), 86.

55 Letter from Zuckerman to friends in Land of Israel, June 20, 1945 [in Yiddish], GFH Archives 3254. See English translation in Zuckerman, *A Surplus of Memory*, 591. The term *paskudne folk* comes from a speech by Chaim Weizmann: "*A kleyn folk ober a paskudne* (a little nation but a nasty one)." A *sheygetz* refers to a Gentile boy.

56 Letter from Zuckerman, GFH Archives 3254.

57 Letter from Krakow to Romania, June 20, 1945, in Zuckerman, *Surplus of Memory*, 592–93; also in Zuckerman, *Yetziat Polin*, 86.

58 Engel, *Bein Shichrur Li-Verichah*, 96.

59 Speech in London at Zionist Congress, August 5, 1945, in Zuckerman, *Yetziat Polin*, 21.

60 Engel, *Bein Shichrur Li-Verichah*, 84, based on protocols of committees in archives of Mercaz Midah of HAHP.

61 Zuckerman, *Yetziat Polin*, 39–40.

62 Zuckerman, *Yetziat Polin*, 50; see also Zertal. On Guzik, see also "In Memoriam: David Guzik," JDC Archives, http://archives.jdc.org/exhibits/in-memoriam/david-guzik/. See also Yochanan Cohen, *Ovrim Kol Gvul*, 413–17 and Yehuda Bauer, *Out of the Ashes: The Impact of American Jews on Post-Holocaust European Jewry* (New York: Pergamon Press, 1989), 75.

63 Zuckerman, *Surplus of Memory*, 576. "The Joint developed after we brought them money from Romania and after Dr. Joseph Schwartz returned. We

established close ties with him, which lasted long after I left Poland, even in matters not connected with Poland."

64 According to Joseph Schwartz, in June/July 1946, the Joint provided $245,000 to the Bricha, 100,000 specifically to Poland. Bauer estimates that $130,000 in cash went to the Bricha in 1945 from the Joint (with another $370,000 being paid to the CCPJ). See Bauer, *Out of the Ashes*, 77.

65 Table from Yochanan Cohen, *Ovrim kol Gvul: HaBrichah, Polin 1945–1946* (Tel Aviv: Zmora-Bitan, 1995), 469.

66 Cholawski, "Partisans and Ghetto Fighters," 249.

67 Cholawski, "Partisans and Ghetto Fighters," 253–54.

68 Cholawski, "Partisans and Ghetto Fighters," 256.

69 In Cholawski, "Partisans and Ghetto Fighters," 256, citing Pachach newspaper *Munich*, 1947–48.

70 See David Cesarani, "Challenging the Myth of Silence: Postwar Responses to the Destruction of European Jewry," in *After the Holocaust: Challenging the Myth of Silence*, ed. David Cesarani and Eric Sundquist (New York: Routledge, 2012), 17. For example, the August 1, 1946, issue of *Farn Folk*: "How Was the Hymn of the Partisans (Zog nit keyn mol) Created"?

71 "European Conference of the World Jewish Congress, London, August 19–23, 1945," AJA, WJC Collection, box A5, file 5, WJC reports, 1944–45, pp. 223–24, http://collections.americanjewisharchives.org/ms/ms0361/ms0361.A005.005.pdf.

72 "The Conference of Jewish Fighters," *Unzer Veg*, vol. 10, December 7, 1945, 2.

73 Leo Schwarz Papers, YIVO Archives, MK 488, roll 9, folder 57, 584. See also "Analysis of Jewish Population in Bavaria, February 1946," Leo Schwarz Papers roll 9, folder 57, 578.

74 "Analysis of Jewish Population in Bavaria, February 1946," Leo Schwarz Papers roll 9, folder 57, 578. While the country of origin for the majority of the Jewish DP population continued to be Poland, by the end of 1946 there were more Jewish refugees arriving from Hungary and Romania. The term "fresh human element" is from Muentz.

75 YIVO Archives, MK 488, Leo Schwarz Papers roll 9, folder 57, 715.

76 The change of Jewish population in the U.S. zone of Germany from Jan. 1946 to Dec. 31, 1946, AJDC calculations, YIVO Archives, MK 488, Leo Schwarz Papers roll 9, folder 57, 713. Population rose from 39,902 to 145,735 (356 percent increase). See appendix on DP demography and population change.

77 See in Avinoam Patt, *Finding Home and Homeland: Jewish Youth and Zionism in the Aftermath of the Holocaust* (Detroit: Wayne State University Press, 2009). The above-mentioned kibbutz groups were named after individuals who participated in the Jewish resistance during the war. In addition to Mordecai Anielewicz, Tosia Altman, Aryeh Vilner, and Yosef Kaplan in Warsaw, Zvi Brandes (b. September 3, 1917, d. August 7, 1943) organized the efforts of the Jewish Fighting Organization in the Zaglembie region. Chaviva Reik (b. 1914, d. November 20, 1944) was born in Slovakia and emigrated to Palestine in 1939 as a member of Hashomer Hatzair. She volunteered to join the parachutists unit and was dropped over Slovakia on September 21, 1944, where she organized Jewish partisan groups to assist in the Slovak national uprising. She was captured and executed on November 20, 1944, at Kremnica.

78 *Ha-Yoman: Yomano shel Kibbutz Lochamei Ha-Getaot 'al shem Tosia Altman* (Givat Havivah: Yad Ya'ari, 1997), 69. Information on the following kibbutz groups is available at the Hashomer Hatzair archives and in the HAHP Archives (123/Hashomer Hatzair/410):

1. Kibbutz *Mordechai Anielewicz*
2. Kibbutz *Chaviva Reik* in Pocking
3. Kibbutz *Tosia Altman*
4. Kibbutz *Aryeh Vilner*
5. Kibbutz *Yosef Kaplan*
6. Kibbutz *Ma'apilim al shem Zvi Brandes* in Feldafing
7. Kibbutz al shem *Fareinigte Partizaner Organizatye* in Vilna (FPO)
8. Kibbutz *BaDerech*
9. Kibbutz *LaMered*
10. Kibbutz *BaMa'avak*
11. Kibbutz *LeShichrur*
12. Kibbutz *Vatikim* in Herzog (July 1946)

13. Kibbutz *Vatikim in Schlifing* (older kibbutz with families)
14. Kibbutz *Bachazit* (older kibbutz with couples and babies)

(There was apparently another kibbutz named after *Shmuel Breslaw* but correspondence between it and the central leadership is not available).

79 Ze'ev Mankowitz, *Life between Memory and Hope: The Survivors of the Holocaust in Occupied Germany* (Cambridge: Cambridge University Press, 2002), 209.

80 Mankowitz, *Life between Memory and Hope*, 209. Mankowitz cites an editorial from the DP newspaper *Unzer Veg*, "Zakhor," vol. 32 (May 10, 1946), 1.

81 Laura Jockusch, *Collect and Record!: Jewish Holocaust Documentation in Early Postwar Europe* (New York: Oxford University Press, 2012), 140, cites Ada Schein, "Everyone Can Hold a Pen: The Documentation Project in the DP Camps in Germany," in David Bankier and Dan Michman, eds., *Holocaust Historiography in Context: Emergence, Challenges, Polemics, and Achievements* (Jerusalem: Yad Vashem, 2008), 126–28.

82 See my article on Abraham Klausner's central role in the postwar organization of the Jewish DP camps, "The People Must Be Forced to Go to Palestine: Rabbi Abraham Klausner and the Surviving Remnant in Postwar Germany," *Holocaust and Genocide Studies* 28, no. 2 (2014): 240–76.

83 See in *Unzer Veg*, vol. 29, April 19, 1946.

84 "A Mitbateilikte Dertsaylt," *Unzer Veg*, vol. 29, April 19, 1946, 3.

85 Mankowitz, "Zionism and the She'erit Hapletah" in Yisrael Gutman and Avital Saf, eds., *She'erit Hapletah, 1944–1948: Rehabilitation and Political Struggle* (Jerusalem: Yad Vashem, 1990), 218; cites Gringauz article, "The Warsaw Uprising, The Age-Old Chain of Jewish Heroism," in *Yiddishe Tsaytung*, no. 29 (97) April 8, 1947, 4.

86 Levi Shalitan, "From Our Agenda: From Masada to Warsaw—The Chain Is Yet Unbroken," *Unzer Veg*, vol. 29, April 19, 1946, 2. Quoted in Mankowitz, "Zionism and the She'erit Hapletah," 219.

87 Levi Shalitan, "Warsaw as a Symbol," in *Dos Fraye Vort*, vols. 29–30, May 3, 1946, 7. Quoted in Zeev Mankowitz, *Life between Memory and Hope: The Survivors of the Holocaust in Occupied Germany* (New York: Cambridge University Press, 2002), 209.

88 Moshe Shertok in *Dos Fraye Vort*, May 3, 1946, 3.

89 See opposing viewpoint of Dr. Wiederman in "The Cult of Heroism," *Dos Fraye Vort*, Sept. 29, 1946.

90 *Unzer Veg*, May 10, 1946, 5.

91 "Anglo-American Sub-Committee Tours Warsaw Ghetto," JTA Daily News Bulletin, February 12, 1946, 1, Jewish Telegraphic Agency, http://pdfs.jta.org/1946/1946-02-12_036.pdf.

92 "Surviving Polish Jews Pay Tribute to Warsaw Heroes on Anniversary of Ghetto Battle," Jewish Telegraphic Agency, https://www.jta.org/1946/04/21/archive/surviving-polish-jews-pay-tribute-to-warsaw-heroes-on-anniversary-of-ghetto-battle.

93 *Dos Naye Lebn*, no. 13 (38), May 1946, 2.

94 "Speech of Yitzhak Zuckerman" in *Dos Naye Lebn*, no. 13 (38), 2.

95 "At the Open Grave of Our Comrades—Heroes of the Warsaw Ghetto Uprising," vol. 1 of *Folkstsaytung*, April 1946, 4; see Slucki, *The International Jewish Labor Bund after 1945: Toward a Global History* (New Brunswick NJ: Rutgers University Press, 2012), 59.

96 "At the Open Grave of our Comrades—Heroes of the Warsaw Ghetto Uprising," vol. 1 of *Folkstsaytung*, April 1946, 4.

97 *Hashomer Hatzair*, vol. 2, April 1946, YIVO Library.

98 Hirsh Glik, "Zog nit Keyn Mol [Never say]," song of the Partisans.

99 *Varsheyer Geṭo oyfshṭand* [Warsaw Ghetto Uprising], 19ṭer April, 1943—19ṭer April, 1947 (Landsberg: Poalei Zion ZS and Dror), 66 pages. Yiddish Book Center Steven Spielberg Digital Yiddish Library, http://www.yiddishbookcenter.org/collections/yiddish-books/spb-nybc210858/varshever-geto-oyfshtand-19ter-april-1943-19ter-april-1947/spb-nybc210858.

100 Cholawski, "Partisans and Ghetto Fighters," 256. See also Yad Vashem Archives, file O.300/55.

101 *Pachach Bulletin in Germany* (Munich), 10/11 (26/27), April 4, 1947, "Dedicated to Warsaw Ghetto Uprising (Erev Pesach)."

102 Dir. and written by Chaim Grade, narrated by Naftali Radenbloom, YouTube, https://www.youtube.com/watch?v=csNnGkC5DJs; USHMM Archives, RG-60.1477 "Warsaw ghetto uprising and postwar immigration

to Israel," https://collections.ushmm.org/search/catalog/irn1004749. Footage of the return of displaced persons to Poppendorf and Jewish youths marching to a memorial ceremony in Warsaw (before the Rapoport statue was erected in April 19, 1948) indicate the film was produced in the latter half of 1947, but before April 1948.

103 According to Meng, *Shattered Spaces*, 124, in 1947, the CKŻP "reinforced this broad message of left-wing heroism by announcing the change of two prominent street names in Muranów: Nalewki street, the heart of the Jewish district's once bustling economic life, was renamed The Ghetto Fighters' Street, and Gęsia street was now called Mordechai Anielewicz street after the leader of the ŻOB." See Marci Shore, "Język, pamięć i rewolucyjna awangarda. Kształtowanie historii powstania w Getcie Warszawskim w latach 1944–1950," *Biuletyn Żydowskiego Instytutu Historycznego* (December 1998): 48.

Chapter 7. The First Published Testimonies of the Surviving Ghetto Fighters

1 Christopher Browning, *Remembering Survival: Inside a Nazi Slave Labor Camp* (New York: Norton, 2010).

2 Jennifer Schuessler, "Survivor Who Hated the Spotlight," *New York Times*, https://www.nytimes.com/2014/11/11/arts/survivor-who-hated-the-spotlight.html?_r=0.

3 Zoe Waxman, *Writing the Holocaust: Identity, Testimony, Representation* (New York: Oxford University Press, 2008), 103 notes the significance of translation from Yiddish and Hebrew texts to English soon after the war—e.g., Borzykowski, Goldstein, Pat, Turkow—all texts dealing specifically with Warsaw.

4 Amos Goldberg, *Trauma in the First Person: Diary-Writing during the Shoah* [in Hebrew] (Or Yehuda: Kinneret Zmora-Bitan Dvir and Ben-Gurion University, 2012). See my review of Goldberg, "'Consider If This Is a Man': Trauma and Diary-Writing during the Shoah," *Yad Vashem Studies* 41, no. 2 (2013).

5 A recently republished version of Edelman's *The Ghetto Fights*, with helpful context and analysis, is Michał Trębacz, ed., *Getto walczy: udział Bundu w*

obronie getta warszawskiego [The Ghetto Fights: The Bund's participation in the defense of the Warsaw Ghetto] (Lodz: Marek Edelman Center, 2015), 65–71.

6 A short excerpt was translated into Hebrew by Zuckerman in Zuckerman and Basok, *Sefer Milhamot*, 168–70.

7 See Katarzyna Zechenter, "Marek Edelman," in *Holocaust Literature*, vol. 1, ed. S. Lillian Kremer (New York: Routledge, 2003).

8 Marek Edelman, *The Ghetto Fights* (New York: American Representation of the General Jewish Workers' Union of Poland, May 1946; Warsaw: Central Committee of the Bund, 1945 [in Polish]). Zofia Nalkowska (1884–1954) was a prominent Polish writer, executive member of the prestigious Polish Academy of Literature in the interwar period.

9 Edelman, *Ghetto Fights*, 18.

10 In Hannah Krall, *Shielding the Flame: An Intimate Conversation with Dr. Marek Edelman, The Last Surviving Leader of the Warsaw Ghetto Uprising* (New York: Henry Holt and Company, 1986), 9.

11 Edelman, *Ghetto Fights*, 26–27.

12 Edelman, *Ghetto Fights*, 27.

13 Edelman, *Ghetto Fights*, 36–37.

14 See Zuckerman, *A Surplus of Memory*, 592–93.

15 Orly Lubin, "Holocaust Testimony, National Memory," in *Extremities: Trauma Testimony and Memory* (Champaign: University of Illinois Press, 2002), 131.

16 Sharon Geva, "'With and Despite the Burden of the Past': 1946 in the Life Story of Zivia Lubetkin," *Moreshet: Journal for the Study of the Holocaust and Anti-Semitism* 14 (2017): 220.

17 Geva, "'With and Despite the Burden of the Past'," 220.

18 Geva, "'With and Despite the Burden of the Past'," 231.

19 Gutterman, *Fighting for Her People*, 355.

20 From Hanoch Bartov, *Dado: Forty-Eight Years and Another Twenty Days* [in Hebrew], part 1 (Tel Aviv: Ma'ariv, 1978), 261; quoted in Gutterman, *Fighting for Her People*, 356.

21 Gutterman, *Fighting for Her People*, 359. As Sharon Geva's research has shown, the timing of Lubetkin's testimony enabled Kibbutz HaMeuchad

to make a leadership claim after the split from Hashomer Hatzair ("With and Despite the Burden of the Past," 236).

22 In Gutterman, *Fighting for Her People*, 362–63, from "Zivia Lubetkin Demands Solace on Behalf of the Diaspora," *Ma'ariv* (n.d.).

23 According to *Mishmar*, June 9, 1946, 4. See Dina Porat, "First Testimonies on the Holocaust," in Dan Michman and David Bankier, eds., *Holocaust Historiography in Context* (Jerusalem: Yad Vashem, 2008), 437. Gutterman cites the *Kibbutz Yagur Bulletin*, June 11, 1946, which counted 6,000 attendees at the conference.

24 Porat, "First Testimonies on the Holocaust," 450.

25 See Zivia Lubetkin, *Biyemei Kilayon UMered* (Tel Aviv: Hakibbutz Hameuhad, 1989), 194, and Neima Barzel, *Sacrifice UnRedeemed: The Encounter between the Leaders of the Ghetto Fighters and Israeli Society* (Jerusalem: HaSifriya Hatziyonit, 1998), 151.

26 Gutterman, *Fighting for Her People*, 367, from *Kibbutz Yagur Bulletin*, June 11, 1946.

27 Zivia Lubetkin, *Aharonim al Ha-Homah*, remarks at the 15th Conference of the Kibbutz HaMeuchad at Yagur, June 8, 1946 (Yagur: HaKibbutz HaMeuchad, 1947).

28 Lubetkin, *Aharonim al Ha-Homa, 3.*

29 Lubetkin, *Aharonim al Ha-Homa*, 4.

30 Lubetkin, *Aharonim al Ha-Homa*, 5.

31 Lubetkin, *Aharonim al Ha-Homa*, 15.

32 Lubetkin, *Aharonim al Ha-Homa*, 20.

33 Lubetkin, *Aharonim al Ha-Homa*, 27. In her Eichmann trial testimony she says this happened on the second day of the revolt and that Rabbi Meisels blessed them; corroborated by Borzykowski, *Between Tumbling Walls*, 57–58.

34 Lubetkin, *Aharonim al Ha-Homa*, 34.

35 Haim Frimer. During the Warsaw ghetto uprising of April 1943 he fought in the combat unit commanded by Berl Broyde, and afterward was in the headquarters bunker at 18 Mila Street. Frimer escaped the fate of his comrades who fell there on May 8, 1943, because on that date he was on a mission outside the bunker. Upon suppression of the uprising, he and others left

the ghetto via the sewers to the Aryan side of Warsaw, went to the Lomianki Forest, and joined the Jewish partisans in the Wyszkow Forest to fight the Germans. See Ghetto Fighters House Archives, http://www.infocenters.co.il/gfh/notebook_ext.asp?book=28995&lang=eng&site=gfh.

36 Lubetkin, *Aharonim al Ha-Homa*, 37. Zivia notes they had a plan in case captured by Germans to send nonfighters out and mingle with them and then ambush Germans so all could escape from the bunker. The other plan discussed was to post guards by the entrances to the bunkers in case the Germans tried to enter. But there Germans did not try to enter.

37 This contradicts Edelman's account, who mentions the story of Lutek Rotblat, who killed his mother, his sister, and then himself.

38 Lubetkin, *Aharonim al Ha-Homah*, 44.

39 Lubetkin, *Aharonim al Ha-Homah*, 50. As Dina Porat's research on Abba Kovner's revenge group demonstrates, some survivors, including members of the fighting underground and the partisans, felt an obligation to avenge the death of the six million before they could continue with their lives.

40 Quoted in the movie *Blue Bird*; cited in Gutterman, *Fighting for Her People*, 374.

41 Nathan Cohen, "Borekh, Shefner," in *YIVO Encyclopedia of Eastern Europe*, http://www.yivoencyclopedia.org/article.aspx/Shefner_Borekh. Shefner managed to escape Warsaw in the first week of September 1939 and reached Vilna. He left Europe in 1940 and arrived in New York in 1941. There he regularly contributed to the *Forverts* and published *Novolipie 7* (1955)—the title being the address of the *Folks-tsaytung* editorial board, which celebrated the lives of the proletarian Jews of Warsaw, who used to gather there regularly.

42 B. Shefner, "Vladka—A Heroine of the Warsaw Ghetto," *Forverts*, June 1, 1946.

43 See also JLC Archives, http://dlib.nyu.edu/findingaids/html/tamwag/wag_025_003/dscref3256.html, and Vladka Meed papers there, JLC Tamiment documents/JLC Tamiment Vladka Meed files/Letter from Vladka to J Pat.pdf. In New York, Benjamin launched his own fur business, while Vladka began writing for the *Forward*. They had two children, Anna (b. 1948) and Steven (b. 1950). When the Miedzyrzeckis were sworn in as

American citizens in the early 1950s they formally changed their names to Benjamin and Vladka Meed. The first edition of Vladka Meed's memoir, *Fun Beyde Zaytn Geto Moyer* was published in New York by the Workmen's Circle in 1948; subsequently published in English as *On Both Sides of the Wall: Memoirs from the Warsaw Ghetto* (New York: Holocaust Library, 1993).

44 USHMMA Archives RG-50.165.0074_trs_en VLADKA MEED.pdf.

45 Rochelle Saidel, "Vladka Meed," in S. Lillian Kremer, ed., *Holocaust Literature: An Encyclopedia of Writers and Their Work* (New York: Routledge, 2003), 819.

46 Vladka starts her "testimony" in August 1942 (this differs from the book version of the memoir [1948], which starts on July 22 and also describes the capture of her own family in greater detail).

47 *Forverts*, June 29, 1946, 2. In Vladka Meed, *On Both Sides of the Wall* (Washington, DC: Holocaust Library, 1993), 47.

48 *Forverts*, July 6, 1946, 2.

49 *Forverts*, July 6, 1946, 7.

50 *Forverts*, September 21, 1946, 2.

51 Meed, *On Both Sides of the Wall (Yiddish)*, 176.

52 *Forverts*, September 21, 1946, 2. Note the book version of *On Both Sides of the Wall* has a description of how Klepfisz died (English version, 142), but not in *Forverts*.

53 *Forverts*, September 21, 1946, 7.

54 Compare *On Both Sides of the Wall* (English version, 147), where this rebuke is absent.

55 In the Yiddish version of the memoir (188), Kazik's party affiliation is not mentioned. Compare Kazik's original report sent from Warsaw on May 24, 1944 (in Simcha Rotem, *Memoirs of a Warsaw Ghetto Fighter* [New Haven CT: Yale University Press, 1994], 163), which does not mention Vladka; he does mention her in the 1994 version of the memoir (in Rotem, *Memoirs of a Warsaw Ghetto Fighter*, 46), which also covers the brushmakers area of revolt and Abrasha Blum and Marek Edelman.

56 See *On Both Sides of the Wall* (Yiddish version, 200; English version, 155).

57 See Philip Friedman and Koppel S. Pinson, "Some Books on the Jewish Catastrophe," *Jewish Social Studies* 12, no. 1 (1950): 83–94.

Chapter 8. Literary and Artistic Representations before the Fifth Anniversary of the Revolt

1 Yael Zerubavel, *Recovered Roots: Collective Memory and the Making of Israeli National Tradition* (Chicago: University of Chicago Press, 1995), 5.

2 See Maurice Hawlbachs, *On Collective Memory* (Chicago: University of Chicago Press, 1992). Originally published as *Les cadres sociaux de la mémoire*, Paris, 1925.

3 The itinerary for many of these visits to Europe also included a stop in the DP camps in postwar Germany. For more on this genre of postwar travel literature, see Monika Adamczyk-Garbowska, "Patterns of Return: Survivors' Postwar Journeys to Poland," Ina Levine Annual Lecture, February 15, 2007, United States Holocaust Memorial Museum, Center for Advanced Holocaust Studies, https://www.ushmm.org/m/pdfs/Publication_OP_2007-10.pdf; and Jack Kugelmass, "Sifting the Ruins: Émigré Jewish Journalists' Return Visits to the Old Country, 1946–1948," David W. Belin Lecture in American Jewish Affairs, vol. 23 (2013), University of Michigan Library, https://quod.lib.umich.edu/b/belin/13469761.0023.001/-sifting-the-ruins-emigre-jewish-journalists-return-visits?rgn=main;view=fulltext.

4 S. L. Shneiderman, *Tsvishn shrek un hofenung: A rayze iber dem nayem Poyln* (Buenos Aires: Tsentral farband fun poylishn Yidn in Argentina, 1947), 50–52, 62. See as quoted in Adamczyk-Garbowska and Kuglemass, *Sifting the Ruins*.

5 Published in Yiddish in 1946 by the Central Yiddish Culture Organization and in English as *Ashes and Fire: On the Ruins of Poland* (New York: International Universities Press, 1947). See Pat, *Ash un Fayer*, 385. See discussion of Pat's travelogue in Michael Meng, "Traveling to Germany and Poland," in Norman Goda, ed. *Jewish Histories of the Holocaust* (New York: Berghahn, 2014), who notes the travelogue must also be read as "an account of emotions expressed by an involved eyewitness," 269.

6 Hal Lehrman, review of *Ashes and Fire*, by Jacob Pat, *Commentary*, July 1, 1948, https://www.commentarymagazine.com/articles/hal-lehrman/ashes-and-fire-by-jacob-pat/.

7 Lehrman, review of *Ashes and Fire*, https://www.commentarymagazine.com/articles/ashes-and-fire-by-jacob-pat/.

8 Pat, *Ash un Fayer*, p. 14.

9 Zvi Kolitz, *Yosl Rakover Talks to God* (New York: Vintage Books, 1999). See introduction by Paul Baade, 50–53. In 1954, *Di Goldene Keyt*, a Yiddish quarterly in Tel Aviv, ran *Yosl Rakover* as an authentic document. The next year, it was broadcast on a Berlin radio station, and was run in the Parisian Zionist journal *La Terre Retrouvée*.

10 Kolitz, *Yosl Rakover Talks to God*; see Paul Baade introduction, 39–41.

11 Kolitz, *Yosl Rakover Talks to God*, 53.

12 See in Gutterman, *Fighting for Her People*, 399–403.

13 *Palestine Post*, April 30, 1947, 3.

14 "Yitzhak Zuckerman in the Land of Israel," *Davar*, April 30, 1947, 8.

15 In "Dapim: HaKibbutz HaMeuchad, Yoman Kibbutz Lochamei HaGetaot," dedicated to Yitzhak Zuckerman after his death, 1981, 61. Reprinted in Zuckerman and Basok, *Sefer Milhamot*, 109–16.

16 Zuckerman, May 9–10, 1947; reprinted in "Dapim: HaKibbutz HaMeuchad," 64.

17 Gutterman, *Fighting for Her People*, 413. See discussion in Tom Segev, *The Seventh Million: The Israelis and the Holocaust* (New York: Hill and Wang, 1993), 449–55. According to Neima Barzel, *Sacrifice Unredeemed: The Encounter Between the Leaders of the Ghetto Fighters and Israeli Society* [in Hebrew] (Jerusalem: The Zionist Library, 1998), survivors chose the name themselves. Kazik arrived in June 1946 after participating in the attempted mass revenge plan in German in April 1946.

18 See Neima Barzel, *Sacrifice Unredeemed*, for example.

19 See Henry Feingold, "Who Shall Bear Guilt for the Holocaust?," in Jonathan Sarna, ed., *The American Jewish Experience* (New York: Holmes and Meier, 1997).

20 See "International Workers Order (IWO) and Jewish People's Fraternal Order (JFPO)," Cornell University Library, Digital Collections, accessed August 8, 2020.

21 In 1950, Fast was called before the House Committee on Un-American Activities and imprisoned for refusing to name other Communist party

members. See Gerald Sorin, *Howard Fast: Life and Literature in the Left Lane* (Bloomington: Indiana University Press, 2012).

22 Baskind, *Warsaw Ghetto in American Art and Culture*, 24.

23 Fast and Gropper, *Never to Forget* (New York: Book League of the Jewish People's Fraternal Order, 1946), 2. In comparison, the epic poem written by Simon Hochberger, *Warsaw Ghetto: Tale of Valor* (Melbourne: Oyfboy, 1946) concludes "the soul of man pay homage to the memory / Of Warsaw's gallant Jews, / And from the hearts of every Jew in all the world / A holy vow descends upon the nameless graves / And rises to the Heavens high: / *Their Sacrifice Shall Not Have Been in Vain! The Jews of Warsaw Died That Israel May Live!*," 35–36.

24 Paul Muni also performed a reading of the ŻOB manifesto at the April 19, 1945, opening of the Jewish Labor Committee exhibition on the Warsaw ghetto. JLC reel 32, folder 13, "Heroes and Martyrs," 338–39. See also in Baskind, *Warsaw Ghetto in American Art and Culture*, 56.

25 See AJHS Archives, records of the American League for a Free Palestine, I-278, https://archives.cjh.org/repositories/3/resources/1634. See also Judith Tydor Baumel, *The "Bergson Boys" and the Origins of Contemporary Zionist Militancy* (Syracuse NY: Syracuse University Press, 2005), 219.

26 Edna Nachshon, "From Geopathology to Redemption: A Flag Is Born on the Broadway Stage," *Kurt Weill Newsletter* 20 (Spring 2002): 5–8, https://www.kwf.org/images/newsletter/kwn201p1-24.pdf#page=5.

27 Stuart Schiffman, "A Stone for His Slingshot," in *Jewish Review of Books*, accessed March 14, 2020, http://jewishreviewofbooks.com/articles/735/a-stone-for-his-slingshot/.

28 See for example *The Jewish Floridian*, September 27, 1946; see also USHMM Library, "The Battle of the Warsaw Ghetto, April 19–June 1, 1943," *Materials for Commemorative Programs on the Anniversary of the Uprising* (New York: Farband of the Labor Zionist Order, n.d.), 62.

29 Jeremy Adam Eichler, "The Emancipation of Memory: Arnold Schoenberg and the Creation of 'A Survivor from Warsaw'," abstract, Columbia University Academic Commons, 2015, https://doi.org/10.7916/D8SB44TJ.

30 Eichler, "The Emancipation of Memory."

31 Marie Syrkin Papers at the AJA Archives, no. 615, http://collections.americanjewisharchives.org/ms/ms0615/ms0615.html#series7.

32 Carole Kessner, "Marie Syrkin," in *Encyclopedia of Jewish Women*, Jewish Women's Archive, https://jwa.org/encyclopedia/article/syrkin-marie.

33 Quoted in Kessner, "Marie Syrkin." As she wrote in the *Jewish Frontier*: "It is a policy of systematic murder of innocent civilians which in its ferocity, its dimensions and its organization is unique in the history of mankind" (November 1942). In 1944 Syrkin also wrote a widely acclaimed book on the American public school system, *Your School, Your Children*.

34 Kessner, "Marie Syrkin." In 1950, Syrkin became the first female professor in an academic discipline at the newly established Brandeis University, where she joined the English faculty and developed the first university course in Holocaust literature and American Jewish fiction.

35 Syrkin, *Blessed Is the Match*, 3–5.

36 Syrkin, *Blessed Is the Match*, 6–7.

37 Syrkin, *Blessed Is the Match*, 24.

38 Syrkin, *Blessed Is the Match*, 147.

39 Syrkin, *Blessed Is the Match*, 162.

40 Syrkin, *Blessed Is the Match*, 168–69.

41 Syrkin, *Blessed Is the Match*, 176.

42 See Aviva Halamish, *The Exodus Affair: Holocaust Survivors and the Struggle for Palestine* (Syracuse NY: Syracuse University Press, 1998).

43 Meyer Levin, review of *Blessed Is the Match*, by Marie Syrkin, *Commentary*, July 1, 1947, accessed March 19, 2020, https://www.commentarymagazine.com/articles/blessed-is-the-match-by-marie-syrkin/.

44 Levin, review of *Blessed Is the Match*.

45 *Furrows*, April 1947.

46 "Memorial to 6,000,000 Murdered Jews of Europe Will Be Erected in New York," Jewish Telegraphic Agency, June 19, 1947, http://pdfs.jta.org/1947/1947-06-19_144.pdf.

47 American Memorial to Six Million Jews of Europe, YIVO Archives RG 1206; see discussion in James Young, *The Texture of Memory: Holocaust Memorials and Meaning* (New Haven: Yale University Press, 1993), 287–89.

48 See in Young, *Texture of Memory*, 288. Young cites an unpublished manuscript of A. R. Lerner, "The Case of the Memorial," Schneiderman Archives, YIVO Archives. Young, 369n4.

49 American Memorial, YIVO Archives RG 1206, folder 2.

50 American Memorial, YIVO Archives.

51 American Memorial, YIVO Archives.

52 Young, *Texture of Memory*, 290.

53 See Avinoam Patt, "Visions of Israel: The Art and Illustrations of Chaim Gross," exhibit catalog, Museum of Jewish Civilization, University of Hartford (CT), April 2013.

54 Hasia Diner, *We Remember with Reverence and Love: American Jews and the Myth of Silence after the Holocaust, 1945–1962* (New York: NYU Press, 2009), 26. See also Rochelle Saidel, *Never Too Late to Remember: The Politics behind New York City's Holocaust Museum* (New York: Holmes and Meier, 1996).

55 Joseph Kermish, *Der Oyfshtand in varshever geto* (Buenos Aires: Tsentral Farband fun Poylishe Yidn in Argentina, 1948).

56 Carrie Friedman-Cohen, "Rokhl Auerbach," in *Encyclopedia of Jewish Women*, Jewish Women's Archive, https://jwa.org/encyclopedia/article/auerbakh-rokhl. For more on Auerbach's work at Yad Vashem, see in particular Boaz Cohen, "Rachel Auerbach, Yad Vashem, and Israeli Holocaust memory," *Polin* 20 (2008): 197–211.

57 Batia Donner, *Natan Rapoport: A Jewish Artist* [in Hebrew] (Jerusalem: Yad Ben Tzvi and Yad Ya'ari, 2014), 82–83.

58 Yisrael Barzilai, *Mishmar*, April 19, 1947, in Donner, *Natan Rapoport*, 83–84.

59 James Young, "The Biography of a Memorial Icon: Nathan Rapoport's Warsaw Ghetto Monument," *Representations* 26, Special Issue: Memory and Counter-Memory (Spring 1989): 69–106. See also Nathan Rapoport personal archives (RG-95–80), USHMM Archives RG-68.182.

60 According to this JDC document, the cost was at least 2.2 million francs, approximately $733,000 in 1949; JDC Archives, http://search.archives.jdc.org/multimedia/Documents/Geneva45-54/G45-54_Count/G45-54_PL_003/G45-54_PL_003_0412.pdf#search=. See Donner, *Natan Rapoport*, 92–93 for a detailed discussion of expenses for monument.

61 Ultimately, the Muranow district would be transformed into a socialist-realist housing district. See discussion in Meng, *Shattered Spaces*, 133. Donner notes in detail the considerations involved over the ideal spot for the monument, along with Marek Edelman's objection to placing the monument at Mila 18: *Natan Rapoport*, 87.

62 From Young, "Biography of a Memorial Icon," 82.

63 Quoted in Young, *Texture of Memory*, 168–69.

64 Cited in Donner, *Natan Rapoport*, 103, from an autobiographical text in Rapoport papers, SZ Archives (written in New York, 1978).

65 Donner, *Natan Rapoport*, 105.

66 "Members of Polish Cabinet Attend Unveiling of Warsaw Memorial to Ghetto Fighters," Jewish Telegraphic Agency, April 20, 1948, accessed March 16, 2020, http://www.jta.org/1948/04/20/archive/bers-of-polish-cabinet-attend-unveiling-of-warsaw-memorial-to-ghetto-fighters.

67 Ibid. For a detailed description of the ceremony, see Donner, *Natan Rapoport*, 119–30.

68 Adolf Berman, "Rocznica wielkiego czynu," *Przełom*, April 19, 1948, 1. Quoted in Meng, *Shattered Spaces*, 128; see Marci Shore, "Children of the Revolution: Communism, Zionism, and the Berman Brothers," *Jewish Social Studies*, n.s., 10, no. 3 (2004): 23–86.

69 "Members of Polish Cabinet Attend Unveiling of Warsaw Memorial to Ghetto Fighters," Jewish Telegraphic Agency.

70 Donner, *Natan Rapoport*, 126, citing autobiographical text in Rapoport papers, SZ Archives.

71 See film from fifth anniversary dedication ceremony, produced by Shaul Goskind and Natan Gross, narrated in Yiddish by Binem Heller, YouTube, accessed April 12, 2018 https://www.youtube.com/watch?v=2ojWM-OMVOQ.

72 Donner, *Natan Rapoport*, 126, based on a protocol of the Central Committee of Polish Jews, ZIH Archive.

73 See Young, *Texture of Memory*, 170.

74 Young, *Texture of Memory*, 170.

75 Donner, 140–41. Both Donner and Mooli Brog in an earlier article on the monument "'Nitsurim be-homot ha-zikaron:' The Warsaw ghetto

memorial as a symbol of destruction and heroism in Poland and Israel" [in Hebrew] (*Alpayim* 14 [1997]: 148–73) note the similarities between Rapoport's monument and François Rude's *The Departure of the Volunteers of 1792* (a.k.a. *La Marseillaise)* visible on the Arc de Triomphe in Paris. See also "Rapoport's Memorial to the Warsaw Ghetto Uprising—A Personal Interpretation," accessed April 2018, https://www.yadvashem.org/articles/general/warsaw-memorial-personal-interpretation.html, for a fine detailed analysis of the monument.

Chapter 9. Warsaw in Israel and America, 1948–53

1 "The Declaration of the Establishment of Israel," Provisional Government of Israel, *Official Gazette* 1, 5 Iyar 5708 / May 14, 1948, p. 1; Knesset, https://www.knesset.gov.il/docs/eng/megilat_eng.htm.

2 See M. Larkin, *The Six Days of Yad-Mordechai* (Givatayim: Peli Printing Works, 1970), 68–71.

3 See in Benny Morris, *Righteous Victims: A History of the Zionist-Arab Conflict, 1881–1999* (New York: Knopf, 1999), 228.

4 See Dina Porat, *The Fall of a Sparrow: The Life and Times of Abba Kovner*, trans. Elizabeth Yuval (Palo Alto, CA: Stanford University Press, 2000) and Michal Arbell, "Abba Kovner: The Ritual Function of His Battle Missives," *Jewish Social Studies* 18, no. 3 (2012): 99–119. On Kovner and revenge, see Dina Porat, *Vengeance and Retribution Are Mine: The Yishuv, the Shoah, and Abba Kovner's Avengers* [in Hebrew] (Haifa: Haifa University Press, 2019).

5 Arbell, "Abba Kovner," 108–9.

6 Emmanuel Sivan, *Dor Tashakh: Mitos, Diyukan ve-Zikaron* (Tel Aviv, Israel: Ministry of Defense, 1991), 76.

7 Hanna Yablonka, *Survivors of the Holocaust: Israel after the War* (New York: New York University Press, 1999), 114.

8 Gutterman, *Fighting for Her People*, 410.

9 *Davar*, April 19, 1949, 1.

10 See Micha Balf, *Unsilenced Voices: Memory and Commemoration of the Holocaust in the Kibbutz Movement* [in Hebrew] (Tel Aviv, Hakibbutz

HaMeuchad, 2008) (Hebrew), 29, and in Gutterman, *Fighting for Her People*, 418.

11 Jacob Pat originally helped them reach Sweden; she had family in Australia and arrived in New York on a transit visa bound for Melbourne, but after connecting with a relative of her late husband, decided to remain in New York where she settled in the Amalgamated Housing in the Bronx, warmly welcomed by many other Bundists. *Forverts, Yiddish Daily Forward*, http://yiddish.forward.com/articles/195915/rose-klepfisz-has-died/.

12 Deborah Lipstadt, *Holocaust: An American Understanding* (New Brunswick NJ: Rutgers University Press, 2016), 32.

13 John Hersey to Mark Nowogrodzki, Oct. 13, 1949, letter in the personal collection of Mark Nowogrodzki, 3. See in Nancy Sinkoff, "Fiction's Archive: Authenticity, Ethnography, and Philosemitism in John Hersey's *The Wall*." *Jewish Social Studies: History, Culture, Society*, n.s., 17, no. 2 (2011): 52–53.

14 Sinkoff, "Fiction's Archive," 67.

15 Sinkoff, "Fiction's Archive," 70. See also Naomi Seidman, "Elie Wiesel and the Scandal of Jewish Rage," *Jewish Social Studies* 3, no. 1 (1996): 1–19.

16 See Eliezer Don-Yehiyeh, "Memory and Political Culture: The Holocaust and Israeli Society," in *Studies in Contemporary Jewry*, vol. 9 (Institute for Contemporary Jewry in the Hebrew University of Jerusalem and Oxford University Press, 1993), 139.

17 For more details on the present location of the forest, see Keren Kayemeth LeIsrael, Jewish National Fund, http://www.kkl-jnf.org/tourism-and-recreation/forests-and-parks/martyrs-forest.aspx. The forest would also become the site of the monument "Scroll of Fire," created by Nathan Rapoport and dedicated in 1968. The forest is off the main highway connecting Tel Aviv and Jerusalem, located near Moshav Kisalon, close to Beit Shemesh.

18 See discussion in Young, *Texture of Memory*, 234. Batia Donner, *Natan Rapoport*, discusses the creation of the monument at Yad Mordecai in even greater detail, 182–214.

19 A report about the Warsaw ghetto uprising, GFH Archives 8964.

20 Z. Segev, *World Jewish Congress*, 201–2.

21 "Martyrs' and Heroes Remembrance (Yad Vashem) Law 5713–1953," Yad Vashem, https://www.yadvashem.or/about/yad-vashem-law.html.

22 May 18, 1953 debate on Yad Vashem Law in Eliezer Don-Yehiyeh, "*Memory and Political Culture*," 142.

23 See discussion in Hannan Hever, *Suddenly the Sight of War: Violence and Nationalism in Hebrew Poetry* (Stanford CA: Stanford University Press, 2016), 110–11, poem trans. Bella Gutterman, 459–60. Rudolf Kasztner (1906–57) was a Hungarian Zionist leader who immigrated to Israel after the war. In 1953, he sued Malkiel Grunewald for libel, after Grunewald published a pamphlet charging that in entering into negotiations with the SS in Hungary in 1944, Kasztner had betrayed Hungarian Jews to save a trainload of nearly 1,700 Jews that included prominent Hungarian Jews and Kasztner's friends and relatives. The trial and subsequent judgment against Kasztner (and his eventual assassination) became known as the "Kasztner Affair."

24 See discussion in Boaz Cohen, *Israeli Holocaust Research: Birth and Evolution* (London: Routledge, 2013), 21. The poem appears in *Davar*, April 30, 1954.

25 Levi Shalitan, "Warsaw as a Symbol," *Dos Fraye Vort* 29–30, May 3, 1946, 7. Quoted in Zeev Mankowitz, *Life Between Memory and Hope: The Survivors of the Holocaust in Occupied Germany* (New York: Cambridge University Press, 2002), 209.

26 Shloime Mendelsohn, "The Battle of the Warsaw Ghetto." For more information on Mendelsohn, who had been one of the Bund leaders in Warsaw before the war and had escaped to Vilna and then Stockholm before reaching New York together with Emanuel Sherer, see Daniel Blatman, *For Our Freedom and Yours*, 27.

27 Havi Dreifuss, "The Leadership of the Jewish Combat Organization during the Warsaw Ghetto Uprising: A Reassessment," *Holocaust and Genocide Studies* 31, no. (2017): 24–60.

28 See "World Jewish Congress delegation travels to Poland to commemorate 75th anniversary of Warsaw Ghetto Uprising," April 19, 2018, World Jewish Congress, https://www.worldjewishcongress.org/en/news/

world-jewish-congress-delegation-travels-to-poland-to-commemorate-75th-anniversary-of-warsaw-ghetto-uprising-4-4-2018.

29 See Samuel Norich, "Letter from Warsaw on the Ghetto Uprising Anniversary," *Forward*, accessed April 19, 2018, https://forward.com/news/399642/letter-from-warsaw-on-the-ghetto-uprising-anniversary/.

Selected Bibliography

Witness Testimonies and Commentary

Apenszlak, Jacob, ed. *The Black Book of Polish Jewry: An Account of the Martyrdom of Polish Jewry under the Nazi Occupation*. New York: American Federation for Polish Jews, 1943.

Auerbach, Rachel (Rokhl). *BeHutzot Varshe*. Tel Aviv: Am Oved, 1954.

———. *Der Yiddisher Oyfshtand Varshe 1943*. Warsaw: Central Committee of Polish Jews, 1948.

Berg, Mary. *The Diary of Mary Berg*. New York: L. B. Fischer, 1945.

Berman, Adolf Avraham. *Me'Yemei Hamachteret*. Tel Aviv: Ha-Menorah Press, 1970–71.

Berman, Basia Temkin. *City within a City*. New York: IP Books and YIVO, 2012.

Bialik, Haim Nahman. "City of Slaughter." Translated by Abraham M. Klein. In *The Complete Works of Hayyim Nachman Bialik*, edited by Israel Efros. Vol. 1. New York: Histadruth Ivrith of America, 1948.

Borzykowski, Tuvia. *Between Tumbling Walls*. Tel Aviv: Ghetto Fighters' House and United Kibbutz Movement, 1976.

Carmi, Aharon, and Chaim Frimer. *From That Inferno (Min HaDeleka Ha-Hi)*. Kibbutz Lohamei HaGeta'ot, 1961.

Dawidowicz, Lucy S. *From That Place and Time: A Memoir, 1938–1947*. New York: Norton, 1989.

Eck, Nathan. "Legend of the Joint in the Ghetto." Country files: Poland. JDC Archives, New York.

Edelman, Marek. *The Ghetto Fights*. Translation of a pamphlet published in Warsaw in 1945 by the Central Committee of the Bund. New York: American Representation of the General Jewish Workers' Union of Poland, May 1946. Reprint, London: Bookmarks, 1990. Bilinguial edition published as *Getto walczy: (Udział Bundu w obronie getta warszawskiego) / The Ghetto Fights: The Bund's Participation in the Defense of the Warsaw Ghetto*, edited by Michał Trębacz. Lodz, Poland: Marek Edelman Center, 2015.

Fast, Howard, and William Gropper. *Never to Forget: The Battle of the Warsaw Ghetto.* New York: Book League of the Jewish People's Fraternal Order, 1946.

Geto in Flamen [Ghetto in flames]. New York: American Representation of the General Jewish Workers' Union in Poland, 1944.

Goldstein, Bernard. *The Stars Bear Witness.* New York: Viking, 1949.

Goskind, Yitzhak, dir. *Von Horvot bis zum Heimland* [From ruins to homeland]. Screenplay by Chaim Grade. 1947. USHMM, courtesy of Yaakov Gross and the Steven Spielberg Jewish Film Archives of the Hebrew University of Jerusalem.

Gross, Natan. *The Fifth Anniversary of the Warsaw Ghetto Uprising.* Documentary film produced by Shaul Goskind and Natan Gross, 1948. Restoration by Realworks. Copies on file at GFHA and USHMM. YouTube.

Grynszpan-Frimer, Pnina. *The Nights Had Been Our Days.* [In Hebrew.] Tel Aviv: Ghetto Fighters House, 1984.

Habas, Bracha. *Letters from the Ghettoes.* Tel Aviv: Am Oved, 1943.

Hazaz, Haim. "The Sermon." In *Modern Hebrew Literature*, edited by Robert Alter. New York: Schocken, 1975.

Hecht, Ben. *A Flag Is Born.* New York: American League for a Free Palestine, 1946.

Hertz, J. S. *In Di Yorn Fun Yiddishn Hurbn.* New York: Unzer Tsayt, 1948.

Hilberg, Raul, Stanislaw Staron, and Josef Kermisz, eds. *The Warsaw Diary of Adam Czerniakow: Prelude to Doom.* New York: Stein and Day, 1979.

Hochberger, Simon. *Warsaw Ghetto: Tale of Valor.* Melbourne: Oyfboy, 1946.

In Heldiszn Gerangl: Der ontejl fun "Bund" in di geto-kamfn [In holy struggle: The participation of the Bund in the ghetto battles]. New York: Unzer Tsayt Farlag, April 1949.

Kaplan, Chaim. *Scroll of Agony: The Warsaw Diary of Chaim A. Kaplan.* Bloomington: Indiana University Press, 1999.

Karski, Jan. *Story of a Secret State.* Boston: Houghton Mifflin, 1944.

Katznelson, Yitzhak. "Dos Lid Fun Oysgehargeten Yiddishn Folk" [Song of the murdered Jewish people]. 1944. New York: YKUF Press, 1963.

Kermish, Joseph. [Josef Kermisz.] *Der Oyfshtand in varshever geto.* Translated from the Polish by Shloyme Lastik. Buenos Aires: Zentral Farband fun Poylishe Yidn in Argentine, 1948.

Kolitz, Zvi. "Yossel Rakovers Vendung Tsu Got." *Di Yiddishe Tsaytung*, Buenos Aires, September 1946. Translated as *Yosl Rakover Talks to God.* New York: Vintage, 1999.

Kovner, Abba. "Reshita shel Ha-Bricha ke-tnuah Hamonit be-eduyotav shel Abba Kovner." *Yalkut Moreshet* 38 (1984).

Kruk, Herman. *The Last Days of the Jerusalem of Lithuania.* Diary. New Haven: Yale University Press, 2002.

Leivick, H. "Der Nes in Geto." In *Nit Gedrukte Drames* [Unpublished works]. Buenos Aires: Congress for Jewish Culture, 1973. Yiddish Book Center digital catalog.

Lest We Forget: The Massacre of the Warsaw Ghetto, A Compilation of Reports. New York: World Jewish Congress, December 1943, 2nd printing.

Lubetkin, Zivia. *Aharonim al Ha-Homah.* Remarks at the Fifteenth Conference of the Kibbutz HaMeuchad, June 8, 1946. Yagur, Israel: HaKibbutz HaMeuchad, 1947.

———. *Biyemei Kilayon UMered.* Tel Aviv: Hakibbutz Hameuhad, 1989.

———. "The Last Days of the Warsaw Ghetto: A Survivor's Account of a Heroic Chapter in Jewish History." *Commentary* (May 1947).

Meed, Vladka. *Fun Beyde Zayten Geto Moyer.* New York: Educational Committee of the Workmen's Circle, 1948. Translated by Steven Meed as *On Both Sides of the Wall.* New York: Holocaust Library, 1993.

Mendelsohn, Moshe. *Kedushah u-Gevruah, Gloiben un Bitokhn* [Sanctity and heroism, faith and confidence]. Chicago: L. M. Stein, 1953.

Mendelsohn, Shloime. "The Battle of the Warsaw Ghetto." Delivered at YIVO, January 1944. New York: YIVO, 1944.

Neustadt (Noy), Melech. *The Warsaw Ghetto Rising.* Tel Aviv: The World Union Poale-Zion (Z.S.)—Hitachduth, February 1944. Dated November 1944.

Niger, Shmuel. *Kiddush Hashem.* New York: CYCO Bikher Farlag, 1948.

Pat, Jacob. *Ash un Fayer: Iber di Hurves fun Poylen.* New York: Central Yiddish Culture Organization, 1946. Translated as *Ashes and Fire: On the Ruins of Poland.* New York: International Universities Press, 1947.

Remember the Warsaw Ghetto. London: Federation of Polish Jews In Great Britain, Nord Press, 1944.

Ringelblum, Emanuel. *Notes from the Warsaw Ghetto: The Journal of Emanuel Ringelblum*. New York: McGraw Hill, 1958.

Rotem (Ratheiser), Simcha (Kazik). *Memoirs of a Warsaw Ghetto Fighter: The Past within Me*. New Haven: Yale University Press, 1994.

Rufeisen-Schuepper, Hila. *Predah Me-Mila 18: Sipurah shel Kasharit* [Farewell to Mila 18: The story of a courier]. Tel Aviv: Lochamei HaGetaot, 1990.

Schoenberg, Arnold. *A Survivor from Warsaw*, op. 46. 1947.

Schwartzbart, Isaac (Ignacy). *The Story of the Warsaw Ghetto Uprising: Its Meaning and Message*. New York: World Jewish Congress, 1953.

Shneiderman, S. L. *Tsvishn shrek un hofenung: A rayze iber dem nayem Poyln*. Buenos Aires: Tsentral farband fun poylishn Yidn in Argentina, 1947.

Stone, Reca. *Revolt in the Ghetto*. Sydney: United Emergency Committee for European Jewry, 1944.

[Jurgen] Stroop Report. May 1943: "Es gibt keinen jüdischen Wohnbezirk in Warschau mehr!" U.S. National Archives and Records Administration website. Translated by Sybil Milton as *The Stroop Report: "The Jewish Quarter of Warsaw Is No More!"* New York: Pantheon, 1979.

Syrkin, Marie. *Blessed Is the Match*. Philadelphia: Jewish Publication Society of America, 1947.

Szwajger, Adina Blady. *I Remember Nothing More: The Warsaw Children's Hospital and the Jewish Resistance*. New York: Pantheon, 1991.

Tuwim Julian. "We, Polish Jews." In *My, Zydzi polscy . . . We, Polish Jews*, edited by Ch. Shmeruk. Jerusalem: Magness Press, 1984.

Varsheyer Geṭo oyfshṭand, 19ṭer April, 1943–19ṭer April, 1947. Landsberg, Germany: Poalei Zion Z.S. and Dror, 1947.

Warsaw Ghetto: Life, Struggle, and Uprising. Exhibition catalogue. New York: YIVO Institute for Jewish Research, 1963.

Wdowinski, David. *And We Are Not Saved*. New York: Philosophical Library, 1985.

Zaretzky, Ronen, dir. *The Last Fighters*. Documentary film. DVD Video, ha-Rashut ha-sheniyah la-ṭeleyizyah ṿela-radio, 2006.

Zuckerman, Yitzhak. *Bageto Uvamered*. Tel Aviv: Beit Lochamei Ha-Getaot, 1985.

———. *A Surplus of Memory: Chronicle of the Warsaw Ghetto Uprising*. Berkeley: University of California Press, 1993.

———. *Yetziat Polin: 'Al ha-Berichah ve'al Shikum ha-Tnu'ah ha-Tnu'ah ha-Halutzit*. Tel Aviv: Beit Lochamei Ha-Getaot, 1988.

Articles and Book Chapters

Aleksiun, Natalia. "Adolf Abraham Berman." In *YIVO Encyclopedia of Jews in Eastern Europe* (online).

———. "Where Was There a Future for Polish Jewry? Bundist and Zionist Polemics in Post–World War II Poland." In *Jewish Politics in Eastern Europe: The Bund at 100*, edited by Jack Jacobs. New York: New York University Press, 2001.

Arbell, Michal. "Abba Kovner: The Ritual Function of His Battle Missives." *Jewish Social Studies* 18, no. 3 (2012): 99–119.

Arendt, Hannah. "Eichmann in Jerusalem." *New Yorker*, February 16, 1963.

Arens, Moshe. "The Jewish Military Organization (ŻZW) in the Warsaw Ghetto." *Holocaust and Genocide Studies* 19 (2005).

Bar, Doron. "Holocaust Commemoration in Israel during the 1950s: The Holocaust Cellar on Mount Zion." *Jewish Social Studies: History, Culture, Society*, n.s., 12, no. 1 (2005): 16–38.

Bauer, Yehuda. "When Did They Know?" *Midstream* 24, no. 4 (1968).

Baumel, Judith Tydor, and Jacob J. Schacter. "The Ninety-Three Bais Yaakov Girls of Cracow: History or Typology?" In *Reverence, Righteousness and Rahamanut: Essays in Memory of Rabbi Dr. Leo Jung*, edited by Jacob J. Schacter, 93–103. North vale NJ: Jason Aronson, 1992.

Berenbaum, Michael. "Some Clarifications on the Warsaw Ghetto Uprising," in *Life in the Ghettos during the Holocaust*, ed. Eric Sterling. Syracuse, NY: Syracuse University Press, 2005.

Blatman, Daniel. "Bund." In *YIVO Encyclopedia of Jews in Eastern Europe* (online).

———. "On a Mission against All Odds: Szmuel Zygielbojm in London (April 1942–May 1943)." *Yad Vashem Studies* 20 (1990): 237–71.

Brog, Mooli. "In Blessed Memory of a Dream: Mordechai Shenhavi and Initial Holocaust Commemoration Ideas in Palestine, 1942–1945." *Yad Vashem Studies* 30 (2002), 297–336.

———. "'Nitsurim be-homot ha-zikaron': The Warsaw ghetto memorial as a symbol of destruction and heroism in Poland and Israel." [In Hebrew.] *Alpayim* 14 (1997): 148–73.

Cesarani, David. "Challenging the Myth of Silence: Postwar Responses to the Destruction of European Jewry." In *After the Holocaust: Challenging the Myth of Silence*, edited by David Cesarani and Eric Sundquist. New York: Routledge, 2012.

Cholawski, Shalom. "Partisans and Ghetto Fighters—An Active Element among *She'erit Hapletah*." In *She'erit Hapletah, 1944–1948: Rehabilitation and Political Struggle*, edited by Israel Gutman. Jerusalem: Yad Vashem, 1990.

Cohen, Boaz. "Rachel Auerbach, Yad Vashem, and Israeli Holocaust Memory." *Polin* 20 (2008): 197–211.

Cohen, Nathan. "Borekh Shefner." In *YIVO Encyclopedia of Eastern European Jews* (online).

Cohen, Raya. "'Against the Current': Hashomer Hatzair in the Warsaw Ghetto." *Jewish Social Studies* 7, no. 1 (2000).

Collomp, Catherine. "'Relief Is a Political Gesture': The Jewish Labor Committee's Interventions in War-Torn Poland, 1939–1945." *Transtlantica* (online), 2014.

Dobroszycki, Lucjan. "Restoring Jewish Life in Postwar Poland." *Soviet Jewish Affairs* 3, no. 2 (1973).

Don-Yehiyeh, Eliezer. "Memory and Political Culture: The Holocaust and Israeli Society." In *Studies in Contemporary Jewry*, 139–62. Vol. 9. Institute for Contemporary Jewry in the Hebrew University of Jerusalem and Oxford University Press, 1993.

Dreifuss, Havi. "The Leadership of the Jewish Combat Organization during the Warsaw Ghetto Uprising: A Reassessment." *Holocaust and Genocide Studies* 31, no. 1 (2017).

———. "Zuckerman: A Witness and a Source, a Leader and a Man." *Yalkut Moreshet* 10 (April 2013), 117–32.

Engel, David. "On Studying Jewish History in Light of the Holocaust." Maurice R. and Corrine P. Greenberg inaugural lecture, United States Holocaust Memorial Museum, April 16, 2002.

———. "The Reconstruction of Jewish Communal Institutions in Postwar Poland: The Origins of the Central Committee of Polish Jews, 1944–1945." *East European Politics and Societies* 10 (1996): 85–107.

Fackenheim, Emil. "The Spectrum of Resistance during the Holocaust: An Essay in Description and Definition." *Modern Judaism* 2, no. 2 (1982).

Feldman, Yael S. "'Not as Sheep Led to Slaughter'? On Trauma, Selective Memory, and the Making of Historical Consciousness." *Jewish Social Studies: History, Culture, Society*, n.s., 19, no. 5 (2013): 159–69.

Friedlander, Henry. "Guilt for the Holocaust." In *The American Jewish Experience*, edited by Jonathan Sarna. New York: Holmes and Meier, 1986.

Friedman, Philip, and Koppel Pinson. "Some Books on the Jewish Catastrophe." *Jewish Social Studies* 12, no. 1 (1950).

Friedman-Cohen, Carrie. "Rokhl Auerbakh." In *Jewish Women's Archive Encyclopedia* (online).

Geva, Sharon. "'With and Despite the Burden of the Past, 1946': The Life Story of Zivia Lubetkin," *Moreshet: Journal for the Study of the Holocaust and Anti-Semitism* 14 (2017).

Goldberg, Amos. "The History of the Jews in the Ghettos." In *The Holocaust and Historical Methodology*, edited by Dan Stone. New York: Berghahn Books, 2012.

Grobman, Alex. "What Did They Know? The American Jewish Press and the Holocaust, 1 September 1939–17 December 1942." In *America, American Jews, and the Holocaust*, edited by Jeffrey Gurock, 331–56. New York: Routledge, 1998.

Gutman, Israel. "The Youth Movement as an Alternative Leadership in Eastern Europe." In *Zionist Youth Movements during the Shoah*, edited by Asher Cohen and Yehoyakim Cochavi. New York: Peter Lang, 1995.

Hilberg, Raul. "The Destruction of the European Jews: Precedents." In *The Holocaust: Origins, Implementation, Aftermath*, edited by Omer Bartov. New York: Routledge, 2000.

Kaplan, Richard. "The Myth of Jewish Passivity." In *Jewish Resistance against the Nazis*, edited by Patrick Henry. Washington DC: Catholic University Press, 2014.

Kermish, Joseph. "Rescue Attempts during the Holocaust." In *Proceedings of the Second Yad Vashem International Historical Conference*, edited by Yisrael Gutman and Efraim Zuroff, 367–98. Jerusalem: Yad Vashem, 1977.

Kessner, Carole S. "Marie Syrkin: An Exemplary Life." In *American Jewish Women and the Zionist Enterprise*, edited by Shulamit Reinharz and Mark A. Raider, 48–64. Waltham MA: Brandeis University Press, 2005.

Kugelmass, Jack. *Sifting the Ruins: Émigré Jewish Journalists' Return Visits to the Old Country, 1946–1948*. Beilin Lecture in American Jewish Affairs, vol. 23. Ann Arbor: University of Michigan, 2013.

Levin, Meyer. Review of *Blessed Is the Match*, by Marie Syrkin. *Commentary*, July 1, 1947.

Lubin, Orly. "Holocaust Testimony, National Memory." In *Extremities: Trauma, Testimony and Community*, edited by Nancy K. Miller and Jason Tougaw, 131–42. University of Illinois Press, 2002.

Mankowitz, Ze'ev. "Zionism and the She'erit Hapletah." In *She'erit Hapletah: 1944–1948: Rehabilitation and Political Struggle*, edited by Israel Gutman and Avital Saf, 211–30. Jerusalem: Yad Vashem, 1990.

Margolis, Rebecca. "Review of the Yiddish Media." In *Nazi Germany, Canadian Responses: Confronting Antisemitism in the Shadow of War*, edited by Ruth Klein. Montreal: McGill-Queens University Press, 2012.

Marrus, Michael. "Jewish Resistance to the Holocaust." *Journal of Contemporary History* 30, no. 1 (1995): 83–110.

Meng, Michael. "Traveling to Germany and Poland: Toward a Textual Montage of Jewish Emotions after the Holocaust." In *Jewish Histories of the Holocaust*, edited by Norman Goda, 266–81. New York: Berghahn Books, 2014.

Nachshon, Edna. "From Geopathology to Redemption: A Flag Is Born on the Broadway Stage." *Kurt Weill Newsletter* 20 (Spring 2002): 5–8.

Ofer, Dalia. "The Past That Does Not Pass: Israelis and Holocaust Memory." *Israel Studies* 14, no. 1 (2009): 1–35.

———. "The Strength of Remembrance: Commemorating the Holocaust during the First Decade of Israel." *Jewish Social Studies* 6, no. 2 (2000): 24–55.

Patt, Avinoam. "The People Must Be Forced to Go to Palestine: Rabbi Abraham Klausner and the Surviving Remnant in Postwar Germany." *Holocaust and Genocide Studies* 28, no. 2 (2014): 240–76.

———. "'We Are Fighting for Three Lines in History . . . It Will Not Be Said That Our Youth Marched Like Sheep to the Slaughter': Writing about Resistance in the Immediate Aftermath of the Holocaust." Paper presented at Beyond Camps and Forced Labour Conference, Imperial War Museum, London, 2015.

Polonsky, Antony. "Warsaw." In *YIVO Encyclopedia of Jews in Eastern Europe* (online).

Porat, Dina. "First Testimonies on the Holocaust." In *Holocaust Historiography in Context*, edited by Dan Michman and David Bankier. Jerusalem: Yad Vashem, 2008.

Ringelblum, Emanuel. "Diary: Thoughts about Resistance and Its Consequences Are Evoked When News about Massacre Reach the Ghetto." In "Emanuel Ringelblum's Notes, Hitherto Unpublished," edited by Joseph Kermish. *Yad Vashem Studies* 7 (1968).

Ronen, Avihu. "The Cable That Vanished: Tabenkin and Ya'ari to the Last Surviving Ghetto Fighters." *Yad Vashem Studies* 41, no. 2 (2013).

Saidel, Rochelle, "Vladka Meed." In *Holocaust Literature*, edited by Lilian Kremer. New York: Routledge, 2003.

Sarna, Jonathan. "The American Jewish Press." In *The Oxford Handbook of Religion and the American News Media*. Oxford: Oxford University Press, 2012.

Schacter, Jacob J. "Holocaust Commemoration Tisha Be-Av: The Debate over Yom Ha-Shoa." *Tradition* 41, no. 2 (2008): 164–97.

Schiffman, Stuart. "A Stone for His Slingshot." *Jewish Review of Books*, March 2014.

Seidman, Naomi. "Elie Wiesel and the Scandal of Jewish Rage." *Jewish Social Studies* 3, no. 1 (1996): 1–19.

Shalev, Ziva. "Tosia Altman." In *Jewish Women's Archive Encyclopedia* (online).

Shlomi, Hana. "*Hitargenut shel Sridei HaYehudim BePolin LeAchar Milchemet HaOlam HaShniyah, 1944–1950.*" In *Kiyum VaShever: Yehudei Polin LeDoroteihem*, edited by Israel Bartal and Israel Gutman. Jerusalem: Merkaz Zalman Shazar, 1997.

Shore, Marci. "Children of the Revolution: Communism, Zionism, and the Berman Brothers." *Jewish Social Studies*, n.s., 10, no. 3 (2004): 23–86.

———. "Język, pamięć i rewolucyjna awangarda. Kształtowanie historii powstania w Getcie Warszawskim w latach 1944–1950." *Biuletyn Żydowskiego Instytutu Historycznego* 4 (December 1998): 48.

Sinkoff, Nancy. "Fiction's Archive: Authenticity, Ethnography, and Philosemitism in John Hersey's *The Wall*." *Jewish Social Studies: History, Culture, Society*, n.s., 17, no. 2 (2011): 48–79.

Slucki, David. "A Community of Suffering: Jewish Holocaust Survivor Networks in Postwar America." *Jewish Social Studies: History, Culture, Society*, n.s., 22, no. 2 (2017): 116–45.

Stola, Dariusz. "Early News of the Holocaust from Poland." *Holocaust and Genocide Studies* 11, no. 1 (1997): 1–27.

Tec, Nechama. *Resistance: Jews and Christians Who Defied the Nazi Terror.* Oxford: Oxford University Press, 2013.

Weinbaum, Laurence. "Deconstructing Memory and History: The Jewish Military Union (ŻZW) and the Warsaw Ghetto Uprising." *Jewish Political Studies Review* 18, nos. 1–2 (2006).

———. "'Shaking the Dust Off': The Story of the Warsaw Ghetto's Forgotten Chronicler, Ruben Feldschu (Ben Shem)." *Jewish Political Studies Review* 22, nos. 3–4 (2010).

Weinberg, Gerhard. "The Final Solution and the War in 1943." In *Revolt amid the Darkness.* Washington DC: United States Holocaust Memorial Museum, 1993.

Werb, Bret. "We Will Never Die: A Pageant to Save the Jews of Europe." *Orel Foundation Online Journal*, August 10, 2010. http://orelfoundation.org/journal/journalArticle/we_will_never_die_a_pageant_to_save_the_jews_of_europe.

Young, James. "The Biography of a Memorial Icon," *Representations* 26. Special Issue: Memory and Counter-Memory (Spring 1989): 79–80.

Zechenter, Katarzyna. "Marek Edelman." In *Holocaust Literature*, vol. 1, edited by S. Lillian Kremer. New York: Routledge, 2003.

Zerubavel, Yael. "The Death of Memory and the Memory of Death: Masada and the Holocaust as Historical Metaphors." *Representations* 45 (Winter 1994): 72–100.

Monographs

Balf, Micha. *Ḳol she-lo ne'elam: 'itsuv zikhron ha-sho'ah ṿe-darkhe hantsaḥatah ba-tenu'ah ha-ḳibutsit* [Unsilenced voices: Memory and commemoration of the Holocaust in the kibbutz movement]. Tel Aviv: HaKibbutz HaMeuchad, 2008.

Bartoszewski, Wladyslaw, and Zofia Lewin, eds. *Righteous among the Nations: How Poles Helped the Jews.* London: Earslcourt Publications, 1969.

Barzel, Neima. *Sacrifice Unredeemed: The Encounter between the Leaders of the Ghetto Fighters and Israeli Society.* [In Hebrew.] Jerusalem: HaSifriya Hatziyonit, 1998.

Baskind, Samantha. *The Warsaw Ghetto in American Art and Culture.* University Park: Pennsylvania State University Press, 2018.

Bauer, Yehuda. *American Jewry and the Holocaust: The American Jewish Joint Distribution Committee, 1939–1945*. Detroit: Wayne State University Press, 1981.

———. *Out of the Ashes: The Impact of American Jewry on Post-Holocaust European Jewry*. New York: Pergamon, 1989.

———. *Rethinking the Holocaust*. New Haven CT: Yale University Press, 2001.

Baumel, Judith Tydor. *The "Bergson Boys" and the Origins of Contemporary Zionist Militancy*. Syracuse NY: Syracuse University Press, 2005.

Beit-Tzvi, Shabtai. *Hatzionut Hapost-Ugandit Bemashber Hashoah* [Post-Uganda Zionism in face of the Holocaust crisis]. Tel Aviv, 1977.

Blatman, Daniel. *Lema'an Heruteinu ve-Herutchem: Ha-Bund be-Polin, 1939–1949*. Jerusalem: Yad Vashem, 1996. Translated by Naftali Greenwood as *For Our Freedom and Yours: The Jewish Labour Bund in Poland 1939–1949*. London: Vallentine Mitchell, 2003.

Browning, Christopher. *Remembering Survival: Inside a Nazi Slave Labor Camp*. New York: Norton, 2010.

Cohen, Boaz. *Israeli Holocaust Research: Birth and Evolution*. New York: Routledge, 2013.

Cohen, Raya. *Ben "sham" le-"khan": Sipurim shel edim la-hurban, Shvaits 1939–1942*. Sifriyat hapalah. Tel Aviv: Am Oved, 1999.

Cohen, Yochanan. *Ovrim kol Gvul: HaBrichah, Polin, 1945–1946*. Tel Aviv: Zemorah-Bitan, 1995.

Dawidowicz, Lucy. *The War against the Jews, 1933–1945*. New York: Holt, Rinehart, and Winston, 1975.

Diner, Hasia *We Remember with Reverence and Love: American Jews and the Myth of Silence after the Holocaust*. New York: New York University Press, 2010.

Dobroszycki, Lucjan. *Survivors of the Holocaust in Poland: A Portrait Based on Jewish Community Records 1944–1947*. Armonk NY: M. E. Sharpe, 1994.

Donner, Batia. *Natan Rapoport: A Jewish Artist*. [In Hebrew.] Jerusalem: Yad Ben Tzvi and Yad Ya'ari, 2014.

Dreifuss, Havi. *Geto Varsha—Sof: April 1942—Yuni 1943* [The Warsaw ghetto—the end: April 1942–June 1943]. Jerusalem: Yad Vashem, 2018.

Engel, David. *In the Shadow of Auschwitz: The Polish Government-in-Exile and the Jews, 1939–1942*. Chapel Hill: University of North Carolina Press, 1987.

Engel, David. *Bein Shichrur Li-Verichah: Nitzulei HaShoah Be-Polin Ve-Hamavak al Hanhagatam, 1944–1946* [Between liberation and flight: The survivors of the

Holocaust in Poland and the struggle over their leadership]. Tel Aviv: Am Oved Press, 1996.

———. *The Holocaust: The Third Reich and the Jews*. New York: Longman, 2000.

———. *Mul Har Ha-ga'ash: Hokrei Toldot Yisrael Le-nochach Ha-shoah*. Jerusalem: Mercaz Zalman Shazar, 2010.

Engelking, Barbara, and Jacek Leociak, *The Warsaw Ghetto: A Guide to the Perished City*. New Haven CT: Yale University Press, 2009.

Friedlander, Saul. *The Years of Extermination: Nazi Germany and the Jews, 1939–1945*. New York: Harper Collins, 2007.

Friedman, Philip. *Martyrs and Fighters: The Epic of the Warsaw Ghetto*. New York, 1954.

Frilling, Tuvia. *A Jewish Kapo in Auschwitz: History, Memory, and the Politics of Survival*. Waltham MA: Brandeis University Press, 2014.

Garbarini, Alexandra, Emil Kerenji, Jan Lambertz, and Avinoam Patt, *Jewish Responses to Persecution, 1938–1940*. Vol. 2. Lanham MD: USHMM/AltaMira Press, 2011.

Gilbert, Martin. *The Righteous: The Unsung Heroes of the Holocaust*. New York: Henry Holt, 2010.

Goda, Norman J. W., ed. *Jewish Histories of the Holocaust: New Transnational Approaches*. New York: Berghahn, 2014.

Goldberg, Amos. *Trauma in the First Person: Diary-Writing during the Shoah*. [In Hebrew.] Or Yehuda: Kinneret Zmora-Bitan Dvir and Ben-Gurion University, 2012.

Gorny, Yosef. *The Jewish Press and the Holocaust, 1939–1945: Palestine, Britain, the United States, and the Soviet Union*. Translated by Naftali Greenwood. New York: Cambridge University Press, 2012.

Grubsztein, Meir, ed., *Jewish Resistance during the Holocaust, April 1968*. Conference Proceedings. Jerusalem: Yad Vashem, 1971.

Gutman, Israel. *Fighters among the Ruins: The Story of Jewish Heroism during World War II*. New York: Bnai Brith Books, 1988.

———*The Jews of Warsaw, 1939–1943: Ghetto, Underground, Revolt*. Bloomington: Indiana University Press, 1982.

———. *Resistance: The Warsaw Ghetto Uprising*. New York: Houghton Mifflin, in association with USHMM, 1994.

Gutterman, Bella. *Fighting for Her People: Zivia Lubetkin, 1914–1978*. Jerusalem: Yad Vashem, 2014.

Halamish, Aviva. *The Exodus Affair: Holocaust Survivors and the Struggle for Palestine*. Syracuse NY: Syracuse University Press, 1998.

Hankin, Saul. "'Brothers and Sisters of Work and Need': The Bundist Newspaper *Unzer Tsayt* and Its Role in New York City, 1941–1944." BA thesis, University of Michigan, April 2013.

Haran, Ronen. "The Source of Reports on the Tragic Results of the Warsaw Ghetto Uprising in Palestine–Eretz Israel." [In Hebrew.] MA term paper, Haifa University, 2013.

Hawlbachs, Maurice. *On Collective Memory*. Chicago: University of Chicago Press, 1992.

Henry, Patrick, ed. *Jewish Resistance against the Nazis*. Washington DC: Catholic University of America Press, 2014.

Hever, Hanan. *Suddenly the Sight of War: Violence and Nationalism in Hebrew Poetry*. Stanford CA: Stanford University Press, 2016.

Hilberg, Raul. *The Destruction of the European Jews*. Chicago: Quadrangle Books, 1961.

Jockusch, Laura. *Collect and Record: Jewish Holocaust Documentation in Early Postwar Europe*. Oxford: Oxford University Press, 2012.

Kassow, Samuel. *Who Will Write Our History? Emanuel Ringelblum, the Warsaw Ghetto, and the Oyneg Shabes Archive*. Bloomington: Indiana University Press, 2007.

Kerenji, Emil. *Jewish Responses to Persecution*. Vol. 4. Lanham MD: Rowman and Littlefield, 2015.

Krall, Hannah. *Shielding the Flame: An Intimate Conversation with Dr. Marek Edelman, the Last Surviving Leader of the Warsaw Ghetto Uprising*. New York: Henry Holt, 1986.

Kurzman, Dan. *The Bravest Battle: The Twenty-Eight Days of the Warsaw Ghetto Uprising*. New York: Da Capo Press, 1993.

Larkin, M. *The Six Days of Yad-Mordechai*. Givatayim: Peli Printing, 1970.

Lazar, Haim. *Matsada shel Varsha*. Tel Aviv: Machon Jabotinsky, 1963.

Leff, Laurel. *Buried by the* Times: *The Holocaust and America's Most Important Newspaper*. Cambridge: Cambridge University Press, 2005.

Levin, Itamar. *Ha-Ḳerav ha-aḥaron: Mered Geṭo Ṿarshah: Ha-sipur ha-amiti*. Tel Aviv: Yediot Aharonot, 2009.

Libionka, Dariusz, and Laurence Weinbaum. *Bohaterowie, hochsztaplerzy, opisywacze: wokół Żydowskiego Związku Wojskowego* [Heroes, hucksters, storytellers: The Jewish Military Organization]. Warsaw: Polish Center for Holocaust Research, 2011.

Lipstadt, Deborah. *Beyond Belief: The American Press and the Coming of the Holocaust*. New York: Macmillan, 1986.

———. *Holocaust: An American Understanding*. New Brunswick NJ: Rutgers University Press, 2016.

Mankowitz, Ze'ev. *Life between Memory and Hope: The Survivors of the Holocaust in Occupied Germany*. Cambridge: Cambridge University Press, 2002.

Mark, Ber. *Uprising in the Warsaw Ghetto*. New York: Schocken, 1975.

Mendelsohn, Ezra. *The Jews of East Central Europe between the World Wars*. Bloomington: Indiana University Press, 1983.

Meng, Michael. *Shattered Spaces: Encountering Jewish Ruins in Postwar Germany and Poland*. Cambridge MA: Harvard University Press, 2011.

Morris, Benny. *Righteous Victims: A History of the Zionist-Arab Conflict*. New York: Vintage, 2001.

Neuman, Eran. *Shoah Presence: Architectural Representations of the Holocaust*. London: Routledge, 2016.

Ofer, Dalia, and Lenore Weitzman, eds. *Women in the Holocaust*. New Haven CT: Yale University Press, 1998.

Novick, Peter. *The Holocaust in American Life*. New York: Houghton Mifflin, 1999.

Patt, Avinoam. *Finding Home and Homeland: Jewish Youth and Zionism in the Aftermath of the Holocaust*. Detroit: Wayne State University Press, 2009.

Person, Katarzyna. *Assimilated Jews in the Warsaw Ghetto*. Syracuse NY: Syracuse University Press, 2014.

Pianko, Noam. *Jewish Peoplehood: An American Innovation*. New Brunswick NJ: Rutgers University Press, 2015.

Porat, Dina. *The Blue and Yellow Stars of David: The Zionist Leadership and the Holocaust*, 1939–1945. Cambridge MA: Harvard University Press, 1990.

———. *The Fall of a Sparrow: The Life and Times of Abba Kovner*. Translated by Elizabeth Yuval. Palo Alto CA: Stanford University Press, 2000.

———. *Vengeance and Retribution Are Mine: The Yishuv, the Holocaust, and Abba Kovner's Avengers*. [In Hebrew.] Haifa: Pardes, 2019.

Porat, Dina, and Mordechai Naor, eds. *Ha-itonut he-yehudit be-Eretz Yisrael nokhah ha-shoah 1939–1945*. Tel Aviv: Tel Aviv University, 2002.

Preiss, Lea. *Displaced Persons at Home: Refugees in the Fabric of Jewish Life in Warsaw*. [In Hebrew.] Jerusalem: Yad Vashem, 2015.

Rosen, Alan. *Sounds of Defiance: The Holocaust, Multilingualism and the Problem of English*. Lincoln: University of Nebraska Press, 2005.

Roskies, David, and Naomi Diamant. *Holocaust Literature: A History and Guide*. Waltham MA: Brandeis University Press, 2013.

Saidel, Rochelle. *Never Too Late to Remember: The Politics behind New York City's Holocaust Museum*. New York: Holmes and Meier, 1996.

Segev, Tom. *The Seventh Million: The Israelis and the Holocaust*. New York: Hill and Wang, 1993.

Segev, Zohar. *The World Jewish Congress during the Holocaust: Between Activism and Restraint*. Berlin: Walter de Gruyter, 2014.

Shandler, Jeffrey. *Jews, God, and Videotape: Religion and Media in America*. New York: New York University Press, 2009.

Shapira, Anita. *Land and Power: The Zionist Resort to Force*. Stanford CA: Stanford University Press, 1999.

Shapiro, Robert Moses, ed. *Why Didn't the Press Shout? American and International Journalism during the Holocaust*. Hoboken: Ktav, 2003.

Sivan, Emmanuel. *Dor Tashakh: Mitos, Diyukan ve-Zikaron*. Tel Aviv: Ministry of Defense, 1991. Slucki, David. *The International Jewish Labor Bund after 1945: Toward a Global History*. New Brunswick NJ: Rutgers University Press, 2012.

Smith, Mark. "The Yiddish Historians and the Struggle for a Jewish History of the Holocaust." PhD diss., University of California at Los Angeles, 2016.

Stauber, Roni. *The Holocaust in Israeli Public Debate in the 1950s: Ideology and Memory*. Portland OR: Valentine Mitchell, 2007.

Stier, Oren. *Holocaust Icons: Symbolizing the Shoah in History and Memory*. New Brunswick NJ: Rutgers University Press, 2015.

Tec, Nechama. *Resistance: Jews and Christians Who Defied the Nazi Terror*. Oxford: Oxford University Press, 2013.

Waxman, Zoe. *Writing the Holocaust: Identity, Testimony, Representation*. Oxford: Oxford University Press, 2008.

Wyman, David. *Abandonment of the Jews: America and the Holocaust, 1941–1945*. New York: Pantheon, 1984.

Yablonka, Hannah. *Survivors of the Holocaust: Israel after the War*. New York: New York University Press, 1999.

Young, James. *Texture of Memory: Holocaust Memorials and Meaning*. New Haven CT: Yale University Press, 1994.

Zertal, Idith. *Israel's Holocaust and the Politics of Nationhood*. Cambridge: Cambridge University Press, 2005.

Zerubavel, Yael. *Recovered Roots: Collective Memory and the Making of Israeli National Tradition*. Chicago: University of Chicago Press, 1995.

Zimmerman, Joshua. *The Polish Underground and the Jews, 1939–1945*. Cambridge: Cambridge University Press, 2015.

Zipperstein, Steve. *Pogrom: Kishinev and the Tilt of History*. New York: Liveright, 2018.

Document Collections

Burstein, Dror, ed. *Without a Single Case of Death: Stories from Kibbutz Lohamei Haghetaot*. Tel Aviv: Beit Lochamei HaGetaot, 2007.

Dawidowicz, Lucy. *A Holocaust Reader*. New York: Behrman House, 1976.

Dror and Rosenzweig, eds. *Sefer Hashomer Hatzair*. Vol. 1, 1913–45. Merhavia, Israel: Sifriat Poalim, 1956.

Friedman, Philip. "Bibliography of the Warsaw Ghetto" in *The Jewish Book Annual*. Vol. 11, 1952–53.

Hertz, J. S., ed. *Zygielbojm-bukh*. New York: Unzer Tsayt Farlag, 1947.

Kermish, Joseph, ed. *Mered Geto Varshah be-Einei ha-Oyev*. Jerusalem: Yad Vashem, 1966.

———, ed. *To Live with Honor and Die with Honor: Documents from the Warsaw Ghetto Underground Archives*. Jerusalem: Yad Vashem, 1986.

Mendes-Flohr, Paul, and Jehuda Reinharz, eds. *The Jew in the Modern World: A Documentary History*. 3rd ed. New York: Oxford University Press, 2011.

Neustadt (Noy), Melech. *Churban ve-Mered shel Yehudei Varsha* [Destruction and rising: The epic of the Jews of Warsaw]. Tel Aviv: Executive Committee of the

General Federation of Jewish Labour in Palestine, 1946. Translated to Yiddish and issued by the same publisher as *Ḥurbn un oyfshṭand fun di Yidn in Varshe eydes-bleṭer un azḳore's*, 1948.

Roskies, David, ed. *The Literature of Destruction: Jewish Responses to Catastrophe.* Philadelphia: Jewish Publication Society, 1988.

———, ed. *Voices from the Warsaw Ghetto: Writing Our History.* New Haven CT: Yale University Press, 2019.

Warsaw Ghetto Resistance Organization Commemoration Journal. New York: WAGRO, 1975, 1978, 1985.

Zuckerman, Yitzhak, and Moshe Basok, eds. *Sefer Milhamot Ha-Getaot* [The book of the ghetto wars]. Tel Aviv: HaKibbutz HaMeuchad, 1954.

Newspapers and Magazines

Admonter Haynt

Al HaMishmar

American Jewish Yearbook, 1943–48

Bund Yedies

Davar

Der Tog

Dos Fraye Vort

Dos Naye Lebn

Farn Folk

Forverts (Jewish Daily Forward)

Furrows

Hashomer Hatzair

Jewish Chronicle

Jewish Frontier

Jewish Telegraphic Agency bulletins

Landsberger Lager Tsaytung

Ma'ariv

Mishmar

The New York Times

Our Journal (*American Council of Warsaw Jews*)

The Palestine Post
Pachach Bulletin in Germany
Unzer Tsayt
Unzer Veg

Archives

American Jewish Archives (AJA), Cincinnati, Ohio
World Jewish Congress (WJC) Collection
American Jewish Committee Archives (AJC), New York, http://ajcarchives.org/main.php
American Jewish Historical Society Archives (AJHS), Synagogue Council of America papers, New York, Center for Jewish History
American League for a Free Palestine Records
Archiwum Zydowskiego Instytutu Historycznego w Polsce [Archives of the Jewish Historical Institute in Poland] (ZIH), Warsaw, http://www.jhi.pl/en/research
Central Zionist Archives (CZA), Jerusalem http://www.zionistarchives.org.il/en/Pages/Default.aspx
Eisenhower Presidential Library and Museum, Abilene, Kansas, https://www.eisenhowerlibrary.gov/research/online-documents/world-war-ii-holocaust-extermination-european-jews
Fortunoff Video Archives for Holocaust Testimonies (FVAHT), Yale University
Ghetto Fighters House Archives (GFHA), Lochamei Ha-Geta'ot, Israel
Haganah Archives, Ha'apalah Project (HAHP), Tel Aviv, Israel
Hashomer Hatzair Archives, Giv'at Havivah, Israel (SZ)
JDC Archives (JDC), Jerusalem
JDC Archives (JDC), New York, https://archives.jdc.org/
Jewish Labor Committee (JLC), Tamiment Archives, Wagner Labor Library, Bobst Library, New York University
United States Holocaust Memorial Museum Archives and Library (USHMMA)
RG 02.208M, Pamietniki Żydów (Memoirs of Jews), 1939–45 (from Jewish Historical Institute, Warsaw)
RG 15.079, Oyneg Shabbes–Ringelblum Archive
RG 15.106, Central Committee of Polish Jews Collection

RG 15.143, Hersh Wasser Collection

RG 15.199M, American Jewish Joint Distribution Committee

RG 50, Oral History Collections

RG 60.5048, Claude Lanzmann Shoah Collection

RG 68.112M, Selected records from the Ghetto Fighters' House (Beit Lohamei Haghetaot)

War Refugee Board Files, Franklin D. Roosevelt Presidential Library and Museum, Marist University, http://www.fdrlibrary.marist.edu/archives/collections/franklin/

Yad Vashem Archives, Jerusalem, M.2

Yad Vashem Archives, Jerusalem, O-55

Yiddish Book Center, Steven Spielberg Digital Yiddish Library, https://www.yiddishbookcenter.org/collections/

YIVO Archives, New York

RG 1206, American Memorial to Six Million Jews of Europe

RG 1400, Bund Archives

RG 294.2, DP Camps in Germany Collection

RG 1258, Philip Friedman Papers

RG 315, H. Leivick Papers

RG 294.1 Leo Schwarz Papers (AJDC-DP Camps)

RG 1454, Shmuel Mordkhe Zygielbojm Papers

Index

Page numbers in *italics* indicate illustrations.

About the Author

Avinoam J. Patt, Ph.D. is the Doris and Simon Konover Chair of Judaic Studies and Director of the Center for Judaic Studies and Contemporary Jewish Life at the University of Connecticut. He is the author of *Finding Home and Homeland: Jewish Youth and Zionism in the Aftermath of the Holocaust* (Wayne State University Press, 2009); coeditor (with Michael Berkowitz) of a collected volume on Jewish displaced persons, *We Are Here: New Approaches to the Study of Jewish Displaced Persons in Postwar Germany* (Wayne State University Press, 2010); and is a contributor to several projects at the USHMM, including *Jewish Responses to Persecution, 1938–1940.* He is also coeditor of an anthology of contemporary American Jewish fiction, *The New Diaspora: The Changing Landscape of American Jewish Fiction* (Wayne State University Press, 2015), and *The Joint Distribution Committee at 100: A Century of Humanitarianism* (Wayne State University Press, 2019). Together with David Slucki and Gabriel Finder, he is coeditor of a new volume, *Laughter After: Humor and the Holocaust* (Wayne State University Press, 2020), and, with Laura Hilton, *Understanding and Teaching the Holocaust.*

www.ingramcontent.com/pod-product-compliance
Lightning Source LLC
LaVergne TN
LVHW040754070826
844660LV00025B/1145

* 9 7 8 0 8 1 4 3 4 8 3 5 2 *